History of the *fourth edition* Canadian Peoples

Volume I | **Beginnings to 1867**

History of the Canadian Peoples

fourth edition

Canadian Peoples

Volume 1 | Beginnings to 1867

Margaret Conrad
University of New Brunswick

Alvin Finkel
Athabasca University

PEARSON
Longman

Toronto

National Library of Canada Cataloguing in Publication

Conrad, Margaret
   History of the Canadian peoples / Margaret Conrad, Alvin Finkel.— 4th ed.

Includes bibliographical references and index.
Contents: v. 1. Beginnings to 1867

ISBN 0-321-27008-8 (v. 1)

   1. Canada—History—Textbooks. I. Finkel, Alvin, 1949– II. Title.

FC164.H57 2005   971   C2004-905508-9

0-321-27008-8

Vice President, Editorial Director: Michael J. Young
Acquisitions Editor: Christine Cozens
Marketing Manager: Cynthia Smith
Developmental Editor: Adrienne Shiffman
Production Editor: Richard di Santo
Copy Editor: Gail Copeland
Proofreader: Martin Townsend
Production Coordinator: Peggy Brown
Permissions Manager: Susan Wallace-Cox
Literary and Photo Research: Amanda McCormick
Page Layout: Janet Zanette
Art Director: Julia Hall
Cover and Interior Design: Miguel Angel Acevedo
Cover Images: *Portrait of Joseph Brant*, George Romney, National Gallery of Canada/8005 (front); *Madeleine de Verchères*, C.W. Jeffreys, Library and Archives Canada/C-010687; C.W. Jeffreys Estate, Toronto (back).

1 2 3 4 5   10 09 08 07 06

Printed and bound in the United States of America.

Contents

Preface   xvii

INTRODUCTION: **Interpreting Canada's Past**   **xix**

What Is History?   xix
The Context Of This Text   xix
Constructing a Text   xx
What's In a Name?   xx
Notes   *xxi*
Selected Reading   *xxi*
Weblinks   *xxi*

PART I: BEGINNINGS   1

CHAPTER 1:   **Canada: A Bird's Eye View**   **2**

The Physical Environment   2
Conclusion   6
Notes   *6*
Related Readings in This Series   *6*
Selected Reading   *6*
Weblinks   *6*

CHAPTER 2:   **The First Nations of Canada**   **7**

Writing Native History   8
First Nations Before 1500   9
Common Cultural Characteristics   10
The First Nations of the Atlantic and Gulf Region   14
The Canadian Shield First Nations   15
The Interior Plains First Nations   18
The Great Lakes-St Lawrence Lowlands First Nations   20
The Western Cordillera First Nations   23
The North's First Nations   25
Conclusion   26
Notes   *26*
Related Readings in This Series   *27*
Selected Reading   *27*
Weblinks   *28*

CHAPTER 3:   **Second Peoples: The European Cultural Heritage**   **29**

A Society in Transition   30
The European Social Order   31
Population   32
Economic Life   33
Women and the Economy   36

The Role of the State 37
Religion 38
Culture and Ideas 40
Portuguese Exploration 41
Spanish Exploration 42
England, Holland, and France 43
Conclusion 45
Notes 45
Related Readings in This Series 46
Selected Reading 46
Weblinks 47

Chapter 4: **The European "Discovery" of Canada to 1632** **48**

Brief Encounters 49
The Role of the Fishery 50
Early British Colonization: The Newfoundland Experience 52
France in America 55
The Founding of Acadia 56
The Fur Trade on the St Lawrence 57
The Founding of Quebec 57
Preaching the Word 58
Crisis on the St Lawrence 61
Conclusion 62
Selected Reading 62
Notes 62
Related Readings in This Series 62
Weblinks 63

Chapter 5: **Natives and Newcomers, 1632–1663** **64**

Civil War in Acadia 65
First Nations and the Church 67
Female Religious Orders 69
The Huron-Five Nations Wars 71
Canada, 1635–1663 74
The Emerging Canadian Social Order 75
New France in Question 77
Conclusion 79
Notes 79
Related Readings In This Series 80
Selected Reading 80
Weblinks 81

Part II: FRANCE IN AMERICA **83**

Chapter 6: **New France Takes Root, 1663–1689** **84**

The Age of Absolutism 84
Absolutism in New France 85
Colonial Administration 89
Paternalism in New France 90

Law and Order   91
Religious Establishment   92
Mercantilism   95
Seigneurialism   97
Conclusion   100
Notes   *100*
Related Readings in This Series   *100*
Selected Reading   *101*
Weblinks   *102*

CHAPTER 7:   The Political Economy of a Strategic Outpost, 1663–1756   103

Controlling the Fur Trade   104
The Hudson's Bay Company   105
Explorations West and South   105
The War of the League of Augsburg   106
The War of the Spanish Succession   108
The Imperial Factor   109
Louisiana and Illinois   110
The Pays d'en Haut   111
Louisbourg   113
Île Saint-Jean   114
The St Lawrence Economy   114
Conclusion   118
Selected Reading   *118*
Notes   *118*
Related Readings in This Series   *118*
Weblinks   *119*

CHAPTER 8:   Social Life in New France   120

Immigration and Society   120
Town Life   122
Municipal Government   123
Arts and Sciences   124
Canadian Peasant Society   125
The Family under the French Regime   127
The Family Economy   129
Class and Society   130
Slavery   133
Labour   135
Conclusion   137
Notes   *137*
Related Readings in This Series   *138*
Selected Reading   *138*
Weblinks   *139*

CHAPTER 9:   Imperial Designs, 1715–1763   140

Enemies and Allies   141
The Beginnings of British Rule in the Atlantic Region 142
The Neutral French   143

Mi'kmaq and Maliseet   144
War of the Austrian Succession, 1744–1748   145
The Uneasy Peace in Acadia, 1749–1755   146
The Southwestern Frontier in Question   147
The British Take the Offensive   149
The Seven Years' War, 1756–1763   152
The Siege of Quebec   153
Surrender and Negotiation   156
Conclusion   156
Selected Reading   *157*
Notes   *157*
Related Readings in This Series   *157*
Weblinks   *158*

PART III: THE ORIGINS OF BRITISH NORTH AMERICA, 1763–1821 — 161

CHAPTER 10: British North America, 1763–1783 — 162

The Conquest and Native Policy   163
The Conquest and Quebec   164
The Quebec Act, 1774   167
Anglicizing Nova Scotia   169
St John's Island   170
Newfoundland and Labrador   171
The American Revolution   172
Quebec in Question   173
The War in the Atlantic Region   174
Conclusion   178
Notes   *178*
Selected Reading   *179*
Related Readings in This Series   *179*
Weblinks   *180*

CHAPTER 11: Redefining British North America, 1783–1815 — 181

The Loyalist Influx   182
Settling the Loyalists   184
The Constitutional Act, 1791   187
Upper Canada, 1791–1812   188
Lower Canada, 1791–1812   190
Agricultural Crisis on the Seigneuries   192
The War of 1812   193
The Maritime Colonies   196
Newfoundland   197
The Legacy of the War of 1812   198
Culture in Colonial Society   199
Conclusion   202
Notes   *203*
Related Readings in This Series   *203*
Selected Reading   *204*
Weblinks   *205*

CHAPTER 12:   **Natives and the Fur Trade in the West, 1763–1821**   **206**

Fur-Trade Rivalries in the Northwest   206
Native Peoples and the Fur Trade   208
The Birth of the Métis Nation   211
The Founding of the Red River Settlement   213
British Columbia: The European Phase   217
Conclusion   219
Selected Reading   *220*
Notes   *220*
Related Readings in This Series   *220*
Weblinks   *221*

PART IV: MATURING COLONIAL SOCIETIES, 1815–1867   **223**

CHAPTER 13:   **The Maritime Colonies, 1815-1867**   **224**

Defining the Maritimes   225
Population Growth   225
The Commercial Economy   228
The Domestic Economy   231
Class and Culture   232
Social Relations in Pre-Industrial Society   232
Religion   233
Emerging Political Cultures   235
Intellectual Awakening   240
Conclusion   242
Notes   *242*
Selected Reading   *243*
Related Readings in This Series   *243*
Weblinks   *245*

CHAPTER 14:   **Newfoundland and Labrador, 1815–1855**   **246**

The Colonial Condition   247
The Migratory Fishery and Settlement   247
The Saltfish Trade   249
Class and Society   252
Political Conflict   253
Labrador   256
The Fate of the Beothuk   257
Conclusion   260
Notes   *260*
Selected Reading   *261*
Related Readings in This Series   *261*
Weblinks   *262*

CHAPTER 15:   **The Canadas: Economy and Society, 1815–1850s**   **263**

Postwar Migration   264
Immigrant Reception   265
Native Peoples in the Canadas   266

Upper Canada: The Countryside   268
Upper Canada: The Cities and Towns   270
Class, Culture, and Conflict in Upper Canada   271
Religion, Leisure, and the Regulation of Morality in Upper Canada   273
Lower Canada: The Countryside   275
Lower Canada: The Cities and Towns   277
Class, Culture, and Religion in Lower Canada   279
Conclusion   280
Notes   *280*
Selected Reading   *281*
Related Readings in This Series   *281*
Weblinks   *283*

CHAPTER 16: Rebellions and Responsible Government in the Canadas, 1815–1860   **284**

The Road to Rebellion in Lower Canada   285
Rebellion in Upper Canada   288
Assessing the Rebellions   294
The Struggle for Responsible Government   294
Responsible Government in Action   297
Land and the Changing Political Order   299
Education for a New Society   299
Conclusion   300
Selected Reading   *302*
Related Readings in This Series   *302*
Weblinks   *303*

CHAPTER 17: The Northwest, 1821–1860s   **304**

The Fur-Trade Monopoly Period, 1821–1849   304
Visions of the Northwest   311
The Northern Fur Trade   312
The Franklin Expedition   312
Conclusion   313
Selected Reading   *316*
Notes   *316*
Related Readings in This Series   *316*
Weblinks   *317*

CHAPTER 18: The Pacific Northwest, 1821–1860s   **318**

The Fur Trade   319
The Close of the Fur-Trade Era   321
Gold Rush Days   324
Settlers and Race Relations   326
British Columbia after the Gold Rush   327
Political Developments   328
Conclusion   329
Notes   *329*
Selected Reading   *330*
Related Readings in This Series   *330*
Weblinks   *331*

PART V: INDUSTRIALIZING CANADA, 1840–1867   **333**

CHAPTER 19: People and Place at Mid-Century   **334**

Small Worlds   335
Communications   336
Colonial Economies   337
Town and Country   338
The Family in Transition   339
Life and Death   340
Gender and Society   341
Class Identities   342
Education   342
Christianity and Culture   343
Race and Racism   344
Sports and Leisure   349
The Creative Arts   350
Conclusion   352
Selected Reading   *354*
Notes   *354*
Related Readings in This Series   *354*
Weblinks   *357*

CHAPTER 20: British North America's Revolutionary Age   **358**

The Industrial Revolution   359
Free Trade, Reciprocity, and Protection   360
Transportation   362
Mobilizing Capital   364
Labour and Industry   365
Law and Industry   367
The Structure of Industrial Capitalism   367
Intellectual Revolutions   369
Conclusion   371
Notes   *371*
Selected Reading   *372*
Related Readings in this Series   *372*
Weblinks   *373*

CHAPTER 21: Society in Transition   **374**

Society in Crisis   374
Poverty in a Cold Climate   375
Social Welfare   376
Social Conflict   376
The Rage for Reform   378
Education Reform   379
The Discovery of the Asylum   381
Public and Private Worlds   382
Women's Rights   384
Nationalism and Colonial Identities   384

Conclusion   387
Related Readings in This Series   *387*
Selected Reading   *387*
Notes   *387*
Weblinks   *388*

CHAPTER 22:   The Road to Confederation   **389**

Nation and Colony   390
The Canadas: Economic Success and Political Impasse   390
The Canadians Make Their Move   392
Great Expectations in the Maritimes   393
The External Pressure for Confederation   396
The American Factor   398
Planning Confederation   399
Selling Confederation   400
The Meaning of Confederation   406
Conclusion   407
Notes   *409*
Related Readings in This Series   *409*
Selected Reading   *410*
Weblinks   *411*

Index   *413*

LIST OF MAPS

MAP 1.1	Canada as seen from a satellite	3
MAP 1.2	The last ice age (Wisconsinan)	3
MAP 1.3	Physiographic regions of Canada	4
MAP 1.4	Canada in the twenty-first century	5
MAP 2.1	Natives at the time of first contact	11
MAP 2.2	Native subsistence at the time of first contact with Europeans	12
MAP 3.1	Western Europe in 1500	31
MAP 4.1	European settlements in North America, 1632	53
MAP 5.1	New France in 1663	77
MAP 6.1	North America, 1697	86
MAP 7.1	North America, 1713	110
MAP 9.1	France in America, 1755	141
MAP 9.2	Nova Scotia/Acadia in the 1750s	143
MAP 10.1	North America, 1763	163
MAP 11.1	British North America, 1783	184
MAP 11.2	British North America, 1791	187
MAP 11.3	The War of 1812	194
MAP 13.1	Maine-New Brunswick boundary claims	225
MAP 13.2	The Maritimes at mid-century	238
MAP 14.1	Newfoundland and Labrador	248
MAP 15.1	The United Province of Canada, 1851	277
MAP 16.1	Sites of the 1837–38 rebellion	292
MAP 17.1	The Western fur trade region circa 1850	305
MAP 18.1	British Columbia, 1870	328
MAP 20.1	Canals and railways in the United Canadas before Confederation	363
MAP 22.1	British North America, 1866	405

LIST OF FIGURES AND TABLES

FIGURE 3.1	Selected European Population Figures (in millions)	32
TABLE 7.2	Colonial Revenues and Expenditures, in livres	115
TABLE 7.1	Fur Exports from Quebec	115
TABLE 7.3	Value of Ginseng Exports	117
TABLE 8.1	Immigration to Canada before 1760	121
TABLE 8.2	Occupational Hierarchy of New France, Based on Conventional Dower	130
TABLE 22.1	Population of British North America, 1851–1871	391

LIST OF BOXES

BIOGRAPHY

Dekanawidah and Hiawatha	22
Étienne Brûlé	59
Marie de l'Incarnation	71
Charles Le Moyne: A Self-Made Nobleman	90
Madeleine de Verchères	107
The Fate of François Bigot	133
Montcalm and Wolfe	155
Joseph and Molly Brant	175
Ezekiel Hart	191
A Tale of Two Maquinnas	218
Enos Collins	229
Shanawdithit	259
Shingwaukonse	269
Papineau and Mackenzie: Rebels with a Cause	290
George Simpson	308
Sir James Douglas	323
Mary Ann Shadd Cary	347
J. William Dawson	370
Emily Jennings Howard Stowe	385
John A. Macdonald: The Changing Face of Toryism in Canada West	394
A.A. Dorion: The Changing Face of Quebec Liberalism	404

A HISTORIOGRAPHICAL DEBATE

Cruelty Versus Germs	44
The Destruction of Huronia	78
Theocratic Tyranny or Benevolent Paternalism?	99
The Status of Women in New France	136
Culture and Conquest	176
The Loyalists	202
The Maritime Economy: The Legacy of Mercantilism in the Maritimes	241
Causes of the Rebellion in Lower Canada	300
Native Women and the Fur Trade	314
Religion and Culture	353
Economic Elites and Confederation	408

MORE TO THE STORY

Diverging Views of Oral Traditions	10
Native Accounts of Creation	17
Peasant Families and the Life Cycle in Early Modern Europe	34
Searching for Asia	52
The Frontier and the Metropolis	65

The Changing Status of Native Women — 69
The Case of Adam Dollard — 73
Social Welfare in New France — 74
Witches and Warlocks in New France — 93
The China Connection — 117
Demography — 121
Élisabeth Bégon, Épistolière — 125
Were the Habitants of New France Truly Peasants? — 127
Life in the Colonial Militia — 147
Early Days in Halifax — 148
Elizabeth and Edmund Doane — 169
Black Loyalist Preachers in Nova Scotia and Sierra Leone — 183
Artists in a New World — 200
The Spread of Disease — 212
Native Agriculture in the Northwest — 216
Joseph Howe on Trial, 1835 — 239
The Seal Fishery — 250
Mummering — 254
Famine in Ireland — 267
Life at a Fur-Trading Post — 306
Romantic Art in a Colonial Setting — 351
The Triumph of Civic Policing in Toronto — 378
Canadians and the American Civil War — 397

Voices from the Past

Dreams and Cree Culture — 19
Columbus and Aboriginal Peoples — 43
The Ferryland Settlement in Newfoundland — 54
Native Assessments of European Society — 61
Governor Denonville Denounces Gangs, 1685 — 95
Wartime Economic Crisis — 109
Shipping a Slave to Louisbourg — 135
Claude Bourgeois Pleads for Relief — 151
The Legend of Brock and the Loyal Militia — 195
The Impact of the Fur Trade on Natives: A Trader's View — 210
Oral History — 226
Drowning a Dog, 1846 — 252
Susanna Moodie Describes an Upper Canadian Charivari — 274
A School Lesson in the 1840s — 296
A View of the Métis — 310
Native Views of European Land Claims — 327
Great Chief Petrokeshig and Oshawana Speak Their Minds — 345
The Annexation Manifesto — 361
Patriotic Poets — 386
The Men Who Voted on Confederation — 403

PREFACE

The fourth edition of *History of the Canadian Peoples* tries to preserve our primary objective of an inclusive history of Canada. In addition to the achievements of the rich and powerful, we include developments in the lives of Aboriginal peoples, women, racial and ethnic minorities, and the poor, who also helped to create the Canada we know today.

Weaving together the rich tapestry of Canada's social, political, and economic story is a daunting task, and, as we note below, we have many people to thank for helping us across the four editions of this text. The fourth edition closely mirrors the structure of the third edition, with the exception of condensing several chapters to reduce the total number from 23 to 22. Although we have adjusted the organization of the chapters, the text remains divided into five parts.

Part 1, "Beginnings," comprises the first five chapters. We begin with an overview of the many millennia of Aboriginal history in Canada, followed by a similarly condensed account of the history of the European invaders and how this influenced their perceptions of the "new land" and its First Nations. Tracing the earliest European involvements in fishing and fur trading in North America, we look at the beginnings of European settlement in the area of today's Canada.

Part 2, "France in America," includes Chapters 6 to 9. These four chapters outline the development of new societies in North America, involving people of French origin, but shaped by an environment in which the role of Aboriginal peoples was crucial. The complex influences of both French imperialism and the local environment provide much of the drama in Part 2, in which near-constant warfare and its aftermath hangs over the efforts of people to shape a livelihood in the "New World."

Part 3, "The Origins of British North America, 1763–1821," Chapters 10 to 12, begins with the British conquests of the remaining French colonies in North America, and the territories of their Native allies. It then focuses on the establishment of British-controlled colonies across the territories of today's Canada, demonstrating both the similarities and the differences among these colonies.

Part 4, "Maturing Colonial Societies, 1815–1867," consists of Chapters 13 to 18, and takes the story of British North America beyond pioneer societies largely based on subsistence or the sale of a single staple to commercial societies perched on the edge of the age of industrialism. We look at the evolving social hierarchies in these societies, and the limits placed upon individuals for reasons of class, gender, or race. We also trace the evolution of democratic thought and institutions in areas initially viewed as colonies of an all-knowing "Mother country."

Part 5, "Industrializing Canada, 1840–1867" covers Chapters 19 to 22, and completes our story. The impact of new technologies, particularly railways, on social life and politics across British North America is central to the story here. We look at the impact on British North Americans of new ideas of the good life, religion, education, social reform, and much else, ending with a discussion of how the various social and political currents of the period shaped the debate on whether British North Americans should create their own nation-state.

In revising and updating this edition, we have maintained the kinds of pedagogical features in the third edition—A Historiographical Debate, More to the Story, Voices from the Past, and Biography—but modified some of the topics covered. Beyond these existing features, we have added an end-of-chapter feature called, "Related Readings in This Series," which directs readers both to complementary articles in *Foundations: Readings in Pre-Confederation Canadian History* and to primary source selections on the accompanying Media Companion CD-ROM. As in the previous edition, timelines appear at the beginning of each chapter to place events in chronological perspective, and we have continued to incorporate several useful weblinks at the end of each chapter.

As you will see, the interior of the fourth edition now has enhanced colour. We have increased the number of photos in the text to maximize this new design and to provide you with further visual support to the narrative.

Our debts to others just keep growing as we pass from edition to edition of this text, and we apologize to those who have contributed but whom we have passed over here. We thank Veronica Strong-Boag, Michael Behiels, Brian Henderson, and Cornelius Jaenen for their role in the initial conceptualization of this project. We owe a particular debt to our editors of the four editions. Curtis Fahey, Barbara Tessman, Dawn du Quesnay, and Adrienne Shiffman contributed immeasurably to the organization, content, and writing of Volume 1.

Many people read and suggested improvements for some or all of these chapters. For the first edition, we thank Veronica Strong-Boag, Michael Behiels, Jim Pritchard, Adrian Shubert, Brian Young, John Dickinson, Douglas Baldwin, and Barry Moody. For the second edition, we thank John Dickinson, Cornelius Jaenen, Gerald Friesen, Mark McGowan, Ruth Brouwer, Graham Decarie, Kathryn McPherson, Norman Hillmer, Marilyn Barber, Jim Miller, Lorne Hammond, Suzanne Zeller, Patricia Dirks, Suzanne Morton, Carmen Miller, Ken Munro, Peter Nunoda, Wendy Mitchinson, Cecilia Danysk, Sharon Myers, Robert Sweeny, and Del Muise. We received helpful input on the third edition from Jim Hiller, John Belshaw (University College of the Cariboo), Roger Hall (University of Western Ontario), Sean Cadigan (Dalhousie University), Catherine Desbarats (McGill University), Linda Kerr (Concordia University College), Rusty Bitterman (Saint Thomas University), Jan Noel (University of Toronto at Mississauga), David Murray (University of Guelph), Ron Stagg (Ryerson Polytechnic University), Jeff Keshen (University of Ottawa), Raymond Huel (University of Lethbridge), Shawn Cafferky (University of Victoria). Norman Hillmer (Carleton University), Jeff Webb (Memorial University), and Cynthia Comacchio (Wilfrid Laurier University).

For the fourth edition, we would like to thank the following reviewers for their contributions and suggestions: Heidi Macdonald (University of Lethbridge), George Davison (College of New Caledonia), Kori Street (Mount Royal College), Clarence Bolt (Camosun College), David J. Hall (University of Alberta), Larry Kulisek (University of Windsor), and Robert Campbell (Capilano College).

Photo and artwork research for the previous editions was done by Maral Bablanian, with Louise McKenzie, Richard Holt, and Madhu Ranadive, and for this fourth edition by Amanda McCormick. Robert Clarke, Barbara Tessman, and Curtis Fahey tried to make our prose as readable as possible in the first edition. Barbara Tessman and Karen Bennett undertook the same objective in the second and third editions respectively. We would also like to acknowledge the efforts of Gail Copeland, the copyeditor for the fourth edition.

Across four editions, secretarial services played an important role. We wish to thank Myrna Nolan, Claire Gemmell, Lorette Kisinski, and Sandra Davidson of Athabasca University; Brenda Naugler and Carolyn Bowlby of Acadia University, and Jan Cleveland of Mount Saint Vincent University for their help with the various editions.

SUPPLEMENTS

Companion Website (www.pearsoned.ca/conrad-finkel): This website is an online study guide that includes self-tests and links to other online resources for further research.

Instructor's Resource CD-ROM (0-321-31184-1): This resource CD-ROM includes the following instructor supplements:

- **Instructor's Manual:** This manual includes chapter-by-chapter lecture outlines, discussion points, assignments, and other resources for instructors.
- **TestGen:** Chapter-by-chapter test questions, including multiple-choice, fill-in-the-blank, short answer, and essay questions, are provided in TestGen format. TestGen is a testing software that enables instructors to view and edit the existing questions, add questions, generate tests, and distribute the tests in a variety of formats. Powerful search and sort functions make it easy to locate questions and arrange them in any order desired. TestGen also enables instructors to administer tests on a local area network, have the tests graded electronically and have the results prepared in electronic or printed reports. TestGen is compatible with Windows and Macintosh operating systems, and can be downloaded from the TestGen website located at www.pearsoned.com/testgen. Contact your local sales representative for details and access.
- **PowerPoints:** PowerPoint presentations highlight the key points in each chapter.
- **Image Archive:** The archive provides selected maps and images from the text in PowerPoint format.

Most of these instructor supplements are also available for download from a password-protected section of Pearson Education Canada's online catalogue, http://vig.pearsoned.ca. Navigate to your book's catalogue page to view a list of those supplements that are available. See your local sales representative for details and access.

Interpreting Canada's Past

In 1829, Shanawdithit, the last surviving Beothuk on the island of Newfoundland, died of tuberculosis. Thirty-eight years later, three British North American colonies united to form the Dominion of Canada. The second of these two events has always had a central place in Canadian history textbooks. The first, until recently, has been ignored. For students of history, it is important to understand why the focus of historical analysis changes and what factors influence historians in their approaches to their craft.

What Is History?

Simply stated, history is the study of the past, but the past is a slippery concept. In non-literate societies, people passed oral traditions from one generation to the next, with each generation fashioning the story to meet the needs of the time. When writing was invented, history became fixed in texts. The story of the past was often revised, but earlier texts could be used to show how interpretations changed over time. Although ordinary people continued to tell their stories, they were considered less important than "official" written histories that reflected the interests of the most powerful members of society. Some of the official texts, such as the Bible and the Koran, were deemed to be divinely inspired and therefore less subject to revision than the accounts of mere mortals.

In the nineteenth century, history became an academic discipline in Europe and North America. Scholars in universities began to collect primary historical documents, compare texts, develop standards of accuracy, and train students to become professional historians. At first, professional historians focused on political and military events that chronicled the evolution of empires and nation-states. Gradually, they broadened their scope to include economic, social, and cultural developments.

The Context of This Text

The authors of this book are university-trained historians, schooled in the theories and methods of what was once called "the new social history." Since the new social history is now more than three decades old, it can no longer be considered new, but its findings have informed our decisions about what to include in this introductory textbook.

Social historians have made a concerted effort to broaden the scope of historical inquiry. To fill the gaps in written documents, they have taken an interdisciplinary approach, drawing upon other disciplines (including archeology, anthropology, demography, and geography) to answer their questions. Such sources as oral traditions and the findings of archeological excavations have enabled historians to explore the lives of the silent majority in past times. When personal computers became widely available in the 1970s, historians were able to more efficiently process large amounts of information found in such sources as censuses, immigration lists, and church registers. The science of demography, which analyzes population trends and draws upon vast quantities of data, has proven particularly useful in helping historians trace changes in family size, migration patterns, and life-cycle choices.

At the same time that new methodologies extended the scope of history, historians were being influenced by new theoretical approaches. Scholars who studied minorities, women, and the working class brought insights from multicultural studies, feminism, and Marxism to their analyses. Canadian history was also enriched by regional studies that integrated the perspectives of the West, North, and Atlantic Canada into the larger national story hitherto dominated by Quebec and Ontario. By focusing on social structures such as class, culture, gender, race, and region, social historians raised new questions about old topics and revolutionized the way Canada's past is perceived.

Social history also has its critics. They argue that it focuses the energy of historians into narrow topics, that it yields interesting but ultimately insignificant findings, and that it destroys the unifying national focus that earlier political studies offered.[1] In response to such charges, we argue that the new social history offers a more comprehensive view of what happened in the past. We also maintain that there cannot be and never was an official version of Canada's history. The claim that there is only one way to view the past is, we believe, as damaging to the historical enterprise as are theories that dismiss history—and the belief that the present can be informed by an understanding of the past—as a figment of the modernist imagination.

CONSTRUCTING A TEXT

From the foregoing discussion, it is clear that history is a dynamic and evolving discipline. Debates rage, methods come and go, new sources are discovered, and different conclusions are drawn from the same body of evidence. We want students who use this text not only to learn about developments in Canada's past but also to gain some understanding of how history is written. At the beginning of and at various points throughout each chapter we cite from primary sources that historians use. We also discuss historiography—that is, reflections on historical interpretation—in sections entitled "A Historiographical Debate." We conclude each chapter with a list of Selected Reading to acknowledge the sources that have informed our thinking and to offer direction for students who wish to explore topics in more depth.

Ultimately our goal is to integrate social and cultural history into the text so that readers can develop a clearer understanding of how economic and political developments influenced the people's lives and vice versa. There is, we maintain, nothing inevitable about historical processes. At times in this text the limitations on an individual's behaviour set by age, class, culture, gender, race, or region may appear to suggest that many, perhaps most, of our ancestors were hopeless victims of forces beyond their control. A closer reading should reveal that people sought in various

ways to transcend the limits placed on their lives. Social struggles of every sort changed or at least sought to change the course of history. As you read this book, we hope that you will gain a greater appreciation of how earlier generations of people in what is now called Canada responded to their environment and shaped their own history.

WHAT'S IN A NAME?

Contemporary political movements that are changing the face of Canada are also forcing historians to think about the words they use. A half-century ago, most textbooks referred to people with black skin as "Negroes." In the 1960s, the term was replaced by "black," and more recently by "African Canadian," despite the fact that not all Africans are black. Similarly, the words used to describe Aboriginal peoples have changed in recent years. "Savages" was quickly dropped from textbooks in the 1960s. Although the misnomer "Indian" has particular applications that seem as yet unavoidable, the preferred terms are now "First Nations" or "Native peoples." "Amerindian" is a scholarly term used to encompass a wide range of Aboriginal cultures.

Women, too, have insisted on being described in more respectful terms. Feminists have objected strongly to the use of the word "girl" when adult women are being discussed, and dismiss "lady" as being condescending or elitist. Because "man" was adequate for the male of the species, "woman," they argued, was the most appropriate term, although some radical feminists prefer a different spelling, such as "wymyn." Only the most hidebound of scholars still insist that the word "man" can be used to describe the entire human species.

Many scholars complained loudly about being asked to abandon words long established in their vocabularies. A few even argued that "political correctness" restricted freedom of speech. We do not hold such views. Since English is a living language and changes over time, we see no reason why it should not continue to reflect the new consciousness of groups in Canadian society. In our view, the words "politically conscious" more accurately describe attempts by groups to name their own experience.

Language, of course, is not only about naming things; it is also about power. Attempts by oppressed groups to find new words to fit their experiences should be seen in the context of their struggles for empowerment. In this text, we attempt to keep up with the changing times while bearing in mind that people in the past used a different terminology. We are also aware that in the future we may revise the words we use, as groups continue to reinvent their identities. Even the word "Canada" has changed its meaning over the past 500 years, and it is our job as historians to shed light on the way this term came to be applied, for a time at least, to all the people living on the northern half of the North American continent.

NOTES

1 The now classic critique of social history in general and the first edition of our text in particular can be found in J.L. Granatstein, *Who Killed Canadian History?* (Toronto: HarperCollins, 1998). For a more nuanced critique see Michael Bliss, "Privatizing the Mind: The Sundering of Canadian History, the Sundering of Canada," *Journal of Canadian Studies* 26, 4 (Winter 1991–92): 5–17. A.B. McKillop offers a thoughtful response in "Who Killed Canadian History? A View from the Trenches," *Canadian Historical Review* 80, 2 (June 1999): 269–99. See also Jocelyn Létourneau, "L'Avenir du Canada: Par Rapport à Quelle Histoire?" *Canadian Historical Review* 81, 2 (June 2000): 230–59 and Linda Kealey et al., "Teaching Canadian History in the 1990s: Whose 'National' History Are We Lamenting?" *Journal of Canadian Studies* 27, 2 (Summer 1992): 129–31.

SELECTED READING

Students interested in the writing of Canadian history should start with the following: Carl Berger, *The Writing of Canadian History: Aspects of English-Canadian Historical Writing Since 1900*, 2nd ed. (Toronto: University of Toronto Press, 1986); Beverly Boutilier and Alison Prentice, eds., *Creating Historical Memory: English-Canadian Women and the Work of History* (Vancouver: UBC Press, 1997); Serge Gagnon, *Quebec and Its Historians: 1840–1920* (Montreal: Harvest House, 1982) and *Quebec and Its Historians: The Twentieth Century* (Montreal: Harvest House, 1985); Ronald Rudin, *Making History in Twentieth Century Quebec* (Toronto: University of Toronto Press, 1997); and M. Brook Taylor, *Promoters, Patriots, and Partisans: Historiography in Nineteenth-Century English Canada* (Toronto: University of Toronto Press, 1989).

More sources on various topics in pre-Confederation Canadian history can be found in M. Brook Taylor, *Canadian History: A Reader's Guide, Vol. 1: Beginnings to Confederation* (Toronto: University of Toronto Press, 1994). Students of Canadian history should also become familiar with four important reference works: *The Dictionary of Canadian Biography* (14 volumes are currently in print covering people who died up to 1920) and *Historical Atlas of Canada*, 3 vols., both published by the University of Toronto Press, Gerald Hallowell, ed., *The Oxford Companion to Canadian History* (Toronto: Oxford University Press, 2004), and *The Canadian Encyclopedia*, 4 vols. (Edmonton: Hurtig, 1988).

WEBLINKS

THE ATLAS OF CANADA
http://atlas.gc.ca/site/index.html

Developed by Natural Resources Canada, this bilingual online atlas offers a collection of maps and related information about all regions of Canada.

CANADA'S DIGITAL COLLECTIONS
http://collections.ic.gc.ca

Canada's Digital Collections is one of the largest sources of Canadian content on the Internet, featuring over 600 collections celebrating Canada's history, geography, science, technology, and culture.

CANADA'S SCHOOLNET
www.schoolnet.ca

This site is designed to connect students and teachers to useful educational resources on the Internet. It features over 7000 learning resources, several interactive features, and a daily information news service on the world of e-learning.

THE CANADIAN ENCYCLOPEDIA
www.thecanadianencyclopedia.com

This electronic version of the Canadian Encyclopedia offers a variety of interactive activities and links.

CANADIAN HERITAGE INFORMATION NETWORK
www.chin.gc.ca

The Canadian Heritage Information Network works with Canadian museums to create, present, and manage Canadian digital content.

CANADIAN INSTITUTE FOR HISTORICAL MICROREPRODUCTIONS
www.canadiana.org/cihm/

This site posts early printed Canadian materials, including books, annuals, and periodicals.

DICTIONARY OF CANADIAN BIOGRAPHY
www.biographi.ca

Hosted by the Library and Archives of Canada, this electronic version of the Dictionary of Canadian Biography facilitates searching across the 14 volumes of the Dictionary currently in print.

HISTORICA
www.histori.ca

This is the home page of Historica, a foundation whose mandate is to provide Canadians with a deeper understanding of their history and its importance in shaping their future.

LIBRARY AND ARCHIVES CANADA
www.collectionscanada.ca

Library and Archives Canada hosts the largest collection of materials related to the nation's history. The site includes electronic resources and research tools. View some exhibits and do some research at this site.

OUR ROOTS
www.ourroots.ca/e/home.asp

The Our Roots project is designed to present an online coast-to-coast record of Canadian local histories.

PARKS CANADA
www.pc.gc.ca

The online home of Parks Canada includes information on Canada's national historic sites.

STATISTICS CANADA
www.statcan.ca

The Statistics Canada website contains a remarkable amount of historical and contemporary data.

VIRTUAL MUSEUM OF CANADA
www.virtualmuseum.ca

This site showcases the distinct culture entrusted in Canadian museums and includes a series of attractive virtual exhibits and an image gallery.

PART I

BEGINNINGS

By the seventeenth century, two peoples without a common history lived in what today is called Canada. The First Nations had been living for millennia in the northern regions of North America, while the Europeans were new-comers. Just like the Europeans, the First Nations had developed complex societies and belief systems. Neither group was very sympathetic to the other's culture or point of view. Part I of this text explores the culture of the two peoples and describes their early interaction to 1663.

CHAPTER 1

Canada:
A Bird's Eye View

Timeline

▶ **80 000 BP**   Last ice age begins
▶ **20 000 BP**   Height of last ice age
▶ **15 000 BP**   Glaciers begin to melt

"For the Beaver people of northern Alberta, Earth's creation began when Muskrat retrieved a speck of dirt from the primordial sea. Muskrat drew a cross on the water's surface, and the cross provided the starting point for a set of paths along the land carved from the dirt. Swan transformed creatures from beyond the sky into earthly forms, and each took up residence along particular pathways. For humans, dependent upon other species for their subsistence, knowledge of the trails that led to animals was essential to survival. This knowledge came from following the necessary rituals intended by the Great Spirit and the spirits of the animals."[1]

Views about the origins of the Earth differ but, for everyone who has ever lived in Canada, the physical environment has been a crucial factor in shaping their life chances and choices. While geography alone does not determine human destiny, it places limits on the possibilities that individuals and groups enjoy. Most of this book focuses on ways people adapted to and transformed their environments and shaped complex societies. In this chapter, we explore some of the features of the physical environment that provided challenges and opportunities to people in various regions as they went about the business of their daily lives.

THE PHYSICAL ENVIRONMENT

Canada is the second largest nation in the world, covering over 7 percent of the Earth's surface. Only Russia is larger. Throughout much of its history, Canada was a cold and inhospitable place, buried under a vast sheet of glacial ice. The last Ice Age reached its maximum extent about 20 000 years ago (see Map 1.2). As the ice moved and melted, it created many of the geographical features we associate with present-day Canada.

MAP 1.1 Canada as seen from a satellite.
RADARSAT data copyright Canadian Space Agency/Agence spatiale canadienne 1999. Received by the Canada Centre for Remote Sensing. Processed and distributed by RADARSAT International.

Geographers have devised several ways of describing the natural environment. They define six major physiographic regions—areas with similar landforms—in Canada: east to west they are the Atlantic and Gulf region, the Great Lakes-St Lawrence Lowlands, the Canadian Shield, the Interior Plains, the Western Cordillera, and the North (see Map 1.3). The typology developed by Statistics Canada and Environment Canada in the 1980s suggests no fewer than 15 "ecozones"—regions distinguished by similar landforms, climate, and vegetation. There are also eight distinct forest regions, although the boreal (northern) forest region, dominated by white and black spruce, accounts for the greater part of Canada's wooded areas.

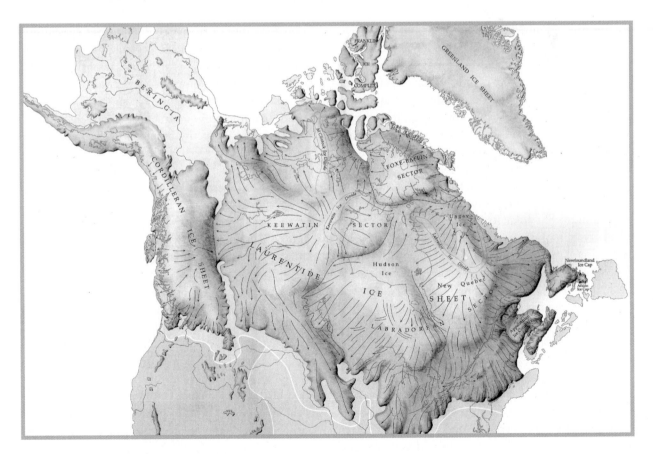

MAP 1.2 The last ice age (Wisconsinan).
Adapted from *Historical Atlas of Canada*, vol. 1 (Toronto: University of Toronto Press, 1987), plate 1

The Atlantic and Gulf region is the northern portion of a physiographic area usually referred to as Appalachia. The Appalachians straddle two national territories, as do most of Canada's other physiographic regions. Encompassing most of the Atlantic region of Canada (except for Labrador, which is part of the Canadian Shield), the Appalachians consist of ancient rounded hills and plateaus with a few large fertile areas, such as the Annapolis-Cornwallis Valley in Nova Scotia. Under the adjacent ocean is the continental shelf, home to what were once thought to be inexhaustible supplies of fish as well as oil and natural gas.

Climate and vegetation vary within the Atlantic and Gulf region. Near the coast, precipitation is heavy and temperatures are less extreme than in the drier inland areas. The island of Newfoundland forms part of the boreal forest, with few deciduous trees amid the conifers. Most of the Maritime provinces, by contrast, lie within the Acadian forest region, which includes both deciduous and evergreen trees. While 80 percent of the Maritimes is forested, only 35 percent of Newfoundland is covered with trees. Population in the Atlantic region has concentrated in the coastal areas and along the St John River. The sea and the rivers yielded much of the food for the region's Native peoples, although hunting and plant gathering also provided important resources for survival. Systematic agriculture developed in the period of European settlement on the flat lowlands of Prince Edward Island and in the fertile valleys and plains of New Brunswick and Nova Scotia.

The Canadian Shield dominates 40 percent of Canada's land mass. Literally a great sheet of Precambrian rock, it represents one of the oldest land formations in the world. Although its hills are interspersed with areas where the land, soil, and drainage offer good farming possibilities, the cool summers and

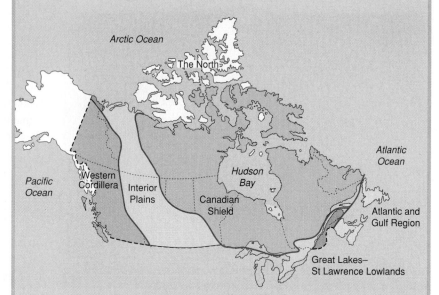

MAP 1.3 Physiographic regions of Canada.

limited number of frost-free days restrict agricultural development. The abundant game in the region's forests supported dispersed Native populations, who faced little competition from European settlers before the nineteenth century. By then, minerals and forest resources in the region attracted commercial interest, as did the hydro-electric potential of the rivers in the twentieth century.

The Interior Plains were created over the course of several ice ages, as flat layers of sedimentary rock were imposed on Shield rock. Flat clay plains intersected by glacial meltwater produced valleys in a region characterized by plains and rolling hills. Although a large portion of the Interior Plains consists of good to excellent soil for farming, climatic conditions limit yields. Winters are harsh; the growing seasons are often short and uncertain. The lack of rain in southwestern Saskatchewan and southeastern Alberta further curtailed agriculture. In any event, the abundant game (especially buffalo) and vegetation in much of the region made a sedentary farming life unnecessary. By the nineteenth century, European farmers began to covet the Interior Plains region, which previously had been of interest only to Europeans involved in fur trading.

MAP 1.4 Canada in the twenty-first century.

The Great Lakes-St Lawrence Lowlands, which includes southern Ontario and southern Quebec, is a region dominated by gentle rolling hills, the product of the last ice age, which ended about 10 000 years ago. As it receded, the ice ground down the sedimentary rock of the Canadian Shield, leaving an area with several major belts of fertile soil, particularly in southern Ontario. The lakes and rivers of the region provided accessible transportation routes for human inhabitants. Before extensive European settlement, deer, rabbit, beaver, bear, fowl, fish, and wild berries abounded, allowing Aboriginal populations to increase steadily. Population growth necessitated further food sources, encouraging some Native groups to begin planting crops in the fertile soil.

Like the Great Lakes-St Lawrence Lowlands, the Western Cordillera sustained a relatively large Aboriginal population. The region consists of a series of six mountain ranges extending through British Columbia and southwestern Alberta. Interspersed with plateaus, rivers, and valleys, the region in the pre-contact period was home to an abundance of freshwater fish, particularly salmon, as well as mountain sheep, bear, and deer. The mountain ranges offered a barrier to contact both among Aboriginal peoples and, later, between European settlers. The temperate climate on the coast and in the southern interior of the Cordillera offers a marked contrast to the climate of the Interior Plains and attracted a large human population.

The North consists of a variety of subregions. Within the subarctic there are areas that might be seen as somewhat colder and less fertile extensions of the Cordillera and the Interior Plains. Further north is the Arctic, home to the Inuit. It is an area of no trees, little soil, and long, harsh winters. The underground permafrost—literally permanent frost—creates special problems for the construction of buildings. Only small concentrations of people dispersed throughout the region could be supported without depleting the caribou, moose, fish, waterfowl, and fur-bearing animals that the regional populations depended upon for survival. Europeans initially regarded the region as a barren wasteland inhospitable for settlement, and suitable only for exploitation of its furs. Over time, its metals and energy resources would lure Europeans into the North.

CONCLUSION

Six regions formed the environment that shaped the experiences of Canada's Aboriginal peoples and challenged early European explorers and settlers.

Geography influenced the size of populations, the economic activities that were undertaken, and the extent to which mobility was required to sustain survival. As we shall see throughout this text, it also inspired the political systems and spiritual beliefs of the peoples who made the northern half of the North American continent their home.

NOTES

1 Robin Ridington, "Technology, World View and Adaptive Strategy in a Northern Hunting Society," *Canadian Review of Sociology and Anthropology* 19, 4 (1982): 474–75.

RELATED READINGS IN THIS SERIES

From *Foundations: Readings in Pre-Confederation Canadian History*
Ken S. Coates and William R. Morrison, "Winter and the Shaping of Northern History: Reflections from the Canadian North," 4–13.

SELECTED READING

Useful introductions to Canadian geography include J. Lewis Robinson, *Concepts and Themes in the Regional Geography of Canada* (Vancouver: Talon, 1989); Lawrence McCann, ed., *Heartland and Hinterland: Canadian Regions in Evolution* (Scarborough, ON: Prentice-Hall, 1987); D.F. Putnam and R.G. Putnam, *Canada: A Regional Analysis* (Toronto: Dent, 1979); and Geoffrey J. Matthews and Robert Morrow Jr, *Canada and the World* (Scarborough, ON: Prentice-Hall, 1985), as well as the three volumes of the *Historical Atlas of Canada* (Toronto: University of Toronto Press, 1987/1990/1993). On the Atlantic region, see Atlantic Geoscience Society, *The Last Billion Years: A Geological Study of the Maritime Provinces of Canada* (Halifax: Nimbus, 2001).

WEBLINKS

GLACIAL ICE
www.entrenet.com/~groedmed/glaciers.html
This site offers a historical overview (with maps) of the glaciers that covered Canada during the Ice Age, as well as a brief introduction to glacier terminology.

home.uleth.ca/vft/crowsnest/iceage.html
This University of Lethbridge site reproduces an illustration of the Cordilleran glacier, which covered much of Alberta and British Columbia.

CHAPTER 2

The First Nations of Canada

Timeline

30 000 BCE	Native peoples begin to inhabit North America
10 000 BCE	Natives use fluted points (sharpened points on a projectile) to kill giant mammals
9000 BCE	Mastodons and mammoths become extinct
5000 BCE	Natives in Labrador build ritual burial mounds; Natives in Alberta use corrals to kill large mammals
4000 BCE	Southern Ontario Natives make use of fish nets, weirs, and grinding implements
1000 BCE	Chiefdoms begin to be established on northwest coast; southern Ontario Natives begin making pottery
900 BCE	Algonkian-speaking groups enter region north and west of Great Lakes, previously the preserve of Siouan speakers
500 BCE	Trade relations established between Natives in southern Ontario and Atlantic region
CE 250	Natives begin using bow and arrow for hunting
CE 500	Horticulture established in southern Ontario
CE 1000	Viking settlements in Newfoundland
CE 1300	Iroquoian societies begin building palisaded villages
CE 1450	Formation of Iroquois Confederacy

Moved seven times in 50 years to make way for mining developments and finally scattered in remote areas, a northern Quebec Cree band were cited by the United Nations in the 1980s as one of the most destitute communities in the developed countries. Militant protests by the Cree finally forced the federal and provincial governments to provide the land and finances to build a permanent community for the 525 band members. The village of Oujé-Bougoumou, designed by First Nations architect Douglas Cardinal, reflects the spiritual, cultural, and environmental values of the Cree. Waste sawdust from area mills heats homes in the community, which are arranged, along with public buildings, in a pattern that emphasize the connectedness of community members, defying modern suburban designs. At the launch of the community's medical clinic, Chief Abel Bossum celebrated the integration of traditional and Western concepts within the community. He asked his listeners to look at the village as a healing centre. "Now we are no longer the 'forgotten Crees.' We are no longer the passive victims of industrial forces, no longer the pathetic, oppressed people seeking the sympathy of others. Instead we have become daring innovators and self-confident planners."[1]

Canada's First Nations have a strong sense of their own identity and the ways in which contact with Europeans partially eroded that sense of identity over several centuries. This chapter outlines their rich history in the period before Europeans arrived in the Americas. By looking at Native societies in the pre-contact period, we can see how they have evolved over thousands of years in a North American environment and understand why history is so important in defining Native identities.

WRITING NATIVE HISTORY

Before the 1960s, Canadian history texts generally began with the "discovery" of the "New World" by European explorers. Arguing that the discipline of history was restricted to archival sources and therefore to literate peoples, historians relegated the study of pre-contact Aboriginal societies to anthropologists and archeologists. Fortunately, such rigid boundaries among disciplines have now begun to break down. "Ethnohistorians," whose background may be in one

of many fields, study First Nations societies by piecing together evidence from European observations, anthropological studies, archeological evidence, and relevant data provided by meteorologists, biologists, and other scientists. In short, ethnohistorians consider all the evidence possible to recreate the lives of the earliest inhabitants of what was to become Canada.

The rich sources consulted by ethnohistorians often pose problems. The oral tradition of the Native peoples, accounts of early fur traders, priests, travellers, and other Europeans, and archeological evidence may each suggest different conclusions. Furthermore, for the hunting and gathering societies of pre-contact Canada—the groups dominating all regions except southern Ontario, the St Lawrence River valley, and the Pacific Coast at the time of European arrival—the archeological record is weak. Time and tides have eroded much of the evidence that could have unlocked the secrets of the past.

Each Aboriginal nation has its own version of its pre-contact history. The tradition of handing down the history orally from generation to generation was firmly established long before the Europeans arrived, and it has continued to thrive. But it is only relatively recently that professional historians have given much credence to oral history. Trained in the European tradition to analyze written documents, historians argued that oral history recreated the past with present-day interests in mind. As American historian James Axtell warns, "myth and history tend to merge." Views that are currently fashionable are easily projected back in time, making them appear to be eternal truths.[2]

Aboriginal historians and many non-Aboriginal scholars now reject the view that written materials are more reliable than oral memories. They note that the documents created by European fur traders, priests, and administrators describing Native societies reflect the

Buffalo Jump, by Alfred J. Miller. For Plains Natives, buffalo were the primary raw material of food, clothing, and almost everything else they used in daily life. First Nations developed a number of ways of killing these large animals, including herding them toward cliffs and then harvesting their carcasses once they had fallen to the ground.
Library Archives Canada/C-000403

Eurocentric biases of their writers. Maori historian Linda Tuhiwai Smith observes pointedly that historians who attempt to delegitimize the Native claims about their own past are far from objective. "Negation of Indigenous views of history was a critical part of asserting colonial ideology, partly because such views were regarded as clearly 'primitive' and 'incorrect' mostly because they challenged and resisted the mission of colonization."[3]

Oral traditions, like written documents, can be distorted by the scholars who record them. For example, until recently most people who studied Native societies were not only of European descent but were almost exclusively men. Women's roles in economic activities, religion, and warfare were given short shrift by male researchers who concentrated on interviews with men in the societies they studied. In recent years gender and ethnic biases in scholarly research have been identified and more women and Native peoples are involved in exploring First Nations history. Nevertheless, researchers must always bear in mind that their own values often play a major role in how they interpret both oral and written historical evidence.

FIRST NATIONS BEFORE 1500

Estimates of the Native population of the Americas at the time of continuous European contact around 1500 have varied greatly, from 30 million to over 100 million. Since most Aboriginal peoples lived in areas of the Americas with warm climates, the territory now called Canada was sparsely settled—scholars estimate a population of between 500 000 (half a million) and two million people. The smaller figure is based on the observations of early European writers, and the larger on estimates (difficult to confirm) of the numbers of indigenous people who might have succumbed to European diseases before direct contact with the invaders. With the 500 000 figure in mind, the distribution of population is estimated to have been 150 000 to 200 000 on the Pacific Coast, 50 000 to 100 000 in the Western Interior, 100 000 to 150 000 in the Great Lakes-St Lawrence Lowlands, and about 30 000 in the Atlantic region.[4]

Although the origins of the First Nations of the Americas are debated, scholars generally argue that they are of Asiatic origin and arrived in the Americas in various waves of migration from 30 000 to 10 000 years ago. The route these pioneers followed was probably across the land bridges that connected Siberia to Alaska during the ice ages. Native peoples themselves often reject the notion that they are descended from people who originated on other continents. Each Native group has a creation myth that explains the origins of the world and its creatures, and these stories have in common the view that life began on the North American continent. As a Mi'kmaq legend claims, they have "lived here since the world began."[5]

At least 50 distinct cultures encompassing 12 language groupings have been identified among Canada's first peoples. The phrase "language grouping" refers to languages with a common origin, not necessarily mutually understandable languages. The Iroquoian-speaking Huron of southern Ontario and the Five Nations Iroquois of New York, for example, spoke languages as different as the Romance languages of French and Portuguese are from one another.

In the sixteenth century, the First Nations lived in societies ranging from the scrupulously egalitarian model of the Athapaskan tribes of the subarctic to the slave-owning, highly stratified societies on the West Coast. Contact with the Europeans would bring dramatic and often unwanted changes to Aboriginal lifestyles, but change and adaptation had always been a feature of their lives. For instance, when the last ice age receded about 10 000 years ago in southern Ontario and northern New York State, the region's only residents appear to have been a few Aboriginal groups hunting caribou. About 6000 years ago, the region's climate had grown warmer, boreal forest had replaced tundra, and deer had supplanted caribou. People began catching fish in nets and weirs (open-work fences) and using milling stones and mortars to grind nuts, berries, and roots. As the food supply became more varied and reliable, the region's population expanded significantly, and trade with other nations brought in copper from Lake Superior and marine shells from the Atlantic coast.

Farming was introduced in the region about 1500 years ago and life became more sedentary than in earlier periods when the search for game forced frequent relocation. When the Europeans made contact with

MORE TO THE STORY

Diverging Views of Oral Traditions

Not surprisingly, Native oral historians and many Euro-Canadian scholars have differing views of the objectivity of Native interpretations of the pre-contact past. Annie Ned, a Yukon elder in her nineties, cooperated with anthropologist Julie Cruikshank to record the history of her people. She told Cruikshank: "I'm going to put it down who we are. This is our Shagoon—our history. You don't put it down yourself, one story. You don't put it yourself and then tell a little more. You put what they tell you, older people. You've got to tell it right. Not you are telling it: it's the person who told you that's telling that story."[6]

While Annie Ned believes that oral histories conserve stories intact from generation to generation, anthropologist Bruce Trigger is largely dismissive of their significance, at least for the study of the Iroquoians. He writes: "Oral traditions do not provide an independent means for studying the history of Iroquoian-speaking peoples. It is of interest when oral traditions confirm other sources of information about the past, but, except when they do, they should not be used even to supple-

ment such sources."[7] Few Native people would agree with Trigger, and many would question the notion that European sources are an "independent means" for the study of Native history.

The question of whether oral history traditions are as valid as the written record is far from simply an academic issue. By the late twentieth century, courts were forced to deal with the competing claims of First Nations oral traditions and the written records of European officials. In 1991, a British Columbia Supreme Court judge issued a verdict in the *Delgamuukw* case that rejected the claims of the Gitskan-Wet'suwet'en Nation to Aboriginal rights to their land. In his decision, he indicated that he discounted the extensive oral history that the Gitskan claimants had included as part of their testimony. For this judge, written historical records were superior to oral history in the eyes of the law. Fortunately for the Gitskan-Wet'suwet'en, the Supreme Court of Canada disagreed and, in 1997, ruled that oral testimony was admissible in efforts by First Nations to establish their rights in court.

---

the Iroquoian-speaking peoples in the late sixteenth century, they encountered palisaded settlements of 1500 to 2000 people. By that time, confederacies of various nations had been formed in an attempt to bring peace to a region that had long been plagued with warfare. Well-crafted pottery suggests that the people had the wealth and leisure time to indulge in pursuits beyond mere survival.

Even in areas where hunting and gathering remained the primary means of obtaining food, dramatic changes had occurred. During an estimated 12 000 years of human habitation on the Prairies, for example, the successive inventions of the spear thrower, the bow and arrow, the buffalo jump, and the buffalo pound increased the time available for spiritual and leisure activities. The spear thrower allowed the hunter to aim more accurately and throw with more force than with the unaided hand; the buffalo pound was a giant corral of brush and hides into which a herd was driven to be systematically killed.

Improved possibilities of subsistence on the Prairies drew newcomers into the region. Three thousand years ago, only Siouan speakers lived on the plains of North America, but by the time of European contact the Blackfoot, who were Algonkian speakers, had come to dominate a portion of the region. The Sioux also disappeared from the thickly forested woodlands and the parklands north and west of the Great Lakes, replaced by Algonkian groups, including the Ojibwa and the Cree, who migrated in search of the caribou. By 1600, the Ojibwa and Cree were the chief inhabitants of Northern Ontario, with the Sioux having been pushed southward and westward.

COMMON CULTURAL CHARACTERISTICS

While change and diversity characterized Native life in the pre-contact period, the various Aboriginal groups shared a number of features. In all Native societies,

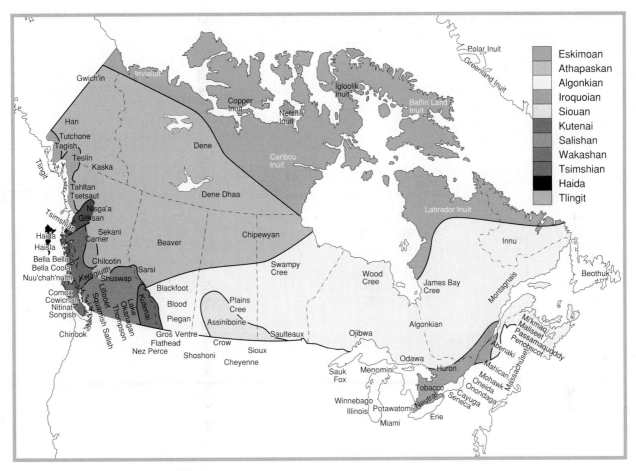

MAP 2.1 Natives at the time of first contact.
Adapted from *Olive Dickason, Canada's First Nations* (Toronto: McClelland and Stewart, 1992), 65

religion, as much as nature, regulated everyday life. Native religions are characterized by a belief in a divinity residing within all living creatures as well as within all natural objects. Because Native religion was all-encompassing, attempts to analyze pre-contact societies have been limited by an inability to comprehend the intricacies of spiritual practices.

First Nations peoples did not see themselves as masters of their environment; rather, they believed that their communion with the spirits was the secret to any successes they might have in staking out a living and achieving happiness. An outside observer might credit the Beaver people of today's northern Alberta with intricate knowledge of the whereabouts of animals and edible plants. The Beaver themselves believed that vision quests and dreams showed them the paths to these animals and plants, and that break-

ing faith with their traditional religious views and practices would result in the disappearance from their lands of their sources of food and other necessities.

A common feature of Native societies was their knowledge of the uses of a wide range of materials found in the natural world. Millennia of experimentation had unlocked an extensive botanical knowledge that was evident in the effective use of plants for medicinal purposes. A familiarity with the properties of various types of wood and other natural materials was displayed in the successful production of means of transportation (including canoes, snowshoes, and toboggans), homes of varying types, cooking utensils, and weapons.

The Aboriginal peoples' knowledge of their environment would prove crucial to the Europeans when they turned their attention to the profits available

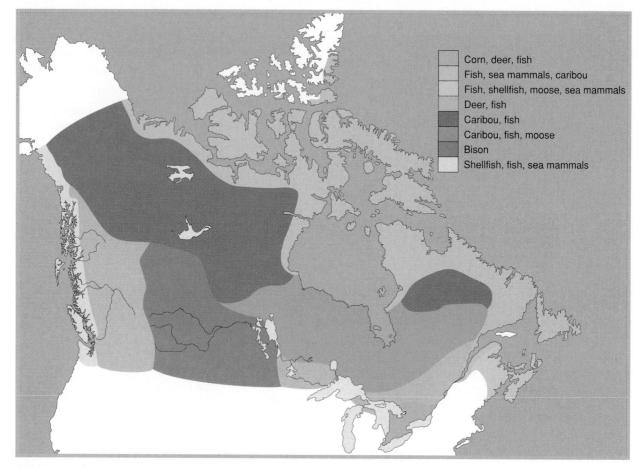

MAP 2.2 Native subsistence at the time of first contact with Europeans.
Adapted from *Historical Atlas of Canada*, vol. 1 (Toronto: University of Toronto Press, 1987), plate 18

Legend:
- Corn, deer, fish
- Fish, sea mammals, caribou
- Fish, shellfish, moose, sea mammals
- Deer, fish
- Caribou, fish
- Caribou, fish, moose
- Bison
- Shellfish, fish, sea mammals

from exploiting the resources of the Americas. Historian Olive Dickason writes:

> Basque whalers availed themselves of Inuit harpooning technology to improve greatly the efficiency of their own techniques; Mi'kmaq . . . sea hunters put their expertise at the service of Europeans to pursue walrus for ivory, hides, and train oil [oil from the blubber of marine animals], all much in demand by the latter; and later Amerindians did the same thing in the production of furs, so much sought after for the luxury trade, as status-conscious Europeans used furs (among other items) as symbols of rank. It has been estimated that by 1600 there may have been up to a thousand European ships a year engaged in commercial activities in Canada's northeastern coastal waters. Such activity would not have been possible without the co-operation and participation of the first nations of the land. When it came to penetrating the interior of the continent, Amerindians guided the way for the European "explorers," equipped them with the clothing and transportation facilities they needed, and provided them with food.[8]

The Native willingness to trade with the Europeans reflected the already established lines of trade among themselves. In the North, First Nations with a local resource not found elsewhere traded for other resources or for manufactured products. Copper, iron, flint, the ivory of walrus, bird feathers, and birchbark canoes all figured in the region's trade. Algonkian hunters in the woodlands traded furs for corn and tobacco grown by Iroquoian-speaking peoples in the Great Lakes region and by the Mandans of the southern plains. Natives on the Prairies journeyed to the summer trade fairs on the Missouri where they could buy handicrafts and dried corn. The first peoples of the Pacific Coast traded products of the sea with inland residents who could supply them with dried meat of caribou and mountain goats, moose hides, and goat-wool blankets.

Excavations at Coteau-du-Lac, near the southern point of the present Ontario-Quebec border, indicate that the earliest inhabitants of the upper St Lawrence engaged in extensive trade to meet their needs. Among the materials found there are projectile points originating in northern Labrador, conch shells from the Gulf of Mexico, and copper from the upper Lake Superior region that was heated and moulded to make tools. Extensive trade routes developed, and when Europeans arrived, Native people introduced them to, and often guided them along, the established water routes, forest paths, and prairie trails. The Europeans would find that many Natives involved in trade had learned the languages of their trade partners and could serve as interpreters between Europeans and a variety of Native groups.

Trade was the peaceful side of relations among Native groups, but warfare between neighbours apparently also occurred in every region. Although some battles had economic causes or were motivated by cycles of revenge, the major motives for warfare were bound up with Native rituals. Warrior males trained and prayed for opportunities to prove their battleworthiness. Others, particularly women and elders, might attempt to restrain warfare, but it was rarely eliminated for extended periods. The limited technology of warfare and the ritualistic motivations for battles reduced the chances of all-out warfare that many European areas experienced in the fifteenth and sixteenth centuries. As in Europe, torture or enslavement of captives was common, but sometimes captives were absorbed into the culture of their captors. Iroquoians, for example, occasionally launched "mourning wars," whose specific purpose was to capture members of other groups who could replace young people who had died prematurely. The captives were treated as if they were members of the victorious nation even though they might have no blood links with their captors.

Aboriginal peoples also seemed to share a relatively relaxed attitude toward sexual and childrearing practices. According to the early European commentators, premarital sex was widely practised in Aboriginal society. Europeans were less shocked by such behaviour, which also occurred in their own societies, than by the fact that Natives expressed their feelings about sex openly and apparently experienced no guilt. European critics believed that divorce in Aboriginal societies was an all-too-easy matter for couples who failed to get along with each other. Europeans also criticized the Native peoples' tolerant attitude toward children. The young were subject to little of the discipline, physical punishment, and exploitation that were typically the lot of children in Europe.

Unlike Europeans, who ruthlessly proscribed erotic encounters between members of the same gender, First Nations people tolerated homosexual relationships. The term *berdache*, the French word for male prostitute, was used by Europeans to describe Aboriginal people who cross-dressed, worked among members of the other gender, and sought same-sex partners in their sexual relationships. Some Native cultures believed that cross-working and cross-dressing women and men actually belonged to a third gender that combined male and female characteristics; but in most cases gays and lesbians simply seem to have assumed the work roles and dress code of the other gender rather than incorporating the behavioural patterns of both men and women.

While the relative influence of men and women in social arrangements varied among Native societies, women generally held far more social power than European women could claim. Although each of the sexes had different economic roles, women generally produced and controlled the food resources of the tribe. Men gained status through their prowess as hunters and protectors of their tribe.

Some First Nations restricted women's role in religious activities. In particular, menstruating women were often forced to absent themselves from ceremonial events. Women may have welcomed this enforced seclusion. As explorer Samuel Hearne observed, among the Athapaskans, menstruation was used by women as justification for taking a holiday from their husbands. Established customs prevented husbands from protesting a woman leaving the tent for four or five days when she claimed to be menstruating, even if she made the argument several times a month.

Women had an important voice among the Athapaskans and other Native groups, but the more valued position of males was reflected in the fact that during times of famine, female infanticide was practised while male infanticide remained rare. Moreover, Athapaskan men could exchange or share wives without the women's consent. When European men arrived in North America, they tended to establish trading relations with First Nations men, thus often enhancing their status.

For all their similarity, First Nations peoples, like Europeans, developed different cultural practices. What follows is a brief overview of the First Nations of Canada at the time of European contact.

THE FIRST NATIONS OF THE ATLANTIC AND GULF REGION

In the fifteenth century, Algonkian-speaking cultures inhabited much of the northern half of the North American continent, including the Atlantic and Gulf region. The Mi'kmaq were the largest group in what is today Atlantic Canada. The region's Algonkian peoples also included the Beothuk in Newfoundland and the Maliseet of what is now southern New Brunswick.

In Newfoundland the harsh climate and rugged terrain limited the potential for population growth. The Beothuk, estimated to number only 1000 in the year 1500, depended heavily on the caribou for food and clothing, which they hunted during the herds' fall migrations. As for other Aboriginal peoples in the Atlantic region, marine resources, such as seals, seabirds, fish, and shellfish, were critical for survival. The Beothuk could travel long distances in distinctive, lightweight birchbark canoes and lived in easily assembled wigwams covered with hides or birchbark. Because they painted themselves with red ochre and were among the first Aboriginal peoples encountered by Europeans, the Beothuk may have inspired the misnomer "Red Indian."

The Mi'kmaq were relatively affluent, living in one of Canada's more favoured geographical areas. Population estimates vary widely, from 3500 to 35 000 before 1500. Whatever archeologists may conclude about their origins, the Mi'kmaq believed themselves to have been placed on the Earth by the supreme deity,

the Great Spirit. A lesser deity, Glooscap, created the natural features of the land during his stay on Earth, and before he departed for the heavens he instructed the Mi'kmaq on how to make tools and weapons. He also foretold the coming of the Europeans.

The Mi'kmaq occupied a territory stretching from the Gaspé Peninsula to Cape Breton Island, taking in present-day Nova Scotia, Prince Edward Island, and northern New Brunswick. Unlike their southern neighbours, they did not establish permanent coastal settlements but migrated to accommodate their seasonal round. Their conical wigwams, dress, and diet were much the same at the time of European contact as archeology suggests they had been 1500 years earlier. Such continuity testifies to a culture extraordinarily well adjusted to its natural surroundings, as well as a relatively stable environment capable of regenerating its resources.

The lives of the Mi'kmaq were governed by the seasons. Each year, when spring approached they set up camp near bays and river mouths and began setting up or repairing their fish weirs in anticipation of the runs of smelt, herring, salmon, and sturgeon. Spring also meant the return of migratory birds in great numbers. Along with the year-round resident ducks and gulls, migratory birds, and their eggs and nestlings, provided an additional source of food. Shellfish, including scallops, clams, mussels, and oysters, added variety to the Mi'kmaq diet. In summer, they hunted seals and walrus that basked on the sandy beaches. The Mi'kmaq also caught dolphins and small whales and fished with baited bonehooks for cod, sea trout, and halibut. As autumn approached they hunted large flocks of migratory birds, and in September they caught eels and dried them for winter use. When the first snow arrived it was time to move inland in search of moose and caribou as well as otter, muskrat, and bear. A severe winter was often the greatest threat to supplies of food resources.

The Mi'kmaq greatly impressed the first European observers, who described them as intelligent, self-reliant, and self-confident. Even missionaries, whose professional mandate was to reconstruct Aboriginal cultures in the image of their own, admitted that these people were peaceable, hospitable, and charitable, displaying little of the greed of European societies. The

Maliseet wigwams depicted in William Robert Herries (1818–45), *Indian Camp, New Brunswick,* **watercolour on paper.**
The Beaverbrook Art Gallery, Fredericton, NB, Canada

Mi'kmaq were relatively egalitarian and they exalted individual liberty. Affluent by the standards of the time, their wealth was evident in the intricate quillwork that adorned their clothing and utensils.

Perhaps because of their relative well-being, the Mi'kmaq may have produced formal governmental structures that went beyond the level of the band— that is, the face-to-face group of people who worked together to guarantee subsistence. Their structures may even have extended beyond the level of the tribe—the collection of bands in a given area—to include the entire Mi'kmaq people. Although the Mi'kmaq practice of choosing a grand chief to preside over all the tribes and seven district chiefs may have developed after European contact, it probably reflected pre-contact relations. The local chiefs were assisted by councils of male elders. Consent rather than coercion kept Mi'kmaq government in place without a state apparatus of courts or police.

The Maliseet, who lived in the southern region of modern-day New Brunswick, had a somewhat different subsistence cycle from that of the Mi'kmaq. At the time of European contact, they had just begun to cultivate corn and pumpkins. Evidence is mounting that they built substantial houses near the seacoast and lived there the year round. Their oval, semi-subterranean "pit houses" were conical structures framed with poles, covered with bark and hides, and held in place by stones at the base. In these small buildings, families worked, ate, and slept.

THE CANADIAN SHIELD FIRST NATIONS

Algonkian peoples also inhabited much of the Canadian Shield, which was, on the whole, less accommodating than the Maritime region to human habitation. In 1500, the nations of the Shield included the Innu (renamed Montagnais and Naskapi by the Europeans), the Ojibwa, the Cree, the Nipissing, and the Algonquin. Most Algonkian peoples lived in dispersed groups of fewer than 400 people who survived by cooperative endeavour. While bands in the region were generally self-governing, most had organized contact with other groups whose culture they shared and with whom they intermarried. Informal alliance systems existed for purposes of warfare. Although these groupings could not create a formal nation in the

European or even Mi'kmaq sense, in modern times many of them have used the term "nation" to describe the bonds that link their members.

The Innu, whose home is in northern Quebec and southern Labrador, hunted caribou and made their tents from caribou skin. The Innu lived lives of rough equality. According to anthropologist Eleanor Leacock, the Innu of southern Labrador made decisions by the consensus of those affected by the decision, and men and women worked closely together to ensure survival. Leacock writes:

> All adults participated in the procuring of food and manufacture of equipment necessary for life in the north. In general, women worked leather and bark, while men worked wood, with each making the tools they needed. For instance, women cut strips of leather and wove them into the snowshoe frames that were made by men, and women covered with birch bark the canoe frames the men made. Women skinned game animals and cured the hides for clothing, moccasins and lodge coverings. Everyone joined in putting up lodges; the women went into the forest to chop down lodge poles, while men cleared the snow from the ground where a lodge was to be erected.[9]

While small groups of Innu men hunted big game away from the local camp, women, responsible for childrearing, hunted small game closer to home. They prepared dried sturgeon mixed with fish oil to provide a high-protein winter food that could be stored for months. Everyone worked together to drive migratory caribou into compounds where they could be speared. Women as well as men became shamans, intermediaries between the people and the spirit world.

In a society without formal laws and systems of punishment, consensus was essential to prevent disunity. Ridicule, rather than corporal punishment, served to sway wayward souls from acting against collective decisions. Although each Innu band of several hundred people had ties with other Innu bands, decisions were usually made at the local rather than the tribal level. Cooperation between bands was also common. A band whose territory became temporarily short of game could hunt within the territory of another Innu band or receive food from that band.

The Ojibwa controlled the northern shores of Lake Huron and Lake Superior from Georgian Bay to the edge of the Prairies. Each Ojibwa band lived in a village of dome-shaped, birchbark wigwams that served as their permanent homes. In times of warfare and during the winter hunt, Ojibwa men left their village; the women remained in the village except when they attended clan feasts or were married to a resident of another village.

Goods and work were shared within bands. Tasks were sex-segregated, and all chiefs and most shamans were male. Men were warriors and hunters of big game such as caribou, elk, and deer, as well as fishers and makers of snares, bows, and arrows. They also built the wigwams. Women hunted small game, gathered wild rice and berries, skinned the animals, prepared all the food, made the clothing, blankets, and cooking vessels, kept the wigwams in good repair, and took all responsibility for children. Before European firearms were available, the Ojibwa hunted animals with snares made of wild hemp, by placing sharp spikes on their path, by using dogs to drive them into water, or by bow and arrow. The bows were made from ironwood or red cedar, the arrows from bone and shell.

Religious beliefs were central to Ojibwa culture. Like many First Nations, the Ojibwa believed that spirits were reflected in all natural phenomena and that each person could enlist the aid of guardian spirits to deal with the natural world and other humans. Among the most feared in the human world were sorcerers who might avenge wrongs by driving the soul from the body or enticing game away from a favourite hunting area. Shamans acted as intermediaries between individuals and the spirits, prescribing herbs that could heal injuries or cure illnesses and indicating the items a hunter should carry in a medicine bag to enjoy success during the hunt.

In their relations with the spirit world, most men did not depend solely on the shamans. They also undertook fasts, which were intended to induce visions, and they served as the audience outside "shaking lodges," small barrel-shaped structures where a diviner would sing and drum to attract spirits. Once these spirits arrived, their presence would cause the lodge to shake and the audience would ask them about the location of game or the fate of relatives. Participants might also entreat the spirits for cures to illnesses.

The Midewiwin, or Grand Medicine Society, played a key role in maintaining and developing the Ojibwa traditional medical-spiritual practices (the two were usually believed to be related). Years of instruction were required before its members reached the highest of its four grades of membership. The annual feast of this society brought together various bands and served as both a social and religious event.

The bands also joined forces on a temporary basis for purposes of warfare. When a band chief wanted to make war against the Sioux, he would send an envoy with pipe and tobacco to invite other bands to participate. Warfare was never within the tribe; it occurred only between the Ojibwa and other nations and was designed to establish control over a particular hunting territory. It also provided the warriors with the opportunity to demonstrate their prowess and was accompanied by a great deal of ritual. Because of the limits imposed by the bow and arrow, the major weapon of the pre-contact period, and the relative equality of the contending groups in battle, few casualties resulted from any encounter.

While the Ojibwa bands hunted separately from one another, intermarriage between them was common, and clans held annual feasts that linked the bands. The feasts were an integral part of the entertainment of the Ojibwa, who also played a variety of ball games, including the forerunner of today's lacrosse and a game called "maiden's ball play," a rough game that was played only by women. Jumping, foot racing, tossing, and gambling were other diversions for a people whose spirituality was never puritanical. Young women were free to engage in premarital sex, but women had no sexual freedom after they married and had little say in the selection of a marriage partner. Rules about marriage, like rules generally, were imposed informally.

North and west of the woodlands Ojibwa lived another Algonkian-speaking nation, the Cree. Almost as populous as the Ojibwa, the Cree had gradually migrated westward, and some of their bands lived west of Lake Winnipeg by the early sixteenth century. Pre-contact populations have been confirmed in the parklands of the Saskatchewan River and the woodlands of Alberta.

MORE TO THE STORY

Native Accounts of Creation

Each Aboriginal Nation has a narrative of how the world began. For the Five Nations Iroquois, the vast land area they lived on was an island on the back of a turtle. Long ago, according to one account, beings similar to humans lived in longhouses in the sky. In the centre of their principal village stood the celestial tree blossoming with lights, the symbols of peace and knowledge. One day a curious woman asked her husband to uproot this tree so she could discover the source of its power. As she bent forward to look into the hole where the tree had once been, she tumbled to a lower world. From the light that now shone through the hole into this lower world, the animals saw her plight. The Canada goose flew down to rescue her and then placed her on the back of the turtle. In this way Great Turtle Island, or North America, came into existence.

Yet another story of the origins of the planet and its creatures is the Cree-Ojibwa tale that suggests the earth had once been destroyed and was recreated by a culture hero named Weesakayjac. The story has some similarities with the biblical story of the flood and Noah's ark. It begins when Weesakayjac carries out a revenge killing of the leader of the powerful underwater cats:

> The remaining underwater cats were very angry when they saw this. They sunk the whole earth. The cats told Weesakayjac they would drown the whole earth and that Weesakayjac would drown too. After this warning, Weesakayjac built a big boat. Then he gathered all the animals. Then the rains came. It rained so much the earth was not visible any more. When the rains finally stopped, Weesakayjac called the water animals together. From the big boat, he wanted one of them to swim to the bottom, to reach the earth.[10]

First the otter, followed by the beaver and the muskrat, make the effort. Finally, the explorations of the wolverine determine that it is safe for the animals to leave the boat. "That's how Weesakayjac made the earth again."[11]

Cree woman fashioning pottery vessels from clay. Many of the items that women made in pre-contact times were displaced by European manufactures in the era of the fur trade.
Courtesy of Manitoba Culture, Heritage and Tourism, Historic Resources Branch

food in a given year, that band would have a right to hunt in the territory of a band that had enjoyed a surplus. Among the Cree, a band that was starving received assistance from a band that was prospering. Large annual Cree tribal gatherings in the summer cemented the bonds that made sharing in times of famine possible. Again, it was the seasons that dictated social arrangements. In the winter, when travel was difficult, it made sense for groups to disperse over the territory of the nation, placing no more people in an area than the wildlife could support. In summer, when travel was easier, gatherings in central locations were feasible.

Like Cree social organization, Cree religious beliefs and rituals diverged from those of their Ojibwa counterparts in many ways. Nonetheless, the two groups shared a belief in the importance of dreams and vision fasts as means of communicating with the spirit world. Both also venerated the dead. The Cree buried their dead in the ground with great lamentation and held annual feasts in honour of the departed.

THE INTERIOR PLAINS FIRST NATIONS

In the pre-contact period, a variety of Aboriginal peoples occupied the territories of the Interior Plains region of North America. Only Siouan-speaking groups lived in the area of present-day Prairie Canada 1000 years ago, but by the time of European contact in the eighteenth century, the Blackfoot, an Algonkian people, had achieved dominance on the northern plains of today's Saskatchewan and Alberta. Siouan groups remained in control of the plains of what is now Manitoba, with the Assiniboine, who probably migrated to the area around 1600, constituting the largest group. The cultures of the Plains peoples of North America varied, but they also had similarities because of a common dependence on the buffalo.

The Blackfoot were an Algonkian nation whose long separation from their eastern counterparts had produced a variant of Algonkian language that could not be understood by other Algonkian speakers. Estimated at about 9000 in the early eighteenth cen-

Because their territory was not as abundant in game as the Ojibwa's, the Cree were more nomadic than their Algonkian neighbours and their bands were smaller. Tipis made of caribou or moose hides, assembled and disassembled by the Cree women, provided them with shelter as they followed the caribou, moose, beaver, and bear. Their sturdy birchbark canoes provided transportation for whole families and their belongings.

The Cree and Ojibwa had no concept of land ownership. Rather, they believed that a particular group had the right to establish primacy in a particular area, giving it the first right to hunt and gather food there each season. It was also understood that if the area hunted by a band did not provide enough

Dreams and Cree Culture

A Plains Cree elder presented a testimony in the 1930s regarding the power of dreams for his people. His emphasis is on the experience of men, but women were equally guided in their lives by the interpretation of dreams.

> The spirit powers may come to you when you are sleeping in your own tipi when you are young. If you want to be still more powerful then you go and fast. The ordinary dreams you have while sleeping are called pawamuwin. They are not worth anything although sometimes you dream of things that are going to happen.

> You can tell a power dream in this way. You are invited into a painted tipi where there is only one man. The crier, who is the Raven Spirit, calls, and many come. I myself knew right away that they were spirit powers. I sat and thought to myself, "That is Horse, that is Buffalo spirit." The one that invited me said, "That's right."

> I was called many times and they always told me the same thing—that I must do more fasting. Each time they invite me to a different painted tipi. Often after I wake up I wonder why they didn't tell me anything. I had nothing to do with girls when I tried to dream.

> Finally, they told me that this would be the last time. They want me to go and fast for eight days. One of them said, "Try hard to finish these eight days, for that will be all." I

> gathered as many offerings as I could. It was during the moon just past [July] and there was plenty of food in camp so I knew the people wouldn't move for a while.

> I promised to stand and face the sun all day and to turn with the sun. Only after sunset would I sit down. I had heard that this was the hardest thing to do and that is why I resolved to do it out of my own mind. I thought that I could help myself a little that way. [By making himself suffer more, he would secure greater blessings.] The sun wasn't very high when I got tired. I suffered all day. I tried all kinds of ways to stand, but I was played out. I raised my hands and cried; I could hardly finish. The sun went down and I just fell over. That was the first day.

> The next morning I got very thirsty. I was not hungry but was thirsty all the time. On the fourth night my brother came with horses to get me. I told him I would stay. He came again on the sixth night but I said I would remain for two more nights. He said, "From the way you look, I may not find you alive."

> All kinds of different spirit powers came to see me every night. Each one who invited me gave me power and songs. Then one gave me the power to make the Sun dance. That is how I got power and how I know many songs. Pretty nearly every night now I sing some of those songs.[12]

tury, the Blackfoot peoples included three tribal groups: Blackfoot, Peigan, and Blood. Before the Europeans arrived, they had begun migrating southward into former Siouan territory, and even before they met Europeans they had used guns and horses acquired by trade with the Cree to gain more Sioux territory by force. The Blackfoot tribes first encountered by the Europeans hunted the plentiful buffalo of the Plains and maintained control over their territory by creating a relatively unified armed force under centralized control. They used warfare to expand their tribal hunting grounds and to capture women who could then be adopted by the tribe to ensure its further population expansion.

Most Blackfoot men belonged to military societies involving several grades of membership according to experience and achievement. The Blackfoot tribes conferred authority upon male chiefs for purposes both of warfare and the hunt. As buffalo hunters, the Blackfoot lived a nomadic existence, following the herds and pitching tipis made of buffalo skin. A late-nineteenth-century missionary, John McDougall, aptly summed up the role of the buffalo in Blackfoot life:

> Without buffalo they would be helpless, and yet the whole nation did not own one. To look at them and to hear them, one would feel as if they were the most independent of all men; yet the fact was they were the most dependent among men. Moccasins, mittens, leggings, shirts and robes—all

buffalo. With the sinews of the buffalo they stitched and sewed these. Their lariats, bridles, lines, stirrup-straps and saddles were manufactured out of buffalo hide. . . . Women made scrapers out of the legbone for fleshing hides. The men fashioned knife handles out of the bones, and the children made toboggans out of the same. The horns served for spoons and powder flasks. In short, they lived and had their physical being in the buffalo.[13]

Worshippers of sun and thunder, the Blackfoot attached special importance to Sun Dance bundles, which, along with medicine bundles, were kept in rawhide bags. They believed that each object in the bag played a role in ensuring good fortune. The transfer of a bundle from one person to another involved an intricate ceremony lasting several weeks as the new owner was exposed slowly to the significance of each item in the bundle and to the visions and songs that justified the object's inclusion.

The deceptively named Sun Dance was an elaborate set of religious ceremonies lasting several days and involving an entire nation. Presided over by a holy woman at a site chosen by a warrior society, it was organized by the extended family of a woman who had publicly promised the Sun Spirit to sponsor the event should the Spirit spare a male relative whose life was in danger. The tribe built a lodge where its various military and secret societies performed dances and rituals in exact sequence. While the Sun Dance was practised before the Blackfoot had direct contact with Europeans, it appears that it did not predate the arrival of the horse, which made hunting easier and left more time for leisure. It is perhaps best viewed as an elaboration of older Blackfoot traditions rather than as a tradition fully in place before the European arrival.

Blackfoot society was less egalitarian than that of the Ojibwa or Cree. Chiefs and male shamans had several spouses and larger tipis than other tribal members since the ceremonial functions performed by these men were thought to require more space and people in the household. Because of male casualties in warfare and the adoption of female captives into the Blackfoot culture, women always outnumbered men. While there were some female shamans, they had no privi-

The Blackfoot holy woman wore this elkskin robe during the Sun Dance. The designs signify the intermediaries responsible for the passage of the spirit world blessings to humans.
Provincial Archives of Manitoba/Edmund Morris 498 (N 15353) c. 1907

leges. First or second wives had higher status than later wives. In the post-contact period, as some leaders acquired many wives, the number of low-status women increased dramatically.

THE GREAT LAKES–ST LAWRENCE LOWLANDS FIRST NATIONS

Although most Aboriginal societies were organized around hunting, gathering, and fishing, the mainly Iroquoian-speaking tribes concentrated in southern Ontario and the St Lawrence valley grew corn, beans, and squash. These nations took advantage of moderate climate and good soils, and were less dependent than other groups on an abundance of game or fish to guard against famine. The sedentary lifestyle encouraged population growth, with the result that the Iroquoian nations—including the St Lawrence Iroquoians, the Huron (in the Lake Simcoe-Georgian Bay area), and the Huron's neighbours, the Petun and the Neutral—together accounted for perhaps 50 000 people in 1500.

Here, too, the seasons governed people's lives. Among the Stadaconans, for example, whose summer home was on the island of Montreal, the women planted crops in the spring and then set off by canoe with their families for the Gulf of St Lawrence, where the men fished and hunted. Families returned home in time for the women to harvest the annual crop.

Interior of a Clallam Winter Lodge, **by Paul Kane.**
© National Gallery of Canada, Ottawa. Transfer from the Parliament of Canada, 1955.

The large palisaded villages and the loose political confederacies of some of the Iroquoian groups marked them off culturally from most hunter-gatherer societies. Another distinctive characteristic was the longhouse. Built of elm bark and attached to wooden frames, the longhouse was 6 metres wide and sometimes over 30 metres long, and within it about 40 members of an extended family lived and shared responsibilities. A village might contain 30 to 50 of these longhouses, each with a row of fires down the middle and bedrooms on both sides. Underground storage pits, usually about 1.25 metres deep and slightly less than 1 metre in diameter, held part of the harvest to protect it from fire and mice. In some villages, chiefs had larger longhouses to accommodate village and war council meetings.

Iroquoian societies were matrilineal (descent was traced through the mother's line) and matrilocal (a man lived with the family of his wife). While women dominated agricultural activities, the men were responsible for providing the smaller portion of the food supply that came from hunting. A minority of men were also involved in intertribal trade. By the sixteenth century, the Huron were extensively involved in barter with a variety of Algonkian groups. Corn,

corn meal, and fishnets were traded for animal skins and fish. Only a small number of families controlled the trade, but the wealth they earned from it was redistributed within the Huron confederacy.

While village or tribal councils involved all men over a certain age, important decisions required the approval of the women. For example, the men might decide to go to war with another tribe, but if the women, who controlled agriculture, refused to supply food for the warriors, there could be no war. Chiefs were men from certain family lines, but the women of the line chose the chief and could replace him if he failed to meet their expectations. Every Huron belonged to a clan, which offered special privileges. Any member of the clan could stay with fellow clan members when passing through a village and could depend upon them for help in a lean crop year.

Burial practices among the Huron were elaborate. About once a decade the remains of the dead were disinterred in the villages and placed in a common burial ground in a ceremony called the Feast of the Dead. This ceremony was believed to make it possible for the souls of the dead, until then interred with their remains, to travel westward to the land of souls. The Huron's land of souls was thought to be much the

Dekanawidah and Hiawatha

The lives of Dekanawidah and his associate Hiawatha illustrate the dynamism of pre-contact First Nations life. But efforts to piece together their life stories also illustrate the difficulties in writing biographies of individuals in pre-literate societies. What we know of Dekanawidah and Hiawatha comes from the stories passed on from storytellers of their own time to later generations of Iroquois. The legends suggest they may have lived as early as the late fifteenth century or as late as a century afterward.

Although Dekanawidah (which means the Peacemaker) was born a Huron in today's southeastern Ontario, he lived his adult life among the Seneca in today's New York. Hiawatha, meanwhile, was born an Onondaga but lived with the Mohawk. We do not know the story of how either man ended up among a different Native group from the one of his birth. But we know they became leaders in their new homelands. These facts alone suggest societies that were in no way static.

Dekanawidah was disturbed by the extent of in-fighting that had developed among Iroquoian-speaking peoples, and concerned that their disunity might entice other First Nations to invade their territories. In his travels, he met Hiawatha, who shared his concerns. The two visited all the Iroquoian groups on the south shores of Lake Erie and Lake Ontario, and possibly along the St Lawrence. They organized a congress of all of these groups. Then, according to tradition, Dekanawidah proposed an elaborate constitution with 117 sometimes quite lengthy clauses dealing with questions of relations among Iroquois peoples and between these peoples and other First Nations. Five groups—the Mohawk, Onondaga, Oneida, Seneca, and Cayuga—smoked the peace pipe to symbolize their acceptance of this constitution.

The constitution, like the legend of Dekanawidah, was preserved orally. It began: "I am Dekanawidah [the Peacemaker] and with the Five Nations' Confederate Lords I plant the tree of the Great Peace."[14] Its many clauses demonstrated an effort to create unity among the Five Nations but at the same time to assure that representatives of the five nations in the Confederacy Council truly spoke for the women and men of these nations. The constitution not only codified elaborate rituals for decision making but also guaranteed each of the nations its religious rights, confirmed women's ownership of the land and soil, and ensured that traditional rights of clans would not be violated. Rules for adoption of individuals and nations into the Five Nations demonstrated that this was not a closed society.

The Iroquois constitution was detailed and sophisticated. It had an influence on the men who drafted the American constitution, particularly Benjamin Franklin.

same as their earthly home—an indication, perhaps, of their positive view of life in their own lands.

The confederacies of Great Turtle Island appear to have been a response to a growing cycle of violence in Iroquoian societies, resulting from blood feuds. The Five Nations Confederacy was the earliest. According to Iroquois legend, it owed its origins to the efforts of Dekanawidah—the "Heavenly Messenger" or "Peacemaker," a Five Nations chief—and his associate, Hiawatha. It proved to be the most effective and enduring of the Iroquoian confederacies, if only because the Five Nations were surrounded by enemies and their members therefore had more incentive to make it work. The Huron and Neutral confederacies, recent phenomena in the period of first contact with the Europeans, did not develop the cohesion evident in the Five Nations Confederacy.

In the confederacies, men chosen by the women of the villages made decisions on war and peace and tried to settle disputes between villages or clans. They were not always effective. Unanimity was required before a decision could be approved, and even then a tribal council that disagreed with a confederacy-level decision could disavow it. The confederacy had no permanent officials, and its decisions required the consent of tribes to be put into effect. It was a loose system of government that made little sense to the recently arrived Europeans.

While individual freedom and collective sharing of tasks and goods characterized Iroquoian society, the increased warfare of the immediate pre-contact period revealed a different side of the society. Warfare appears to have been on the rise because the young warriors had become more militant in their demands to be allowed to demonstrate their prowess in battle. Prisoners were often tortured, and sometimes captured warriors were cooked and eaten in ceremonies suggesting that cannibalism, where it involved a captured warrior, had been given religious approval within the culture. Still, casualties in battles between Iroquoian groups were relatively light, and women and children taken as prisoners were generally adopted as equals rather than enslaved by the tribe that captured them.

THE WESTERN CORDILLERA FIRST NATIONS

The coastal societies of British Columbia stand apart from all other First Nations. Of the twelve language families that have been identified for pre-contact Canada, six are exclusive to British Columbia. With a combined population of perhaps 200 000 people in the eighteenth century, the coastal societies included the Tsimshian on the northern mainland, the Coast Salish on the southern mainland and Vancouver Island, the Southern Kwakiutl (or Kwakwaka'wakw) on the east coast of Vancouver Island, the Haida of the Queen Charlotte Islands, and the Nootka (or Nuu'chah'nulth) on Vancouver Island's west coast. These groups constituted the most affluent Native societies of pre-contact Canada, and their social structure is often attributed to this affluence.

Although different in many ways, all West Coast nations were chiefdoms characterized by social hierarchies that resembled the ordered patriarchal societies of Europe more than the relatively egalitarian Aboriginal societies of the rest of Canada. The chief, always a man, was regarded as a priest who owed his position of power and wealth to the gods. Generally holding his position by virtue of family descent and ruling between 100 and 500 people, the chief controlled the distribution of the resources of the community and took a larger proportion of the community's goods for his own use. Below the chief in the hierarchy were certain members of his family, members of

A Pacific Coast First Nations chief wearing a headdress and woolen trade blanket. A chief inherited the right to wear inherited symbols of his clan.
Library and Archives Canada C-074711

several other wealthy leading families, free men (that is, non-slaves) and their families, and finally slaves.

The potlatch, a feast during which individuals distributed portions of their property in the form of gifts, reduced disparities somewhat and emphasized the connection between all free men and women of the tribe. It demonstrated that property belonged to the community even if custom dictated that its use was not equally shared. Status was indicated by a family's generosity at potlatch time. Ironically, the accumulation of goods for this ceremony encouraged aggressive competition between potlatches, and the elaborate rituals governing gift giving ensured that the social system reproduced itself.

By redistributing wealth, potlatches legitimized the social structure and served diplomatic roles as well. Within a tribe, the potlatch ensured that no free person was reduced to poverty and obviated the need for formal policing mechanisms that might have been required if some members were forced to resort to thievery to survive. Among tribes, potlatches between chiefs allowed one chief to demonstrate his control over an area by granting lavish wealth derived from it. Thus, potlatches served as a diplomatic way to stake out territory and fend off potential rivals.

Slaves, usually women and children captured in wartime (adult male captives were killed), were almost universally excluded from the potlatches. Although slaves worked alongside free people, their slave status was a badge of shame. Generally, a tribe would pay a ransom to free tribal members enslaved by an enemy nation, but slaves captured in forays far from the tribal home of their captors might never be freed; their slave status passed to their children. The treatment of slaves varied. In some villages there was little distinction between the slaves and free people except at potlatch and marriage time. In other villages there was mistreatment of slaves, but the tendency was exaggerated by European observers, particularly missionaries, who were convinced that slaves were both eaten and used in ceremonial sacrifices. Native oral tradition rejects these claims and insists that cannibalism was taboo and only animal flesh was used in ceremonies.

A favourable geographical location and ingenious use of local resources created wealthy societies on the northwest coast of North America. Plants, almost exclusively gathered by women, and plentiful stocks of fish, particularly salmon and halibut, and shellfish provided the staples of the coastal diet. The coastal peoples built weirs to divert fish so they could be easily harpooned or netted. The men made harpoons of wood with barbs of bone or horn from local animals. While the men fished, the women prepared the catch, preserving large quantities by smoke-drying. The women cooked food in pit ovens that they dug in the ground.

Abundant timber allowed the Native peoples of the coast to build large homes for extended families. Among the Tsimshian, for example, homes made of massive timbers from red cedar measured 15 by 16.5 metres. A central pit, 9 by 1.5 metres, served as the main living space, where women cooked and everyone ate and relaxed. Recreation for coastal nations included wrestling, weightlifting, tug-of-war, foot races, and gambling.

The free women wove intricate baskets from red and yellow cedar and the flexible roots of the spruce. They also made textiles from mountain-goat wool, dog wool, and the down of ducks and other birds. Men and women learned different skills. While the women wove, the men worked in stone and wood. The woodwork was particularly impressive, consisting of elaborately decorated totem poles and masks, house façades, feast dishes, canoes, storage boxes, helmets, and even cradles and chamber pots.

Aboriginal societies of the West Coast had varying resources, religious beliefs, and marriage practices. While the Nuu'chah'nulth were whalers, the Haida lived off sea otters, sea lions, fur seals, and fish. The Haida and Tsimshian were matrilineal societies: the children inherited their line of descent, and thus their position in society, from their mothers. Women in these two societies generally enjoyed a higher status than women in the other coastal groups, which traced descent through the father's line. In all coastal societies, pubescent girls were secluded for lengthy periods, restricting their freedom during a stage of life when few restraints existed for males.

Coastal peoples worshipped gods of the forests, mountains, and beaches, but they also believed that sinister forces resided in nature—sea monsters, ferocious birds in caves, ogres in the forest, and thunderbirds on mountains that could swoop down on any prey. To fend off such monsters, a person had, among other things, to carry out periodic fasts, to avoid sexual relations, and to scrub the body with branches. Shamans, both men and women, were the intermediaries between the Natives and the spirit world. Long years of training taught them how to perform rituals that would cure diseases, which were believed to be the result of souls wandering or the intrusion of foreign objects into the body at the whim of malevolent spirits.

While the coastal societies had developed cultures vastly different from those east of the Rockies, the village-based societies of the plateau (that is, the southern interior of British Columbia and the mountain regions of southwestern Alberta) were generally characterized by looser, more democratic structures similar to the ones further east. First Nations such as the Interior Salish, which included the Shuswap, the Lillooet, and the Kutenai, organized their societies in ways that resembled Plains societies far more than coastal societies. Lacking the rich concentration of resources that coastal nations enjoyed, the interior peoples were more nomadic and more egalitarian. Yet the Interior Salish shared many of the coastal peoples' spiritual and cultural practices, including the potlatch.

Band-level chiefs in these societies rarely appropriated more of the product from the hunt or salmon fishing than other members of the tribe. Distinctions among families were uncommon, and slavery was not practised. Among both the Carrier and Sekani of east-central British Columbia, hunting grounds and fishing spots were commonly owned by the band.

The Carrier women enjoyed a status equal to that of men. Indeed, if recent field research can be accurately projected backward into the pre-contact period, elder women were regarded as greater repositories of wisdom than elder men. Women participated in key subsistence activities, including salmon fishing, snaring, trapping, and hunting. While most of the salmon fishing was done by men, it was the women who filleted, smoked, and stored the fish and made fish eggs into dried cakes that often were used as trade items.

subarctic were marked by cooperation in the tasks required for eking out a subsistence in a harsh terrain. A group that had experienced a bad year could count on aid if it moved to an area where a local surplus existed. Work was sex-segregated, as it was among the Algonkian groups, but again there is little to suggest that women's work was less valued than men's. While the men hunted big game, women trapped smaller animals and prepared clothing from moose hides and rabbit skins. Women also carted the band's goods as groups moved from place to place in winter. Both women and men could become shamans.

The Athapaskans believed that, at one time, animals such as the crow and the wolf spoke and behaved like humans. They therefore felt it necessary to know details of the past of these animals as well as of plants so they could understand their nature and how they must be treated. An elaborate mythology detailing this past was passed from generation to generation.

By the sixteenth century, the Thule people, ancestors of today's Inuit, enjoyed undisputed control of the tundra region beyond the tree line from Labrador to the Yukon. The Thule, nomadic but originally concentrated in the western Arctic, had gradually followed the caribou to spread their domain as far as the Atlantic. Speaking their own language, Inuktitut, they were alone among the First Nations of Canada to have claimed a home on

THE NORTH'S FIRST NATIONS

A variety of Aboriginal societies whose people spoke Athapaskan languages lived in the northern regions of today's four western provinces and in the Northwest Territories and Nunavut. Harvesting local resources of the subarctic, such as fish, small game, caribou, trees, and berries, the Athapaskans lived in self-sufficient groups of about 20 or 30 related people. Tribal organization did not exist, and even band-level organization was only temporary: a coming together of people to carry out a specific task.

The lives of members of the Athapaskan groups of the western

Inuit costume.
Library and Archives Canada/PA533606

two continents when the Europeans first arrived. Until political pressures in the nineteenth century forced them to choose to live either in Greenland or Canada, the Inuit moved freely between the Canadian Arctic and Greenland in search of whale, caribou, and seal.

The sealskin-covered kayaks and umiaks of the Inuit were their main sea transportation; dog sleds provided land transport. With the bow and arrow and the spear thrower they caught their prey and fended off the rare intruder who might dispute their control of the far North. Although they maintained their physical distance from the other Native groups in North America, the Inuit had religious beliefs and followed cultural practices that had much in common with those of other hunter-gatherer cultures such as the Athapaskans. Like these groups, the Inuit carved out their subsistence in a harsh environment. Their famous igloos, winter homes made of ice and snow, alternated as residences with summer houses that had frames made of whalebone and driftwood and roofs covered with baleen from whales and then sod.

Although the northern peoples lived in a less favourable environment than other Aboriginal peoples, they possessed rich cultures. They developed songs and dances to celebrate their subsistence activities, beating drums made of caribou skins with sticks to accompany the dancers. Gambling, football, archery, and club-throwing were among their leisure activities. They also made every effort to bring beauty into their lives. Author Keith J. Crowe notes:

> They tattooed their bodies and embroidered their clothing with beads of horn or soapstone, with the quills of goose and porcupine, with moosehair or strips of weasel skin. Some made toothmark patterns on birchbark containers. Some people painted their skin tents and shirts with paint made from red ochre or black graphite. Any possession, a wooden bowl, a horn dipper, or a knife, might be decorated in some way. Painting, carving, embroidery, tassels, fringes and beads, dyeing, and bleaching were all used.[15]

CONCLUSION

Throughout thousands of years, Aboriginal peoples not only adapted to various geographical environments but also carved out rich, dynamic lives and relationships. As part of this process, they defined their earthly existence by developing vibrant spiritual beliefs, which also changed over time. In the fifteenth century, when Europeans began to come regularly to the shores of the Americas, the resident nations entered relationships with people whose social values, religious beliefs, and cultural practices were at sharp variance with their own.

NOTES

1 Canada, Royal Commission on Aboriginal Peoples, *Report*, vol. 3 (Ottawa: Government of Canada, 1996), chapter 4, section 7.2.

2 James Axtell, *The Invasion Within: The Contest of Cultures in Colonial North America* (New York: Oxford University Press, 1985), 14–15.

3 Linda Tuhiwai Smith, *Decolonizing Mythologies: Research and Indigenous Peoples* (London: Zed Books, 1999), 29.

4 Arthur J. Ray, *I Have Lived Here Since the World Began: An Illustrated History of Canada's Native People* (Toronto: Lester/Key Porter, 1996), 21.

5 Ibid.

6 Julie Cruikshank, *Life Lived Like a Story* (Vancouver: UBC Press, 1992), 278.

7 Bruce G. Trigger, *The Children of Aataentsic: A History of the Huron People to 1660* (Montreal: McGill-Queen's University Press, 1987), 19–20.

8 Olive P. Dickason, *Canada's First Nations: A History of Founding Peoples from Earliest Times* (Toronto: Oxford University Press, 1997), xii.

9 Eleanor Leacock, "Women in Egalitarian Societies," in *Becoming Visible: Women in European History*, ed. Renate Bridenthal, Claudia Koonz, and Susan Stuard, 2nd ed. (Boston: Houghton Mifflin, 1987), 22–23.

10 James R. Stevens and Chief Thomas Fiddler, *Legends from the Forest* (Toronto: Penumbra Press, 1991), 22.

11 Ibid.

12 David G. Mandelbaum, *The Plains Cree: An Ethnographic, Historical and Comparative Study* (Regina: Canadian Plains Research Centre, 1979), 160–61.

13 John McDougall, *Saddle, Sled, and Snowshoe* (Toronto: William Biggs, 1896), 261–62.

14 Ronald Wright, *Stolen Continents: The "New World" Through Indian Eyes* (Toronto: Penguin, 1993), 120.

15 Keith J. Crowe, *A History of the Original Peoples of Northern Canada* (Montreal: McGill-Queen's University Press, 1991), 22.

RELATED READINGS IN THIS SERIES

From *Foundations: Readings in Pre-Confederation Canadian History*

"Constitution of the Iroquois Nations: The Great Binding Law, Gayanashagowa," 14–34.

From **Media Companion CD-ROM, Volume I**

Mide'wiwin Origin Narrative:
The Story of Crow

SELECTED READING

Sections of the following books grapple with general problems involved in studying the history of Native peoples: Arthur J. Ray, *I Have Lived Here Since the World Began: An Illustrated History of Canada's Native People* (Toronto: Lester/Key Porter, 1996); Olive P. Dickason, *Canada's First Nations: A History of Founding Peoples from Earliest Times* (Toronto: Oxford University Press, 1997) and *The Myth of the Savage and the Beginnings of French Colonialism in the Americas* (Edmonton: University of Alberta Press, 1984); J.R. Miller, *Skyscrapers Hide the Heavens: A History of Indian-White Relations in Canada* (Toronto: University of Toronto Press, 1994); Bruce Trigger et al., *The Cambridge History of the Native Peoples of the Americas* (Cambridge: Cambridge University Press, 1996); Bruce G. Trigger, *Natives and Newcomers: Canada's "Heroic Age" Reconsidered* (Montreal: McGill-Queen's University Press, 1985); James Axtell, *The Invasion Within: The Contest of Cultures in Colonial North America* (New York: Oxford University Press, 1985); Calvin Martin, ed., *The American Indian and the Problem of History* (New York: Oxford University Press, 1987); Cornelius Jaenen, *Friend and Foe: Aspects of French-Amerindian Cultural Contact in the Sixteenth and Seventeenth Centuries* (Toronto: McClelland and Stewart, 1976); Eleanor Leacock and Nancy Lurie, eds., *North American Indians in Historical Perspective* (New York: Random House, 1971); and Barry Gough and Laird Christie, eds., *New Dimensions in Ethnohistory* (Ottawa: Canadian Museum of Civilization, 1991).

The historical geography of Native settlement is outlined in R. Cole Harris, ed., *Historical Atlas of Canada*, vol. 1, *From the Beginning to 1800* (Toronto: University of Toronto Press, 1987). An accessible overview of the pre-contact period can be found in Robert McGhee, "Canada Y1K: The First Millennium," *The Beaver* (December 1999/January 2000): 8–17.

Broad coverage of Aboriginal societies in the eastern half of Canada is found in Bruce Trigger, *Handbook of North American Indians*, vol. 15, *The Northeast* (Washington: Smithsonian Institute, 1978), and A.G. Bailey, *The Conflict of European and Eastern Algonkian Cultures, 1504–1700* (Toronto: University of Toronto Press, 1969). On Atlantic Canada, see James A. Tuck, *Newfoundland and Labrador Prehistory* (Ottawa: National Museum, 1976) and *Maritime Provinces Prehistory* (Ottawa: National Museum, 1984); Harold E.L. Prins, *The Mi'kmaq: Resistance, Accommodation and Cultural Survival: Case Studies in Cultural Anthropology* (Fort Worth: Harcourt Brace, 1996). On the Beothuk see Ingeborg Marshall, *A History and Ethnography of the Beothuk* (Montreal: McGill-Queen's University Press, 1996).

The early history of what later became Quebec and Ontario can be found in two studies by J.V. Wright: *Quebec Prehistory* (Ottawa: National Museums of Canada, 1980) and *Ontario Prehistory: An Eleven Thousand Year Archaeological Outline* (Ottawa: National Museums of Canada, 1981). Among important works on the Huron are Bruce Trigger, *The Children of Aataentsic: A History of the Huron People to 1660* (Montreal: McGill-Queen's University Press, 1987) and Conrad Heidenreich, *Huronia: A History and Geography of the Huron Indians, 1600–1650* (Toronto: McClelland and Stewart, 1971).

On the Iroquois see Ronald Viau, *Enfants du néant et mangeurs d'âmes: Guerre, culture et société en Iroquoisie ancienne* (Montreal: Boréal, 1997) and by the same author, *Femmes de personne: Sexes, genres et pouvoirs en Iroquoisie ancienne* (Montreal: Boréal, 1997). On the Ojibwa, influential works include Charles A. Bishop, *The Northern Ojibwa and the Fur Trade* (Toronto: Holt, Rinehart and Winston, 1974), and Peter S. Schmalz, *The Ojibwa of Southern Ontario* (Toronto:

University of Toronto Press, 1991). The Cree tell their own story in Freda Ahenakew and H.C. Wolfart, eds., *Kohkominawak Otacimowiniwawa—Our Grandmothers' Lives, as Told in Their Own Words* (Saskatoon: Fifth House, 1992). Studies of Cree religious and cultural life include Harold Cardinal and Walter Hildebrandt, *Treaty Elders of Saskatchewan; Our Dream Is That Our Peoples Will One Day Be Clearly Recognized as Nations* (Calgary: University of Calgary Press, 2000); Jennifer Brown and Robert Brightman, eds., *The Orders of the Dreamed: George Nelson on Cree and Northern Ojibwa Religion and Myth* (Winnipeg: University of Manitoba Press, 1988); and David G. Mandelbaum, *The Plains Cree: An Ethnographic, Historical and Comparative Study* (Regina: Canadian Plains Research Centre, 1979). Blackfoot life is discussed in Oscar Lewis, *The Effects of White Contact upon Blackfoot Culture with Special Reference to the Role of the Fur Trade* (Seattle: American Ethnological Society, 1942), and Treaty 7 Elders and Tribal Council with Walter Hildebrandt, Sarah Carter, and Dorothy First Rider, *The True Spirit and Original Intent of Treaty 7* (Montreal and Kingston: McGill-Queen's University Press, 1996). See also Irene Spry, "The Great Transformation: The Disappearance of the Commons in Western Canada," in *Man and Nature on the Prairies*, ed. Richard Allan (Regina: Canadian Plains Research Centre, 1976): 21–45.

On the pre-contact history of Pacific Coast Natives, see Chief Earl Maquinna George, *"Living on the Edge": Nuu-Chah-Nulth History from an Ahousat Chief's Perspective* (Winlaw, BC: Sono Nis, 2003); Erna Gunther, *Indian Life on the Northwest Coast of North America, as Seen by the Early Explorers and Fur Traders during the Last Decades of the Eighteenth Century* (Chicago: University of Chicago Press, 1972); Helen Codere, *Fighting with Property: A Study of Kwakiutl Potlatching and Warfare, 1792–1930* (New York: American Ethnological Society Monograph, 1950); and the early chapters of Mary-Ellen Kelm, *Colonizing Bodies: Aboriginal Health and Healing in British Columbia, 1900–1950* (Vancouver: UBC Press, 1998).

An excellent overview of pre-contact Native life in northern Canada is provided in Keith J. Crowe, *A History of the Original Peoples of Northern Canada* (Montreal: McGill-Queen's University Press, 1991). Also useful are John Bennett and Susan Rowley, *Uqalurait: An Oral History of Nunavut* (Montreal: McGill-Queen's University Press, 2004); Renée Fossett, *In Order to Live Untroubled: Inuit of the Central Arctic, 1550 to 1940* (Winnipeg: University of Manitoba Press, 2001); Kerry Abel, *Drum Songs: Glimpses of Dene History* (Montreal: McGill-Queen's University Press, 1993); Kenneth Coates, *Canada's Colonies: A History of the Yukon and Northwest Territories* (Toronto: Lorimer, 1985) and *Land of the Midnight Sun: A History of the Yukon* (Edmonton: Hurtig, 1988). A highly readable examination of ancient northern peoples is Robert McGhee, *Ancient People of the Arctic* (Vancouver: UBC Press, 1996). An excellent oral history is Julie Cruikshank, *Life Lived Like a Story* (Vancouver: UBC Press, 1992).

On Native sexuality, see Gary Kinsman, *The Regulation of Desire: Homo and Hetero Sexualities*, 2nd ed. (Montreal: Black Rose Books, 1996), and Evelyn Blackwood, "Sexuality and Gender in Certain Native American Tribes: The Case of Cross-Gender Females," *Signs* 10, 1 (Autumn 1984): 27–42.

WEBLINKS

VARIOUS ABORIGINAL SITES
Mi'kmaq:
mrc.uccb.ns.ca
Beothuk:
www.mun.ca/rels/native
Ojibwa:
www.picriver.com
Blackfoot:
www.head-smashed-in.com
Haida:
www.civilization.ca/aborig/haida/haindexe.html
These sites offer cultural and historical information.

ROYAL COMMISSION ON ABORIGINAL PEOPLES
www.ainc-inac.gc.ca/ch/rcap/index_e.html
This government of Canada site allows access to the text of the RCAP.
www.ainc-inac.gc.ca/ch/rcap/sg/sg4_e.html#20
The 1996 Royal Commission on Aboriginal Peoples notes that "Rendering accurately the history of a cross-cultural relationship is not simple or straightforward," and includes a discussion of the "Conceptions of History" on this site.

CHAPTER 3

Second Peoples: The European Cultural Heritage

Timeline

1337–1453 Hundred Years' War between Britain and France

1348–49 Black Death

1444 Portugal begins African slave trade

1492 First voyage of Columbus to the Americas

1497 John Cabot "discovers" Newfoundland

1521 Hernando Cortés conquers Aztec Empire

1532–33 Francisco Pizarro conquers Inca Empire

1562–98 Religious warfare in France

1607 Virginia colony established

1612 Beginnings of Dutch settlement on Hudson River

1620 Puritan settlement in Massachusetts

In 1601, the government of Queen Elizabeth I legislated "An Acte for the Reliefe of the Poore." It required every parish in England to appoint "overseers of the poor" who would collect property taxes to provide the funds required to take care of the poor. The overseers had the task of separating out the "deserving poor" from "sturdy beggars" whom the state regarded as unemployed as a result of laziness. "Sturdy beggars" and their families were to be placed in spartan institutions called workhouses, where they would have to earn their daily bread by putting in many hours a day of hard labour. While some of the "deserving poor" would be provided relief in their own homes, most would be required to enter poorhouses, institutions in which they would be required to participate in domestic labour but would not be overworked in the manner of workhouse inmates. Destitute elderly people, physically and mentally handicapped persons, widows, and, sometimes, whole families ended up in crowded poorhouses, which, over time, became indistinguishable from workhouses. With the growth of towns and cities, old feudal arrangements, in which landlords were expected to care for tenants and labourers, were breaking down. Both the state and the church stepped into the breach, trying at once to fend off mass starvation and to maintain the existing social hierarchy.[1]

Queen Elizabeth I, by Robert Peake. Queen of England from 1558 to 1603, she presided over England's rise to the position of the world's major naval power. Once it controlled the seas, England began to take an earnest interest in establishing colonies that could be exploited for the benefit of the Mother Country.

Queen Elizabeth I in procession with her Courtiers (c.1600/03) from *Memoirs of the Court of Queen Elizabeth* after an oil attributed to Robert Peake (c.1592–1667) at Sherborne Castle, published in 1825 (w/c and gouache on paper), Essex, Sarah Countess of (d.1838). Private Collection, The Stapleton Collection; www.bridgeman.co.uk

This chapter explores the character of European societies in the early period of European exploration and settlement of the Americas—that is, roughly from 1500 to 1700. Our objective in this chapter is to assess the cultural baggage that Europeans brought with them as they entered what they called the "New World." By understanding their world view, we can better understand why they interacted with the First Nations in certain ways and created communities quite unlike those they found in North America. Over time, of course, the new environment changed European perspectives. Nonetheless, the values of the "metropolis"—that is, their European homelands—would continue to play an important role in the lives of all people living in North America.

A SOCIETY IN TRANSITION

At the time of overseas exploration and settlement, societies throughout Western Europe were in transition. A social order characterized by agricultural self-sufficiency and rigid hierarchies was giving way to a new order in which trade and impersonal market-based relationships were becoming increasingly important. Although a landowning aristocracy continued to dominate society, new leaders were emerging in urban centres whose wealth came from organizing the trade that linked far-flung territories. This new elite was allied with increasingly powerful monarchs. Their attempts to constrain the power of the aristocracy led to the emergence of nation-states, wherein government bureaucracies, rather than individual landlords, made the rules that ordinary people were forced to obey.

European society also supported a small class of intellectuals who challenged traditional values. Their growing curiosity about how the universe worked led them away from the teachings of the Roman Catholic Church and produced both the knowledge and some of the incentive to search for undiscovered lands. Even universities, most of which began as church-sponsored institutions, became hotbeds of intellectual ferment. Courses in law, medicine, science, and philosophy transformed the way people thought about their world and laid the foundations for professions that would help define the modern age.

In this age of transition, Europe was a complex continent. Not only did incredible opulence live side by side with grinding poverty, but religious devotion co-existed with greed and bloody warfare; humanist interest in scientific advance and new forms of artistic and architectural expression coincided with religious and racial bigotry; and the acceptance of female monarchs in many nation-states stood in contrast to the profound oppression of women in society at large. These contradictory tendencies often fuelled new ideas and encouraged new directions.

MAP 3.1 Western Europe in 1500.

THE EUROPEAN SOCIAL ORDER

In the thirteenth century, a minor English baron, the Lord of Eresby, employed "a steward, a wardrober, a wardrober's deputy, a chaplain, an almoner, two friars, a chief buyer, a marshal, two pantrymen and butlers, two cooks and larderers, a saucer, a poulterer, two ushers and chandlers, a baker, a potter, and two furriers, and each had their own boy 'helpers.'"[2] Households of this kind—and it was the household of a minor baron—had not always been a feature of European life.

As a response to population pressures, egalitarian hunting-and-gathering societies in Eurasia gave way to agricultural settlements between 10 000 and 2000 years ago. Gradually, religious and military castes formed and society became more rigidly stratified. Slaves captured from enemies usually occupied the bottom rung of the social order, and everyone else was forced to conform to the demands of military and religious authorities. Patriarchal ideology, which stressed women's subordination to men, and young people to adult males, complemented the hierarchical notions that were replacing older egalitarian practices.

Between the years 900 and 1400, much of European society was locked into reciprocal, though unequal, obligations that historians have labelled the feudal system. Men of the elite classes had the right to bear arms, and relations among them were formalized through military allegiances secured with religious pledges. At the top of the social pyramid within a given region was the king, who granted control over huge estates to a small number of powerful nobles in return for military allegiance.

The vast majority of the people—the serfs—were legally subordinated to the military castes. In return for paying tribute to the noble, they received military protection from him and tenure on a small plot within his estate, or manor. While tribute was initially paid by working three days a week in the noble's fields, a variety of rental arrangements gradually replaced this system of forced labour. The growth of towns offered serfs the possibility of escape from the feudal manor and its obligations.

As forced labour began to give way to rental obligations, serfs became tenants who paid fixed rents, whether in money or in kind, to the nobles who became landlords. The Black Death of 1348–49 and the subsequent plagues that drastically reduced the populations of many countries encouraged landowners to increase incentives to their tenants. In France in the late fifteenth century, many noblemen, short of farm workers, hived off parts of their estates as land grants to peasants who would also work the noble's land. Wages for farm work were relatively generous because of the difficulty of getting enough labourers. The lands granted were usually too small to provide peasant families with an independent livelihood, but the combination of wage work on the manor and the crop from their own smallholding allowed the peasants to improve their standard of living.

Population increases in France in the 1500s restored the relative power of the landlords, or seigneurs, over the tenants and peasants who worked their land. As per capita food production dropped, landowners, blessed with a larger labour force than required to harvest their crops, reduced the wages of farm workers while increasing the price of grain. Rural workers in the Paris region are estimated to have had only half the purchasing power in 1550 that they had enjoyed in 1450. Many peasants were forced to sell their smallholdings, and landless, unemployed tenants often turned to theft to survive. In addition to falling wages and rising food prices, French peasants and tenants faced tax increases imposed by the French monarchy. Only in the late seventeenth century did the balance between prices and wages again begin to tip in favour of farm workers.

POPULATION

In the sixteenth century, Europe was home to an estimated 100 million people. Owing to the opening up of new lands to agriculture and to a decline in epidemics, the states that established empires in the "New World" counted about 39 million people in 1600, an increase of 7 million in a century.

The population increase was a departure for a region of the world hitherto ravaged by famine, epidemics, and warfare. Epidemics were often the by-product of famine. Large stores of grain could help people weather one year of drought, but two dry years in a row usually brought famine. In the Nantes region of France, for example, there were repeated famines from 1528 to 1545 in the wake of grain shortages, and many deaths from starvation. Starving populations living in unsanitary conditions became easy prey for germs. Contagious diseases such as diphtheria, typhoid fever, smallpox, whoop-

ing cough, and tuberculosis killed large numbers of people before running their course. Maladies without a modern equivalent often cut a deadly swath: in England in 1486, 1507, 1518, 1529, and 1551, "sweating sickness" claimed thousands of lives. Its victims developed fits of shivering and sweated profusely, dying within hours of the onset of symptoms. The greatest scourge was the "plague," which periodically ravaged Europe. Its most spectacular occurrence was the Black Death, a form of bubonic plague, which was responsible for the death of about 25 million Europeans out of a total of approximately 80 million in the mid-fourteenth century.

The famines that led to epidemics were not always the result of crop failure. Warfare often left famine in its wake as plundering soldiers dispossessed peasants. Wars within Europe were fought for territorial aggrandizement, over questions of honour, and, in the sixteenth and seventeenth centuries, over religion. Once the monopoly of the armed nobility, warfare in the age of exploration was generally waged by mercenaries—that is, soldiers paid by monarchs trying to centralize power in their own hands. By hiring standing armies of infantrymen, kings and queens could avoid dependence on their noble cavalrymen for military power.

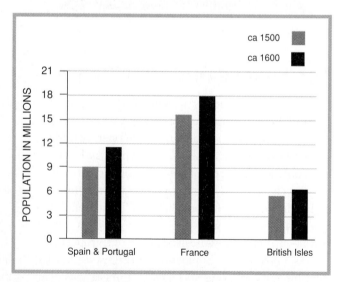

FIGURE 3.1 Selected European Population Figures (in millions)
Source: Carlo M. Cipolla, *Before the Industrial Revolution: European Society and Economy, 1000–1700*, 2nd ed. (New York: Methuen, 1980), 4

Until the second half of the seventeenth century, attempts to control relations between soldiers and civilians were limited. Poorly provisioned, soldiers were expected to force peasants to feed and house them, and they often repaid their hosts with massacre, torture, and rape. They sometimes carried epidemics into the lands that they invaded. Even when wars ended, the peasantry was often harassed by laid-off soldiers who had no source of income and terrorized local populations to gain tribute.

The Thirty Years' War (1618–48), an orgy of religious warfare that embroiled most of the states of Europe, provides a particularly brutal example of the impact of warfare on civilians. The war claimed the lives of 350 000 soldiers and millions of civilians. In the areas of heaviest fighting, the population declined from 21 million to 13.5 million. Monarchs had proved unable to restrain their rival armies from destroying crops and livestock and raping and murdering innocent farm folk. The extent of the mayhem in that war encouraged monarchs to enforce rules on troops regarding their relations with civilians.

Though unarmed, peasants sometimes reacted violently to either invaders or their rightful rulers, whose heavy exactions of rents, taxes, and church dues made provision against famine difficult. Peasant revolts were suppressed brutally where necessary, but still occurred frequently in early modern Europe. Although limited communication among peasants in various regions made a full-scale peasant rebellion unlikely, spontaneous local eruptions when famine threatened were frightening to European elites. Usually the peasants had no revolutionary objectives; they merely asked for "just prices" (that is, prices fixed at an affordable level) and for lower rents and taxes.

In a society where so many people were poor, life expectancy was short—about 45 years for those who survived the first year of life—and death in the first year was common. A third of all children born alive died before reaching their first birthday in seventeenth-century French towns. Rather than breastfeeding their own babies, well-off women hired poor women to suckle their young. These ill-fed women thereby suffered the dilemma of being unable to nourish their own child and their employer's children at the same time.

ECONOMIC LIFE

In 1600, the majority of the people in Europe, including areas where feudalism had disintegrated, remained on the land. About 75 percent of the people in most countries were dependent for their livelihood on the farming of small and usually rented landholdings. Although crop yields had improved slowly from 1000 to 1600, farming was a precarious occupation. According to historian Carlo Cipolla, "The land produced little because seeds were not selected, crop rotation and implements were primitive, pesticides were unknown, and last, but not least, manure, the only known fertilizer, was always in very short supply."[3] Animal husbandry practices were also primitive, and peasant diets were low in protein.

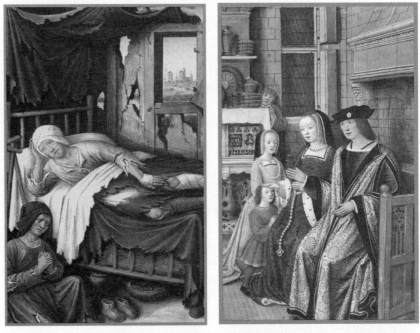

These miniatures by Bourdichon, c. 1490, illustrate the contrast in the living conditions of the poor and wealthy classes in French society. Left, *L'état de pauvreté*; right, *L'état de richesse*.
Masson 91, 93/École nationale supérieure des beaux-arts, Paris

MORE TO THE STORY

Peasant Families and the Life Cycle in Early Modern Europe

What was life like for a typical European peasant born about 1600? The birth would take place at home, perhaps with a midwife helping the mother to deliver her child. For the first year or so the baby would be swaddled and largely unable to explore surroundings, except visually. Because the mother could not leave her field or home duties to take care of a baby, and fathers did not take care of babies, the child would either be cared for by an older sibling or left unsupervised for much of the time. A grandparent might be present in the household, but the nuclear family had already largely replaced the three-generation and extended-family households that some historians claim were common in earlier periods.

Older children would accompany their mother to the fields. Both mother and father would discipline the children sternly, using physical beatings to enforce warnings that youngsters, who could not always be watched by a working parent, must avoid the fire, the river, the forest, and wild animals.

Girls and boys would receive parental instruction regarding their respective gender-based chores. In 1600, formal education in a school was unlikely for all but the most privileged children. By the age of seven, the girl or boy would be a full-time worker in the household economy: girls cooked, sewed, cleaned, fetched, did field work, and supervised younger siblings; boys joined their fathers in doing the back-breaking work of primitive farming. After work there would be no privacy in the small hut. Everyone slept in one room, and the parents made little effort to copulate out of sight of the children.

In an increasingly commercial economy where families needed cash both to pay rents and taxes and to buy items they did not make for themselves, many children (in England a majority) would leave home between the ages of seven and fourteen to work for a wealthier farmer or a noble, the girls as servants, the boys as labourers. Increasingly, children might also be formally apprenticed to a skilled artisan to learn a trade such as tailoring, blacksmithing, or shoemaking. A typical boy and girl would spend their adolescence in households away from home. Even if they stayed at home, the odds were that, before they reached adulthood, one or both of their parents would be dead. So, too, would perhaps half of their siblings.

While working in service, a girl earned a small wage. She sent most of her income home but kept some of it as a dowry for her marriage. A boy in service would also accumulate some savings. Somewhere between the ages of 24 and 28, young adults would be prepared to marry and settle down on a small plot of rented land, often on the estate where the groom's parents had rented property. Both men and women tried to choose a partner who would be an asset in the struggle to eke out a living. Family and friends would be consulted, but anyone who had been separated from parents for a long time would probably be sufficiently independent to make the final choice.

After the marriage ceremony, which was usually performed by a minister but represented a community opportunity for a rowdy party, the young couple would continue to follow an endless round of work activities, except now within their own household. They would also begin to have babies. If both partners managed to live to about the age of 45, the woman would bear seven or eight children, with three or four of them surviving to adolescence. Coitus interruptus and sexual abstinence, as well as ingestion of plant substances reputed to abort pregnancies, were employed in attempts at contraception.

Although their economic partnership and their children might cause this couple to feel a strong bond, both spent much of their work time and leisure time in the company of other members of their own sex within the community. Men

A Country Wedding, by Bruegel the Elder, c. 1565.
Kunsthistorisches Museum, Vienna

worked together in the fields and spent their rare free time at the alehouse, while women gathered around a neighbour's fire, working and talking while their children had an opportunity to play. If parents lived to an age where they became too frail to farm alone, they might hand over the farm to one of the children in return for bed and board. The chances of living to a ripe old age were, in any case, slim, and most peasants worked the fields until they died.

Peasant life followed a seasonal rhythm that changed little over centuries. The cycle of heavy work in spring, summer, and early autumn was followed by riotous merrymaking after the harvest and preceded by early spring carnivals. Restricted to their local communities, peasants participated reluctantly in the cash economy with rents and taxes. Ravaging wars, pestilential plagues, crop failures, and highway robbery added to the uncertainty of daily life. The church offered some consolation through its sacraments, its liturgical calendar tied to the agricultural cycle, and the promise of a better life after death.

By 1600, population growth forced people to leave settled communities for new areas where infertile land often guaranteed poverty. Average standards of living fell. While landlords in earlier times had been concerned that their labour supply might decrease if they raised rents too high, they could now charge what an overpopulated market would bear. Unable to both pay their rent and feed themselves, many farm families looked to places other than their fields for income. Women spun or wove wool or hemp supplied to them by urban-based textile merchants through the so-called "putting-out system," while men and children worked as field labourers on nobles' estates.

A worrying side effect of increased population in a society of low-yield agriculture was that peasants attempted to gain more land by chopping down forests. Governments belatedly passed a variety of decrees designed to stop or slow down the removal of trees and the inevitable soil erosion that followed. Such legislation was often indifferently implemented, because alternative short-term solutions to the problems of peasant hunger eluded authorities bent on preserving the outlines of the hierarchical social order. A general lack of interest in the environmental impact of economic decisions would be carried by Europeans into the Americas as well.

While the farm family attempted, by working as a unit, to use its resources to scrape by, many city and town residents in 1600 lived in a state of permanent desperation. Towns had begun as relatively compact places where guilds—collective organizations of workers involved in particular trades—made rules that ensured good remuneration and limited competition for their members. By 1400, there were guilds for brewers, weavers, ironmongers, masons, bakers, and hatmakers, among others. Their main markets were the nobility and church officials, sectors of society that craved the high-quality products of guild artisans. Gradually, as wealth accumulated in the towns, a merchant class arose that also had considerable disposable income for the purchase of luxuries.

By the sixteenth century, the migration of landless people to cities had weakened guild arrangements. Instead of recruiting apprentices, who eventually could set up their own shops, the budding capitalists hired waged workers who would remain dependent on bosses for a livelihood. The well-being of the common labourer was always in jeopardy. Finding work, even at low wages, was often difficult. At the end of the seventeenth century, an estimated 10 percent of the French population were beggars. At the same time in England, which, as we have seen, had instituted a Poor Law to provide some aid to the poor, about one-quarter of the population were chronically poor and underemployed.

At the bottom of the social order in the towns and the countryside were the slaves, whose numbers were significant even before the Europeans began subjecting millions of Africans to slavery. In the mid-1300s, Tartars, Circassians, Chinese, Jews, Mongols, and Russians were bought and sold in Venice, a crossroads for European commerce in human beings.[4] In Venetian Crete, clergymen of both the Catholic and Orthodox churches as well as officials, professionals, and even some fishers held slaves. Young males were sold to the Turkish sultan to be used as cannon fodder or to nobles in Crete and Cyprus seeking labour for their fields. Teenage girls, including Christian ones, were sold in Africa, Italy, southern Spain, and southern France as domestic servants or concubines. In 1442, a Venetian gentleman settled his debts to a shipwright by handing him a Russian girl.

Although the standard of living of the majority of the population was deteriorating in the sixteenth century, it was an age of economic growth. Wealth was being concentrated in the hands of the rich. This development was, it seems, a prerequisite for an expanding market economy and the colonization and exploitation of "discovered" areas. According to historian Ralph Davis: "It was their demand, for good quality woolen and linen cloths, furs, silks, wine, armour, ornaments and other luxuries, that promoted some concentration in industry and in specialized agriculture, expanded the international market economy, and gave opportunities to economic enterprise, outlets for accumulating capital, and scope for experimenting with new economic institutions."[5]

WOMEN AND THE ECONOMY

The expansion of economic specialization and market relations played an important part in changing the position of European women in the fifteenth and sixteenth centuries. While the patriarchal organization of society was long-established in Europe, the degree of subordination of the women of various social classes had fluctuated from era to era. Opportunities for townswomen and aristocratic women were declining in the sixteenth century, and male authorities were advocating a limited sphere of activities for women. In contrast, the status of the great mass of rural women in the household economy remained much the same, although women who broke social norms were more likely than ever to be punished, as the large number of witchcraft trials attested.

Until the early fifteenth century, women were allowed to become members of most guilds. Their presence was especially obvious in areas such as weaving, needlemaking, yarn spinning, and hatmaking, where dexterity rather than strength was a key to success. Women were employed in metallurgical works in France and in the Arsenal of Venice making sails. From 1365 to 1371, relatively equal numbers of men and women were employed in the building yard of Périgord College in Toulouse, France.

Occupational equality between the sexes began to break down when journeymen in guilds, finding themselves less able to become masters, turned on female employees in an attempt to limit competition and improve their chances of advancement. Barring women had the double effect of keeping out competitors and emphasizing the exclusivity of a trade, as did the exclusion of men of illegitimate birth and sons of serfs. So, in 1649, Frankfurt hatmakers kept out not only women but also all journeymen trained in Fulda, because Fulda hatmakers employed women and therefore presumably tainted male employees in the town. Widows of tradesmen had once assumed almost automatically the duties of their husbands, but by the sixteenth century they found themselves increasingly blocked by the guilds. In Frankfurt, in 1624, a widow of a stonemason asked guild permission to keep her late husband's shop in operation; she was rejected on the grounds that women were not proper masters and could effectively control neither a shop nor journeymen.

Kept out of guilds, women worked in hospitals and orphanages, as midwives, in public baths (until these were closed down in the sixteenth century along with brothels), and as domestics. In most cities, 15 to 20 percent of the adult population were in domestic service, with women accounting for most of this number. Poor women sold small items—pretzels, nuts, wooden implements, cookies, candles, herbs, lace, firewood—that they could make or gather. Women were also barred from universities and increasingly unable to use designations, such as "physician," which before the sixteenth century were not reserved for graduates of universities.

With only minor exceptions, women also lacked the capital and connections to become merchant capitalists involved in the expanding global trade of the fifteenth and sixteenth centuries. The consequences were serious. As Merry E. Wiesner suggests: "It was exactly the occupations with formal education, political functions, capital investment, or international connections, such as physicians, merchants, bankers, lawyers, government officials and overseas traders, that were gaining in wealth, power and prestige."[6]

THE ROLE OF THE STATE

In feudal times the lords of the manor enjoyed as much or more power over their domains as the monarchs and dispensed justice to their serfs and artisans as they saw fit. The monarch's role was largely limited to arbitrating territorial disputes and leading the nobles in times of war. As warfare increased and standing armies replaced the army of nobles, kings and queens attempted to limit the powers of the landowners and centralize lawmaking in their own hands. It was a gradual process, but by the late seventeenth century the long-established notion that kings ruled by "divine right" rather than at the pleasure of the nobility had become a central argument in royal propaganda favouring centralization of power.

After policies had been established by a council of ministers answering to the monarch, a centralized government bureaucracy implemented the rulings across the territory. Courts appointed by the monarch's advisers, rather than the nobles, enforced royal decrees on everything from commerce to personal morality. Royal prisons, workhouses, and asylums demonstrated the monarch's ability to penalize those whose behaviour fell afoul of the norms established from above.

Although many nobles tried to defend their former privileges and even won some concessions, many more were absorbed into the court as advisers, military specialists, or simply part of the monarch's personal circle. The increasing reach of the monarchy in France was evident in the vast increase in the number of royal officials. In 1515, Francis I employed about 8000 officials throughout a far-from-unified French kingdom; by the end of the seventeenth century, Louis XIV paid the salaries of over 11 times as many officials to impose his will on his 20 million subjects.

The increasingly powerful monarchs of France, England, Spain, Portugal, and Holland used their armies in attempts to gain control of as much territory as possible. Although most peasants continued to think of themselves solely as part of a local community, the trading classes and intellectuals in the cities increasingly identified themselves as citizens of the larger territory controlled by their monarch. The nation-state, an entity peculiar to Europe, had come into being.

The new political order represented by the nation-state proved a boon to trade. In the period when nobles and petty princes enjoyed as much power as or more power than monarchs, trade had been an expensive and even dangerous undertaking. A merchant wanting to pass from one town to another would confront armed men and tax collectors at every turn, which at times made relatively short-distance trade as difficult as trade across borders. For those who attempted to trade on a larger scale, the presence of pirates, uninhibited by governmental forces, also created endless hazards. The emergence of national monarchies with taxation powers and armies capable of humbling nobles and pirates alike offered improved conditions for trade.

The nation-state, which created a bond between monarchs and merchants at the expense of nobles, went beyond the breaking down of internal and external trade barriers and the provision of protection for merchants. It also played an entrepreneurial role. Arsenals, the largest manufacturing centres in the period, were in state hands, and sometimes so was shipping. Private-sector growth also owed much to the expansion of the state. Kings and queens, busily making war to expand their territory, convert heathens, and extract new wealth, needed loans from bankers, arms from munitions makers, and cloth from textile merchants to clothe their armies. The profits made by both private and state entrepreneurs from such ventures were reinvested and permitted greater concentrations of wealth and greater specialization.

Monarchs and nobles who sponsored overseas ventures hoped that those activities would increase national wealth and make a better life possible for a restive peasantry, as well as provide work for the growing army of unemployed townspeople. For some, the idea of establishing colonies in areas seized from Aboriginal inhabitants was appealing partly because of the possibility of unloading surplus people in the new territories. There the new arrivals could both feed themselves and pay taxes to the mother country, while at the same time defending the country's conquered

Cathedral of Cologne.
German National Tourist Office

RELIGION

The Roman Catholic Church had established its dominance throughout most of Europe during the Middle Ages, ruthlessly suppressing heretics. Led by the pope, regarded as Christ's earthly representative, the church had received royal recognition of various rights: to dictate the religious beliefs of all the monarch's subjects, to collect tithes to support the church's personnel, and to build and maintain its grandiose cathedrals. In his efforts to maintain a united Christendom, the pope sometimes fought both monarchs and nobles. By 1500, increasingly powerful monarchs asserted their right to control the behaviour of all citizens, including members of the church hierarchy.

The church was a hierarchical and patriarchal organization that mirrored the larger society. Archbishops, bishops, and cardinals, who generally purchased their titles, lived comfortable lives that had little in common with the poverty that faced parish priests and cloistered nuns. The tithes that everyone was forced to pay to the church went disproportionately to the building and upkeep of magnificent cathedrals and the opulent homes of church officials.

In the sixteenth century, the rising tide of nationalism and monarchical ambitions, added to long-simmering resentment against the church's corruption, brought a permanent rupture to western Christendom. The emerging wealthy classes of merchants, craftsmen, and professionals remained devout Christians, but they questioned why a considerable amount of their profits should go to maintaining an expensive bureaucracy. Ancient church laws against moneylending also offended the new capitalists. While the laws could be circumvented, their very existence seemed to condemn activities that formed the basis of a commercial society.

Martin Luther, a priest in the German town of Wittenberg, led the challenge against the papacy in 1517. Soon Europe was in a state of religious upheaval. Along with certain monarchs eager to assert unrivalled authority within their territories, the dissenters created rival "Protestant" churches that disputed the Roman Catholic Church's religious

territories from would-be interlopers. They might also help spread the Christian faith, which, like capitalism and nationalism, fuelled the European drive for overseas expansion.

monopoly. This "Reformation" of Christianity was unacceptable to the Catholic Church, which encouraged its supporters to suppress the dissenters. Wars between Catholics and Protestants sometimes ended with only one variant of Christianity being allowed within a monarch's territory.

In England in the 1530s, Henry VIII declared his Church of England to be outside the pope's jurisdiction. After an initial attempt to suppress the Catholic Church, a degree of official toleration was allowed. In France, the battle between Catholics and Protestants (there called Huguenots) resulted in almost constant warfare from 1562 to 1598. A temporary truce between the two faiths occurred in 1598 when King Henri IV created a strong central government and granted, by the Edict of Nantes, toleration to non-Catholics. This tol-

Constantinople, **by Jacobo Negretti Palma. Founded by Constantine the Great in 330 as the new capital of the Roman Empire, Constantinople became the centre of Christendom in the East once the destruction of the Roman Empire in the fifth century led to a separation of the Christian communities of Western Europe from areas eastward. In 1453, the Ottoman Turks seized control of the city, renamed it Istanbul, and made Islam its official religion.**
The Taking of Constantinople (oil on canvas) by Palma II Giovane (Jacopo Negretti) (1548–1628), Palazzo Ducale, Venice, Italy. Bridgeman Art Library

eration was never total and disappeared entirely with the revocation of the edict in 1685. Royal orders that only Catholics be allowed to settle in France's colonies, such as Canada and Acadia, demonstrated the continuation of discrimination against religious dissenters in France.

Unable to countenance rival versions of Christianity, western Europeans could hardly be expected to countenance rival religions. Practising Jews were expelled from England in 1290 and from France in 1394. They would be gradually allowed to return to both countries in small numbers and to play an important role in the commerce of these two nations. In 1492, Spain expelled Jews as well as Muslims, who had invaded the Iberian peninsula as early as the eighth century. Venice became a destination for many Jews fleeing these places, but it too began to persecute its Jews in the 1570s. Jews often hid their faith and faked conversions to Christianity to be allowed to stay in countries where their religion had been proscribed. Others resettled in Eastern Europe,

in Constantinople, or wherever a temporary welcome might be found.

European intolerance also manifested itself further afield. Christians regarded Islam as no better than paganism and the Muslim occupation of the Holy Lands of the Middle East as an affront to their Christian faith. From the late eleventh century to the mid-thirteenth century, Christians tried in vain to recapture the Holy Lands in a series of crusades.

If greed and bloody-mindedness had been its only face, Christianity would not likely have commanded the allegiance of European peoples. Religious orders dedicated to carrying Christ's message of hope to rich and poor, heathen and convert, played an important missionary role both at home and abroad. Following the Protestant revolt, the Roman Catholic Church made a concerted effort to correct past abuses. Two of the Catholic orders that emerged in this context, the Jesuits and the Ursulines, were destined to play an important role in the history of the European occupation of North America.

The militant Society of Jesus, or the Jesuits, was imbued with the mystical devotion of its Spanish founder, Ignatius Loyola, and was organized along quasi-military lines. Fervent in their view that Catholics must be absolutely obedient to the pope, the Jesuits founded schools and universities and became active in foreign missions in an effort to rekindle the Catholic flame that the Reformation had dimmed.

The Ursulines, founded by Angela Merici in Italy in 1535, just as the Jesuits were beginning their work, were devoted to teaching girls. These women took vows of chastity but initially taught uncloistered, in their own homes. Believing that girls must be educated in the Catholic faith so they would not become Protestants and pass on heresies to their children, the church accepted the Ursulines' work but demanded that they perform it within the cloister—that is, within institutions owned and controlled directly by the church. After many battles the Ursulines capitulated.

Not all female religious orders followed the example of the Ursulines. In the seventeenth century, congregations of uncloistered women proliferated and began to receive grudging acceptance by the church, which needed all the help it could get in its deadly competition with Protestants. In France, for example, the pope gave official recognition to teaching congregations of *dévotes*, women who devoted their lives to the church but remained outside the cloister. Despite its continued patriarchal views, the Catholic hierarchy allowed both its nuns and the dévotes to open schools, hospitals, asylums, and orphanages in an attempt to make the church integral to the lives of its adherents. New France would feel the influence of this women's movement in the church, both in its cloistered form (the Ursulines) and its dévote form (the Soeurs de la Congrégation de Notre-Dame and the Soeurs Grises).

CULTURE AND IDEAS

Church anxieties about the need to vigorously propagate the faith reflected concerns about the broad questioning of existing knowledge that characterized the period after 1400. Beginning in the Italian city-states, a Renaissance (or rebirth) of interest in the classical scholars and societies of ancient Greece and Rome sparked debates—initially in elite intellectual circles—about beliefs that the church held unassailable.

With the revival of ancient learning, scholars began to challenge the prevailing notion that the Earth was the centre of the universe and the sun revolved around it. In 1543, a Polish clergyman-physician named Nicolaus Copernicus dared to suggest that the Earth was simply a planet that, along with other planets, revolved around the sun. Galileo Galilei, a Venetian, built a telescope in 1609 and used it to make observations that corroborated Copernicus's theory. He was forced by the Catholic authorities to recant his discovery, but the die had been cast and a whole new astronomy born.

Other thinkers joined the astronomers in challenging received wisdom about how the universe operated. In his 1637 *Discourse on Method*, the French philosopher René Descartes claimed that there were discernible and immutable mechanical laws of nature. The Renaissance thinkers nominally accepted the traditional Catholic view that held individuals to be ranked in hierarchical order, with their place in the universe fixed by God, but they increasingly embraced a secular individualism that would soon fracture the traditional social structure. Whether it was a Machiavelli expounding a secular political science or a da Vinci designing machines to make human flight possible, Renaissance intellectuals recognized few boundaries in the topics they explored.

Women were rarely the beneficiaries of the ideas of Renaissance men. The chief male writers and painters of the period, both following and influencing the merchants who sponsored their creative work, revived classical notions of a public sphere exclusive to males and a private, domestic sphere to which women's lives must be devoted. Not surprisingly, some women challenged those who tried to restrict their freedom. In 1405, the Italian-born French humanist Christine de Pisan produced a work entitled *The Book of the City of Ladies* in which she exhorted women to refute denigrations of women by following such models as the Virgin Mary; Clotilda, who brought Christianity to the Franks; and Queen Esther, who prevented the genocide of the Assyrian Jews. Among the aristocracy, some women courtiers—members of the royal entourage—painted, wrote, and composed, resisting attempts to limit their sphere of activity.

Misogynist notions were widespread in European society. For women who were both poor and out of step with the behaviour prescribed for their sex, the consequences were sometimes fatal. Single women whose babies were stillborn, a common enough occurrence at a time when infant mortality rates were high, were often executed for committing infanticide; the burden of proof for proving innocence was placed on the hapless mother. Older women whose behaviour offended neighbours were often accused of practising witchcraft. Between 1500 and 1750, over 100 000 women in Europe faced this accusation, and about 60 000 were executed.

The Renaissance witnessed a spate of inventions as intellectual inquiry led to a search for solutions to technical problems. For many centuries before the Renaissance, Europeans had demonstrated a willingness to apply inventions, although many of the new ideas were imported from elsewhere. Between the sixth and eleventh centuries, for example, Europeans adopted the windmill from Persia, the spinning wheel, gunpowder, and paper from China, and the compass from the Arabs. At the same time, Europeans took ancient inventions that had been little applied and made them crucial to their economy. Water mills, which had been prohibited by the Romans as labour-saving devices that reduced human employment, were enthusiastically embraced. In the Middle Ages, Europeans even combined their knowledge of Chinese manual manufacture of paper with their knowledge of water mills and used mills to process pulp.

Historians have debated why Europeans were so willing, compared with other peoples, to search for applications for inventions. The general turmoil in the period after the break-up of the Roman Empire no doubt was a factor: there were no longer powerful authorities who could join rulers elsewhere in the world to prohibit new inventions. Also, the interminable warfare over the possession of land encouraged technological experimentation as each party dreamed of gaining a military advantage over its rivals. Thus, in China, where emperors held a monopoly over the means of war, gunpowder was used to make firecrackers. In Europe, it was used to make deadly weapons.

Military and commercial imperatives encouraged improvements in navigation. The introduction of full-rigged ships in the fifteenth century meant that ships could go faster and no longer needed to wait for the most favourable breeze before sailing. In the same century, the Portuguese developed greater knowledge of the winds in the Atlantic and invented the quadrant to measure latitude. Innovation in the techniques of naval construction, navigation, and armament production was a major factor in the successful overseas expansion of Europe.

Technology was a key to exploration, but it does not explain why Europeans in particular ventured to uncharted areas of the globe. Both the Chinese and the Arabs had the technology to enable them to explore the world. Economic motives peculiar to Western Europe provided some of the motivation: Islam barred the best land and sea routes to Asia as well as to the grain and timber of south Russia. But Europeans were hardly alone in being motivated by hopes of economic gain. Ultimately the reason for the European quest to explore the globe may rest in the scope for curiosity of the peoples of that continent—a curiosity exemplified by the Renaissance. Elsewhere, powerful rulers sufficiently suppressed such curiosity so that people could not act upon their dream of finding a "new world."

PORTUGUESE EXPLORATION

The leader in European expansion was Portugal. Like Spain, Portugal had been under Muslim control for several centuries and its leaders in the early-modern period were particularly disdainful of "infidels." The desire to liberate the Holy Lands from Muslim control remained a key component of Portuguese state policy long after the crusading zeal had passed in other European states. As in the earlier crusades, Portugal's religious goals in the East blended with its commercial objectives. Gradually, undermining Muslim control of the Indian spice trade became more clearly the aim of the Portuguese Crown than the retaking of Jerusalem from the heathens.

With the monarchy and the merchants allied in search of new territories, it was not long before Portugal had spread its tentacles throughout many parts of the world. Portuguese vessels reached the Gulf of Guinea in 1440 and soon began carrying back slaves, gold, and ivory from Africa. In 1487, Bartolomeu Diaz, a Portuguese navigator, sailed around the Cape of Good Hope. Ten years later his countryman, Vasco da Gama, sailed directly from Africa to India, returning in 1498 to Lisbon with jewels and spices. At its height, the Portuguese commercial empire encompassed more people than any previous trading block in recorded history. Historian Fernand Braudel notes:

> The Portuguese had from the start sent their ships to India, then beyond to the East Indies, China and Japan. They also organized the great slave trade between Africa and America, not to mention the clandestine export of silver from Potosi by way of the overland routes of Brazil and, even more, by Buenos Aires and the little boats of the Rio de la Plata. This added up to an immense and complicated system, drawing on the economy of the whole world.[7]

Portuguese successes left corpses and misery in their wake. The marks of Portugal's seizure of the spice trade were "cities bombarded, ships pillaged and sunk, and appalling cruelties—the slicing off of noses and ears—inflicted on enemies real or imagined."[8] On the Canary Islands, the Portuguese wiped out the indigenous peoples, the Guanches, who numbered about 100 000. Those who did not die of diseases or in resistance to Portuguese occupation were enslaved and shipped to places such as Madeira, where they laboured to early deaths on Portuguese sugar plantations. In Brazil, the gentle Tupi-Guarani faced much the same fate.

The Portuguese slave traders brought African slaves in the millions to the Americas, using them to replace the decimated indigenous peoples of Brazil. Others they sold to British, French, and Spanish plantation owners. Although the African slaves survived in larger numbers in the Americas than did Aboriginal slaves, their death rate was high and the treatment they received was often cruel. Commenting on Iberian attitudes toward Africans, historian G.V. Scammell observes:

> Slavery was to be the Africans' lot since they were of the race that carried, as the Book of Genesis recorded, the burden of Noah's curse on the offspring of Canaan, son of Ham, and so [were] destined to toil forever in the service of others. They were supposedly captured in what were considered to be "just wars" against societies of evil practices—though in fact most were acquired from pagan or infidel dealers. Their enslavement was accordingly legitimate, and the price they had to pay to become Christians. Crude prejudice reinforced this convenient erudition. Africans looked and smelled differently to Europeans, and were commonly and offensively naked. Above all they were black, the colour that proclaimed the enormity of their ancestors' sins, and the colour popularly identified with evil in a civilization already conscious of the superiority of whiteness.[9]

SPANISH EXPLORATION

Spain hoped to outstrip the wealth of its Iberian neighbour by finding a passage to the riches of Asia. By the middle of the sixteenth century, Spain was the major European power in the "New World." Its conquests began modestly with Columbus's short-lived attempts to establish Caribbean colonies in the 1490s. A Genoan by birth, Columbus won the support of King Ferdinand and Queen Isabella of Spain for his plans to find a northwest passage to Asia. Far off course, he landed on an island that he named Hispaniola (now Haiti and the Dominican Republic). Mistakenly thinking that he had come ashore in India, he called the island's inhabitants Indians, a misnomer that has survived to this day (although not without controversy) as a description of the first peoples of the Americas.

Between 1519 and 1521, Hernándo Cortés conquered Mexico and destroyed the Aztec Empire. The Aztecs ruled a vast empire won by conquest, and their architectural and political triumphs impressed Cortés. Their weapons could not match European guns and swords, and the resentment of the peoples they had subjugated ensured that no popular uprising would defend the Aztec military caste against the light-skinned intruders from overseas. Weakened by diseases to which they had no immunity, the Aztecs were soon on the defensive.

The Spanish invasion, conducted by fewer than 1000 soldiers, was made easier by the initial unwillingness of Montezuma, the Aztec ruler, to fight. A prophecy that the Aztec god Quetzalcoatl would return that year coincided with Cortés's arrival. Montezuma therefore invited the Spaniard to enter his capital, on the site of today's Mexico City. After making Montezuma his prisoner, Cortés seized power and incorporated local rulers into his own conquistador authority. Spain named Cortés governor and

Columbus and Aboriginal Peoples

Columbus's observations to Ferdinand and Isabella about the "Indians" and their potential use to Spain reveal a great deal about European attitudes toward the Aboriginal peoples that they encountered. Viewing them as pacific and generous, he declared them to be excellent candidates for slaves. He also concluded that the resources of their lands could be exploited at will by the Spanish Crown.

> They are all . . . unprovided with any sort of iron, and they are destitute of arms, which are entirely unknown to them. . . . No one refuses the asker anything that he possesses, on the contrary, they themselves invite us to ask for it. They manifest the greatest affection toward all of us, exchanging valuable things for trifles, content with the very least thing or nothing at all. . . . I make this promise to our most invinci-

ble sovereigns, that if I am supported by some little assistance from them, I will give them as much gold as they have need of, and in addition spices, cotton, and mastic, which is found only in Chios, and as much aloes-wood, and as many heathen slaves as their Majesties may choose to demand.[10]

Columbus was eager to profit from his discovery: in 1495 he shipped 550 Aboriginal slaves to Europe. About 200 of them died on the voyage, and most of the rest died soon after they reached Spain. He had no permission from the Spanish monarchs to engage in the slave trade; indeed, he was supposed to be attending to the conversion of these Amerindians to Christianity.

---

captain-general of New Spain, an area that included most of what is now Mexico, and Cortés lost little time in forcing many of his new subjects to labour in the silver mines to enrich their new masters. Although exploited by the Aztecs, the indigenous peoples of Mexico had achieved a population of some 27 million by 1500. After 150 years of European exploitation and diseases, that number fell to about one million.

Cortés was soon followed by other conquistadores who had control of the upper Amazon basin. Initially concerned mainly with the silver and other precious metals of South and Central America, the conquistadores quickly found that there was even more money to be earned by harnessing the agricultural abilities of their new subjects. Huge haciendas, or plantations, run by Spanish overlords yielded crops for export and for the feeding of a growing Spanish population. As Aboriginal populations died out, particularly in the Caribbean, African slaves were imported to replace them. By 1600, Spanish rule extended over what is now the southwestern United States, Mexico, Central America, the Caribbean islands, Venezuela, Colombia, Ecuador, Peru, Chile, and coastal Argentina and Uruguay.

ENGLAND, HOLLAND, AND FRANCE

Over time, other nations followed the lead of Portugal and Spain. In the English port of Bristol, fishing interests active in the North Atlantic commissioned Giovanni Caboto (John Cabot), an Italian navigator with an apparent knowledge of land beyond the "ocean sea," to carry out a voyage of exploration in uncharted territories. It is not surprising that the men of Bristol would engage an Italian seaman. Italy was the heartland of intellectual, cultural, and commercial activity in Europe, and its navigators were employed by Portugal, Spain, and France as well as England to make pioneering transatlantic voyages.

After Cabot's 1497 "discovery" of "the new isle"—which became known as Newfoundland—French fleets joined the Portuguese and Spanish ships in making regular visits to the Atlantic fishing grounds. England itself at first remained largely content to fish off Iceland but, following the defeat of the Spanish Armada in 1588, became bolder in its overseas ventures. In 1607, a new Virginia colony was established by a joint stock company with a royal charter. Poor people from England were indentured—that is,

A HISTORIOGRAPHICAL DEBATE

Cruelty Versus Germs

Historians have noted the extent to which contact with Europeans resulted in the decimation of Aboriginal populations. They have also suggested that Europeans treated the indigenous peoples with unusual cruelty. Can these two observations be linked? Some historians think that microbes alone devastated the Aboriginal peoples. Others suggest that the cruel treatment meted out by Europeans contributed significantly to a physical weakening of Native people and allowed the diseases to take their deadly course.

Historian Alfred W. Crosby, while not minimizing the European exploitation of the First Nations, suggests that it was the unplanned European biological attack on the Americas that accounted for most deaths. While Aboriginal peoples were familiar with venereal syphilis, polio, some varieties of tuberculosis, hepatitis, and encephalitis, they had no experience of or immunity to smallpox, measles, diphtheria, whooping cough, chicken pox, bubonic plague, malaria, typhoid fever, cholera, yellow fever, influenza, and other infectious diseases that the Europeans brought with them. As a result, whole communities often disappeared or declined precipitously even before European contact had altered their lifestyles.

Crosby observes that Europeans who wanted to enslave the Natives could not have been happy to see their labourers dying like flies. There were a few diseases that passed the other way—from Amerindians to Europeans—but these were not deadly. Had they been, the ability of the Europeans to conquer the Americas might have been curtailed. The failure of the Crusades, Crosby notes, was in large part attributable to the vast numbers of Crusaders who succumbed in the Muslim lands to diseases from which they had as yet no natural protection. Combatants, in any case, were unaware of their biological impact as they intruded on new regions. Crosby adds:

> Neo-Europeans did not purposely introduce rats, and they have spent millions and millions of pounds, dollars, pesos and other currencies to halt their spread—usually in vain. The same is true for several other varmints in the Neo-Europe—rabbits, for instance. This seems to indicate that the humans were seldom masters of the biological changes they triggered in the Neo-Europes.[11]

Other historians, while not disputing that European biological warfare in the Americas was generally unintentional, argue that it is only a partial explanation for the decimation of Native populations. They point to the deliberate cruelty of European labour practices. Europeans cared little about the people they found in the Americas and exploited them ruthlessly, importing African slaves when indigenous labourers were too few or too unwilling to perform the services required. On the island of Hispaniola, under both Columbus and his successors, the local people were worked to death in gold mining and on building projects. The same tragedy was repeated in Puerto Rico, Cuba, the Leeward Islands, and the Bahamas.[12]

The germ theory, while important, fails to explain differential death rates among Native groups in contact with Europeans. In regions such as Canada, the decline in population, while considerable, was simply not on the same scale as in Mexico, for instance. In Canada, as well, the impact of infectious diseases on population levels has varied dramatically, with some First Nations recovering their population numbers within a generation after an epidemic, while others never recovered at all.[13] An important body of recent historical work has challenged the notion that population losses, especially in the long term, were solely or mainly the result of First Nations bodies lacking immunity to germs that Europeans carried. Mary-Ellen Kelm, for example, studying the health of First Nations in British Columbia, stresses that European colonizers robbed Natives of the resources that had provided their traditional sustenance, and criminalized their traditional healing arts and related spiritual practices. First Nations resisted such efforts to control their minds and bodies, but colonialism nonetheless exacted a heavy toll in Native lives and health.[14] Maureen K. Lux, in a parallel study of the health of Prairie First Nations, argues that the Natives of this region proved well able to adapt to the fur trade with Europeans. In the settlement period, however, the bison disappeared and the implementation of their treaties with Canada failed to provide for their basic human needs. Starvation and poor living conditions resulted in many deaths. But the Canadian authorities blamed the victims for this state of affairs. "As the diseases of poverty rushed in, those who administered their lives would frame disease as a function of their race and their supposed 'stage of civilization.' From that point on, Christianity and assimilation were the paths to good health. That the people were nearly destroyed in the process was rarely seen as a fault of the policy; rather it was the fault of the people's character and customs—of their 'race.' " [15]

committed to long-term contracts—by the Virginia Company to farm on their estates. As incentive to servitude, they were promised freedom and land at the end of their contracts.

Tobacco crops raised in Virginia found markets throughout Europe, and eventually African slaves were imported to do most of the plantation work and provide household domestic labour. The British Royal African Company, founded in 1663, was given a monopoly over British trade with Africa, including the slave trade, which quickly became the most profitable arm of its business. The success of Virginia encouraged other colonial ventures. The Puritans, Protestants who regarded the official Church of England as being too close to Catholicism in its rituals and too worldly in its outlook, began colonizing Massachusetts in 1620. This was the beginning of European settlement in the area known as New England, on the northeastern seaboard of today's United States.

Holland, the leading sea power of northern Europe in the seventeenth century, also made earnest colonization efforts in the Americas. Englishman Henry Hudson, in the employ of the Dutch East India Company at the time, discovered the river that bears his name in 1609. Within a few years Dutch settlements began to appear on the Hudson and Delaware Rivers. The Dutch West India Company, established in the 1620s, brought settlers, and New Netherlands, the name given to the Dutch settlements in today's New York and New Jersey, had a population of 10 000 by 1664.

The Dutch colonists conducted a profitable trade with the local inhabitants, first the Mahicans and then the Iroquois (Five Nations). But agricultural expansion in New Netherlands, as in the English colonies, soon led to efforts to seize Native lands. For all its expansion, New Netherlands was largely undefended. England took advantage of this weakness and seized control of the region in 1664. They renamed the capital, known as New Amsterdam to the Dutch, New York.

France had also begun to seek colonies. It failed in half-hearted attempts to establish settlements on the St Lawrence in 1541–42 and in Florida in the 1560s and tended to look on the Americas as a source for resources, mainly fish and furs. Rivalries in Europe eventually convinced successive French kings that overseas settlements were necessary to ensure imperial supremacy. Sugar in the West Indies and fish and furs in North America provided powerful incentives to colonize in the "New World."

CONCLUSION

As feudalism gave way to a social order characterized by competing monarchical states, expanding trade, growing intellectual curiosity, and religious diversity, Europe became the likely candidate for overseas expansion. Population pressures provided monarchs with an incentive to search for new resources and later to support the founding of colonies. The trade-oriented capitalists of the rising cities provided encouragement and finance for such ventures. Finally, Renaissance intellectuals inspired both the theoretical speculations and the technological advances that made the search for new areas of the globe appear possible and desirable. In sum, the interests of nation building, trade, and science conspired to create the European "age of discovery."

NOTES

1 Anthony Brundage, *English Poor Laws 1700–1930* (Houndmills, Basingstoke, Hampshire: Palgrave, 2003), 5.

2 Carlo M. Cipolla, *Before the Industrial Revolution: European Society and Economy, 1000–1700*, 2nd ed. (New York: Methuen, 1980), 78. An almoner is an ecclesiastic attached to a noble household.

3 Ibid., 125.

4 G.V. Scammell, *The World Encompassed: The First European Maritime Empires, c. 800–1650* (London: Methuen, 1981), 107.

5 Ralph Davis, *The Rise of the Atlantic Economies* (London: Weidenfeld and Nicolson, 1973), 16.

6 Merry E. Wiesner, "Spinning out Capital: Women's Work in the Early Modern Economy," in *Becoming Visible: Women in European History*, ed. Renate Bridenthal, Claudia Koonz, and Susan Stuard, 2nd ed. (Boston: Houghton Mifflin, 1987), 245.

7 Fernand Braudel, *The Mediterranean and the Mediterranean World in the Age of Philip II*, vol. 1 (New York: Harper Torchbooks, 1975), 227.

8 Scammell, 236.

9 Ibid., 257.

10 L.S. Stavrianos, *A Global History from Prehistory to the Present*, 5th ed. (Englewood Cliffs, NJ: Prentice-Hall, 1991), 403.

11 Alfred W. Crosby, *Ecological Imperialism: The Biological Expansion of Europe, 900–1900* (Cambridge: Cambridge University Press, 1986), 192.

12 Eduardo Galeano, *Open Veins of Latin America: Five Centuries of the Pillage of a Continent* (New York: Monthly Review Press, 1973).

13 Ann Hering, "Toward a Reconsideration of Disease and Contact in the Americas," *Prairie Forum*, 17, 2 (Fall 1992): 153–65.

14 Mary-Ellen Kelm, *Colonizing Bodies: Aboriginal Health and Healing in British Columbia, 1900–50* (Vancouver: UBC Press, 1998).

15 Maureen K. Lux, *Medicine That Walks: Disease, Medicine, and Canadian Plains Native People, 1880–1940* (Toronto: University of Toronto Press, 2001), 19.

RELATED READINGS IN THIS SERIES

From Media Companion CD-ROM, Volume I
The Malleus Maleficarum
The Life of Glukel of Hameln

SELECTED READING

Good overviews of early modern Europe include George Huppert, *After the Black Death: A Social History of Early Modern Europe* (Bloomington: Indiana University Press, 1998); Euan Cameron, ed., *Early Modern Europe: An Oxford History* (Oxford: Oxford University Press, 1999); Peter Musgrave, *The Early Modern European Economy* (New York: St Martin's Press, 1999); Carlo Cipolla, *Before the Industrial Revolution: European Society and Economy, 1000–1700*, 2nd ed. (New York: Methuen, 1980); Fernand Braudel, *Civilization and Capitalism, Fifteenth–Eighteenth Century*, 3 vols. (New York: Harper and Row, 1983–86); and Immanuel Wallerstein, *The Modern World System*, vol. 1, *Capitalist Agriculture and the Origins of the European World Economy in the Sixteenth Century* (New York: Academic Press, 1974). Critical attempts to explain why Western Europe developed differently from other parts of the world include J.M. Roberts, *The Triumph of the West* (London: BBC Books, 1985), and Jared Diamond, *Guns, Germs, and Steel: The Fates of Human Societies* (New York: Norton, 1999).

On the growth of trade and of exploration, see Ralph Davis, *The Rise of the Atlantic Economies* (London: Weidenfeld and Nicolson, 1973); G.V. Scammell, *The World Encompassed: The First European Maritime Empires, c. 800–1650* (London: Methuen, 1981) and *Ships, Oceans, and Empires: Studies in European Maritime and Colonial History, 1400–1750* (Aldershot, Hampshire: Variorum, 1995); and J.D. Tracy, ed., *The Rise of Merchant Empires: Long-Distance Trade in the Early Modern World, 1350–1750* (Cambridge: Cambridge University Press, 1990). Changes in warfare are detailed in W.H. McNeill, *The Pursuit of Power: Technology, Armed Force and Society Since A.D. 1000* (Chicago: University of Chicago Press, 1984). On the Crusades, see Malcolm Billings, *The Cross and the Crescent* (London: BBC Books, 1987). On the attitudes and behaviours of the early European explorers in the Americas, see Anthony Pagden, *Lords of All the World: Ideologies of Empire in Spain, Britain and France c. 1500–1800* (New Haven: Yale University Press, 1995); Cecil H. Clough and P.E.H. Hair, *The European Outthrust and Encounter: The First Phase c. 1400–c. 1700* (Liverpool: Liverpool University Press, 1994); and Eduardo Galeano, *Open Veins of Latin America: Five Centuries of the Pillage of a Continent* (New York: Monthly Review Press, 1973). See also Alfred W. Crosby, *Ecological Imperialism: The Biological Expansion of Europe, 900–1900* (Cambridge: Cambridge University Press, 1986), and Ronald Wright, *Stolen Continents: The "New World" since 1492* (Toronto: Viking, 1992). On the slave trade, see James Walvin, *Black Ivory: A History of British Slavery* (London: HarperCollins, 1992).

Important regional studies include Fernand Braudel, *The Mediterranean and the Mediterranean World in the Age of Philip II*, 2 vols. (New York: Harper Torchbooks, 1975, 1977); Kenneth R. Andrews, *Trade, Plunder and Settlement: Maritime Enterprise and the Genesis of the British Empire, 1480–1630* (Cambridge: Cambridge University Press,

1985); C.R. Boxer, *Race Relations in the Portuguese Colonial Empire, 1415–1825* (Westport, CT: Greenwood Press, 1985); Lyle N. McAlister, *Spain and Portugal in the New World, 1492–1700* (Minneapolis: University of Minnesota Press, 1984); R.J. Knecht, *French Renaissance Monarchy: Francis I and Henry II*, 2nd ed. (London: Longman, 1996); Henry Heller, *Iron and Blood: Civil Wars in Sixteenth-Century France* (Montreal: McGill-Queen's University Press, 1991); and Fernand Braudel, *Identity of France* (London: Collins, 1988).

The literature on social life includes Fernand Braudel, *Civilization and Capitalism, Fifteenth–Eighteenth Century*, vol. 1, *The Structures of Everyday Life* (London: Collins, 1983); Philippe Aries and Georges Duby, eds., *A History of Private Life*, vol. 2, *Revelations of the Medieval World* (Cambridge: Harvard University Press, 1988) and *A History of Private Life*, vol. 3, *Passions of the Renaissance* (Cambridge: Harvard University Press, 1989).

The history of European women of this period is probed in Merry E. Wiesner, *Women and Gender in Early Modern Europe* (Cambridge: Cambridge University Press, 1994). Women in the Catholic Church are the subject of Elizabeth Rapley, *The Dévotes: Women and Church in Seventeenth-Century France* (Montreal: McGill-Queen's University Press, 1990). On the persecution of alleged witches, see Brian P. Levack, *The Witch-Hunt in Early Modern Europe*, 2nd ed. (London: Longman, 1995).

On the Renaissance, significant works include Trevor Cairns, *Renaissance and Reformation* (Cambridge: Cambridge University Press, 1987); J.H. Salmon, *Renaissance and Revolt: Essays in the Intellectual and Social History of Early France* (Cambridge: Cambridge University Press, 1987); J.R. Hale, *Renaissance Europe: The Individual and Society* (Berkeley: University of California Press, 1971); Gene Brucker, *Renaissance Florence* (Berkeley: University of California Press, 1983); and Donald R. Kelly, *Renaissance Humanism* (Boston: G.K. Hall, 1991). On the Reformation and Counter-Reformation, see Martin D.W. Jones, *The Counter Reformation: Religion and Society in Early Modern Europe* (Cambridge: Cambridge University Press, 1995), and Simon Schama, *The Embarrassment of Riches: An Interpretation of Dutch Culture in the Golden Age* (New York: Knopf, 1987). The debate on the relationship between religious ideas and the rise of capitalist institutions has sparked several important works, including Max Weber, *The Protestant Ethic and the Spirit of Capitalism* (London: Unwin, 1980); R.H. Tawney, *Religion and the Rise of Capitalism* (Magnolia, MA: Peter Smith, 1984); and A.O. Hirschman, *The Passions and the Interests: Political Arguments for Capitalism before Its Triumph* (Princeton: Princeton University Press, 1977).

WEBLINKS

CRUSADES

www.georgetown.edu

Select the "Crusades" category on this site to access an extensive listing of resources and links on the subject of the Crusades.

NICOLAUS COPERNICUS

www-groups.dcs.st-and.ac.uk/~history/Mathematicians/Copernicus.html

This site offers a brief biography of Copernicus. Many related weblinks are listed.

CHRISTOPHER COLUMBUS

www1.minn.net/~keithp/index.htm

The Columbus Navigation Homepage provides information on navigation history as well as general material on Columbus and his voyages.

CHAPTER 4

The European "Discovery" of Canada to 1632

Timeline

1000	Viking settlements in Newfoundland
1534–35	Jacques Cartier's voyages to the Gulf of St Lawrence region
1541–43	Cartier, followed by Roberval, makes unsuccessful colonization attempt at Quebec
1562–98	Religious warfare in France
1605	Establishment of Port Royal
1608	Establishment of Quebec
1610	Cupid's Cove settlement
1611	Jesuits establish a mission in Acadia, the first religious mission in the Americas
1615	Récollets arrive in New France
1620	Ferryland settlement
1625	Jesuits arrive in Quebec
1629	William Alexander establishes Scottish settlement at Port Royal; English occupy Quebec
1632	Acadia and Canada return to French control

"They emerged from their hiding place and, when they were spotted by the strangers, the response was very favourable. This was the Indians' first encounter with white people. They could not understand their language . . . The whitemen took the Indians aboard . . . When they arrived on the ship, they saw many strangers. From the expressions on the strangers' faces, they could tell they were welcome aboard.

"This is where the Indians saw the whiteman smoking using pipes. They were given tobacco to smoke; they were given matches. They were also introduced to a gun. Now a gift was made to the Indians in the form of a gun."[1]

First Nations oral traditions suggest that Natives initially believed that they could establish harmonious relations with the Europeans who arrived in their midst. So, for example, a story that has passed down to the Cree of Kashechewan on James Bay suggests that the first encounter of their people with Europeans occurred when two Natives saw signs of strangers at the mouth of the Churchill River. The Natives hid but then decided to greet the newcomers.

Fish and furs first attracted Europeans to the northern half of North America. Initially this meant only annual forays from Europe, but a variety of political and economic interests gave rise to efforts to settle in the Americas. In their competition for power and glory, European monarchs saw overseas colonies as a way to gain political advantage. Always short of money, monarchs hoped to build their empires on the cheap. They therefore granted monopolies over the increasingly lucrative fur trade to entrepreneurs who in return would agree to sponsor settlement and often Christian missions as well in the "New World."

For the most part, humble folk, rather than monopolists, were recruited to settle in the colonies. Their lot was often a hard one. European settlement gradually took root in North America, but many early colonies collapsed in the face of daunting challenges. Only when Europeans learned to adapt to the alien environment could they actually survive in it.

Native peoples had no need to "discover" today's Canada, nor did they have to adapt to an environment that they knew very well. Their biggest challenge was to determine the intentions of the Europeans and to adapt to the technology, diseases, and values they brought with them. This chapter focuses on the objectives of early European explorers and settlers, and the initial impact of the newcomers on the long-established inhabitants.

BRIEF ENCOUNTERS

Evidence suggests that intermittent contact between the First Nations of the Americas and various peoples from abroad may have occurred well before the voyage of Columbus. A twelfth-century carving found in southern India has a figure holding a cob of corn, a plant that at the time grew only in the Americas. As early as 5000 years ago, the peanut, another American plant, was grown in southeastern China, while two varieties of chickens believed to be native to Asia were being raised in the Americas when the Spanish arrived in the sixteenth century.

One of the more compelling stories of Asian travel involves five Buddhist monks reputed to have spent 40 years in the Americas in the fifth century CE. According to the Annals of the Chinese Empire, in 499, Hwui Shan, one of the monks, provided the emperor with an extensive description of lands far to the east of China. His account of the indigenous cultures there suggests that Fu-sang, as he called the territory he explored, included today's Mexico and California.

If there was any contact before the tenth century between the First Nations of the Americas and people from other continents, the cultural impact on both sides was negligible, and historians tend to discount the legends describing such encounters. The first contact leading to a settlement that has been confirmed by archeological evidence involved Greenlanders and dates from the end of the tenth century.

The Norse, or Vikings, of Greenland were kin to the Scandinavians who ruled much of Northern Europe in the ninth and tenth centuries. These seafaring people had settled in Iceland late in the ninth century. Around 982, Eirik the Red, a ruffian expelled by the Icelanders, established a settlement in Greenland. In 986, a Norwegian merchant-shipowner, Bjarni Herjolfsson, was blown off course while travelling to the new settlement and found himself travelling along an unknown coastline. His reports led to attempts to settle in the newfound lands.

According to Norse sagas, Leif Eiriksson, a son of Eirik the Red, was the first to lead an expedition to the coasts described by Herjolfsson. Leif identified three distinct areas of North America. The first, a land of rock and ice that he called *Helluland*, was probably Baffin Island. The second, *Markland*, flat and wooded, was almost certainly part of southern Labrador. Leif then reached a country he called *Vinland*, which he described as having grassy meadows and well-stocked rivers. The expedition wintered in Vinland before returning to Greenland.

The sagas indicate that Leif made several later expeditions, and that Thorfinn Karsefni attempted to establish a settlement in Vinland. The settlement included women as well as men, and some children were born there, perhaps the first children of European descent to be born in the Americas.

While the site of Vinland is still much disputed, the discovery in 1961 of a Norse habitation at L'Anse-aux-Meadows suggests a Newfoundland location. But archeologists at the habitation have discovered butternuts, which do not grow further north than present-day New Brunswick. As a result of this and other evidence, scholars have concluded that L'Anse-aux-Meadows was probably a base camp, from which the Vikings travelled into the Gulf of St Lawrence, along the coasts of Nova Scotia and New Brunswick, and perhaps beyond.[2]

The Viking settlements failed to take root in Vinland. While the area offered better agricultural prospects than either Iceland or Greenland, it was already settled. Hostilities quickly developed with the people living in the region, whom the Norse called *Skraelings*, a derogatory term meaning "wretches" or "savages." The Vikings were a people of military prowess, but European weaponry at the end of the

L'Anse-aux-Meadows. Site of a Norse habitation in Newfoundland, L'Anse-aux-Meadows has been named a UNESCO World Heritage Site.
Jonathan Hayward/CP

tenth century was not as superior to its Native counterparts as it would be 500 years later. Lacking both the numbers and the military might to subdue the local residents, the Vikings retreated to Greenland. The Beothuk, Mi'kmaq, Innu, and Inuit peoples who came into contact with these ill-mannered European intruders were probably not significantly affected by this troublesome interlude.

THE ROLE OF THE FISHERY

The peoples of the northeastern parts of the North American continent saw little more of Europeans until the end of the fifteenth century, when they were inadvertently "discovered" by adventurers searching for sea routes to Asia. Although a few Bristol fishermen may have begun catching cod off Newfoundland around 1480, it was John Cabot's reports of a vast cod fishery off the shores of the "new isle" that sparked widespread European interest in the Americas.

Europe's sixteenth-century population had rebounded from the decline caused by the Black Death, but the peasantry remained desperately poor. Their diet lacked sufficient protein, a problem that could be partly rectified by the abundance of codfish

from the new fishing grounds. For Roman Catholics, who endured 153 meatless days a year, cod was an especially prized commodity. By 1580, over 400 Portuguese, Spanish, Basque, and French ships, with combined crews of about 10 000, were fishing cod in the waters off Newfoundland. As late as 1760, shipments of cod bulked larger in France's imports from New France than furs, and the fishery employed far more people than the fur trade.

Conducted exclusively by Europeans for the European market, the cod fishery did not require interaction with Aboriginal peoples. Nevertheless, it created the conditions for contact. Fishermen at first came ashore only for firewood and drinking water, but it was not long before a "dry fishery" developed, involving the cleaning and salting of the fish on land. The dry fishery required a stay of two or three months on shore, and by the seventeenth century it resulted in hired hands staying over winter on the island of Newfoundland and elsewhere in the Atlantic region to protect favoured fishing sites.

Although France, Spain, and Portugal continued to use the "green-cure" method of preserving the fish aboard ship, England lacked the ready access to salt that those countries enjoyed. Its fishermen favoured the dry fishery, which required far less salt than green-curing did. As a result, the English were more likely than their continental counterparts to linger on shore and winter in North America. Few, however, gave much thought to settling permanently in what they considered a harsh environment.

In the early years of contact, friendly trade was common between the Europeans in the fishing industry and the First Nations. Europeans traded iron pots, kettles, and glass beads, among other items, for the furs that the Native peoples were wearing. Trade goods made life easier for the Natives who acquired them and were held in high regard, as evidenced by their abundance in the bur-

Cod fishing and drying by the French in the eighteenth century.
Elizabeth Melau/Library and Archives Canada/C05230

ial sites of eastern nations. They were also traded to tribes further west by the Mi'kmaq, Innu, and other First Nations in contact with Europeans. By 1530, iron goods had reached the upper St Lawrence, and before the end of the century they had penetrated Huron territory.

Fishers sold the furs they acquired to hatters in Europe. The trade picked up noticeably in the last two decades of the sixteenth century, when a rage for broad-brimmed beaver-felted hats took hold among the fashionable set on the continent. As the Baltic sources of fur were exhausted, demand suddenly outstripped supply, leaving North America as the principal source for furs. A race soon developed to secure Aboriginal trading partners.

While the cod fishery and the fur trade were the chief economic activities linking Europeans to North America, the hunting of walrus and whales was initially of equal significance. The Portuguese on Sable Island and Spanish Basques on the islands of the Gulf of St Lawrence were the first walrus-hunters, joined by the French on Chaleur Bay, Prince Edward Island, and the Magdalen Islands before 1570.

One of the earliest and most successful whaling operations in the "New World" was conducted in the Strait of Belle Isle by the Basques. Their primary base was located at Red Bay on the southern coast of Labrador. At the height of the industry from the 1540s to the 1580s, some 30 Basque ships and 2500 men came annually to hunt and process right and bowhead whales. The Basques gradually depleted the whale stocks off Labrador and abandoned Atlantic whaling entirely by the end of the century. Spain annexed Portugal in 1580 and the fortunes of both countries declined after the English defeat of the Spanish Armada in 1588. In the wake of the Basques came French, English, and German whalers, searching for the profits from whale oil, which lit most of Europe's lamps, and baleen, the large horny plates that took the place of teeth for whales and bolstered European dresses of the period.

The lure of wealth from the pursuit of walrus and whales led to some dubious colonization schemes. In 1598, a Breton nobleman, Marquis Troilus de la Roche, established a small settlement on Sable Island with 40 freed prisoners and 10 soldiers. The colonists

MORE TO THE STORY

Searching for Asia

While fish and furs were the attractions for most of Europe's early excursions to North America, the search for the Northwest Passage—which had alerted Europeans to these resources in the first place—continued to motivate expeditions to the Americas. Most of the European knowledge of the northern territories resulted from the continued search for a sea passage that would link the Atlantic to the Pacific and lead to the wealth of China and the East Indies. In 1576, 1577, and 1578, for example, explorer Martin Frobisher sailed west from Greenland in search of the elusive passage. He entered the bay that today bears his name and charted much of the eastern Arctic. Digging for ore on Baffin Island, Frobisher found little of value but did capture some Inuit, whom he offered to the king of England as evidence of his miraculous explorations.

Like Frobisher, Sir Humphrey Gilbert raised funds from English merchants who believed the passage existed and could guarantee their trading fortunes. In 1583, on his second voyage across the Atlantic, Gilbert took possession of Newfoundland in the name of England and made plans to establish a colony. Within two months, Gilbert had drowned at sea, and the only ship remaining of the original five that had sailed with him returned home. From 1585 to 1587, John Davis made three voyages along the Arctic coast to search for the passage and wrote sympathetically of the Inuit he encountered. Henry Hudson, working first for the Dutch and later the English, ascended the Hudson River in 1609 before braving the dangers of Hudson Strait the following year and sailing into Hudson Bay. Three centuries would elapse before the expedition of Norwegian Roald Amundsen (1903–06) finally traversed the Northwest Passage.

The Last Voyage of Henry Hudson, by John Collier. This explorer's name has been given to a bay, a river, and a strait as a result of his explorations in 1609 and 1610.
Hudson's Last Voyage, c.1881, Collier, John (1850-1934). Royal Academy of Arts, London, UK; www.bridgeman.co.uk

hunted the walrus, in demand for its ivory and oil, but mutinied when food supplies failed to arrive in 1602. The colony was subsequently abandoned.

EARLY BRITISH COLONIZATION: THE NEWFOUNDLAND EXPERIENCE

Between 1610 and 1630, the English made several attempts to establish settlements in Newfoundland. Most ended in failure. Because there were no quick profits to be made, the merchants and philanthropists who sponsored these colonization efforts were unable to raise the capital they needed to ensure the success of their ventures. The generally impoverished people from England, Wales, and Ireland who were recruited to settle Newfoundland in this period were among the earliest European immigrants to North America. With nothing at home to return to, they survived in Newfoundland by fishing, raising a few animals, growing turnips and cabbages, and trading for other essentials with the ships that, without fail, arrived every summer to engage in the cod fishery.

In 1610, the London and Bristol Company sponsored England's second overseas plantation (the first was in Virginia) at Cupid's Cove, Conception Bay. The settlement was designed to serve as a base for the Newfoundland fishery and trade in furs with the

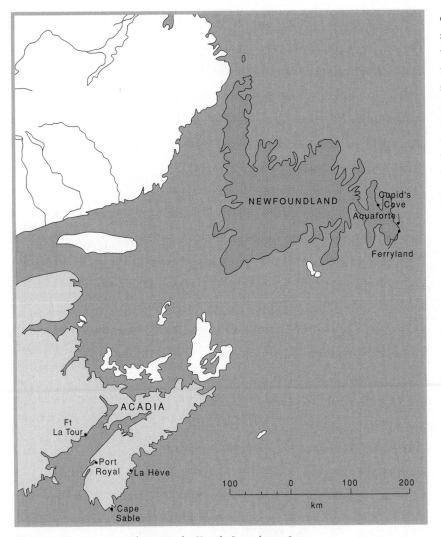

MAP 4.1 European settlements in North America, 1632.

colonizers. Sir William Vaughan, a Welsh lawyer and scholar, tried unsuccessfully to establish a settlement at Aquaforte, and in 1620 sold off sections of his property to Sir George Calvert (later Lord Baltimore). As England's secretary of state for the colonies, Calvert was influential. He was also wealthy. His mercantile interests included a variety of colonial ventures, including the Virginia Company and the East India Company. Within a year of setting his sights on Newfoundland, he laid the foundations for one of the best capitalized colonization projects in North America.

Ferryland, with its sheltered harbour and good drying areas, had been an English fishing station since the sixteenth century. Calvert recruited mostly Roman Catholic settlers—he was himself a convert to Roman Catholicism—but he permitted both Protestant and Catholic clergy to minister in the colony. Religious bickering was the least of the problems that dogged the venture. French privateers and an outbreak of scurvy made the winter of 1628–29 unbearable, causing Calvert to withdraw his active interest in the colony and leave its operation to family agents. All the Catholic settlers in the total population of under 150 people departed either for England or English colonies further south, including Maryland, which was Calvert's next colonizing venture.

While a small number of Protestant settlers remained, they were soon caught in a crossfire between the Calvert family and the family of David Kirke. Having received royal recognition of his claims, Kirke forcibly seized Calvert's properties in 1639. Interested mainly in the fishery, Kirke also promoted agriculture and the production of salt. His widow, Sarah Kirke, was in charge when a Dutch squadron

Beothuk. Between 1610 and 1612 John Guy, a merchant from Bristol, brought out 39 men and 12 women. The colonists cleared land, planted gardens, and built homes, surrounding their small settlement with a palisade protected by mounted guns.

Although the colony's early years were quite promising, problems soon developed. The settlement was harassed by pirates, agriculture proved difficult, and the Beothuk were not eager to trade in furs. Nor were the migratory fishermen enthusiastic about settlement on one of their prized fishing coves. These factors, added to internal dissension, led to the plantation's break-up in the early 1620s.

To recoup some of its investment, the London and Bristol Company sold tracts of land to other potential

The Ferryland Settlement in Newfoundland

Throughout its early history, Ferryland, like other small colonies in Newfoundland, was faced with the daunting challenge of creating a defensible, agriculturally productive settlement that could provision the dry fishery of the area. In 1622, an optimistic Captain Edward Wynne, appointed commander of the settlement by Sir George Calvert, wrote to his superior indicating the steps taken to achieve these objectives:

> After Christmas, we imployed our selves in the woods especially in hard weather, whence we got home as many boord-stocks, afforded us above two hundred boords and above two hundred timber trees besides. We got home as much or as many trees as served us to palizado into the Plantation about foure Acres of ground, for the keeping off of both man &; beast, with post and rayle seven foote high, sharpened in the toppe, the trees being pitched upright and fastened with spikes and nayles. We got also together as much fire wood, as will serve us yet these two moneths. Wee also fitted much garden ground for seede, I meane, Barley, Oates, Pease, and Beans. For addition of building, we have at this present a Parlour of foureteene foote besides the chimney, and twelve foote broad, of convenient height, and a lodging chamber over it; to each a chimney of stone worke with staires and a staire case, besides a tenement of two rooms, or a storie and a halfe, which serves for a store house till we are other wise provided. The Forge hath been finished this five weekes: The Salt-worke is now almost ready. . . . We have also broken much ground for a Brew-house roome and other Tenements. We have a wharfe in good forwardnesse towards the Low-water-marke.[3]

Attempts by such would-be colonizers to recreate their Old World culture in North America often flew in the face of colonial realities. As Calvert himself noted in a letter to Charles I when he decided "to shift to some other warmer climate of this new worlde," the winters were a formidable obstacle to settlement in Ferryland: "from the middest of October, to the middest of May there is a sadd face of wynter upon all this land, both sea and land so frozen for the greatest part of the tyme as they are not penetrable, no plant or vegetable thing appearing out of the earth untill it be about the beginning of May nor fish in the sea besides the ayre is so intolerable cold as it is hardly to be endured."[4]

virtually destroyed the colony in 1673. The Dutch, at war with Britain from 1672 to 1674, had recaptured New Amsterdam (New York) in 1673 and used it as a base to attack other British colonies. Two years later, the population was estimated at over 150.

More attacks by Dutch pirates followed in the 1670s and 1680s. After a brief respite, attacks began again, this time by France, which captured the colony in 1696 and deported all the settlers. Although the British reasserted control the following year, they provided no military protection, with the result that the settlement was destroyed repeatedly in the eighteenth century. It was nonetheless rebuilt each time and by 1800 was one of the major English settlements in Newfoundland.

Jacques Cartier at Hochelaga, by C.W. Jefferys.
Library and Archives Canada/C70257, detail

FRANCE IN AMERICA

Whereas English settlement in Newfoundland was an outgrowth of the fishery, French colonization in eastern North America was prompted by visions of much greater riches. The successes of Spain and Portugal in finding wealth in Central and South America stirred hopes in the French court of finding similar riches through overseas ventures.

In 1534, Francis I commissioned Jacques Cartier, a sea captain from St Malo, to discover and claim for France the fabled lands where gold and other precious metals were to be found. Cartier undertook three voyages to North America between 1534 and 1541. The only gold he found was iron pyrite or "fool's gold," which he mistook for the real thing. His attempt at colonization was also a failure, owing in large part to his duplicitous dealings with the Aboriginal peoples.

Cartier was a product of European society, which treated all non-Christian people with disdain. He left a detailed record of his travels that revealed much about early encounters between Natives and newcomers. In the Baie des Chaleurs area, Cartier traded with Mi'kmaq who appeared familiar with Europeans and proved anxious to trade their furs for iron wares and other European commodities. After leaving the Baie des Chaleurs, Cartier sailed into Gaspé Bay and encountered a hunting party of Iroquoians from the village of Stadacona, located at the present site of Quebec City. Troubles began when he claimed the Stadaconans' territory for Francis I and erected an imposing cross.

Donnacona, the Stadaconan chief, objected to the presence of the cross. According to Cartier, Donnacona "made us a long harangue, making the sign of the cross with two of his fingers, and then he pointed to the land all about, as if he wished to say that all this region belonged to him, and that we ought not to have set up this cross without his permission."[5] In response, Cartier took Donnacona captive and only freed him when he proved more amenable. The chastened chief gave reluctant consent to Cartier's plan to take two of the chief's sons to France for a year.

Returning in September 1535, Cartier again behaved arrogantly. The Stadaconans, perhaps trying to preserve their status as intermediaries between Natives further inland and the Europeans, expressed displeasure at Cartier's wish to travel up the St Lawrence. Cartier ignored their wishes and sailed as far as Hochelaga, the site of present-day Montreal. The Hochelagans welcomed the French to their fortified villages and offered them lavish gifts, but they had little interest in acquiring European goods. Disappointed, Cartier took leave of his hospitable hosts after only one day.

Cartier returned to Stadacona, where he and his crew spent a difficult winter. Twenty-five of the European party of 110 died of scurvy before Native remedies prevented the rest from succumbing as well. The Stadaconans understood the curative powers of a broth and a poultice made from the bark and needles of the *anneda* (possibly white cedar), which is rich in the vitamin C needed to prevent scurvy.

Cartier showed his gratitude by seizing Donnacona, two of his sons, and seven others to accompany his party back to France. There, they were paraded through the streets of several cities. The kidnapping of Aboriginal people for this purpose was a common practice among European explorers eager to convince monarchs and merchants that they had truly discovered new lands full of untold riches. Cartier assured Donnacona that the king of France would handsomely reward him for his visit.

Cartier returned five years later as the leader of an advance party for Jean-François de La Rocque de Roberval, a nobleman who was commissioned to found a permanent settlement near Stadacona. Nine of the ten Stadaconans had died in France, but Cartier, without the survivor along to contradict him, explained that all ten had become great princes. By this time, the Stadaconans were not disposed to assist Cartier's colonists, who spent a rough winter and then headed home with a cargo of fool's gold. Deserted by his lieutenant, Roberval tried nonetheless to re-establish a settlement at the same site during the winter of 1542–43. The charms of his settlers, most of them ex-convicts, found little favour among the Stadaconans, and after a scurvy-ridden winter they too departed.

For several decades thereafter, France gave up on the idea of settlement so far north in the Americas. Failed attempts at settlement in Florida and Brazil (where the Portuguese and Spanish defended their exclusive claims), followed by 40 years of religious warfare, absorbed attention that might otherwise have been bestowed upon the vast territories of Canada. There was no rationale for settlement in the northern part of North America as long as the region's only profitable economic activity was the cod fishery. But by 1600, the dramatic increase in demand for furs had changed the French perspective.

THE FOUNDING OF ACADIA

After establishing temporary religious peace in 1598, Henri IV was determined to have France emulate Spain and Portugal in establishing permanent colonies in the Americas from which wealth and prestige could be derived. In 1603 he granted Pierre du Gua de Monts, a distinguished Protestant soldier and administrator, a 10-year monopoly of trade in the Atlantic region. In return, de Monts promised to settle 60 colonists a year and to promote Roman Catholicism among the Native peoples. In the long run, de Monts' attempts to comply would result in the permanent establishment of European settlement in the Maritime region of Canada, but in the short term his ventures proved disastrous.

In 1604, de Monts and 78 colonists, all male, wintered on an island at the mouth of the St Croix River on the present border between Maine and New Brunswick. Unlike Roberval's convicts, de Monts' colonists were mainly gentlemen, artisans, and mariners. Among them was Samuel de Champlain, who would become a towering figure in Canadian exploration and colonization. The rigours of a Canadian winter defeated these men: 35 died of scurvy.

In the spring, de Monts decided that the site was not promising for agriculture and moved across the Bay of Fundy to the shore of the Annapolis Basin. Only three of the surviving St Croix settlers were prepared to spend another winter in Acadia, but de Monts recruited new colonists for the settlement, which was named Port Royal. The cooperation of the Mi'kmaq, who showed the settlers how to avoid scurvy and survive northern winters, proved invaluable.

In the spring of 1606, the governor of Port Royal, Jean de Poutrincourt et de Saint-Just, brought skilled workmen as well as several aristocratic relatives and friends who would play important roles in the development of New France. These included his son, Charles de Biencourt; a cousin from Paris, Louis Hébert, who was an apothecary and horticulturalist; a cousin from Champagne, Claude de Saint-Étienne de La Tour, and his 14-year-old-son Charles; and Marc Lescarbot, a lawyer from Paris who recorded the activities of this charmed circle in his *Histoire de la Nouvelle France*, published in 1618. Mathieu d'Acosta, an African, who was subsequently described as an interpreter of "Acadian tongues," or Aboriginal languages, is also believed to have been involved in the Port Royal settlement.

The French planted wheat, built a grist mill, raised cattle, and grew fruit and vegetables. Delighting in the warmer winters at Port Royal, they developed innovative responses to the challenges of survival. Champlain founded *l'Ordre de Bon Temps*, its chief purpose to oblige each man to take turns providing game and fish for the table.

De Monts lost his trade monopoly in 1607, but by then the small colony was, however precariously, on its feet. Inspired by the idea of a colonial estate, Poutrincourt secured a grant of the Port Royal area. In 1610, he and Biencourt returned to Acadia with some 20 colonists, including a priest, Jessé Fléché. Membertou, an elderly Mi'kmaq chief, had maintained the habitation during the absence of the French and was apparently eager to accommodate Poutrincourt's colonial ambitions. In short order, Fléché baptized Membertou and 20 members of his family, and traders bartered for the much desired furs. Armed with evidence of both financial and spiritual success, Biencourt returned to France to secure further support for the colony.

He managed to find a patron in the person of the Marquise de Guercheville, but her support was tied to the condition that the Jesuits, who had become influential at the French court, would control missionary work in Acadia and become partners in the trade. In May 1611 Biencourt returned to Port Royal with 36 colonists and two Jesuit priests, Pierre Biard and Énemond Massé, the first mission by a French religious order in the Americas. Quarrels soon erupted between Biencourt and the Jesuits. Determined to see the Jesuits triumph, the Marquise financed an expedition to move the Jesuits from Port Royal to Saint-Sauveur, a new colony established on a site opposite what is now known as Mount Desert Island on the Penobscot River in Maine.

Alarmed by developments on their northern flank, the governor of the English colony of Virginia instructed Samuel Argall to attack the French settlements. In the fall of 1613 he burned and looted Saint-Sauveur and Port Royal. Returning the following year to find complete devastation, Poutrincourt took most of the colonists back to France. Only Biencourt, his cousin Charles de Saint-Étienne de La Tour, and a few others stayed on.

The Mi'kmaq and Maliseet, who had traded furs with Europeans for generations before French settlement took root, developed close ties with the French who lived among them. Not only did they gradually reconcile their beliefs with those of the persistent Roman Catholic missionaries in their midst, they also entered marriage relationships with the newcomers. Following the death of Biencourt in 1623, the direction of the colony was entrusted to Charles de La Tour, who with his father Claude continued to make Acadia home. Charles married a Mi'kmaq woman, who was likely the daughter of a local chief. Later blessed by a Récollet priest, the union produced three daughters, all of whom were baptized; one eventually entered a convent in Paris.

French claims to Acadia were directly challenged by Sir William Alexander, a Scot who in 1621 received from James I a grant of "New Scotland," defined as extending from the St Croix to the St Lawrence. After his first attempt to found a colony failed, Alexander persuaded the king in 1624 to create 150 knights-baronets, who, in return for payment, would receive a title and a land grant of 30 000 acres. Although small colonies were established in 1629 at Port-aux-Baleines on Cape Breton Island under the command of Lord Ochiltree and at Port Royal under Sir William Alexander's son (also named William), they both were short-lived. Within months of its founding, Ochiltree's settlement was destroyed by a French expedition. Alexander's colony survived by making accommodation both with the Mi'kmaq and Claude de La Tour.

THE FUR TRADE ON THE ST LAWRENCE

Meanwhile, de Monts and Champlain had directed their attention toward the St Lawrence, where the fur trade had better prospects for success. The fur trade reached the First Nations along the St Lawrence well before France colonized the area. In 1559, French traders established a trading post at Tadoussac, where the Saguenay River flows south into the St Lawrence. By the beginning of the seventeenth century, over 1000 Algonquin, Innu, and Maliseet arrived each year at Tadoussac to trade with French fisher-traders.

By that time, the Iroquoian peoples whom Cartier had met had vanished from the area. Their fate is unknown and a source of much speculation. One hypothesis argues that they were dispersed by the Algonkian peoples of the area, while another suggests that they were absorbed, willingly or by force, into either the Huron or Five Nations Iroquois. It seems unlikely that they left of their own accord. Presumably, the Algonkians in the region, who traded with the Mi'kmaq, would have been in a position, with their new hatchets and axes and perhaps a musket or two, to chase away peoples minimally involved with European traders. Because some groups traded with Europeans while others were excluded, the relative equality of arms in the past had given way to dramatic imbalances. Yet another possibility is that contact with the Europeans in the Cartier period may have resulted in the spread of mortal diseases, causing the thin ranks of the survivors to flee to other territories to escape a scourge that seemed inexplicable.

The Native peoples were absolutely necessary to fur traders: only they knew the terrain in which beaver could be trapped at just the right time. Beaver down was thickest in winter when the animals inhabited remote lakes and streams, their lodges well hidden. Pelts worn as clothing lost their long guard hairs and became glossy and supple through contact with body oil and perspiration. They were thus ideal for felting by Parisian hatters. European experience with Aboriginal peoples elsewhere might have suggested enslaving the Natives to ensure that they became a pliant, reliable, cheap labour force. But, unlike plantation workers and miners, fur trappers did not work in large numbers in a small area, so the European traders had to treat them with some consideration.

THE FOUNDING OF QUEBEC

The north shore of the St Lawrence became the focus of the French Empire in North America. By the time Quebec was founded in 1608, the area was known as

Canada, derived from the Huron word "kanata" meaning village or settlement. The borders of Canada were never firmly set during the French regime. The term was loosely used, even in official correspondence, as a synonym for New France, but as Jesuit Father Pierre Baird pointed out as early as 1616, "Canada . . . is not, properly speaking, all this extent of country which they now call New France; but it is only that part which extends along the great River Canada [soon to be called the St Lawrence] and the Gulf of St Lawrence."[6]

As de Monts' lieutenant, Samuel de Champlain chose the site of today's Quebec City as the new base of operations in Canada. It had several advantages. In addition to spectacular natural defences, it was also close to the lands of the Native peoples who traded at Tadoussac, where trade continued in violation of de Monts' fur-trading monopoly. Although Champlain soon became obsessed with making Quebec a settled, Christian community on a European model, his goal in 1608 was simply to monopolize the St Lawrence fur trade.

Quebec's beginnings were modest and inauspicious. Of twenty-five men who wintered there in 1608–9, only nine were alive the following spring after scurvy had taken its toll. The credit for the colony's survival belongs in large part to Champlain. Frustrated in his efforts to revive the court promise of a commercial monopoly, de Monts was prepared to abandon Quebec, but Champlain persevered. As he would several times over the next quarter-century, Champlain travelled to France to seek court and financial support for the struggling St Lawrence colony. A new commercial monopoly was established and Quebec was saved, with Champlain becoming the lieutenant of the monopolist who replaced de Monts.

What little we know about Champlain's origins comes mostly from his own writings, which are almost devoid of references to his personal life. What is apparent is that by the time he arrived in North America he was a devout Roman Catholic and an accomplished navigator and mapmaker. He held no official position in de Monts' initial entourage, receiving the title of lieutenant only in 1608. A robust, ebullient man, he persuaded his French audiences that a colony on the St Lawrence would soon pay dividends in the form of a Northwest Passage to Asia as well as mineral discoveries in the colony and opportunities to convert Native peoples.

Although Champlain never became the formal governor of Quebec, he had effective charge over its civil administration, enforcing the king's laws and overseeing relations with the Native peoples. He also invested a substantial sum in the colony, using the proceeds from a dowry he received when he married a 12-year-old French girl, Hélène Boullé, in 1610. Champlain, who was about 40 at the time, agreed not to consummate the marriage for two years. His wife joined him in the colony in 1620 but remained for only four years.

The Algonquin who controlled the territory where Quebec was founded did not reside permanently in the region. Nonetheless, their power was very real, and the French needed their consent for the establishment of a settlement. After that consent was obtained, Champlain demonstrated his good will toward his prospective commercial partners by agreeing in 1609 to act as their military ally in an ongoing war with the Five Nations Iroquois. That alliance also led to contact with the Huron allies of the Algonquin and to direct involvement in a battle against the Iroquois in 1615.

Within a short time, Indian and European rivalries had intertwined. The Huron became partners with the Algonquin and the Innu in a military-commercial alliance with the major French fur-trading interests. The Five Nations Iroquois became fur suppliers to the Dutch at New Amsterdam (New York City) and Albany. This alignment strengthened the French resolve to encourage continued Huron hostility toward the Iroquois. Otherwise, northern nations, for whom the Huron on Georgian Bay and the Algonquin on the upper Ottawa River acted as intermediaries, might barter furs to Natives who traded with the European rivals of the French.

PREACHING THE WORD

The French did not count on military alliances alone to cement their relations with their First Nations trading partners. For European monarchs, including the French kings, it was important to give the colonizing ventures in newly explored territories a higher pur-

BIOGRAPHY

Étienne Brûlé

Hoping to better the understanding between the French and their Native allies, as well as to create a supply of interpreters to carry on the fur trade, Champlain encouraged the men in his charge to live with Native allies and learn their languages. The first to volunteer was Étienne Brûlé. While still in his teens, Brûlé had been one of the nine survivors of the difficult winter of 1609, and he went on not only to learn the Huron language but also to adopt Huron dress and customs. In turn, he was effectively adopted by the Natives, who complained nonetheless that he used the relative sexual freedom of Native society to practise uncontrolled lechery. While serving as an interpreter for French traders with the Natives, Brûlé most likely became the first European to see Huronia, Lake Ontario, Lake Superior, and today's state of Pennsylvania. He was also branded a traitor for collaborating with the English after they seized Quebec in 1629. About 1633, for reasons unknown, the Huron turned against him, killing and eating him. This adventurous Frenchman became the prototype for the many young men who would live among the Native peoples later in the century, engaging in the fur trade and adopting, for a time, Native language and ways.

This recent painting depicts Champlain and his interpreter, Étienne Brûlé, with a party of Huron on Lake Simcoe in 1615.
Rogers Communications Inc.

pose than the extraction of wealth. The Christianizing of the Natives became that purpose. Fur traders, initially leery of imposing representatives of a foreign religion on their trading allies, found that the missionaries could be useful in strengthening relations between the French and particular Native groups as well as in instilling European notions of regular work habits. Apart from conversion of the Natives, the church would serve as a cultural link with France within the colony, counselling settlers to obey both divine law and the laws of His Majesty the King. Religious orders, both of women and men, became the exclusive providers of education, health, and charity services to the colonists.

Conversion of the First Nations to Christianity was never an easy task. Each Aboriginal group had its own well-established religious beliefs, and little in Aboriginal experience suggested that one set of religious views and practices must apply to all peoples. Moreover, they believed themselves to be morally superior to the Europeans, among whom they thought that thieves and drunks, whose actions contradicted Christian values, abounded. Their usual response to the Christians' universal claims was: "Such is not our custom; your world is different from ours; the God who created yours did not create ours."[7]

The first group of missionaries in Quebec reaped little success from their conversion efforts. The Récollets, who began arriving in 1615, were convinced that Aboriginal peoples must be Europeanized if they were to become Christians. Although the Récollets conducted missions among Algonkian tribes, they had difficulty adjusting to their migratory lifestyle. The sedentary agricultural Huron villages near Georgian Bay seemed a more likely base for their missionary efforts. Huronia was a significant location in both commercial and strategic terms: it was the point of exchange between the southern agricultural nations and the northern nomadic hunters. From these villages in the Great Lakes basin, travellers could have

"Teaching parishioners to say their catechism, using ideograms." Missionary Chrestien LeClercq prepared this illustration to celebrate the work of the Gaspé mission at Miscou. Established in 1633 to convert the local Natives, the mission was destroyed by English privateers from New York in 1690.

Library and Archives Canada/NL22323

1620s, commented favourably on the skilled craftwork of the women and men, particularly their pottery, canoe making, and weaving. The Huron were sober and healthy; the ravages of European liquor and disease had not yet reached them. Sagard considered them the aristocracy of the Aboriginal peoples because they were sedentary and agricultural, while he likened the roaming Innu to the poor of Europe. If the Huron were Christians, Sagard thought, these would be families among whom God would take pleasure to dwell. Their tolerance, a virtue little practised in Europe, caused Sagard's co-religionist, Joseph Le Caron, to conclude: "No one must come here in the hope of suffering martyrdom . . . for we are not in a country where the natives put Christians to death on account of their religion." On the contrary, they "leave everyone to his own belief."[8] Sagard also found much to criticize about the Huron. While they were generous to a fault, they were also, in his opinion, unclean, ill-mannered, revenge seeking, incorrigible liars, and shameless belchers.

All of Sagard's remarks, like those of his fellow missionaries, must be treated with caution. By virtue of their occupation, the missionaries were likely to exaggerate the flaws of the culture they wished to destroy, and they tended to overlook the flaws of the culture they wished to impose in its place. Still, they did at times favourably compare Native to European customs, such as the Huron practice of warriors carrying their own food when they went on the warpath. Sagard remarked, "If Christians were to cultivate the same frugality they might maintain very powerful armies at smaller cost and make war on enemies of the Church and of the Christian name without oppressing the people or ruining the country, and God would not be so greatly offended as He is by the majority of our soldiers who seem, to a good man, rather people without God than Christians born to be raised to heaven."[9]

Nonetheless, the missionaries believed that they had more to teach the Native peoples than vice versa. In 1625, Jesuits began arriving in Quebec, ostensibly to aid the Récollets with their missionary work but in reality to supplant them as the principal missionaries to the Natives. The work of both groups was rudely interrupted when an English expedition captured Quebec in 1629.

access by waterways and relatively easy portages to the far western plains, the Mississippi River, and even Hudson Bay. It was a logical point from which to start building a Laurentian commercial empire, a missionary network, and a chain of military fortifications.

The missionaries found aspects of Native society both to praise and criticize. While they denounced the relative power of women, the permissive upbringing of children, and the sexual freedom among youth, they acknowledged Native hospitality and generosity. Brother Gabriel Sagard, writing of the Huron in the

CRISIS ON THE ST LAWRENCE

The English attack could not have taken place at a worse time. In 1627, when the population of Quebec was only 107, Champlain's efforts to build a colony on the St Lawrence received a boost from France. Cardinal Richelieu, Louis XIII's chief minister, engineered a new trade monopoly, designed to encourage trade, settlement, and missionary activity. Known as the Compagnie de la Nouvelle France or Compagnie des Cents Associés (Company of One Hundred Associates), it was granted lands from Florida to the Arctic Circle, a perpetual monopoly of the fur trade, and a monopoly of all other commerce except the fisheries for 15 years. In return the monopoly holders would be required to settle at least 200 Catholic colonists a year for 15 years and fund missionary activities. Prominent nobles and merchants were among the 100 associates who invested in the company, which represented the largest colonization effort ever attempted by France.

Unfortunately, the venture got off to a poor start. War broke out between England and France just as the Company of One Hundred Associates was under-taking its first overseas initiatives. David Kirke and his four brothers, financed by London merchants and commissioned by Charles I to displace the French from "Canida," seized Tadoussac and captured the company's ships carrying 400 colonists, off Gaspé. Blockaded by the English, Quebec surrendered in July 1629. A few French colonists stayed, but most of the fur traders, led by Champlain, departed.

In 1632 Canada and Acadia were restored to France by the Treaty of Saint-Germain-en-Laye. This treaty established an important pattern of European intrusion in the Americas: while battles in North America might temporarily determine who exercised control, longer-term authority would be decided in Europe through negotiations among the imperial powers. Charles I of England, who had married the sister of the king of France, refused to return the captured territories in North America until his brother-in-law had paid his sister's full dowry. In such negotiations, the colonies in today's Canada were mere pieces on a chess board, to be moved about according to the strategic and personal interests of the imperial players. The views of the colonists themselves would matter little when larger interests of empire were at stake.

Native Assessments of European Society

During France's brief occupation of a portion of Brazil, the French conquerors brought three Tupinambas to Rouen in 1562. The Tupinamba, asked for an assessment of French society, indicated that "they had noticed that there were among us men full of and gorged with all sorts of good things, and that their other halves were beggars at their doors, emaciated with hunger and poverty; and they thought it strange that these needy halves could endure such an injustice, and did not take the others by the throat, or set fire to their houses."[10]

Similarly, Sauvignon, an 18-year-old Huron, who accompanied Samuel de Champlain on a trip to France in 1611, judged that country unfavourably. He noted the "great number of needy and beggars" in France, "saying that if [they] had some intelligence [they] would set some order in the matter, the remedies being simple."[11]

The Mi'kmaq, according to the *Jesuit Relations*, "consider themselves better than the French. 'For,' they say, 'you are always fighting and quarreling among yourselves; we live peaceably. You are envious and are all the time slandering each other; you are thieves and deceivers; you are covetous and are neither generous nor kind; as for us, if we have a morsel of bread we share it with our neighbor.' "[12]

Conclusion

Colonization had modest beginnings in Canada and Acadia. In 1632, Ferryland, Acadia, and Quebec each included roughly 100 permanent settlers. Yet certain patterns of European penetration of First Nations territory had been firmly established. First, the intense rivalries among European countries, particularly Britain and France, had been transported to the New World. Second, the Europeans and Natives were developing trade relations where both sides perceived a benefit. Third, the Europeans had no intention of simply leaving the Natives to live as they wished in their ancestral homes. The religious orders were committed to conversion of the Natives to Christianity and European ways.

Notes

1 John S. Long, "Narratives of Early Encounters between Europeans and the Cree of Western James Bay," *Ontario History* 80, 3 (September 1988): 231.

2 Robert McGhee, "Contact between Native North Americans and the Medieval Norse: A Review of the Evidence," *American Antiquity* 49, 1 (1984): 4–26; Thomas H. McGovern, "The Archeology of the Norse North Atlantic," *Annual Review of Anthropology* 19 (1990): 331–51.

3 Joseph R. Smallwood, ed., *Encyclopedia of Newfoundland and Labrador*, vol. 2 (St John's: Newfoundland Book Publishers, 1984), 53.

4 George Calvert to King Charles I, 19 August 1629, in Gillian Cell, *Newfoundland Discovered: English Attempts at Colonization, 1610–1630* (London: Hakluyt Society, 1982), 295–96.

5 *The Voyages of Jacques Cartier*, trans. and ed. H.P. Biggar (Ottawa: King's Printer, 1924), 65.

6 W. Kaye Lamb, "Canada," *The Canadian Encyclopedia*, vol. 1 (Edmonton: Hurtig, 1988), 322.

7 James P. Ronda, "We Are Well as We Are: An Indian Critique of Seventeenth-Century Missions," *William and Mary Quarterly*, 3rd series, 34 (1977): 77.

8 Joseph Le Caron, *Au Roy sur la Nouvelle-France* (Paris: n.p., 1626), 68.

9 Father Gabriel Sagard, *The Long Journey to the Country of the Huron* (Toronto: Champlain Society, 1939), 153.

10 James Axtell, "Through Another Glass Darkly: Early Indian Views of Europeans," in *Out of the Background: Readings on Canadian Native History*, 2nd ed., ed. Ken Coates and Robin Fisher (Toronto: Copp Clark, 1996), 25–6.

11 Ibid., 26.

12 A.G. Bailey, *The Conflict of European and Eastern Algonkian Cultures 1504–1700: A Study in Canadian Civilization*, 2nd ed. (Toronto: University of Toronto Press, 1969), 14.

Related Readings in This Series

From *Foundations: Readings in Pre-Confederation Canadian History*

Ramsay Cook, "1492 and All That: Making a Garden out of a Wilderness," 35–48.
Alan Gordon, "Heroes, History, and Two Nationalisms: Jacques Cartier," 49–65.

From Media Companion CD-ROM, Volume I

Letter from Lagarto to John the Third, King of Portugal
Examination of Newfoundland Sailors Regarding Cartier
The Mission in New France, 1612
Champlain

Selected Reading

On the Norse explorations, see P.H. Sawyer, ed., *The Oxford Illustrated History of the Vikings* (Oxford: Oxford University Press, 2000), and William Fitzhugh and Elizabeth I. Ward, eds., *Vikings: The North Atlantic Saga* (Washington: Smithsonian Institution Press, 2000). A recent work on John Cabot is Peter Edward Pope, *The Many Landfalls of John Cabot* (Toronto: University of Toronto Press, 1997). On Frobisher, see Robert McGhee, *The Arctic Voyages of Martin*

Frobisher (Montreal and Kingston: Canadian Museum of Civilization/McGill-Queen's University Press, 2001).

Cartier's account of his explorations is found in *The Voyages of Jacques Cartier*, trans. Henry Percival Biggar, ed. Ramsay Cook (Toronto: University of Toronto Press, 1993). Useful texts on Samuel de Champlain include Francine Légaré, *Samuel de Champlain, père de la Nouvelle-France* (Montreal: XYZ, 2003), and Edward Gaylord Bourne, ed., *Samuel de Champlain, Algonquians, Hurons and Iroquois: Champlain Explores America, 1603–1616*, trans. Annie Nettleton Bourne (Dartmouth, NS: Brook House Press, 2000).

The major surveys in English of the history of New France are W.J. Eccles, *The Canadian Frontier, 1534–1760* (New York: Holt, Rinehart and Winston, 1969) and *The French in North America, 1500–1783* (Markham, ON: Fitzhenry and Whiteside, 1998). A detailed study of New France before 1663 is Marcel Trudel, *The Beginnings of New France, 1524–1663*, trans. Patricia Claxton (Toronto: McClelland and Stewart, 1973). Rich details on the social history of Montreal are found in Louise Dechêne, *Habitants and Merchants in Seventeenth Century Montreal* (Montreal: McGill-Queen's University Press, 1992).

The early history of Acadia is covered in John G. Reid, *Acadia, Maine, and New Scotland: Marginal Colonies in the Seventeenth Century* (Toronto: University of Toronto Press, 1981); Naomi E.S. Griffiths, *The Contexts of Acadian History, 1686–1784* (Montreal: McGill-Queen's University Press, 1992) and *The Acadians: Creation of a People* (Toronto: McGraw-Hill Ryerson, 1973); Sally Ross and Alphonse Deveau, *The Acadians of Nova Scotia: Past and Present* (Halifax: Nimbus, 1992); Elizabeth Jones, *Gentlemen and Jesuits* (Halifax: Nimbus Publishing, 2002); and Andrew Hill Clark, *Acadia: The Geography of Early Nova Scotia to 1760* (Madison: University of Wisconsin Press, 1968). Newfoundland in the seventeenth century is discussed in Gordon W. Handcock, *So Long as There Comes Noe Women: Origins of English Settlement in Newfoundland* (Milton: Global Heritage Press, 2000); Gillian Cell, *Newfoundland Discovered* (London: Hakluyt Society, 1982); and H.A. Innis, *The Cod Fisheries: The History of an International Economy* (Toronto: University of Toronto Press, 1978). On whaling, see Daniel Francis, *A History of World Whaling* (Markham, ON: Penguin, 1990).

There is a growing literature on early European-Native relations in Canada. Some of these texts are referred to in Chapter 2. Additional sources include Denys Delâge, *Amerindians and Europeans in the American Northeast, 1600–1664* (Vancouver: UBC Press, 1993); L.C. Green and Olive P. Dickason, *The Law of Nations and the New World* (Edmonton: University of Alberta Press, 1989); Cornelius Jaenen, *The French Relationship with the Native People of New France and Acadia* (Ottawa: Indian and Northern Affairs Canada, 1984); Bruce G. Trigger, *Natives and Newcomers: Canada's "Heroic Age" Reconsidered* (Montreal: McGill-Queen's University Press, 1986); and E.S. Rogers and Donald B. Smith, eds., *Aboriginal Ontario* (Toronto: Dundurn Press, 1994). On early missionaries to New France, see John Webster Grant, *Moon of Wintertime: Missionaries and the Indians of Canada in Encounter since 1534* (Toronto: University of Toronto Press, 1984).

WEBLINKS

JACQUES CARTIER
www.win.tue.nl/~engels/discovery/cartier.html

This page, part of Discoverers Web, has a biography of Cartier and links to related sites.

FUR TRADE
collections.ic.gc.ca/hbc/catex6.htm

This address leads to the Hudson's Bay Company's Digital Collection, based in the Manitoba Museum of Man and Nature. The site offers images of artifacts of the fur trade, as well as links to the rest of the collection and its history.

THE COD FISHERY
http://collections.ic.gc.ca/cod/index.htm

This site provides an overview of the history of the northern cod fishery.

ST CROIX ISLAND
http://collections.ic.gc.ca/saintcroixisland/
http://collections.ic.gc.ca/ile-ste-croix

These two sites provide a detailed history of the short-lived French settlement on St Croix Island in 1604–05.

INVESTIGATING FERRYLAND
http://www.heritage.nf.ca/avalon/arch

This site explores the history and recent archeological investigations of the Ferryland settlement in Newfoundland.

CHAPTER 5

Natives and Newcomers, 1632–1663

Timeline

▶ **1635**	Death of Champlain
▶ **1639**	Ursulines arrive in New France
▶ **1642**	Founding of Montreal
▶ **1649**	Destruction of Huronia
▶ **1654**	English seize Acadia

Aenons was a Huron leader who objected to the Jesuits opening a mission in Huronia. His objections were recorded in *Jesuit Relations*, the journal prepared by the Jesuits to propagandize their efforts to spread the Christian faith to First Nations. The Jesuits made note of Aenons' views so that supporters of the Jesuits' work would understand the uphill struggle faced by Christians in attempting to convert the "heathen" Natives.

> When you speak to us of obeying and acknowledging as our master him whom you say has made Heaven and earth, I imagine you are talking of overthrowing the country. Your ancestors assembled in earlier times, and held a council, where they resolved to take as their God him whom you honor, and ordained all the ceremonies that you observe; as for us, we have learned others from our own Fathers.[1]

Nor was Aenons alone in doubting the wisdom of rejecting traditional First Nations religion in favour of Catholicism. An unidentified Huron, responding to continuing Iroquois attacks on Huronia in the 1640s, told the Jesuits:

> You tell us that God is full of goodness, and then, when we give ourselves up to him he massacres us. The Iroquois, our mortal enemies, do not believe in God, they do not love the prayers, they are more wicked than the Demons—and yet they prosper; and since we have forsaken the usages of our ancestors, they kill us, they massacre us, they burn us—they exterminate us, root and branch. What profit can there come to us from lending ear to the Gospel, since death and the faith nearly always march in company?[2]

The Huron, like most other Aboriginal peoples, willingly engaged in the fur trade with the Europeans. They hoped to acquire trade items that seemed useful within the terms of their established cultures. Yet trade with the Europeans brought more than material goods. It brought missionaries, diseases, and alcohol. It also led to a deep questioning of Native cultural practices and created internal divisions in their societies. The social values of European fur traders, settlers, and missionaries were also called into question by the colonizing experience. In the frontier environment, they found that the forces of repression that enforced relationships in the metropolis were noticeably weaker. This chapter explores the relative influence of the frontier and the metropolis on both the Natives and newcomers to New France.

CIVIL WAR IN ACADIA

Following the Treaty of Saint-Germain-en-Laye, the French government was determined to re-establish control over Acadia. The new attitude on the part of France became apparent when Cardinal Richelieu appointed Isaac de Razilly to take the surrender of Port Royal in 1632—with a force of three ships and 300 men—and further commissioned him as the royal lieutenant general in New France. During the next three years, Razilly, with his lieutenants Charles de

---

MORE TO THE STORY

The Frontier and the Metropolis

Throughout this text, in order to better understand the dynamics of a given society, it is helpful to bear in mind two key questions. Where is the locus of decision making in the society? What are the influences that produce social change? Historians have developed the concepts of frontier and metropolis to analyze societies and formulate answers to these questions.

Within the context of the European exploration and settlement of what was to become Canada, the frontier includes the natural environment as well as the human inhabitants in the "New World." We could study the frontier in isolation, without reference to the impact of the power or the ideas of the metropolis, or "mother country." An emphasis on the frontier allows us to see how immigrants adapted their ideas and practices to a new environment, and how they were influenced by both geography and their encounters with the First Nations. Taken to its extreme, however, this perspective treats the colonists as if their lives began when they left their homelands. It ignores the continuing importance of imperial powers in shaping the ideas and institutions of the colonies. Moreover, it treats the Native peoples as if their lives and attitudes were unaffected by colonialism.

At the other end of the continuum, we could study metropolitan institutions as if they were puppet-masters controlling the lives of the colonists and the First Nations. Emphasis on the metropolis reminds us that imperial powers actively intervened in their colonies and that metropolitan ideas were important in shaping people's responses to a new society. If we focus on the roles of various institutions, both political and economic, we can also see that there is a chain of metropoles that can shape the lives of individuals. So, for example, the government in Paris might give orders to Montreal institutions, which in turn exerted power on the fur traders and First Nations in western Canada. Used exclusively, an emphasis on the power of the metropolis ignores the frontier influences that also moulded behaviour.

In the 1960s historian W.J. Eccles noted that although metropolitan authorities were successful in planting French institutions in New France, colonial conditions encouraged modifications. Thus, the French government was able to ban participation by lawyers in legal matters to make the costs of seeking justice cheaper for people in New France than it was in France. While colonial officials defended a rigid social hierarchy that resembled that of France, they felt compelled to respond sympathetically to popular pressures that might have been dealt with in France by repression. For example, grassroots opposition to church "tithes" (compulsory dues) at the high levels experienced by French peasants resulted in official decisions to impose substantially lower tithes in New France. The relative impact of metropolis and frontier also changed over time. In the early years of settlement, the frontier experience demanded adjustments to institutions and practices that by the eighteenth century were no longer necessary.

Madame de La Tour's active role in defence of her family's claim to Acadia demonstrates the atypical roles that women sometimes played in New France despite the growing public power of men over women in European centres.
The Story of Acadia by James Hannay (Kentville Nova Scotia: Dominion Atlantic Railway), New Brunswick Museum, St John, NB

Menou d'Aulnay and Nicholas Denys, laid the groundwork for a lasting Acadian colony. Razilly established his main base at La Hève on the south shore of Acadia, which was better suited to his military and commercial interests than Port Royal. Denys engaged in fishing, lumbering, and fur-trading activities, concentrating his efforts at Canso, Saint-Pierre (St Peters), and Nepisiquit on the Bay of Chaleur.

Razilly managed to maintain harmonious relations with Charles de La Tour, who also claimed title to Acadia. Staying out of Razilly's way, La Tour conducted major trading operations from his bases at Cape Sable and on the St John River and dealt separately with the Compagnie des Cent Associés, which had authority over all of New France. Following Razilly's death in 1635, his successor, Charles de Menou d'Aulnay, proved less accommodating to La Tour's claims. D'Aulnay was interested in agricultural settlement and made Port Royal the centre of his colonization efforts and immediately challenged La Tour's rights to trade in Acadia.

The battle between the d'Aulnays and the de La Tours for control of early Acadia was a complicated affair that pitted two families against one another in a struggle for status and wealth. While Charles de La Tour and Charles de Menou d'Aulnay were the key participants in the feud, their wives were also important players. Charles de La Tour's second wife, Marie, arrived in the colony in 1640 and settled in La Tour's fort on the St John River, across the Bay of Fundy from Port Royal. Active in defence of the family claim to Acadia, she travelled to France in 1643 to plead—unsuccessfully—her husband's case against charges that he had plotted with the English to place the colony in their control in return for driving d'Aulnay away.

Meanwhile, d'Aulnay razed La Tour's settlement at Cape Sable in 1641. In 1645, while Charles was in Boston purchasing arms and supplies, he attacked La Tour's fort on the St John River. Marie took command of the fort's 45 or so men and for five days withstood a siege by a larger, better-armed force. She surrendered in return for a promise from d'Aulnay to spare her men—a promise quickly broken. She died of unknown causes several weeks later, while still d'Aulnay's captive. Charles de La Tour took refuge in Quebec.

The victorious d'Aulnay drowned in 1650, leaving an estate heavily in debt. His chief creditor,

Emmanuel Le Borgne, seized Port Royal and attacked other settlements in the region. D'Aulnay's widow, Jeanne Motin, battled creditors in the courts and even married Charles de La Tour in a fruitless effort to secure her claims. The La Tours were joined in opposition to Le Borgne by Nicolas Denys, who by this time had substantial interests in the fishery and the fur trade between Canso and the Gaspé.

Civil war in Acadia was averted in 1654 by an English force led by Robert Sedgwick, who plundered Port Royal and other settlements and took La Tour prisoner. The English government agreed that La Tour could reoccupy his posts in Acadia on the condition that he swear allegiance to England and pay off his huge debts to Boston and other English creditors. To raise the money he needed to satisfy his captors, he sold most of his rights in Acadia to Thomas Temple (who became governor in 1662) and William Crowne. The English remained in control of Acadia until 1667 when, by the Treaty of Breda, the colony was returned to France.

Despite the difficulties, the European population in Acadia had reached about 400 by the mid-seventeenth century. Both d'Aulnay and La Tour recruited settlers, many of them indentured labourers and domestics. While many servants left once they had served their indenture, those who remained behind soon took root. The seizure of Port Royal by New Englanders in 1654 caused the French settlers in the area to move upriver. When French rule was restored, the "Acadians" had become accustomed to trading with New Englanders and resisting the demands of authorities, whether French or English. This independent spirit would continue to grow in a region that remained at the crossroads of conflicting imperial claims.

Although the Mi'kmaq still outnumbered Europeans in Acadia in the 1650s, their culture was being fundamentally altered. Depletion of game occurred early in the Mi'kmaq territories. By the mid-seventeenth century, there had been several famines; moose in Cape Breton (Île Royale) had become extinct and so had elk on Mission Island. Fur-bearing animals, killed in larger numbers to accommodate the traders' demands, became harder to find. The Mi'kmaq increasingly bought clothes from the Europeans, and as European cottons, woollens, and kettles replaced local manufacture, Native women's crucial production roles broke down. The men's skills in crafting items from stone and other indigenous materials also diminished. While some traditions survived, French missionaries increasingly defined familial, sexual, and property arrangements.

Resource depletion led the Mi'kmaq to cluster around the French settlements, where they consumed unfamiliar foods such as peas, prunes, and bread. As elsewhere in North America, alcohol also became a staple of Mi'kmaq diets. The resulting physical deterioration may have contributed to their vulnerability in the face of European-imported diseases. By the end of the seventeenth century, Mi'kmaq numbers had declined to between 2000 and 3000. Kinship groups collapsed as disease decimated the population. The Mi'kmaq had not been forced by Europeans to change their way of life; they had merely engaged in trade with outsiders whose goods they wished to acquire. Eventually, the loss of their resource base meant that the Mi'kmaq lacked the option of returning to their old lifestyle.

Historians now tend to be cautious in using the term "dependence" in discussing Native relations with the Europeans because it implies that the First Nations became charity cases or that they were victims rather than actors in their relations with the newcomers. In the case of the Mi'kmaq, neither was the case. If the Mi'kmaq had become dependent on French goods, the French were as dependent upon them for their survival: until the French were forced out of North America, the Mi'kmaq served as invaluable military allies against New England.

FIRST NATIONS AND THE CHURCH

The return of Canada and Acadia to France in 1632 resulted in a redoubling of efforts to Christianize Aboriginal peoples. In the first half of the seventeenth century, Acadia was an open field for competing clerical orders. Récollet, Jesuit, and Capuchin priests conducted missions among the Mi'kmaq and Maliseet. The Capuchins were particularly active, sending at least 40 priests and 20 lay brothers to Acadia between 1632 and 1656.[3] Most priests spent only a few years in the region, but they achieved their goals: the Mi'kmaq and Maliseet gradually reconciled their beliefs with those of the persistent Christians in their midst.

French political intrigues decreed that the Jesuits but not the Récollets would be allowed to return to Canada. In 1639, they built a headquarters called Sainte-Marie in Huronia to oversee their village missions. Jérome Lalement, the superior of the mission, conceived of such a centre as a means both of reducing missionary economic dependency on the Huron and of providing Christian Huron with a place of worship away from their pagan fellows. By 1648, Ste-Marie-Among-the-Hurons boasted 18 priests and 46 lay assistants. Few of the Christian converts, however, agreed to abandon their villages and traditional customs and relocate to Ste-Marie. Ste-Marie was burned to the ground by the Jesuits in 1649 to avoid its desecration by the Iroquois after the dispersal of the Huron.

The Jesuits also encouraged Christian Natives from several tribes to move to Sillery, a Jesuit-sponsored reserve outside of Quebec established in 1638. Here it was hoped that the new converts would farm under the guidance of the Jesuits and be free of contamination by "pagan" influences.

The first inhabitants of Sillery failed to adapt to a sedentary agricultural life, and soon alcohol and disease introduced by European intruders sent the reserve into a steep decline. Huron refugees from the Huron-Iroquois war gave it a more stable existence after 1650. They punished drunks and absentees from mass and proved especially harsh with women who clung to traditional notions of their rights. One young woman, whose parents were converts, was publicly whipped for yielding to advances from a traditionalist, while another woman was chained by one foot for having refused to obey her husband.

Initially the Jesuits, like the Récollets, sought to transform the Aboriginal peoples into Christian farmers and to undermine their existing beliefs and practices. They quickly realized that their emphasis on forced assimilation was failing and became more flexible in their approach to missionary work. They settled among the first peoples, allowing themselves to be adopted by families, and accepted that, in some circumstances, hunting must be combined with, rather than replaced by, farming. Syncretic religious practices, linking Native religious traditions with Christianity, were tolerated. So, for example, the

Jesuits acknowledged the practice of resuscitating a dead person by permitting a living relative to adopt the dead person's name and children. In return, Christian Natives were required to recognize Christian notions of death in the speeches that accompanied the resuscitation ceremony.

The Jesuits also encouraged the Native use of rosaries, crucifixes, Christian medals, and rings as good luck charms. Indeed, the Jesuits tried to make use of Native preferences for public-relations purposes. Charles Garnier, writing in 1645 from Huronia to his brother, a monk in France, asked for pictures of a beardless Jesus, including one of him as a youth of 18. He stressed that, to make the maximum impression on the Natives, the pictures chosen should have Jesus, Mary, and happy souls in white while others should be dressed in bright red or blue. The agony of a man damned in the eyes of God, Garnier noted, should be portrayed in graphic detail: a huge dragon twisted around him, and two horrible demons jabbing him with an iron harpoon while a third demon scalped him.

The Natives were impressed that the Jesuits, with their European technology, could foresee eclipses, and they wondered if the priests could also predict the weather and the appearance of enemies. As pre-literates, Natives were fascinated by books and writing. According to Gabriel Sagard, they found it remarkable that Europeans could make thoughts travel great distances using scribbled notes.

Notwithstanding the impression made by the missionaries on the Native peoples, the extent of real conversions in the early years of Jesuit proselytizing is difficult to determine. Some converts were zealots who spurned their relatives and refused to participate in traditional religious ceremonies. Others may have accepted conversion to improve their trading position with the French traders, who regarded Christianized Indians as more reliable partners. In Huronia, for example, only the Christianized Natives received muskets in their trade with the French.

The persistence of the Jesuits and their desire for martyrdom impressed even those most resistant to their teachings. Several Jesuit priests were captured by the Iroquois and tortured to death, while others died less romantically of exposure, drowning, disease, or exhaustion. Jesuits were aware that the Natives, at least in the beginning, regarded them as strange and lacking in survival skills; and they knew that the "Savages" were determined to assert their superiority over Europeans. As Father Jean de Brébeuf, who would become one of the most celebrated martyrs, indicated in a letter to his superiors in France in 1637: "If you could go naked, and carry the load of a horse upon your back, as they do, then you would be wise according to their doctrine, and would be recognized as a great man, otherwise not."[4]

The Jesuits were convinced that formal education would socialize Native peoples to European ways. Paul Le Jeune, superior of the Canadian Jesuit missions, founded a Jesuit college at Quebec to teach lessons in Christianity to Indian boys, among whom he hoped to find potential priests. Not surprisingly, Aboriginal families were not enthusiastic supporters of this endeavour. The Jesuits had to bribe parents to part with their children and then cater to their pupils' whims in order to retain them. Father Le Jeune complained: "They must be well lodged and well fed; and yet these Barbarians imagine that you are under great obligation to them. I add still more: generally, presents must be made to their parents and, if they dwell near you, you must help them to live, part of the time."[5]

FEMALE RELIGIOUS ORDERS

Following the European practice of gender segregation, the Jesuits did not accept girls in their schools. It was therefore necessary to call on female teachers to found schools for girls in the colony. The call was heeded by Marie de l'Incarnation, an Ursuline and the first of many energetic religious women to immigrate to New France. The Jesuits encouraged the Natives of Sillery to send their daughters to the Ursulines' school, informing them that the nuns were the daughters of French chiefs. Requiring the girls to board at school so they could be shielded from any non-Christian influences, the Ursulines taught them prayers and simple lessons. Some of the girls were fascinated by the devout women from France and sought to emulate them; but most tried to run away from their authoritarian European teachers.

While missionary attempts to convert Natives to European ways met with hostility from both men and women, the latter had particular reasons to defend their traditions. Missionary proscriptions on premarital sex and divorce and the value placed on a family life centred on nuclear, male-headed households threatened women's considerable power within Native societies. Indeed, several Huron men who became Christians were barred from their longhouses by their angry mothers-in-law. The women were rejecting, among other things, the European view that lineage must be determined patrilineally—that is, through the male line—and that non-marital sex must be forbidden so men could be certain about the paternity of offspring. Innu women knew that the Jesuits were behind the system of electing male captains, who would then attempt to impose Christian morality on the whole

The Changing Status of Native Women

Innu women who summered along the St Lawrence River were accustomed to holding their own councils. In 1640, a group of them were surprised to be summoned before a council composed of three male captains. The captains were Christian converts, chosen in a Jesuit-sponsored election. According to the women, who related their experience to the Jesuits: "They treated us so rudely that we were greatly astonished. 'It is you women,' they said to us, 'who keep the Demons among us; you do not urge to be baptized. . . . When you pass before the cross you never salute it, you wish to be independent. Now know that you will obey your husbands and you young people know that you will obey your parents, and our captains, and if any fail to do so, we will give them nothing to eat.'"[6]

One hundred years earlier, if a group of Innu men had demanded that the women accept subordinate status and that children be obedient, they would have been dismissed as madmen possessed by evil spirits. Their threat to withhold food would have been meaningless in a society that required its members to take collective responsibility for obtaining and preparing food. After a century of contact with Europeans, the status of Innu women had clearly declined significantly.

The First Ursulines in Canada. The Ursulines, moved by religious devotion, became the first European teachers of girls in New France.
National Gallery of Canada/15852

learned the nursing skills that in Quebec would endear her to the sick and to those wounded in the wars with the Iroquois. She came to Canada in 1641 as a single woman in her thirties. A year later, under the leadership of Sieur de Maisonneuve, Montreal (initially called Ville Marie) was founded by the Société de Notre-Dame, a religious organization that planned to make their settlement an outpost of strict piety in North America. Only those who could demonstrate their complete devotion to the Catholic Church's teachings would be permitted to settle within the new community.

Jeanne Mance was among the pioneers of Montreal. She founded the Hôtel-Dieu, the first hospital in Ville Marie. As a member of the Société de Notre-Dame, Mance was also able to persuade a wealthy French woman to finance a plan to bring several Soeurs Hospitalières from La Flèche to Ville Marie in 1657. When Ville Marie needed money to hire soldiers for its battles with the Iroquois, Mance went to France to persuade her patron of the urgency, even though she had recently fallen and had to be carried about in France on a stretcher.

Marguerite Bourgeoys founded the colony's first teaching community, the Soeurs de la Congrégation de Notre-Dame, a body of secular teachers who, she claimed, were guided by the Virgin Mary herself. She modelled her congregation on the non-cloistered Sisters of Charity in France, and concentrated on educating children from poorer families. She appears to have had some success: illiteracy rates in early New France were lower than in France. The Congrégation travelled wherever it was needed to educate children because, as Bourgeoys observed, the Virgin was never cloistered and travelled wherever she was needed to do a good deed. The idolization of Mary—a central feature of religious and cultural life in New France—strengthened these pioneer religious women when bishops tried to control their institutions. The Soeurs

group. As a result, many of the women made little secret of their contempt for the new order.

While many Native women continued to assert their traditions, a coterie of women zealots, imitating the nuns, gained notoriety. They whipped each other, wore hair shirts, mixed ashes in their food, stood naked in snowstorms, and put glowing coals between their toes. Some worked to aid the poor and sick, and eventually some were allowed to join the French women's religious houses. None, however, survived to enjoy a fruitful religious career.

The Native converts were often inspired by the example of the French women who joined religious orders attached to the Roman Catholic Church and played important public roles in New France as teachers and caregivers. In addition to Marie de l'Incarnation and her Ursuline sisters, Jeanne Mance and Marguerite Bourgeoys stand out as particularly noteworthy. Both were heirs to the Counter-Reformation creation of non-cloistered religious orders for women. Jeanne Mance was moulded by an Ursuline education in her youth. As a member of a society of religious women who devoted their lives to charitable work in her home city of Langres, she

Marie de l'Incarnation

Marie de l'Incarnation was one of the most complex individuals to travel to New France in the early days of European settlement. Born Marie Guyart in Tours in 1599, she had a willingness to let her visions guide her life—much like the Natives whose religion she sought to displace. Visions led her as a young widow to put her 12-year-old son in a boarding school and join the cloistered Ursulines. Another vision persuaded her to heed the call of Paul Le Jeune for nuns to open a school for Native girls in Quebec.

Like many of her Ursuline and Jesuit counterparts, she was a religious zealot who lived a life of excruciating discipline. According to one biographer: "She wore a penitential shirt with knots and thorns, slept on a hair mattress that kept her always half awake, and sometimes rose at night to chastise herself, first with thongs, later with a whip of nettles. . . . She ate wormwood with her food, holding the bitterness in her mouth, and sometimes approached the fire to burn her skin."[7]

The founder of Canada's first school for Indian girls was more than just an otherworldly self-flagellator. She had managed a large shipping company for her brother-in-law for a decade before devoting herself fully to Christ, and the administrative skills she had acquired proved invaluable in her religious endeavours. First she found a wealthy patron, Marie-Madeleine de La Peltrie, who funded and accompanied Marie and two other Ursulines to New France in 1639. Then she supervised the building of a school for Native and French girls and a convent for the nuns. When the convent burned down in 1650, she had a larger convent built to replace it. At the time of her

Marie de l'Incarnation, as portrayed by C.W. Jeffreys.
Library and Archives Canada

retirement as superior in 1669, her convent housed between 50 and 55 people. Of these, 22, including four lay sisters and three novices, were members of the religious community.

de la Congrégation de Notre-Dame, for example, successfully resisted efforts of the first bishop, François de Laval, to have their order cloistered and even opened a primary school in the town of Quebec, the seat of his diocese.

THE HURON-FIVE NATIONS WARS

Religious interference in the lives of Native peoples, however destructive, was overshadowed by the more serious impact of European germs and weapons. In the late 1630s, smallpox and measles wrought devastation among the French fur-trade allies, particularly the Huron and Innu. Huron numbers were reduced by between one-half to two-thirds, leaving only 10 000 Huron in the early 1640s. Death on this scale robbed the Huron of many of their leaders and played havoc with the delicate social arrangements of the four tribes of the loose Huron Confederacy.

These arrangements had already suffered the strains of quite different responses to the Jesuit teachings and presence. Two of the tribes were receptive to the Jesuits while the other two proved hostile. Opponents of the "black robes" accused the missionaries of practising black magic to unleash deadly diseases. Only a threatened cut-off of French trade saved the

Jesuits from expulsion from Huronia, underlining the dependence of the missionaries on the men of commerce. But the rift between the traditionalists and the Christian minority increased. The converts increasingly refused to have their family members buried in non-Christian sites and even refused to fight alongside non-Christian Huron in battles against enemies.

Those enemies would destroy Huronia in 1649. The Five Nations Iroquois had become dependent on the fur trade, but they had exhausted fur supplies within their own territory and began to seek new supplies in the lands to the north. For their part, the Huron and their allies on the Ottawa and St Lawrence rivers were determined to preserve their monopoly as go-betweens for the trappers and the French.

In the 1640s, the Five Nations attempted to disrupt the annual flotilla of Huron canoes that made the long journey from Huronia to Quebec and back again. In 1642, for example, a Mohawk party massacred Huron returning from Quebec to Huronia. Although the Five Nations had suffered the ravages of epidemic diseases resulting from contact with the Europeans, they had been free of European religious influence and so were able to maintain a cohesiveness that religious rivalries had undermined among the Huron. They were also better armed, because their Dutch allies in New Netherlands increasingly traded guns for furs, whereas the French insisted that guns be traded only to the Christian minority among the Huron.

When the attacks on Huron fur convoys proved unsuccessful in forcing the Christianized Huron to bend to their demands for access to furs, the Iroquois launched direct attacks on Huronia itself. An attack in 1648 was repulsed, but not without significant Huron casualties. In 1649, the Iroquois broke through Huron defences. Caught by surprise, the Huron were unable to organize a concerted defence. Terrorized by a hitherto unheard-of concentration of enemy warriors, and internally divided, they burned their villages and dispersed. Some traditionalists simply surrendered to the Iroquois, who proved willing to adopt them into their tribes. Most residents of Huronia took the lead of the converts who followed the Jesuits to Christian Island. Even there, they were dogged by disaster. A drought on the desolate island made it impossible to replace the crops abandoned in Huronia. A winter of starvation left 5000 people, half or more of the remaining Huron population, dead.

A majority of the Huron who survived the winter of devastation on Christian Island joined their ancient enemies, the Five Nations Iroquois. The new arrivals introduced Christianity to the Iroquois and had a strong influence. While the Five Nations remained at war with the French, by the end of the seventeenth century a large percentage of the Mohawk had established themselves in Christian settlements near Montreal. Many of the Huron who did not join the Iroquois in 1650 went to live among the Petun and Neutral Indians, only to face another Iroquois raid and dispersal later that year. Again the Iroquois absorbed most of the survivors, and many of this expanded Iroquois nation settled in the former territories of the Huron and their allies, as trappers rather than farmers. Not all of the Huron were absorbed by the Five Nations. About 600 Huron resettled near Quebec, where they were given aid by the religious orders. A small but crucial group moved westward to live among nations that had once supplied them with furs to sell to the French.

For the Iroquois, the destruction of Huronia meant they could

This wampum belt depicts the formation of the Iroquois League of Five Nations. From right to left, or east to west, are the Mohawk, Oneida, Onondaga, Cayuga, and Seneca. Wampum were shell beads used to signify value in Native trade. But they were more than the Native equivalent to European money. For the Iroquois, wampum embodied spiritual powers that aided traders to determine fair exchanges.
Courtesy of the Woodland Cultural Centre, Brantford, ON

The Case of Adam Dollard

At age 25, Adam Dollard des Ormeaux, a soldier and recent immigrant to New France, was the leader of a group of 17 Frenchmen who, with the aid of Algonquin and Huron allies, attempted to ambush a party of Iroquois hunters along the Ottawa River in April 1660. Surprised by a large contingent of Iroquois at the foot of Long Sault rapids, for a week Dollard and his men attempted to fend off their attackers. All the Frenchmen died. An even larger group of their Native allies suffered the same fate.

These facts are not in dispute, but historical narrative is not just a presentation of facts. It is also an interpretation of events and, as such, is influenced, consciously or unconsciously, by the political beliefs of the historian. In the case of the battle of the Long Sault, the motivation of Dollard has intrigued historians who hold differing views of the event's significance. For some historians, particularly religiously inclined French-Canadian nationalists writing in the period before the Second World War, the defenders of the Long Sault were martyrs to the cause of New France, motivated by a desire to free the colony from the Iroquois threat.

Other historians, perhaps less sympathetic to the nationalist cause, or wanting to emphasize the predominance of commercial over religious interests in New France, suggest that the young men were greedy adventurers trying to capture a shipment of Iroquois furs, oblivious to the danger—in the form of Iroquois retribution—they might thereby create for the colony. Until recently, there were few challenges to the Eurocentric assumption that the Iroquois had their sights trained upon the colony. The recent work of historians who have set out to study the First Nations perspective on historical events suggests that the Iroquois target was not the colony at all but their Native enemies.

There is a particular challenge in determining the motivation of Dollard and his comrades because none of the French-Canadian or Native victims of Long Sault recorded their aims. Historians have had to infer their motivation from their own particular understandings of the society of early New France and surrounding Native societies. Ascribing motivation is one of the challenges of writing history. Sometimes all the historian can do is make an educated guess, especially when people left no records—or when the accuracy of the records they did leave is in doubt. In the same way that the historian must evaluate a source to determine its bias and validity, readers must be aware of the underlying political objectives or perspectives of historians and how these can affect their interpretations of events.

establish settlements in new territories and trap furs to supply their Dutch and English partners. Algonkian peoples and the remnants of the Huron still gathered furs from the nations in the western Great Lakes area and, with French aid, could still impede Iroquois access to the better fur-bearing territories. The Ojibwa were also a factor in frustrating Iroquois goals. In the period of Huron dominance of the fur trade, they had been exclusively trappers on the parklands and plains. Now they saw an opportunity to become go-betweens. Using French arms, the Ojibwa succeeded in driving the Iroquois out of former Huron territory in the late seventeenth century, and many of them stayed to settle in that territory. Others moved north and west and served as go-betweens for the French traders and the Dakota and Assiniboine, two Siouan-speaking groups, as well as the Cree west of Lake Superior.

For the struggling St Lawrence colony, the loss of Huronia had grave commercial, military, and even agricultural consequences. Before 1649, the French involved in the fur trade could receive furs in the colony without ever setting foot in the upper country where the furs originated. In addition, their allies had protected them against hostile Iroquois; now those allies were gone. It would be several decades before their replacements would become a match for the Iroquois, who had begun to torch crops and kill settlers in an effort to force fur traders to recognize them as the exclusive sellers of furs to Europeans.

As a result of the collapse of Huronia, the French were forced to develop new fur-trade strategies. They began to send young men of the colony to live in the upper country to help the remaining Native allies fend off the Iroquois and to make contact with Native trappers to ensure they were not won over by the Aboriginal allies of rival European nations. French voyageurs rather than Natives would be in charge of the flotillas bringing furs from the interior to the St Lawrence colony. Faced with hostile Iroquois, the colony would require military reinforcements from France on a large scale. The dispersal of the Huron demonstrated that New France could not survive simply as a small fur-trading post. From the 1660s on this reality would prove crucial in French policy making regarding the colony.

Canada, 1635–1663

The French colony based on the St Lawrence was in no position to control the chaos in the interior. Although Champlain had returned to Quebec in 1633, he died two years later. His efforts to make Quebec a settled agricultural community rather than simply a fur-trading post had yet to bear much fruit. He had recruited a few farmers, and his French patrons had contributed a few more, but the colony's total population in 1635 was only about 400. This number included some individuals who had taken up land, as well as officials and missionaries. The majority were inden-

tured labourers who had been imported to build housing and work the land. Most of these labourers would return to France at the end of their contracts.

The Compagnie de la Nouvelle France made efforts to fulfil its charter pledges to bring colonists to New France, but the fur trade, which was meant to provide the capital to sustain their efforts, let them down. When profits collapsed in the face of Iroquois attacks on the Huron fur flotillas in the 1640s, the company sublet the fur trade to the Communauté des Habitants, an organization composed of several leading members of the colony. Although the Compagnie de la Nouvelle France retained administrative control of the colony, it lost interest in colonization efforts.

After Champlain's death, the French court vested authority over civil administration in the colony to a governor, and in 1647 a council was named to direct trade and control justice in consultation with the governor. The governor enjoyed an effective veto over the council, and the conflict for political power lay between the governor and the Compagnie de la Nouvelle France. In 1659, the company obtained a ruling from France that gave it the greatest authority

More to the Story

Social Welfare in New France

By 1663, Roman Catholic organizations had established the foundations of a network of social welfare institutions in New France. Schools and hospitals operated in Quebec and Montreal. By the end of the century, so too did a variety of almshouses that sheltered the destitute.

The Church depended upon the support of the wealthy in order to provide services to the destitute. It was therefore unsurprising that both schools and hospitals reinforced social-class structures in the colony. While Marguerite Bourgeoys trained the future wives of habitants to be good housekeepers, the Ursuline schools taught music, art, singing, and foreign languages to the prospective wives of bourgeois men. The Jesuits provided a classical education for the sons of wealthy parents while running a vocational school for less fortunate boys. Nor was education universal. Only about 10 percent of the habitants of 1760 were literate.

The hospitals established by the nuns, beginning with a hospital at Quebec in 1639, provided services to both rich and poor. But the rich were housed in a separate wing of the hospital and received deluxe services for which they paid handsomely. The poor, by contrast, experienced spartan conditions on crowded wards. For the most part, the wealthy avoided the hospitals, where contagious diseases spread rapidly, and hired doctors to attend their needs in their own homes.

The religious communities worked tirelessly for the individuals whom they served. But it would be an imposition of today's secular values on the past to conclude that they were advocates of social justice. Historian Allan Greer observes:

> . . . the aim was not to solve "social problems." The accent was on the act of alms-giving and on its spiritual significance to the giver, rather than the needs of the recipient. The religious were not necessarily expected to adjust their handouts when times were hard, and they certainly did not aim to eliminate poverty. Accordingly, we find indigent people begging in the streets while widows of military officers occupy comfortable lodgings at the hospital.[8]

over the administration of justice in the colony, making power arrangements hopelessly confusing.

A shadowy presence in the emerging colony was the Compagnie du Saint-Sacrement, a secret organization of religious zealots who fought growing secularism in France and saw in North America a virgin territory that could be consecrated to God. Leading figures in this organization formed the Société de Notre-Dame, which founded Montreal in 1642.

The influence of the zealots at court secured the appointment in 1659 of the Jesuit-trained François de Laval-Montigny as New France's first bishop. Laval was a devoted servant of the sick and poor of the colony, but he was also a domineering individual who expected, as the emissary of both pope and king, to be obeyed by the civil authorities, the missionaries, and the colonists. Laval's moralistic crusades against blasphemy, gambling, and fornication were of little interest to the civil authorities, and his threat to excommunicate any French colonists who traded liquor with the Natives enraged both the governor and the fur traders. Together they convinced the French authorities that this action could cause France's Native partners to seek new European allies—which would destroy not only the French fur trade but also the central reason for the colony's existence. Even the religious orders, which had for years governed themselves in the colony without aid of a bishop, resented Laval's interference and sometimes defied his orders.

By the early 1660s, the Roman Catholic Church was a towering presence in the colony. Religious orders of both men and women ran all the schools and hospitals. Meanwhile, the colonists, though respectful toward the church authorities, were demonstrating signs of the free-spiritedness common in frontier societies, where authorities lack the structures and personnel to enforce obedience to their will. Huronia's tragic end and the independent-mindedness of the colonists indicated limits to church power outside the institutional realm.

THE EMERGING CANADIAN SOCIAL ORDER

Despite the challenges it faced, Canada by 1660 was taking on the trappings of a settled European community. Two-thirds of the 3035 settlers in the colony resided in the countryside and depended on farming

for their livelihood. Land had been granted on the basis of the seigneurial system: the Compagnie de la Nouvelle France granted estates to seigneurs who in turn granted farms freely to censitaires, who paid feudal dues. Narrow strip farms stretching along the St Lawrence made up a seigneury.

The seigneurial system differed from the crumbling feudalism of France in that it did not include military obligations; all land was granted without charge, and all obligations between seigneur and censitaire were stipulated in a notarized contract. Moreover, the landholdings of individual farmers, who were called habitants rather than peasants, were far larger than those held by tenant farmers in France. By 1663, 69 seigneuries had been granted, with members of the nobility holding title to 84 percent of the land. The largest seigneury included almost half the land granted, and seven families related by blood held most seigneurial land.

French politics recognized three "estates": the clergy, the nobles, and the commoners. In Canada, the first two estates included 78 and 96 members, respectively, in 1663. This left 94.3 percent of the population in the third estate. Although 68 percent of the population were members of farm or labourer households, 796 people were members of bourgeois families, including public servants, merchants, non-noble seigneurs, and master artisans.

Immigrants from 30 French provinces lived in Canada in 1663, but three western provinces—Normandy, Perche, and Aunis—provided half of the colonists. Their social origins are less well known than their geographical origins, but it is likely that most, apart from the clergy and the original residents of Montreal, had come to better their economic circumstances. For the younger sons of nobles, this meant the opportunity to become landowners; for habitants, some of whom had been landless labourers or peasants in France, it meant a chance to gain a real living from farming.

The modest immigration to New France has sometimes been attributed to a French unwillingness to emigrate, but in the sixteenth century about 250 000 French migrated to bullion-rich Spain, where jobs were available at high wages. New France offered no such attraction. The prohibition on dissenters entering the colony also limited potential immigration to New France, a colony that had little appeal to most French people in any case because of its cold winters

The Habitant Farm, by Cornelius Krieghoff.
National Gallery of Canada/2036

contrast, settlers in New France were often enticed with large land grants. In 1634, for example, the seigneur Robert Giffard convinced several French families to settle on his seigneury of Beauport near Quebec by offering each family 840 acres of land and part of the harvest of his own farm. In practice, a family could expect to clear only two acres a year, and the work of felling trees and preparing land for crops was backbreaking. The first homes were tiny one-room cabins. They had little or no furniture and what did exist was home-made. Oiled paper substituted for glass windows, and the clay chimneys and cold winters often led to destructive fires. Colonists learned quickly to become as self-sufficient as possible, which bred habits of independence, a certain pride in unskilled versatility, and opposition to any trade or artisanal organization and restriction.

In 1660, a third of the population of Canada lived in the three towns of the colony: Quebec, founded 1608; Trois-Rivières, 1635; and Montreal, 1642. By

and the stories of its fearsome Native peoples. Not surprisingly, then, the West Indies colonies—France seized control of Guadeloupe and Martinique from Spain in 1635—drew more French immigrants than did the St Lawrence.

Frontier conditions helped to create a society in which the classes mixed relatively freely during this early period of colonization. The small population was united both by external threats to the colony's survival and by the need to clear land as quickly as possible. Nobles and bourgeois secured servants from Europe through indentures of usually three to five years, although enforcement of the contracts sometimes proved difficult. Initially, most indentured servants and labourers returned home at the end of their contracts, but after 1650, as more seigneuries opened up for prospective habitants, a slight majority of immigrants chose to remain permanently in the colony.

Peasants in France eked out a living on a few acres of land and faced execution if they tried to supplement an insufficient diet by hunting or fishing on a noble's land. By

Working a canoe up a rapid on the Ottawa River. The route followed by voyageurs in the 1600s remained in use until the nineteenth century, when this drawing was produced.
Newberry Library, Chicago

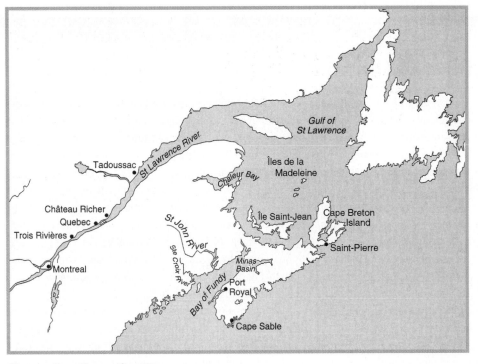

Map 5.1 New France in 1663.

their lives trading in the bush. Most had liaisons with Native women while they lived in the upper country. Some remained in the Great Lakes basin and never returned to Quebec. Others abandoned their Native wives when they returned to the Laurentian settlements, but a few brought their wives back with them. Champlain and, for a time, the Jesuits, promoted interracial marriages as a means of encouraging assimilation. "Our sons shall marry your daughters and together we shall form one people," Champlain proclaimed.

While the men who had lived among the First Nations rarely rejected their own religion in favour of Native religious beliefs, few behaved piously upon their return to the colony. Their drinking, rioting, and gambling, which influenced the activities of other colonists, became the cause of many an unenforceable decree and countless Sunday sermons. In a curious paradox, New France became a society marked by notable excesses of both piety and secular enjoyment.

NEW FRANCE IN QUESTION

Despite concerted efforts between 1632 and 1663, the future of New France looked uncertain. Acadia, with its development impeded by the battles of rival French claimants, was in English hands. Quebec, subject to raids by the Mohawk, was embattled, as a fragile peace negotiated with the remaining four Iroquois nations in the 1650s unravelled. The Iroquois, whose trade links were with the Dutch and the English, controlled the territories once settled by the Huron and their allies, who had been solidly in France's camp.

The dispersal of Huronia—an event demonstrating the destructive impact of European imperial rivalries and religion on intertribal and intratribal

1663, Quebec, the most highly developed centre, could boast a church, seven chapels, a college, a convent school for girls, a hospital, nine mills, a brewery, and a bakery. The city was surrounded by five forts that protected area residents.

The Native peoples had a significant impact on the foods eaten by the early settlers, on the transportation methods they employed, and even on their dress. They also had an impact on the colonists' attitudes toward life. Indian corn (maize); pumpkins; beaver flesh, tails, and feet; and the meat of moose, bears, dogs, and feathered game supplemented the colonists' more familiar food items, at least in the earliest years of the colony's development. Tobacco, an indigenous crop that garnered great interest among Europeans, was also grown in New France. The French found Native inventions such as the birchbark canoe, toboggan, and snowshoes to be invaluable. Native medicine helped remedy scurvy and other ailments, although European haughtiness prevented the French from taking advantage of the full cornucopia of Native cures.

One group of colonists was particularly influenced by the free-spirited behaviour of the Native peoples. These were the young men who spent a good part of

The Destruction of Huronia

What caused the destruction of Huronia? At one level the answer is simple. The Five Nations Iroquois, with an estimated 500 guns in their possession, dispersed an enemy that could count on only 120 guns. French policy regarding provision of weapons to the Native peoples was inconsistent from region to region, but in Huronia only Christian converts received guns. In 1648, only about 15 percent of the Huron were nominal Christians, and a disproportionate number of those had the job of transporting furs to the French colony. Given the lack of guns, Huronia, including its Christians, became more vulnerable to Iroquois attack.

For historian Cornelius Jaenen, there is no conclusive evidence that Iroquois raiders made much use of guns in their attacks on the Huron. They may instead have resorted mainly to the traditional tomahawk and torch to terrorize their Huron and French enemies. Employing solid military tactics involving concentration of forces, surprise, and sustained attack, they moved quickly from one village to the next before the Huron could assemble and mount a counter-offensive. Since their opponents were already bitterly divided between Christians and traditionalists, their tactics were effective.[9]

Some scholars have maintained that arming the Huron would have been unnecessary if European trade rivalries had not promoted Huron-Iroquois hostility. Anthropologist George Hunt argued in 1940 that the Huron and the Five Nations Iroquois, sharing common origins, were unnatural enemies and that the fur trade created new and more intense rivalries between Native groups.[10] While Hunt's general point regarding the impact of the fur trade on the motivations for intertribal conflicts has merit, few researchers accept his claim that the Iroquois and Huron were on good terms in the immediate pre-contact period.

Geographer Conrad Heidenreich suggests that Iroquois desperation and guns alone do not explain their success in vanquishing the Huron. The cohesiveness of the Five Nations Iroquois, whose contact with Europeans was largely restricted to traders, was in contrast to the disunity of the Huron, whose society had been less integrated than the Five Nations to begin with and became even less so as a result of religious division and the removal of recognized leaders by diseases.[11] Anthropologist Bruce Trigger is still more emphatic in pinpointing Jesuit activities as the cause of the destruction of Huronia.[12] In contrast, Jesuit historian Lucien Campeau argues in the order's defence that the Iroquois destroyed both the Petun and the Neutral; and the Petun had only sporadic contacts with the Jesuits, while the Neutral had none at all. It was Iroquois guns, Campeau says, not cultural and religious confusion, that destroyed the Huron, just as those guns also brought down the other two nations.[13]

A Huron writer suggests an interesting counter-thesis. Georges Sioui argues that the Iroquois understood the Europeans' threat to the Native way of life and so became engaged in a war of liberation against the French. Because they suffered huge losses of life in this war, they could only survive as a people by absorbing new members into their nations, by force if necessary. For Sioui, the large-scale adoption by the Iroquois of the Huron, Petun, and Neutral was not the unintended consequence of the attack on Huronia, but indeed the objective of the attack. Sioui also maintains that historians of European origin have exaggerated the toll of the Iroquois wars on Huron lives to disguise an essential fact: that European diseases, and not Native warfare, were responsible for the sharp decline of Native populations.[14]

American historian Daniel Richter supports Sioui's view that the chief aim of the Iroquois was to take captives, but his research questions Sioui's claims that such an aim was part of an Iroquois effort to build Native resistance against Europeans. "Mourning wars"—that is, wars meant to take captives to replace population losses among their own people—were part of ancient Iroquois tradition, Richter argues. The decimation caused by European diseases simply intensified such warfare. Moreover, the mourning wars did not promote unity among the Iroquois; the Five Nations fought among themselves for the right to various groups of captives.[15]

relations—made changes in the organization of both trade and the colony necessary. If the French wished to retain control of the colony and the western fur trade, they would need more military strength and a greater population in the colony as well as a direct presence in the west. The growth of England's American colonies, whose European population stood at about 70 000 in 1660, also emphasized the vulnerability of the St Lawrence colony, which had a mere 3000 settlers.

Grumbling from within the colony convinced Louis XIV's government in 1663 that the oligarchy controlling the Compagnie de la Nouvelle France was incapable of directing effective colonization. The company's property, administrative, and monopoly trade rights were revoked and replaced with royal government—that is, administration by state officials responsible to the Crown. A new era in the history of New France was about to begin.

Conclusion

After nearly a half-century of effort, France had fallen badly behind in the competition to establish North American colonies. Canada and Acadia were little more than fur-trade outposts, vulnerable to internal dissension and external assault. They produced no great riches for the empire, nor were they high on the list of overseas destinations sought by French emigrants, who would rather risk contracting malaria in the French West Indies than suffer a winter in New France. If the northern colonies were to thrive, they needed strong leadership and infusions of capital. Louis XIV, the so-called "Sun King," would provide both—at least for a time.

Notes

1 Quoted in James P. Ronda, "'We Are Well As We Are': An Indian Critique of Seventeenth-Century Christian Missions," *William and Mary Quarterly*, 3rd series, 34 (1977): 77.

2 Ibid., 77–78.

3 Luca Codignola, "Competing Networks: The Roman Catholic Clergy in French North America, 1610–58," *Canadian Historical Review* 80, 4 (December 1999): 539–84.

4 S.R. Mealing, ed., *The Jesuit Relations and Allied Documents* (Toronto: McClelland and Stewart, 1963), 50.

5 Reuben Gold Thwaites, ed., *The Jesuit Relations and Allied Documents*, vol. 12 (Cleveland: Burrows Brothers Co., 1896–1901), 105–7.

6 Ibid., vol. 18, 47.

7 Joyce Marshall, ed. and trans., *Word from New France: The Selected Letters of Marie de l'Incarnation* (Toronto: Oxford University Press, 1967), 5.

8 Allan Greer, *The People of New France* (Toronto: University of Toronto Press, 1997), 46.

9 Cornelius Jaenen, *The French Relationship with the Native People of New France and Acadia* (Ottawa: Indian and Northern Affairs Canada, 1984).

10 George T. Hunt, *The Wars of the Iroquois* (Madison: University of Wisconsin Press, 1967).

11 Conrad Heidenreich, *Huronia: A History and Geography of the Huron Indians, 1600–1650* (Toronto: McClelland and Stewart, 1971).

12 Bruce G. Trigger, "The Jesuits and the Fur Trade," in *Sweet Promises: A Reader in Indian-White Relations in Canada*, ed. J.R. Miller (Toronto: University of Toronto Press, 1991), 15–16; Bruce G. Trigger, *The Children of Aataentsic: A History of the Huron People to 1660* (Montreal: McGill-Queen's University Press, 1987).

13 Lucien Campeau, *La Mission des Jésuites chez les Hurons, 1634–1650* (Montreal: Éditions Bellarmin, 1987).

14 Georges Sioui, *For an American Autohistory: An Essay on the Foundations of a Social Ethic* (Montreal: McGill-Queen's University Press, 1992).

15 Daniel K. Richter, *The Ordeal of the Longhouse: The Peoples of the Iroquois League in the Era of European Colonization* (Chapel Hill: University of North Carolina Press, 1992).

RELATED READINGS IN THIS SERIES

From *Foundations: Readings in Pre-Confederation Canadian History*

James P. Ronda, "'We Are Well As We Are': An Indian Critique of Seventeenth-Century Christian Missions," 66–78. Karen Anderson, "Commodity Exchange and Subordination: Montagnais-Naskapi and Huron Women, 1600–1650," 79–89.

From Media Companion CD-ROM, Volume I

The First Year, 1640
Ossossané Afflicted with the Contagion, 1637
Instructions to the Fathers of Our Society Who Shall Be Sent to the Hurons, 1637

SELECTED READING

The readings for Chapter 4 also cover many of the topics in this chapter. Discussions of the debate on the relative influence of the frontier and the metropolis in New France are found in Michael S. Cross, ed., *The Frontier Thesis and the Canadas: The Debate on the Impact of the Canadian Environment* (Toronto: Copp Clark, 1970); W.J. Eccles, *France in America*, rev. ed. (East Lansing, MI: Michigan State University Press, 1990); and John A. Dickinson and Brian Young, *A Short History of Quebec*, 3rd ed. (Montreal and Kingston: McGill-Queen's University Press, 2003). For a biography of Champlain's successor, consult Jean-Claude Dubé, *The Chevalier de Montmagny: First Governor of New France* (Ottawa: University of Ottawa Press, 2004). On the fate of the Huron, see Daniel K. Richter, *The Ordeal of the Longhouse: The Peoples of the Iroquois League in the Era of European Colonization* (Chapel Hill: University of North Carolina Press, 1992), and Georges Sioui, *For an American Autohistory: An Essay on the Foundations of a Social Ethic* (Montreal: McGill-Queen's University Press, 1992). On the fate of the Iroquoian nations more generally, see José António Brandao, ed., *Nation Iroquoise: A Seventeenth-Century Ethnography of the Iroquois* (Lincoln: University of Nebraska Press, 2003). A Mi'kmaq's account of his people's post-contact history is Daniel N. Paul, *We Were Not the Savages: A Mi'kmaq Perspective on the Collision of European and Native Civilizations* (Halifax: Fernwood Publishing, 2000). The impact of contact on the lives of Aboriginal women is explored in Eleanor Leacock, "Montagnais Women and the Jesuit Program for Colonization," in *Rethinking Canada: The Promise of Women's History*, 3rd ed., ed. Veronica Strong-Boag and Anita Clair Fellman, (Toronto: Oxford University Press, 1997). On the early history of residential schooling, see J.R. Miller, *Shingwauk's Vision: A History of Native Residential Schools* (Toronto: University of Toronto Press, 1996). Church perspectives both on Native-European relations and conditions in New France are found in S.R. Mealing, ed., *The Jesuit Relations and Allied Documents* (Ottawa: Carleton University Press, 1990); Joyce Marshall, ed. and trans., *Word from New France: The Selected Letters of Marie de l'Incarnation* (Toronto: Oxford University Press, 1967); Raymond Brodeur, ed., *Mystique et missionaire: Marie Guyart de l'Incarnation* (Québec: Les Presses de l'Université Laval, 2003); Patricia Simpson, *Marguerite Bourgeoys and Montreal, 1640–1665* (Montreal: McGill-Queen's University Press, 1997); and Father Gabriel Sagard, *The Long Journey to the Country of the Huron* (Toronto: Champlain Society, 1939). A work of synthesis is Cornelius Jaenen, *The Role of the Church in New France* (Toronto: McGraw-Hill Ryerson, 1976). For a recent study of missionary endeavours in this period see Carol Blackburn, *Harvest of Souls: The Jesuit Missions and Colonialism in North America, 1632–1650* (Montreal: McGill-Queen's University Press, 2004), and Luca Codignola, "Competing Networks: The Roman Catholic Clergy in French North America, 1610–58," *Canadian Historical Review* 80, 4 (December 1999): 539–84.

Apart from the general texts, works with information on the social history of early New France include R. Cole Harris, "The Extension of France into Rural Canada," in *European Settlement and Development in North America: Essays on Geographical Change in Honour and Memory of Andrew Hill Clark*, ed. James R. Gibson (Toronto: University of Toronto Press, 1978). On the society of origin of the first European colonists of Acadia and New France, a lively account is Pierre Goubert, *The Ancien Regime: French Society, 1600–1750* (Paris: Colin, 1969).

On women in early New France, there is good general information in the Clio Collective, *Quebec Women: A History*, trans. Roger Gannon and Rosalind Gill (Toronto: Women's Press, 1987), as well as Isabel Foulché-Delbosc, "Women of Three Rivers: 1651–1663," in *The Neglected Majority: Essays in Women's History*, vol. 1, ed. Susan Mann Trofimenkoff and Alison Prentice (Toronto: McClelland and Stewart, 1977), and Jan Noel, "New France: Les Femmes Favorisées," in *Rethinking Canada*, ed. Strong-Boag and Fellman, 28–50.

WEBLINKS

MARIE DE L'INCARNATION

www.library.upenn.edu/exhibits/rbm/kislak/religion/mincarnation.html

The site contains a portrait and a biography of Marie de l'Incarnation. Other links are available.

JEANNE MANCE

www.collectionscanada.ca/heroes/h6-224-e.html

This is a short biography of Jeanne Mance on the Canadian heroes page at the Library and Archives Canada Web site.

JEAN DE BRÉBEUF

www.sfo.com/~denglish/wynaks/wn_stmar.htm

This site gives a brief description of events at Ste-Marie-Among-the-Hurons.

www.rockies.net/~spirit/charlene/huroncarol.html

For information on the Huron Carol, written by Jean de Brébeuf, see this site. Links to other sites relating to Huron culture are included.

First Nations and Europeans had each established complex, evolving societies over the millennia and each group judged the other through lenses shaped by its own history and social values. While this ethnocentrism resulted in misunderstandings, it produced a partnership in the fur trade from which both sides seemed to benefit. It also increased competition among the First Nations and Europeans for advantage in the fur trade, sometimes with disastrous results. Neither the Huron, who were nearly wiped out by disease and warfare, nor the Europeans, who faced scurvy and attacks from European rivals, could have anticipated the horrors that the coming together of the two worlds precipitated. Yet by 1663 the fur trade, together with the North Atlantic fisheries, had inspired Europeans to establish settlements in the area of present-day Canada and, for better or worse, they were mobilizing to stake a permanent claim to what to them was a "New World."

FRANCE IN AMERICA

Between 1663 and 1763, the French built an empire in North America and then lost most of it to Great Britain. New France at its height included Newfoundland and Acadia, and extended along the St Lawrence and the Great Lakes, into the Prairies, and down the Mississippi. Valued for the commerce (mostly in fish and furs), prestige, and military might it brought to the French monarchy, New France never attracted many settlers. Only close alliances with Native peoples enabled France to lay claim to such a vast domain. When wars erupted between Great Britain and France for dominance in Europe, they inevitably spilled into the colonies. France was defeated during the Seven Years' War but left a legacy of French settlement in North America that remains to this day.

CHAPTER 6

New France Takes Root, 1663–1689

Timeline

1661	Louis XIV takes control of affairs of state in France
1662	France establishes a base at Placentia to protect its Atlantic fishery
1663	Royal government established in New France; Bishop Laval establishes a seminary in Quebec
1663–73	Over 2000 immigrants arrive in New France
1664	English capture New Amsterdam from the Dutch
1665	Carignan-Salières regiment and Intendant Jean Talon arrive in New France
1666	Marquis de Tracy invades Mohawk territory
1669	Colonial militia established
1670	Governor Grandfontaine arrives at Port Royal
1685	Edict of Nantes revoked

"The hundred girls that the King sent this year have just arrived and already almost all of them are married. He will send two hundred more next year and still others in proportion in the years to come. He is also sending men to supply the needs of the marriages, and this year fully five hundred have come, not to speak of the men that make up the army. In consequence, it is an astonishing thing to see how the country becomes peopled and multiplies. It is said that His Majesty intends to spare nothing, being urged by the seigneurs that are here, who find the country and living here delightful in comparison with the West Indies whence they come, where the heat is so extreme one can scarcely live."[1]

In this letter to her son Claude, written in October 1665, Marie de l'Incarnation described some of the developments that were dramatically altering the French settlements along the St Lawrence River. King Louis XIV was determined to develop an overseas empire and, beginning in the early 1660s, took steps to address the problems facing the colony. He sent out settlers, provided military protection, and introduced much-needed political and economic reforms. By the end of the seventeenth century, Canada was emerging as the heart of a vast colonial empire—*La Nouvelle France*—that extended from Hudson Bay to the Gulf of Mexico.

THE AGE OF ABSOLUTISM

The transformation in the fortunes of New France came as a direct result of Louis XIV's decision in 1661 to assume personal charge of state affairs. This was a significant event, not only for France and its colonies but also for Europe as a whole. From the time that nation-states had begun to take shape in the late Middle Ages, monarchs and nobles had competed for supremacy. Louis XIV effectively brought an end to the competition by creating a complex bureaucracy to administer state affairs and by making royal favour rather than lineage and landowning the chief source of power. The old aristocracy (*noblesse d'épée* or *de sang*) and the new elite created by royal favour (*noblesse de robe*) were drawn to the king's fabulous court at Versailles, the largest and most opulent structure in Europe. There they could be kept under the king's watchful eye.

By centralizing military, legal, and financial administration and domesticating the aristocracy, Louis XIV emerged as an absolute ruler. All power was embodied in the king, and all the lower orders—aristocracy, merchants, artisans, and peasants—were subordinate to him. Even the Roman Catholic Church in

Louis XIV and His Heirs, by Nicolas de Largillière. So successful was Louis XIV in establishing his absolutist regime that other European monarchs tried to imitate his policies, but no one managed to outshine the "Sun King," and the period of his long reign (1643–1715) is often referred to as "the age of Louis XIV." Despite crippling losses on the battlefield toward the end of his rule, and a society periodically racked by famine and heavy taxation, the Sun King bequeathed one of the most powerful nations on Earth to his successor, Louis XV (1715–74), who is probably the child in this portrait.
Reproduced by the permission of the Trustees of the Wallace Collection, London

France collaborated in this consolidation of power, advancing the theory of the divine right of kings to justify the new political order. This theory proclaimed the monarch to be God's direct representative on Earth. Few dared to defy the double-barrelled authority of state and church.

There were, of course, a number of limitations to the exercise of royal authority. The king was his own first minister, but his policies were only as good as the advice he received from the ministers, secretaries, courtiers, clergy, family members, and mistresses who surrounded him. In the early years of the reign of Louis XIV, one of the most influential royal officials was Jean-Baptiste Colbert. He was controller-general of finances (1662–83) and, after 1669, minister of colonial and maritime affairs as well. To enhance the glory of the monarch, Colbert was determined to

reform national finances, promote economic self-sufficiency, and build a colonial empire with a navy to defend it.

ABSOLUTISM IN NEW FRANCE

The impact on New France of developments in France was immediate. By 1663, military, bureaucratic, and ecclesiastical elites within the French state had taken up the task of securing the colonial foundations laid by private entrepreneurs, merchant associations, and missionaries. The outburst of royal enthusiasm lasted only a decade before more pressing matters in Europe diverted the attention of the king and his ministers. Nevertheless, by the 1670s the structures and policies of absolutism had been firmly implanted and, with only minor changes, would serve New France for nearly a century.

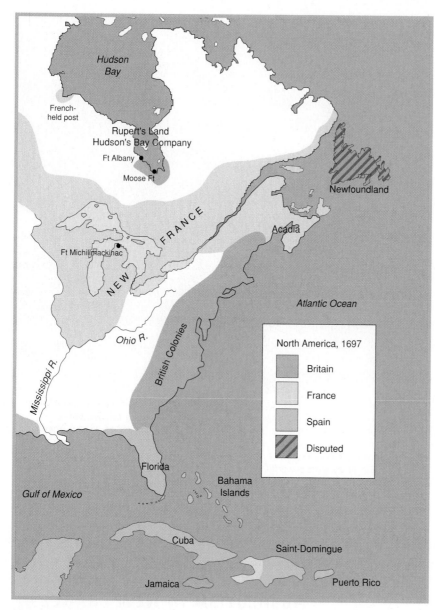

MAP 6.1 North America, 1697.
Adapted from W.J. Eccles, *France in America* (East Lansing, MI: Michigan State University Press, 1972), 61

Although warfare with the dreaded Iroquois Confederacy would break out again before the end of the century, two decades of relatively good relations gave French authorities the breathing space they needed to transform their St Lawrence colony.

Another matter for the king's immediate attention was the small population of the colony. Recognizing that young families constituted the best method of stimulating sustained population growth, the royal government dispatched nearly 800 women, known as the filles du roi, to the colony. Most of the filles du roi were orphans, plucked from the state-sponsored institution in Paris that looked after the disadvantaged peoples of French society. In an effort to ensure that the women had good health and morals, officials arranged for them to be chaperoned by nuns.

Within a few months of their arrival, most of the women had found husbands in a colony where bachelors outnumbered marriageable European women six to one. Women were essential to maintaining the household economy upon which basic survival depended in pre-industrial societies. As a result, they were eagerly sought as marriage partners and had some say in choosing whom to marry. Some 15 percent of those who signed a marriage contract changed their minds before going to the altar. Despite the short period of courtship, the filles du roi had stable marriages; only four women formally requested separation from their hastily chosen husbands. Thirty of the women returned to France without marrying and one, Madeleine de Roybon d'Alonne,

The royal government's most immediate problem was military security. In 1665, Alexandre de Prouville, Marquis de Tracy, and 1200 troops, most of them members of the Carignan-Salières regiment, arrived in the colony. In the following year, two expeditions were launched into Mohawk country. The European-trained army suffered more casualties than it inflicted, but the show of force had the desired effect. The Five Nations sent delegates to Quebec and agreed to keep the peace.

forsook a formal marriage to become the mistress of the notorious adventurer Chevalier de la Salle.

In the decade following the declaration of royal government, the colony also became home to a significant number of French soldiers. The members of the Carignan-Salières regiment, for instance, were encouraged to settle in the colony, and about 400 of them did so. Indentured servants (engagés), in contrast to their counterparts in earlier years, now more often chose to stay in New France once they had fulfilled their contractual obligations. Between 1663 and 1673, over 2000 immigrants arrived, nearly doubling the population of the colony and laying the foundations for stable community development.

With the increase in marriages, the peculiar demographic features of New France began to give way to patterns that resembled those of old France. The average age of marriage for women rose, the number of widows increased, and even the times of the year when weddings took place changed. In the early days of the immigrant ships, ceremonies were held soon after the boats arrived, usually between August and October. By the end of the century, marriage customs in New France, as in France, followed the rhythms of agricultural work, with weddings taking place in October (after harvest and before Advent) or in winter before Lent.

The royal government, eager to increase the population base of New France, was not content to let nature take its course. For a short time it offered bonuses for families of 10 or more children and imposed penalties on people outside the church who clung to the single life. Evidence suggests that these "carrot and stick" policies had little impact on family formation. As in France, couples in New France did not practise birth control and, on the average, had a child every two years. Lower mortality rates, a higher standard of nutrition, less exposure to epidemic diseases, and a lower age of marriage for women than in

The Arrival of the Filles du Roi, by Arthur E. Elias.
Library and Archives Canada/C-029486

France are the factors that seem to account for the rapid growth of the population to 15 000 by the end of the century and to 70 000 by 1763.

While French communities were spreading along the banks of the St Lawrence, Aboriginal peoples adapted as best they could to the aliens in their midst. A few Innu stayed close to Quebec, where they became dependent upon French foodstuffs, but the majority moved into the region around Tadoussac, their traditional summer encampment. Huron and Ottawa Valley Algonquin, threatened by the Iroquois, settled near Montreal and Quebec. As soon as the peace was signed in 1666, Mohawk and Oneida began moving into the Montreal region. Abenaki from New England, pushed by war and English immigration, migrated northward in the 1670s. By 1685, there were over 2000 Natives living on seigneurial lands of the St Lawrence, and that number would double by the 1750s.

Acadia

Acadia was theoretically subject to the same policies as Canada, but in practice it experienced royal authority quite differently. Held by the English between 1654 and 1667, the colony missed Louis XIV's brief burst of enthusiasm for colonial development. A governor, subordinate to the governor general based in Quebec, was finally appointed in 1670. With a motley garrison of 50 soldiers and 60 new settlers to augment the fewer than 500 people already living there, Governor Hector d'Andigne de Grandfontaine was expected to maintain the king's authority over an area that today roughly corresponds to the Maritime provinces of Canada and part of the state of Maine.

The French officials sent to Acadia seemed at a loss to define their role. Initially, they were even unable to fix upon a site for their administration, migrating around the Bay of Fundy before finally returning to Port Royal. Significantly, the French settlers, who quickly gained a reputation for their independent spirit, escaped the close scrutiny of authorities by moving up the Bay of Fundy to settle at Beaubassin in the 1670s and to the shores of the Minas Basin in the 1680s. Other smaller fishing settlements were maintained throughout the region, which attracted seasonal visits from European fishing fleets.

Not surprisingly, given its small population and dispersed settlement, Acadia lacked the institutional development that characterized the St Lawrence colony. Although 55 seigneuries were granted in the region, rents were rarely collected. The few priests in Acadia sometimes took on legal duties in the absence of judicial officers. Without an effective military presence, the Acadians were reluctant to make enemies. They established amicable relations with the Abenaki, Mi'kmaq, and Maliseet in their midst and, in defiance of official injunctions, traded regularly with the New Englanders, who regarded Acadia as their northern outpost.

Dykeland agriculture emerged as a distinctive feature of Acadia. Instead of clearing the forests for planting, the settlers reclaimed the marshlands built up by the high tides of the Bay of Fundy. This difficult engineering feat produced rich soil that sustained cattle and crops in abundance. The Sieur de Dièreville, a merchant who visited the colony in 1699, described the process by which the marshland soil was reclaimed from the sea:

> To grow wheat the marshes which are inundated by the Sea at high Tide, must be drained; these are called Lowlands & they are quite good, but what labour is needed to make them fit for cultivation!

> The ebb & flow of the Sea cannot easily be stopped, but the Acadians succeed in doing so by means of great Dykes.... Five or six rows of large logs are driven whole into the ground at the points where the Tide enters the Marsh & between each row other logs are laid, one on top of the other, & all the spaces between them are so carefully filled with well-pounded clay, that the water can no longer get through. In the centre of this construction, a Sluice is contrived in such a manner that the water on the Marshes flows out of its own accord, while that of the Sea is prevented from coming in. An undertaking of this nature, which can only be carried on at certain Seasons when the Tides do not rise so high, costs a great deal, & takes many days, but the abundant crop that is harvested in the second year, after the soil has been washed [of the salt] by Rain water compensates for all the expense. As these lands are owned by several Men, the work upon them is done in common.[2]

Newfoundland

Newfoundland offered no such agricultural potential. Its wealth existed in the vast quantities of cod found on the offshore "banks." Economically more important to France than beaver, cod supported a thriving bank fishery, based in the French ports of Le Havre, Honfleur, and Les Sables-d'Olonne. It supplied green-cured fish (or "green fish") to the huge market in and around Paris and along the Loire. Ships from the other major fishing ports produced dried cod for the southern European market. In 1664, the bank fishery accounted for about a third of the French fleet.

Appreciating the value of cod to the French economy, Colbert was quick to commission a study of the fisheries and to impose regulation on them. By a 1670 ordinance, boys under 12 could not be hired on fishing crews, and fishermen who had completed five or six seasons were made liable for service in the royal navy. An ordinance in 1681 required a surgeon on every vessel with a crew of 20 or more, and another ordinance in 1694 called for a chaplain as well. Few surgeons or chaplains seemed to be attracted to such a demanding calling, but the sons of peasants from western France did enter the lucrative industry, becoming fishermen, sailors, and, in a few cases, pioneer settlers in North America.

In 1662 Colbert had chosen the ice-free port of Placentia, on the south coast of the Avalon Peninsula of

A view of Placentia Harbour, July 17–September 5, 1786 from *The Log Book of His Majesty's Ship Pegasus*, p. 72. Artist: James S. Meres (1766/1767–1836).
Library and Archives Canada/C2523

Newfoundland, to serve as a base to protect the much-valued fishery. Served by a governor and a few administrators, troops, and missionaries, it soon attracted settlers to its shore properties. By the end of the century, Placentia consisted of 40 resident fishing families and served a France-based fishing fleet of over 400 vessels, employing an estimated 10 000 men. Like the men in the fisheries who could be forced to serve on naval vessels in time of war, Placentia also had military potential, a fact that did not go unnoticed by the English based in St John's, the major centre on what was now called the "English shore" of the Avalon Peninsula.

COLONIAL ADMINISTRATION

Under royal government, New France was administered in much the same way as a province in France, with modifications adapted to the colonial reality. Because of its distance from the centre of power, New France was not as directly ruled in practice as in theory. Instead, a kind of government by correspondence was established: royal commands and bureaucratic directives were sent to Quebec, and replies from the colony would find their way to the royal court at Versailles each navigational season. The time lag, which was sometimes more than a year, often meant that state policies were hopelessly outdated by the time they had been formulated and had reached their destination.

The administration of New France was also spared the practice, common in France, of selling government jobs. The practice of purchasing offices, or *venality*, brought money into the government's coffers.

While it attracted a number of men of proven ability to the service of the state, it could also lead to crippling inefficiency and corruption. In New France, with a few exceptions, offices were not purchased. They were awarded on the basis of influence or merit and held "at the king's pleasure." If officials failed to perform to the satisfaction of the king or his minister, dismissal was certain, as several administrators found to their chagrin.

Although New France escaped the system of venality, it was not immune to other practices that today would be considered corrupt. Administrators throughout the French Empire used their positions for personal gain, often lining their own pockets at the expense of the state. Nepotism, or patronage based on family relationship, was rampant. All but one of the 15 intendants in New France were relatives or clients of two French administrative families, the Colberts and the Phélypeaux.

Colonial Officials

The chief officer in New France was the governor general based in Quebec. Always a military man, and usually a member of the old aristocracy (*noblesse d'épée*), the governor general controlled the military forces in the colony and was responsible for relations with the First Nations. Local governors in Montreal and Trois-Rivières reported to him, as did, in theory at least, governors located in Port Royal and Plaisance. With the arrival of the Troupes de la Marine in the 1680s, New France always had a substantial military force that the governor general could use to protect the colony from external attack and to quell any civilian unrest. The military establishment was also a significant source of revenue for the colony.

As in France, the intendant in New France was the chief provincial administrator, responsible for finance, economic development, justice, and civil administration. Intendants, usually members of the new aristocracy (*noblesse de robe*), represented the efforts of the king to bring bureaucratic efficiency and centralized control to bear on distant provinces. By the eighteenth century, the intendant, like the governor general, was assisted by delegates in the main districts as well as a number of minor officials such as royal notaries, road surveyors, and customs officials.

Both the governor general and the intendant sat on the Sovereign Council, an appointed body modelled upon the provincial *parlements* in France. Its main functions were to serve as the court of appeal from the lower courts, to issue decrees for the governance of the colony in line with royal instructions, and to register the royal edicts that served as the constitutional framework for the colony. As the population grew, the number of councillors rose from the original five in 1663 to seven in 1675 and twelve in 1703. The Sovereign Council also included the bishop of the Roman Catholic Church and an attorney general who was trained in law and was a member of the bar at the Parlement of Paris. In 1703, at the behest of the king, the name was changed from Sovereign to Superior Council, reflecting the more modest role that the absolute ruler expected this colonial institution to play.

In the early years of royal government, the powers of the governors and intendants were inadequately defined. By 1675, the duties of senior officials were clarified, and thereafter the political structures worked reasonably well. Since the duties of the governor general and intendant were so hopelessly entwined, any personality clash between the two senior officials could spell disaster for the administration of the colony. Both men sat on the highest court in the colony; governors general were responsible for military policy while intendants supplied and paid the troops; intendants often meddled in Native policy because of their interest in advancing the colonial economy; and competition for patronage brought everyone into potential conflict.

BIOGRAPHY

Charles Le Moyne: A Self-Made Nobleman

The son of a French innkeeper, Charles Le Moyne arrived in New France in 1641 at the age of 15. He worked for the Jesuits for a time and then became a fur trader, interpreter, and soldier. In 1654, he married a commoner, Catherine Thierry, and they had twelve sons and two daughters. Le Moyne, who became one of the most successful merchants in Montreal, distinguished himself in the wars against the Iroquois and received small seigneuries before being raised to noble status in 1668. Four years later, he was granted the seigneury of Longueuil. As members of a noble family, Le Moyne's sons easily found commissions in the military. His eldest son, Charles, was named Baron de Longueuil in 1700 and received the coveted Croix de Saint-Louis in 1703. Another son, Pierre Le Moyne d'Iberville, had a distinguished military career. Yet another, Jean-Baptiste, usually known by his noble title, Bienville, was a long-time governor of Louisiana.

PATERNALISM IN NEW FRANCE

Power in the age of absolutism was exercised by the social elite. Any notion of authority emanating from the people was anathema to men such as Louis XIV and Colbert. Indeed, Colbert abolished the system whereby elected syndics from the major towns brought the concerns of the people to the Sovereign Council. Nor were people allowed to sign petitions. At the same time, the habitants were encouraged to take their problems to their superiors, both civilian and spiritual, and, on major issues, colonial authorities were instructed to convene consultative assemblies and report recommendations. While the advice thus rendered need not be acted upon, it was often in the best interest of absolute rulers to listen to the concerns of the people they governed.

Under the old regime, power may have been narrowly focused, but it was usually exercised with a sense of responsibility toward all classes of society. Such an approach, called paternalism, was particularly obvious in New France, where special circumstances—pioneer hardships, Iroquois hostility, and colonial rivalries—often elicited a sympathetic response from royal authority. To some extent, this sympathy reflected the recognition that frontier conditions made enforcement of edicts difficult. A memorandum dated 1663, for example, explained: "The general spirit of government ought to lean in the direction of gentleness, it being dangerous to employ severity against transplanted peoples, far removed from their prince, and to hazard using an absolute power founded only on their obedience, because having once found a means of resisting they would quickly forget respect and submission."[3] Obviously, a paternalistic approach was more likely to bring positive results than was a naked show of force.

Paternalism, as practised in New France, made it possible for the colony to be granted exceptions from the general rules prevailing in the mother country. For instance, the North American colonists were spared the crushing burden of taxation that was levied on the people of France on the grounds that frontier conditions made it difficult for them to pay their share.

Frontier conditions also produced institutional responses that were unique to North America. In 1669, Louis XIV ordered the governor general to enrol all male habitants between the ages of 16 and 60 into militia companies. The Iroquois threat and colonial rivalries made such an innovation necessary for the defence of the colony. With a company in every parish, everyone had easy access to a militia captain, a man chosen from the parish to lead the militia in times of war and to report local concerns to the intendant in times of peace. Ordinances from the civil authorities were also passed down this military hierarchy, in a society where the privileges of the elite were carefully assigned and jealously guarded.

LAW AND ORDER

In 1664, Louis XIV decreed that the Custom of Paris—the legal code used in the Paris region of France—would be the basis for the civil law of the colony. The Sovereign Council served as supreme court in the colony, hearing appeals from royal courts established in major towns. On rare occasions, wealthy colonists appealed their cases to the Conseil des Parties in France. The intendant appointed all court officials, supervised the court system, and had wide legal authority, including judging cases under 100 livres if all par-

ties agreed and intervening in cases where he felt justice was not being done. A few seigneurial and church courts existed in the colonies but, as in France, they were subordinate to royal policy.

It was in the royal interest to keep legal proceedings cheap and accessible. In France, the cost of going to court, driven high by efforts on the part of judges and lawyers to enrich themselves, deterred many people from seeking justice. Legal reforms introduced in New France included the barring of lawyers from the courts. According to one commentator, this policy had the desired effect: "I will in no wise say whether justice is more untainted or disinterested than in France, but at least if it is sold, it is much cheaper. We do not pass through the squeezing of the lawyers, the grasp of attorneys, nor the claws of the clerks; that vermin has not yet affected Canada. Each pleads his own cause, the decision is expeditious and it is not bristling with bribes, costs and expenses."[4]

While reforms made the courts more accessible in New France, justice was not free. Nor was it always expeditiously or equally rendered. There was a fixed schedule of court costs as well as fees for bailiffs and witnesses. Access to the system was always easier for the elite. Excepting some female servants who had been seduced by their employer or his son and had borne a child out of wedlock, domestic servants, apprentices, and slaves never brought charges against their masters. People in the countryside faced the added burden of travelling to one of the towns where the cases were heard. The peasantry, which made up about 80 percent of the population, comprised only 18 percent of the litigants who came before Quebec's royal court, which was known as the *Prévôté*.

Violence, bloodshed, and death were facts of colonial life, and the criminal law in New France, as in all of Europe in the seventeenth century, was harsh. Under the French regime, criminal law recognized three categories of crimes: crimes against God, such as heresy, blasphemy, and sorcery; crimes against the Crown, such as treason, sedition, rebellion, desertion, duelling, and counterfeiting; and crimes against person or property, such as murder, suicide, rape, slander, libel, theft, and arson. The French inquisitorial system of justice was based on the interrogation of the accused, and the final decision as to guilt or innocence was rendered by the judge, not, as in the British system, by a jury of peers.

Depending upon the seriousness of the charges, the accused might even be subjected to judicial torture, *la question extraordinaire*, to extract a confession.

Since harsh sentences were meant to act as a deterrent to potential criminals, they were conducted in public and with considerable fanfare. There were three categories of punishment—capital, infamous, and pecuniary—and within each a judge had some latitude. For capital crimes, death could be brought about by beheading, strangulation, burning at the stake, quartering, amputation of the limbs, mutilation, or some combination of these methods. Members of the nobility condemned to death had the privilege of being beheaded rather than hanged. The total number of people executed in Canada during the French regime was eighty-five, six of them broken on the wheel. Infamous punishment included humiliation on a wooden horse, in the stocks, or at the pillory, and might also include exile or loss of civil rights. Pecuniary punishment consisted of fines or confiscation of property.

Although the law set forth brutal punishments for a wide range of offences, the judges in New France were often lenient on appeal. They also showed a marked reluctance to order that individuals have their tongues cut out for blasphemy, be drawn and quartered for passing counterfeit money, or have a fleur-de-lis branded on their cheek for a first offence of selling brandy to Natives. Had they pushed the law to the limit, many more people in New France would have been mutilated than actually was the case.

RELIGIOUS ESTABLISHMENT

Louis XIV kept a tight rein on the institutional church in his realm. Not only did he persecute all non-Catholics, but he also resisted any attempts on the part of the pope to interfere in the functioning of the church on French soil. This relationship of church and state in New France reflected an ideology known as Gallicanism. In the French context, Gallicanism meant that the church was organized on a national scale, with all clergy answering to their superiors up the hierarchy through bishops and archbishops, who, in turn, were responsible to the king. The king, not the pope, nominated all church officials in France and controlled the rules and membership of all religious communities.

As ruler by divine right, Louis XIV claimed to be the supreme protector of the church, and any person or group opposing his claims was ruthlessly persecuted. Protestants, Jews, and Jansenists, the latter a puritanical group within the Catholic Church, bore the brunt of his zeal for spiritual uniformity. With the revocation of the Edict of Nantes in 1685, which had granted Protestants limited toleration in France, 1 000 000 Huguenots were faced with forced conversion to Catholicism. Many chose instead to leave France, taking their skills and their ambitions with them. New France suffered the same intolerance. Quebec's wealthiest merchant, Gabriel Bernon, was a Protestant and so was obliged to return to France in this new atmosphere of intolerance. He soon moved to the English colonies, where he continued to trade with his acquaintances in Canada.

The influence of the Roman Catholic Church—so important in the early years of colonization—continued after 1663, but, not surprisingly given the absolutist goals of Louis XIV, the relation of church and state changed. The church in New France emerged as the handmaiden of the state, charged with maintaining schools, hospitals, and charitable institutions, sustaining the social order by preaching obedience and submission, and cementing Native alliances through missionary endeavours.

New religious communities, especially those reporting directly to Rome, were discouraged from operating in the colony. While the period before the proclamation of royal government witnessed a veritable explosion of religious orders—Récollets, Jesuits, Soeurs Hospitalières, Ursulines, Soeurs de la Congrégation de Notre-Dame, Sulpicians, and, in Acadia, the Capuchins—only two major new communities appeared in New France in the next century: the Frères Hospitaliers (or Brothers of Charity) in Montreal and Louisbourg, and the Soeurs Grises (or Grey Nuns).

The most notable development after 1663 was the creation of a parish system to serve the needs of the expanding community. Following his arrival in 1659, Bishop Laval began the process of carving out parishes. In 1663, a seminary to train priests was established in Quebec and the tithe was introduced to support the

Witches and Warlocks in New France

Marie de l'Incarnation, writing to her son in 1668, described a case in which a young woman was "possessed by the devil," apparently when a young man, recently arrived from France, was refused permission to marry her. According to Marie de l'Incarnation, the young man "attempted to gain by spite what he could not obtain by fair means," using the offices of "certain magicians and sorcerers that had come from France." She continued:

> To be brief, the girl, who was continually pursued and agitated by demons, was put in a room in the hospital where sick persons are also kept, and, by the order of Monseigneur [Laval], Mother de Saint-Augustin was set to watch over her. . . . The good mother watched over the girl day and night. By day the demon did not appear, but he worked his ravages at night, agitating the girl greatly and from time to time giving her views of the magician, who appeared to her accompanied by many others. But all these hellish flies could never prevail over the girl, since they were always driven away by the one to whom the Church had committed her. Enraged because Mother de Saint-Augustin guarded the girl's purity with such care, the demons appeared to her in hideous forms and beat her outrageously. The wounds and bruises that marked her body were enough to show that they were realities and not illusions. . . . Finally, the demons and magicians withdrew, through the intercession of this holy man [Father de Brébeuf], who had spilled his blood for the upholding of the Faith in this country.[5]

Portrait of Mother Louise Soumande de Saint-Augustin, by Dessaillant, 1708. Mother de Saint-Augustin was the first superior of the Hôpital-Général de Québec. Although the religious leaders in the early years of settlement came from France, by 1760 all nuns in New France had been born in the colony.
Les Augustines de la Misericorde de Jésus du Monastère de l'Hôpital-Général de Québec

This incident points to the church's importance in fostering stability in a colony where the rigours of frontier life might easily have led to social unrest. In contrast, the Protestant community of Salem, Massachusetts, was racked in 1692 by a series of trials against people, most of them women, accused of being witches and warlocks. When the episode finally ended, 20 of the accused had been executed and 100 were awaiting trial. No such panic occurred in New France, primarily, it seems, because most people in the colony believed fervently in the ability of church authorities to exorcise demons. Nor would the church hierarchy in New France have allowed accusations to get out of hand, as they certainly did in Salem.

church establishment. Institutions to take care of the poor, orphaned, and indigent—*bureaux des pauvres* and *hôpitals-généraux*—appeared in the colony before the end of the seventeenth century. Like the schools and hospitals, they were initiated and administered by the religious orders.

Despite the church's status in the colony, the parochial system developed slowly, and the bishop won few battles in confrontations with the secular authorities. Colbert was suspicious of clerical officials and even went to the length of sending the Récollets back to the colony in 1670 in an attempt to reduce the power of the Jesuits, who had been influential in the appointment of Laval. The Sulpicians, who became seigneurs of Montreal in 1663 and built their own seminary, also challenged the bishop's authority.

Instructions from France deprived the bishop of his role in appointing and dismissing, jointly with the governor general, the members of the Sovereign Council, and authorized the intendant to discourage the bishop from attending council meetings. When Laval asked that the tithe be set at one-thirteenth of

Portrait of Jean-Baptiste de la Croix de Saint-Vallier, Bishop of Quebec.
Les Augustines de la Misericorde de Jésus du Monastère de l'Hôpital-Général de Québec

the produce of the land, parishioners objected and it was set at one-twenty-sixth and on cereals alone, not the entire agricultural output. As a result, the church was dependent upon state subsidies for as much as one-third of its revenue.

It took some time for the church to get established in the countryside. When Laval's successor, Jean-Baptiste de la Croix de Saint-Vallier, arrived in Quebec in 1688, there were 21 priests resident in the parishes, of whom 12 lodged with parishioners because there was as yet no rectory. In only six localities was the tithe sufficient to assure a modest living. Until the eighteenth century, priests were often itinerant, visiting a parish for a few weeks each year rather than residing there permanently. Even at the end of the French regime, with 114 parishes to serve, there were only 169 priests, including the seminary, missionary, and chaplaincy personnel.

The church also struggled against the superstitions and questionable religious practices of their often uneducated flock. Bishop Saint-Vallier, sensing the lack of rigour in parish religious life, published a *Rituel*, or service book, for his priests and a catechism for the instruction of children and Native people. In the eighteenth century, the church faced an even greater challenge in the growing secular orientation of social life.

Despite slow beginnings and seemingly endless obstacles, parish priests gradually became a significant presence in the countryside. They presided over the religious ceremonies that marked every stage of an individual's life. For many of the settlers, religious rituals offered much-needed comfort and reassurance in the face of the unfamiliar and often terrifying realities of colonial life. The priest also served as a key adviser to the *fabrique*, the board of trustees of the parish.

In addition to their religious duties, priests kept parish registers, which today provide us with valuable vital statistics, and they even drew up legal documents. They also provided some of the basic education that country folk received. Ultimately the parish priest, recruited among the local population and trained in the seminary at Quebec, would identify with his parishioners much more than with the bishop, who, with the exception of Laval, spent more time in France than in his diocese.

Local boys were recruited for the seminary, but they were less welcome among the regular orders that drew their members mainly from France. Before the conquest, only three Canadians entered the Jesuit order, and none became Sulpicians. No Canadian was appointed bishop or superior of a major religious order during the French regime. Although Canadian-born priests served the rural parishes in increasing numbers, there was always a shortage of clergy. At the end of the French regime, almost one-half of the clergy were still of French origin. In contrast, fully 20 percent of the girls in noble families in New France entered the convent—a reflection, it seems, of parental strategies designed to pass as much of the family estate as possible to sons.

Although the institutional church lost some of its political power under Louis XIV, there is no question about the influence that the Gallican brand of Roman Catholicism had on the colony. Virtually everyone belonged to the Roman Catholic Church, and those who did not were required by law to conform to its practices. Christian values and prejudices permeated the laws and customs of the colony and were imposed, when there was an opportunity to do so, upon the Aboriginal peoples. Although Protestants were allowed to return to the colony in the eighteenth century, they posed no threat to the Roman Catholic Church, which remained the only institutional church in New France throughout the French regime.

MERCANTILISM

Nowhere was the hand of the royal government more visible than in the economic development of New France. Under Louis XIV and Colbert the economic policy known as mercantilism reached its supreme expression. France's overseas colonies, according to this theory, were important only to the extent that they provided France with a market for French manufactures and the raw materials that the kingdom would otherwise have to import from foreign countries. By so doing, colonies would contribute to the imperial goal of increasing exports, reducing imports, and building up a substantial budgetary surplus.

Colbert reasoned that the fur trade in New France had a detrimental influence on stable colonial development. He therefore set out to create a compact colony on the St Lawrence, a place with a diversified economy based on the exploitation of its primary resources of agricultural land, timber, fish, and minerals. The fur trade would be carried on by a company carefully controlled by the state. Once firmly rooted, the colony was expected to provide a range of raw materials to sustain the French economy.

The chief instrument for executing Colbert's goals for the colony was the intendant, one of the two most powerful royal officials in the colony. Jean Talon, the first intendant to arrive in New France, proved equal to the task defined by Colbert. During his terms

VOICES FROM THE PAST

Governor Denonville Denounces Gangs, 1685

Both religious and civil authorities in New France were alarmed by the influence of the frontier on the culture of young men in the colony. In 1685 Governor Denonville expressed his concern to the Minister of Marine and Colonies:

> Monsieur de la Barre has suppressed a certain gang called the Chevaliers, but he has not taken away its manners or disorders. A way of dressing up like savages, stark naked, not only on carnival days but also on all days of feasting and debauchery, has been treated as

a clever action and a joke. These manners tend only to maintain the young people in the spirit of living like savages and to communicate with them and to be eternally profligate like them. I cannot express sufficiently to you, Monseigneur, the attraction that this savage life, of doing nothing, of being restrained by nothing, of following every whim and being beyond correction, has for the young men.[6]

of office (1665–68, 1670–72) he worked energetically to establish the colony on a firm economic base and explore the potential of the local resources. He promoted the development of agriculture, supervising the distribution of imported horses, cattle, sheep, and goats among the settlers, and encouraged the cultivation of hemp and flax. In an effort to reduce the dependency on imported wines and liquor, he ordered that a brewery be built. He laid the foundations for Canada's first shipyard at Quebec and envisioned the colony's vast timber resources being transformed into the casks, barrels, tar, potash, and soap required by the settlers. When he learned of deposits of iron near Trois-Rivières and coal on Île Royale (Cape Breton), he planned their development.

Talon also explored the possibility of "triangular" trade with France's West Indies possessions of Guadeloupe and Martinique. In 1667, wood, fish, seal oil, and dried peas were sent directly to the West Indies, and the vessel then loaded sugar bound for France, from which metropolitan goods would be shipped back to New France. This trading pattern failed to thrive to the extent that Colbert had hoped, in part because Canada was isolated in winter and proved to be a weak link in the system. Besides furs it had no commodities that the other colonies could not get more easily elsewhere. The West Indies, like Acadia, had direct year-round contact with France and easy access to illicit trade with foreign nations. Talon's efforts to provide France with ships and naval stores such as masts, planking, tar, and cordage also failed because colonial products could not successfully compete with supplies from Northern Europe.

Historians debate the extent to which the mercantile practices of the French state retarded colonial economic development. It was certainly the case that royal policy frowned on colonial economic initiatives, especially if they threatened industries already well established in France. In 1703, for example, when the flax and hemp harvests in Canada had been particularly successful, the royal government refused to send weavers to the colony because metropolitan manufactures might be threatened by a robust textile industry. Three years later, royal instructions reiterated restrictions on colonial manufactures that would compete with those of France and expressly prohibited trade with the English colonies and direct trade with other French colonies.

Despite such injunctions, the exceptions to mercantile restrictions in New France were many and significant. Colbert had approved of Talon's efforts to develop direct trade with the French West Indies. In wartime, trade with other French colonies, usually in foodstuffs, was encouraged. Even trade with foreign nations was permitted when the demands of the empire—and the fur trade—dictated it. Exceptions could also be made "in the interest of the poor people" to ensure the availability of basic necessities.

Because both bureaucrats and merchants in New France supported an economic system based on protection rather than free trade, conflicts between the mother country and the colonies over mercantile restrictions did not develop to the same extent as they did in the Anglo-American colonies. Moreover, France lacked the resources and the will to stop any illicit activities that occurred in North America. Trade along the Montreal-Albany-New York route, for instance, was rarely curtailed. It offered a welcome outlet for an often oversupplied fur market and was an important source of income for Native allies on reserves near Montreal. Similarly, Acadians traded with nearby New Englanders without much interference from metropolitan authorities.

Even the restrictions on textile manufacturing could be circumvented by those with imagination and initiative. In 1705, Montreal businesswoman Agathe de Saint-Père, Madame de Repentigny, ransomed nine English weavers who were being held captive by Native allies and put them to work on looms that she had built for their use. Soon she had turned her home into a workshop, complete with apprentices, making "linen, drugget, twilled and covert-coating serge."

Canadians also showed initiative in overcoming one of the ongoing difficulties of a colonial economy: the chronic shortage of specie, or hard money. Government expenditures were covered by money sent annually from France, but this source proved less than reliable. In 1685, Intendant Jacques de Meulles used playing cards as promissory notes to pay the troops and labourers when the ships failed to arrive from France until late in the season. This ingenious solution also enabled the authorities to carry on nor-

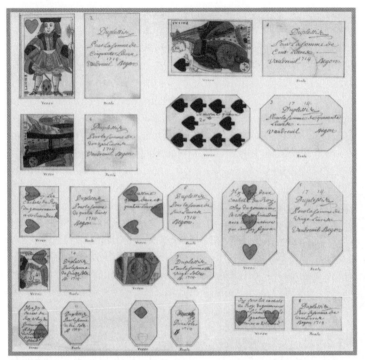

Beginning in 1684, intendants sometimes used playing cards, inscribed with a certain value, when they ran out of currency. The cards were refundable when the funds from the king arrived.
Library and Archives Canada/C117059

mal transactions when money was short during pro-longed periods of war. It also had its disadvantages. When paper currency was redeemed at less than its face value following the War of the Spanish Succession, those who held playing cards suffered a severe financial loss. France was itself too far in debt to worry about the fortunes of the colonials. A similar and much deeper discounting of paper currency also occurred after the Seven Years' War in the 1760s.

SEIGNEURIALISM

In pre-industrial Europe, agriculture was the main-spring of economic life, and the peasant household was the basic economic unit. Seigneurialism was the typical landholding system in France and the structure around which peasant agriculture took shape in Canada. According to seigneurial theory, all the land belonged to the Crown, which made grants of estates, or seigneuries, to the privileged orders—that is, the church and the nobility.

The seigneur was required to maintain a household on his estate and develop it with the help of peasant farmers, called censitaires. This term derived from the annual fees known as *cens et rentes* that the peasants paid for the privilege of working the land for them-selves and their seigneur. Notaries in New France called such lots concessions, or habita-tions, and thus the people who lived on them became known as habitants. The seigneur could require his censitaires to work a certain number of days on his property, or demesne. He could also require that they grind their wheat in his mill for a price (*banalités*) and pay a fee (*lods et ventes*) if the concession changed hands. In these ways, the wealth of peasant labour was accumulated by the seigneur in the time-honoured manorial tradition.

As it developed in the colony, seigneurial-ism was intended to accomplish a number of objectives: to provide the colony with a basic land-survey system; to perpetuate a traditional class structure; to establish a legal framework for relations between privileged landowners and dependent peasant families; and to develop a system for recruiting and settling immi-grants. Not all of these objectives were achieved. Apart from the religious communities that ultimately accounted for about one-quarter of the 185 seigneuries granted (making the church the largest seigneur in the colony), few seigneurs were successful immigration agents. To prevent land speculation, seigneurs and cen-sitaires were obliged to bring the land into production or forfeit their grants. In 1711, royal decrees known as the Arrêts de Marly threatened to revoke undeveloped seigneurial grants and censitaire concessions. They also froze seigneurial dues at levels that remained in place until after the British conquest.

The traditional survey system quickly adapted to the geography of the Laurentian lowlands. Instead of a three-field system encircling a village, as was typical in traditional feudal jurisdictions in Europe, the grants conformed to the river, becoming long, narrow trape-zoids fronting along the St Lawrence River and other waterways. The Jesuits experimented with circular-shaped seigneuries near Quebec, but this style failed to

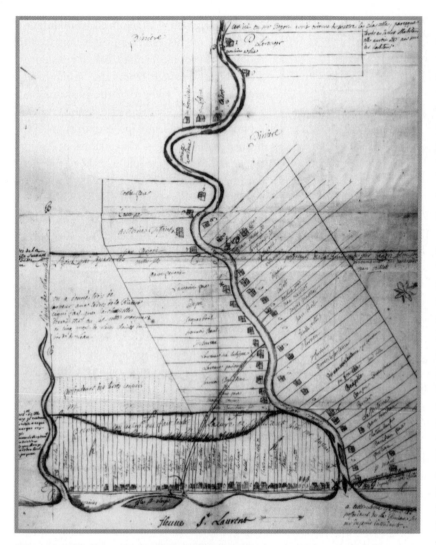

This survey of Batiscan, a seigneury belonging to the Jesuits, shows the names of the settlers and the buildings erected along rivers and roads.
Archives Nationales, Paris: Section Outre-Mer (Colonies)

frontage—access to a variety of soils and vegetation: marshlands for fodder near the river, rich heavy soils for cereals, upland meadows for grazing, woodlots for fuel, and timber at the upper reaches of the property. One disadvantage was that villages were slow to develop under such a system, and services, both commercial and religious, were often underdeveloped in the rural countryside.

Although the seigneurial system succeeded in reflecting the conservative class structure favoured in the age of absolutism, social distinctions and upper-class privileges were somewhat blunted in New France. Especially in the early years of settlement, some seigneurs were almost as poor as their censitaires. As a result, they were unable to provide such customary services as a grist mill and church. Once a seigneury had 30 or 40 well-established censitaires, it became profitable, and traditional seigneurial privileges—such as hunting and fishing rights, ownership of ferries and common pastures, and the reservation of building stone or wood supply—became carefully guarded.

Social custom reinforced the status of the seigneur. The front pew of the parish church was reserved for the use of the seigneur and his family, the family received communion before all others, and if the seigneur was also a patron founder of the parish church he would be mentioned in the weekly prayers. Nevertheless, the foundation of the old nobility was never allowed to develop in New France. Seigneurs had no official military role, as they did under the feudal regimes of Europe. Indeed, in New France seigneurs were not always nobles; even if they were ennobled, most could not claim hereditary privileges from time immemorial. They, like the new nobility in France, owed their status to the kind offices of the king.

catch on. Seigneurial grants were on average 10 times longer than they were wide, and tenant grants were similarly strip-like. When the first line of farms, or *côte*, was full, a second line, or *rang*, was opened along a road running behind the first settlements.

For a pioneer community, there were many advantages to this type of survey. In addition to being inexpensive to run, it permitted farmers to live near their own fields and to each other. It gave them access to fish and other marine life and to the best transportation route in the colony. By cutting across the ecological boundaries that tended to run parallel to the river, it gave each farmer—at least those with river

A Historiographical Debate

Theocratic Tyranny or Benevolent Paternalism?

The noted American historian Francis Parkman, writing in the late nineteenth century, portrayed the inhabitants of New France as ignorant, superstitious, downtrodden colonials crushed under the heavy weight of stifling mercantilist restrictions, metropolitan intervention, an oppressive and despotic monarchy, and an even more powerful and fanatical church. He asserted that the "fault" of the absolutist monarchy and authoritarian church "was not that they exercised authority, but that they exercised too much of it, and, instead of weaning the child to go alone, kept him in perpetual leading strings, making him, if possible, more and more dependent, and less and less fit for freedom."[7]

Similar views of colonial rule were perpetuated by both British imperial and English-Canadian historians until quite recently. Among the French-Canadian historians, Canon Lionel Groulx, in formulating his views of the dominant role of the church in colonial life, came closest to the Parkman interpretation. However, Groulx celebrated rather than criticized New France's authoritarianism. He described a "proper subordination" of the state to the church in the laying down of "the foundations of the social and political order" of his future Quebec.[8]

At the opposite pole of the debate was Guy Frégault's interpretation of French rule as benevolent paternalism. According to Frégault, colonial administration concerned itself with poor relief, hospitalization and medical care, welfare provisions, building regulations, price controls, and the supervision of the church's charitable and educational institutions. Land was free, and there was no direct taxation. Although New France was not Utopia, it could stand favourable comparison with New England.[9]

It was William J. Eccles who documented and refined this interpretation, to the point that New France emerged as an embryonic welfare state in which the health, safety, security, and contentment of the population was a major concern of the governing class. As Eccles stated, "The basic premise, not merely of royal policy, but of all social institutions—indeed the basic premise upon which society in New France rested—was individual and collective responsibility for the needs of all."[10]

This concern for the welfare of the community should not be confused with democracy: in France the Estates-General had not met since 1614, and there were no elected assemblies in the French colonies. Still, the people of New France were not completely pow-

erless. Royal edicts contrary to the interests of the colonists were never implemented; the council at Quebec did not register and proclaim them, and delayed action by asking for further instructions and suggesting amendments in the time-consuming process of government through annual correspondence.

There were also avenues for the expression of popular will in the colony in the form of consultative assemblies. Moreover, several historians have noted that the colonists did not seem entirely submissive, or as respectful of their social superiors as convention required. Eccles attributes this behaviour to the relative independence of the colonial farmer, to the influence of the Native peoples and fur traders, and also to the slow implantation of social distinctions.

Cornelius Jaenen concludes, in his study of the role of the church in Canada, as does Charles O'Neill about Louisiana,[11] that the clergy was frustrated in its attempts to dominate either socially or politically: "The colonists were far from docile, subservient, downtrodden, inarticulate, priest-ridden peasants. Contemporary documentation shows them to be remarkably independent, aggressive, self-assertive, freedom-loving and outspoken individuals."[12] Terence Crowley, in examining popular disturbances in the colony, found that people demonstrated against what they considered to be unfair impositions, or against government inaction to remedy perceived injustices such as hoarding or profiteering. They protested the abuse of power but did not rebel against constituted authority.[13]

New France, then, appears to have been neither a theocracy nor a tyranny. The clergy may have wielded great power in the period before 1663, but royal authority would soon assert itself in line with Gallican principles of the mother country. As for royal power, it was attenuated by a wide ocean, a cumbersome bureaucracy, and the relative unimportance of the colony. It was also more successful than private enterprise in populating and sustaining the colony in a difficult northern climate. The social legislation that Eccles underscores flowed not only from what Frégault and others called paternalism, but also from Catholic social teaching regarding the responsibilities of elites, just price, and charity. According to the prevailing views of the period, the common good should have priority over individual interest and advantage. The coming of British rule would introduce a different philosophy while providing an element of continuity.

In New France, the bulk of the seigneur's income came from trade, military service, and government positions, not from the rents extracted from tenants. So significant was commercial activity to the social structure of the colony that a special ordinance, issued in 1685, made it possible for the colonial nobility to engage in trade. In France, such involvement in pursuits "beneath one's station" had led to the loss of noble status. Thus, especially in the early years, the elite in New France was a fusion of noble and middle-class elements, and the *bourgeois-gentilhomme* was a typical member of the colonial upper class.

CONCLUSION

Between 1663 and 1689, French institutions took root in North America. French immigrants, though few in number, learned to adapt to their new environment and actually began to thrive. With church, state, military, and commercial institutions firmly in place—thanks to the will of Louis XIV—Canada was emerging as the heart of a genuine "Nouvelle France." Acadia and Newfoundland were outposts of Canada, prized for their strategic location and the rich fisheries off their coasts. Preoccupied by affairs at home, Louis XIV showed little inclination to expand his North American empire beyond these modest beginnings. The outbreak of war in Europe in 1689 changed everything.

NOTES

1 Marie de l'Incarnation to her son, 29 October 1665, cited in *Word from New France: The Selected Letters of Marie de l'Incarnation*, ed. and trans. Joyce Marshall (Toronto: Oxford University Press, 1967), 314–15.

2 Cited in Allan Greer, *The People of New France* (Toronto: University of Toronto Press, 1997), 95–96.

3 Library and Archives Canada, MG1, series CIIA, vol. II, p. 48, anonymous memorandum on colonization [1663].

4 Cited in André Vachon, "Le Notaire en Nouvelle-France," *Revue de l'Université Laval* 10, 3 (1955–56): 235.

5 Joyce Marshall, ed. and trans., *Word from New France*, 343–44.

6 Library and Archives Canada, MG1, series C11A, vol. VII, p. 46, Governor Denonville to Minister of Marine and Colonies, 13 November 1685, cited in Cornelius Jaenen and Cecilia Morgan, *Material Memory: Documents in Pre-Confederation History* (Don Mills, ON: Addison Wesley Longman, 1998), 35.

7 Francis Parkman, *The Old Régime in Canada*, vol. 1 (Toronto: n.p., 1899), 199.

8 Abbé Lionel Groulx, "Ce que nous devons au catholicisme," *Action française* (November 1923), cited in *Emerging Identities: Selected Problems and Interpretations in Canadian History*, ed. Paul W. Bennett and Cornelius Jaenen (Scarborough, ON: Prentice-Hall, 1986), 72.

9 Guy Frégault's views are summarized in *Canadian Society in the French Régime* (Ottawa: Canadian Historical Association, 1968).

10 W.J. Eccles, *Essays on New France* (Toronto: Oxford University Press, 1987), 39.

11 Charles O'Neill, *Church and State in French Colonial Louisiana: Policy and Politics to 1732* (New Haven, CT: Yale University Press, 1966).

12 Cornelius Jaenen, *The Role of the Church in New France* (Toronto: McGraw-Hill Ryerson, 1976), 155.

13 Terence Crowley, "'Thunder Gusts': Popular Disturbances in Early French Canada," *Canadian Historical Association Historical Papers* (1979): 11–32.

RELATED READINGS IN THIS SERIES

From *Foundations: Readings in Pre-Confederation Canadian History*
R. Cole Harris, "The Seigneurial System in Canada during the French Regime," 94–97.

From Media Companion CD-ROM, Volume I
The King's Girls, 1665
Jean Talon
New France: A Crown Colony, 1663

SELECTED READING

The age of Louis XIV is described in Pierre Goubert, *Louis XIV and Twenty Million Frenchmen* (New York: Random House, 1970) and Roger Mettam, *Power and Faction in Louis XIV's France* (Oxford: Basil Blackwell, 1988). The standard biography of the Sun King is J.B. Wolf, *Louis XIV* (New York: Norton, 1968).

On New France, see W.J. Eccles, *The French in North America, 1500–1783*, rev. ed. (Markham, ON: Fitzhenry and Whiteside, 1998), as well as Eccles's earlier *The Canadian Frontier, 1534–1760* (New York: Holt, Rinehart and Winston, 1969), *Canada under Louis XIV, 1663–1701* (Toronto: McClelland and Stewart, 1964), and *The Government of New France* (Ottawa: Canadian Historical Association, 1965). See also Jacques Mathieu, *La Nouvelle-France. Les Français en Amérique du Nord, XVIᵉ-XVIIIᵉ siècle. 2ᵉ édition* (Sainte-Foy: Les Presses de l'Université Laval, 2001); Leslie Choquette, *Frenchmen into Peasants: Modernity and Tradition in the Peopling of French Canada* (Cambridge, MA: Harvard University Press, 1997); H. Charbonneau et al., *The First French Canadians: Pioneers in the St Lawrence Valley* (Newark: University of Delaware Press, 1993); Marcel Trudel, *An Initiation to New France* (Toronto: Holt, Reinhart and Winston, 1968); Dale Miquelon, *The First Canada to 1791* (Toronto: McGraw-Hill Ryerson, 1994); and Cornelius Jaenen, *The French Regime in the Upper Country of Canada in the Seventeenth Century* (Toronto: Champlain Society, 1996). On Acadia, see Naomi Griffiths, *The Contexts of Acadian History, 1686–1784* (Montreal: McGill-Queen's University Press, 1992).

Aspects of social and institutional developments in New France are summarized in Peter N. Moogk, *La Nouvelle France: The Making of New France—A Cultural History* (East Lansing, MI: Michigan State University Press, 2000); Alan Greer, *The People of New France* (Toronto: University of Toronto Press, 1997); R. Cole Harris and John Warkentin, *Canada before Confederation* (Toronto: Oxford University Press, 1974), chap. 2; and John A. Dickinson and Brian Young, *A Short History of Quebec*, 3rd ed. (Montreal: McGill-Queen's University Press, 2003), chaps. 2 and 3. Volume 1 of R. Cole Harris and Geoffrey J. Matthews, *Historical Atlas of Canada* (Toronto: University of Toronto Press, 1988) provides a wealth of information on Native and European society under the French regime, as do vols. 1–4 of *Dictionary of Canadian Biography* (Toronto: University of Toronto Press, 1966–79).

Studies on the seigneurial system include Colin M. Coates, *Les transformations du paysage et de la société au Québec sous le régime seigneurial* (Sillery: Septentrion, 2003); Sylvie Dépatie, Mario Lalancette, and Christian Dessureault, *Contributions à l' étude du régime seigneurial canadien* (Montreal: Hurtubise HMH, 1992); R. Cole Harris, *The Seigneurial System in Canada: A Geographical Study* (Madison, WI: University of Wisconsin Press, 1966); Marcel Trudel, *The Seigneurial Regime* (Ottawa: Canadian Historical Association, 1956). On the church in New France see Cornelius Jaenen, *The Role of the Church in New France* (Toronto: McGraw-Hill Ryerson, 1976) and the early chapters of Roger Magnuson, *A Brief History of Quebec Education* (Montreal: Harvest House, 1980). Important insights on economic development in this period can be found in Louise Dechêne, *Habitants and Merchants in Seventeenth-Century Montreal* (Montreal: McGill-Queen's University Press, 1992) and *Le Partage des subsistances au Canada sous le régime français* (Montreal: Boréal, 1994). Other specialized studies include Jack Verney, *The Good Regiment: The Carignan-Salières Regiment in Canada, 1665–1668* (Montreal: McGill-Queen's University Press, 1991); Danielle Gauvreau, *Québec: Une ville et sa population au temps de la Nouvelle-France* (Montreal: Presses de l'Université du Québec, 1991); Louis Lavallée, *La Prairie en Nouvelle-France, 1647–1760: Étude d'histoire sociale* (Montreal: McGill-Queen's University Press, 1992); Lorraine Gadoury, *La noblesse de Nouvelle-France: Familles et alliances* (La Salle, QC: Hurtubise HMH, 1992); Marie-Aimée Cliche, *Les Pratiques de dévotion en Nouvelle-France* (Sillery, QC: Les Presses de l'Université du Québec, 1991); André Lachance, *Crimes et criminels en Nouvelle-France* (Montreal: Boréal Express, 1984) and *Les marginaux, les exclus et l'autre au Canada aux XVIIᵉ et XVIIIᵉ siècles* (Montreal: Fides, 1996); Jean-Charles Falardeau, "The Seventeenth Century Parish in French Canada," in *French Canadian Society*, ed. Marcel Rioux and Yves Martin (Toronto: McClelland and Stewart, 1964); and Jonathan Pearl, "Witchcraft in New France in the Seventeenth Century: The Social Aspect," *Historical Reflections* 4 (1977).

On women, see the Clio Collective, *Quebec Women: A History*, trans. Roger Gannon and Rosalind Gill (Toronto: Women's Press, 1987); Alison Prentice et al., *Canadian Women: A History*, 2nd ed. (Toronto: Harcourt Brace, 1996); Karen Anderson, *Chain Her by One Foot: The Subjugation of Women in Seventeenth-Century New France* (London: Routledge, 1991); Jan Noel, "New France: Les femmes favorisées," in *Rethinking Canada: The Promise of Women's History*, 3rd ed., ed. Veronica Strong-Boag and Anita Clair Fellman (Toronto: Oxford University Press, 1997), 33–56; Yves Landry, *Orphelines en France, pionnières au Canada: Les Filles du roi au XVIIᵉ siècle* (Montreal: Leméac, 1992); an article summarizing his main findings, "Gender Imbalance, les Filles du Roi, and Choice of a Spouse in New France," in *Canadian Family History: Selected Readings*, ed. Bettina Bradbury (Toronto: Copp Clark Pitman, 1992), 14–32; Marcel Trudel, *Les écolières des Ursulines de Québec, 1639–1686: Amérindiennes et canadiennes* (Montreal: HMH, 1999).

On historiographical questions, see Serge Gagnon, *Quebec and Its Historians: The Twentieth Century* (Montreal: Harvest House, 1984); Dale Miquelon, *Society and Conquest: The Debate on the Bourgeoisie and Social Change in French Canada, 1700–1850* (Toronto: Copp Clark Pitman, 1977); Ronald Rudin, *Making History in Twentieth-Century Quebec* (Toronto: University of Toronto Press, 1997); and Roberta Hamilton, *Feudal Society and Colonization: The Historiography of New France* (Gananoque, ON: Langdale Press, 1988).

WEBLINKS

PLACENTIA
http://www.pc.gc.ca/lhn-nhs/nl/castlehill/index_e.asp
This is the Parks Canada site for historic Castle Hill at Placentia.

NEW FRANCE
http://www.civilization.ca/vmnf/vmnfe.asp
The Virtual Museum of New France Web site offers a wealth of information on economic, social, and political developments in the colony.

ACADIE
http://www.umoncton.ca/etudeacadiennes/centre/cea.html
The Centre d'études acadiennes Web site offers information and links to a wide range of sources on Acadian history and culture.

CHAPTER 7

The Political Economy of a Strategic Outpost, 1663–1756

Timeline

1670	England grants charter to Hudson's Bay Company
1672–74	Jolliet and Marquette explore the northern Mississippi
1673	Fort Frontenac established at Cataraqui
1682	La Salle reaches Gulf of Mexico
1687	Governor Denonville sends army to quash the Seneca
1689	Iroquois attack on Lachine
1689–97	War of the League of Augsburg
1690	Sir William Phips captures Port Royal and leads an unsuccessful expedition against Quebec
1694	D'Iberville's forces capture St John's
1697	D'Iberville's forces capture Fort York
1701	Treaty of Montreal signed by delegates of French and Native allies with Iroquois; Louisiana founded
1702–13	War of the Spanish Succession
1710	English capture Port Royal
1711	Walker expedition fails to reach Quebec
1713	Treaty of Utrecht awards Newfoundland, Acadia, and Hudson Bay territory to the British
1715–74	Reign of Louis XV
1720	Construction of Louisbourg begins; "Mississippi bubble" bursts
1726	France sends a small detachment of soldiers to Île Saint-Jean
1732	La Vérendrye begins his search for a "western sea"
1744–48	War of the Austrian Succession

"In this memoir I shall consider Canada strictly as an unproductive frontier. . . . I will ask if a land, although sterile and a cause of great expenditure, can be abandoned if by its strategic position it provides its inhabitants with a great advantage over its neighbours.

This is precisely the case with Canada. We cannot deny that this colony has always been a burden to France and that it will probably continue to be so for a very long time to come. But it is also the most powerful obstacle we can use to check English ambitions."[1]

By 1750, when Governor Roland-Michel Barrin de La Galissonière wrote this statement, the fur trade, Native alliances, even social policy in New France were increasingly being dictated by strategic considerations. The challenge of European rivals—in particular the Protestant English and Dutch—for power in Europe and overseas colonies had become the determining factor in French colonial policy.

Strategic considerations flew in the face of Colbert's plans for a compact colony on the St Lawrence. In 1663, New France extended westward only a short distance beyond Montreal. By the beginning of the eighteenth century, the French had not only explored and laid claim to more than half of the North American continent, but had also begun consolidating their empire by forging alliances with the Native nations. The fur trade alone would not have justified such dramatic imperial ambitions. There were, after all, limits to the numbers of furs required to keep Europeans fashionably clad. But when the fur trade became the vehicle for advancing French power at the expense of its European rivals, the potential for growth was limited only by the will of the French state to foot the bill.

As this drawing suggests, religious authorities in the colony were opposed to the sale of alcohol. Civil authorities, however, tolerated the traffic in spirits because it was a popular commodity in the fur trade.
Archives départementales de la Gironde, Bordeaux

CONTROLLING THE FUR TRADE

When the Iroquois threat was reduced in 1666, furs again began moving through Montreal. Dreams of great wealth, coupled with stiff competition, drove young men to make the hazardous journey into the *pays d'en haut*, the area around the Great Lakes, to cut out Native middlemen whose demands for compensation struck the Europeans as too steep. By the end of the 1660s, Michilimackinac, at the northern tip of Lake Michigan, had become the focus for the fur trade in the interior, but it was only a short time before competition pushed French traders farther west. Missionaries and explorers also traded in furs to finance their costly activities. Even Talon justified fur trading on these grounds, assuring Colbert that the

explorers he sent to find minerals and the rumoured western sea would be self-financing.

In addition to the pressure to push ever westward, the fur trade created social problems that troubled authorities: the use of alcohol as a major trade item and the loss to the colony of so many young men who entered the trade, often in defiance of the law. Colbert introduced regulations to control both the sale of alcohol to Natives and to limit the role of the coureurs de bois, as the unlicensed fur traders were called, in the fur trade, but his efforts proved futile.

By the 1670s, it was plain for all to see that alcohol had become a principal commodity in the fur trade. The church, in particular, complained about the deleterious effects that the brandy trade had upon the Natives. In 1678, the intendant was ordered to convene a consultative assembly of leading laymen to advise on the matter. Significantly, no churchmen were invited and, although the evils of the traffic in liquor were deplored, those assembled recommended against major restrictions on the trade. If the French curtailed the trade in alcohol, it was reasoned, the Natives would simply turn to the English for their supply, and the French fur trade would collapse. A royal edict issued the following year forbade carrying brandy to Native dwellings but otherwise respected the wishes of the fur traders.

The problem of the coureurs de bois was equally contentious. By 1680, over 600 coureurs de bois were trading in the interior, in defiance of repeated ordinances. Attempts to have the Natives bring their furs to Montreal had failed miserably. Again the church was involved in the debate over how to handle the problem, this time expressing concern about the impact of the fur trade on the moral fibre of young men in the colony. Coureurs de bois, by definition outlaws, often became too fond of the brandy they traded and had sexual relations with Native women without benefit of marriage.

Both religious and civil authorities also fretted about the effect on the colony of the absence of so many of its young men. They argued that farms and families were being neglected, church attendance and tithes ignored, and the fabric of community life weakened by men who failed to return promptly to the colony when ordered repeatedly to do so. It is perhaps not surprising that young men were attracted to frontier life. Not only could they sometimes find companionship there, but they could also make a good living and escape the censure of the authorities who were overzealous in their efforts to impose control over the activities of the colony's population.

Admitting failure in the attempts to control the interior trade, Louis XIV issued two edicts on the matter in 1681: one granted amnesty to all coureurs de bois if they would return immediately to the colony; the other set up a system of trading permits, called congés, each of which initially permitted one canoe and three men to engage in the upcountry trade. The illicit traders paid little attention to the edicts, and the congés soon became little more than a source of revenue for the governor and intendant who sold them to the colonists.

THE HUDSON'S BAY COMPANY

The efforts of French officials to control the fur trade inadvertently gave the king of England an excuse to award a charter to the Hudson's Bay Company. In 1660, two St Lawrence-based traders, Pierre-Esprit Radisson and his brother-in-law Médard Chouart, Sieur des Groseilliers, returned from a trading expedition north of Lake Superior with a plan to ship furs to Europe through Hudson Bay. French officials refused to countenance such a proposal, and added insult to injury by accusing Radisson and Groseilliers of illegal trading. The pair took their idea to New England and eventually to England, where a group of merchants agreed to finance an expedition to Hudson Bay. The *Nonsuch* and its intrepid crew spent the winter of 1668–69 at the mouth of the Rupert River on James Bay, and returned to England the following summer with a cargo of high-quality furs.

By 1670, English investors had created a company and applied for a charter from Charles II giving them a monopoly of all the territory drained by rivers flowing into Hudson Bay. The area, called Rupert's Land in honour of Prince Rupert, a cousin of the king and the company's first governor, included nearly one-third of the territory of present-day Canada. Largely ignorant of the size of their grant or the numbers of people already living there who could be deemed to have a prior claim, the Hudson's Bay Company would

eventually make huge profits from their North American holdings. In the meantime, because the English had also recently taken control of New York from the Dutch, they were well placed to restrict the French to a narrow band on the St Lawrence.

Throughout most of the seventeenth century, the Baymen confined themselves to posts on the shores of Hudson Bay, while French traders based on the St Lawrence moved steadily westward in their search of furs. In 1682, Canadian entrepreneurs, assisted by an overland military expedition led by the Chevalier de Troyes, captured the English posts on Hudson Bay. Since France and England were technically at peace, Louis XIV was obliged to return the trading posts to the English, but the contest between the St Lawrence and Hudson Bay traders continued.

EXPLORATIONS WEST AND SOUTH

In 1671, Talon sent an expedition, which included the Jesuit Charles Albanel, into the Hudson Bay region and another under fur trader Daumont de Saint-Lusson into Lake Superior country in search of a route leading to the Pacific. Louis Jolliet, another experienced fur trader, was commissioned in 1672 to follow up on earlier efforts by Sulpician priests François Dollier de Casson and René de Bréhant de Galinée to find the rumoured river that flowed into the Gulf of Mexico. Jolliet was joined at Michilimackinac by Father Jacques Marquette, and together they explored the Mississippi as far as the mouth of the Arkansas River.

Talon returned to France in 1672, two years before Jolliet found his way back to the colony. By that time the initiative for territorial expansion had been seized by Louis de Buade, Comte de Frontenac, the new governor general of New France. A military man of great personal ambition, Frontenac defied Colbert's instructions. In 1673, he had a fortified trading post built at Cataraqui (present-day Kingston) and obtained rights for his friend René-Robert, Chevalier de La Salle, to build posts and to trade in the valley of the Mississippi River. La Salle finally reached the Gulf of Mexico in 1682, but he had disturbed Native and European fur traders with his irascible behaviour and aggressive trading activities.

The Iroquois, in particular, were alarmed by La Salle's alliances with their enemies, the Illinois. The Seneca attacked La Salle's fort at St Louis in 1684. Governor La Barre, as deeply involved in the fur trade as Frontenac had been, sent an expedition to intimidate the Iroquois but was forced to accept a humiliating peace. La Barre was recalled for his failure, and his successor, the Marquis de Denonville, sent another expedition in 1687. This time the troops—832 regulars, 900 militiamen, and 400 Indian allies—had more success. English fur traders sent by Governor Thomas Dongan of New York were intercepted and the Seneca were subjected to a "scorched earth" policy. To guard French access to the Illinois country, a blockhouse with a garrison of 100 soldiers was built at the mouth of the Niagara. Nevertheless, the Iroquois were still in control of the southern interior and posed a real threat to New France.

In August 1689, 1500 Iroquois descended on Lachine, putting 56 homes to the torch and killing their captives, sometimes after torturing them. The tactics of the Iroquois were no better or worse than those of the French in this period of history. Instructing Denonville to eliminate the Iroquois "barbarians," Louis XIV demanded that captured warriors be sent to France, where they would become slaves for the Mediterranean fleet. Some 36 Iroquois were seized for this purpose in 1687. In the same year, La Salle was murdered, apparently by his own men.

THE WAR OF THE LEAGUE OF AUGSBURG

While the Iroquois were threatening the outlying settlements of Canada, Louis XIV had become embroiled in a European war. Throughout the 1670s, he harassed the Dutch and then began asserting his right to occupy territories on the border of France and the United Provinces of the Netherlands. The so-called Glorious Revolution, which put the Protestant ruler of the United Provinces, William of Orange, and his wife Mary on the English throne in 1689, spelled disaster for Louis XIV's ambitions to expand French borders and to champion the cause of Roman Catholicism in Europe. The Dutch ruler was able to bring England into a defensive alliance known as the League of Augsburg.

War in Europe made it easier for Governor Frontenac, who had returned to the colony in 1689 for a second tour of duty, to launch retaliatory raids against the English in New England and New York in an effort to convince them to abandon their alliance with the Iroquois. Although the border raids had the desired effect—the English trading base at Albany was temporarily rendered ineffective—they also brought a direct attack on Quebec.

The expedition against New France by land and sea was the idea of the feisty New Englanders who in the spring of 1690 attacked and looted Port Royal in Acadia and then attempted to take Quebec. While the force sent overland soon collapsed, Sir William Phips, with his armada of 34 ships and 2000 men, appeared below the walls of Quebec in October 1690. With winter approaching and smallpox ravaging his troops, Phips was forced to withdraw without achieving his objective. Frontenac is said to have responded to the demand to surrender with the words: "I have no reply to make to your general other than from the mouths of my cannon and muskets." So pleased was Louis XIV by the lifting of the siege that he struck a medal to commemorate the occasion. Its inscription read: "France in the New World Victorious, Quebec 1690." The medal was restruck by the French mint in 1967 at the time of General Charles de Gaulle's visit to Canada, an echo to his famous statement at the time: "Vive le Québec libre!"[2]

French bravado in the colonies continued to reap rewards. In 1694, the Canadian-born naval captain Pierre Le Moyne d'Iberville captured and burned St John's as well as a large number of English fishing bases along the coast of Newfoundland. He then proceeded to Hudson Bay where he captured Fort York from the Hudson's Bay Company one week before peace was negotiated in Europe. In the colony itself, civilians, including women such as Madeleine de Verchères, distinguished themselves by showing exceptional initiative in the face of Iroquois attacks. The War of the League of Augsburg ended in 1697 with the Treaty of Ryswick without any territorial losses to the French Empire in North America.

Frontenac and his ambitious fur-trading friends used the war to justify building more fortified posts in the interior. By 1695, French traders had made direct

Madeleine de Verchères

In 1692 Madeleine de Verchères, a 14-year-old girl, became a hero when she helped to defend her community downriver from Montreal from an Iroquois attack. Her father, a seigneur and army officer, and her mother, who had repulsed a similar attack two years before, were absent at the time of the attack. According to the story, which became more exaggerated as time went on, she was pursued and quickly overtaken by the Iroquois, who seized her by the kerchief she was wearing around her neck. She loosened the scarf and ran into the stockade on her father's seigneury. "I went up on the bastion where the sentry was," she later explained. "I then trans-formed myself, putting the soldier's hat on my head, and with some small gestures tried to make it seem that there were many people, although there was only this soldier."[3] She fired a cannon shot to warn others in the settlement that they were under attack and to summon aid. The Iroquois retreated when armed troops arrived from Montreal the following day.

There seems to be little doubt that young Madeleine showed initiative under difficult circumstances and there were good reasons for her to do so. At the time of this incident, she had already lost two brothers and two brothers-in-law to Iroquois attacks. Later in life she told an embellished version of her story to secure a pension. As Colin Coates has noted in his study of Verchères, her story was forgotten for over a cen-tury after her death in 1747. Following the rediscovery of her manuscript letters in the 1860s, "she reappeared, not only as a historical figure, but also as a national icon, a heroic symbol of the 'golden age' of French Canada."[4] She was recast in public memory as Quebec's Joan of Arc, championing nationalist sen-timent in the province against formidable foes.

Madeleine de Verchères, by C.W. Jeffreys.
Library and Archives Canada/C-010687. Reproduced with permission of C.W. Jeffreys Estate, Toronto

contact with the Sioux and the Assiniboine, tradition-al enemies of France's allies, the Ottawa. For a time it seemed as if the Iroquois would become allied with the aggrieved Ottawa, and together the groups would force the French out of the interior and perhaps out of North America. Frontenac realized his strategic blun-der soon enough to launch a blow to the heart of Iroquois territory. In 1696, an expedition destroyed the villages of the Onondaga and the Oneida.

Meanwhile, orders came from Versailles that no more congés were to be issued and that all western trading posts except St Louis in the Illinois country were to be closed down.

The near-century of warfare between and among Natives and newcomers in North America prompted a general desire for peaceful relations. In September 1700, delegates from four Iroquois tribes (the Mohawk stayed away) made peace at Montreal with

Signing ceremony for the Grand Peace of August 4, 1701, watercolour by François Girard.
F. Girard/© Videanthrop

western base from Michilimackinac to Detroit as part of the strategy to intimidate the Iroquois and contain the English.

These developments signalled a dramatic shift in colonial policy, one that was dictated by France's relations with foreign powers, both Native and European. From now on, economic aspects of the fur trade were superseded by military considerations. The posts that France had planned to abandon in 1696 were to be maintained, and new ones were to be established. The fur trade would help cement Native alliances, while the coureurs de bois, with their skills in Native relations and guerrilla warfare, would become agents of the Crown. This turn of events, driven by developments in Europe, put the final nail in the coffin of Colbert's earlier dream of a compact colony on the St Lawrence.

the Huron, Abenaki, and Ottawa who lived on reserves in the colony. In July of the following year, over 1300 Natives from 32 nations assembled near Montreal to negotiate peace among themselves and renew their alliances with the French. By the Treaty of Montreal, the French recognized the Iroquois as an independent nation and in return the Iroquois promised to remain neutral in any war between France and Britain.

THE WAR OF THE SPANISH SUCCESSION

As people in North America were sorting out their relations, France became embroiled in another war. This time, Louis XIV hoped to establish his grandson on the throne of Spain, thus uniting two of Europe's great empires. As a pre-emptive move, Pierre Le Moyne d'Iberville was dispatched in 1698 to the mouth of the Mississippi to lay claim to the region for France. Three years later, he was ordered to establish a colony there. Louisiana was to become the final link in a chain of posts reaching from the St Lawrence to the Spanish empire in Mexico. Antoine Laumet de Lamothe Cadillac, another prominent member of the beaver aristocracy, also convinced the Minister of Marine and Colonies to move the

The War of the Spanish Succession broke out in 1702 with England and France ranged on opposing sides. Although unwilling to antagonize anew the recently subdued Iroquois, Governor Vaudreuil had no hesitation in attacking settlements on the New England frontier. Raiding expeditions conducted by the Canadian militia and their Native allies in 1703 and 1704 wreaked havoc in outlying settlements and flooded New France with prisoners, many of them slaves of their Native captors. From the Deerfield raid alone, over 100 hostages were taken. In Newfoundland, English fishing communities were again the object of brutal raids. The greatest devastation occurred when a force of 450 Canadians and their Native allies under Daniel d'Auger de Subercase, Governor of Plaisance, spent the winter of 1705 burning, looting, and taking no fewer than 1200 prisoners on the "English shore."

The people who survived the Newfoundland raids could do little by way of retaliation, but the New Englanders, once again, struck back. In 1703, 1704, and 1707 they attacked the outlying settlements in Acadia, taking hostages of their own, but achieved no strategic objective. Finally, in 1710, a force of 1500

Wartime Economic Crisis

After more than two decades of almost continuous warfare, New France in 1712 faced a serious financial crisis. Prices had skyrocketed, hard cash had evaporated, and colonial administrators were forced to pay the troops with playing cards that they hoped would be redeemed by the imperial treasury. As this communication from the Minister of Marine and Colonies in 1712 indicates, the colonies could expect little help from France:

> A number of people from Canada have told me this year that it will in future be absolutely impossible to find the means of supporting the troops and meeting ordinary expenses if the treasurers general do not honour the bills of exchange when they fall due, and that the large

quantity of cards issued in the country brings them into disrepute, which causes goods to quadruple in price, since [these cards] give the traders nothing but bills of exchange which go dishonoured, which ruins them in interest charges and brings suffering to the entire colony. I accept the truth of all these facts, but the unfortunate state of the kingdom in the past several years has prevented His Majesty from meeting both his expenses and those it was indispensable for him to make, on the other hand, to defend himself against the enemies of the state. . . . The King is not in a position to provide for the colony.[5]

British and colonial troops assisted by the marines and a company of grenadiers captured Port Royal, which was defended by its recently appointed governor, Daniel d'Auger de Subercase, with a garrison of 258 soldiers. The English launched an ambitious attack led by Sir Hovenden Walker on Quebec in 1711, but they were forced to abandon their invasion following heavy losses of men and ships in the treacherous currents and shoals of the lower St Lawrence River.

With the exception of Port Royal, the French suffered few losses in North America and inflicted considerable damage on English settlements and posts in New England, Newfoundland, and the Hudson Bay area. But European considerations dictated the terms of the peace. To secure the Bourbon dynasty on the Spanish throne, Louis XIV was forced to make concessions in the Treaty of Utrecht, which ended the war. Colonial territory was thrown into the balance. France agreed to abandon Hudson Bay, Acadia, and Newfoundland to the British and to recognize British authority over the Iroquois Confederacy. France retained fishing rights on the north coast of Newfoundland as well as two islands protecting the entrance to the Gulf of St Lawrence: Île du Cap-Breton (soon to be rechristened Île Royale) and Île Saint-Jean (Prince Edward Island).

On the surface, the losses seemed inconsequential. France had invested little energy in developing these lost outposts of its emerging continental empire, and

they had brought in little or no direct wealth. For New France, however, the signs were ominous: European interests alone seemed to determine the fate of colonies in the Americas. The impact on Acadia was more profound. Following the Treaty of Utrecht, Acadie/Nova Scotia became what John Reid and others call a "hybrid colony,"[6] based on Mi'kmaq tolerance, Acadian accommodation, and haphazard attempts by British and French governments to exert influence. It was only a matter of time before the delicate balance of power would be called into question.

THE IMPERIAL FACTOR

The death of Louis XIV brought a five-year-old child, Louis XV, to the throne of France. Between 1715 and 1723, Philippe, Duc d'Orléans, acted as regent for the young king. As a tool for an aristocracy determined to regain its power, the duke restored the authority of the parlements and replaced bureaucrats on the councils with eminent aristocrats who pursued their own supposedly enlightened policies. Even Protestants and Jews would be tolerated as long as they kept silent in public. On one issue, however, the duke carried on the Sun King's tradition: colonies were valued only to the extent that they enhanced the wealth of France and restrained the growth of rivals to French imperial power.

As it turned out, the Regency ushered in three decades of peace in which France moved to consolidate

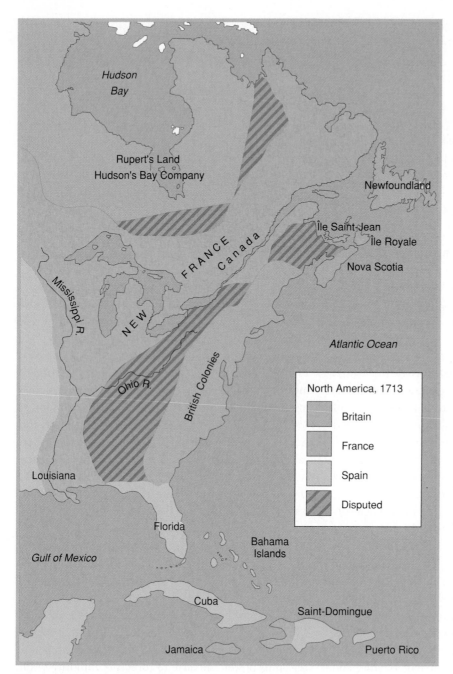

Map 7.1 North America, 1713.
Adapted from W.J. Eccles, *France in America* (East Lansing, MI: Michigan State University Press, 1990), 122.

rose to prominence. The British would have much to reckon with when they faced France again on the colonial battlefield.

Louisiana and Illinois

In the years immediately following the Treaty of Utrecht, Louisiana was in desperate straits. Officially a regional jurisdiction, subordinate to officials in Quebec, Louisiana was in practice directly administered from France, often with the help of Canadian-born officials. Even the seasoned Canadians found Louisiana a difficult challenge. In the first two decades of its existence, a high death rate from disease and famine conditions gave the colony a bad name and caused surviving troops and settlers to desert to nearby Spanish or English colonies. Freehold land tenure, offered as an inducement, brought little response. The colony produced no needed raw materials for the mother country; indeed, ships had trouble reaching the colony through the treacherous Gulf of Mexico and the swampy, mosquito-infested Mississippi Delta.

The situation was further complicated by a disastrous scheme put to the Duc d'Orléans by the clever Scottish financier John Law. Law proposed to establish a government-sponsored central bank that would issue paper notes, expand credit, and encourage investment in a new trading company for the French colonies. By tying the bank to the Compagnie des Indes—another monopoly company with control over colonial enter-

its North American empire. The forts along the Mississippi route between Louisiana and Canada were reoccupied and garrisoned, and the fur trade was subsidized to help sustain Native alliances. In the northwest, Canadian traders outflanked the Bay traders and set up trading networks with new nations in the far west. On Île Royale, the fortified town of Louisbourg prises, including the trade in furs, tropical produce, and slaves—and predicting vast profits from the new colony of Louisiana, Law encouraged speculative investment in his project. The "Mississippi bubble" burst in 1720, as did the pocketbooks of many investors, undermining confidence in new colonial ventures.

Despite the odds, Louisiana survived, but only because the French state willed it so. In 1722, the seat of government was moved from Mobile to New Orleans, considered a healthier site. Between 1719 and 1729, 6000 African slaves were brought to the colony to do the hard work required to establish and develop the economy. By 1739, the colony's exports included pitch, tar, furs, and hides; eventually tobacco, silk, indigo, cotton, and rice were added. Troupes de la Marine were sent to defend the colony, and Ursuline, Jesuit, Carmelite, and Capuchin orders ministered to the spiritual and social needs of the settlers. By 1746, there was a white population of over 4000, one-fifth of them soldiers. The cost to the Crown of this ambitious colonization project was staggering: 20 million livres by 1731 and 800 000 livres a year thereafter to sustain the strategic outpost.

In 1717, the Illinois country was attached administratively to Louisiana. Sporadic military campaigns against the Fox nation slowed development, but by 1731 the Illinois country was home to 108 non-Native families, most of them originally from the Montreal area, as well as 44 soldiers, several missionaries, and scores of traders. Twenty years later, the population had reached over 3000, including 1536 French and 890 African and Native slaves. By that time, large slave-worked estates were shipping wheat, flour, corn, cattle, and swine to Louisiana and the French West Indies.

THE PAYS D'EN HAUT

On the northwest frontier, the French aggressively pursued trading alliances with the Natives in the Abitibi-Temiskaming region, along the north shore of

La Vérendrye, Canada's Farthest West, 1732, **by John Inness.**
Library and Archives Canada/C-146611

Lake Superior, and into the Prairies. The man who played the biggest role in establishing the French presence on the Prairies was Pierre Gautier de Varennes et de La Vérendrye.

While serving as commander of a fur-trading post at the mouth of the Nipigon River, La Vérendrye heard from a variety of Aboriginal sources about a "muddy lake" and a "great river" to the west. In the spring of 1730, a chief of the Kenisteno, called La Martleblanche by the French, promised to guide La Vérendrye to these mysterious bodies of water, which he hoped would lead to the Pacific. La Vérendrye sought and secured from Louis XV a commission to find the Pacific Ocean and a monopoly of the trade in the territories claimed by the Hudson's Bay Company. In the summer of 1732, La Vérendrye, two of his sons, a priest, and at least 16 voyageurs joined an Aboriginal war party of 50 canoes on a journey into the interior.

Over the next 10 years, La Vérendrye and his sons established a chain of trading posts stretching from Lake Superior to the heart of the western plains: Fort St Pierre (Rainy Lake), Fort St Charles (Lake of the Woods), Fort Maurepas (on the Winnipeg River), Fort Rouge (at the junction of the Red and Assiniboine rivers), Fort La Reine (Portage La Prairie), Fort Dauphin (on Lake Manitoba), Fort Bourbon (on Lake

This watercolour by Mark Catesby in 1724 is one of the earliest European depictions of the buffalo that inhabited the western plains. A source of food, clothing, and housing for Native peoples of the Plains, buffalo were so numerous that explorers and fur traders claimed that they were obliged to chase them away from their encampments.

Windsor Castle, Royal Library. © 1992 Her Majesty Queen Elizabeth II, RE 26090, detail

regime's main benefits from his frontier activities.

Although La Vérendrye's party never found the Pacific, one of his sons reached the foothills of the Rockies. La Vérendrye himself lost his fur-trade monopoly and died a poor man in 1749. Nevertheless, he left a significant legacy. French trading posts in the interior were a more convenient source of supplies for Native peoples than the distant posts on Hudson Bay. Only the limited capacity of canoes, the principal vehicle of inland trade, restricted the ability of the French to totally undermine the commercial activities of the Bay traders.

Following La Vérendrye's death, Governor La Jonquière ordered Jacques Le Gardeur de Saint-Pierre to take possession of La Vérendrye's posts, establish new ones, and continue the search for the elusive Western Sea. In 1754, Louis La Corne, who succeeded Le Gardeur, built Fort Saint-Louis, near the forks of the Saskatchewan River, which became the limit of French expansion under the French regime. The English might well claim sovereignty over their posts on Hudson Bay, but they would have considerable difficulty controlling their inland supply routes. So aggressively did the French pursue their trading enterprises that the Bay men were forced to send their own traders into the interior. In 1754, Anthony Henday embarked on a journey that took him to the site of what is today Edmonton, Alberta, in an effort to persuade the Natives to bring their pelts to the Hudson's Bay Company posts.

By the mid-eighteenth century, Canada's commercial hinterland consisted of most of the interior of the continent. Two main entrepôts, Detroit and Michilimackinac, served as headquarters for merchants, traders, and Jesuit missionaries as well as transshipment points. Detroit also had a garrison of troops and a summer population of over 400 people. Outside

Winnipegosis), and Fort Pascoyac (on the Saskatchewan River). The success of the effort depended upon alliances with the Cree and the Assiniboine and their long-standing rivals, the Ojibwa and the Dakota. Eager to maintain good relations with the First Nations, La Vérendrye chose several young men from each post to live with the local tribes and permitted two of his sons to be adopted by the Cree. He also shipped Sioux slaves back to the colony and boasted that this trade in humans was one of the French the fort, 500 settlers made a good living supplying the fur-trade network from their productive farms. The Jesuit mission at Detroit served a resident population of 2600, primarily Ottawa, Petun, and Potawatomi, the largest Aboriginal concentration in the Great Lakes basin.

LOUISBOURG

Following the loss of Newfoundland, France decided to build a base on Île Royale. Named in honour of the king, Louisbourg was designed to protect the St

Lawrence entrance to France's continental empire and provide a North American base for the lucrative fisheries. Like Louisiana, Louisbourg was an expensive venture, costing nearly 20 million livres to establish. Construction of the fortified town began in 1720. Although it fell both times it was attacked and was never very effective in protecting the St Lawrence, Louisbourg soon became a major fishing port and a thriving entrepôt for the North Atlantic trade.

Even before the ink was dry on the Treaty of Utrecht, Louisbourg had a population of 116 men, 10 women, and 23 children, all of whom had moved from Placentia, Newfoundland, in 1713. The remainder of the evacuees arrived the following year. It proved more difficult to persuade the Acadians to leave their prosperous farms on the dyked marshlands of the Bay of Fundy for the rocky soil of Île Royale. The prospect of freehold land tenure—there would be no seigneuries on Île Royale—was no boon to the Acadians, who had enjoyed the benefits of, if not official title to, free land for nearly a century. Only 67 Acadian families immigrated to Île Royale between 1713 and 1734. Most of them lived in areas outside the town where they could farm and fish for their subsistence.

During Louisbourg's short history under French rule, the majority of people who lived there came directly from France. Men involved in the fishery and navy often wintered in the town, some of them marrying local women and setting down roots. As in other French colonial possessions, the military were well represented, making up one-quarter to one-half of the population. The Récollets, Frères Hospitaliers, and Soeurs de la Congrégation de Notre-Dame located in the community.

Although most of the residents were Roman Catholics, Louisbourg attracted people from a variety of ethnic and religious backgrounds. A significant proportion of the fishing community was drawn from the Basque-speaking region of southern France, and between 1722 and 1745 about 20 percent of the garrison consisted of German and Swiss soldiers of the Karrer regiment. Louisbourg's inhabitants included black and Native "servants," a few Irish, Scots, and Spanish sojourners, and at least one Jew. By the 1740s, there were over 2000 residents in the town, and the population of the island had grown to over 5000.

This medal, one side of which shows the head of Louis XV, was struck to commemorate the founding of Louisbourg in 1720.
Parks Canada, Fortress of Louisbourg

The first people on the spot, the primarily Newfoundland-born settlers from Placentia, took up the choice beach lots and the best land grants in and around Louisbourg. These fishing proprietors (*habitants-pêcheurs*) dominated the island's economy and helped to maintain a spirit of independence in the town. They also controlled the Superior Council until 1745, holding four of the five council positions. As in Canada, the leading officials in Louisbourg (a lieutenant-governor and commissaire-ordonnateur) were from France.

Louisbourg was a cosmopolitan place. Open to sea traffic for much of the year—fogs permitting—it was the single most productive fishing port on the North Atlantic, harvesting some 150 000 quintals of fish annually by 1720. An average of 154 ships a year called at the port, a number exceeded in North America only by Boston, New York, and Philadelphia. Although fish and fish oil were the only locally generated exports, the wharves in Louisbourg harbour were awash with manufactured goods, fishing supplies, and foodstuffs from France; molasses, sugar, and rum from the West Indies; foodstuffs and building supplies illegally shipped from New England; and foodstuffs and forest products from Canada. There was a sixfold increase in French seaborne commerce in the years between 1710 and 1740, and Louisbourg was one of the major beneficiaries of this growth.

ÎLE SAINT-JEAN

French authorities also made efforts to entice the Acadians to move to Île Saint-Jean, but with no better results than they had on Île Royale. Why would they leave their hard-won dykeland farms to start over again on the tree-covered soils, however fertile, of Île Saint-Jean? In 1719, the islands of Saint-Jean, Miscou, and Magdalen were granted to the Comte de Saint-Pierre with the stipulation that he settle the territory. The following year his Compagnie de l'Île Saint-Jean sent out over 250 colonists who established themselves at Port LaJoie (near present-day Charlottetown), Havre Saint-Pierre (St Peter's), and other coastal locations. Like most private ventures sponsored by France, this one failed within a few years and the settlers drifted away.

To confirm French sovereignty, in 1726 the governor of Louisbourg was ordered to send over an armed detachment—all of 30 men—to occupy Saint-Pierre's dilapidated buildings at Port LaJoie. During the 1730s Jean-Pierre Roma, an energetic Parisian merchant, established fishing operations on the island. He built roads to connect his base at Trois-Rivières with Havre Saint-Pierre and Port LaJoie, and attracted settlers to the island. According to a census taken in 1735, there were 432 colonists on Île Saint-Jean, about a third of them of Acadian origin. Roma hoped to establish a thriving fishing and trading centre. Had the War of the Austrian Succession not intervened, he may well have succeeded in his goal.

THE ST LAWRENCE ECONOMY

By the eighteenth century, most of Canada's population was colonial-born, but the economy of the St Lawrence colony was still largely shaped by the interests of the mother country. Canada's strategic importance to the French Empire in North America accounted for two of the three main sources of investment in the colony: the fur trade and the military. Agriculture, the third pillar of the St Lawrence economy, also benefited from the need to supply the troops stationed in the colony and at the interior posts.

The Fur Trade

Fur remained Canada's chief export and was the focus for French-Native relations. Although the supply of beaver continued to decline from overtrapping in the eighteenth century, other fur-bearing animals more than took up the slack. The slaughter in the wilderness netted over 250 000 pelts a year in 1728, rising to over 400 000 by the 1750s.

Montreal was the pivot of the trade, which reached far into the interior of the continent and back across the Atlantic to La Rochelle in France. Each year the convoys of canoes set out from Montreal for the *pays d'en haut* laden with items for the fur trade and supplies for the long journey and the interior posts. In the upper country, the trade developed on a three-tier system. Forts Frontenac and Niagara operated as king's posts in direct competition with British interlopers and their agents at Oswego. To ensure its success, the trade at these posts was heavily subsidized by the state. At Detroit, and Michilimackinac and other garrisoned posts, the trade was controlled through congés, or licences, but there were still unlicensed coureurs de bois operating in their own interests or on behalf of unnamed merchants and royal officials. At Green Bay and posts west of Sault Ste Marie—the *mer de l'ouest* region where the trade was now the most lucrative—monopolies were leased by the Crown to military officers and a few merchants, who used their privileges to enrich themselves.

Furs were also traded illegally. To avoid customs duties and export controls, furs shipped on the accounts of colonial officials were loaded onto fishing vessels at Kamouraska or the Gaspé or unloaded clandestinely in France before reaching La Rochelle. Other traders bypassed Quebec by shipping out of New Orleans, or even New York via Oswego and Albany. The trade through New York was officially condemned but unofficially winked at because of its many advantages. These included sizable profits, immediate payments, and access to English trade commodities, which were eagerly sought by Canadians and Natives alike.

The necessity of satisfying their Native allies was an ongoing challenge. Manufacturers at Montpellier, Montauban, Carcassonne, and Rochefort in France made goods specifically for the fur trade. Far from being blindly exploited, taken in by inferior quality and short measure, the Native traders were discrimi-

TABLE 7.2 Colonial Revenues and Expenditures, in livres

Year	Income	Expenditures
1713	442 348	445 455
1715	548 246	548 243
1720	381 499	381 499
1725	393 577	393 594
1730	496 253	494 217
1735	485 852	520 484
1740	417 968	503 766
1745	500 038	1 337 722
1750	904 722	1 774 715

Source: Cornelius Jaenen and Cecilia Morgan, *Material Memory: Documents in Pre-Confederation History* (Don Mills, ON: Addison Wesley Longman, 1998), 90.

nating in taste and value, and they commanded and received goods of acceptable standards.

An ancillary activity associated with the strategic role of the colony and the fur trade was the military establishment. Although it is impossible to separate the exact amounts that were spent maintaining troops and fortifications from the general Crown expenditures in New France, most years the military had the lion's share of the appropriations. When the colony was put on a wartime footing in 1744, the annual budget soared. The French government also spent large sums on arming and equipping the Canadian militia, which was of direct benefit to the colonists, and on presents to their Aboriginal allies. In wartime, the Crown provided subsistence for the families of the Native auxiliaries, who fought side by side with the colonial militia and the regular troops.

Economic Initiatives

Other than furs, few colonial resources proved successful as exports. Although sawmills became a familiar site on the Canadian landscape—there were 52 in operation by 1752—they produced squared timber and lumber primarily for local use. Shipbuilding proved more successful. By the 1730s, colonists were building 150- and 200-ton vessels. A royal bounty of three livres per ton stimulated investment, and in most years Canadians completed eight to ten vessels that qualified for the subsidy. With the expansion of the West Indies trade, ships were built in the colony

TABLE 7.1 Fur Exports from Quebec

(number of pelts)

Year	Beaver	Other pelts	Total
1728	101 840	157 234	259 074
1732	106 929	176 078	283 007
1733	147 235	163 178	310 413
1735	118 353	187 035	305 388
1736	123 372	183 042	306 414
1737	82 524	273 609	356 133
1739	88 751	236 539	325 290
1754	88 301	320 327	408 628
1755	99 332	315 973	415 305

Source: H.A. Innis, *The Fur Trade in Canada: An Introduction to Canadian Economic History* (Toronto: University of Toronto Press, 1927), 153–54.

specifically to carry flour, wood products, and stoves to the West Indies.

Military vessels were also built in the colony. In 1731, orders were placed for the construction of ships-of-the-line at the royal shipyards on the St Charles River near Quebec. Ten warships were built for the French navy in the 1740s and two more in the 1750s. Appropriately, the first warship launched was christened *Le Canada*, but the pride of the shipyards was *Le Caribou*, a 700-ton man-of-war. In the 1750s, four naval vessels were built to patrol Lake Ontario.

In comparing New France's shipbuilding industry with that of nearby English colonies, contemporaries and later historians judge it a failure. Admittedly, there were problems. The imported skilled workers, sent to the colony under contract, complained that they had poor housing and unfair working conditions compared with the Canadians, who were sometimes better-paid and given leave during inclement weather. In 1741, the disgruntled immigrant workers underlined their discontent by bringing construction activities to a halt. Intendant Gilles Hocquart responded by imprisoning the mutinous workers in irons, a measure that quickly brought an end to their protest. Constituted authority was prepared to deal harshly with insubordination from the lower orders, and in pre-industrial society there was little working-class consciousness that might have induced the Canadian workers to cooperate with their metropolitan brothers to protect their collective economic interests.

The ships built in the colony also cost too much. In part this was because of the corruption that characterized state activities in New France. Many expenses not associated with construction activities were charged to the company. An even bigger problem was the quality of the final product, which rotted quickly. Without proper facilities for drying and storing the lumber, it was exposed to the elements and soon deteriorated. Moreover, colonists rapidly depleted the supply of hard oak and pine in the St Lawrence lowlands and were forced to use less sturdy timbers, which led to an inferior product. While the colonials lacked the resources and skills to construct the huge 500-ton ships required by the navy, they had no difficulty producing the thousands of fishing boats, coastal vessels, and bateaux that served their local needs.

In the eighteenth century, mining got underway in Île Royale, where coal reserves near the ground surface were easily exploited. With the age of steam still a century away, coal was used primarily as a source for heat and could not as yet form the basis of a booming industry. Denys La Ronde spent 25 000 livres bringing equipment and two German experts to explore the possibilities of exploiting the copper deposits in the Lake Superior region, but little came of the venture.

Iron was a basic commodity for people in pre-industrial Europe, and Canada had an excellent source on the banks of the St Maurice River about 12 kilometres from Trois-Rivières. In 1730, a Montreal merchant, François Poulin de Francheville, opened a bog-iron plant to provide the colony with forged iron for stoves, cauldrons, pots, axeheads, and the small tools and implements required in the colony. After his death in 1735, the ironworks were taken over by François-Étienne Cugnet. With a royal subsidy of 100 000 livres, Cugnet began full-scale production, but within five years the company was bankrupt and the state assumed management of the forges. As a state enterprise, the company occasionally made a profit. In 1747, the ironworks began experimenting with steel making and cannon founding with a view to supplying the military, but such efforts had barely got off the ground before the conquest.

Like the shipyards, the St Maurice ironworks were less than a complete success as an economic venture, and for some of the same reasons. Skilled workers had to be imported and mistakes were made in the construction and layout of the plant. One investigation also revealed that a number of people drew large salaries without having much to do with the ironworks. Clearly, capitalist notions of efficiency were not always uppermost in the minds of those pioneering such enterprises. In any case, industrial capitalism had yet to transform the way that people worked and planned their manufacturing ventures. What is significant is that the French state supported these new efforts in its colonies and that a new way of thinking about economic activities was beginning to take shape in the North Atlantic world.

MORE TO THE STORY

The China Connection

Although the fur trade was the golden goose of the St Lawrence economy, the colonists briefly made fortunes on ginseng, a plant that grew wild in the region. The ginseng root was much prized in Asia for its reputed medicinal, restorative, and aphrodisiac properties. It came to the attention of the Jesuits through correspondence with their counterparts in Manchuria, where the root was harvested by the peasants. Father Joseph-François Lafitau at the Caughnawaga (Kahnawaké) reserve, near Montreal, identified the plant in the neighbouring woods. By 1721, Canadian ginseng shipped to France was being sold in Canton, China. The market boomed in the late 1740s when a regular trade was established through the Compagnie des Indes, which obtained the exclusive right to sell ginseng in the Orient.

With the value of the trade at La Rochelle approaching 20 percent of the revenues from the fur trade, ginseng fever struck the colony. Even the religious communities sent their domestic servants and slaves to gather the precious root. When preparing his report on colonial agriculture, the engineer Louis Franquet remarked that the Canadian farmers were neglecting their harvests and could not find Natives willing to help them because everyone seemed bent on making quick money by gathering ginseng.

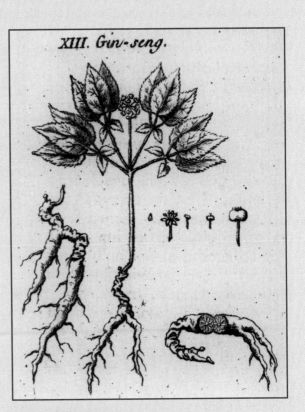

Etching of ginseng, 1744.
Library and Archives Canada/C103993

TABLE 7.3	Value of Ginseng Exports

Year	Value in livres
1747	12 900
1748	10 125
1749	76 300
1750	65 562
1751	152 100
1752	484 120
1753	33 000

Source: Brian Evans, "Ginseng: Root of Chinese-Canadian Relations," *Canadian Historical Review* 61, 1 (March 1985): 1–26.

As with so many colonial ventures, the ginseng boom was a short one. In 1751, the Compagnie des Indes refused to purchase the stocks accumulating in La Rochelle, and by 1752 ginseng was selling for only nine livres a pound in Canton. Because of its inferior quality, the Chinese refused to purchase the Canadian product. Thereafter the Compagnie des Indes would buy only properly harvested and treated roots. A very modest trade continued until the conquest, by which time the plant had been hunted virtually to extinction. Abbé Raynal, who frequently commented on colonial affairs, noted: "The colonists were severely punished for their excessive rapaciousness by the total loss of a branch of commerce, which if rightly managed, might have proved a source of opulence."[7]

CONCLUSION

Between 1663 and 1744, France had laid the foundation for a vast North American empire based on trade and Native alliances. The losses sustained by the Treaty of Utrecht were balanced by the construction of Louisbourg, a growing French presence on the St Lawrence, and expansion into the Great Lakes and Mississippi regions. Life in a strategic outpost was always precarious but, as we shall see in the next chapter, it had its advantages, at least for those with ambition.

NOTES

1 "Memorandum on the Colonies in North America, 1750," cited in *Emerging Identities: Selected Problems and Interpretations in Canadian History*, ed. Paul W. Bennett and Cornelius Jaenen (Scarborough ON: Prentice-Hall, 1986), 40.

2 Dale Miquelon, *The First French Canada: To 1791* (Toronto: McGraw-Hill Ryerson, 1994), 61, note 6.

3 André Vachon, "Jarret de Verchères, Marie-Madeleine," *Dictionary of Canadian Biography*, vol. 3, *1741–1770* (Toronto: University of Toronto Press, 1979), 308–13.

4 Colin Coates, "Images of Heroism and Nationalism: The Canadian Joan of Arc," in Colin M. Coates and Cecilia Morgan, *Heroines and History: Representations of Madeleine de Verchères and Laura Secord* (Toronto: University of Toronto Press, 2002), 41.

5 Cited in Guy Frégault, "La colonisation du Canada au XVIIIe siècle," *Cahiers de l'Academie canadienne-française* 2 (1957): 53–81.

6 John Reid et al., *The "Conquest" of Acadia, 1710: Imperial, Colonial and Aboriginal Constructions* (Toronto: University of Toronto Press, 2003), 208.

7 Brian Evans, "Ginseng: Root of Chinese-Canadian Relations," *Canadian Historical Review* 61, 1 (March 1985): 17.

RELATED READINGS IN THIS SERIES

From *Foundations: Readings in Pre-Confederation Canadian History*

Colin M. Coates, "Images of Heroism and Nationalism: The Canadian Joan of Arc," 116–134.

From Media Companion CD-ROM, Volume I

Hudson's Bay Company Charter, 1670
Report of La Vérendrye, 1730
Impact of the Fur Trade on the People of New France

SELECTED READING

In addition to the works by W.J. Eccles, Louise Dechêne, Alan Greer, Jacques Mathieu, Dale Miquelon, Peter Moogk, and Marcel Trudel cited in the previous chapter, see André Vachon et al., *Taking Root: Canada from 1700 to 1760* (Ottawa: Public Archives of Canada, 1985) for a survey of developments in New France in the eighteenth century. Two biographies offer insights into developments in New France in the seventeenth century. W.J. Eccles, *Frontenac: The Courtier Governor* with an introduction by Peter Moogk (Lincoln: University of Nebraska Press, 2003), and Martin Fournier, *Pierre-Esprit Radisson, Merchant Adventurer, 1636–1701* (Montreal: McGill-Queen's University Press, 2003). Colin Coates puts the career of Madeleine de Verchères in perspective in Colin M. Coates and Cecilia Morgan, *Heroines and History: Representations of Madeleine de Verchères and Laura Secord* (Toronto: University of Toronto Press, 2002). French-Native relations are discussed in Gilles Havard, *The Great Peace of Montreal of 1701: French-Native Diplomacy in the Seventeenth Century* (Montreal: McGill-Queen's University Press, 2001). The conquest of Acadia is the focus of an important new collection of essays: John Reid et al., *The "Conquest" of Acadia, 1710: Imperial, Colonial and Aboriginal Constructions* (Toronto: University of Toronto Press, 2003). On the history of Louisbourg, see Christopher Moore, *Louisbourg Portraits: Life in an Eighteenth-Century Garrison Town* (Toronto: Macmillan, 1982), and two books by A.J.B. Johnson, *Control and Order in French Colonial Louisbourg, 1713–1758* (East Lansing: Michigan State University Press, 2001) and *Religion in Life at Louisbourg* (Montreal: McGill-Queen's University Press, 1984). See Georges Arsenault, *The Island Acadians, 1720–1980* (Charlottetown: Ragweed, 1989) for information on the early history of Île Saint-Jean. This period in Newfoundland history is covered in Olaf Uwe Jansen, "The French Presence in Southwestern and Western Newfoundland Before 1815," in André Magord, dir., *Les Franco-Terreneuviens de la péninsule de Port-au-Port* (Moncton: Chaire d'études acadiennes, Université de Moncton, 2002) and the relevant chapters of Patrick O'Flaherty, *Old Newfoundland: A History to 1843* (St John's: Long Beach Press, 1999). On the "upper country," see Gilles Havard, *Empire et métissage: Indiens et Français dans le Pays-d'en-Haut, 1660–1715* (Sillery: Septentrion, 2003); Charles J. Balesi, *The Time of the French in the Heart of North America, 1673–1818* (Chicago: Alliance Française, 1992); Joseph L. Peyser, *Letters from New France: The Upper Country, 1686–1783* (Urbana: University of Illinois Press, 1992); and Richard Wright, *The Middle Ground: Indians, Empires, and Republics in the Great Lakes Region, 1650–1815* (Cambridge: Cambridge University Press, 1991). On economic matters, see François Brière, *La pêche française en Amérique du nord au xviiiᵉ siècle* (Montreal: Fides, 1990); Harold Innis, *The Fur Trade in Canada: An Introduction to Canadian Economic History* (Toronto: University of Toronto Press, 1927); John F. Bosher, *The Canada Merchants* (Oxford: Oxford University Press, 1978); Cameron Nish, *Les bourgeois-gentilhommes de la Nouvelle-France, 1729–1748* (Montreal: Fides, 1975); Kathryn A. Young, *Kin, Commerce, Community: Merchants in the Port of Quebec, 1717–1745* (New York: Peter Lang, 1995); Jacques Mathieu, *La Construction navale royale à Québec, 1739–1759* (Quebec: Société historique de Québec, 1971) and *Le commerce entre la Nouvelle-France et les Antilles au xviiiᵉ siècle* (Montréal: Fides, 1981); Réal Boissonnault, *Les forges du Saint-Maurice, 1729–1883* (Quebec: Parcs Canada, 1983); Cameron Nish, *François Cugnet: Entrepreneur et enterprises en Nouvelle-France* (Montreal: Fides, 1975); James Pritchard, "The Pattern of French Colonial Shipping to Canada before 1760," *Revue française d'histoire d'outre-mer* 63, 231 (1976); Gratien Allaire, "Fur Trade Engagés, 1701–1745," in *Rendezvous: Selected Papers of the North American Fur Trade Conference 1981*, ed. Thomas C. Buckley (St Paul, MN: Minnesota Historical Society, 1984), and "Officiers et marchands: les sociétés de commerce des fourrures, 1715–1760," *Revue d'histoire de l'Amérique française* 40, 3 (1987).

WEBLINKS

PIERRE-ESPRIT RADISSON
www.collectionscanada.ca/heroes/h6-236-e.html

This Library and Archives Canada site offers a biography, a brief bibliography, and additional links.

TREATY OF UTRECHT
www.geocities.com/Yosemite/Rapids/3330/constitution/utrecht.htm

A portion of the treaty text relating to Newfoundland is available on this site.

LOUISBOURG
collections.ic.gc.ca/louisbourg/enghome.html

This is an outstanding site, providing a wealth of information on the fortress and the time period. There is an extensive subject index of site resources. Online access is available to parish records of births, marriages, and deaths from 1713 to 1758.

SAINT MAURICE IRONWORKST
http://www.pc.gc.ca/lhn-nhs/qc/saintmaurice/index_e.asp

This is the Parks Canada Web site for the Forges du Saint-Maurice National Historic Site of Canada.

CHAPTER 8

Social Life in New France

Timeline

1702–3	Smallpox epidemic in Quebec
1709	Slavery recognized in New France
1716	Kahnawaké founded
1717	Merchants allowed to form associations
1721–49	Over 700 petty criminals sent to New France
1753	Grey Nuns receive official recognition

"The common man in Canada is more civilized and clever than in any other place in the world that I have visited. On entering one of the peasant's houses, no matter where, and on beginning to talk with the men and women, one is quite amazed at the good breeding and courteous answers which are received, no matter what the question is. . . . Frenchmen who were born in Paris said themselves that one never finds in France among the country people the courtesy and good breeding which one observes everywhere in this land. I have heard many native Frenchmen assert this."[1]

When Peter Kalm—a European scientist and university professor—visited the English and French colonies in 1749–50, he was especially impressed by New France. He found productive farms, happy peasants, and a sophisticated governor (Roland-Michel, Barrin de la Galissonière) who regaled Kalm with his theories on "ways of employing natural history to the purposes of politics, the science of government."[2] These conditions represented everything that an enlightened eighteenth-century gentleman found desirable. Kalm's judgments also reflected a view held by many visitors to the colony: that a distinctive Canadian culture was emerging on the banks of the St Lawrence. Although it was definitely French in tone and structure, New France differed from a province of old France, just as the regions of France differed from each other.

IMMIGRATION AND SOCIETY

Canada, the St Lawrence colony where most immigrants to New France settled, was not a carbon copy of the European social order. Although there was enough grinding poverty in France to make emigration a tempting option, few peasants chose to start a new life overseas. Most merchants and aristocrats, even if they spent some time in the colonies, had no incentive to retire there. In the

150-year period prior to the conquest, some 27 000 foreign-born individuals spent some time in Canada, but most were sojourners. Nearly two-thirds of them went back home. Who, then, stayed in the colony?

For many citizens of France, the colonies represented a place that drew only the poor, criminal, or highly motivated. This view has some basis in fact. People moving permanently to Canada tended to be concentrated into a few specific occupational groups. The most likely settlers were either soldiers released from military service (3300) or engagés (1200) committed to a specific term of service, usually three years. Neither soldiers nor contract labourers had much say in where they served, but most had the option of either staying in New France or returning home. Over half of the 1500 women who migrated to Canada were filles du roi. Some 1000 salt smugglers and other petty criminals were sent to Canada, and at least 200 of them stayed.

Other than some 500 clergy, most of them in the male religious orders, self-financing immigrants

MORE TO THE STORY

Demography

Demography is a social science that analyzes population trends and is concerned with factors relating to births, marriages, deaths, and migrations of peoples. While present-day data-gathering techniques give demographers plenty of information upon which to base their conclusions, the sources for earlier periods are often elusive. Happily, the bureaucratic nature of the French regime had the unintended result of providing historians with a variety of sources—censuses, parish records, marriage contracts, confirmation lists, indenture agreements, death certificates, for example—that can be used to reconstitute the general trends in immigration, family formation, and life expectancy. From such sources, demographers have determined immigration patterns for Canada.

Historian Peter Moogk offers the following statistical summary:

TABLE 8.1	Immigration to Canada before 1760
Soldiers	3300
Acadians	1800
Women from France	1500
Indentured servants	1200
Slaves	900
British subjects	650
Other European foreigners	525
Male clergy	500
Self-financed immigrants	250
Transported prisoners	200
Total	10 825

Source: Peter Moogk, *La Nouvelle France: The Making of New France—A Cultural History* (East Lansing: Michigan State University Press, 2000), 113.

This summary of a census taken in Acadia in 1686 indicates that census takers were interested not only in the human population but also in the amount of cleared land, the number of farm animals, and the firearms held in the colony.

Archives nationales, Paris, Section Outre-Mer, Série G1, vol. 466, no. 10

accounted for no more than 250 people. A few were *fils de famille*, a general term for debauched sons sent abroad. To save themselves further embarrassment, influential families could obtain a royal *lettre de cachet* to send the offending child to prison or into exile without a trial. While a few errant sons stayed, most of them, like the other immigrants, left the colony.

Four times as many men as women, and as many urban as rural people, chose Canada as their home. Nearly all immigrants were single; only one man in twenty and one woman in five were married or widowed. Most were relatively young. Although immigrants came from all regions of France, Paris and the areas immediately surrounding embarkation ports such as La Rochelle, Rouen, St Malo, and Dieppe contributed a disproportionate number of settlers.

Most immigrants were French citizens, but 525 Europeans from areas outside of France fetched up in the colony. So, too, against their will, did 900 slaves, both Native and African. In addition, 650 British subjects, over 500 of them captives of raids on English colonies or vessels, settled in Canada, as did 1800 Acadians who escaped to the St Lawrence region following the initial deportation order in 1755. In total, as Table 8.1 indicates, nearly 10 000 Europeans immigrated to Canada. Another 500 settled in Acadia. Over a quarter of the immigrants came in just two decades: 1660–69 and 1750–59. Louisbourg at its height was home to over 4000 people, but most of them left following the conquests of 1745 and 1758.

By the end of the French regime about 4000 Native people had also settled in Canada, most in reserves around Quebec and Montreal. The church played an important role in drawing Natives to the colony. In 1676, for example, the Jesuits established a mission at La Prairie for Aboriginal Christians, most of them Iroquois. They moved several times before finally settling at Sault St-Louis, or Caughnawaga (Kahnawaké), in 1716. There they grew through natural increase and adoptions. Among the latter were Natives captured during wars, captives from British colonies, and French foundlings and children born out of wedlock. In the 1750s, 30 families from Kahnawaké, including a part-African Abenaki named Louis Cook, moved to St Regis-Akwesasné on Lake Francis to be nearer to the Iroquois in what is now the state of New York.

TOWN LIFE

About 20 percent of the people in New France lived in urban communities. Closely linked to France through church, state, and commercial institutions, the major colonial towns were quick to reflect the social and intellectual currents transforming European society. The Marquis de Montcalm, writing in 1757, judged Quebec to be the equal of most French towns. Visitors to Montreal and Louisbourg were often surprised by the vibrant urban life they encountered.

Located on one of the most imposing sites in North America, Quebec never failed to impress the first-time visitor. As the capital of New France and the chief port of Canada, Quebec had grown from a population of 500 in 1660 to 10 times that size a century later. Importers and artisans mixed in Lower Town, while administrative and religious institutions were concentrated in Upper Town. Dominating all was the Château Saint-Louis, the residence of the governor general. At the rear of the town stood the intendant's palace, which served as his official residence and the meeting place for the Superior Council, the Quebec Prévôté, and the Admiralty Court. Stone fortifications ran behind the town from the St Lawrence to the St Charles river. By 1750 many of the houses in the town were also built of stone, a result of a ban on new wooden structures following a disastrous fire in 1726.

Quebec was a busy place, especially in the late spring and early summer when the ships began arriving from France. On weekly market days people from the countryside crowded the town's narrow streets. In backyards throughout Quebec, but especially in the expanding precincts of Upper Town, people grew gardens, kept live animals, and built their privies. Pigs and cattle commonly wandered the streets unattended. When citizens wanted to discard refuse, they simply spread it on the unpaved streets, thus adding new odours to those already wafting from the open sewers that carried the town's liquid sludge to the river's edge. Such practices were common to all colonial communities and in no way detracted from Quebec's pre-eminent position in New France. The town was home to the highest-ranking officials in church and state as well as over 350 artisans representing more than 30 different crafts. On religious holidays, Quebec could mount the most impressive processions, with all ranks of society accounted for.

By the middle of the eighteenth century, Quebec was a "tenant's town,"[3] with over half of the town's population renting rather than owning their dwelling places. The mobility of the population and the competitive economic climate made it difficult for labourers and artisans to earn enough money to purchase a home. While widows in Quebec had the highest rate of home ownership, they were also the most likely people to rent out rooms. The favourite time for moving to new lodgings was in the first week in May, when spring encouraged new beginnings.

Montreal was Canada's second-largest town, with over 4000 inhabitants in the mid-eighteenth century. By that time, it had lost much of its earlier religious tone and taken on the trappings of a frontier garrison town, dominated by soldiers and men of the fur trade rather than by the Sulpicians. Flanked by Mount Royal and protected by a stone wall, Montreal, like Quebec, made an impressive site. Its island location was surrounded by prosperous farms and Native communities. During the summer, Natives from the interior were frequent visitors. Rich and rowdy, especially when brigades were assembling for, or arriving from, the *pays d'en haut*, Montreal may have been less dignified than Quebec, but it was a more lively place.

The intendant's palace at Quebec, 1761.
Richard Short/National Archives of Canada/C360

By the 1740s, Louisbourg was a handsome town, reflecting the most advanced thinking in urban planning and defensive strategy. On top of the town's highest hill stood the major public buildings, all constructed in stone. The royal fleur-de-lis graced the elegant bell tower that capped the imposing citadel. A thick stone and mortar rampart, with outer rings of ditches and earthworks, encircled the town. Around the harbour, gun batteries were mounted with heavy cannon to ward off enemy attack. With a population of over 4000, and even more in the summer when the fishing fleets and merchant traders were in port, Louisbourg hummed with activity.

MUNICIPAL GOVERNMENT

Because there was no municipal government in New France, the royal courts also exercised administrative functions. A series of 42 by-laws issued by the Sovereign Council in 1676 constituted what today would be called a municipal code for Quebec. Included in this code were ordinances establishing a town market and setting the prices of essential commodities such as meat and bread. Building standards, fire protection, and town planning were also covered in the code. Because human and animal wastes constituted a major health hazard, by-laws were eventually passed to regulate their removal. Poverty, begging, vagrancy, and prostitution were also subject to regulation. Vagrants, for example, were prohibited from remaining in the town without permission of the authorities, and the town's poor were not allowed to beg without a certificate of poverty signed by a priest or judge.

The growing incidence of prostitution in the port town of Quebec resulted in a 1676 by-law forbidding all citizens to harbour women of dubious morals, as well as pimps and madams. In the previous year, an unusually high number of prostitutes arrived in the colony from France. A judgment handed down in August 1675 sentenced two of these women to banishment and fined their customers 10 livres. Another prostitute, Anne Bauge, was freed by the lieutenant general of the Prévôté, but he was relieved of his duties and Bauge was subsequently banished from Quebec for three years. Jailed in 1678 for violating her banishment, she was released upon the appeal of her husband on the grounds that the couple were soon to leave for France.

As the size and complexity of town life increased, so too did the number of vagabonds and foundlings. In the 1730s, the state's cost of maintaining *enfants bâtards* in Canada became a cause for concern: nearly 5000 livres for Quebec and nearly 8000 livres in Montreal. The Crown responded by reducing the stipend for the care of the infants, but it was clear from their numbers and the proliferation of other proscribed activities—including maintaining mistresses, drinking, gambling, and prostitution—that colonial society reflected the relaxed moral values that also characterized French society in this period.

In Montreal, the care of foundlings became one of the prime concerns of the Soeurs Grises, or Grey

France bringing the faith to the Indians of New France, 1670, attributed to Claude François, also known as Frère Luc. This depiction is believed to be the first large painting undertaken in the colony.
Musée des Ursulines, Quebec

Nuns, a religious community that received official sanction from the king in 1753. Founded by Marie-Marguerite d'Youville, the Soeurs Grises devoted their energies to the care of the sick and poor. The problem of abandoned infants led them to take in about 20 babies a year. A death rate among the unfortunate foundlings of 80 percent—typical of such institutions in Europe—underscored the fragility of life in institutional settings in the pre-industrial world.

By modern standards, the people of colonial towns were remarkably law-abiding. Tavern brawls and the occasional duel between officers were de rigueur, but the presence of the Troupes de la Marine made law and order a relatively easy matter for authorities.

ARTS AND SCIENCES

The towns were the centres of the intellectual life in New France. In addition to the religious orders that had long provided the colonies with a high standard of education and social services, there developed a class of civilian intellectuals, both French and colonial-born, whose interests reflected the preoccupations of the Enlightenment philosophers of France. Two eighteenth-century medical doctors, Michael Sarrazin and Jean-François Gauthier, for instance, sent reports on the natural history of Canada to the Academie Royale des Sciences in Paris.

Other than travel accounts and a few plays in verse for special occasions, Canadians produced little formal literature. Marie-Élisabeth Bégon (commonly referred to as Élisabeth), a resident of Montreal, excelled in the eighteenth-century art of letter writing, but few emulated her example. With France on the cutting edge of European intellectual life in the eighteenth century, the colonial elites relied heavily upon their mother country for the ideas that animated their dinner conversations. They neither produced their own newspaper nor bothered to import a printing press.

Painting, sculpture, and architecture were stimulated in New France by the demands of the growing urban elite, as well as by church and state. While much of the fine furnishings that graced the elegant homes and public buildings of the towns came from France, local artisans also practised their skills in fine crafts. Surviving ex-votos, portraits of notable citizens, beautifully carved

Élisabeth Bégon, Épistolière

Élisabeth Bégon (1696-1755), the wife of a colonial official, was a prolific letter-writer who reported the details of daily life in New France. From her letters, it is clear that some elite families in the colony had advanced views of education for girls. Bégon reported in 1749 that she was teaching her granddaughter, Marie-Catherine de Villebois de la Rouvillière, "everything she wants to learn." This included "the history of France, Rome, geography, basic reading in French and Latin, writing, verses, history. . . ." Bégon noted that Marie-Catherine had little interest in the usual educational program for girls that emphasized sewing and housekeeping. "I leave her alone," Bégon revealed, "preferring her to learn her lessons, rather than to do household work—she will learn that when I decide."[4]

Bégon also made pointed comments about her acquaintances. For example, she noted that "Madame Vassan, whose husband left her at her father's house when he went to Fort Frontenac, found she did not have enough freedom there. She has taken rooms at Martel's where she has found her match in her own lady servant, who is just as wild as she is; she is out night and day."[5]

Private correspondence such as that of Élisabeth Bégon is an invaluable source of information for historians attempting to understand the way people thought and acted in the past.

Élisabeth Bégon.
Library and Archives Canada/C010599

pine furniture, and locally crafted silver plate all testify to the rich level of material culture that was produced in eighteenth-century New France.

CANADIAN PEASANT SOCIETY

Trade, services, and artisan production in the towns engaged only a small proportion of the Canadian population. By the mid-eighteenth century, over 80 percent of Canadians lived in the rural countryside, where they farmed the soil. Most of the people living in rural areas were Canadian-born. Although the fur trade still attracted the young and unmarried men, most fur traders came from the towns of Montreal and Trois-Rivières, not from the seigneuries. Meanwhile, many of the common immigrants to the colony, whether engagés, salt smugglers, soldiers, or free pioneers,

gradually found themselves absorbed into the countryside where a peasant culture had taken root.

In the early years of settlement, the process of creating a farm from the tree-covered banks of the St Lawrence was back-breaking work. At best a peasant family could clear two *arpents*—roughly one hectare—a year, and a farm of thirty to forty arable arpents was the most that could be expected from a lifetime of labour. The children of the first generation had an easier task. Not only were they used to the hard work involved, but they could also live at home while starting their new farms. By the mid-eighteenth century, seigneurial farms had spread along both sides of the St Lawrence and down the Richelieu River. A second and sometimes even a third *rang* of seigneuries was being carved out behind original grants. Parish churches, a few seigneurial manors, and many small peasant houses dotted the landscape.

The houses of peasants were usually constructed of squared logs, whitewashed, and topped with a thatched or cedar roof. Their ground floors, averaging eight by six metres, were divided into two or three rooms. Manor houses tended to be more imposing and often built of stone, especially in the older, more established regions. Besides the main house, a manor would usually include a wooden barn with a central threshing floor and bays for storing hay and grain, stables for horses and cattle, a shed, an outdoor oven, and perhaps other small structures for specific functions.

A typical peasant farm in the eighteenth century might consist of 100 arpents, about 10 times the size of a peasant holding in France—although not all of this land was cleared or arable. Heavy yields would be produced for the first decade, after which they would drop dramatically. Rapid soil depletion necessitated the clearing of more forest land on the upper reaches of the riverfront farm. Wheat was the chief cereal crop, but Canadians also grew flax, oats, barley, and peas. At the interior posts the colonists learned to grow corn, the staple crop of the Iroquois nations. Almost every farm in the St Lawrence valley had kitchen gardens planted with onions, cabbage, beans, carrots, lettuce, radishes, beets, parsnips, and a variety of herbs.

Around Montreal, which had more fertile soils and a longer growing season than Quebec, apple, pear, and plum trees, as well as melons and pumpkins, did particularly well. Tobacco was harvested in the sandy soils around Trois-Rivières, but most kitchen gardens throughout the colony included some tobacco among their plantings. By the end of the French regime, horses, cattle, and sheep grazed on the marshes and uplands, and pigs and poultry roamed the farmyards. A 1709 ordinance stipulating that no person was to keep more than two horses and a foal seems to have been ignored. Canadians raised horses for farm work and transportation and even for racing. Despite injunctions from intendants that crop rotation, fertilization, and selective breeding be practised, most peasants produced mixed crops for their own subsistence and not for a specialized market. On the seigneuries around Quebec and Montreal, farmers made a systematic effort to respond to market demands and often had grain surpluses to export.

One of the biggest difficulties facing the peasant farmers was the fact that wheat was not ideally suited to the soil and climate of the St Lawrence lowland. Early frosts, smut, rust, drought, or infestations of grasshoppers and caterpillars reduced wheat yields. In years of poor harvest—17 times between 1700 and 1760—flour had to be imported. In 1749, hungry peasants congregated in the towns. Intendant François Bigot, reminded of the periodic bread riots in France, quickly opened the storehouses and enacted regulations to prohibit begging and vagrancy.

By the third generation of settlement, families began developing strategies to avoid excessive subdivisions of their holdings. Such a prospect loomed large because the Custom of Paris required that all children in non-noble families share equally in inheritance, whereas in noble families a larger portion of the estate was bestowed upon one heir. The peasants responded to the problem in a variety of ways. One strategy involved an arrangement whereby one or two children acquired the family farm; the others took their inheritance in cash or kind and could then move to outlying regions individually or in groups. This process brought people from different seigneuries together in a new settlement. Yet another approach was to send the older children to other seigneuries with their moveable inheritance while the parents entered into a contract, usually with the youngest son still under the parental roof, requiring him to care for his parents in their old age in return for the farm. This donation among the living heirs enabled the family to avoid inheritance laws.

Finally, in areas where farms had become too small to ensure subsistence, peasants made attempts to supplement farm income by gaining winter employment on government construction projects or in the fur or timber trade. It was usually the more prosperous families whose sons turned to wage labour. A few even managed to take up trades permanently and set up shop in the villages that had begun to develop in the rural countryside. The most prosperous censitaires bought farms from their poorer neighbours for their children, while the original owners moved to new settlements. Although undeveloped concessions were free, no one could enter farming without money to buy the tools, animals, and seeds needed to get started and enough provisions to last until the first crops were harvested.

MORE TO THE STORY

Were the Habitants of New France Truly Peasants?

This question, posed by historian Allan Greer, is not easy to answer. In New France rural farmers were commonly called "habitants" rather than "peasants," a sign that they may have been evolving into a class of independent producers. Greer does not accept this reasoning. By drawing upon the work of scholars who study peasant life, Greer distills five characteristics that, he argues, define peasants both in old and New France:

1. Peasants are small-scale agricultural producers who use simple equipment to grow crops and raise animals.
2. They generally work as a family.
3. Economically they are self-sufficient to a large degree, but not completely.
4. They possess the means of production, particularly land, even if they do not own them.
5. They are dominated and exploited, some of what they grow being appropriated to support the privileged class.[6]

   The habitants in New France were in a similar position in the social hierarchy as French peasants, but they experienced feudal practices in different ways. Although they paid annual dues to the seigneur, tithes to the church, and taxes to the state like their counterparts in France, the habitants were subject to much lower levels of taxation, were better housed, and rarely encountered the prospects of famine, a fate common among the peasantry in many regions of France. There is also general agreement that French peasants were more deferential to authority than their colonial counterparts, who were notorious for their lack of discipline. The widespread availability of land may help to account for this spirit of independence, which was typical of the lower classes generally in North America.

At the same time, many peasants in New France had great difficulty raising a crop that sustained their household needs. As a result, the exactions of seigneurs, clerics, and state bureaucrats, while not a large percentage of the crop, constituted an oppressive burden. Most peasants in New France had fewer material possessions than their French cousins, and were destined to remain near the bottom of the social hierarchy. They also had much lower literacy rates than their immigrant ancestors.

By the mid-eighteenth century, the peasants had become the solid base of the colony that Colbert had once hoped for. Following the surrender of New France to the British in 1763, the fur-trade frontier would be controlled by British traders, the military establishment would be staffed by foreigners, and the towns would be transformed by an influx of English-speaking administrators, soldiers, and merchants. But the farming communities along both sides of the St Lawrence would remain intact and largely French in culture—just as they are today.

THE FAMILY UNDER THE FRENCH REGIME

Among all the people of European origin in New France—whether they were on the peasant farm, in the artisan shop, or in the governor's mansion—the family was the fundamental social unit. It was in the family that most of the colony's production took place, where services were administered, and where pain and pleasure alike were experienced. Even on the frontier, families thrived. Commandants, for instance, often took their wives and children with them to the interior posts or formed close relationships with Aboriginal women.

Canadian women married at a younger age than their European counterparts. In France, in the eighteenth century, the average age of marriage for women was 25; in New France, it was 22. There was little appreciable difference in the average age of marriage for men, which was 26 in both France and in the colony. In New France, men remarried within a year or two after losing a wife, women after three years of widowhood. Coureurs de bois often took Native companions and produced Métis children. No doubt owing to the influence of the church and the relatively young age of marriage for women, illegitimacy rates were low, only 10 or 12 per 1000 compared to much higher rates

Couple in Sunday clothes.
City of Montreal. Records Management and Archives. (BM7/42498.34-2-4-1)

in the twentieth century. Sex was officially for procreation, not pleasure, although prostitution flourished in the larger towns, where a population of unmarried soldiers and labourers provided a ready market.

Canadian families were large. Because of the younger age of marriage, Canadian women had more children on the average than women in France. A woman who survived her childbearing years in the eighteenth century could expect to give birth to about seven or eight children. In Acadia, where the age of marriage was lower than on the St Lawrence, the average family was even larger. Families provided most of the social services that were taken up by the state in the twentieth century. Children were born at home with the assistance of an experienced midwife, and

much of the education in practical and productive skills took place under the watchful eye of parents. When people were sick or injured they were treated in their homes. Without a family, an individual was forced to rely on the church-operated public institutions.

Weddings were social events, surrounded by Christian and pagan customs. The rituals included the charivari, a noisy gathering of young people in the community under the window of a recently married couple. If the marriage were socially questionable—a widow who had remarried too soon after the death of her husband, or a couple of too unequal age—the affair could take a menacing tone. Occasionally couples married *à la gaumine*, without the benefit of clergy, and common-law relationships were even more likely to take place on the fur-trade frontier, where marriage *à la façon du pays* reflected Native customs and the absence, or defiance, of priestly injunctions. The church frowned on all such unions. It also discouraged marriages with Protestants or non-Christians, or of a couple too closely related, and it proscribed all homosexual relations.

Death was a frequent visitor to families in pre-industrial society. Urban areas were particularly dangerous places to live, with their high vulnerability to the epidemics that periodically ravaged the colony. In 1702–3, an outbreak of smallpox in Quebec took the lives of 350 people—nearly 20 percent of the town's population. Accidental and violent deaths were also commonplace. Historian Allan Greer notes that of the 4587 deaths recorded by priests in the seventeenth century, 51 people were struck by lightning, 299 died in war, 71 were crushed by trees or other falling objects, 37 froze to death, 69 were killed by fire, and 1302 drowned.[7]

Because of the high death rate, marriage partners could expect their unions to last only 15 or 20 years or so before the Grim Reaper took one of them away. Women and children were the most vulnerable. On average, one in four children died in the first year of life, and childhood diseases prevented a good many of the rest from reaching the age of 15. It was a relatively common occurrence for women to die in childbirth, which meant the death rate for women between the ages of 15 and 49 was higher than the rate for men in the same age group.

THE FAMILY ECONOMY

In pre-industrial society, families were important economic units, with everyone working together to ensure collective survival. No peasant farm could thrive without the work of all members: father, mother, and children. Land was most commonly received through inheritance, or seigneurial grant, not through purchase. For elite families, protection or patronage first went to members of the family—as exemplified by the adeptness of families such as the Colberts at finding positions for their relatives within the Ministry of Marine. In 1704, Governor Vaudreuil wrote to the minister on behalf of his own children: "I have eight boys and a girl who need the honour of your protection. Three of them are ready for service. I entered the musketeers when I was as young as my oldest. I hope you will have the goodness to grant to me for him the company of the Sieur de Maricourt who has died."[8]

Marriage was also a business partnership to which a woman brought a dowry in return for her husband's patronage. Dowries varied in amount according to class and, especially among the peasantry, might be largely in kind—household linen, items of furniture, clothes, or livestock. When her husband died, a woman was expected to continue living in the manner to which she had become accustomed in marriage. The law of dower was an attempt to ensure that this was the case. Marriage contracts sometimes stated that a wife would receive a fixed dower no matter what outstanding debts were held against her deceased husband's estate. A woman without a fixed dower was entitled to the "customary dower," that is, "the enjoyment" for life of one-half the husband's estate, but she was obliged to pay the outstanding debts and the dues on the land, and she was required to maintain the real property so it could pass intact to her husband's heirs.

Like society as a whole, families in New France were hierarchical, with the father at the apex of the hierarchy. Unless a wife made a special contract, all of her possessions were controlled by her husband. Children belonged first to their fathers, and they could not marry without his consent until the age of 25 for daughters and 30 for sons. Because marriage was so critical to the family's economic well-being and social status, it was an event that could not be entrusted to the wishes of consenting partners alone.

The colony's approaches to childrearing and education were transplanted from France. Because so many children died in infancy, parents tried to avoid strong emotional attachments to their babies, and grieving parents found consolation in the popular belief that their deceased infants became angels who interceded on their behalf in heaven. Particularly in elite families, swaddling, wetnursing, and early toilet-training were part of the infant regime. To inculcate respect for authority, obedience, and discipline, corporal punishment was liberally administered. The religious orientation of French education reinforced authoritarian practices. Children were taught to emulate their teachers in their devotion to self-discipline, abstinence, and fasting. When children were disobedient, they were threatened with the fiery hell and terrifying demons of eternal damnation.

Despite the seemingly harsh discipline, most families enjoyed a reasonable level of domestic harmony. The need for peasant families to function as a unit of production coupled with religious teachings encouraged cooperative behaviour. In the eighteenth century, church teachings increasingly focused on the infant Jesus and the Virgin Mary, and offered a less disciplinarian approach to those in subordinate positions within the family than had prevailed in the seventeenth century. Gradually, too, the examples of Native childrearing practices may also have had an impact. French commentators often remarked on the fact that Aboriginal peoples treated their children with affection and kindness rather than strict discipline reinforced by violence.

Such remarks may well have reflected the growing tendency to see Native people in a more positive light. The idea of the "noble savage" appealed to those who perceived with increasing clarity the flaws in the social system of the *ancien régime*. According to several intendants, Canadian youth showed a remarkable lack of discipline and were prone to an independent spirit. Freedom and independence would soon become the watchwords for revolutionary groups throughout Europe and North America. No doubt the authorities were reading things into the behaviour of Canadians that reflected their own growing concerns.

CLASS AND SOCIETY

There is no indication that New France in the eighteenth century had become more egalitarian than society in Europe, or that social distinctions had become less pronounced. Indeed, quite the reverse seems to be true. As the population grew and as communication across the Atlantic became more reliable, the values of Europe seem to have taken root more firmly than ever. The emphasis on class and rank under the *ancien régime*, and the privileges that went with such distinctions, eventually led to violent revolution in France in 1789. In New France, the conquest intervened before a revolution could occur, neatly removing the top echelons of the French ruling elite and substituting British conquerors.

Social structure in New France was not built on economic differences alone. Rather, social rank dictated economic behaviour. Social position, achieved by birth or influence, demanded a particular way of life, and people in New France, whether they could afford to or not, lived on a scale deemed appropriate to their rank. Those who did otherwise were widely scorned. Governor Jean de Lauson, for example, was criticized by his contemporaries because he lived without a personal servant and ate only pork and peas, like a common artisan or peasant. Peasants who used their horses for racing rather than farm work earned disapproving comments from authorities.

For many members of the colonial elite, maintaining the outward show of their status often kept them on the edge of bankruptcy. Those below them, in contrast, could live simply while accumulating wealth. One tanner in Quebec, for example, possessed only 82 livres of clothing and furniture when he died but held promissory notes to the amount of 4312 livres. Wealth, of course, usually went hand in hand with rank. Those higher up on the social ladder had access to more forms of wealth, including seigneurial grants, military appointments, and commercial opportunities.

TABLE 8.2 Occupational Hierarchy of New France, Based on Conventional Dower

Ranking by average dower	Other occupations
1. The Elite (2000–8000 livres per annum)	
Commissioned military officers	Senior clergy and nuns
Senior judicial and administrative officers	
2. Honourable Employments (800–1500 livres)	
Architects	Minor clergy
Master builders in stone	Wholesale merchants
Silversmiths	Royal notaries
Non-commissioned officers	
3. Good Trades (600–750 livres)	
Hatmakers	Land surveyors
Surgeons	Hussiers
Shoemakers	
4. Modest Occupations (425–500 livres)	
Metalworkers	
Woodworkers	
Private soldiers	
5. Base Occupations (400 livres or less)	
Stonemasons	Food retailers
Tenant farmers	Carters
Tailors	Sailors
	Hired servants

Source: Peter Moogk, "Rank in New France: Restructuring a Society from Notarial Documents," *Histoire sociale/Social History* 7, 15 (May 1975): 43.

While a great gulf existed between the nobility and the common folk, there was a precisely defined pecking order among the members of the middle classes. Fine craftsmen distinguished themselves from those who practised more common trades, and royal officers had more status than municipal officials. Rituals and ceremonies observed throughout the colony reinforced this hierarchy. In a church the benches were assigned so that the elite sat closest to the front, with the middle classes behind them. The lower orders sat or stood at the back. People dressed, lived in homes, and behaved in public in ways that "befitted their station." Women usually derived their status from their husbands' positions.

The Colonial Elite

At the top of the social hierarchy in New France was the *noblesse*, a class of military officers, administrators, and the highest-ranking church officials holding letters patent of nobility. Nobles in the colonies—unlike those in France—were allowed to engage in trade without being stripped of their titles. It was also possible, by combining seigneurial, military, commercial, and administrative functions in a way that would draw the attention of the king, for an ambitious young commoner to achieve noble status. As individuals rose up the social scale, they also often managed to "marry up," especially in a second or third marriage—although upward mobility was easier in the seventeenth than in the eighteenth century. It was also easier in the early years of settlement for individuals to claim noble status that they did not have. In 1684, those who used the title *écuyer* (esquire) in legal documents were ordered to give proof of their pretensions. They were fined if they made false claims.

Because its families were large, the nobility was more than able to perpetuate itself, even though few colonials were ennobled in the eighteenth century. The restrictions on upward mobility did not, however, stop those in the upper echelons of the middle class from seeking the trappings of noble life. By 1760, nearly 50 percent of the seigneurs in the colony were members of the middle class. The middle class also sought places in the Troupes de la Marine for their sons, but these positions, too, became increasingly rare over the course of the eighteenth century. With only 112 positions in the officer corps and 56 cadetships, commissions in the Troupes were the objects of bitter competition among the leading families of the colony.

The church also reflected the rigid class system that prevailed. While the Quebec seminary recruited most of its students from the colony, it was not an institution that advanced the careers of peasant boys. Most of the recruits came from wealthier middle-class families. Toward the end of the French regime, there was a marked increase in sons of artisans entering the priesthood, but only 2 of the 195 ordained colonial-born priests between 1611 and 1760 were sons of common farmers.

Its aristocratic ethos and military flavour made New France distinct from its English neighbours. The colony came by its snobbish image honestly. After all, the court of Versailles was the centre of diplomatic life in Europe, French was the common language of the European elite, and the French army was the envy of absolute rulers everywhere. The strategic role defined for the colony, with its garrisoned towns and interior fur-trading posts, enhanced the arrogance of its ruling class. During the French regime, both the Canadian-born and the transient French elite in the colony puffed up their fortunes so they could do what all self-respecting nobles aspired to: build a fashionable château in France and enjoy the good life.

The elite were not the only ones inspired by the aristocratic ideal. Peasants had virtually no chance of moving up the social scale in eighteenth-century New France. They nevertheless aped the values of their social superiors and enjoyed being lords of their domain, even if that was only a seigneurial concession. Nor were they excluded, as were most Europeans in this period, from military conscription. With the colony at war or under threat of hostility for much of the eighteenth century, the military ethos penetrated deeply into the social fabric.

Merchants

All colonists had the right to engage in trade. In 1706, foreign merchants were permitted to set up shop in the colony. Thanks to mercantilism, the colony relied on France for a number of crucial commodities: cloth and clothing, wines and brandies, guns, powder and lead, utensils, salt, and a variety of luxury goods. A score of importers in Montreal and Quebec did a comfortable business bringing in merchandise from France and selling it to the 100 or more *négociants*—traders, outfitters, and shopkeepers—whom Intendant Hocquart believed to be double the number the colony could support.

Merchants in Quebec were active in organizing their own interests. In 1708, they established a bourse, an organization similar to a board of trade, and rented a house for its activities. A royal decree of 1717 authorized the merchants in Montreal and Quebec to meet every day in a suitable place to carry out their business and to make representations to the king on matters of policy that would benefit their trading activities. In a 1719 communication to the king, this tightly knit community of Canadian merchants made specific reference to their colonial origins, claiming to "have had great-great-grandfathers, great-grandfathers, grandfathers, their fathers, in this colony."9

By the 1740s, François Havy and Jean Lefebvre, representing the firm of Dugard in Rouen, were the most powerful merchants in Canada. They retailed goods in both Quebec and Montreal, invested in sealing expeditions along the Labrador coast, and exported wheat to Louisbourg. Smaller merchants in the towns and countryside stocked important items and made their living by retailing. So, too, did a few pedlars who travelled the seigneuries along the river. Like the First Nations, Canadians were becoming discriminating consumers and could not be sold inferior products, a trait that earned them the accusation of being vain.

Women played a significant and direct role in the commercial life of New France. They worked with their husbands in commercial and artisan establishments and operated businesses as diverse as taverns and sawmills. Some women became active in trade when their husbands were away on business or died prematurely. Marie-Anne Barbel, for instance, took over her husband's business interests when he died in 1745, continuing his partnership in a fishing concession and his fur-trade operations. Just as any man would do in similar circumstances, she traded properties, established new businesses, and took her adversaries to court. She continued to make a comfortable living for herself and her unmarried children until her death at the age of 90.

In addition to the private trade, which occupied at least 15 vessels each year out of La Rochelle, the Crown shipped supplies to the colony to support its military establishment and related state activities. This was a highly profitable trade for the metropolitan merchants and their Canadian contacts. Supplies for colonial troops were brought at cheaper prices, and the Crown bore the risks of the voyage—shipwreck, piracy, spoilage, and capture in wartime. Even if the ship were lost at sea or the cargo spoiled, the contractor would receive his commission. In some cases, contractors could also draw upon naval stores and sailors to outfit their ship.

La Rochelle and Rouen were the dominant ports in the trade with New France in the first half of the eighteenth century. During the 1750s, Bordeaux took on special significance. Intendant François Bigot organized a ring with Bordeaux merchants and Canadian collaborators to monopolize the lucrative supply trade. Members of this charmed circle amassed large personal fortunes by mismanaging military appropriations and defrauding the colonists. In addition to Bigot, the principal culprits were Governor Vaudreuil the Younger and Joseph Cadet, *munitionnaire* (supplier of the Ministry of War).

In all, 22 millionaires emerged from this operation. Bigot headed the list with a fortune of 29 million livres, followed by Governor Vaudreuil with 23 million and Cadet with 15 million. The military elite in the colony generally accounted for 35 million livres, the bureaucrats attached to the intendant's office for 79 million, and those in charge of the stores for another 20 million—although they were millionaires in paper money only. When the Seven Years' War ended and the bills of exchange were discounted to the tune of 85 percent, the wealth of these rascals was greatly deflated. Nevertheless, excessive profiteering weakened the colonial economy.

Bigot had developed his skills while stationed at Louisbourg, which was also a place where officials found easy opportunities for lining their pockets. In this busy entrepôt, clandestine trade was particularly lucrative. Port registers indicate that the greatest number of vessels clearing the harbour were from the English colonies and the West Indies. Even the vessels owned by Louisbourg residents were often of New England origin.

The Fate of François Bigot

François Bigot was born in 1703 in the Bordeaux region of France. The Bigot family had risen to prominence over three generations, and young François was probably attracted to the marine department because his cousin had briefly served as its chief minister. Known for his passion for gambling and pretty women, as well as for his ambition, Bigot was appointed financial commissary to Louisbourg in 1739 and intendant to Canada in 1748. Bigot had no great desire to live in the colonies, but he saw service there as an opportunity to make his fortune. In taking advantage of his posting, he was no different from other colonial officials. He nevertheless differed from most of them because he was brought to trial for his corrupt administrative practices.

Following the surrender of Canada, Bigot and many of his former business associates were arrested. The state needed a scapegoat for the loss of the colony, and the activities of Bigot's circle were so outrageous that they had reached the ears of the highest authorities in France. By exposing Bigot, the king could also justify the decision to default on the colonial debts that had been accumulated during the war. Bigot spent nearly two years in the infamous Bastille before being brought to trial in 1763. A tribunal of 27 magistrates handed down a 78-page indictment, announcing Bigot's permanent banishment and the confiscation of all of his property. Several of Bigot's close associates were also heavily fined.

Shortly before the judgment was delivered, Bigot moved to Switzerland, where he lived under an assumed name. Although not destitute, he lived less elegantly than he had planned, and he suffered from poor health. He died on 12 January 1778 at Neuchatel. As requested in his will, he received a modest burial: "I desire that my body be buried in the cemetery at Cressier without any pomp, just as the poorest person in the parish would be."[10]

Artisans

Artisans produced most of the colony's goods and services and trained others in the skills of their trade. In urban areas of France, guilds controlled the progression from apprentice to journeyman and master craftsman and regulated the quality of their work, but the Crown restricted the operation of guilds in the colonies and reserved the supervision of all manual trades to itself. When master roofers in Quebec asked in 1729 for *la jurande*, or the right to control the standards of their trade, the Superior Council rejected their request on the grounds that there were no legally constituted master craftsmen in the colony with the exclusive rights to pursue a particular trade.

In the absence of guilds, the state regulated, as corporate bodies, the bakers, butchers, surgeons, midwives, and notaries. The church was permitted to exercise regulatory authority over the activities of itinerant schoolmasters and private tutors. The state also encouraged the religious activities of these corporate groups. Within each trade, *confréries*, or fraternities, organized annual religious observances in honour of the craft's patron saint. While such organizations had the potential for collective political action, they remained essentially religious and social institutions.

The guild system was already breaking down in Europe by the time that colonists began moving to North America. Throughout the colonies, the ideal was to be free to work as needs determined. A few colonists in New France entered partnerships to learn a trade, and apprenticeship was still common, but these arrangements were often short-lived. Journeymen, those who had served their apprenticeship and were required to practise their trade as a wage earner for a period (usually six years) before becoming a master craftsman, virtually disappeared in New France. Most shops were small family affairs consisting of a master who worked with the help of his wife and older children, and perhaps one or two apprentices. They produced goods on order, not in large quantities, striving for honest subsistence and, if possible, an easy living, rather than ever-increasing wealth.

SLAVERY

In pre-industrial society, the problem of securing a reliable labour force had resulted in a variety of work-inducing institutions, including seigneurialism, indentured labour, and slavery. All of these forms of labour took root in New France, albeit under somewhat modified circumstances.

Slavery was common in many Aboriginal societies around the world, including North America, but it became a very different institution when it was transplanted to the commercial colonies of the Americas. Black slavery, in particular, developed insidious characteristics. As slavery became equated with skin colour, racial stereotyping soon followed. Eventually it became difficult for any black person to be other than a slave, and the distinction between servant and slave, once narrow, widened precipitously.

Both Native and African peoples were employed as slaves in New France. While the numbers are difficult to determine, historians estimate that about 400 blacks were enslaved in Canada in the period between 1690 and 1760 and at least 216 in Louisbourg. African slaves were more common in Louisiana, the Illinois country, and the French West Indies than in Canada where Native slaves formed a slight majority of the enslaved population. Enslaved Natives began arriving in the colony in the late 1680s when French explorers and fur traders purchased a number of Pawnee in the Mississippi region. The French called all slaves of Native origin *panis* (Pawnee), but they took slaves from a number of First Nations.

During the French regime, Canadians on several occasions asked the Crown to dispatch African slaves to the colony to help relieve the perpetual labour shortage. Such shipments were never forthcoming, in part because of the curious belief of the period that Africans were especially ill-suited to northern climates. Most African slaves who came to Canada and Île Royale were purchased from one of the other French colonies or picked up as "prizes" in raids on the English colonies. In Canada, male slaves worked as common labourers; female slaves were employed in domestic service.

Slave owners remained uncertain of the status of their chattels, especially Native slaves, until 1709 when Intendant Jacques Raudot proclaimed slavery to be legal. Black slaves throughout the French Empire were governed by the Code Noir. Under its provisions, slaves could be bought and sold as property, but their owners were obliged to house, feed, and clothe them properly and care for the aged and infirm. Slaves were to be encouraged to marry, and all of them were to be instructed and baptized in the Roman Catholic religion. Although masters could whip their slaves,

they could not imprison or execute them without recourse to the courts. Women, who constituted slightly more than half of the enslaved population, were not to be sexually exploited, nor were children to be sold separately from their parents before reaching adolescence.

Slaves, whether black or Aboriginal, were expensive. The price of a black slave ranged between 200 and 2400 livres and averaged about 900 livres. Native slaves were worth less, about 400 livres, no doubt because of the greater supply and the likelihood of them running away. Because of their cost, slaves were purchased only by the wealthier colonials. Governor Charles de Beauharnois, for instance, owned 27. Marguerite d'Youville, founder of the Soeurs Grises, owned several slaves, as did Bishop Laval. Institutions operated by the church often relied heavily on the labour of their unhappy chattels. Like all moveable property, slaves could be passed on by inheritance. Charles Le Moyne, the first Baron de Longueuil, left seven slaves when he died—a mother and father and their five children. He instructed that they be divided between his two sons.

Both black and Native slaves had an appallingly short life expectancy: 17.7 years for Natives and 25.2 for Africans, compared with nearly 50 for white colonials. Slaves could marry only with the permission of their owners, and their children became the master's property too. Baptismal records usually record only the master's name, not that of the mother. Nearly 60 percent of slave children were born out of wedlock, sometimes fathered by other slaves, more likely by the master or the master's son, who often had no compunction about exercising the *droit de seigneur* on a chattel slave. As a result, Métis and mulatto children were relatively common in the elite families who owned slaves. Blacks and Natives were encouraged to marry each other, and 45 of these "mixed" marriages were recorded.

Few records have survived of slave resistance to their treatment. An exception is the case of Marie-Joseph Angélique who, when threatened with sale, set fire to her owner's house and ran away. She was caught and condemned to death for defying her master. A more positive case is recorded in 1753 in Louisbourg, where Jean-Baptiste Cupidon, a free black servant, purchased the freedom of his future bride Catherine

Shipping a Slave to Louisbourg

Throughout the Americas, if slaves showed any sign of resistance they were often sold to new owners. In 1753 the following letter was sent from a merchant in the French colony of Martinique in the West Indies to the Louisbourg firm of Beaubassin and Silvain. It reveals the degree to which slaves were treated as just another commodity to be bought and sold.

> I have put aboard the Ste Rose a Negro by the name of Toussaint, to ask that you get rid of him for me at any

price. He belongs to one of my friends who wants to get [him] out of these islands because of the excessively strong habits he has here. Please do me the pleasure of rendering him the service of having him remain in Louisbourg, and of selling him to someone who will never bring him back here. He is a baker by trade. As for the price of the sale, you can use it for whatever you think best, whether cod or something else.[11]

from her owner for 500 livres, a sum equal to more than a year's wage for a common labourer or artisan.

LABOUR

Much of the work in New France conducted outside the family context was done within the structure of feudal obligations. Seigneurs could extract dues from their censitaires, who were also required to work a stipulated number of days on the seigneur's demesne. In addition, the Crown imposed the *corvée*, a requirement to work a certain number of days on public works. These obligations remained an important feature of the work world in New France and, indeed, would be carried on for many years after the conquest.

Merchants or administrators requiring a fully committed workforce commonly used indentured labour, contracted for a specific period. The fur trade's engagés, or voyageurs, were usually recruited in the colony, as many as 400 a year. Perhaps because of the profits to be made and the adventure associated with the trade, it seems there was little difficulty finding enough young men willing to take the arduous trip into the

interior. However, it then became difficult to find the extra hands required at harvest time or to help build the roads that were becoming increasingly necessary as the population moved inland. Because of the shortage of labourers, the Crown permitted soldiers in the colony to work for wages when they were not needed for military duties.

The shortage of labour led to the arrival of one of the largest groups of eighteenth-century immigrants: men convicted of petty crimes. During the Regency period, Governor Vaudreuil had asked the Duc

Acadians Repairing Dykes.
History Collection/Nova Scotia Museum NSM 871202

The Status of Women in New France

Historians disagree about how to interpret the status of women in New France. Jan Noel has argued that the unusual conjunction of cultural heritage, demographic features, and economic conditions combined to make women in the colony "femmes favorisées."[12] She cites examples of 20 outstanding women in business, church, and politics who made their mark on the colony's history, and she comments on the level of education—usually better than that of men in the colony—and the range and freedom of action that colonial women enjoyed. Such examples, Noel maintains, suggest that women in New France had more opportunities than did their contemporaries in New England and Europe, and more even than women in the nineteenth century. More recently Terence Crowley echoes Noel's point that the role played by women in the church hierarchy "contrasted sharply with the situation in British possessions to the south," and "allowed them to make a vital contribution to colonial development."[13]

There is considerable evidence to back up this position. In particular, the female religious orders produced women of outstanding intellectual achievements and administrative abilities. Marie de l'Incarnation, Jeanne Mance, and Marguerite Bourgeoys stand shoulder to shoulder with Champlain, Maisonneuve, and Laval for their pioneering activities in the New World. Moreover, women were often instrumental in raising the money needed for commercial and religious ventures in the colonies. For example, Hélène Boullé, who married Champlain at the age of 12, was an heiress whose dowry financed her husband's early expeditions. Another woman, Madame la Marquise de Guercheville, never came to the New World but used her wealth to finance Jesuit activities in Acadia. When she became suspicious of the motives of the fur traders in charge of developing Port Royal, she purchased (with her husband's permission) de Monts's rights in New France. She held title to Acadia until she relinquished her claims to the Compagnie de la Nouvelle France in 1627.

Micheline Dumont, one of the authors of a collective history of Quebec women, takes issue with this perspective. She maintains that women in the seventeenth century may have played a unique role because of the exceptional circumstances prevailing in the infant colony, but that by the eighteenth century their status had become more like that of their sisters in France.[14] And while it is true that women in New France were sometimes forced to do the tasks traditionally assigned to men, they saw their fate as an aberration, not a step toward some ideal of liberation. Madeleine de Verchères, for instance, who claimed to have organized the defence of her village against an Iroquois attack in 1692, argued for a pension on the grounds that she was an unusual woman with "feelings which lead me to glory, just like many men." Most women, she implied, would not aspire to such acts of heroism.

Dumont also cautions historians not to confuse privileges based on class with the experience of all women. As in France, elite women in New France had considerable scope for action under the laws of the ancien régime, especially when they acted on behalf of their husbands or in segregated religious orders. Marie de La Tour fought to the death to defend her absent husband's fort in Acadia in 1645, but such leadership was expected of wives in this period. In New France, women may have stretched the boundaries of the limitations placed upon them, but at no time were those boundaries ever erased. Others have added that no woman ever served as governor, bishop, intendant, military commander, notary, sovereign councillor, or judge, and as far as we can tell no one ever argued that they should have done so.

Finally, by emphasizing exceptional women, Dumont argues, historians often overlook the significant contribution that women made to colonial society through their productive and reproductive work within the family. In pre-industrial European and colonial society, the family was the fundamental unit of economic life. The bearing and rearing of children, the growing and preparing of food, the making of cloth and warm clothing, and the nursing and nurturing of family and friends—all carried on almost exclusively within the domestic setting—were fundamental to the survival of the family, the community, and the colony.

Even if Dumont's cautions are correct, it remains the case that women in New France functioned in a different environment than the one that prevailed in France or even in nearby New England. The important institutional roles played by the church and state, the significance of the fur trade and the military establishment, the absence of deeply rooted traditions, the influence of First Nations, and perhaps even the particular cultural practices brought by the few thousand immigrants selected from French society to settle in North America: all these elements combined to produce, if not a totally new society, at least a considerably altered one.

Perhaps women in New France were not so much *favorisées* as challenged to adapt their traditional notions of gender roles to the colonial environment. The same could be said for men, whose roles were also reshaped by the colonizing experience. Together in New France, French women and men became Canadiennes and Canadiens, whose differences from their counterparts in old France became the cause for comment, and sometimes conflict, during the course of the eighteenth century.

d'Orléans to have his officials send out poachers, counterfeiters, and salt smugglers as a source of labour for the colony. In the 1730s, these unfortunates, who had often committed no more serious crime than to attempt to circumvent the dreaded salt tax (*gabelle*), were still being rounded up and sent to Quebec.

Available records indicate that more than 700 salt smugglers and other petty criminals arrived in New France between 1721 and 1749. They do not seem to have been treated much differently from engagés. A dispatch from the Minister of Marine in 1739 announced that, of 81 salt smugglers sent to Canada, all had either been incorporated into the troops or distributed to individuals or communities offering good contracts. They were not hardened criminals and were regarded in the colony, where the salt tax was not levied, as individuals possessing a great deal of initiative, creativeness, and independence of mind.

CONCLUSION

By 1750, most of the people in New France had been born in North America and were beginning to call themselves "Canadians" and "Acadians." With little more than a century of colonial settlement behind them, they had succeeded in adapting to a new climate, creating an uneasy alliance with their Aboriginal neighbours, and making North America their home. They may have been subjects of the French king and schooled in the ways of the old country, but they had also become citizens of their own new world.

NOTES

1 Peter Kalm, *Travels in North America*, vol. 2, ed. Adolph B. Benson (New York: Dover Publications, 1966), 558.

2 Ibid.

3 Yvon Desloges, *A Tenant's Town: Quebec in the Eighteenth Century* (Ottawa: National Historic Sites Parks Service, Environment Canada, 1991), 106.

4 Élisabeth Bégon, 9 January 1749, cited in the Clio Collective, *Quebec Women: A History*, trans. Roger Gannon and Rosalind Gill (Toronto: The Women's Press, 1987), 61.

5 Ibid., 20 February 1749.

6 Allan Greer, *Peasant, Lord and Merchant: Rural Society in Three Quebec parishes, 1740–1840* (Toronto: University of Toronto Press, 1985), xi.

7 Allan Greer, *The People of New France* (Toronto: University of Toronto Press, 1997), 24.

8 John F. Bosher, "The Family in New France," in *Readings in Canadian History: Pre-Confederation*, 3rd ed., ed. R. Douglas Francis and Donald B. Smith (Toronto: Holt, Rinehart and Winston, 1990), 117.

9 Cited in André Vachon et al., *Taking Root: Canada from 1700 to 1760* (Ottawa: Public Archives of Canada, 1985), 235.

10 J.F. Bosher and J.-C. Dubé, "Bigot, François," in *Dictionary of Canadian Biography*, vol. 4, *1771 to 1800* (Toronto: University of Toronto Press, 1979), 59–70.

11 Kenneth Donovan, "Slaves in Île Royale," *Acadiensis* 25, 1 (Autumn 1995): 22.

12 Jan Noel, "New France: Les Femmes Favorisées," in *Rethinking Canada: The Promise of Women's History*, 3rd ed., ed. Veronica Strong-Boag and Anita Clair Fellman, (Toronto: Oxford University Press, 1997), 33–56.

13 Terence Crowley, "Women, Religion and Freedom in New France," in *Women and Freedom in Early America*, ed. Larry Eldridge (New York: New York University Press, 1997), 110–11.

14 Micheline Dumont, "Les femmes de la Nouvelle-France: Étaient-elles favorisées?" *Atlantis* 8, 1 (Fall 1982): 118–24; see also the Clio Collective, *Quebec Women: A History*, trans. Roger Gannon and Rosalind Gill (Toronto: Women's Press, 1987).

Related Readings in This Series

From *Foundations: Readings in Pre-Confederation Canadian History*

Fernand Ouellet, "Free or Exploited? The Peasant before 1850," 98–115.

Christopher Moore, "Charles Renaut's Letter," 135–47.

Peter Kalm, excerpts from *Travels in North America, 1749*, 148–54.

From Media Companion CD-ROM, Volume I

Frontier Farm in Lower Canada

Grey Nuns Convent

Coureur de Bois

Governor Vaudreuil

Trade in Quebec City: General Trade of the Country and of His Majesty's Domain, 1709

The City of Montreal

Selected Reading

In addition to the works cited in Chapters 5 and 6, see André Lachance, *La vie urbaine en Nouvelle-France* (Montreal: Boréal Express, 1987) and *Vivre, aimer et mourir en Nouvelle France: La Vie quotidienne aux XVIIᵉ et XVIIIᵉ siècles* (Montreal: Libre Expression, 2000); Hubert Charbonneau, *Vie et mort de nos ancêtres* (Montreal: Les Presses de l'Université de Montréal, 1973) and *The First French Canadians* (Urbana: University of Illinois Press, 1993); and Lorraine Gadoury, *La famille dans son intime: Échanges épistolaires au sein de l'élite canadienne du XVIIIᵉ siècle* (Montreal: Hustubise HMH, 1998). Music in New France is discussed in Élisabeth Gallat-Morin and Jean-Pierre Pinson, *La Vie musicale en Nouvelle-France* (Quebec: Éditions du Septentrion, 2003). On religious life see Marie-Aimée Cliché, *Les pratiques de dévotion en Nouvelle-France* (Quebec: Presses de l'Université Laval, 1988). A selection of Élisabeth Bégon's correspondence can be found in *Lettres au cher fils*, ed. Nicole Deschamps (Montreal: Hurtubise, HMH 1972).

Articles that explore specific topics include John F. Bosher, "The Family in New France," in *Readings in Canadian History: Pre-Confederation*, 3rd ed., ed. R. Douglas Francis and Donald B. Smith (Toronto: Holt, Rinehart and Winston, 1990); Allan Greer, "The Patterns of Literacy in Quebec, 1745–1899," *Histoire sociale/Social History* 11, 22 (Nov. 1978); Terence Crowley, " 'Thunder Gusts': Popular Disturbances in Early French Canada," *Historical Papers/Communications historiques* (1979) and "Women, Religion and Freedom in New France," in *Women and Freedom in Early America*, ed. Larry Eldridge (New York: New York University Press, 1997); John Dickinson, "Reflexions sur la police en Nouvelle-France," *McGill Law Review* 32, 2 (1987); Kenneth Donovan, "Tattered Clothes and Powdered Wigs: Case Studies of the Poor and Well-to-Do in Eighteenth Century Louisbourg," in *Cape Breton at 200: Historical Essays in Honour of the Island's Bicentennial, 1785–1985*, ed. Kenneth Donovan (Sydney: University College of Cape Breton Press, 1985); Lilianne Plamondon, "A Businesswoman in New France: Marie-Anne Barbel, the Widow Fornel," in *Rethinking Canada: The Promise of Women's History*, ed. Veronica Strong-Boag and Anita Clair Fellman (Toronto: Copp Clark Pitman, 1986); Louise Dechêne, "L'Évolution du régime seigneuriale au Canada: le cas de Montréal aux XVIIᵉ et XVIIIᵉ siècles," *Recherches sociographiques* 12, 2 (1971); and Yves Zoltvany, "Esquisse de la Coutume de Paris," *Revue d'histoire de l'Amérique française* 25, 3 (1971). On slavery in New France, see Marcel Trudel, "Ties That Bind," *Horizon Canada* (1985); Kenneth Donovan, "Slaves and Their Owners in Île Royale, 1713–1760," *Acadiensis* 25, 1 (Autumn 1995): 3–32; and André Lachance, "Les esclaves aux 17ᵉ et 18ᵉ siècles," in *Les Marginaux, les exclus et l'autre au Canada aux XVIIᵉ et XVIIIᵉ siècles* (Montreal: Fides, 1996), 201–08.

WEBLINKS

Upper Town

www.pc.gc.ca/progs/spm-whs/itm2-/site9_E.asp

This site offers a brief description of the historic section of Quebec, with links to other significant historic locations in and around the city.

Soeurs Grises

www.newadvent.org/cathen/07031a.htm

This page is an excerpt from the New Catholic Encyclopedia on the origins of the Soeurs Grises of Montreal.

Code Noir

www.tlfq.ulaval.ca/axl/amsudant/guyanefr1685.htm

This site offers the text of the Code Noir in French.

Census Data on New France

estat.statcan.ca

E-STAT, Census Canada's Web site, offers a way to explore census data on New France.

CHAPTER 9

Imperial Designs, 1715–1763

Timeline

1715–74	Reign of Louis XV
1726	British sign treaty with Mi'kmaq at Annapolis Royal
1744–48	War of the Austrian Succession
1745	Louisbourg conquered by British and Anglo-American force
1746	D'Anville Expedition
1747	Battle of Grand Pré
1748	Treaty of Aix-la-Chapelle
1749	Halifax founded
1752	Treaty of Peace and Friendship with the Mi'kmaq
1755	Fort Beauséjour falls to British
1755–62	Expulsion of the Acadians
1756–63	Seven Years' War
1758	Louisbourg recaptured by the British
1759	Conquest of Quebec
1760	Articles of Capitulation signed in Montreal
1760–61	Mi'kmaq and Maliseet sign peace treaties with British authorities in Nova Scotia
1763	Treaty of Paris; Royal Proclamation

"Open your eyes, Canadians, to your own interests, all communication with the Ocean being blocked, what can you expect of an army, weak, beaten and dispirited; without hope or resource, with a great army of disciplined troops in the heart of the country, another at its gates, nearly all posts in the upper country captured and abandoned.

"We exhort you eagerly to have recourse to a people, free, honest and generous, ready to stretch out its arms to you, to set you free from a harsh despotism, and to enable you to enjoy with them the comforts of government, just, mild and equitable. For if you do not profit by this advice, you must expect the most rigorous treatment, which is permissible by law."[1]

When the British captured Quebec in September 1759, it was still unclear whether they would conquer Canada. This proclamation of 15 November 1759 suggests that military governor James Murray, who was in command of the British forces in Quebec, had his hands full maintaining order in the walled town. Through threats and promises, he hoped to secure the victory and follow it up with surrender of the French concentrated in Montreal, but only time would tell which side would receive the much-needed reinforcements from their mother country. The destiny of New France hung in the balance during the fall and winter of 1759–60.

In the eighteenth century, the contest for supremacy in Europe was played out around the world, and nowhere were the battles more viciously fought than in North America. Between 1744 and 1763 a state of almost constant warfare scattered the Acadians to distant ports, sealed the fate of New France, and profoundly altered the relationships between Natives and newcomers. The War of the Austrian Succession set the ball rolling.

ENEMIES AND ALLIES

The long period of relatively peaceful relations between 1713 and 1744 had given Great Britain and France a chance to position themselves for the next stage of their longstanding military rivalry. On the surface, the British had the upper hand in North America. Their colonies had grown in population and wealth, while the French holdings remained sparsely settled and economically dependent upon their mother country. In theory, when the British colonies con-

scripted human resources for war, they could draw upon a population base of nearly one million people; French possessions, including Louisbourg and Louisiana, had less than one-tenth that number.

Balanced against this demographic reality was the Native population of North America. The Treaty of Utrecht in 1713 gave Britain control over Iroquois territory and the Hudson Bay region, but the new rulers had been slow to develop formal policy with respect to the people living in these areas. France, in contrast, had been aggressive in pursuing Native alliances. By the 1740s, most of the interior of the continent and the Atlantic frontier were occupied by First Nations loosely allied with France.

The success of the French in developing alliances with the First Nations was a result, in part, of Louis XIV's decision to use the fur trade as a diplomatic tool. By supplying the Natives with manufactured items,

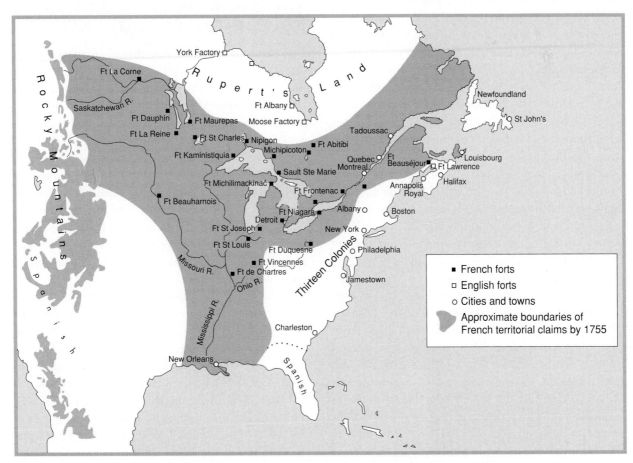

MAP 9.1 France in America, 1755.
Adapted from J.L. Finlay, *Pre-Confederation Canada: The Structure of Canadian History*, 3rd ed. (Scarborough, ON: Prentice-Hall, 1989), 68.

including the weapons they needed for hunting and fighting, the French became valued trading partners. Early in their colonization experience, the French had learned that Aboriginal peoples would accept neither European claims to land ownership and sovereignty nor French laws and taxes. If alliances were to succeed, the French were obliged to recognize the original inhabitants of North America as "free and independent people" with title to their ancestral lands. Alliances embodying such provisions were signed with much pomp and ceremony and were reinforced by the annual distribution of "King's presents." These agreements remained secure only as long as the French were willing to accept the fact that they were partners and protective patriarchs, not overlords.

Natives had their own reasons for entering into alliances with the foreigners in their midst. They enjoyed the increased material wealth that resulted from trade and used European alliances to enhance their power in relation to other Native nations. Moreover, after many years of contact, Aboriginal peoples found their cultural practices gradually transformed. Especially in the eastern regions of North America, First Nations had been drawn into family relationships with Europeans and converted to Christian beliefs. Even had they wished to do so, they would have found it difficult to disentangle themselves from the Europeans who had made North America their home. They also recognized that wars among European nations were often waged on their ancestral lands, making it impossible for them to remain neutral. This reality was most obvious in the Atlantic region and the Ohio territory, where the settlement frontier was fast encroaching on a "middle ground" of joint European-Native occupation.

Like the European nations, the First Nations were not uniform in their response to military alliances. The Iroquois initially tried to remain neutral and profit from European rivalries. Their strategic geographical location between the French and British colonies, and the hard lessons learned in the wars of the seventeenth century, made this the logical approach to take. In Acadia and the Ohio-Mississippi region, First Nations tended to form alliances with the French because of the threat that expanding Anglo-American settlement posed to their territorial claims. The Iroquois who

sought sanctuary in the French missions understood this reality when they stated in 1754:

> Brethren, are you ignorant of the difference between our Father [the French] and the English? Go see the forts our Father has erected, and you will see that the land beneath his walls is still hunting ground, having fixed himself in those places we frequent, only to supply our wants; whilst the English, on the contrary, no sooner get possession of a country than the game is forced to leave it; the trees fall down before them, the earth becomes bare, and we find among them hardly wherewithal to shelter us when the night falls.[2]

For the First Nations as much as for the French in North America, the rise of the British Empire and the birth of the United States of America in the second half of the eighteenth century would force major adjustments.

THE BEGINNINGS OF BRITISH RULE IN THE ATLANTIC REGION

Nowhere was the three-way struggle for power more intense than in the Atlantic region. According to the Treaty of Utrecht, the French ceded "All Nova Scotia or Accadie, comprehending its ancient boundaries," to Britain. Those "ancient boundaries" soon became the subject of dispute. France tried to make the best out of a bad bargain by claiming that Acadia meant only the Nova Scotia peninsula. The British argued that the traditional French definition of Acadia included the area north of the Bay of Fundy. The dispute was eventually submitted to arbitration, but in the meantime Britain and France jockeyed for control over the borderland region, which was a critical territorial link in both colonial empires.

The British were initially slow to establish a major presence in their Atlantic colonies. Following the 1710 capture of Port Royal, renamed Annapolis Royal in honour of Queen Anne, a garrison of fewer than 500 British and colonial soldiers was stationed in Nova Scotia. British fishing fleets returned to St John's, which had been sacked twice by the French during the war, but the official policy remained one of discouraging settlement in Newfoundland. With only a few British settlers and servants in Newfoundland—fewer than 3000 year-round residents in 1713—a population of about

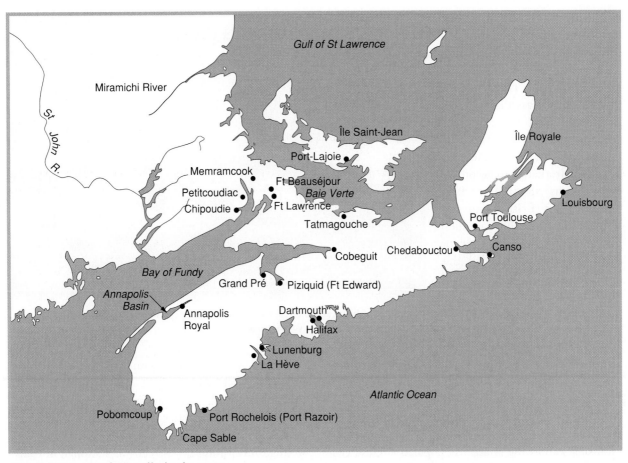

MAP **9.2** Nova Scotia/Acadia in the 1750s.

2000 Roman Catholic Acadians in Nova Scotia, and hostile Beothuk, Mi'kmaq, and Maliseet throughout the region, there was little incentive to establish an apparatus of colonial administration.

In 1717, the British made a feeble attempt to mould the region into a coherent administrative unit by appointing Colonel Richard Phillips governor of Placentia and Nova Scotia. He lost his authority over Placentia when Captain Henry Osborn became governor of Newfoundland in 1729, but Phillips retained his Nova Scotia posting until 1749. Neither official was permanently resident in the colony he governed. In the three decades following the Treaty of Utrecht, British settlement in the Atlantic region consisted of a few soldiers, merchants, and officials at military outposts and several hundred fishing families scattered along a vast coastline. The most obvious British presence was a seasonal one: fleets of fishing vessels based from May to October off Canso and the eastern coast of Newfoundland.

THE NEUTRAL FRENCH

By the Treaty of Utrecht, the Acadians were granted the liberty "to remove themselves within a year to any other place, as they shall think fit, together with their moveable effects." Those who decided to remain were to be "subject to the Kingdom of Great Britain" and permitted "to enjoy the free exercise of their religion, according to the usage of the church of Rome, as far as the laws of Great Britain allow the same." Most of the Acadians opted to remain on their farms in the Bay of Fundy region. Acadia had changed hands several times during the previous century, and it was possible that their homeland could once again be returned to France.

British officials tried to persuade the Acadians to take an oath of allegiance, but their new subjects made it clear that any oath of loyalty must include explicit guarantees that they not be required to take up arms against the French and Mi'kmaq. Such a provision was the only practical alternative to becoming the victims in the crossfire between the British and the French and their Native allies. In 1729 and 1730 Governor Phillips verbally conceded this exemption when he administered an oath of allegiance to men over 15 years of age in many Acadian settlements. British authorities were thus forced to admit defeat in their efforts to procure an unqualified oath of allegiance from people they sneeringly dubbed the "neutral French."

A view of Louisbourg as seen from the lighthouse during the siege of 1758.
P. Ince/Library and Archives Canada/C5907

The three decades following the conquest of 1713 must have seemed, in retrospect, a golden age to the Acadians. Family life flourished, population grew, economic opportunities beckoned, and the hand of authority was light. Settlement expanded up the Shepody, Petitcoudiac, and Memramcook estuaries, and along the eastern shore from Baie Verte to the Baie des Chaleurs. With the establishment of Louisbourg, the Acadians had an alternative to the Boston market for surplus products from their farms and fisheries. Hard work and a healthy climate gave them a better-than-average chance of reaching old age surrounded by an expanding network of kin. By 1750, there were over 9000 Acadians in "Nova Scotia or Accadie" and 3000 more scattered throughout the rest of the region.

Although most of the Acadians stayed well out of the way of their new masters, a few ambitious families made the most of the situation. Marie Madeleine Maisonnat, for example, married Huguenot officer William Winniett, who soon became prominent in the economic and political life of Nova Scotia. Their large family of seven sons and six daughters extended the influence of the Winnietts throughout the colony.

Similarly, Agathe Saint-Étienne de La Tour married, in succession, two British officers stationed in Annapolis Royal. Her sons from the first marriage, Simon and John (baptized Jean-Baptiste) Bradstreet, both secured commissions in the British army. As a young officer, John Bradstreet was stationed in Canso and became engaged in smuggling goods to Louisbourg. He was captured by the French when Canso was attacked in 1744. Upon his release he turned his knowledge of Louisbourg to his advantage by advising Governor William Shirley of Massachusetts about conditions at the French fortress, and he participated in its capture in 1745.

MI'KMAQ AND MALISEET

The biggest problem facing the British in their recently acquired Atlantic colonies was the hostility of the Mi'kmaq and Maliseet. Allied with the Abenaki, who comprised the first line of defence against the New England settlers moving up the Atlantic seaboard, the Mi'kmaq and Maliseet fought on land and sea to preserve their traditional territorial rights. They also remained steadfast in their French alliances. After nearly 150 years of French missionary activity, most of them were practising Roman

Catholics, and some had intermarried with the Acadians. They resisted making political alliances with the British, whose religion and language were foreign to them.

Although the Treaty of Utrecht made no mention of any territorial rights of Natives in the Atlantic region, British authorities tried to insist that the Natives in the region, like the Acadians, swear an oath of allegiance to the British Crown. In return they were offered the same privileges that the Acadians enjoyed in religious matters and government-sponsored trading posts called "truck-houses." The Natives were not impressed with the proposal. They had never sworn allegiance to the French, and they had no intention of doing so to the British. Moreover, they had little need of trading posts because they usually obtained better prices from the French in Louisbourg or from the ships that arrived in their inshore waters every spring.

When the French learned that the British were attempting to exert control over the Natives in the Atlantic region, they moved quickly. Count Jerome de Pontchartrain, as Minister of Marine, sent Canadian-born missionary Antoine Gaulin to persuade the Mi'kmaq to move to Île Royale. Like the Acadians, the Mi'kmaq were reluctant to do so, except on a seasonal basis to receive their "presents" from the French. Political priests were key to maintaining Native alliances. In addition to Gaulin, who served the region from 1689 to 1731, Pierre-Antoine-Simon Maillard orchestrated French-Mi'kmaq relations from his base on Chapel Island, Île Royale, from 1735 to 1758. Jean-Louis Le Loutre, whose missions included the Acadians as well as Mi'kmaq from 1737 to 1755, was so effective in his political activities that the British finally put a price on his head.

The Mi'kmaq needed little encouragement from the French to challenge the British presence in Nova Scotia. In 1720, they drove the New England fishing fleet out of Canso, justifying their act as protecting the land that God had given them. During the summer of 1722, the Mi'kmaq were reported to have captured 36 trading vessels in the waters off Nova Scotia. The New Englanders and the British authorities in Nova Scotia were quick to retaliate. For the next three years, the New England-Nova Scotia frontier was embroiled in a bloody "Indian War." In the summer of 1724, the

Mi'kmaq even attacked Annapolis Royal, burning part of the town and killing several British soldiers.

Finally, in December 1725, peace treaties were concluded in Boston and Falmouth (in present-day Maine); they were ratified at Annapolis Royal the following year. These agreements included recognition of British sovereignty over "Nova Scotia or Accadie." Since the Mi'kmaq could not read English, their understanding of the treaty was based on verbal negotiations. Historian William Wicken maintains that what was important was how the words of the treaty were translated from English into Mi'kmaq by the two Acadian interpreters who facilitated the negotiations. Under the French regime, the Natives in the Maritime region continued to see themselves as allies, not subordinates to the French Crown and, Wicken argues, it is "reasonable to assume that the delegates understood their words on the basis of Mi'kmaq history, not British."[3] The Treaty of 1726 thus became the basis for a classic stand-off in which each side interpreted the agreement in ways that the other failed, or refused, to do.

WAR OF THE AUSTRIAN SUCCESSION, 1744-1748

The test of Acadian neutrality and Native alliances came in 1744, when the lack of a male heir in the Hapsburg line provoked a war in Europe over the succession to the Austrian throne. Britain and Holland supported the claims of the Archduchess Maria Theresa, while France and Prussia opposed her right to rule. Three weeks before the news reached Annapolis Royal and Boston, Governor Le Prévost Duquesnel at Louisbourg learned that war had been officially declared. Following his instructions from France, Duquesnel authorized privateers to attack New England shipping, dispatched a force to capture Canso, and made plans to attack Annapolis Royal.

Inevitably, the New Englanders were alarmed by these developments on their northeastern frontier. Under the direction of Governor William Shirley of Massachusetts, a volunteer militia of 4300 men led by William Pepperell was organized to attack Louisbourg. A squadron from the West Indies under the command of Commodore Peter Warren provided naval support. In the spring of 1745, the New Englanders pounded the mighty fortress for seven weeks before forcing its surrender on 17 June. In 1746, the French sent a squadron of 54 ships carrying 7000 men, commanded by the Duc d'Anville, to recapture Louisbourg. The expedition was dogged with bad luck and retreated without even reaching its objective. The expedition was testimony to the decline of the French navy, which no longer had the ships or the experienced commanders needed to protect its North American empire.

With communications between France and its North American colonies at the mercy of the British fleet, the French colonials were left to pursue their own wartime strategies. Authorities in Quebec took steps to secure their frontiers by launching raids against New York and Massachusetts, and increased the volume of trade and present-giving among their Native allies. On their eastern front, 300 militiamen under Captain Louis Coulon de Villiers embarked on a classic guerrilla campaign against Annapolis Royal. They made their way through heavy winter snows to Grand Pré, where they encountered 500 New England troops quartered in Acadian homes. Alerted by several Acadians, de Villiers and his men surrounded the houses where the New Englanders were sleeping, killed 70 of them, including their leader Colonel Arthur Noble, and forced the rest to surrender.

The "Massacre of Grand Pré," as the English called it, put the Acadian strategy of neutrality in serious jeopardy. While it was clear that some of the Acadians had warned Noble about the French presence in the area, he had not believed them. After the event, when the English discussed Acadian policy, it would be the "treacherous informers" and "traitors," not those who had maintained a desperate neutrality, who would be remembered.

Further reprisals were temporarily averted when the two sides agreed to a negotiated peace. By the Treaty of Aix-la-Chapelle in 1748, Britain and France agreed to restore their captured possessions. This policy meant that France gave up its conquests in the Netherlands and India in return for Louisbourg. The New Englanders were appalled by Britain's apparent lack of concern for their safety and well-being and insisted that their northeastern frontier be properly defended.

THE UNEASY PEACE IN ACADIA, 1749–1755

All sides—French, British, and Native—moved immediately to strengthen their positions for the war that was certain to come very soon. Again the activity was particularly intense in the Atlantic region. In 1749, the French reoccupied Louisbourg, and the British, aware of resentment in their colonies, decided to build a fortified base on the Nova Scotia peninsula. In the spring of 1749, Edward Cornwallis led an expedition of 2500 soldiers, settlers, and servants to found Halifax on the shores of Chebucto Bay.

As governor of Nova Scotia, Cornwallis was determined to bring the Aboriginal peoples under his authority. The Maliseet and their allies the Passamaquoddy on the north shore of the Bay of Fundy were prepared to reconfirm the Treaty of 1726 with Cornwallis and his emissaries, but the Mi'kmaq were defiant. They resumed their attacks against the British on land and sea and harassed the British base at Halifax, which was located on one of the Mi'kmaq's favourite summer encampments. Cornwallis responded by offering a reward of 10 guineas for every "savage taken or his scalp." The Mi'kmaq in turn declared war on the British for having settled their lands without permission and for undertaking to exterminate them. A formal declaration of war was drawn up with the help of Abbé Maillard and Abbé Le Loutre.

The declaration of hostilities by the Mi'kmaq gave the French the opportunity they were looking for to extend their influence in the region. In 1750, they built Fort Beauséjour north of the Missaguash River on the Isthmus of Chignecto. Cornwallis reacted quickly, dispatching Lieutenant-Colonel Charles Lawrence and two regiments with orders to construct a fort within sight of Beauséjour. Meanwhile, the Mi'kmaq continued to attack the British. In 1751, they even conducted a successful raid on the new community of Dartmouth across the harbour from Halifax. Cornwallis's successor, Peregrine Hopson, managed to persuade a few Mi'kmaq to sign his treaty of peace and friendship in 1752, but it had little impact. With more than 1000 Acadian men within two days' march of Fort Beauséjour, and 400 Native allies encamped at nearby Baie Verte, the French had proved once again that they were masters of war in time of peace.

Life in the Colonial Militia

The feats of bravery and endurance of Canadian militiamen have become the stuff of legend. In the eyes of their enemies, the Canadians possessed superhuman abilities. They were capable of travelling hundreds of kilometres in the dead of winter, their knowledge of the terrain equalled that of their Native allies, and they were crack shots with their flintlock muskets. As experts in *la petite guerre* (guerrilla warfare), they had few equals.

A Canadian militiaman going into battle on snowshoes.
Library and Archives Canada/C1854

They were also noted for their cunning and cruelty. In the early years of settlement, they commonly attacked their enemies at night, sometimes burned their captives in their homes, and spared neither women nor children. Although the cruelty of border raids abated considerably in the eighteenth century, the Canadian militia remained widely respected and feared.

The French authorities made every effort to keep their militia in top fighting condition. After 1669, every Canadian male between the ages of 16 and 60 who was capable of bearing arms was subject to conscription and monthly military training. In 1752, when Governor Ange de Menneville Duquesne discovered that the militia was not up to scratch, he ordered weekly exercises and required that each soldier have a rifle, a full powder horn, and at least 20 bullets. Militiamen wore civilian clothes and were thus spared the expense of buying a costly uniform. The young men who cut their teeth on the gruelling fur-trade expeditions into the pays d'en haut clearly had the advantage over their farm-based cousins in the militia, but most men in the colony were accustomed to hunting and knew the basics of frontier survival.

Few men, it seems, tried to shirk their military responsibilities, and many men aspired to the social and political rewards that went with the unpaid position of militia captain. During the siege of Quebec, even the students at the seminary formed their own company, which was nicknamed "Royal Syntax." The old feudal emphasis on military loyalties coupled with the desperate attempt to save the cherished homeland meant that almost all male colonists were willing to serve.

Following the conquest of Canada, British commanders and British traditions dulled the Canadian enthusiasm for military exploits, but during the French regime the Canadian militia was, René Chartrand argues, the best fighting force on the continent.[4]

THE SOUTHWESTERN FRONTIER IN QUESTION

In Canada, Governor La Galissonière made impressive plans for defending French interests in North America. He sent a detachment to the mouth of the St John River, strengthened the forts in the Lake Champlain region, and dispatched a military expedition under Pierre-Joseph Céloron de Blainville into the Ohio Valley. Friendly Iroquois were gathered at La Présentation (Odgensburg, New York) by Sulpician priest Abbé Picquet to serve as a buffer between New France and New York. To protect their communications from Fort Frontenac to Fort Niagara, the French put a small fleet on Lake Ontario. Fort Rouillé was built in 1750 at present-day Toronto, site of a strategic portage.

MORE TO THE STORY

Early Days in Halifax

Halifax, founded in 1749, represented Britain's first serious attempt to colonize the French possessions acquired by the Treaty of Utrecht of 1713. Named after the chief officer of the Board of Trade and Plantations, the garrison town attracted a curious mix of immigrants, including artisans from London and soldiers and sailors discharged from the recent war. Soon after they arrived, many of the military men disappeared on vessels bound for Boston, but in their place came New Englanders attempting to escape debt or indenture and merchants eager to profit from the vast sums of money being invested in the frontier colony.

The capital of Nova Scotia, Halifax represented the latest thinking in urban planning. The town was laid out according to a rigidly symmetrical model plan, with rectangular streets moving up the steep slope from the waterfront. In the centre was the Grand Parade, which served as the focus of community life. An Anglican and a Presbyterian church faced the parade grounds alongside storehouses for munitions. On the land-ward side, the town was protected by a palisade and five forts, while water approaches were secured by three batteries. A common burial ground was located just outside the palisade.

In year-round communication with the North Atlantic world, Haligonians were kept informed about the latest developments by their local newspaper, the *Halifax Gazette*, founded in 1752. Its four pages of cramped print was by no means the principal vehicle of communication in Halifax. Since most people could not read or write, news was conveyed by word of mouth, and major events were announced by the town crier. Gossip travelled quickly through Halifax's compact streets, helped along by an abundance of taverns—estimated at as many as 100 by 1760—where merchants, administrators, soldiers, and civilians mingled regularly.

In its first decade, Halifax was a divided and unhappy community. Old and New Englanders nurtured ancient grudges and spawned new grievances. Merchants and government officials clashed over contracts and public policy. Into this fractious community stepped a Jersey-born merchant, Joshua Mauger, who took advantage of the chaos to gain ascendancy over both the economy and political institutions of the colony. Using his vast wealth gained from the West Indies trade and smuggling with Louisbourg before its capture in 1758, he advanced credit to the merchants in Halifax and soon became their indispensable patron.

Mauger's influence in London and Louisbourg made him a major player in administrative circles. Moreover, his monopoly of the manufacture of rum, protected from imports by a high customs duty, ensured that his wealth and influence would both continue to increase. By the 1760s, Mauger was so powerful in London that he could secure the dismissal of governors and other officials who challenged his authority.

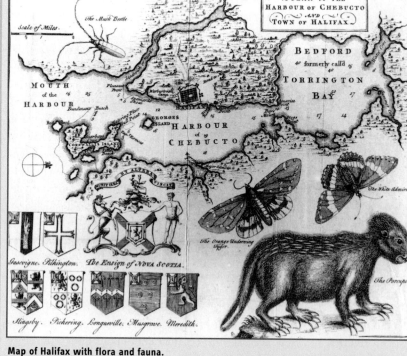

Map of Halifax with flora and fauna.
Nova Scotia Archives and Records Management PANS N-9893

With British activity in the interior undermining Native alliances, it was imperative that the French act decisively. The scope of Anglo-American ambitions was revealed by the creation of the Ohio Company in 1748. Sustained by capital invested by London merchants and such powerful Virginia families as the Lees, Fairfaxes, and Washingtons, the Ohio Company planned to make vast profits by selling half a million acres to land-hungry settlers.

In 1752, a new governor, the Marquis de Duquesne, arrived at Quebec with orders to drive the British out of the Ohio. Duquesne sent 300 Troupes de la Marine, 1700 Canadian militia, and 200 allied Natives into the Lake Erie region to construct a road to the headwaters of the Ohio and establish forts at strategic locations. In 1753, Governor Robert Dinwiddie of Virginia sent George Washington to the region to officially protest French activities, but the delegation received a polite rebuff from French commander Jacques Saint-Pierre at Fort Le Boeuf (present-day Waterford, Pennsylvania). Fort Duquesne, built early in 1754 on the site of present-day Pittsburgh, stood as a symbol of French control over the region.

Washington returned in the spring of 1754 with a small detachment of militia to order the French out of the Ohio territory. When they encountered a French scouting party, led by Ensign Joseph de Jumonville, they attacked it, killing Jumonville and nine of his men. Such an attack at a time when the British and French were officially at peace brought a swift reaction. On 3 July, a force from Fort Duquesne, led by Jumonville's brother, Louis, caught up with Washington's party, which had taken refuge in a crude shelter aptly named Fort Necessity. After a bruising assault that lasted nine hours, Washington surrendered. He and his surviving men were allowed to retreat in safety, but by the terms of the capitulation agreement the Virginians promised to abandon all claims to the disputed Ohio territory.

THE BRITISH TAKE THE OFFENSIVE

The success of the French on the frontier forced the Anglo-American colonies into cooperation. In 1755, they launched a four-pronged attack against the outer defences of New France: Fort Beauséjour in Acadia, Fort Frédéric on Lake Champlain, Fort Niagara in the Great Lakes region, and Fort Duquesne. Major-General Edward Braddock and two regiments of regulars were sent by Britain to assist the colonial effort.

France in the meantime had sent out Jean-Armand, Baron de Dieskau, with 3000 Troupes de Terre. Like the Troupes de la Marine, they were placed under the governor, who in 1755 was Pierre de Rigaud de Vaudreuil. The son of an earlier governor of the colony, he was the first Canadian-born appointee to the highest position in the colonial administration. Vaudreuil's strategy was to launch surprise attacks at various points along the American frontier. Guerrilla raids would keep the colonists terrorized, unnerve the British soldiers, put the enemy on the defensive, and take advantage of one of France's major assets: its Native alliances.

Major-General Braddock himself led the force that was organized to capture Fort Duquesne. Unused to frontier conditions, he failed miserably. A detachment of 108 colonial regulars, 146 Canadian militia, and 600 Natives defeated Braddock's army with little difficulty. Two-thirds of Braddock's 2200 men, and Braddock himself, were killed or wounded, while the French and their allies left the field with only 43 casualties. Braddock's papers, which revealed the plans for the other campaigns, were among the equipment abandoned by the British.

Governor Shirley of Massachusetts led the expedition against Fort Niagara, but his force of 2400 colonial militia was dissolved by disease and desertion before it reached its objective. The thrust toward Lake Champlain was blunted by a force led by Dieskau. Only on the Nova Scotia frontier were the British successful. A colonial militia of nearly 2500 men under the command of Lieutenant-Colonel Robert Monckton captured Fort Beauséjour on 12 June 1755 after a brief siege. With only 160 regular soldiers, and 300 Canadian militia and hastily conscripted Acadians, the French commander's position was hopeless.

The Acadian Deportation

On 1 May, even before the fall of Beauséjour, British authorities had decided to expel the Acadians living north of the Missaguash River. New Englanders would be placed in this borderland district to serve as a barrier

Fort Beauséjour.
Capt. John Hamilton/Library and Archives Canada/C-002707

between the remaining Acadians in peninsular Nova Scotia and the Canadians on the St Lawrence. On 25 June, this policy was approved by the governing council in Halifax.

The fate of the remaining Acadians was still to be decided, but it was unlikely that they would continue to live as they had since 1713. Although the Acadians captured at Fort Beauséjour protested that they had been forced to fight against their will—and the articles of capitulation had granted them pardon—the authorities in Halifax were no longer willing to give them the benefit of the doubt. With rumours circulating in the colony that the French were preparing to launch a counterattack, Lieutenant-Governor Charles Lawrence decided to act immediately to force the Acadians to do his bidding or face the consequences.

In July, delegates from the Acadian communities in peninsular Nova Scotia were summoned to Halifax and ordered to take an unqualified oath of allegiance. They refused to do so, promising only to remain neutral. Told that deportation would be the consequence of their refusal to take an unqualified oath, they stuck stubbornly to their position, even when given another chance to reconsider.

Unfortunately for the Acadians, the strategies they had pursued in the past would no longer work. While these negotiations were taking place, word of Braddock's defeat reached Halifax and panic spread throughout the town. The decision to deport the remaining Acadians was taken by Lawrence and his council on 28 July. It was a military decision, made by colonial authorities faced with the responsibility of defending a frontier colony. Although it clearly lacked humanity, it would solve the problem of the "neutral French" once and for all.

Lawrence moved quickly. Orders were sent to the military commanders at Chignecto, Piziquid, and Annapolis Royal instructing them to seize the men and boys as well as the boats, so that the women and children would not try to escape. As soon as it could be arranged, transports from Boston would take them away. All Acadian land and livestock became the property of the Crown. The deportees could take only the goods they could carry with them. Their destination would be other

British colonies in North America, where they would be scattered like leaves before the wind.

Terror swept through the Acadian communities as the awful reality dawned. At Chignecto the men were summoned to Fort Cumberland (formerly Fort Beauséjour) to be told of their fate and held in captivity; 80 of them escaped by digging a tunnel and fleeing with their families into the nearby woods. The Acadians near Piziquid were imprisoned in Fort Edward. At Grand Pré, the parish church served as a makeshift prison until the transports arrived. Annapolis Royal was a different story. There the Acadians had prior warning, and many managed to escape before the authorities issued their fatal order. Whether free or captive, no Acadian was spared the horror of what followed. The British soldiers put Acadian homes, barns, and churches to the torch and rounded up their cattle. In a few turbulent days in the late summer of 1755, the golden age of Acadian life came to a tragic end.

The departure brought more heartbreak as extended families and neighbours were separated and the land they so loved was left behind. In his diary, Colonel John Winslow described the pitiful scene as men "went off Praying, Singing & Crying, being Met by the women & Children all the way . . . with Great Lamentations upon their Knees praying, etc." For Winslow, who had seen much during his military career, it was "the worst peace [sic] of Service that Ever I was in."[5]

The horrors of the deportation did not end there. Authorities in the British colonies, with no idea that they were expected to receive hundreds of refugees, offered them little assistance. A few colonies even refused to accept their quota of "boat people" and sent them on their way. For many Acadians, their deportation from Nova Scotia marked the beginning of a lifetime of wandering that took some of them the length of North America and others to the West Indies, to Britain, or back to France. Nowhere did they feel at home. Even in France they felt like strangers and begged to be returned to the "New World" where they had been born.

Nor were the heart-rending events of 1755 the end of the deportations. In 1756, Lawrence ordered some 200 people in the Pubnico area of peninsular Nova Scotia to be shipped off to Boston. In 1758, after the fall of Louisbourg, the 3500 Acadians on Île Royale and Île Saint-Jean were sent to France. Three years later, another 300 Acadians in the Miramichi area were exiled. In all, about 11 000 of an estimated 13 000 Acadians had been removed from their native land. Many had died, including those drowned when their boats capsized during their endless wanderings. Eighteen hundred of them escaped to Canada, where they were among the most determined defenders of

Claude Bourgeois Pleads for Relief

Although there are no letters or diaries written by the deported Acadians, their desperate conditions while in exile prompted several petitions to authorities for relief. This petition, dated 24 May 1756, from Claude Bourgeois to the civil authorities in Massachusetts, was signed with an X, indicating that he found someone to help him write his plea for assistance.

Claude Bourgeois, your Petitioner, one of the late French inhabitants of Nova Scotia, was sent with his family to Amesbury by order of the General Court [of Massachusetts], where he has resided constantly with his wife and six children; and begs leave to represent to your Honours, that about four weeks ago ten or twelve men came and took away from him two of his daughters, one of the age of 25 years and the other 18, that his daughters were at that time employed in spinning for the Family, the poor remains of the Flax of wool which they had saved from Annapolis. Your Petitioner having fetched his Daughters home again, the Town have withheld their subsistence so that fourteen Days past he has received nothing at all to prevent them from starving, and the owner of the house where he lives threatens that he shall pay the rent of it by his children's labour. Your petitioner prays your Honours to relieve him under these circumstances, and your Petitioners shall ever pray, etc.[6]

the colony during its siege in 1759–60. Many of those who were dumped in the southern colonies made their way to Louisiana, where their descendants, called Cajuns, still live. Those who remained in Nova Scotia survived by hiding out in the woods and living with the Mi'kmaq. A few were rounded up and used as prison labour in the colony during the war.

The lesson of the deportation was not lost on the Canadians and their Native allies. They could now expect the worst from the British, who, it was clear, would take whatever measures were necessary to gain the upper hand in North America. Although the Acadian deportation had not been authorized by Lawrence's superiors in Britain, they had little difficulty in sanctioning it. Lawrence was not reprimanded for his controversial action; on the contrary, he was promoted from lieutenant-governor to governor of Nova Scotia in July 1756.

The departure of the Acadians made the Mi'kmaq more vulnerable to Lawrence's efforts to conquer them. In May 1756, he authorized both military forces and civilians to "annoy, distress, take, and destroy the Indians inhabiting different Parts of this Province" and offered "a reward of thirty pounds for every male Indian prisoner above the age of sixteen years, brought in alive; or for a scalp of such male Indian twenty-five pounds, and twenty-five pounds for every Indian woman or child brought in alive."[7] The final battle for the control of the border colony had begun in earnest.

THE SEVEN YEARS' WAR, 1756–1763

In 1756, warfare on the frontiers of New France finally merged into a larger contest, known as the Seven Years' War. It was essentially a continuation of the War of the Austrian Succession, this time with France

The Expulsion of the Acadians at Fort Amherst.
Permission of the artist, Lewis Parker, courtesy of Parks Canada

and Austria pitted against Britain and Prussia. Fought both in Europe and its colonies, this war would profoundly alter the balance of power in North America and open the way for a dramatic confrontation between Britain and its American colonies.

When war was declared, the Canadians moved quickly to secure the approaches to their colony. In 1756, Dieskau's successor, Louis-Joseph, the Marquis de Montcalm, led a successful expedition against Oswego, thus blocking British entry to the Great Lakes. In the following year, another campaign down the Lake Champlain route resulted in the capture of Fort William Henry. After the surrender, Montcalm's Native allies fell on the retreating British forces, killing 29 and taking over 100 prisoners.

This incident added fuel to the fire of intense hatred that was building in the Thirteen Colonies against their adversaries. On the frontier, French and Native raiding parties had made life intolerable for the English colonists. Governor Vaudreuil informed his superiors in 1756 that one of his commanders had been "occupied more than eight days merely in receiving scalps; that there is not an English party but loses some men, and that it was out of his power to render me an exact report of all the attacks our Indians made."[8]

Oswego and Fort William Henry were important victories for Montcalm, but they brought criticism from Vaudreuil, who felt that the European style of warfare was too formal for frontier conditions. As commander of the Troupes de la Marine, the militia, and Native forces, Vaudreuil championed the flexible guerrilla tactics of his army and was afraid that the conventional European fighting techniques used by Montcalm and his Troupes de Terre would lead to disaster.

In 1757 William Pitt's accession as prime minister brought new energy to the British cause. Pitt focused military strategy on the colonies, directing British troops in large numbers—at least 23 000—and naval resources to the conquest of New France. While the Canadians were experts in frontier wars, they were more vulnerable to the formal campaigns envisioned by Pitt. If the British blockaded the northern coastline, the colonials would be required to provision their military and civilian population without help from France. Withstanding a prolonged siege would be virtually impossible.

As the British converged on the colony in 1758, the conflict between Montcalm and Vaudreuil intensified. Montcalm, with a force of 3600 men, won another major victory at Carillon (Ticonderoga) against a massive British army of 15 000 men, but he remained convinced that the best strategy was to abandon outlying defences and concentrate all available manpower on the St Lawrence heartland. Vaudreuil continued to insist that the outlying forts be defended and that guerrilla tactics were the best way of keeping the British troops divided and defeated. Montcalm was so discouraged by the situation in North America that he asked to be recalled. Instead, he was promoted to lieutenant-general, a rank that made him supreme

commander of all French forces in North America. Vaudreuil was now required to submit to the dictates of his superior officer and watch his Canadian forces become secondary to the Troupes de Terre from France.

While Vaudreuil and Montcalm were quarrelling over strategy, Louisbourg had been captured for the second time by the British. Jeffrey Amherst led a force of over 13 000 men who took the fortress, defended by 4000 soldiers, on 26 July 1758 after a seven-week siege. With the British navy under Admiral Edward Boscawen preventing the French from receiving provisions or reinforcements, there was little that people in Louisbourg could do other than keep the British engaged long enough to prevent a campaign against Quebec that summer.

THE SIEGE OF QUEBEC

It was clear that the British were circling ever closer on their prey. Following the capture of Louisbourg, the British occupied Île Saint-Jean (now anglicized as St John's Island) and squelched any remaining Mi'kmaq and Acadian resistance in the Atlantic

The View of the Taking of Quebec.
Library and Archives Canada/C-001078

region. In August, Colonel Bradstreet took Fort Frontenac, effectively cutting the French supply line to the Ohio region. The French were forced to blow up Fort Duquesne to prevent it from falling into British hands. In June 1759 the Royal Navy under the command of Vice-Admiral Charles Saunders appeared on the St Lawrence. As well as 18 000 sailors, the expedition carried over 8600 seasoned troops under the command of General James Wolfe. The siege of Quebec had begun.

The arrival of the British on the St Lawrence made it impossible for the French to hold the interior. On 25 July, Fort Niagara surrendered after a siege of three weeks and Fort Rouillé was destroyed to prevent its capture by the British. Similarly, Fort Carillon and Fort Frédéric were blown up by the French as they retreated before an advancing army led by Jeffrey Amherst, who had become chief of the British forces in North America. The French commander Bourlamaque entrenched his troops at Île-aux-Noix on the Richelieu River, his last line of defence against the capture of Montreal.

Conditions in Quebec had become desperate even before British ships appeared on the St Lawrence. While Montcalm and his friends indulged themselves in the good times of the casino, ballroom, and banquet hall, the ordinary people faced rationing and even starvation. The presence of nearly 16 000 regular, militia, and Native soldiers added pressure to the limited supplies of food available in the colony. Prices had risen dramatically for any commodities that were still available, and even horses were being slaughtered to feed hungry mouths. Crop failure and an outbreak of typhus added to the misery. Only the arrival of 22 supply ships from France in May 1759 made it possible to feed the soldiers and civilians in the town until the fall harvest.

The British reasoned that the capture of Quebec would ensure the eventual surrender of the entire colony, but success would not come easily. Although the British succeeded in taking Pointe Lévis across the river from Quebec and laid waste to much of the surrounding countryside, they failed to land on the left flank of the town. Nor could they cut communications to the main supply base at Batiscan, 80 kilometres upstream from Quebec. Wolfe's forces launched an artillery bombardment from their base on Pointe Lévis, but the walled town remained invincible. Repeated landing attempts were driven back by a combined force of 4000 regular French troops, up to 10 000 Canadian militiamen, and 1000 Native warriors. In each encounter the British suffered heavy casualties.

By early September, the town of Quebec, but not its protective walls, lay in ruins, and what was left of its frightened population was threatened by starvation. Montcalm made plans for an eventual retreat to distant Louisiana. The British were equally demoralized. Over 1000 soldiers had been laid low with dysentery in an unsanitary base hospital, General Amherst's forces were stalled at Lake Champlain, and Wolfe's staff officers were becoming discouraged as their commander became ill and increasingly frustrated at his lack of success. With fall rapidly approaching, Vice-Admiral Saunders was afraid his fleet would be caught in the ice of an early winter. Unless something happened soon, the Canadian climate would dictate the outcome of the battle of Quebec.

Good luck rather than good management determined victory. On the night of 12 September, Wolfe managed to land nearly 4500 men at Anse-au-Foulon, a cove about three kilometres above Quebec. They scrambled up a steep cliff to the Plains of Abraham, where they stood in battle array on the morning of 13 September.

From a tactical point of view, the Battle of the Plains of Abraham was a blundering fiasco for both the French and the British. Wolfe ordered his men to form two lines below a crest of higher ground to await the French army, which arrived breathless from Beauport. With few rations, no reserves, and only one field gun, his position was tenuous. Montcalm could have waited for the British to charge uphill against his winded troops, or he could have remained within the stout walls of the town until reinforcements under Bougainville arrived from Batiscan to attack the British from the rear. He did neither. Instead, he lined up his troops outside the town walls and ordered them to charge in three columns. This strategy severely limited the number of men who could fire at any one time and resulted in the breaking of the charge under a withering British volley. As the French retreated in disarray to the protection of the town, Montcalm was mortally wounded and Wolfe lay dead on the battlefield.

Montcalm and Wolfe

THE MARQUIS DE MONTCALM

Born in 1712 to a distinguished family in France, Louis-Joseph de Montcalm was commissioned as an ensign in the Hainault Regiment at the age of nine. He began his active military career in 1732 after being educated at home. His tutor found him stubborn and opinionated, a view shared by his colonial nemesis, Governor Vaudreuil. Married in 1736 to Angelique-Louise Talon de Boulay, the daughter of another aristocratic family, Montcalm rose easily through the military ranks and was knighted in 1743. He saw plenty of military action in Europe during the War of the Austrian Succession. Claiming long service (31 years, 11 campaigns, and 5 wounds), he applied for and in 1753 received a substantial pension from the government.

Montcalm might have ended his days enjoying the tranquil life of a gentleman at his château at Candiac. Instead he responded to the call to serve in New France following Dieskau's capture in 1755. Montcalm arrived in Quebec in May 1756 and never returned to his native land. He died in the early morning hours of 14 September following his defeat on the Plains of Abraham, and was buried in a shell crater under the floor of the chapel of the Ursuline nuns.

JAMES WOLFE

Born in 1727, James Wolfe was educated in Westerham and Greenwich, England. He received his first military appointment in the 1st Regiment of Marines, in which his father was a colonel. Like Montcalm, Wolfe saw action on the European continent during the War of the Austrian Succession. He also participated in the Battle of Culloden against the Scots in 1746 and was stationed in Scotland after the war. It was perhaps during the Scottish campaign that Wolfe developed the tough military policies for which he became infamous in New France. Following the capture of Louisbourg, in which he showed himself to be a gifted officer, Wolfe urged "an offensive and destructive" war in the region to prevent the Canadian "hell-hounds" from securing an advantage. He personally helped to lay waste to the settlements and fisheries in what is now northern New Brunswick and the Gaspé region as a prelude to the campaign against Quebec.

Despite his poor health, he was chosen by Sir William Pitt to command the expedition against the heart of New France. Like Montcalm, Wolfe died in the conflict, but, unlike his beaten adversary's, Wolfe's reputation grew after the Battle of the Plains of Abraham. Many portraits and statues of Wolfe were produced to commemorate the hero of the hour, none more widely circulated than that by Benjamin West depicting, in a highly idealized style, Wolfe's death.

The Marquis de Montcalm.
Library and Archives Canada/C27665

The Death of General Wolfe, by Benjamin West.
National Gallery of Canada/8007

Casualties were heavy on both sides—658 for the British and 644 for the French. Despite the retreat of the French, the British still held only the Plains of Abraham. Nevertheless, the war-weary inhabitants of the town, as well as the jaded Troupes de Terre, were eager to surrender. On 19 September, the French troops left the fortress of Quebec, their flags unfurled, torches lit, drums beating, and fifes playing. The British navy returned home, and a garrison under Brigadier James Murray was left behind in the shambles of the old capital. They faced a cold winter, short rations, and a devastating outbreak of scurvy. Whenever they ventured outside the walls of the town for food or firewood, the British were attacked by Canadian militiamen and their Native allies, who also harassed anyone caught collaborating with the conqueror.

In the spring, a contingent of 7000 men under the Chevalier de Lévis, who had succeeded Montcalm, attempted to retake Quebec. Murray then made the same tactical blunder as Montcalm. Instead of waiting for an assault on the walled fortress, he ordered his troops to meet the French at Sainte-Foy. The British charged without success, were routed by a bayonet charge, and fled in disarray to Quebec. The arrival of the British navy with reinforcements prevented Lévis from following up his victory. Sainte-Foy was the last major engagement of the war. Although the French won that battle, they lost the war and the colony.

SURRENDER AND NEGOTIATION

Governor Vaudreuil surrendered New France to General Amherst on 8 September 1760. Although Amherst refused to grant the honours of war to the French troops, he responded in a practical way to Vaudreuil's pleas for leniency in dealing with the conquered Canadians. Under the Articles of Capitulation, everyone who wished to do so could leave the colony and take their possessions with them. Those who remained were granted security of property and person. Canadians were granted freedom to practise their Roman Catholic faith, but the status of enforced tithing remained in doubt. Amherst refused Vaudreuil's request to permit the king of France to name the Roman Catholic bishop of the colony, and he reserved decision on the rights of the Jesuits,

Récollets, and Sulpicians to continue their ministries. In contrast, the female religious orders were granted their customary privileges.

The Acadians who had sought refuge in Canada were given permission to go to France, but they were specifically excluded from the guarantees against deportation that were given to the French and Canadians. Afraid that the British would deprive the conquered people of their valuable human property, Vaudreuil secured guarantees for the continuance of black and Aboriginal slavery and the right of owners to bring up their slaves "in the Roman Religion." Vaudreuil also attempted to protect his Native allies from the wrath of the conqueror. Article XL provided that "Indian allies" of the French were to be "maintained in the lands they inhabit" and were not to be "molested" for having fought against the British.

Until the peace treaty was signed in Paris on 10 February 1763, New France was ruled by martial law. The British gave some thought to exchanging their conquered territory for Guadaloupe, but the Treaty of Paris confirmed British possession of all of New France, except for Saint-Pierre and Miquelon. The French were also granted permission to fish on the Treaty Shore of Newfoundland. Louisiana, which had not been a theatre of war, was divided along the Mississippi, with Britain receiving the eastern section and navigational rights to the mighty river. In a separate treaty, France ceded the area west of the Mississippi to its ally Spain.

During the negotiations, France showed surprisingly little interest in regaining Canada, which philosopher Voltaire dismissed as "a few acres of snow." As well, the French took some pleasure in the prospect of a full-scale confrontation erupting between Britain and its Thirteen Colonies, now that the French threat on the continent had been eliminated. In all of these negotiations the Natives were not represented, and their homelands were parcelled out to European powers as if North America were an empty frontier ripe for exploitation.

CONCLUSION

Britain emerged from the Seven Years' War as the dominant imperial power in North America. As we will see in the next chapter, its efforts to administer the colonial possessions met with failure on all sides. Not only did the British find themselves fighting a war with the First Nations on the frontier, but they also faced a rebellion in their colonies. The attempt to impose British political and legal institutions in Quebec also failed. As the British responded to these troublesome colonial realities, their policies increasingly resembled those of their French predecessors. Like the French, the British found themselves fighting the Thirteen Colonies, forging Native alliances, and resorting to aristocratic paternalism in a desperate attempt to maintain their North American empire.

NOTES

1 "Ordinances, Proclamations. . . Issued by the Military Governors of Quebec, Montreal and Trois Rivières from the Capitulation of Quebec Until the Establishment of Civilian Government. . . ." Cited in *The French Canadians, 1759–1766: Conquered? Half Conquered? Liberated?* ed. Cameron Nish (Toronto: Copp Clark Publishing Company, 1966), 43.

2 W.J. Eccles, *The Canadian Frontier, 1534–1760* (New York: Holt, Rinehart and Winston, 1969), 158.

3 William C. Wicken, *Mi'kmaq Treaties on Trial: History, Land, and Donald Marshall Junior* (Toronto: University of Toronto Press, 2002), 98.

4 See René Chartrand, "Death Walks on Snowshoes," *Horizon Canada* (1987), 1:260–64.

5 Cited in Barry Moody, *The Acadians* (Toronto: Grolier, 1981), 72–73.

6 Sally Ross and Alphonse Deveau, *The Acadians of Nova Scotia: Past and Present* (Halifax: Nimbus, 1992), 66.

7 Cited in Daniel N. Paul, *We Were Not the Savages: A Mi'kmaq Perspective on the Collision between European and Native American Civilizations* (Halifax: Fernwood, 2000), 146.

8 G.F.G. Stanley, *New France: The Last Phase, 1744–1760* (Toronto: McClelland and Stewart, 1968), 147.

RELATED READINGS IN THIS SERIES

From *Foundations: Readings in Pre-Confederation Canadian History*
Naomi E.S. Griffiths, "1755–1784: Exile Surmounted," 155–73.

From Media Companion CD-ROM, Volume I
Treaty of 1725
Drafting the Oath of Allegiance at Annapolis Royal
Governor Charles Lawrence, "To the Governors of the Continent," August 11, 1755
The Death of General Wolfe
Louisbourg Under Siege, 1758
Articles of Capitulation

SELECTED READING

On Native-European relations in the eighteenth century, see texts by Olive Dickason, J.R. Miller, and Arthur Ray cited in Chapter 2. See also L.S.F. Upton, *Micmacs and Colonists: Indian-White Relations in the Maritimes, 1713–1867* (Vancouver: UBC Press, 1979); Richard White, *The Middle Ground: Indians, Empires, and Republics in the Great Lakes Region, 1650–1815* (Cambridge: Cambridge University Press, 1991); Cornelius J. Jaenen, "French Sovereignty and Native Nationhood during the French Regime," *Native Studies Review* 2, 1 (1986); Olive Dickason, "Amerindians between French and English in Nova Scotia, 1713–1763," *American Indian Culture and Research Journal* 10, 4 (1986): 31–56, and "Louisbourg and the Indians: A Study in Imperial Race Relations," *History and Archeology* 6 (1976): 1–206; Jennifer Reid, *Myth, Symbol, and Colonial Encounter: British and Mi'kmaq in Acadia* (Ottawa: University of Ottawa Press, 1996); and Stephen E. Patterson, "Indian-White Relations in Nova Scotia, 1749–1761: A Study in Political Interaction," *Acadiensis* 23, 1 (Autumn 1993): 23–59.

On the military and imperial history of the eighteenth century, see I.K. Steele, *Guerrillas and Grenadiers: The Struggle for Canada, 1689–1760* (Toronto: Ryerson Press,

1969); George F.G. Stanley, *New France: The Last Phase, 1744–1760* (Toronto: McClelland and Stewart, 1968); James Pritchard, *The Anatomy of a Naval Disaster: The 1746 French Expedition to North America* (Montreal: McGill-Queen's University Press, 1995); Kenneth Banks, *Communications and the State in the French Atlantic, 1713–1763* (Montreal: McGill-Queen's University Press, 2002). On the events leading up to and including the Seven Years' War (known as the French and Indian War in the United States) see three recent publications: Daniel Marston, *The French-Indian War, 1754–1760* (Oxford: Osprey Publications, 2002); Denis Vaugeois, *The Last French and Indian War* (Montreal: McGill-Queen's University Press, 2003); and Peter D MacLeod, *Les Iroquois et la guerre de Sept Ans* (Montreal: VLB éditeur, 2000). C.P. Stacey's classic study of the capture of Quebec is available in a new edition: *Quebec 1759: The Siege and the Battle* (Toronto: Robin Brass Studies, 2002). See also Guy Frégault, *Canada: The War of the Conquest*, trans. Margaret M. Cameron (Toronto: Oxford University Press, 1969). The careers of Montcalm and Wolfe are judicially assessed by W.J. Eccles in the *Dictionary of Canadian Biography*, vol. 3.

On the Acadians, see Nicolas Landry and Nicole Lang, *Histoire de l'Acadie* (Sillery: Septentrion, 2001); Naomi Griffiths, *The Acadians: Creation of a People* (Toronto: McGraw-Hill Ryerson, 1973) and *The Contexts of Acadian History, 1686–1784* (Montreal: McGill-Queen's University Press, 1992); Andrew Hill Clark, *Acadia: The Geography of Early Nova Scotia to 1760* (Madison: University of Wisconsin Press, 1968); and Sally Ross and Alphonse Deveau, *The Acadians of Nova Scotia: Past and Present* (Halifax: Nimbus, 1992). Earle Lockerby offers details on the appalling death rate of the Acadians deported from Île Saint-Jean in "The Deportation of the Acadians from Île St-Jean, 1758," *Acadiensis* 27, 2 (Spring 1998): 45–94. Jean Daigle, ed., *Acadia of the Maritimes: Thematic Studies* (Moncton: Chaire d'études acadiennes, Université de Moncton, 1995) brings the Acadian odyssey up to the twentieth century. J.B. Brebner, *New England's Outpost: Acadia before the Conquest of Canada* (New York: Columbia University Press, 1927), and George A. Rawlyk, *Nova Scotia's Massachusetts: A Study of Massachusetts-Nova Scotia Relations, 1630–1784* (Montreal: McGill-Queen's University Press, 1973), offer valuable insights on geopolitical developments in the Atlantic region in the early eighteenth century. On Newfoundland in this period see Jerry Bannister, *The Role of the Admirals: Law, Custom and Naval Government in Newfoundland, 1699–1832* (Toronto: Osgoode Society and University of Toronto Press, 2002). See also the relevant chapters in Phillip A. Buckner and John G. Reid, eds., *The Atlantic Region to Confederation: A History* (Toronto: University of Toronto Press, 1994).

WEBLINKS

EDWARD CORNWALLIS
www.schoolnet.ca/aboriginal/treaties/maritim5-e.html

This page provides portions of the text of the maritime treaties signed between Edward Cornwallis and representatives of the Chinecto and St John's tribes.

FORT ROUILLÉ
schools.tdsb.on.ca/jarvisci/toronto/rouille.htm

This site describes the French settlement of 1750 at Fort Rouillé in what is now Toronto.

MI'KMAQ TREATIES
mrc.uccb.ns.ca/treaties.html

These treaties are currently under judicial review.

A SOLDIER'S ACCOUNT OF THE CAPTURE OF QUEBEC, 1759
www.militaryheritage.com/quebec1.htm

This site includes the journal of a sergeant-major who participated in the capture of Quebec in 1759.

A LETTER DESCRIBING THE CAPTURE OF QUEBEC, 18 SEPTEMBER 1759
www..lib.uwaterloo.ca/discipline/SpecColl/archives/holmes/holmes.html#letter

This University of Waterloo Library site includes the transcription of a letter describing the capture of Quebec. It was written by Rear-Admiral Charles Holmes, third in command under James Wolfe.

PART II SUMMARY

In the century from 1660 to 1760, France established several distinct communities in North America. Acadia, largely ignored by France in the seventeenth century, and, after 1713, a British colony called Nova Scotia, sustained, through dykeland farming and fishing, a small but relatively prosperous population. Canada, the headquarters of France's North American fur trade, received more attention from the mother country, particularly from 1663 to 1672, and became home to an even larger farm population. While the demands of the fur trade could have been met by a compact colony with strategic alliances with several Native groups, France's imperial policies after 1698 dictated a strategy of vigorous colonial expansion. From a full-blown colony in Louisiana and a fortress in Louisbourg to an expanding set of thinly populated trading posts across much of the western three-quarters of the continent, France was on the move in North America until the 1750s. The Seven Years' War brought an end to the French regime in North America and marked the high point of British power in North America.

THE ORIGINS OF BRITISH NORTH AMERICA, 1763–1821

The Seven Years' War sealed the fate of New France, but Great Britain had difficulty governing its North American colonies old and new. In 1776 most of the British colonies along the Atlantic seaboard declared independence and fought a successful war to establish their claim. Britain and the world were forced to recognize a new nation—the United States of America—in 1783. Within a decade Great Britain was again at war with France and, for a brief time (1812–14), with the United States. The French Revolutionary and Napoleonic Wars dragged on from 1793 to 1815. Meanwhile, the "old regime" that had characterized European nations and their colonies was being rapidly swept away. The American and French Revolutions signalled the birth of the "modern" era characterized by liberal democratic political systems, industrial capitalism, and new social values. Despite its embarrassing losses in North America, Great Britain emerged as the dominant power in this new world order. The remaining British North American colonies, for better or worse, would be defined in the crucible of this revolutionary age.

CHAPTER 10

British North America, 1763–1783

Timeline

▶ **1763**	Treaty of Paris; Royal Proclamation
▶ **1763–65**	Pontiac's Revolt
▶ **1759–67**	New England Planters arrive in Nova Scotia
▶ **1764**	Acadians permitted to settle in Nova Scotia
▶ **1767**	St John's Island granted by lottery to British proprietors
▶ **1769**	St John's Island given colonial status
▶ **1770**	George Cartwright builds his first fur-trading and fishing base in Labrador
▶ **1770–71**	Moravians establish mission in Labrador
▶ **1774**	Quebec Act; First Continental Congress
▶ **1775**	Palliser's Act, Newfoundland
▶ **1775–76**	American invasion of Quebec
▶ **1776**	The United States declare independence from Great Britain
▶ **1778**	France enters the war as an ally of the United States
▶ **1783**	American Revolutionary War ends

"Why do you suffer the white men to dwell among you?. . . Why do you not clothe yourselves in skins, as your ancestors did, and use the bows and arrows, and the stone-pointed lances, which they used?. . . You have bought guns, knives, kettles, and blankets, from the white men, until you can no longer do without them; and what is worse, you have drunk the poison firewater, which turns you into fools. Fling all these things away. . . and as for these English . . . you must lift the hatchet against them."[1]

So spoke Pontiac, the Ottawa chief in the Detroit region who led an armed uprising against the British in 1763. The British conquest of New France not only brought unwelcome changes for the colonists; it also marked a new stage in Native-European relations. Pontiac's insights came too late to save his people or himself. Although the First Nations living along the Anglo-American frontier scored spectacular successes against the hated British, they were soon forced to surrender the posts they had captured. Their dependence on European guns, ammunition, and even food made it difficult for them to sustain a prolonged campaign once their French allies could no longer help them.

Pontiac himself became a victim of the confusion and desperation of his people, who resented the fact that he finally agreed to peaceful relations with the British and monopolized all the attention of the white authorities. In 1769, he was assassinated by the nephew of a Peoria chief in Cahokia. His death, according to historian Richard White, was "a monument to the limits of chieftainship."[2]

THE CONQUEST AND NATIVE POLICY

The transfer of New France to British control was as traumatic for the Aboriginal peoples of North America as it was for the Canadians. With the rivalry of the British and French removed, the Natives could no longer play one side against the other to their advantage. The price of furs plummeted, the quality and quantity of European trade goods declined, and the custom of giving annual presents in recognition of military alliances was abandoned. With the Aboriginal peoples now at the mercy of Anglo-American speculators and land-hungry settlers, their very survival was at stake.

Aware of the potential for disaster in their Native policy, the British developed a new approach to relations with the First Nations, drawing upon lessons learned from their French rivals. They had observed, for example, the necessity of respecting Native self-government and the value of trading alliances. In addition, they saw how important it was to maintain a unified approach. They knew that by permitting each colony to pursue its own Native policy they had nearly lost their strategic advantage to the French. In 1755, Britain established an Indian Department, the initial step in its attempt to impose a coordinated imperial policy on Aboriginal people.

Britain's new Native policy was first implemented in Nova Scotia. The fall of Louisbourg and Quebec signalled the end of Aboriginal ascendancy in the region. Without a source of supply for arms and ammunition, the Maliseet, Passamaquoddy, and Mi'kmaq made their peace with their conquerors in a series of treaties signed in 1760 and 1761. In a ceremony held at his farm near Halifax, on 25 July 1761, Lieutenant-Governor

Jonathan Belcher informed one group of Mi'kmaq that they were "in full possession of English protection and Liberty."[3] What Belcher really meant was that they were subjects of the British king and bound by British laws. Belcher was instructed to draw up a proclamation forbidding encroachment on Native lands, which he obediently did, but he refused to publicize it because, as he told his superiors: "If the proclamation had been issued at large, the Indians might have been incited . . . to have extravagant and unwarranted demands, to the disquiet and perplexity of the New Settlements in the province."[4]

The Royal Proclamation of 1763

The Royal Proclamation of October 1763 was a further manifestation of Britain's new Native policy. A decree of the Crown, not a law of Parliament, the proclamation set out the policy for governing the newly acquired territories and for relations with

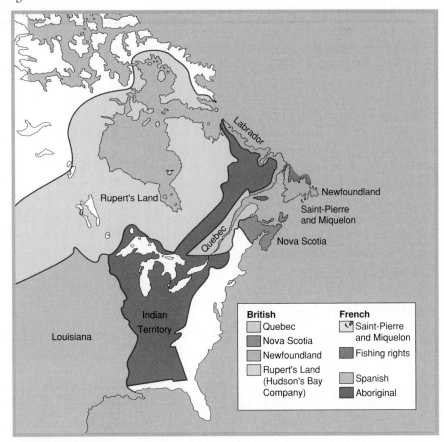

MAP 10.1 North America, 1763.
Adapted from *Historical Atlas of Canada*, vol. 1 (Toronto: University of Toronto Press, 1987), plate 42

Native people in North America. Canada was reduced in size (see Map 10.1) and renamed Quebec. The eastern part of the colony was placed under the jurisdiction of Newfoundland, while the interior region west of the Allegheny Mountains was declared to be Indian territory. By firmly entrenching the concept of Native title to the hinterland, the Proclamation marked a major milestone in European–First Nations relations and is rightly regarded as a great charter of Native rights.

According to the Proclamation, any lands that had "not been ceded to or purchased" by Britain were reserved for "the said Indians." The British "strictly" forbade any individual, "on Pain of our Displeasure," to purchase Native land. If Natives wished to sell their land, they could do so only through the British Crown "at some public Meeting or assembly of the said Indians, to be held for the Purpose by the Governor or Commander in Chief of our Colony." And only those who held a licence from the governor could trade with the Native people.

The provisions of the Royal Proclamation of 1763 were of little immediate consequence to the Native nations on the frontier who were facing deprivation and even starvation. Under Britain's streamlined policy, trade was confined to a limited number of designated posts, and annual gift giving was abandoned. The policy proved a dismal failure. The new shortage of guns and ammunition brought particular hardship to the Aboriginal nations that had come to depend upon them. Encouraged by French traders still resident in the interior, the First Nations prepared to strike at the hated British in their midst. During the summer of 1762, a war belt and hatchet circulated among the disaffected peoples. By the following spring a border war had erupted.

Pontiac's Uprising

One of the principal leaders of the uprising was the Ottawa chief Pontiac, who hoped for the return of French forces to aid his people and appealed to his fellow warriors to wipe the "dogs dressed in red" from "the face of the earth." Always ingenious guerrilla fighters, the Natives captured most of the posts in the upper Mississippi and Ohio River basins and killed over 2000 settlers. Detroit held out because the com-

mander had been warned of the attack. It took the British nearly two years to regain control of the frontier. In desperation, Amherst even considered resorting to biological warfare. He suggested that his commanders might use smallpox-infected blankets "to extirpate this execrable race," and at least one officer, Captain Ecuyer at Fort Pitt, acted on this suggestion.[5]

The sequel to Pontiac's revolt was mounting pressure on the British to resume the fur trade out of Montreal as a means of maintaining Native goodwill. Through the mediation of William Johnson, the superintendent of Indian affairs in the Mohawk Valley, efforts were made to define a boundary for Indian territory. More than 3000 Natives, mostly Iroquois and their allies, met with Johnson at Fort Stanwix in 1768 to establish a permanent boundary between white settlements and Indian hunting grounds. Since neither the Iroquois nor the British could control the people they claimed to bargain for, the new boundary line was widely ignored. As independent traders and settlers clashed with Native communities, the Anglo-American frontier dissolved into chaos. William Johnson's nephew, Guy Johnson, was instrumental in convincing the British to exert more control over the region by placing the Ohio territory under the jurisdiction of Quebec in 1774.

THE CONQUEST AND QUEBEC

Debates about the meaning of the conquest of Quebec make it difficult to sort out what actually took place in the years immediately after the British assumed control. Undoubtedly, the destruction caused by a victorious foreign army, followed by the imposition of the conqueror's rule, constituted a traumatic series of events. But it was by no means the conquest alone that determined the fate of the Canadiens (as they had come to be called) in subsequent years. As the British experimented with various administrative policies, groups within the new British colony of Quebec began to assert themselves, and developments in the larger North Atlantic world continued to influence the course of events.

In the aftermath of the conquest, between 2000 and 3000 people moved to France—mostly administrators, merchants, and military leaders—but the bulk of the colonists remained. Most of the 70 000 people living in Canada had been born in the colony; some of them traced their Canadian ancestry back several generations. They had little choice but to accept the fact that they were now British subjects by conquest. Required to take an oath of allegiance to the British king, they did so with little resistance. Their conquerors had taken the precaution of disarming them, and the fate of the Acadians was still fresh in their minds.

The colony remained under military rule and military occupation until 1764. James Murray maintained a strict discipline among his occupying forces and a lenient policy toward the conquered people. A fiery Scot with 20 years of military service behind him, he was still only 39 years old when he became the most powerful man in the colony. His decisions respecting colonial policy would have a major impact on how the conquered colony developed under British rule.

Murray introduced a form of military rule that resembled the political system under the French regime. He governed with an appointed council and subordinates in the three jurisdictions of Quebec, Trois-Rivières, and Montreal. Since the chief military officers all spoke French and French laws were respected, the transition to British authority was eased considerably. Murray granted new commissions to former militia captains, and most of them adequately performed the required duties.

The British distrusted Roman Catholics, particularly the Jesuits, who were notorious around the world for their political intrigues. The capitulation agreement reflected this distrust by stipulating that only the parish priests and female religious orders could continue their activities. Male religious communities were forbidden to recruit new members and would gradually die out. If they had wished to do so, the British could have crippled the Roman Catholic Church by refusing to appoint a successor to Bishop Pontbriand, who had died in 1760. Without an official head of the church, no priests could be consecrated, and in short order the whole structure of the institutional church would crumble. However, Murray recognized the critical role played by the church in the social and spiritual life of the colony. Accordingly, he collaborated in having Abbé Jean-Olivier Briand whisked off to France to be consecrated by French bishops in 1764. As "Superintendent of the Romish Religion," Briand had full episcopal powers. For the time being at least, the institutional structure of the church remained intact.

Like the French administrators before him, Murray relied upon the church to perform necessary social services. He also expected the priests to counsel their flocks to submit to their new masters. Briand and most of those who served under him proved obedient, motivated not only by their fundamental respect for authority but also by the knowledge that the fate of the church would be determined by the goodwill of the conquerors.

Economic Policy

The economic crisis induced by a generation of warfare and profiteering was perhaps the biggest problem facing the conquered colony. Not surprisingly, the merchants who had made the biggest profits were among those who quickly decided to leave. Those who stayed found themselves

This engraving is one of 12 views of Quebec City based on drawings by Richard Short, a naval officer with the British fleet in 1759. It offers evidence of the effects on the city of months of British bombardment, during which one-third of the buildings were destroyed and many more so badly damaged that they had to be pulled down.
Library and Archives Canada/C350

unable to compete with the British and New England merchants who arrived in the wake of Wolfe's army. Although there were not many of them—the immigrant British population remained under 1000 in the decade following the conquest—they had the connections, the capital, and the competitive edge over their French rivals in the British mercantile system. Because the rules of mercantilism required that colonial trade be confined solely to the mother country, the Canadians' contacts in France, which once counted for everything, were now worthless.

Inflation and monetary problems threatened the general economic stability of the colony. During the final years of the French regime, paper money had flooded the market, and prices had skyrocketed. The British introduced hard currency, imposed price controls, and regulated the supply of necessities. Paper money was registered and, although heavily discounted, gradually disappeared from circulation.

In the early years of the occupation, the sympathy shown by Murray and his army surprised the Canadians, who had been encouraged to expect the worst from their conquerors. The military paid in hard cash for the supplies it commandeered, and when there was a shortage of essential supplies in the colony the British made military stores available to civilians. Even Murray felt compelled to comment to his superiors on the "uncommon generosity" displayed by his men toward "these poor deluded people." According to Murray, British soldiers contributed to a fund to help the Canadians from which "a quantity of provisions was purchased and distributed with great care and assiduity to numbers of poor families, who, without this charitable support, must have inevitably perished."[6] Soon after the conquest, orders had to be issued to stop the soldiers from marrying Canadian women without permission from their commanders. Clearly, the attitudes of at least some of the conquered people were softening toward the conqueror.

Civilian Rule

With the Treaty of Paris signed, British officials began to make plans to incorporate New France into the British colonial empire. James Murray was appointed governor of a compact British colony, which would be called Quebec. While armed with detailed instructions on the requirements of the new civilian administration, Murray was offered no special advice on how to deal with the cultural differences of the new subjects. Quebec was to become a colony like most of the others in North America, ruled by a governor advised by an appointed council and an elected assembly. British law would be introduced and justices of the peace appointed at the local level. Since Roman Catholics were denied political rights under British law, only the few hundred Protestants in the colony would be eligible to vote and hold public office. The thinking behind such policy—if there was any thinking at all—seems to have been that the conquered subjects would be easily assimilated into the language and religion of the conquering people.

Both Murray and his successor, Sir Guy Carleton, quickly realized that British institutions were not suited to the newly conquered colony. The Canadians complained about the cost and complexity of the British legal system as well as the harsh penalties it imposed for minor offences. Because only Protestants could serve as lawyers, jurors, justices of the peace, and judges, cultural antagonism soon coloured the judicial process. Murray eased the tension by permitting Roman Catholics to practise law and serve on juries, but it was clear that the conquered people longed for a return to the French civil code.

As British institutions began to take root, the whole structure of Canadian society was put in jeopardy. The seigneurs, for instance, found themselves in a precarious position. Although they retained ownership of their estates, their seigneurial privileges were less secure under British law. Even more damaging to their status was the loss of income derived from their military and political offices, which had previously supplemented their seigneurial dues.

Canadian merchants also faced predictable difficulties in their attempts to adjust to the British mercantile system. While a few of them made a successful switch from French to British suppliers, the British merchants usually had the upper hand in securing military contracts, credit, and cargo space. British merchants in Montreal also quickly gained primacy in the fur trade, and like the French before them they emerged as the chief rivals of the Hudson's Bay Company traders. Canadian personnel proved valuable as guides, interpreters, and labour in the fur trade, but they no longer commanded the posts or determined trade policy.

For the majority of people, the problems facing the privileged classes were manifested only indirectly. The freeze in seigneurial dues during the last half-century of the French regime no longer applied, and some seigneurs desperately tried to shore up their declining income through exorbitant rent increases, but this practice only became widespread when seigneurial dues were sanctioned in law in 1774. In the years immediately following the conquest, agricultural production increased and the population grew at a rapid rate. These were not the best of times for Canadian peasants, but they were certainly not the worst.

The old aristocratic ideal as reflected in the seigneuries appealed to British administrators. For Murray, the system stood in sharp contrast to the grasping commercialism typical of the small knot of British and New England merchants in the urban centres. Murray informed the Board of Trade in London:

> Little, very little, will content the New subjects; but nothing will satisfy the licentious fanatics trading here but the expulsion of the Canadians, who are perhaps the bravest and the best race upon the face of the globe, a race, who could they be indulged with a few privileges which the laws of England deny to Roman Catholics at home, would soon get the better of every national antipathy to their conquerors, and become the most faithful and most useful set of men in this American empire.[7]

In an effort to prevent the British minority from using its power to exploit the Canadians, Murray postponed calling an assembly. The English merchants were outraged. They were also annoyed both by the restrictions on the fur trade that Murray enforced and by his obvious attempts to conciliate the conquered Canadians. In 1765 their criticisms of the governor led to his recall. Sir Guy Carleton arrived in Quebec in 1766 prepared to address the concerns of the small British community in the colony, but he soon adopted the views of his predecessor.

Both men were influenced to a considerable degree by the larger political forces emerging on the North American continent. With France no longer a threat to their development, the Anglo-American colonists were less willing to accept colonial policies defined exclusively with British interests in mind. Like Charles Lawrence, the official in Nova Scotia responsible for the Acadian expulsion, Murray and Carleton were military men charged with protecting their colony in the event of war. Yet the strategic factor coupled with their own aristocratic values caused them to reach a different conclusion than that of the governor of Nova Scotia. The conquered Canadians would make better patriots, they reasoned, than the rebellious, republican-minded Anglo-American colonists.

THE QUEBEC ACT, 1774

Carleton's views were reflected in the Quebec Act, passed by the British Parliament in 1774. Designed to strengthen the traditional elites in the colony, the act was based on the mistaken belief that those elites would ensure the loyalty of the masses in time of war.

Portrait of novelist Frances Brooke, painted in 1771 by her friend Catherine Read. Between 1763 and 1768, Frances Brooke, one of Britain's leading literary figures, lived in Quebec and produced the first novel written in what would become Canada. *The History of Emily Montague*, published in London in 1769, described the rich social life that prevailed in administrative and military circles in Quebec. As the wife of the Reverend John Brooke, who served as garrison chaplain, Frances Brooke was in a good position to observe the behaviour of her social set. The rapid rise in literacy in the English-speaking world in the second half of the eighteenth century meant that there was a larger audience for written material designed to entertain as well as educate.
Library and Archives Canada/C117373

To that end, the tithes of the church were guaranteed, the seigneurial system was legally recognized, and French civil law was reintroduced in the colony, although English criminal law would remain in force. The status of the colonial elite was enhanced by the decision to permit Roman Catholics to participate in colonial government. Under the Quebec Act, the colony was to be ruled with the advice of an appointed council rather than an elected assembly. Canadians could be appointed to the council, but all councillors would serve at the pleasure of the governor. No rabble-rousing assembly like the ones that existed in the colonies of Massachusetts and Virginia would stir up problems for imperial authorities in Quebec.

This cartoon, which appeared in *London Magazine* in July 1774, is a satirical comment on the religious implications of the Quebec Act. With the devil looking on, British politicians and Anglican priests support a bill that lifts some of the restrictions on Roman Catholics in Britain's North American colony.
Library and Archives Canada/C38989

The Quebec Act also dramatically increased the size of the colony. Quebec's boundaries were extended southwest into the Ohio territory, eastward to include Labrador, and north to the borders of Rupert's Land. Here, too, strategic interests seem to have dominated the thinking of British authorities. What better way to forestall the greedy Anglo-American settlers eyeing the fertile lands of the Ohio frontier than to attach the region to the fur-trade interests of Montreal? If anyone could establish some semblance of order in the region, it was the Montreal traders.

Similarly, Quebec was the nearest administrative centre to Labrador and the northern fur-trade frontier. These areas were virtually empty of permanent European settlement, and Britain hoped to keep them that way. By Palliser's Act of 1775, Newfoundland was barred to settlement and North American-based fishing interests. Not surprisingly, many Anglo-Americans saw both the Quebec Act and Palliser's Act as deliberate attempts on the part of the mother country to restrict their access to the rich resources of the North American continent. The Ohio Valley was particularly contentious. For many colonists, it represented the next agricultural frontier. Important colonial leaders had speculated in the lands in the region, no one more so than Virginian plantation owner and politician George Washington, who would later become the first president of the United States of America.

By 1774, the British had virtually re-established the old regime in Quebec. Their reasons for doing so were practical. With another war in North America a virtual certainty, it was important to ensure the security of this strategically located and potentially rebellious colony. Secret instructions to Carleton indicated that, in the long run, the British authorities hoped to whittle away the legal and clerical concessions of the Quebec Act, but in the meantime those concessions would serve to placate the Canadian elite.

There is little doubt that the seigneurs and clerical leaders were pleased by the restoration of their traditional privileges, but other segments of Quebec society were less enthusiastic. Although delighted with the extension of the boundaries of their fur-trade empire, the Protestant merchants resented the loss of their democratic right to an elected assembly they could dominate. The habitants also had mixed feelings about an act that left them more beholden than ever before to the seigneurs and clergy. Would not an elected assembly work for the ordinary people in a colony where there were fewer than 1000 British immigrants and a Canadian elite that survived only through the intervention of the conqueror?

ANGLICIZING NOVA SCOTIA

British authorities were more open to developing elected institutions in Nova Scotia. Following the capture of Louisbourg in 1758, they forced a reluctant Governor Lawrence to call an elected assembly and issue a proclamation inviting prospective immigrants to the frontier colony. A second proclamation in 1759 outlined the rights guaranteed in the new Nova Scotia: two elected assembly members for each settled township, a judicial system like the one in New England, and freedom of religion for Protestant dissenters.

With these matters seemingly settled, over 8000 New Englanders responded to Lawrence's call. Known as "Planters," the old English term for settlers, they created a new New England in the western portions of the old colony of Nova Scotia. Fishing families from Massachusetts moved into the sheltered bays and harbours of Nova Scotia's south shore; farming families from Connecticut, Rhode Island, and Massachusetts filled up the townships located in the Annapolis Valley and around the Isthmus of Chignecto. James Simonds, James White, and William Hazen, New England merchants associated with Joshua Mauger, established trading operations near the mouth of the St John River in what is now New Brunswick. A group of farmers from Essex County, Massachusetts, squatted further up the river on land that was occupied by Acadians and Maliseet. Helped by Joshua Mauger's intervention, the New Englanders received title to the land and promptly named their settlement Maugerville in honour of their champion.

By the end of the 1760s, the New England migration had slowed to a trickle. Land speculation contributed to the decline: in one 17-day period in 1765, some 1.2 million hectares of land had been granted, leaving little arable land for potential settlers. The opening of the western territories in 1768 also pulled New England settlement in a westerly rather than a northerly direction. By that time, well over half the 14 000 people in Nova Scotia could trace their origins to New England. With their dissenting religious views, penchant for trading, and fierce individualism, the Planters brought a distinctly "Yankee" culture to the shores of Nova Scotia.

MORE TO THE STORY

Elizabeth and Edmund Doane

Elizabeth and Edmund Doane were enterprising New England Planters who settled in Barrington, Nova Scotia. According to family tradition, the Doanes dismantled their two-storey house in the Cape Cod community of Eastham and loaded it, together with their seven children, livestock, and provisions, on a boat for the journey to Nova Scotia. Bad weather and shipwreck dogged their journey northward in the fall of 1761, but they finally reached Barrington the following spring.

In addition to running their own farm, they kept a shop that held accounts for 50 of the community's families. Elizabeth Doane also served as doctor and midwife for her neighbours. When the Doanes began to talk of returning to New England because of hard times in the pioneer community, their neighbours encouraged them to stay by suggesting that Elizabeth Doane submit a petition for a land grant in her own name. Her petition, dated 13 May 1770, stated: "Elizabeth Done Being Destitute of Accommdation of Land to Set a House upon But am Nevertheless free and willing to Exert my facilities and Skil [in physic and surgery and midwifery] and having a Love for the People . . . Request the favour of . . . a Small tract of Land." Thirty-eight proprietors of the Township of Barrington—all men—signed her petition, and her grant was approved. Elizabeth Doane continued to provide medical care for her Barrington neighbours for many years, and when she became too old to make house calls by foot, two men carried her in a basket suspended by a pole across their shoulders. She died in 1798 at the age of 82.[8]

As settlers took over much of the land in the Maritimes, the Mi'kmaq, whose craft and hunting skills are showcased in this early nineteenth-century drawing, lost access to much of their land.
National Gallery of Canada/6663

The New Englanders were only the largest of several immigrant groups to locate in Nova Scotia in the two decades following the expulsion of the Acadians. Indeed, the Acadians themselves became one of the largest groups of "planters" in their former homeland—though not in the areas that they had previously inhabited. In 1764, the British agreed to permit the Acadians to stay in Nova Scotia on condition that they take an oath of allegiance. This decision served as a signal for those in hiding to lay claim to land and for those in exile to return to their beloved "Acadie."

By 1775 Nova Scotia had been transformed into a colony of pioneer settlements. In addition to New Englanders and Acadians, its rich cultural mosaic included German- and French-speaking Protestants from continental Europe, many of them based in Lunenburg; fish merchants and their employees from the Channel Islands located in areas of the Gaspé and Cape Breton; Yorkshire English who took up land in the Chignecto region; Irish, both Protestant and Roman Catholic, who settled in several locations throughout the colony; and, with the arrival of the *Hector* in Pictou harbour in 1773, the first of successive waves of Scottish immigration.

St John's Island

Scots made up a significant portion of the British pioneers on St John's Island. Of great interest to land speculators once it was confirmed as a British possession in 1763, the island was surveyed into 67 townships by Captain Samuel Holland in 1764. Three years later, in one of the most spectacular "lotteries" in Canadian history, the British government gave 64 of the lots to favourites of the king and court in London. According to the conditions of the grants, the proprietors were required to bring out Protestant settlers, improve their properties, and sustain early colonial administration through the payment of land taxes, known as quitrent.

As in New France, there was a twofold purpose in resorting to this method of planting colonies. One was to maintain a conservative social structure that placed power and wealth in the hands of a colonial elite. The other consideration was to have private initiative bear the cost of colonial settlement. Theoretically there was little risk involved in delegating authority in this way. If the proprietors failed to fulfil the conditions of their grants, their titles could be escheated, or cancelled, and the ownership of the land would revert to the Crown.

Unfortunately for St John's Island, the proprietors did not fulfil the conditions of their grants, nor did the normal processes of escheat prevail. The proprietors used their influence to have a separate administration for the island proclaimed in 1769. In 1770, Governor Walter Patterson arrived in the colonial capital, named Charlottetown in honour of the queen, and by 1773 the first assembly was elected. Thereafter any policy for land reform had to be approved by the colonial legislature as well as by British authorities. Since proprietorial interests had strong supporters both on the island and in Britain, movements to improve the land system were easily frustrated. The lottery of 1767 thus marked the beginning of the great "land question" that would bedevil Island society until the proprietorial system was abolished in the 1870s.

In their initial flush of enthusiasm, several proprietors made serious efforts to fulfil their settlement obligations. Many of the proprietors were Scots, who recognized that conditions in the Highlands—a disintegrating clan structure, overcrowding on meager tenant properties, and rising rents—made emigration an attractive option. The first Scottish settlers, recruited by Captain Robert Stewart for Lot 18, arrived on the *Annabella* in 1770. Tenants from Ulster were tempted by what seemed like reasonable terms for leasing land, and a colony of London Quakers established a base at Elizabethtown. In the early years of settlement, lack of provisions, social conflict, and crop failures—plagues of mice were a recurring menace—threatened survival. Many who could afford to do so left their farms for better opportunities elsewhere. Nevertheless, St John's Island had nearly 1500 residents by 1775 and, in the words of historian J.M. Bumsted, "appeared to be teetering on the brink of success."[9]

NEWFOUNDLAND AND LABRADOR

Notwithstanding official policy discouraging settlement, Newfoundland in the eighteenth century drew a steady stream of immigrants from the homeports of the British fleet and the south coast of Ireland where crews were recruited for the fishing season. The advantages of wintering in Newfoundland were obvious to the fishermen. They could get a head start on the fishery in the spring, protect their shore bases from interlopers, and live without tax or trouble on a sheltered patch of the coastline. By 1775, over 12 000 people called themselves "Newfoundlanders," a term apparently used as early as the 1760s.

In the eighteenth century, the shore-based fishery grew steadily, while the catch of the migratory fleet declined. Recognizing the obvious, British merchants sent an increasing number of "sack ships"—the large ocean carriers of the eighteenth century—to purchase the product of the resident fisheries for their European markets. By the 1750s, New Englanders were competing with British merchants in supplying Newfoundlanders with manufactured goods, provisions, and rum in return for fish, which they sold in

Esquimaux Lady, by John Russell. In the mid-1700s, Mikak, an Inuit woman, and her son were kidnapped and taken to England by British marines intent on rounding up a group of Natives suspected of plundering a whaling station. After she returned home, Mikak served as a guide to the first Moravian missionaries when they arrived at Nain in 1770.
Institut und Sammlung für Völkerkunde der Universität Göttingen

the West Indies. This activity contravened the British navigation acts that restricted colonial trade to British vessels, but as long as the acts were not enforced in Newfoundland waters, New England and foreign vessels could trade with impunity.

Following the Seven Years' War, Britain took steps to establish tighter control over the Newfoundland fishery. In 1764, laws were passed giving British authorities more power to arrest smugglers. A customs house was built at St John's to collect duties on imports, followed by a Court of Vice-Admiralty to handle disputes relating to trade. Between 1762 and 1770, Captain James Cook and his successor Michael Lane carried out a survey of Newfoundland, providing the British with a more accurate picture of the colony over which they officially had control.

The imperial thrust was epitomized in the person of Captain Hugh Palliser, who became governor of Newfoundland in 1764. He expelled as many as 5000 fugitives during his four-year tenure, challenged the rights of "owners" of shoreline property, and, in his well-meaning efforts to protect Native people, even seized the bases of the Labrador seal fishermen. In the so-called Palliser's Act of 1775, the British government reaffirmed its commitment to discourage settlement in Newfoundland and increase the competitive edge of the British-based fishing fleet. Like many of Britain's imperial policies in this period, Palliser's Act flew in the face of colonial reality and only consolidated the growing resentment within the older British North American possessions.

Labrador, dominated by a population of Inuit and Innu, also opened to outside influences following the Seven Years' War. In 1770 George Cartwright built a fur-trading and fishing base at Cape Charles and later moved to Sandwich Bay. He was followed by other British-based companies, but it was not until 1834 that the Hudson's Bay Company built its first trading post at Rigolet. Until that time, Moravian missionaries of the United Brethren, a highly disciplined Protestant sect, were the major European presence in Labrador. The first of several Moravian missions in Labrador was founded at Nain in 1770–71. The Moravians established schools, taught practical skills, provided medical services, and kept close control over the trade of the region.

THE AMERICAN REVOLUTION

While the British government wrestled with administrative issues relating to the colonies that had been ceded by France in 1713 and 1763, the 13 colonies further south along the Atlantic seaboard were beginning to challenge imperial authority. There, the celebrations that marked the victory against France and Spain in 1763 soon gave way to howls of protest as the British government introduced measures to pay off its war debt and recover the costs of maintaining a North American empire that now stretched from Hudson Bay to Florida.

The Proclamation of 1763 restricting settlement and trade in the Native territory west of the Appalachians became an early cause for grievance in the colonies. In short order it was followed by three even more contentious pieces of legislation: the Sugar Act (1764) imposing tariffs on a wide range of luxury goods such as sugar, coffee, and wines imported into the American colonies; the Stamp Act (1765) placing an excise tax on printed documents such as newspapers, legal documents, licences, and even playing cards; and the Quartering Act (1765) requiring colonial legislatures to house and feed British troops sent to North America.

Colonial Americans quickly organized resistance against what they claimed was a conspiracy to subvert the liberties of all British subjects. In the summer of 1765, a paramilitary group calling themselves the Sons of Liberty began using violence to intimidate colonial officials trying to enforce the odious regulations. In October, delegates attended an intercolonial Stamp Act Congress in New York where they passed a series of resolutions condemning the British policy of taxing people without their consent. Although the Stamp Act was eventually withdrawn, the British government continued to pass legislation imposing taxes on the colonies. Tensions between British soldiers and colonial Americans reached a fever pitch in March 1770 when British troops fired into a Boston mob killing five people.

Three years later, another action in Boston against taxation, this time on imported tea, precipitated the final round of conflict leading to war. On 16 December 1773, Patriots disguised as Mohawks boarded three East India ships laden with tea and dumped their cargo into Boston harbour. The British government responded with a series of measures collectively known as the Coercive Acts and dubbed the Intolerable Acts by the aggrieved colonists. The legislation closed the port of Boston, suspended the Massachusetts legislature, and placed the colony under military rule. In May, General Thomas Gage arrived in Boston to replace civilian governor Thomas Hutchinson.

British policy as expressed in the Quebec Act and Palliser's Act was included among the grievances cited by the Americans against their mother country. By annexing the Ohio country to Quebec, granting privileges to Roman Catholics, and restricting access to the Newfoundland fisheries, British authorities had simply gone too far.

In September 1774, delegates from 12 colonies—all except for Newfoundland, St John's Island, Nova Scotia, Quebec, and Georgia—met in Philadelphia to coordinate a response to Britain's arbitrary colonial policy. The First Continental Congress demanded the repeal of the Coercive Acts. When Britain refused to back down, the colonial militia was placed on alert. British troops dispatched to capture a weapons depot at Concord in April 1775 confronted the Patriot militia at Lexington. A second military engagement took place at Bunker Hill on 17 June. As Massachusetts erupted in bloody violence, a Second Continental Congress voted to raise an army under George Washington to defend "American liberty." After driving the British out of Boston, they planned to march on Quebec.

QUEBEC IN QUESTION

This decision to invade Quebec was based on a number of assumptions. There was every reason to expect that the Canadians would be eager to throw off the yoke of their recent conquerors, and a few of the English-speaking merchants were sympathetic to the republican cause. If spontaneous uprisings erupted in support of the invading armies, all to the good. Nova Scotia was also home to a sympathetic population, fully half of New England origin, but the colony was impossible to attack without supporting seapower. The British forces in Quebec, however, might succumb during a winter siege.

In September 1775, an army of 2000 men led by Richard Montgomery moved down the Lake Champlain-Richelieu River route toward Montreal. The plan was to take Montreal and proceed to Quebec, where they would meet another army under Benedict Arnold, which was marching overland along the Kennebec and Chaudière Rivers. Because Carleton had sent half of his garrison to assist General Gage in Boston, he was left with only 600 regulars for the defence of his colony. The fate of Quebec hung on the reaction of the colonists to the invading forces.

To Carleton's dismay, Montgomery's troops met considerable support as they moved down the well-worn route along Lake Champlain and the Richelieu River toward Montreal. The citizens of the city capit-

ulated without a fight, and Carleton himself narrowly escaped capture as he fled to Quebec. In Quebec, Carleton found the people more disposed to repel the invading forces. Their popularity had quickly dwindled when they commandeered supplies without compensation and desecrated Roman Catholic shrines and churches. By the time winter had set in, few Canadiens saw the Anglo-Americans as their liberators.

Like Wolfe before him, Montgomery had difficulty breaching the natural defences that surrounded Quebec. A desperate attack launched on the evening of 31 December failed. Montgomery was killed during

Prior to the invasion, the Americans flooded Quebec with propaganda to persuade Canadians to join their democratic cause. It is difficult to assess what impact their call to arms had on the common people. What was clear is that one of the issues fuelling the war was democratic idealism, which contrasted sharply with the monarchical traditions of European nations.
Library and Archives Canada/C111468

the encounter and Arnold was wounded. In May 1776, the Americans beat a hasty retreat when British ships arrived bearing 10 000 troops. The large military force also guaranteed the good behaviour of the civilian population. Carleton's successor, Sir Frederick Haldimand, handed out stiff sentences to those who resisted the hated military corvée and kept a close watch on anyone suspected of disloyalty.

During the nine-month occupation by the Americans, Carleton found little to criticize about the behaviour of the seigneurs and clerical officials. They had enthusiastically supported his efforts to raise a colonial militia to save the colony from republicanism. In contrast, the habitants, who were experiencing the second war on their native soil in two decades, were reluctant to fight. Both sides in the conflict were led by English-speaking Protestants whose goals seemed to have little relevance to the lives of ordinary people. While a few habitants voluntarily participated in the fighting on both sides, most of them waited out the conflict, selling supplies to those who offered hard cash, and preserving their neutrality as long as possible.

The British element in the colony was no more reliable than the habitants. Some of the merchants acted as informers for Montgomery. As the war dragged on, fur traders such as Peter Pond found it a convenient time to make a trip into the interior to discover new customers and communication routes. Pond established a post on Lake Athabasca in 1778 at the behest of the Chipewyan, who were particularly aggressive in courting trading partners. The Montreal traders were soon tapping the furs along the Peace and Mackenzie rivers as well.

While the Natives in the Northwest were spared involvement in the war, others were not so fortunate. Like the Canadians, the Iroquois had armies marching across their territories and, again like the Canadians, they were divided about what to do. Joseph Brant and his Mohawk followers and some Seneca, as well as the Iroquois of the Caughnawaga and St Regis reserves, fought with the British. The Oneida and Tuscarora, perhaps influenced by their ties with Congregational ministers, leaned toward the Americans. The Onondaga and Cayuga remained neutral until 1779, when American troops invaded their territory. This provoked them into retaliatory raids on American set-

tlements. With their homelands at stake, the Natives proved to be among Britain's most effective combatants, although they were fighting for themselves, not for any European power.

Carleton's failure to pursue the retreating militiamen meant that the Americans lived to fight another day. On 4 July 1776, the Thirteen Colonies declared independence from Britain. When Britain's forces were defeated in the battle of Saratoga in 1777, its European enemies could not resist the chance to strike a mortal blow. France joined the fray in 1778, followed by Spain the next year. With France as an ally of the Americans, another invasion of Quebec was planned, but because neither side could agree on who should rule the colony if it were captured, Quebec was spared a second invasion.

THE WAR IN THE ATLANTIC REGION

Like Quebecers, people in the Atlantic region were forced to choose sides. Newfoundland's situation was perhaps the most clear-cut. Its fisheries were part of the great triangular trade dominated by Great Britain. It would have been economic suicide to cut the ties that bound that trade together. Even if Newfoundlanders had chosen to take the side of the Thirteen Colonies, they would have had difficulty doing so in any formal way. There were no local institutions on the island that could respond to an invitation from the Continental Congress to join in the crusade for liberty.

Halifax was similarly a creation of the imperial system, and the people there considered British soldiers an economic boon rather than a social irritant. In the outlying regions of the colony, there was much sympathy for the rebel position but little enthusiasm for battle. A religious revival led by Henry Alline in the townships settled by New England Planters attracted as much, if not more, attention as the secular battles raging around them. On St John's Island, the inhabitants were too busy putting down roots to participate in a war for independence.

Still, for most people in the Atlantic region, the issues fuelling the conflict were sharply drawn. To take up with the wrong side could result in the loss of property, position, and even life itself. Seizure of rebel

Joseph and Molly Brant

Mary Brant—generally known as Molly—and her brother Joseph were members of a powerful Mohawk family who allied themselves with the British during the Seven Years' War. In 1758, as a young man of 15, Joseph Brant took part in Abercrombie's campaign to invade Canada. He subsequently joined Indian superintendent Sir William Johnson in the capture of Niagara in 1759 and participated in the siege of Montreal the following year. It was around this time that Molly Brant attracted Johnson's attention. Their first child was born in 1759, and before Johnson's death in 1774 they had seven more children who survived infancy. Molly Brant presided over Johnson's household in the Mohawk Valley and proved a valuable partner in his fur-trade and diplomatic activities. In his will Johnson left his estate to his white son, John, and gave Molly Brant a good portion of land, a black female slave, and £200. With her legacy she opened a store, which sold rum and other trade items to her people.

When the American Revolutionary War broke out, Joseph and Molly Brant allied themselves with the British. Joseph Brant led a force of Native and white soldiers in frontier battles, which included campaigns against the Oneida and Tuscarora, who had sided with the United States. Like white Americans, the Six Nations experienced the American Revolution as a civil war. Meanwhile, Molly Brant helped to provision the Loyalist forces and kept them informed about rebel activities. In 1777, the victorious Oneida took revenge on the Mohawk. Molly's home was looted and she took refuge at Onondaga (near Syracuse, New York) and later at Niagara. As head of the Six Nations matrons, she exercised her considerable influence to prevent the Mohawk from wavering in their support of the British. During the darkest days of the war, she went to Carleton Island, New York, to convince her discouraged people there to continue the fight. According to Alexander Fraser, the commander in the region, Molly Brant was instrumental in keeping the warriors in line. Their "uncommonly good behaviour is in great measure to be ascribed to Miss Molly Brants Influence over them, which is far superior to that of all their Chiefs put together," he concluded.

When the war ended, Molly Brant moved to Kingston, where Governor Haldimand had a house built for her use. She was also awarded an annual pension of £100, the highest paid to an Aboriginal ally. Joseph Brant, embittered by Britain's decision to relinquish sovereignty over all the territory east of the Mississippi to the Americans, tried in vain to forge a confederacy that would, by war or diplomacy, produce a better deal for his people.[10]

***Portrait of Joseph Brant*, by George Romney, painted during Brant's visit to Britain in 1776.**
National Gallery of Canada/8005

property by British soldiers or attacks by New England privateers could wipe out a generation of hard-earned subsistence. Few of the pioneer colonists could risk such a fate, and as a result behaved cautiously.

Raids by New England privateers were a feature of the war for most people living in the seabound Atlantic colonies. In November 1775, privateers landed in Charlottetown, plundering homes, seizing provisions, and carrying away the colony's leading officials, including the acting governor, Phillips Callbeck. Most raids were similarly selective, leaving all but targeted victims unmolested, but such activities did little to endear pioneer settlers to the revolutionary cause. Virtually every outpost settlement from Yarmouth Township to Labrador was visited by privateers, an indication that republican forces perceived the northern colonies as an extension of the British frontier of influence in North America rather than as allies in the cause.

The presence of a British fleet in the North Atlantic during much of the war discouraged George Washington from any serious thought of invading the region. There was a brief flurry of rebel activity in the fall of 1776 when Jonathan Eddy, a member of the Nova Scotia assembly for Cumberland, and John Allan, a Scottish-born resident in the area, led a force of nearly 180 men against the British garrison at Fort Cumberland (formerly Fort Beauséjour). Eddy's ranks included 19 Natives from the St John River area and about 40 Acadians prepared to use the occasion to strike at their British conquerors. The rest were mostly New England-born settlers. While the attack was easily repulsed by soldiers sent from Halifax, the tension among settlers in the area around Fort Cumberland resulted in bloodshed, looting, and litigation that continued for over a decade.

After the defeat of British forces at Saratoga in 1777, the scene of fighting moved to the middle and southern American colonies. Thereafter the North Atlantic colonies became even more British in orientation. The increased military presence in colonial capitals, the profit to be gained by supplying British troops, and the influx of Loyalists fleeing from rebel-held strongholds sealed the fate of Nova Scotia and St John's Island.

In 1781 the British army under Lord Cornwallis suffered a crushing defeat at Yorktown, Virginia. Two years later in another treaty negotiated in Paris, the British agreed to recognize the independence of the United States, a decision that would have profound

A HISTORIOGRAPHICAL DEBATE

Culture and Conquest

Historians have little difficulty agreeing upon the immediate impact of the conquest on the Canadians. As stated most bluntly by Susan Mann Trofimenkoff, "Conquest is like rape."[11] Scholars are less likely to agree upon the long-term impact of such a traumatic event.[12] As with most historical debates, events in the present very often shape the way historians view this critical moment in Quebec's history. There were other conquests in Canadian history—for instance, that of Acadia in 1710-13 and the centuries-long subordination of the First Nations—but the conquest of Quebec has generated the most comment because many historians see it as a causal factor in the problems facing the Québécois in the nineteenth and twentieth centuries.

Early French-Canadian historians were inclined to see the conquest as a tragedy that blunted the colony's cultural and institutional development. Conservative in their political philosophy, they argued that New France was devastated when the leading citizens departed for France following the conquest and French political structures were replaced by "barbaric" British institutions. In the words of one of French Canada's first historians, François-Xavier Garneau, "The evils they had previously endured seemed light to them compared to the sufferings and humiliations which were in preparation, they feared, for them and their posterity."[13]

A contrasting view, popular among nineteenth-century clerics, saw the hand of God in a conquest that spared Quebec the evils—in particular the liberalism and atheism—of the French Revolution. Only a few liberal French-Canadian historians, such as Benjamin Sulte, saw virtue in the conquest because Britain replaced absolute rule with constitutional government. This view had been typically argued by anglophone historians, most notably Francis Parkman, who maintained, "A happier calamity never befell a people than the conquest of Canada by British arms."[14] For Parkman, the most important theme in history was the broadening of liberty as represented in the Protestant Reformation, representative institutions, and laissez-faire economic policies. New France, with its Roman Catholic hierarchy, authoritarian political institutions, and mercantile economy, clearly had, in his view, little to offer to the progress of Western civilization.

As the Industrial Revolution began drawing more and more Canadiens into the ranks of the urban working class, conservative historians in Quebec gradually made the habitant farmer the hero of New France. It was in the countryside that the seeds of French-Canadian nationalism were well and truly planted, they argued, and where Christian virtues remained uncorrupted. Abbé Lionel Groulx, writing in the interwar years, even claimed that the French Canadians were a superior race, purified by the fires of the conquest and guided throughout by the steady influence of the Roman Catholic Church. In Groulx's estimation, the Québécois were "perhaps the purest race on the whole continent," a characteristic not easy to verify by demographic evidence, but one that clearly meant much to him.[15]

Quebec entered a period of rapid social and economic transformation following the Second World War; *la survivance* in the countryside was no longer enough, and the interpretations of the conservative school were squarely challenged. Maurice Séguin, an influential historian at the Université de Montréal, called upon Canadiens to lift themselves from the paralyzing hold of the "agrarian retreat." For Séguin, Canada under the *ancien régime* was "colonization in the full sense of the term," while the conquest was a "catastrophe" forcing the Canadiens back on an ever-declining agricultural economy. "The solution to Quebec's problems," he maintained, "would be a return to the kind of integral colonization we had before 1760." His call to action inspired many of the students who attended his classes: "Let us take the land, but also the forest, the mines, the watercourses, the fisheries; in a word; all the resources of our country, their processing and their trade, if we want to save our nationality by ensuring its unrestricted economic life."[16]

Two of Séguin's colleagues at the Université de Montréal, Guy Frégault and Michel Brunet, were the most articulate advocates of what became known as the "Montreal School." Frégault concluded that New France was, like all colonies, dependent upon imperial investment, but its evolution was "normal" within the context of North American colonial development. The Canadian community in 1763, however, was "conquered, impoverished, socially decapitated, and politically in bonds," while "French colonization, more vital than ever, was conclusively halted."[17]

Michel Brunet went even further. Drawing directly upon Marxist theory, which held that the bourgeoisie was the dynamic class in capitalist society, he explored the impact of the conquest on the Canadian middle class in the 30 years following the conquest. He concluded that French-Canadian business people were unable to hold their own against their English competitors. For Brunet, the excessive emphasis on agriculture, the domination of social and intellectual life by the Roman Catholic Church, and the distrust of democracy all stemmed from the "decapitation" of the Canadian society in 1763.[18]

The Montreal School's position reflected contemporary concerns over the English domination of the Quebec economy. By the 1960s, they were politically linked with the *nationalistes* who were seeking independence for Quebec. Historians at Université Laval in Quebec City, who were branded as "federalists" for their historical interpretations, challenged the views put forward by the Montrealers. Jean Hamelin led the way, calling into question the notion that there was a dynamic middle class in pre-conquest New France. "The essential fact on this subject that emerges from the intendants' correspondence," he maintained in 1960, "is the poverty of merchants and traders as a group throughout the period of French rule." For Hamelin, "The absence in 1800 of a vigorous French-Canadian bourgeoisie . . . emerges not as a result of the Conquest but as the culmination of the French regime."[19]

Hamelin's views were echoed by Fernand Ouellet, who accepted the finding that there was a weak middle class in the pre-conquest period. Unlike Hamelin, however, Ouellet concluded that this fact was irrelevant to the economic condition of French Canadians in the post-conquest period. For Ouellet, the profound changes wrought by the Industrial Revolution were reasons enough for the economic underdevelopment that characterized Quebec in the nineteenth and twentieth centuries. In recent years, most historians have followed Ouellet's lead in moving away from overly deterministic interpretations of the conquest. While welcoming the rich historical evidence marshalled for the debate, they resist seeing it as having value except in revealing more about life as it was lived in the eighteenth century.

implications for what was left of "British" North America. Although the victorious Americans suggested that the British might want to withdraw completely from North America, they never seriously considered such a policy. The boundary was set at the St Croix River in the east, vague highlands along the Quebec border to the 45th parallel, and then a line running along the St Lawrence and through the middle of the Great Lakes. Because the maps used during the negotiations were faulty, it would take more than half a century of negotiation to determine the exact border between the two emerging nations.

CONCLUSION

Between 1763 and 1775, the British tried to impose order on their North American colonies but their efforts ended in failure. They lost 13 of their most valued colonies and were left with only the possessions that they had acquired from France by treaties signed in 1713 and 1763. There is no easy answer as to why

Quebec, Newfoundland, Nova Scotia, and St John's Island failed to become part of the new United States of America. A series of developments—the failure of an American invasion of Quebec in 1775–76 and the attack on Fort Cumberland in Nova Scotia in 1776; the presence of British troops and naval power; and the caution of the people, many of whom had personal experience of the Seven Years' War—seems to have combined to keep them within the British sphere of influence.

As we will see in the next chapter, the impact of the American Revolutionary War was as great on the North American colonies that remained in the British Empire as it was on those who joined the new United States of America. A flood of immigrants, a reorganized colonial administration, and a new boundary line followed in the wake of the war. In one crucial decade, the British Empire in North America was reduced to a shadow of its former self, and the foundations of a second transcontinental nation on the North American continent were tentatively laid.

NOTES

1 W.J. Eccles, *The Ordeal of New France* (Montreal: Canadian Broadcasting Service, 1966), 142.

2 Richard White, *The Middle Ground: Indians, Empires, and Republics of the Great Lakes Region, 1650–1791* (Cambridge: Cambridge University Press, 1991), 313.

3 L.S.F. Upton, *Micmacs and Colonists: Indian-White Relations in the Maritimes, 1713–1867* (Vancouver: UBC Press, 1979), 58.

4 G.P. Gould and A.J. Semple, eds., *Our Land: The Maritimes* (Fredericton: Sainte Annes Point Press, 1980), 177.

5 White, 288.

6 Cited in Eccles, 139.

7 Governor James Murray to the Lords of Trade, 29 October 1764, cited in *Documents Relating to the Constitutional History of Canada, 1759–1791*, part 1, ed. A. Shortt and A.G. Doughty (Ottawa, 1918), 231.

8 Phyllis Blakeley, "And Having a Love for the People," *Nova Scotia Historical Quarterly* 5, 2 (June 1975): 172–73.

9 J.M. Bumsted, *Land, Settlement, and Politics on Eighteenth-Century Prince Edward Island* (Montreal: McGill-Queen's University Press, 1987), 64.

10 See Barbara Graymont, "Koñwatsiãtsiaiéñni," in *Dictionary of Canadian Biography*, vol. 4, *1771 to 1800* (Toronto: University of Toronto Press, 1979), 416–18; and Barbara Graymont, "Thayendanegea," in *Dictionary of Canadian Biography*, vol. 5, *1801 to 1820* (Toronto: University of Toronto Press, 1983), 803–12.

11 Susan Mann Trofimenkoff, *The Dream of Nation: A Social and Intellectual History of Quebec* (Toronto: Gage, 1982), 31.

12 For a summary of the debate, see Dale Miquelon, ed., *Society and Conquest: The Debate on the Bourgeoisie and Social Change in French Canada, 1700–1850* (Toronto: Copp Clark Pitman, 1977); "The Conquest of 1760: Were Its Consequences Traumatic?" in *Emerging Identities: Selected Problems and Interpretations in Canadian History*, ed. Paul Bennett and Cornelius Jaenen (Scarborough, ON: Prentice-Hall, 1986), 76–105; and Serge Gagnon, *Quebec and Its Historians: The Twentieth Century* (Montreal: Harvest House, 1985), 53–89.

13 François-Xavier Garneau, *History of Canada, from the Time of Its Discovery till the Union Year (1840–1841)*, vol. 2, trans. Andrew Bell (Montreal: n.p., 1860), 84–86.

14 Francis Parkman, *The Old Regime in Canada*, vol. 2 (Toronto: n.p., 1899), 205.

15 Lionel Groulx, *Lendemains de conquête* (Montreal: n.p., 1920), 234–35, cited in *Emerging Identities*, ed. Bennett and Jaenen, 90.

16 Maurice Séguin, "La Conquête et la vie économique des Canadiens," *Action nationale* 28 (1947), cited in Miquelon, *Society and Conquest*, 78.

17 Guy Frégault, "La colonisation du Canada au XVIIe siècle," *Cahiers de l'Académie canadienne-française* 2 (1957): 53–81.

18 Michel Brunet, *La Présence Anglaise et les Canadiens* (Montreal: Beauchemin, 1958).

19 Jean Hamelin, *Économie et société en Nouvelle-France* (Quebec: n.p., 1960), cited in Miquelon, *Society and Conquest*, 105, 114.

Related Readings in This Series

From *Foundations: Readings in Pre-Confederation Canadian History*

Peter Moogk, "'The Apples Do Not Fall Far From the Tree': The Legacy of New France in Modern Canada," 178–92.

From Media Companion CD-ROM, Volume I

Royal Proclamation of 1763
James Murray
Letter from Governor Murray, 1764
Petition of French Subjects to the King, 1773

Selected Reading

On Quebec following the conquest, see A.L. Burt, *The Old Province of Quebec* (Ottawa: Carleton University Press, 1933; reprint 1968); Hilda Neatby, *Quebec: The Revolutionary Age, 1760–1791* (Toronto: McClelland and Stewart, 1966); Fernand Ouellet, *Social and Economic History of Quebec*, trans. Robert Mandron (Toronto: Gage, 1980); Allan Greer, *Peasant, Lord and Merchant: Rural Society in Three Quebec Parishes, 1740–1840* (Toronto: University of Toronto Press, 1985); Philip Lawson, *The Imperial Challenge: Quebec and Britain in the Age of the American Revolution* (Montreal: McGill-Queen's University Press, 1989); Roch Legault, *Une élite en déroute: Les militaires canadiens après la Conquête* (Outrement: Athéna, 2002); and José Iguartua, "A Change in Climate: The Conquest and the Marchands of Montreal," *Canadian Historical Association Historical Papers* (1974): 115–43. Debates surrounding the conquest are usefully summarized and discussed in Cameron Nish, ed., *The French Canadians, 1759–1766: Conquered? Half Conquered? Liberated?* (Toronto: Copp Clark Pitman, 1966) and Dale Miquelon, ed., *Society and Conquest: The Debate on the Bourgeoisie and Social Change in French Canada, 1700–1850* (Toronto: Copp Clark Pitman, 1977).

Native issues are discussed in the books by Dickason, Miller, Ray, Reid, Upton, and Wright, cited earlier, as well as Howard H. Peckham, *Pontiac and the Indian Uprising* (Chicago: Russell, 1971); Robert J. Surtees, "Canadian Indian Treaties," in *Handbook of North American Indians 4: History of Indian-White Relations*, ed. Wilcomb Washburn (Washington, DC: Smithsonian Institution, 1988); and William C. Wicken,

Mi'kmaq Treaties on Trial: History, Land and Donald Marshall Junior (Toronto: University of Toronto Press, 2002).

Overviews of settlement in British North America in the eighteenth century can be found in R. Cole Harris and Geoffrey J. Matthews, *Historical Atlas of Canada*, vol. 1, *From the Beginning to 1800* (Toronto: University of Toronto Press, 1987) and R. Cole Harris and John Warkentin, *Canada before Confederation* (Toronto: Oxford University Press, 1974). For the larger context, see J.B. Brebner, *The North Atlantic Triangle* (Ottawa: Carleton University Press, 1968); John J. McCusker and Russell R. Menard, *The Economy of British North America, 1600 to 1798* (Chapel Hill, NC: Duke University Press, 1985); D.W. Meinig, *The Shaping of America: Atlantic America, 1492–1800* (New Haven, CT: Yale University Press, 1986); and Bernard Bailyn, *Voyagers to the West: A Passage in the Peopling of America on the Eve of the Revolution* (New York: Knopf, 1986).

Developments in the Atlantic region are covered in relevant chapters of Phillip A. Buckner and John G. Reid, eds., *The Atlantic Region to Confederation: A History* (Toronto: University of Toronto Press, 1994); W.S. MacNutt, *The Atlantic Provinces: The Emergence of Colonial Society, 1713–1857* (Toronto: McClelland and Stewart, 1965); and Margaret R. Conrad and James K. Hiller, *Atlantic Canada: A Region in the Making* (Toronto: Oxford University Press, 2001). Specialized studies include Andrew Hill Clark, *Three Centuries and the Island: A Historical Geography of Settlement and Agriculture in Prince Edward Island* (Toronto: University of Toronto Press, 1959); J.M. Bumsted, *Land, Settlement and*

Politics on Eighteenth-Century Prince Edward Island (Montreal: McGill-Queen's University Press, 1987); Jerry Bannister, *The Role of the Admirals: Law, Custom and Naval Government in Newfoundland, 1699–1832* (Toronto: Osgoode Society and University of Toronto Press, 2002); and Patrick O'Flaherty, *Old Newfoundland: A History to 1843* (St John's: Longbeach Press, 1999). The post-expulsion Acadian odyssey is described in Jean Daigle, ed., *Acadia of the Maritimes: Thematic Studies* (Moncton, NB: Chaire d'études acadiennes, Université de Moncton, 1995) as well as books cited in Chapter 9.

New England's influence on the Maritime region is explored in two classic volumes by J.B. Brebner: *New England's Outpost: Acadia before the Conquest of Canada* (New York: Columbia University Press, 1927) and *The Neutral Yankees of Nova Scotia* (New Haven, CT: Yale University Press, 1937). George A. Rawlyk, *Nova Scotia's Massachusetts: A Study of Massachusetts-Nova Scotia Relations, 1630–1784* (Montreal: McGill-Queen's University Press, 1973) also offers useful insights. Articles in *They Planted Well: New England Planters in Maritime Canada* (Fredericton: Acadiensis Press, 1988), *Making Adjustments: Change and Continuity in Planter Nova Scotia, 1759–1800* (Fredericton: Acadiensis Press, 1991), and *Intimate Relations: Family and Community in Planter Nova Scotia, 1759–1800* (Fredericton: Acadensis Press, 1995), all edited by Margaret Conrad, offer wide-ranging perspectives on this early wave of anglophone immigrants. The Yorkshire settlers are the subject of James D. Snowdon, *Footprints in the Marsh Mud: Politics and Land Settlement in the Township of Sackville, 1760–1800* (Sackville, NB: Tantramar Heritage Trust and R.P. Bell Library Maritime Literature Reprint Series, 2000). The Scots in the region are covered in Donald MacKay, *The People of the Hector* (Toronto: McGraw-Hill Ryerson, 1980) and J.M. Bumsted, *The People's Clearance: Highland Emigration to British North America, 1770–1815* (Winnipeg: University of

Manitoba Press, 1982). The German and French Protestants who were transported to Nova Scotia have received detailed treatment in Winthrop Bell, *The "Foreign Protestants" and the Settlement of Nova Scotia* (Toronto: University of Toronto Press, 1961), republished in 1991 by Acadiensis Press.

Useful surveys of the American Revolution include Edward Countryman, *The American Revolution* (New York: Hill and Wang, 1985); Robert Middlekauff, *The Glorious Cause* (New York: Oxford Universal Press, 1982) and E.S. Morgan, *The Birth of the Republic* (Chicago: University of Chicago Press, 1977). The American invasion of Canada is discussed in George F.G. Stanley, *Canada Invaded, 1775–1776* (Toronto: Hakkert, 1973); Robert McConnell Hatch, *Thrust for Canada: The American Attempt on Quebec in 1775–1776* (Boston: Houghton Mifflin, 1979); and Gustav Lanctot, *Canada and the American Revolution, 1774–1783* (London: Harrap, 1967). See also Barbara Graymont, *The Iroquois in the American Revolution* (Syracuse, NY: Syracuse University Press, 1972); Isabel Thompson Kelsay, *Joseph Brant, 1743–1807: Man of Two Worlds* (Syracuse, NY: Syracuse University Press, 1984); and Richard White, *The Middle Ground: Indians, Empires, and Republics in the Great Lakes Region, 1650–1815* (Cambridge: Cambridge University Press, 1991). The Maritimes during the American Revolution are the focus of George A. Rawlyk and Gordon Stewart, *A People Highly Favoured of God: The Nova Scotia Yankees and the American Revolution* (Hamdon, CT: Archon Books, 1972) and J.M. Bumsted, *Henry Alline* (Toronto: University of Toronto Press, 1971). The Eddy Rebellion of 1776 is well chronicled in Ernest Clarke, *The Siege of Fort Cumberland: An Episode in the American Revolution* (Montreal: McGill-Queen's University Press, 1995). Boundary disputes resulting from the war are discussed in Francis M. Carroll, *A Good and Wise Measure: The Struggle for the Canadian-American Border, 1783–1842* (Toronto: University of Toronto Press, 2001).

 ## WEBLINKS

TREATY OF PARIS (1763)

odur.let.rug.nl/~usa/D/1751-1775/7yearswar/paris.htm

This site offers an English translation of the text of the treaty.

THE QUEBEC ACT (1774)

www.solon.org/Constitutions/Canada/English/PreConfederation/qa_1774.html

This site provides the English text of Articles 1–18 of the Quebec Act.

"PLANTERS"

ace.acadiau.ca/history/plstcntr.htm

Sponsored by the Planter Studies Centre at Acadia University, this site provides information on the history of the New England residents who migrated to Nova Scotia between 1759 and 1774. Internal links lead to brief articles on Planter architecture and artifacts.

CHAPTER 11

Redefining British North America, 1783–1815

"[Our] fate seems now decreed, and we left to mourn out our days in wretchedness,—[no] other recourse . . . but to submit to the tyranny of exulting enemys, or settle a new country. I am one of the number, that gladly would embark for Nova Scotia, was it either prudent or proper, but I am told it will not do for me at present[.] What is to become of us, God only can tell. . . ."[1]

Timeline

1783	American Revolutionary War ends and Loyalists move to British North America
1784	New Brunswick and Cape Breton established as separate colonial jurisdictions
1789	French Revolution begins
1791	Constitutional Act creates the colonies of Upper and Lower Canada
1793	Upper Canada act against slavery
1793–1815	French Revolutionary and Napoleonic Wars
1796	Maroons transported to Nova Scotia
1799	St John's Island renamed Prince Edward Island
1805	Parti canadien established
1806	The newspaper Le Canadien founded
1809	Labrador placed under jurisdiction of Newfoundland
1812–14	War of 1812
1815	Black refugees arrive in the Maritimes
1817	Rush-Bagot Treaty
1818	Anglo-American Convention

In this letter to her cousin Benjamin Marston, written in April 1783, Sarah Winslow describes the uncertainty that she and other Loyalists faced at the end of the American Revolutionary War. The Winslow family had been well-established in the colony of Massachusetts but the war changed everything. After considering their options, the Winslows eventually moved to New Brunswick, a British colony that was created in 1784 to accommodate those who remained loyal to Great Britain.

When the American Revolutionary War ended, many of those who had supported the British cause were forced to flee. Branded as "Tories" or "Royalists" by the triumphant American patriots, at least 70 000 self-styled "Loyalists" left the United States to start their lives over again. Those who could afford to do so, about 2000, moved to England, and others found their way to Africa and the West Indies. The majority had little alternative but to locate in the closest British territories in North America. At least 35 000 moved to Nova Scotia and another 15 000 to Quebec. Although their suffering during the first years was genuine, they were luckier than many refugee peoples. They were given land, provisions, and temporary shelter; a few, among them the Winslows, eventually received compensation for their losses from the British government. Whatever their individual experiences, the

Loyalists represented a significant immigrant population to the remnants of "British" North America. Many of the refugees had a strong sense of political entitlement and played a major role in laying the foundations for a second transcontinental North American nation.

THE LOYALIST INFLUX

While historians often discuss the Loyalists as if they were a homogeneous group, they were as socially and culturally diverse as the society they came from. Many of the Loyalist grantees were soldiers disbanded from volunteer and regular regiments. Others were refugees who had burned their bridges behind them when they sided with the British; still others were opportunists attracted by the British promise of free land and provisions for three years in what was left of British North America. Over half of the Loyalists were women and children whose fortunes were dictated by family decisions to support the British cause. A number of widows whose husbands had served in the war were included in the land grants. Like most pioneer women, Loyalist women were forced to adjust to the circumstances thrust upon them and raise their families in conditions not of their choosing.

A disproportionate number of the Nova Scotia Loyalists came from urban centres, such as Boston, New York, and Charleston, where British armies had been stationed at various times during the war. Unsuited to the hardships of pioneer life, they were tempted to sell their land and ship out. Port Roseway, renamed Shelburne, in Nova Scotia, was perhaps the most extreme example of Loyalist mobility. Its population of nearly 10 000 in 1783 had dwindled to less than 1000 a decade later. In contrast, many of the refugees who flooded into Quebec were farmers from upstate New York and the back country of Pennsylvania and New England, who were better prepared for the challenges that confronted them on the frontier.

The greatest number of Loyalists were drawn from the lower and middle classes of labourers, farmers, artisans, and merchants. Although a few highly placed colonial officials and Harvard-trained professionals moved to Nova Scotia and Quebec, most of the wealthy Loyalist elite went to Britain or the West

Indies. Nor were the pretensions of a few Loyalists well received by the mass of refugees. When 55 prominent Loyalists petitioned for estates in Nova Scotia of 5000 acres rather than the basic allowance of 100 acres for each head of household and 50 for each family member, there was such an outcry that British officials were forced to bow to the wishes of the majority.

Culture as well as class divided the Loyalists. While most of the migrants were colonial-born, 10 percent were recent immigrants from Britain and elsewhere. Ethnic and religious minorities were particularly visible among the refugees. People of Dutch, German, and Huguenot ancestry swelled the Loyalist ranks. During the war, pacificist groups, such as the Quakers, were particularly vulnerable to Patriot demands that people take sides, with the result that they became Loyalists by default.

Slave-holding Loyalists brought their "property" with them, and over 3000 free black Loyalists chose to settle in Nova Scotia. During the war, the British had encouraged slaves to leave their rebel masters by promising them their freedom if they fought in British regiments. Black Loyalists were offered land, but were given smaller grants in less desirable areas and became the objects of hostility and violence during the tension-ridden early years of settlement. In 1792, nearly 1200 black Loyalists chose to leave the Maritimes when offered passage to the new colony of Sierra Leone in Africa.

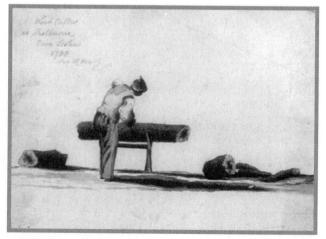

This painting by William Booth shows a black woodcutter in Shelburne, Nova Scotia, in 1788.
Library and Archives Canada/C40162

Black Loyalist Preachers in Nova Scotia and Sierra Leone

Shelburne, Nova Scotia, was the initial destination of nearly half of the free black Loyalists. Pushed to the opposite shore of the harbour, they founded a community named Birchtown in honour of the British commander in New York who had signed their embarkation certificates.

Religious leaders played an important role in the African-American community. Many of the Birchtown settlers were under the pastoral care of the Methodist minister Moses Wilkinson, a former slave. Blind from birth, he was a fiery and persuasive preacher who inspired Boston King, another black Loyalist, to take up the ministry. King was appointed to the Methodist society in Preston, near Halifax, in 1791. Another member of Wilkinson's congregation, John Ball, became an itinerant Methodist preacher in the colony.

After the arrival of the Loyalists, one-quarter of the Methodists in Nova Scotia were African Americans, a fact that did not go unnoticed by the denomination's founder, John Wesley. In a letter to the white Methodist Loyalist James Barry in July 1784, Wesley noted: "The work of God among the blacks in your neighbourhood is a wonderful instance of the power of God; and the little town they have built is, I suppose, the only town of negroes that has been built in America—nay perhaps in any part of the world, except only in Africa."[2] Wesley vowed to keep his black followers supplied with religious books and encouraged white Methodists to "give them all the assistance you can in every possible way."

Not all the citizens of Birchtown were Methodists. The Reverend John Murrant attracted about 40 families to the evangelical Anglican sect known as the Huntingdonians, named after Countess Huntingdon who funded their missions. When Murrant left Nova Scotia in 1791, his successor as chief pastor to the black Huntingdonians was Birchtown resident Cato Perkins. David George, by far the most controversial and successful of the black Loyalist preachers in the Shelburne area, was Baptist. Converted to the Baptist faith while still a slave in Georgia, George was a founding member, in 1773, of North America's first African-American church, Silver Bluff

Baptist, in South Carolina, and the first slave to serve as its pastor. When the Revolutionary War broke out, he escaped to the British lines and came to Shelburne in 1784. His meetings were attended by both black and white settlers, but rioting soldiers tore down his house and drove him out of the town. Birchtown residents, it seems, also found his message too radical and forced him to return to Shelburne.

In addition to their emphasis on salvation through faith rather than good works, Baptists also insisted on adult rather than infant baptism and baptism by immersion rather than by sprinkling. By adopting these beliefs and practices, Baptists defied the teachings of established churches and were widely perceived as encouraging opposition to law and order. As George's following grew and his fame spread, he incurred the hostility of people who liked neither his message nor the colour of his skin. In New Brunswick, the lieutenant-governor insisted that he preach only to black people. Riots broke out when he baptized a white couple in Shelburne.

The dream of a "promised land," where they could escape prejudice, own property, and live independently, had inspired black Loyalists to move to Nova Scotia. This dream also led nearly 1200 of them to emigrate to Sierra Leone in 1792. Assisted by philanthropists in Britain who believed that blacks would have a better life in their African homeland, they were also encouraged by their religious leaders to make this last pilgrimage. Over one-third of the blacks in Shelburne, including virtually all of David George's congregation as well as most of Moses Wilkinson's Methodists and Cato Perkins' Huntingdonians, accepted the challenge. The members of Boston King's Methodist chapel in Preston also joined the exodus.

Despite their short sojourn in Nova Scotia, the black Loyalist ministers and their followers had a significant impact on the colony. They left a legacy of literacy, religious conviction, and self-help in both of their adopted homelands, and to this day in Sierra Leone the descendants of the black Loyalists are identified by their Nova Scotia heritage.

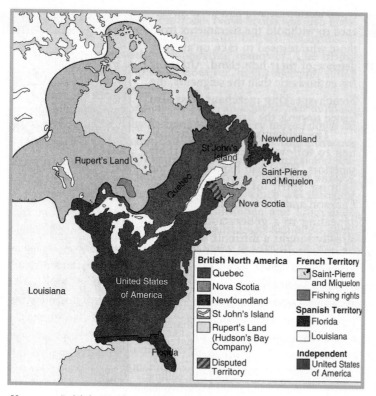

MAP 11.1 British North America, 1783.

Map legend:

British North America
- Quebec
- Nova Scotia
- Newfoundland
- St John's Island
- Rupert's Land (Hudson's Bay Company)
- Disputed Territory

French Territory
- Saint-Pierre and Miquelon
- Fishing rights

Spanish Territory
- Florida
- Louisiana

Independent
- United States of America

SETTLING THE LOYALISTS

Establishing the Loyalists in their new homeland posed a huge administrative challenge. In Nova Scotia, Governor John Parr moved quickly to escheat unoccupied land that had been granted in the colony and to carve out townships for the immigrants, but delays in securing land title and much-needed provisions caused enormous frustration. When Loyalists on the St John River complained that Halifax was too remote from their concerns, the British government responded by reorganizing colonial administration. In 1784, the old province of Nova Scotia was reduced in size and two new colonies were created: New Brunswick and Cape Breton, with capitals at Fredericton and Sydney respectively. By that time, two cities—Shelburne and Saint John—and dozens of villages—Aylesford, Digby, Gagetown, Guysborough, Rawden, Ship Harbour, Sussex Vale—had emerged from the forest-covered landscape.

Governor Walter Patterson of St John's Island tried to lure Loyalists to his estates there, but few wanted to begin their new lives as tenant farmers. Since there was no effort to escheat unsettled land on the island, most of the refugees looked elsewhere for a place to live. Over half of the 500 Loyalists on the island were disbanded soldiers who had been stationed there during the hostilities.

For the Mi'kmaq and Maliseet, the migration of the Loyalists to the Maritimes represented yet another threat to their access to fish and game. Aboriginal leaders petitioned for land, which was sometimes granted but then stolen by squatters who knew that authorities would not object. In 1783 the Mi'kmaq chief John Julien obtained a licence of occupation for 8100 hectares on the Miramichi River, but half of it was gone by 1807 when the government finally got around to establishing the Eel River Reserve. Many of the Acadians living in the lower St John River Valley also found their land granted away. Once again dispossessed, they were offered grants further up the river in the Madawaska region.

In Quebec, Governor Frederick Haldimand diverted many of the Loyalist immigrants to the north shore of Lake Ontario. Here, he believed, they would be safer from American attack than in the Eastern Townships, where they had originally hoped to settle. Another war might come at any time, and it would be difficult for British forces to protect such an exposed frontier. Before he could establish settlements in what would become the province of Ontario, Haldimand was obliged to secure the agreement of Natives living in the region.

First Nations had been neither consulted nor involved in the negotiations ending the war. Under the terms of the peace treaty, the British ceded all territorial claims south of the Great Lakes to the United States. This left the Natives living there at the mercy of land-hungry American settlers, who were no longer restrained by the provisions of the Royal Proclamation of 1763. Pressured by their desperate Native allies and the merchant community of Montreal who had lost a lucrative fur trade frontier, the British continued to occupy the western posts south of the Great Lakes until Aboriginal policy in the region could be determined.

Encampment of the Loyalists at Johnstown a New Settlement, on the Banks of the River S.t Laurence in Canada, taken from [...] marked in the Plan

A sketch of a Loyalist Camp near Cornwall by James Peachy.
Library and Archives Canada/C-002001

Fearing another frontier war like the one that had erupted in 1763, Governor Frederick Haldimand made arrangements for a tract of land along the Grand River, which the Mississauga Ojibwa had recently relinquished, to be provided for the Mohawk and other members of the Six Nations and their allies who wanted to move to British-held territory. A census taken in 1785 indicates that over 1800 Aboriginal Loyalists moved to the colony of Quebec, including 400 Mohawk, several hundred Cayuga and Onondaga, and smaller groups of Seneca, Tuscarora, Delaware, Nanticoke, Tutelo, Creek, and Cherokee.

Until the 1780s, the present-day southern Ontario peninsula was the homeland of the Ojibwa, Ottawa, and Algonquin, collectively called the Anishinabeg, a word meaning "true human beings." These nations had a history of nearly two centuries of contact with Europeans. When approached by Haldimand, they relinquished control over some of the best agricultural land in British North America, often for seemingly little in return. The Mississauga, for instance, exchanged a strip of land near Fort Niagara for "three hundred suits of clothing" in 1781. By 1788, most of the rest of the land north of Lake Ontario had been ceded in return for guns, ammunition, clothing, and other material items. While the British believed they were engaging in real-estate deals, the First Nations expected to share the land with the Loyalist refugees. They could scarcely imagine that in less than a century millions of white settlers would claim the land as their own.

In 1784, surveyors began laying out townships in the St Lawrence-Bay of Quinte area. Five of the townships went to John Johnson's Royal Yorkers, who arranged themselves in cultural groupings: Catholic Highlanders, Scottish Presbyterians, German Calvinists, German Lutherans, and Anglicans. Other townships in the region were allotted to Major Edward Jessup's corps, Robert Rogers's corps, and refugees from New York organized under Captain Michael Grass and Major Peter Van Alstine. Loyalists arriving from the frontier districts of New York and Pennsylvania settled around Fort Niagara. Others located at Sandwich (present-day Windsor) and across the river at Amherstburg, where they mingled with French settlers already long established near Fort Detroit. Loyalists also settled in established communities: Saint-Jean, Chambly, Yamachiche, Pointe-Claire, Sorel, Gaspé, St Armand, Foucault, and Montreal.

When the British finally agreed to evacuate the fur-trading posts south of the Great Lakes by Jay's Treaty in 1794, settlers moved from Detroit to British-controlled territory. These were the last "real" Loyalists. By that time, the colony had also become

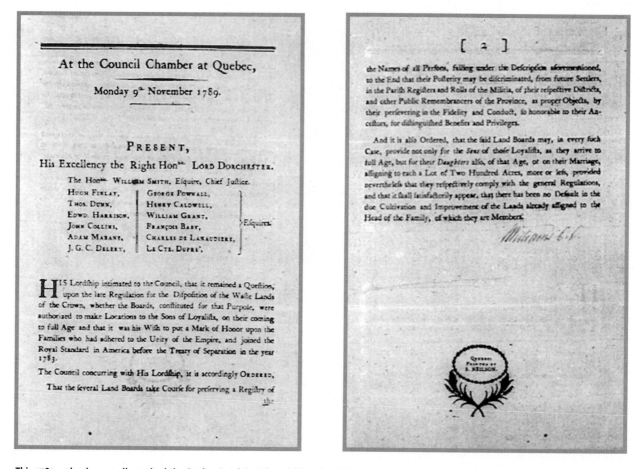

This 1789 order-in-council required the Quebec Land Boards, which assigned land to new settlers, to keep a registry of persons "who had adhered to the United Empire." Such persons and their children were eligible for certain benefits and privileges not granted the population at large.

Library and Archives Canada/C130528, C130529

the destination of "late Loyalists," residents of the United States who had second thoughts about staying in the new republic and who were attracted by generous land grants in the new colony of Upper Canada.

As in Nova Scotia, there was tension among the Loyalists who moved to Quebec. Many of the settlers resented the pretensions of their former military officers, who received larger land grants and attempted to establish themselves in positions of authority. In addition, the 84th Regiment had received especially generous grants, a preferential treatment that piqued the jealousy of those less favoured. Carleton, who had been knighted for his service during the American Revolution and returned as governor of Quebec in 1786, reduced dissatisfaction by increasing land grants all around, but the pressure for constitutional reform

would not go away. Among the most vocal critics of the status quo in British North America were the English merchants in Quebec. They remained stoutly opposed to the provisions of the Quebec Act, which denied them access to the full range of British legal and political institutions.

Petitions from both sides in the debate over the future of Quebec were sent to the authorities in London, who were now more disposed to listen to their disaffected colonists. In the aftermath of the American Revolution, support for liberalism had grown quickly in Europe. Even France, the supreme symbol of absolute government, was awash with debates about the power of the people. When a popular revolution broke out in France in 1789, colonial officials in London moved quickly to try to find a safe middle ground between unbridled democracy and despotic government.

THE CONSTITUTIONAL ACT, 1791

In 1791, the British Parliament passed the Constitutional Act, the third attempt to establish institutions for Quebec in as many decades. By this act, Quebec became two colonies: Upper and Lower Canada. In Upper Canada where the English-speaking Loyalists made up the majority of the population, British laws, including freehold land tenure, prevailed. Lower Canada, with its overwhelmingly French-speaking population, retained the seigneurial system and French civil law. As compensation to the English settlers in Lower Canada, provision was made for freehold tenure outside of seigneurial tracts, and the Eastern Townships were opened for settlement.

Each colony was granted a bicameral legislature, with an appointed legislative council and an elected assembly. Anyone with a 40-shilling freehold in rural areas or who paid rent at the rate of 10 pounds per annum was qualified to vote. Because of the availability of land in North America, a larger proportion of the men in the colonies could vote than in Great Britain. In theory, women with the requisite property qualifications could also vote, but they rarely held property in their own name, and even if they did, the franchise was considered a male prerogative. A special oath of allegiance was devised to permit Roman Catholics to vote and hold public office.

The Constitutional Act represented an attempt on the part of British authorities to stem the tide of republican sentiment sweeping the North Atlantic world. To do so they hoped to blunt the power of the elected assembly by strengthening the institutions embodying monarchical and aristocratic ideals. The monarchy was represented by a governor in Lower Canada and a lieutenant-governor in Upper Canada, while the aristocracy was represented in appointed legislative and executive

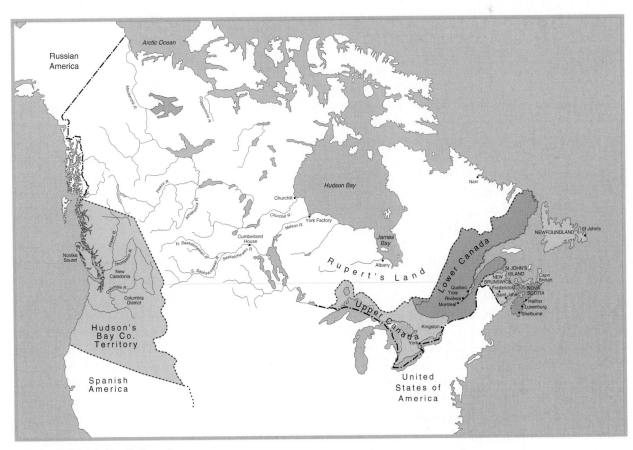

MAP 11.2 British North America, 1791.

councils. The governor (or lieutenant-governor), acting on behalf of the Crown, appointed individuals to the legislative council, which could introduce its own bills and veto all bills originating in the assembly. Because the members of the legislative council held office for life, were granted huge tracts of land, and were even eligible for titles, they were clearly meant to become the nucleus of a colonial aristocracy. The governor was also authorized to appoint an executive council to advise him on colonial matters. As was the case with the legislative councils, the men chosen to serve on the executive councils tended to hold office for life and were in a strong position to pursue their self-seeking policies.

The powers of the governor added more control over the activities of the assemblies. A governor could withhold consent from a bill passed by the colonial legislature; or he could reserve it for consideration by British authorities, who could disallow the bill within two years of its passage. He could also dismiss an assembly whose policies he found not to his liking. Reserves of Crown land and funds from Britain ensured that there would be sources of independent revenue to sustain the governor's independence from monies granted by the assembly.

Under the act, one-seventh of the land granted in every township was reserved for "the Support and Maintenance of a Protestant Clergy." The wording was vague and would soon be subject to much debate, but the intent was clear. In Upper Canada there would be an established church, presumably the Church of England, to add strength to the monarchical principle. The separation of church and state, a policy favoured by democrats everywhere by the end of the eighteenth century, was still too radical a concept for British colonial policy makers.

Colonial officials hoped that the granting of an elected assembly would encourage the colonists to tax themselves to pay the cost of local improvements and ensure their loyalty in the event of another war. The test would come all too soon. A popular revolution broke out in France in 1789 and three years later the triumphant republicans set out to export their revolutionary ideals. Britain and other European monarchies went to war to stop them. When Napoleon seized control of his war-ravaged country in 1799, he, too, took on his European rivals. The French Revolutionary and Napoleonic Wars finally ended in 1815, but not before

they had induced a nasty little sideshow in North America, known as the War of 1812.

UPPER CANADA, 1791–1812

Nowhere was loyalty more of an issue than in Upper Canada. In the years from 1791 to 1812, the population of the frontier colony increased ninefold, with most of the new residents coming from the United States. Immigration from the former Thirteen Colonies had been encouraged by Upper Canada's first lieutenant-governor, John Graves Simcoe (1792–98). In Simcoe's estimation, the Americans who came to Upper Canada to farm would again become loyal subjects of the king if administrators took care to cultivate British institutions in the colony.

Simcoe had commanded a Loyalist unit, the Queen's Rangers, during the American Revolution and was eager to recreate British institutions in the backwoods of British North America. He appointed officials with views similar to his own and, in return for their services, granted them vast tracts of land that they held for speculative purposes. Along with the Clergy and Crown reserves, these grants constituted a major grievance for early immigrants. New settlements, instead of being compact, were generally widely dispersed, making the provision of local services such as roads and schools costly, and separating neighbours by inconvenient distances. In 1839, when Lord Durham reviewed the state of surveyed land in Upper Canada, he found that over half of it had been either granted to "classes of grantees whose station would preclude them from settling in the wilderness" or set aside as Clergy reserves.[3]

The badges of elite membership were a land grant along with a government post and membership in the Law Society of Upper Canada, which controlled entry into the legal profession in the colony. Living in large, comfortable homes, the elite hired servants and educated their children in private schools. Their male children generally also joined the elite. William Jarvis, for example, owed his appointment by Simcoe as provincial secretary and registrar to his rank as an officer in the Queen's Rangers. A generation later his son Samuel was deputy provincial secretary and chief superintendent of Indian affairs, while his other son, William, became sheriff of Gore District. Women in

***York*, by Elizabeth Francis Hale, 1804.**
Library and Archives Canada/40137

elite families lived more restricted lives. Following the injunctions of an emerging cult of domesticity among the British middle class, women of means in Upper Canada were expected to marry sons of other elite families and make motherhood, household work, and charity their major preoccupations.

In the early years of Upper Canada, the land-rich political elite was concentrated in York (renamed Toronto in 1834), a site selected as the capital in 1793 because it was less vulnerable to American attack than Newark where the capital had originally been located. Kingston, the largest town, boasted only 50 houses. The majority of people lived in the countryside. Compared to most colonies, rural residents were well served by roads. The British government paid the cost of building a network of military roads—Yonge Street, for example—that became commercial routes as well.

Simcoe established a system of local government along British lines that provided a framework for legal and social services. Upper Canada was divided into districts, which were in turn divided into townships. The township became the unit of local administration, and

its property owners elected the men who assessed property values for tax purposes, collected these taxes, and oversaw the highways. As in the Maritime colonies, these unpaid local officials were less important than the justices of the peace, appointed by the lieutenant-governor. The justices of the peace levied local taxes, appointed district treasurers, and superintended the building of jails and highways and the sale of liquor licences. Determined to rid the new colony of the scourge of slavery, Simcoe was the moving spirit behind an act against slavery in Upper Canada in 1793.

In the early years of settlement, the British government provided most of the funds that sustained the colonial economy. Government jobs and contracts, dispensed at the discretion of the lieutenant-governor and officials appointed by him, helped to create local oligarchies loyal to the government throughout Upper Canada. Not surprisingly, opposition to this privileged elite soon found a voice in the elected assembly. Simcoe left the colony in 1798 but his successors were confronted by a population increasingly distrustful of their rulers.

In the Upper Canadian Assembly, challenges to the government's authority before 1812 were usually identified closely with three Irish-born men: William Weekes, Robert Thorpe, and Joseph Willcocks. While misgivings about Britain's brutal suppression of an Irish uprising in 1798 and the subsequent Act of Union (1801) between Great Britain and Ireland had initially kindled these men's criticism of colonial governance, their focus was on the heavy hand of appointed officials in Upper Canada. Their supporters were united by a sense of grievance rather than by ethnicity.

LOWER CANADA, 1791–1812

In Lower Canada, governors used patronage to sustain the power of an English-speaking elite, despite the overwhelming preponderance of French-speaking people in the colony. Some members of the English elite were merchants who had made their fortunes in the fur trade. After 1800, this wealth was supplemented by investments in local industries such as brewing and distilling as well as the burgeoning timber trade.

Equivalent in importance to oil in the twentieth century, timber was essential to the successful prosecution of overseas trade and global wars. Until the 1790s, the British navy relied primarily on Baltic suppliers for timber. This source was seriously restricted when Napoleon entered into alliances with Russia, Prussia, Sweden, and Denmark in 1807. Britain moved quickly to raise duties on foreign timber, thereby offering some guarantee of long-term protection for capitalists prepared to invest in colonial production. By 1810, 74 percent of exports from Lower Canada were forest products. Furs, which accounted for 76 percent of exports in 1770, made up less than 10 percent of export receipts in 1810. British demand for squared timber also encouraged other ventures, such as John Molson's steamboat service on the St Lawrence and the beginnings of a Quebec shipbuilding industry.

With commercial connections in Great Britain, English-speaking merchants and capitalists had a major advantage over their French counterparts. Anglophones who had made money in the fur trade bought seigneuries both to gain access to timberlands and to earn income from habitants' dues. By 1812, an estimated two-thirds of the seigneuries were in the hands of English-speaking merchants. The predominantly English-speaking merchant group of Montreal also accumulated about 2.5 million hectares of land outside the seigneurial belt, granted by the Crown under the "leader and associate" system. A leader received 2500 hectares for every farmer he settled on a 500-hectare farm; the leader's grant supposedly repaid his costs of both recruiting and transporting settlers and provisioning them until they could grow

When this sketch was drawn in 1786, rue Notre-Dame was one of Montreal's major thoroughfares, lined with the homes of officials, merchants, professionals, and master artisans.
Molson Archives/Library and Archives Canada, detail

their first crop. In practice the leaders, many of them wealthy merchants, provided the government with inflated lists of alleged settlers and generally provided few services to the real settlers.

Most of the new settlers moved north from the New England states. By 1812, about 20 000 of them had been enticed by promises of free land in the Eastern Townships south and east of Montreal. Because they received their lands in freehold tenure, the settlers did not have to contend with the seigneurial system, but they did have to cope with rocky soil, poor transportation, and huge areas of wilderness set aside for Clergy reserves, Crown reserves, and speculative purposes. The modest lives of these immigrants underscore the fact that only a small proportion of the English-speaking residents of Lower Canada, who in 1812 numbered 50 000 or about 15 percent of the population, were wealthy.

The French-speaking majority included only a small number of wealthy merchants and seigneurs. With commercial avenues blocked, there was a dramatic growth in the number of French-speaking professionals in the early nineteenth century. The leaders of the Roman Catholic Church welcomed priests fleeing the excesses of the French Revolution, who staffed a number of the new classical colleges in the colony. Although the colleges were designed to train a native-born priesthood, about 50 percent of the classical-college graduates sought employment in secular occupations, using their academic talents to become notaries, lawyers, journalists, and clerks. The socially ambitious continued to look to the purchase of a seigneury as a badge of their success. For instance, Louis-Joseph Papineau, who became the leader of the opponents of the government after 1815, was the son of a notary who purchased a seigneury called Petite Nation on the Ottawa River in 1801.

Frustrated by their failure to penetrate the government bureaucracy, the French-speaking middle class became increasingly nationalistic. Its members saw themselves as the natural leaders of French Canada. Through the Parti canadien, established in 1805, they focused upon the elected House of Assembly as a forum for demanding greater popular

BIOGRAPHY

Ezekiel Hart

Ezekiel Hart was born in Trois-Rivières in 1770, the son of a Jewish merchant. There were fewer than 100 Jews in the Canadas before 1800, but their number included enterprising and prosperous individuals. Hart and his two brothers had run a successful brewery and potashery before Ezekiel established his own import-export business and a general store and began to purchase a great deal of land. In 1807, Hart won a by-election in Trois-Rivières, but the Parti canadien, regarding him as a supporter of the government, declared him ineligible to serve. The following year, Hart was re-elected and took the Christian oath of office required of members, but the assembly majority argued that his adhesion to the Jewish faith invalidated his oath.

Although Governor James Craig supported Hart's right to take his seat in the assembly, the colonial secretary confirmed that Jews were unable to serve in British legislatures. Catholics in Britain suffered from the same legal restrictions as Jews, so it was ironic that the mainly Catholic assemblymen of Lower Canada embraced the British ban on Jews in government. In 1832, with religious toleration established in British law, Ezekiel Hart's son Samuel won a seat in the Lower Canadian Assembly and became the first Jew to hold a seat in a British legislature.

The Parti canadien's rejection of Ezekiel Hart may suggest that the Canadiens were anti-Semitic. Anti-Semitism was indeed widespread in Christian societies in the nineteenth century, as it had been earlier. But Hart had been elected on both occasions by an electorate that was predominantly French-speaking. The Parti canadien, in turn, was most likely using Hart's Jewishness as a pretext to exclude a rich merchant suspected of being a supporter of the governor. The judge rejected by the same assembly was, after all, a Canadien. Nevertheless, the Parti canadien's willingness to use a man's religion as an excuse to ban him from its midst demonstrates that the party was not prepared to defend individual freedom of conscience.

control over government. Supportive of the seigneurial system, and initially favourable to church control over education and social services, most members of the Parti canadien saw the Assembly as a tool for cultural survival. It could be used to protect French Canada's laws and language, limit the power of the merchants, and ensure that economic development was not controlled from abroad.

In 1806, the nationalists had their own newspaper, *Le Canadien*, edited by Pierre Bédard and François Blanchet. It was used to denounce the administration of Governor James Craig and assert the right of the assembly to shape policy for the colony. Craig retaliated in 1810 by imprisoning the editors and dissolving the assembly for a second straight year, which forced new elections. Since war with the United States seemed imminent, British authorities moved in 1811 to replace Craig with a more conciliatory governor, but this only postponed what became the norm in all British North American colonies: confrontation between elected and appointed officials.

Agricultural Crisis on the Seigneuries

By the beginning of the nineteenth century, commercial and demographic pressures were transforming the peasant economy based on the seigneuries. Farmers in Lower Canada exported a million bushels of wheat in 1802 but the colony would soon relinquish its place as the breadbasket of British North America to Upper Canada. Secret instructions to the governor accompanying the Constitutional Act forbade the expansion of the seigneurial system beyond the boundaries established in 1791. As the population on the seigneuries grew, land in some areas became subdivided to the point where farm units were unproductive.

Most habitants lacked the funds necessary to buy land and were therefore forced to seek alternative ways of making a living. In many farm families, fathers and sons pursued seasonal work in the fur trade, at lumber camps, on canal construction, or in shipbuilding, while women took responsibility for farm management. Agriculture under these circumstances remained largely for family subsistence rather than for commercial profit.

While men who could not be supported on the farms might find employment in the timber trade, fisheries, or fur trade, women had fewer options. Many women became domestic workers in the cities; others became prostitutes. In the city of Quebec, with a population of only about 14 000 in 1810, 400 to 600 prostitutes, native-born and immigrant, tried to earn a living off their bodies, relying particularly on the members of a local British garrison that averaged close to 2500 men from 1810 to 1816.

The agricultural crisis was most evident in areas where it was difficult to engage in farming for export. In Sorel, along the Richelieu River, at least one-third of the adult male population in the 1790s contracted with the North West Company (NWC) to work in the western fur trade. Some two-thirds of these went west during the growing season. Wheat, the exportable crop, would not grow well in the Sorel area. When the NWC merged with the Hudson's Bay Company in 1821 and implemented large layoffs, Sorel was thrust into poverty.

Similarly, in the Gaspé where farming was often marginal, over 5000 individuals in 1800 depended for most of their income on the Robins and other Channel Island families who bought their fish for resale in Britain. Unable to subsist on agriculture, Gaspésiens depended for their survival on merchants who paid them not in cash but in credits, which could be redeemed only at the merchants' stores. Above all, in Lower Canada after 1806, it was seasonal work for lumberjacks, teamsters, drivers, and raftsmen in the timber trade that added cash to hard-pressed subsistence-agriculture households.

Overpopulation and outdated agricultural practices were not the only problems facing the habitants. While the impact of seigneurial dues on the habitants is much debated for the post-conquest period, evidence in some areas suggests that they had a crippling effect. In the Richelieu region, for example, over half of the habitant's agricultural surpluses were remitted to the seigneur. This situation left little possibility of saving for the poor crop years that, because of wheat-fly infestations, became more frequent in Lower Canada after 1800. It also made it difficult for habitants to invest in new farming practices that were revolutionizing agriculture in other areas of North America and Europe.

The British officials tended to dismiss poverty in Quebec as the fault of its allegedly unprogressive victims. This was a distortion of reality. Both before and after the conquest, the Canadiens demonstrated an ability to take advantage of market opportunities. Furthermore, whatever the anti-materialist ideology of their church, the Canadiens were far from other-worldly. Rather, their problems were rooted in the failure of the British either to fix seigneurial dues, which had been done before 1760, to prevent gouging, or to grant free lands to capital-short farmers. British policies—or the lack thereof—on these fronts stymied the Canadiens economically and stimulated their desire for political reforms.

THE WAR OF 1812

In 1812, demands for political reform were temporarily halted when war was declared between Great Britain and the United States. Although the issues that ultimately led to war—Native policy on the frontier and the rights of neutral shipping on the high seas—directly affected the British North American colonies, they were handled by authorities in London. So, too, was the military side of the war. British troops assisted by their Native allies living in American territory did most of the fighting. Even the resolution of the conflict was negotiated between Britain and the United States without taking British North American interests into consideration. Nevertheless, the war created powerful mythologies, especially in the two Canadas, reinforcing conservative ideology among the elite in Upper Canada and nationalism among the French-speaking middle class in Lower Canada.

The main goal of the United States in the war was to seize Britain's thinly populated North American colonies. Since the Canadas seemed the easiest target—the Maritimes could be protected by the British navy—they became the object of attack. The fact that so many Upper Canadians had immigrated from the United States convinced some American authorities that the capture of Upper Canada would be a "mere matter of marching." On the eve of leading his army into Upper Canada, American General William Hull issued a declaration indicating that he came to liberate the people of Upper Canada from the yoke of British oppression, not to conquer them.

Most Upper Canadians appear to have opposed the idea of breaking links with Great Britain, but a significant minority supported the American cause.

During the course of the war, several hundred American immigrants in Upper Canada moved back to the United States to avoid being called upon to fight their former homeland. Many who remained in the colony pointedly took no role in the fighting until it became clear that Great Britain was prepared to make a major commitment to defence. In the final analysis, about 11 000 colonists were active in the militia, poorly trained as it was, while members of the elite received officer commissions.

Despite the enlistments, the military commander, Major-General Isaac Brock, regarded the population as defeatist. He informed his superiors in 1812:

> My situation is most critical, not from any thing the enemy can do, but from the disposition of the people—The population [of Upper Canada], believe me, is essentially bad—A full belief possesses them that this Province must inevitably succumb. This prepossession is fatal to every exertion—Legislators, Magistrates, Militia, Officers, all, have imbibed the idea, and are so sluggish and indifferent in all their respective offices that the artful and active scoundrel is allowed to parade the Country without interruption, and commit all imaginable mischief. . . . Most of the people have lost all confidence—I however speak loud and look big."[4]

To demonstrate that Britain could win a war with the Americans, Brock authorized an assault on Michilimackinac soon after war was declared. This aggressive posture won the British the support of the Native peoples of the Ohio Valley, who united under the Shawnee chief Tecumseh after receiving promises that Britain would seek to win the return of this vast area to Native control. With Native help, Brock seized Detroit, but then his luck ran out.

At a battle in October 1812, on the heights above the village of Queenston, in the Niagara region, Brock and 28 of his men were killed. His army, which included 1000 British regulars, 500 Iroquois, and 600 Upper Canadian militia, nevertheless carried the day. Over 900 Americans were taken prisoner when they were trapped by reinforcements from Fort George led by Major-General Roger Hale Sheaffe. The victory, following the earlier capture of Detroit, helped to raise the morale of the Upper Canadians and stiffen their resolve to resist the invaders.

In the following year, the Americans under Commodore Oliver Perry defeated the British fleet in

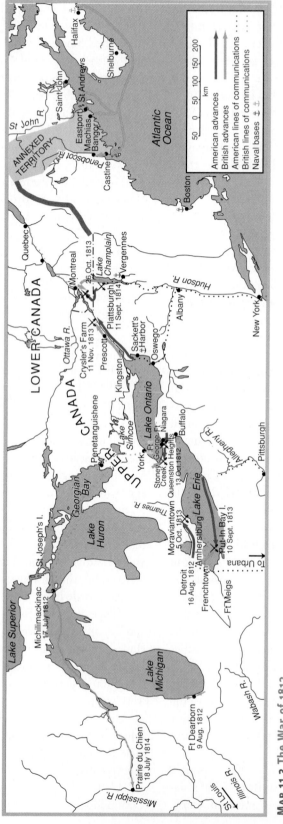

MAP 11.3 The War of 1812.
Adapted from D.G.G. Kerr, *Historical Atlas of Canada*, 3rd ed. (Scarborough: Nelson, 1975), 38

The Legend of Brock and the Loyal Militia

Following the Battle of Queenston Heights, Upper and Lower Canadians began singing the praises of brave General Brock and the loyal militia who supposedly saved British North America from the invading Americans. Brock, whose harsh judgments of the Canadian militia are quoted in this chapter, may not have been entirely in agreement with this effusive outburst, which appeared in the *Montreal Gazette* on 26 October 1812:

> The intelligence received last week from [Upper Canada] is such as cannot but call forth the astonishment, the gratitude, and the applause of all classes of His Majesty's Subjects in British America when we consider the number of assailants, compared to that of the little band of heroes who so nobly defended this devoted portion of the British Empire and the brilliant results of their exertions at Queenston on the 13th. . . . The Historian in handing down to posterity the details of this historic achievement will dwell with rapture on the undaunted courage displayed and the unshaken loyalty evinced by a little army not exceeding 800 British subjects against an enemy at least three times their numbers, and while he bedews with merited regret the memory of the illustrious Chief and his heroic companions who so nobly fell on this glorious day, he will inscribe the name of BROCK on the imperishable list of British Heroes and class the victory that resulted among the most brilliant events which adorn the page of British History. —Our fellow subjects in the United Kingdom

Battle of Queenston Heights.
Library and Archives Canada/C-000276

will, no doubt, duly appreciate the splendid exertions of their Canadian brethren, and will freely confess that they are worthy of the King whom they serve and the Constitution which they enjoy, and that the men who have come forward so cheerfully in defence of the cause of their country and who have conspicuously distinguished themselves in sharing with British Troops in the capture of Michilimackinac and Detroit, and in this latter glorious defeat of the enemy at Queenston, are well entitled to the friendship and protection of their mother-country.—May the union between Britain and such heroic descendants be eternal. . . .

Lake Erie at the Battle of Put-in-Bay in September 1813. This victory forced the British to abandon Detroit. Soon thereafter, the American army defeated British forces under Lieutenant Brock's successor, Colonel Henry Proctor, at Moraviantown. Tecumseh died in the battle, which undermined the effect of the Native alliance. Meanwhile, the American army ranged freely in the western peninsula, burning Newark (Niagara-on-the-Lake) to the ground before departing in December 1813. On the eastern frontier, American forces had been unable to capture Kingston and thereby gain control of Lake Ontario. As a conso-

lation prize, they occupied York for a few days in the spring of 1813, and torched its parliament buildings. The British in turn razed sections of Washington, DC, in August and attacked Buffalo in the state of New York on 30 December.

In Lower Canada, the squabbles between the Parti canadien and the governor were set aside as both factions united to defend the colony. The Lower Canadian Assembly authorized the new governor, Sir George Prevost, to conscript manpower and to keep as many as 6000 men in the field for a full year. The Roman Catholic Church, under Bishop

Two Ottawa chiefs who had come from Michilimackinac, Lake Huron, to hold discussions with Crown representatives in York, 1813.
Library and Archives Canada/C-114384

Joseph-Octave Plessis, supported the British cause. In October 1813 a force of about 1300 men, consisting of the French Canadian Voltigeurs under Lieutenant-Colonel Charles de Salaberry and 150 Iroquois, fended off 4200 undisciplined, poorly trained American recruits who crossed the river Châteauguay en route to Montreal.

In 1814, battles in the Niagara peninsula exhausted both sides. The bloodiest occurred in pitch darkness at Lundy's Lane, not far from Queenston Heights, on 25 July 1814. British regulars, assisted by the militia, confronted American troops, who could barely be seen in the dark. By morning the casualties on both sides were enormous. While the Upper Canadian authorities touted Lundy's Lane as a glorious victory, it actually confirmed the pattern of rough equivalence between the two sides and deepened war-weariness in both Washington and London.

THE MARITIME COLONIES

Unlike Upper and Lower Canada, the Maritime colonies were spared invading armies during the War of 1812. Their assemblies also included men who criticized the authoritarian nature of governors and their appointed advisors, but the wartime atmosphere that prevailed for more than two decades and widespread loyalist sentiment meant that there was no systematic movement for reform.

Meanwhile, opportunities stimulated by the war had a transforming effect on the region's economy. As alternative sources of supply were cut off, Atlantic colonies found a ready market for their timber, fish, and foodstuffs. The timber trade reached boom proportions, and shipbuilding and the carrying trade made promising beginnings. In St John's Island (renamed Prince Edward Island in 1799) and other fertile areas of the Maritimes, farmers were spurred to greater production. There were even signs that the Maritimes could become a major player in the lucrative West Indies trade.

New Brunswick's economy was boosted by Napoleon's blockade of the Baltic timber supply. Between 1805 and 1812, the fir and pine timber reaching Britain from New Brunswick increased more than twentyfold. Businessmen, many of them based in the Scottish port city of Greenock, brought their capital, labour, and technology to the shores of the Miramichi and St John rivers. By 1815, forest products accounted for nearly two-thirds of the colony's exports and Saint John began to rival Halifax in population and wealth. Control over Crown lands and the revenue of the timber trade became issues that would dominate New Brunswick's social and political life long after the wars that prompted the timber boom had come to an end.

The War of 1812 also expanded the potential for privateering, which had been carried on against French shipping, with more or less success, throughout the Napoleonic Wars. Thirty-seven vessels from the Atlantic colonies engaged in privateering activities during the conflict, recording 207 captures. The *Liverpool Packet* was the champion of the privateering fleet, taking 50 "prizes," most of them from Massachusetts. These captures helped to line the pockets of ambitious Halifax merchants who bought the vessels at prize courts and sold them at a profit. The war also inspired moments of great excitement. In June 1813, for example, Haligonians were treated to the spectacle of the HMS *Shannon* arriving with the USS *Chesapeake* in tow following a brief engagement off Boston harbour. The following year, a British army under Sir John Sherbrooke occupied part of the coast of present-day Maine, providing more opportunities for commercial profit.

The wars with France and the United States encouraged more black immigration to the Maritimes. In 1796 some 550 Maroons from Jamaica, freedom fighters who had lost their most recent battle in their 140-year war against the British, arrived in Halifax, where they were put to work on the town's fortifications. They, like many black Loyalists before them, decided to relocate in Sierra Leone. Over 2000 African Americans who fought for the British in the War of 1812 were brought to the Maritimes. After spending a difficult winter in Halifax, they were finally settled in communities outside the city. Preston and Hammonds Plains absorbed most of the immigrants; as many as 500 settled at Loch Lomond in New Brunswick. After the abolition of the slave trade in 1807, slavery was not upheld in the courts and gradually died out in the Maritimes.

View of Saint John, New Brunswick, 1814, by Joseph Brown Comingo (1784–1821). Saint John was incorporated in 1785, soon after the arrival of the Loyalists, and became a thriving port during the Napoleonic Wars.
New Brunswick Museum, Saint John, NB

NEWFOUNDLAND

Newfoundland was transformed by two decades of war. With the decline in the number of West Country vessels sent to the Grand Banks and inshore fishery, Newfoundlanders increasingly dominated the salt-fish trade. Their dominance was further augmented by the exclusion of the French and Americans from the Newfoundland fishery. During the wars, St Pierre and Miquelon were occupied by British troops and the French Treaty Shore was patrolled, bringing the French fishery to a standstill. The wars also encouraged economic diversity, including a lucrative seal fishery and a local shipbuilding industry.

With opportunities beckoning to those willing to work, Newfoundland attracted immigrants. Among them were merchants and fishing crews determined to avoid wartime restrictions and impressment. By 1815, the population of the colony had reached 20 000, and St John's had emerged as the commercial capital of the North Atlantic fisheries. As historian Shannon Ryan put it, Newfoundland "had always been a fishery based around an island." Now, with the French and Napoleonic Wars serving as a catalyst, it "would finally become a colony based on the fishery."[5]

A colony in all but name and status, Newfoundland had also expanded its territorial jurisdiction. In 1809, Labrador, which had been part of Quebec/Lower Canada since 1774, was re-annexed to Newfoundland. This was a result, in part, of imperial policy developed for the protection of Labrador, but it was also a reflection of the growing presence of Newfoundlanders in the Labrador inshore and seal fisheries. Since Europeans were confined largely to the coast, the inland boundary between Lower Canada and Labrador remained undefined and the matter remained unsettled until the twentieth century.

THE LEGACY OF THE WAR OF 1812

While the War of 1812 receives little attention in British and American textbooks, it features prominently in most accounts of Canadian history.

Especially in Upper and Lower Canada where most of the battles were fought, the failure of the United States to capture the less powerful British colonies became a source of pride and the inspiration for a remarkable number of commemorative heritage sites. Historical memory also dimmed with the passage of time. In many Canadian accounts of the war, the fact that British regulars did much of the fighting became less significant than the role played by the brave colonial militia in such battles as Queenston Heights and Châteauguay. The war was even seen in retrospect as the seedbed of Canadian nationalism, with English and French Canadians cooperating to push back the aggressive Americans.

The War of 1812 also deeply affected political values in the colonies. Along with the American Revolution, it served as a rationale in Tory thought for maintaining a hierarchical, class-stratified society rather than an egalitarian one. The alternative to British rule and British class structures, it was argued, was a slide into atheist republicanism and even annexation to the United States.

Conservatives in the Canadas used the war to justify appointing to public office only an elite loyal to British institutions and values. As a result, those who could claim Loyalist credentials often received special treatment from the authorities. Men embellished their record of military service to demonstrate that they had earned the right to special consideration from the government. Reflecting prevalent notions of gender relations, they presented themselves as heroic men who were protecting their families against the depredations of predatory Americans. A cult developed around the fallen British general, Sir Isaac Brock, who was presented as the very embodiment of the manly virtues to which loyal colonial men aspired. It was rather more difficult for a woman to take advantage of her contributions to the military effort to receive favours from the state, as Laura Secord would learn. In 1813, she had walked through enemy lines from Queenston to Beaver Dams to warn British troops of an impending American assault. Efforts both by her husband and herself to elicit government patronage on the basis of this service yielded a 100 pound reward from the Prince of Wales in 1860 and later generations, for their own reasons, would come to venerate Secord.

American expansionism, exemplified by the War of 1812, offered government in the postwar period a pretext to suppress dissent. Anyone who railed against land speculators and Crown and clergy reserves was held to be disloyal. So, for example, the government jailed and eventually deported Robert Gourlay, a Scottish immigrant who in 1817 published a survey of settler complaints and began to rally the population behind a campaign for major land reforms. After 1814, the government also actively discouraged American immigration to Upper Canada and, for a time, placed the political and property rights of Americans in the colony in doubt. Most new settlers who arrived in the Canadas after the War of 1812 would come from Britain, not the United States.

With the passage of time, the War of 1812 also became significant because it was the last official war between Great Britain and the United States. By the Treaty of Ghent, signed 24 December 1814, both parties agreed to return any enemy territory that they had occupied. Two agreements reached after the war helped to establish peaceful relations between the United States and Britain in North America. The Rush-Bagot agreement of 1817 limited the number of armed vessels on the Great Lakes and Lake Champlain to those required to control smuggling. In the same year, agreement was reached over the disputed islands in Passamaquoddy Bay. Boundaries were further clarified by the Anglo-American Convention of 1818, in which the 49th parallel was recognized as the boundary between the Lake of the Woods and the Rockies, and the disputed territory on the Pacific coast was to be subject to joint occupation until an agreement could be reached. American rights to the inshore fisheries of the Atlantic region were also restricted.

Although the United States and Britain never again declared war on each other, both sides continued to see the other as a potential enemy. Military bases were constructed and strengthened on both sides of the border over the next century. Between 1826 and 1832, the British built the Rideau Canal linking Kingston and Ottawa as an alternative water route to the vulnerable international section of the St Lawrence River between Montreal and Kingston. The route of the Intercolonial Railway, built in the 1870s, was also chosen with military considerations in mind.

This was yet another legacy for British North America of the War of 1812.

CULTURE IN COLONIAL SOCIETY

While war and rumours of war dominated colonial society between 1783 and 1815, it was also a period in which high culture took root. The arrival of the Loyalists and the prosperity associated with the French and Napoleonic Wars encouraged the refinement, literary output, and scholarly debate—aspects of a new intellectual awakening known as the Enlightenment—that was increasingly animating the North Atlantic world.

Many of the Loyalists had enjoyed the amenities of urban life and they were impatient to establish churches, schools, and newspapers in their new homeland. Only a minority of them belonged to the Church of England, but the structure of the established church of Britain was strengthened by the Loyalist presence. In 1787, Charles Inglis, the Loyalist rector of Trinity Church in New York, was consecrated as the first Church of England bishop of Nova Scotia, with jurisdiction over all the British North American colonies. The first overseas bishop in the British Empire, Inglis was eager to enhance the status of Anglicanism in the colonies. He supported the founding in 1789 of King's College in Windsor, Nova Scotia, as an exclusive institution for sons of the Anglican elite and backed various missionary efforts—most of them futile—to draw the mass of the population from their dissenting religious views. In New Brunswick, the Loyalists were instrumental in founding the Provincial Academy of Arts and Sciences, which received its charter as the College of New Brunswick in 1800.

As a "consolation to their distress," many educated Loyalists turned to literature. They produced poems, essays, and sermons and were avid readers of British fiction and advice books. In 1789, John Howe, a Loyalist from Massachusetts, and William Cochran, an Anglican clergyman and classical scholar, attempted to provide a forum for colonial writers. Although their *Nova Scotia Magazine*, published in Halifax, lasted less than two years, it ranks as the first literary journal in the British North American colonies. By the late 1780s, there were two bilingual newspapers in Quebec: the *Quebec Gazette* and the *Montreal Gazette*. The latter was the more radical of the two, advocating greater social equality, public education, and restrictions on the powers of the church.

With the Loyalists came the full range of eighteenth-century political ideologies, which raised the level of political debate. The Loyalist elite was unable to curtail the liberal tendencies taking root in the era of the American and French revolutions, but they added weight to the conservative side of the political spectrum. In rare cases they also proved far-sighted. William Smith, a Loyalist from New York who became chief justice of Quebec, proposed a federated British North America under a "governor-general" to serve as a "showcase of the continent." His "grand design" for the British colonies in North America was a little premature, but it had merits that would eventually be recognized by colonial politicians.

In the years during and following the American Revolutionary War, voluntary organizations emerged in colonial towns. Service organizations, such as the Charitable Irish Society, and private clubs, such as the Masonic Lodge, were established and informal literary salons, popular in Britain, became a feature of polite society. In the summer of 1791, a debating club christened the Robin Hood Society—its name was later changed to the Montreal Society—was formed. Among the topics of debate were the "duty of electors" and the relative merits of marriage and celibacy.

As one of the major military bases in the British Empire and an emerging commercial centre, Halifax reflected many of the cultural trends of the times. Several of the town's finest public buildings were also constructed in this period. New Hampshire-born Loyalist Sir John Wentworth, who served as lieutenant-governor of Nova Scotia from 1792 to 1808, and his wife Frances oversaw the construction of Government House, an elegant Georgian mansion that still serves as the official residence of the lieutenant-governor of the province.

Between 1794 and 1799 Halifax was also the home of Prince Edward, who commanded the garrison. He, along with his mistress, who was publicly addressed as Madame St Laurent, brought glamour and excitement to Halifax social life. Struck by "the miserable state of all the works and public buildings," the prince devoted

MORE TO THE STORY

Artists in a New World

Native artists in British North America produced intricate carving, beading, baskets, and painted skins. By the eighteenth century, Europeans were systematically collecting Native artwork, some of which found its way into galleries and museums.

The first European artists in the colony were soldiers, draftsmen, and natural scientists who had received some training in drawing. Because drawing was the only method of creating a visual record before the introduction of photography in the mid-nineteenth century, it was a valuable skill taught in many professions.

Eighteenth-century European-born artists were trained to impose a rigid order on their subject matter, omitting any details that might offend European sensibilities. The idealized North American environment can be seen in the work of Richard Short, a purser with James Wolfe's expedition.

Joseph Frederick Wallet DesBarres was a Swiss-born army officer who, together with Samuel Holland and James Cook, surveyed most of the Atlantic region in the period following the Seven Years' War. DesBarres included landscape views in his much-praised *Atlantic Neptune*, a four-volume guide to navigation in the region. In their detail and colour, the paintings of Thomas Davies represent a departure from the topographic watercolours done by students of the military academy. Davies was posted in the British colonies from 1755 to 1790, and his

A painted robe, Sioux type.
Canadian Museum of Civilization/CMC 74-7928

***View of the River La Puce Near Quebec in Canada, 1792*, by Thomas Davies.**
National Gallery of Canada/6274

***Miniature of Jane Harbel Drake*, by Joseph Brown Comingo.**
New Brunswick Museum, Saint John, NB/989.13.1

work, such as *View of the River La Puce*, offers an exceptional visual record of the eighteenth-century landscape.

By the eighteenth century, it had become fashionable among the middle class in Europe and North America to have their portraits painted. It was difficult to make a living solely as a portrait artist in British North America, in part because members of the colonial elite often travelled either to Britain or the United States to have their portraits painted by the most widely acclaimed artists of the period. The first colonial-born portrait artist in the Atlantic region was Joseph Brown Comingo, from Lunenburg, Nova Scotia. Although little is known about his artistic training, he worked extensively throughout Nova Scotia and New Brunswick, painting both portraits and landscapes. His miniatures, such as the one of Jane Harbel Drake, were particularly popular in the eighteenth and early nineteenth centuries.

One of British North America's most accomplished artists was William Berczy. Born in Wallerstein (Germany), in 1744, Berczy arrived in 1794 in Upper Canada, where he was involved in various colonization schemes. During his sojourn in the colony, he supplemented his income by painting miniatures and portraits. His portrait of Joseph Brant is considered an accurate portrayal of the Mohawk chief, and art historian Dennis Reid argues that Berczy's *The Woolsey Family*, painted in 1809, is "one of the few exceptional Canadian paintings" of the early nineteenth century.

In the private schools that flourished following the arrival of the Loyalists, young ladies received training in the "polite" accomplishments of drawing and watercolour painting. Women were also occasionally taught to draw by their formally trained fathers and brothers. Because they had few practical outlets for their work, women rarely earned a living from their artistic endeavours, and very few signed pieces of their work have survived the ravages of time and neglect.

***The Woolsey Family, 1809*, by William Berczy.**
National Gallery of Canada/5875

his considerable energy to overhauling Halifax's defences and was instrumental in the construction of three exquisite round structures: St George's Anglican Church, the Old Town Clock, and the Prince's Lodge Rotunda. Elevated to the peerage as the Duke of Kent in 1799, Prince Edward later became the father of Victoria, Queen of England from 1837 to 1901.

CONCLUSION

Between 1783 and 1815 the social, economic, and political ties linking Upper and Lower Canada and the Maritimes to Great Britain became stronger. The immigration of Loyalists and settlers from Great

Britain helped to anglicize the colonies, while the French and Napoleonic Wars drew them more fully into the British mercantile system of production and trade. In the Canadas, the War of 1812 encouraged commitment to the British parliamentary system rather than its republican counterparts in the United States and France. With a thriving fishery and growing population, Newfoundland and Labrador began to take on the trappings of the other colonies of settlement. The rest of British North America—the great Northwest and the Arctic—as we shall see in the next chapter, were also increasingly subject to the world's greatest empire.

A HISTORIOGRAPHICAL DEBATE

The Loyalists

No immigrant group in the history of Canada has attracted more historical controversy than the Loyalists, who represented a thick slice of North American society: white, black, and Native; rich and poor; liberal and conservative. Most Loyalists were ordinary people who happened, for a variety of reasons, to become refugees during the American Revolution, but this was not the dominant historical interpretation for most of the two centuries following the revolution.

Loyalists were so useful in providing English Canadians with a sense of identity that historians now talk about a Loyalist "myth." A myth is an instrument for self-identification, drawing its justification from an ideological interpretation of the past. The search for a "usable past" is not unique to Canada, but the case of the Loyalists offers an excellent example of how a nation's history can become distorted when historians set out to create a past rather than to analyze it.

Writing in 1898, Henry Coyne, a fellow of the Royal Society of Canada, offered one of the more extreme claims for his subjects: "[T]he Loyalists, to a considerable extent, were the very cream of the population of the Thirteen Colonies," Coyne opined. "They represented in very large measure the learning, the piety, the gentle birth, the wealth and good citizenship of the British race in America, as well as the devotion to law and order, British institutions, and the unity of the Empire."[6] This passage includes

some of the essential elements of the Loyalist tradition as defined by historians Murray Barkley and Norman Knowles: the elite origins of the refugees, their loyalty to the British Crown, their suffering and sacrifice in the face of hostile conditions, their consistent anti-Americanism, and their divinely inspired sense of mission.[7] Historians could emphasize any aspect of this cluster of attributes as the need arose. Thus, during the period when Loyalists were claiming compensation for what they had left behind when they fled the revolution, historians focused on loss and suffering. In the late nineteenth century, when Loyalist centennial celebrations coincided with a revival in British imperial sentiment, historians singled out their sense of mission. By the twentieth century, the Loyalist experience was used to explain why Canada, unlike the United States, had maintained a continuing colonial association with Britain, while at the same time sustaining liberal political values and institutions.

As with most myths, many of these claims contain a grain of truth. A few Loyalists were members of the colonial elite, and a good number of the refugees developed an unshakable loyalty to all things British. A few suffered unspeakable violence and hardship. Many of them were committed to liberal political principles. But other aspects of the tradition are harder to justify. Research suggests that immigrants from Britain were just as loyal as the refugees of the American

Revolution. The records also show that many Loyalists—probably up to 20 percent—returned to the United States once it was safe to do so. Other Loyalists participated in the War of 1812 on the side of the United States. So much for their loyalty and committed anti-Americanism.

In using their history to justify claims to superiority, descendants of the Loyalists abused the truth and actually diminished their status in the eyes of their non-Loyalist neighbours. At the same time, the definition of Loyalist descent became so broad that by the twentieth century most Anglo-Canadians who bothered to do so could find a Loyalist ancestor somewhere in their family tree. In New Brunswick, where the Loyalist myth was particularly pervasive, even descendants of Irish immigrants passed themselves off as Loyalists.

While those aspiring to Loyalist roots may be forgiven for exaggerating aspects of their family past, historians should not be judged so lightly. Many textbooks still present the Loyalists as the first anglophone immigrants to present-day Canada, conveniently ignoring more than 50 000 English settlers already living in the British colonies by 1783. The scholars who argue that the Loyalists planted the seeds of Canadian liberalism or conservatism in British North America usually fail to take into account not only the larger context of political discussion that prevailed throughout the North Atlantic world, but also the political values brought to British North America by other immigrants in the second half of the eighteenth century.

NOTES

1 Sarah (Sally) Winslow to Benjamin Marston, 10 April 1783, Winslow Family Papers, vol. 2, part 1, p. 67, Archives and Special Collections, University of New Brunswick.

2 James W. St. G. Walker, *The Black Loyalists: The Search for a Promised Land in Nova Scotia and Sierra Leone, 1783–1870* (New York: Longman, 1976), 73.

3 *Lord Durham's Report: An Abridgement of Report on the Affairs of British North America by Lord Durham*, ed. Gerald M. Craig (Toronto: McClelland and Stewart, 1963), 119.

4 Cited in Gerald M. Craig, *Upper Canada: The Formative Years, 1784–1841* (Toronto: McClelland and Stewart, 1963), 70–71.

5 Shannon Ryan, "Fishery to Colony: A Newfoundland Watershed, 1793–1815," *Acadiensis* 12, 2 (Spring 1983): 52.

6 J.H. Coyne, "Memorial to the U.E. Loyalists," *Niagara Historical Society Pamphlets*, No. 4 (Niagara-on-the-Lake, 1898), cited in L.F.S. Upton, *The United Empire Loylists: Men and Myths* (Toronto: Copp Clark, 1967), 138.

7 Murray Barkley, "The Loyalist Tradition in New Brunswick," *Acadiensis* 4, 2 (Spring 1975): 3–45 and Norman Knowles, *Inventing the Loyalists: The Ontario Loyalist Tradition and the Creation of a Usable Past* (Toronto: University of Toronto Press, 1997).

RELATED READINGS IN THIS SERIES

From *Foundations: Readings in Pre-Confederation Canadian History*

Norman Knowles, "'Chiefly Landholders, Farmers and Others': The Loyalist Reality," 193–201.
Ann Gorman Condon, "The Family in Exile: Loyalist Social Values after the Revolution," 202–10.
George Sheppard, "'Cool Calculators': Brock's Militia," 211–232.

From Media Companion CD-ROM, Volume I

The Exodus to Grand River
The Constitutional Act, 1791
Loyalists
Boston King
Jay's Treaty
Legislative Assembly of Lower Canada
Loyalist Farm in Upper Canada
Treaty of Ghent
Letter from English-Speaking Merchants to the Governor

Selected Reading

There is an extensive literature on the Loyalists. In *The United Empire Loyalists: Men and Myths* (Toronto: Copp Clark Pitman, 1967), L.S.F. Upton discusses the historiographical issues that haunt the topic. Specialized studies that avoid most of the historiographical traps include Norman Knowles, *Inventing the Loyalists: The Ontario Loyalist Tradition and the Creation of a Usable Past* (Toronto: University of Toronto Press, 1997); Esther Clark Wright's *The Loyalists of New Brunswick* (Wolfville, NS: Wright, 1955); Neil MacKinnon, *This Unfriendly Soil: The Loyalist Experience in Nova Scotia, 1783–1791* (Montreal: McGill-Queen's University Press, 1989); Marion Robertson, *King's Bounty: A History of Early Shelburne* (Halifax: Nova Scotia Museum, 1983); Robert L. Dallison, *Hope Restored: The American Revolution and the Founding of New Brunswick*, The New Brunswick Heritage Series, vol. 2 (Fredericton: Goose Lane Editions and the New Brunswick Heritage Project, 2003); David Bell, *Early Loyalist Saint John: The Origins of New Brunswick Politics* (Fredericton: New Ireland Press, 1983); Ann Gorman Condon, *The Envy of the American States: The Loyalists of New Brunswick* (Fredericton: New Ireland Press, 1984); Phyllis R. Blakeley and John N. Grant, eds., *Eleven Exiles: Accounts of Loyalists of the American Revolution* (Toronto: Dundurn, 1982); Robert S. Allen, *The Loyal Americans: The Military Role of the Loyalist Provincial Corps and Their Settlement in British North America, 1775–1784* (Ottawa: National Museums, 1983); Bruce Wilson, *As She Began: An Illustrated Introduction to Loyalist Ontario* (Toronto: Dundurn, 1981); and James J. Talman, ed., *Loyalist Narratives from Upper Canada* (Toronto: Champlain Society, 1946). The black Loyalist experience is described in James Walker, *The Black Loyalists: The Search for a Promised Land in Nova Scotia and Sierra Leone, 1783–1870* (1976; reprinted, Toronto: University of Toronto Press, 1992); William Spray, *The Blacks in New Brunswick* (Fredericton: Brunswick Press, 1972); and Ruth Holmes Whitehead and Carmelita A.M. Robertson, eds., *The Life of Boston King: Black Loyalist, Minister, and Master Carpenter* (Halifax: Nimbus Publishing, 2003). Literary issues are discussed in Gwen Davies, "Consolation to Distress: Loyalist Literary Activity in the Maritimes," in *Studies in Maritime Literary History* (Fredericton: Acadiensis Press, 1991), 30–47. On Loyalist women, see Mary Beth Norton's pioneering article, "Eighteenth-Century American Women in Peace and War: The Case of the Loyalists," *William and Mary Quarterly* 3, 33 (1976): 386–409, and Janice Potter-MacKinnon, *While Women Only Wept: Loyalist Refugee Women* (Montreal: McGill-Queen's University Press, 1993). Overviews are provided by Christopher Moore in *The Loyalists: Revolution, Exile and Settlement* (Toronto: Macmillan, 1984), and Wallace Brown and Hereward Senior, *Victorious in Defeat: The Loyalists in Canada* (Toronto: Methuen, 1984).

Quebec in the aftermath of the American Revolution is covered in A.L. Burt, Allen Greer, Fernand Ouellet, and Hilda Neatby, cited in Chapter 10, as well as Philip Lawson, *The Imperial Challenge: Quebec and Britain in the Age of the American Revolution* (Montreal and Kingston: McGill-Queen's University Press, 1989), and F. Murray Greenwood, *Legacies of Fear: Law and Politics in Quebec in the Era of the French Revolution* (Toronto: University of Toronto Press, 1993).

The social history of early Ontario is examined in a variety of excellent essays in J.K. Johnson and B. Wilson, eds., *Historical Essays on Upper Canada: New Perspectives* (Ottawa: Carleton University Press, 1989) and an earlier volume, *Historical Essays on Upper Canada* (Ottawa: Carleton University Press, 1975). On elite formation in the colony, see Johnson's *Becoming Prominent: Regional Leadership in Upper Canada, 1791–1841* (Montreal: McGill-Queen's University Press, 1989), and Bruce Wilson, *The Enterprises of Robert Hamilton: A Study of Wealth and Influence in Early Upper Canada* (Ottawa: Carleton University Press, 1983). The colony's economic history is surveyed in Douglas McCalla, *Planting the Province: The Economic History of Upper Canada, 1784–1870* (Toronto: University of Toronto Press, 1993). The gendered public discourse of Upper Canada is explored in Cecilia Morgan, *Public Men and Virtuous Women: The Gendered Language of Religion and Politics in Upper Canada, 1791–1850* (Toronto: University of Toronto Press, 1996). On women in Upper Canada, see Elizabeth Jane Errington, *Wives and Mothers, School Mistresses and Scullery Maids: Working Women in Upper Canada, 1790–1840* (Montreal: McGill-Queen's University Press, 1995); and Katherine M.J. McKenna, *Anne Murray Powell and Her Family, 1755–1849* (Montreal: McGill-Queen's University Press, 1994). On Upper Canadian politics, see Gerald Craig's *Upper Canada: The Formative Years* (Toronto: McClelland and Stewart, 1963); David Mills, *The Idea of Loyalty in Upper Canada, 1784–1850* (Montreal: McGill-Queen's University Press, 1988); and Jane Errington, *The Lion, the Eagle, and Upper Canada: A Developing Colonial Ideology* (Montreal: McGill-Queen's University Press, 1987).

For Lower Canada, Fernand Ouellet, *Lower Canada, 1791–1840: Social Change and Nationalism* (Toronto: McClelland and Stewart, 1980) and his *Economic and Social History of Quebec* (Toronto: Macmillan, 1981) provide abundant information as well as suggestive interpretations of the economic, social, and political history of Quebec during this period. Jean-Pierre Wallot, *Un Québec qui bougeait: trame socio-politique au tournant du XIXᵉ siècle* (Trois-Rivières: Boréal Express, 1973) offers a view of Lower Canada's economy and society before 1815 at variance with Ouellet's. An earlier study, more sympathetic to the British merchants, is Donald Creighton, *The Empire of the St Lawrence* (Toronto: Macmillan, 1956). Case studies of rural life are found in Allan Greer, *Peasant, Lord, and Merchant: Rural Society in Three Quebec Parishes, 1740–1840* (Toronto: University of Toronto Press, 1985). On the English-speaking minority, see Ronald Rudin, *The Forgotten Quebecers: A History of English-Speaking Quebec, 1759–1980* (Quebec: Institut québécois de recherche sur la culture, 1985).

The causes of the War of 1812 are assessed in Harry L. Coles, *The War of 1812* (Chicago: University of Chicago Press, 1965). Military aspects of the war are dealt with both in Coles and G.F.G. Stanley, *The War of 1812: Land Operations* (Toronto: Macmillan, 1983). On the social impact of war, see George Sheppard, *Plunder and Profit, and Paroles: A Social History of the War of 1812 in Upper Canada* (Montreal: McGill-Queen's University Press, 1994). A two-volume popular history of the war is Pierre Berton, *The Invasion of Canada, 1812–1813* and *Flames across the Border, 1813–1814* (Toronto: McClelland and Stewart, 1980; 1984).

Developments in Atlantic Canada in this period are covered in Buckner and Reid, Conrad and Hiller, MacNutt, and Bannister, cited earlier. See also Sean T. Cadigan, *Hope and Deception in Conception Bay: Merchant-Settler Relations in Newfoundland, 1785–1855* (Toronto: University of Toronto Press, 1995), and three books by Julian Gwyn: *Ashore and Afloat: The British Navy and the Halifax Naval Yard before 1820* (Ottawa: University of Ottawa Press, 2004), *Frigates and Foremasts: The North American Squadron in Nova Scotia Waters, 1745–1815* (Vancouver: UBC Press, 2003), and *Excessive Expectations: Maritime Commerce and the Economic Development of Nova Scotia, 1740–1870* (Montreal and Kingston: McGill-Queen's University Press, 1998). The significance of privateering for the Maritimes in this period is summarized in Daniel Conlin: "They Plundered Well: Planters as Privateers, 1793–1805," in *Planter Links: Community and Culture in Colonial Nova Scotia*, ed. Margaret Conrad and Barry Moody (Fredericton: Acadiensis Press, 2001), 20–35. The Maroon and black refugee migration in this period is covered in the two volumes by John N. Grant: *The Maroons in Nova Scotia* (Halifax: Formac, 2002) and *The Immigration and Settlement of the Black Refugees of the War of 1812* (Dartmouth: Black Cultural Centre for Nova Scotia, 1990).

WEBLINKS

EDWARD WINSLOW'S LETTERS
http://atlanticportal.hil.unb.ca/acva/en/winslow/
index.php

This University of New Brunswick site includes letters written to and from Massachusetts Loyalist Edward Winslow, who settled in New Brunswick after the American Revolution.

JAY'S TREATY
www.earlyamerica.com/earlyamerica/milestones/
jaytreaty/

This site begins with a description of the treaty, and allows access to an online readable reproduction of the treaty text.

THE CONSTITUTIONAL ACT, 1791
www.collectionscanada.ca/confederation/
h18-2088-e.html

This Library and Archives Canada site offers a description of the act and access to the text in both English and French.

AFRICAN NOVA SCOTIANS IN THE AGE OF SLAVERY AND ABOLITION
www.gov.ns.ca/nsarm/virtual/africanns

An online exhibit developed by the Nova Scotia Archives & Records Management on African Nova Scotians. It focuses mainly on the period between the founding of Halifax in 1749 and the coming into force in 1834 of the act that abolished slavery in the British colonies.

CHAPTER 12

Natives and the Fur Trade in the West, 1763–1821

Timeline

1741	Bering and Chirikov explore North Pacific
1772	Samuel Hearne reaches Arctic Ocean
1778	The Nuu'chah'nulth of Nootka Island encounter Captain Cook; Peter Pond establishes post on Lake Athabasca
1783	North West Company formed
1790	Nootka Sound Convention
1793	Alexander Mackenzie reaches Pacific by overland route
1794	Jay's Treaty
1811	David Thompson descends the Columbia to its mouth
1812	Establishment of Red River settlement
1821	Merger of Hudson's Bay Company and North West Company

In 1837, the Select Committee on Aborigines in the British House of Commons concluded frankly that British colonialism had "incurred a vast load of crime." The committee noted that "by taking possession of their hunting grounds . . . we have despoiled them of their means of existence." Despite this indictment of British behaviour, the committee asserted that colonies must remain the destination of the "superabundant populations of Great Britain and Ireland."[1]

While First Nations in today's western Canada would eventually also regard the growing European presence in their midst as "a vast load of crime," they were far more positive in the early years of their contact with the foreigners. In the period from 1763 to 1821, Natives continued to vastly outnumber the Europeans throughout the Northwest and British Columbia, and they became willing, often enthusiastic, participants in the fur trade. This chapter explores the motives of both Natives and Europeans in the Western fur trade, and the extent to which each controlled the direction of events in the period after the British had chased the French out of North America and its fur trade.

FUR-TRADE RIVALRIES IN THE NORTHWEST

According to the charter granted by Charles II in 1670, the Hudson's Bay Company had exclusive trading privileges in the area drained by rivers flowing into Hudson Bay. The Company initially confined its posts to the shores of Hudson Bay—Moose Factory, Albany, York Factory, and Churchill—relying on Native middlemen to bring in furs from afar. They were forced to abandon this strategy when the French on the St Lawrence began to invade their hinterlands in the 1730s. By the 1750s the French operated a network of posts that extended as far as the forks of the Saskatchewan River, limiting the supply of furs that reached the Bay posts.

In response, the Bay ventured inland. In 1754, Anthony Henday, a labourer and netmaker at York Factory, volunteered to explore the interior. Travelling in the company of a group of Cree, he made contact with the Plains nations and returned in 1755 with not only detailed maps but also a rich supply of furs. He was possibly the first European to reach the foothills of the Rocky Mountains. His original journal was severely edited because in it he chronicled his sexual relationship with his "Indian wife," which

A Hunter-Family of Cree Indians at York Fort, drawn from nature, 1821, by Peter Rindischer.
Library and Archives Canada/C-001917

offended the sensibilities of some Bay Company officials. He nevertheless proved the profitability of making contact with distant tribes and of using Native guides and interpreters as partners. After his initial foray, Bay Company traders made annual visits to the plains and parkland regions of Rupert's Land in pursuit of furs.

By this time the Natives living on the Plains had already adapted the horse to their hunting and fighting needs. The Blackfoot, Cree, and Assiniboine acquired horses through trade with First Nations to the south and had formed a strong trade alliance. Once they were in direct contact with the Europeans, the Plains peoples were able to acquire firearms that also contributed to their roles as hunters and warriors. The Cree-Blackfoot alliance became a casualty of the struggle to achieve dominance in the fur trade, and their firearms were more likely to be turned on each other than on the European fur traders.

Like the First Nations, Europeans competed among themselves for dominance in the fur trade. Indeed, the British conquest of New France resulted in an intensification of competition rather than its termination. Even before the Treaty of Paris was signed in 1763, traders from New York, New England, and

Scotland moved to Montreal and began to occupy French posts in the interior. Pushing aggressively north and west, they extended their range to the outer reaches of the continent.

At first, the area south and west of the Great Lakes was the favoured area for fur-trade operations. The American Revolution forced fur traders to reconsider their strategy. With the Americans determined to open the west to settlement, many fur traders were convinced that their long-term future lay in developing the northwest of the continent. Many First Nations in the southwest formed alliances with the British during the American Revolution to defend their homelands from the onslaught of white settlement.

As the traders established posts in the Northwest, they were welcomed by Natives. The Chipewyan were particularly aggressive in courting trading partners. They encouraged Peter Pond, a trader connected with Montreal merchants, to establish a post on Lake Athabasca so that they did not have to venture to Fort Prince of Wales or York Factory. In 1778, Pond acquiesced. Montreal traders were soon tapping the main fur-producing areas along the Athabasca, Peace, and Mackenzie rivers. In 1789, Alexander Mackenzie, exploring on behalf of the North West Company of

Samuel Hearne.
HBCA Documentary Art P-167 (N5353); *Mr. Samuel Hearne, Late Chief at Prince of Wale's Fort, Hudson's Bay* (Churchill). Engraving, coloured, 1796

Montreal, reached the Arctic Ocean along the river that bears his name.

Not to be outdone, the Hudson's Bay Company opened its first interior post in 1774, at Cumberland House some 800 kilometres from Hudson Bay. By that time, Bay men were crisscrossing the West in their efforts to outdistance their rivals based in Montreal. Like their Montreal counterparts, the Bay traders explored areas new to Europeans. In 1772, for example, Samuel Hearne reached the Arctic Ocean by way of the Coppermine River and put an end to speculation about a water passage from Hudson Bay to the Pacific.

Competition between the river and the bay led to the proliferation of trading posts. In 1774, there were only 17 posts in the Northwest—7 belonging to the Hudson's Bay Company and 10 to the St Lawrence traders. By 1804, there were 430 posts. Scarcely a Native living in the Northwest was more than 200 kilometres from a trading post.

The Montreal traders largely bested the Bay men in the battle for furs. In the winter of 1783–84, the leading Anglo-American traders in the western territories pooled their resources with the Montreal merchants who marketed their furs abroad. Together they formed the North West Company (NWC) to supply trade goods to "wintering partners"—the leaders of the trade in the interior—as well as to market the furs shipped from the trading posts to Montreal. The main Montreal partners were Benjamin and Joseph Frobisher and Simon McTavish, who held more shares than did the "wintering partners." In the years that followed, the western fur trade would make fortunes for these and other Montreal businessmen—fortunes invested in land, the timber trade, and other ventures in Lower Canada.

The new company's main advantages over the Hudson's Bay Company (HBC) were its experienced French-Canadian voyageurs, its Native-style birch-bark canoes, and its wintering partners. In a short time, however, the HBC had built and put into operation large numbers of York boats, flat-bottomed vessels made of spruce and rowed by eight men with long oars. The experienced boatmen hired for the purpose were found mainly in the Orkney Isles north of the Scottish coast. To match the wintering partners of the "Nor'Westers," the HBC placed its posts in the hands of inland masters. Although these traders, unlike the wintering Nor'Westers, did not initially share in profits, they were permanently stationed in the interior. The two rival companies, pitting London against Montreal capital, continuously expanded their operations until they finally merged in 1821.

NATIVE PEOPLES AND THE FUR TRADE

For Native peoples, it mattered little whether their furs went to London or Montreal merchants. Their goal remained the receipt of as many high-quality goods as possible for their furs at a conveniently located post. During the period of HBC-NWC competition, this goal was often met. Economic advantages as well as aggressive attempts by the companies to enlist new groups of Natives to their respective sides drew an ever-expanding number of nations into the trade. A new "middle ground" of Native-European culture soon developed. The companies depended upon the Natives as trappers and providers of local food. Living in proximity to them, company employees often married Native women.

In Northern regions competition among the companies was often more of a curse than a blessing, and fur-trader "marriages" to Native women sometimes appeared to the Dene as forced confinement of the women rather than willing partnerships. A trader would simply use force or intimidation to acquire a woman whom he wanted to live with, rather than seek her consent or the consent of her family. Taking advantage of the smaller concentrations of people and relative lack of firearms in the North, traders imposed a harsher regime than they dared among the more populous and better-armed First Nations further south. The companies often used threats and beatings, as opposed to more attractive trade goods at better rates of exchange, to prevent Natives from dealing with a competitor.

The North West Company was particularly notorious in this regard. After the Hudson's Bay Company began to establish posts in the Athabasca District in 1790, the Nor'Westers had little hesitation in employing violence against both their competitor and their Native suppliers to try to maintain as much of their former monopoly in the region as possible. The violence reached new levels between 1798 and 1804, when the XY Company, a loose grouping of traders who had broken from the NWC, attempted to gain a foothold in the region. Though the XY group returned to the NWC fold by 1804, the violence in the North continued.

Some Dene groups responded to trader violence by withdrawing from the trade. From the early days of contact, many tribes had refused to become part of the fur trade and appeared to live happily enough without the white man's goods. While withdrawal from the trade was the usual response to a pattern of fur-trader violence, retaliation was not uncommon. In the Fort Chipewyan area, at the turn of the nineteenth century, there were several incidents of Dene murders of traders deemed to have treated the Natives abusively.

If such abuse was less common further south, it was not always the case that First Nations that participated in the fur trade got what they bargained for. The Ojibwa of what is now northwestern Ontario

experienced a cycle that would be repeated for many tribes on the parklands and plains of the West in the era of the HBC's monopoly. In the late eighteenth century, the Ojibwa were indispensable to the traders north and west of Lake Superior not only as trappers, but also as guides to the many superficially similar rivers of the area, as providers of venison, and as labourers on the supply boats. They were able to command good prices for their furs and to influence the location of trading posts. Continuing as ever to hunt big game and to provide themselves with most of the necessities of life, the Ojibwa valued the trade in beaver pelts for the firearms and metal utensils that made their lives easier. The easy partnership would not last. From 1804 onward, there were reports that beaver were becoming scarce in the region trapped by the Ojibwa. Soon it became clear that big game in the area was also disappearing.

Reports of death from starvation and rumours of cannibalism underlined the gravity of the situation. With few furs to sell and food supplies low, the Ojibwa had to work harder and to travel further in search of game. This was an ironic outcome of the fur trade, given that European goods had once been attractive because they reduced the amount of work necessary for survival. Overtrapping and overhunting had jeopardized Ojibwa independence. Many of them moved west to the Plains where they could continue to hunt and trap, while those who remained behind were increasingly dependent upon the fur-trade companies for survival. Once they became indebted to the companies, their lives became an endless round of trying to pay off debts. Although Ojibwa communities maintained cooperative patterns and traditional religious customs, there were signs of cultural erosion. The young who were reared in poverty often showed little respect for elders, whom they saw as poor providers.

Some of the Ojibwa adapted to the new circumstances by turning to the cultivation of corn and potatoes, both for subsistence and for exchange with the fur traders. At Lake of the Woods and Red Lake, substantial gardens had been established by the 1820s. Agriculture had not been practised in the western interior in the early fur-trade period, and it was not the traders but the Ottawa nation moving westward with the trade who introduced it into the region. Growing food provided a livelihood only for a tiny minority of

The Impact of the Fur Trade on Natives: A Trader's View

In 1774, Samuel Hearne, a former officer in the Royal Navy, was placed in charge of Cumberland House, a post set up by the Hudson's Bay Company to compete with the Montreal traders for customers among the First Nations. He had proved his mettle by surviving in the Canadian interior and dealing on a friendly basis with the Aboriginal people during a 1900-kilometre journey in 1771–72 that led him as far as the Arctic Ocean. His description of the Chipewyan in the early 1770s reflects the views of a trader who admired the Natives and had few illusions about the impact of the fur trade on their society:

> The real wants of these people are few, and easily supplied; a hatchet, an ice-chisel, a file, and a knife, are all that is required to enable them, with a little industry, to procure a comfortable livelihood, and those who endeavour to possess more, are always the most unhappy, and may, in fact, be said to be only slaves and carriers to the rest, whose ambition never leads them to anything beyond the means of procuring food and clothing. It is true, the carriers pride themselves much on the respect which is shown to them at the Factory; to obtain which they frequently run great risques of being starved to death in their way thither and back; and all they can possibly get for the furrs they procure after a year's toil, seldom amounts to more than is sufficient to yield a bare subsistence, and a few furrs for the ensuing year's market; while those whom they call indolent and mean-spirited live generally in a state of plenty, without trouble or risque; and consequently must be the most happy, and, in truth, the most independent also. It must be allowed that they are by far the greatest philoso-phers, as they never give themselves the trouble to acquire what they can do well enough without. The deer they kill, furnishes them with food, and a variety of warm and comfortable clothing, either with or without the hair, according as the seasons require; and it must be very hard indeed, if they cannot get furrs enough in the course of two or three years, to purchase a hatchet, and such other edge-tools as are necessary for their purpose. Indeed, those who take no concern at all about procuring furrs, have generally an opportunity of providing themselves with all their real wants from their more industrious countrymen, in exchange for provisions, and ready-dressed skins for clothing.
>
> It is undoubtedly the duty of every one of the company's servants [employees] to encourage a spirit of industry among the natives, and to use every means in their power to induce them to procure furrs and other commodities for trade, by assuring them of a ready purchase and good payment for every thing they bring to the Factory; and I can truly say that this has ever been the grand object of my intention. But I must at the same time confess, that such conduct is by no means for the real benefit of the poor Indians; it being well known that those who have the least intercourse with the Factories [posts], are by far the happiest. As their whole aim is to procure a comfortable subsistence, they take the most prudent methods to accomplish it, and by always following the lead of the deer, are seldom exposed to the gripping hand of famine, so frequently felt by those who are called the annual traders.[2]

the Aboriginal population; most Natives continued to rely on hunting, fishing, and trapping even as local resources diminished. They tended to see agriculture as at best a supplementary source of food and income.

The experience of the Blackfoot was different from that of the Ojibwa. By about 1730, the Blackfoot had come into indirect contact with the European presence when they received their first horses from the Shoshoni, another Plains nation, and firearms and iron from the Cree and Assiniboine. At the time, the Blackfoot lived on the northern plains of Saskatchewan, but their new weapons and an outbreak of smallpox among the Shoshoni allowed them to expand south and west and eventually to dominate southern Alberta as well as Montana. As the Piegan, followed by the Blood and Blackfoot, pushed west to the foothills of the Rockies, the Shoshoni and Kutenai were forced across the mountains.

During his travels to the West in 1754, Anthony Henday encountered the Blood, one of the groups that made up the Blackfoot Confederacy. They made clear their lack of interest in journeying from their territory to trade in furs. Their livelihood, they noted, was the buffalo hunt, and their territorial expansion was focused on areas where buffalo were plentiful. In 1787, David Thompson was sent by the HBC to persuade the Blackfoot to bring furs to company posts on the South Saskatchewan River, but he met with the same response.

By the 1790s, the Blackfoot apparently had a change of heart. As the HBC and NWC built posts on the northern fringe of Blackfoot country, this once aloof nation began to bring wolf and fox skins to trading posts, although they still refused to trap beaver. The major item that the Blackfoot traded with the Europeans quickly became pemmican, a mixture of dried buffalo and berries that became the mainstay of officers and employees at fur-trade posts as other game became less plentiful.

The Blackfoot, unlike the Ojibwa, did not become dependent on the Europeans during the fur-trading period because the large number of buffalo in their territory continued to provide them with self-sufficiency in food, clothing, and much else besides. They were not interested in either the Europeans' food or, for a long period, clothing—the women in particular refused to respond to the traders' blandishments to purchase their woollens—so the Blackfoot traded for guns, powder, awls, iron, beads, tobacco, and liquor. The traders were pleased but sometimes puzzled that the Blackfoot had agreed to trade with them. Fur trader Daniel Harmon wrote in 1804: "Those Indians who reside in the large Plains are the most independent and appear to be the happiest and most contented of any People upon the face of the Earth. They subsist on the flesh of the Buffalo and of the skin they make the greatest part of their cloathing which is both warm and convenient."[3]

To some extent, the trade was profitable for the Blackfoot. It allowed them to expand their territory, increase the size of their tipis and buffalo corrals, and generally to prosper. At the same time, their self-sufficient economy was slowly transformed into an increasingly commercial one, and tendencies toward inequality dating from the pre-contact period were reinforced. The traders from the two companies, wooing the Blackfoot tipi by tipi, encouraged a degree of individualism that eroded the unity of the tribes.

As a result of these developments, the scale of warfare increased dramatically. Young men were the chief victims of an increasingly violent society. The balance in numbers of men and women evident at the time of David Thompson's 1787 visit gave way in two generations to a three-to-one preponderance of women over men. While the men who survived were often able to marry four or even eight wives and live in huge tipis, the women were not as fortunate. A sorority of wives had characterized polygamy in an earlier period when most men had one or two wives. With larger numbers of wives, that tendency broke down. Beyond a third or fourth marriage, new wives were regarded almost as slaves, were excluded from the Sun Dance, and were otherwise discriminated against.

Still, by the 1820s the Blackfoot remained in control of their destiny and regarded the fur trade as beneficial. Other tribes of the parklands and plains, unlike the Ojibwa of Northern Ontario, felt the same way. Apart from the Blackfoot, the major groups in the area that now forms the southern half of the Prairie provinces were Cree, Ojibwa, and Assiniboine, many of them immigrants during the fur-trade period. All had experienced a degree of cultural change after moving onto the Plains, mainly through the adoption of a number of the beliefs and rituals of the original Plains nations. The Sun Dance, for example, was adopted by all the new residents of the northern plains. While missionaries settled among these nations and attempted to convert them to Christianity, the Natives were as yet under little compulsion to accept beliefs and practices that they found unconvincing. For one Native group, however, the question of cultural identity was inevitably complicated. This was the Métis, whose heritage was both Indian and European.

THE BIRTH OF THE MÉTIS NATION

The term Métis theoretically refers to "mixed-blood" people—that is, people whose known ancestral heritage is a mixture of European and Native Indian. In practice, only a fraction of mixed-blood individuals ever identified themselves as Métis. During the

MORE TO THE STORY

The Spread of Disease

While the Natives could choose what elements of European culture they wished to adopt, they had little ability to control the pathogens that Europeans brought into their midst.

Mulks, a Squamish elder who spoke only his Coast Salish mother tongue, was about 100 years old in 1896 when he recounted the Squamish people's tale of a smallpox epidemic that had ravaged the peoples of the Strait of Georgia in the period before they had ever seen any Europeans. The master of an Anglican college in Vancouver, who transcribed the account that the Squamish translators provided, wrote:

> A dreadful skin disease, loathsome to look upon, broke out upon all alike. None were spared. Men, women and children sickened, took the disease and died in agony by hundreds, so that when the spring arrived and fresh food was procurable, there was scarcely a person left of all their numbers to get it. Camp after camp, village after village, was left desolate. The remains of which, said the old man, in answer to my queries on this head, are found today in the old camp sites or midden-heaps over which the forest has been growing for so many generations. Little by little the remnant left by the disease grew into a nation once more, and when the first white men sailed up the Squamish in their big boats, the tribe was strong and numerous again.[4]

The epidemic of which Mulks spoke was the Pacific coastal leg of a smallpox pandemic among Natives of the Americas that broke out in central Mexico in 1779. Spreading rapidly north and south, smallpox killed half the people of the Assiniboine, Ojibwa, Cree, and Blackfoot nations. By 1782 it had reached the northern plains, leaving its deadly mark on the Chipewyan, and had crossed the Rockies to devastate First Nations in southern British Columbia, few of whom had yet encountered a white man. Captain George Vancouver, exploring the territory around Puget Sound and the Strait of Georgia in the early 1790s, was astonished by the number of deserted villages with hundreds of human skeletons lying on the beaches.

The expanding fur trade across the Plains helps to account for the speed with which the epidemic moved. In the seventeenth century, Spanish traders sold horses to Natives in Mexico and today's American southwest. By the 1780s, the horse had become an essential part of the lives of Plains First Nations. Making land-based trade across the continent easier than ever, the horse culture opened up new trading patterns that linked people across vast distances. It also opened up a pathway for pathogens such as smallpox and diphtheria, bringing to the Plains the tragedies that had already befallen the Natives east of the Great Lakes. While smallpox's course was slower in British Columbia, where many of the coastal nations remained relatively isolated from other Native groups, the fur trade would eventually introduce all the western First Nations to a variety of diseases that would take a heavy toll in human lives.

Yet the indigenous peoples of the Western Cordillera, the Interior Plains, and the North survived the onslaught of disease and generally remained enthusiastic participants in the fur trade. Such enthusiasm was particularly evident among the Métis, who owed their very existence to the fur trade.

French regime, intermarriage between white men involved in the fur trade and Native women was so common that one demographer suggests that as many as 40 percent of French-Canadians in Quebec today have at least one Native ancestor. Children of part-Native descent who integrated into Quebec society did not develop a sense of being members of a separate nation, nor did the offspring of Native-white liaisons who rejoined the tribes of their mothers.

The term Métis, then, is probably most usefully applied to persons who were members of mixed-blood communities and whose sense of identity was with other mixed-bloods rather than with a particular Native or European group. Before the end of the French regime, sizable Métis communities had sprung up in the territory of the upper Great Lakes, and more such communities developed in the area of the modern-day Prairie provinces during the years that followed.

Liaisons between fur traders and Native women were frowned upon by the Catholic Church and forbidden by the HBC. The church could have little impact upon young men who lived much of their lives in the interior, but the HBC was somewhat more successful in restraining its employees—at least until competition from the North West Company forced it to relax its regulation that only officers of posts could have sexual relations with Native women. This was an enforceable policy while the HBC restricted its operations to a small number of forts along Hudson Bay, but it later became a detriment in attracting employees to winter at inland posts.

Native society approved of marriages between its women and European traders; such unions were consistent with pre-contact practices in which intertribal marriages cemented trade and military relationships between groups. Both in the French regime and afterward, the traders often proved fickle marriage partners. When it came time to retire, they would often abandon long-term relationships that had produced many children. In the French period, most of the abandoned Native wives and their children were reintegrated into their former communities. Later, as it became common both for the traders and First Nations to move frequently, Native women could no longer easily return home, and many of them and their children became dependent upon the fur-trade posts for their survival. As the numbers of mixed-blood women increased, they became the preferred marriage partners for white fur traders.

Meanwhile, the Métis men played a special role in the plans of the two fur-trade companies. For the most part, the sons of British employees, whether officers or clerks, were hired as labourers at the posts. The French-speaking Métis, who had started their own settlements, were valued as providers of pemmican, as boatmen, and as guides. Significantly, all the jobs reserved for Métis were low in status and pay. Even the Métis sons of officers or partners were blocked from advancement.

The Métis communities developed cultural patterns that set them apart from both Native and Euro-Canadian culture. The offspring of the French developed their own language, Michif,

which combined French and the Plains Cree language in almost equal quantities. English-speaking Métis also developed their own language, Bungi, a combination of Cree with the Scots dialect of the Orkneys. The dances of the Métis combined the intricate footwork of Natives with Scottish and French forms, including reels and jigs. In the Red River area, Métis travelled in carts with "dished"—saucer-shaped—wheels to avoid getting stuck in the prairie mud. The carts were made entirely of wood, the parts bound together by wet rawhide that shrank after drying and proved particularly sturdy. The Métis women, maintaining the leather-work skills of their Aboriginal ancestors, used beads rather than porcupine quills to decorate the coats, belts, and moccasins they produced. Later the women of the Plains nations also adopted this practice.

THE FOUNDING OF THE RED RIVER SETTLEMENT

Although the Métis played a crucial role in the life of the two rival fur-trade companies, they were not consulted by the HBC when it established the Red River settlement near present-day Winnipeg. The settlement's origins reflected a convenient mix of philanthropic and commercial objectives. Lord Selkirk, a Scottish landowner and peer in the British House of Lords, regarded with concern the fate of Scots

Red River cart.
Library and Archives Canada/C61689

The Selkirk Settlement, begun in 1812, was the first European agricultural settlement in western Canada.
Library and Archives Canada/C-008714

Highlanders deprived of their land by his fellow landowners who wanted land for sheep enclosures. He also had sympathy for impoverished Irish whose revolt against British rule in 1798 had been bloodily suppressed. Selkirk began to promote colonization as a commercial venture that would not only enrich its promoters but also rid Great Britain of a surplus population for which the new industrial order offered no employment. In 1808 and 1809, Selkirk and a group of associates purchased a third of the HBC's shares and used their voting power within the company to promote an agricultural settlement in the Red River valley. Selkirk's partner, Andrew Colvile, argued that the settlement could help provision the western fur trade, reducing the costs associated with getting supplies from Britain.

That settlement began modestly in 1812 with 35 people, whose numbers were reduced by scurvy the first winter. Although the settlers were able to survive with the help of local Saulteaux (Ojibwa), their early attempts at farming were disastrous. They did not begin to sow viable crops until the late 1820s.

While the experienced HBC fur traders viewed Selkirk's settlement derisively, the Nor'Westers suspected that it was a ploy to create a strategic outpost that could disrupt their company's river links between Montreal and the interior. The Métis, with several large settlements in the area, also believed that the Red River colony threatened their future, and NWC traders encouraged them in this view. As it turned out, the actions of the colony's governor, Miles Macdonnell, suggested that the Nor'Wester and Métis suspicions were justified. With poor crops and more settlers arriving annually, the fledgling colony was dependent on pemmican supplies for its survival. In January 1814 Macdonnell issued a proclamation against the export of pemmican from the vast region—known as Assiniboia—that had been placed under his control as a potential area of settlement. This proclamation threatened the NWC's supplies and confirmed fears about the real purposes of the colony. It was also a blow to the Métis, who were the main producers and exporters of pemmican.

The Métis had another reason to dislike Macdonnell. Emulating the Plains nations, the Métis hunted the buffalo by running them on horseback, a practice that was gradually driving the animals away from the lower Red River. Wanting to avoid a situation in which the colony would depend on Natives and Métis for provisions, Macdonnell issued a proclamation in July 1814 forbidding the running of buffalo. This confirmed the Métis view that the settlement would not recognize their rights in the region.

The NWC encouraged the Métis to respond belligerently to these provocations. Nor'Wester Duncan

Cameron named three prominent Métis "captains" and in 1816 made one of them, Cuthbert Grant, "Captain-General of the Métis." The militia led by these captains solidified the sense of identity among the Métis of the Prairies.

In 1815, the NWC's intrigues forced Macdonnell to leave the settlement, which was being besieged by Métis attackers. His interim replacement, Peter Fidler, a long-time fur trader and father to a large Métis family, capitulated to Métis demands to disband the colony, but the colonists had only been gone a few months before they returned under new leadership and with reinforcements. Governor Robert Semple, like his predecessor, was insensitive to Métis interests and antagonistic toward the NWC. He reinstated the pemmican ban and, to make it last, ordered the seizure of Fort Gibraltar, the NWC's post in the Red River area, in March 1816.

In retaliation, the Métis under Grant seized pemmican from HBC posts on the Qu'Appelle River to provision the Nor'Westers on Lake Winnipeg. On their way to the Nor'Westers, Grant's Métis militia were surprised by Semple and a group of armed colonists at a place called Seven Oaks. Semple, misjudging the numbers under Grant's direction, demanded that the Métis disarm. In the ensuing confrontation, Semple and twenty of his men were killed; on Grant's side, there were only two casualties.

Lord Selkirk, determined to punish the Métis as well as the Nor'Westers, whom he blamed for the Métis aggressiveness, hired Swiss mercenaries to improve the colony's defences. He also had Grant and other Métis leaders charged with murder and forced to appear before Canadian courts, but no one was convicted. Selkirk's actions against several NWC officials were similarly unsuccessful.

The court rulings confirmed the finding of a British-appointed commission that no premeditated Métis massacre of Selkirk settlers had occurred at Seven Oaks. In his report William Bachelor Coltman, the principal commissioner, concluded that the Selkirk party had fired the first shot. Coltman believed that the Métis had subsequently killed wounded men rather than taking prisoners, and he suggested that the heavy casualties of the HBC men were the result of their "standing together in a crowd, unaccustomed to the use, of fire-arms, or any of the practices of irregular warfare" while they faced "excellent marksmen, advantageously posted in superior numbers around their opponents."[6]

Until recently, the conclusions of Coltman and the courts did not prevent most Manitoba historians from treating the Seven Oaks incident as a massacre. The discrediting of the Métis formed part of the narrative of the conquest of "savagery" by "civilization" and could be used to mask the reality of dispossession of Native lands.

For First Nations in the Red River area, the beginnings of dispossession occurred subtly. William Coltman, while in the Red River area, agreed to a request from Lord Selkirk to negotiate a treaty between the Crown and the Cree and Ojibwa of the area so that Selkirk could acquire lands that he wanted for his settlement. In return for allowing Europeans to settle designated pieces of land that stretched from two to six miles from the banks of the Red and Assiniboine rivers, the First Nations received a "quit-rent," initially set at 200 pounds of tobacco per year. The Natives understood the deal as an annual lease of lands, while Selkirk understood the transaction as a surrender for all time of a portion of Native lands to the Europeans. This cultural clash in the interpretation of treaties would be repeated time and again. For Natives, land was a gift of the Creator, a sacred trust. It was not a commodity and could not be sold. For Europeans, by contrast, with the feudal system behind them, everything was potentially a commodity, and land was no exception.

Merger of the Hudson's Bay Company and the North West Company

The competition between the HBC and NWC nearly ruined both companies financially and placed a severe strain on fur-bearing animals and game in the Northwest. Political pressures in Britain, as well as these economic pressures, forced the two companies to merge in 1821. The new company took the Hudson's Bay Company's name and was required by the British Parliament to end the use of liquor as a trade item in the fur trade. Fast on the heels of the merger came massive layoffs as rival posts were consolidated.

Native Agriculture in the Northwest

While archeological research suggests that in the pre-contact period, agriculture was practised in the Northwest as far north as today's Lockport, Manitoba, it had ceased during the early fur-trading period, probably because corn, tobacco, and other cultivated products had become available through trade. Trade goods received from the Europeans in exchange for furs were, in turn, traded with agricultural nations further south. As the availability of both fur-bearing animals and game declined in areas under Ojibwa control, many Native peoples tried to adapt to the new circumstances by taking up agriculture.

The Ottawa resident on the Red River in the village of Netley Creek reintroduced agriculture to the Northwest in 1805 after receiving seed from trader Alexander Henry. They planted Indian corn, potatoes, and other crops. In turn the Ottawa taught the Ojibwa, migrants from parklands areas with no farming tradition, how to plant corn. Initially the HBC and the NWC discouraged Indians from planting crops, fearing it would diminish their participation in the fur trade. Later, as game became more scarce in the region, it was accepted that Native farmers could contribute to the traders' food requirements. Agriculture spread among the Ojibwa despite the early lack of enthusiasm on the part of fur traders. South of Lake Manitoba corn was the major crop; north of the lake it was potatoes. While no group gave up the hunt and became completely sedentary, agricultural sites often became the centre of ceremonial gatherings for the Ojibwa. A description by HBC trader William Brown in 1819 indicates the impact of agriculture on Ojibwa life, including the division of labour by gender:

> A considerable number of the Indians particularly those of Fort Dauphin, and the Manitoba, have ground under cultivation, and raise a great many Potatoes, but that is their only crop. . . . Those of the Manitoba. . . [cultivate] on an Island towards the North end of the

Lake, they have erected there what they call a Big Tent, where they all assemble in spring, hold Councils and go thro' their Religious Ceremonies—The soil here is excellent and each family has a portion of it under cultivation, which the women and old men remain, and take care of during the summer—while the young men go a hunting—In the fall of the year when they are going to abandon the place, they secure that part of the produce, under ground till spring, which they cannot carry along with them—During favourable years, they generally make a considerable quantity of maple sugar, part of which they also put in Cache—The Big Tent is constructed in the form of an arch, and consists of a slight frame of wood covered on the outside with the bark of the pine tree, and lined in the inside with bulrush mats. It is 60 ft. long—15 ft. wide—and 10 ft. high.[5]

There was commercial corn production in the region between Lake Superior and Lake of the Woods, where big game had dwindled dramatically, leaving both Natives and traders with a diminished food supply. The Ottawa were innovators in this region, as they had been on the Red River. In 1812, they began growing crops on Garden Island, their first agricultural site in the Lake of the Woods area, and by 1819 the women were growing corn, potatoes, pumpkins, onions, and carrots. Ojibwa agricultural sites soon followed. After mid-century, in the period of rapid European settlement, missionaries believed they could speed up the process of "civilizing" and "Christianizing" the Native peoples by encouraging them to take up agriculture. Such a belief was a departure from earlier in the century when agriculture had provided a means by which the Ojibwa and Ottawa of the Northwest, faced with a declining resource base, retained their culture in the face of threats to their independence.

The Selkirk settlement, where poor crops, floods, and locusts were driving away many settlers, received a much-needed boost from the arrival of many of these discharged employees. Henceforth, large numbers of retired HBC men, usually the fathers of Métis families, would choose to spend their declining years with their families as farmers in the Red River settlement. The strengthening of the settlement was only one of the far-reaching consequences for Western Canada of the amalgamation of the two rival fur-trading companies.

BRITISH COLUMBIA: THE EUROPEAN PHASE

Coastal Trade

West of the Rockies, European contact came later and under different conditions. Recent evidence suggests Sir Francis Drake, who had circumnavigated the globe between 1578 and 1580, explored coastal British Columbia on a secret mission for Elizabeth I in 1579. Unfortunately, his maps, drawn up in cryptograms to prevent them being intelligible if they fell into the hands of rival Spain, were forgotten after both he and Elizabeth were dead.

The continuous European history in British Columbia began in 1778 when Captain James Cook surveyed the northwest coast in his search for the elusive Northwest Passage from Hudson Bay to the Pacific. Before that time, Russian and Spanish explorers had approached the region from opposite directions. In separate expeditions, the Russians Vitus Bering and Aleksei Chirikov explored the Alaska coast in 1741, their explorations leading to the sea otters' silky furs becoming available to an appreciative market in Russia and China. A growing Russian presence on the Pacific coast led the Spanish to send expeditions from San Blas, their naval base in Mexico, to search for interlopers and establish a Spanish claim to the region. In 1774, Juan Perez sighted what would become known as the Queen Charlotte Islands and traded with the Haida, who sailed out to meet his ship. The coastal Natives had traded among themselves for at least three millennia and needed no coaxing to make exchanges with newcomers bearing products made of metal. The following year, Juan Francisco de la Bodega y Quadra officially claimed the North Pacific coast for Carlos III of Spain.

In 1789, the Spanish sent Captain Esteban Jose Martinez to establish a fortified base at Nootka Sound, where Cook had landed in 1778. War over the North Pacific coast was avoided in 1790 with the Nootka Sound Convention, which permitted joint occupation of the Pacific coast north of San Francisco. Five years later, the Spanish abandoned their fortified base on Nootka Sound.

By that time, Europeans and Aboriginal peoples had taken stock of each other and found a common ground of interest in the exchange of material goods.

During his four-week stay with the Nuu'chah'nulth (Nootka) in 1778, Cook and his crew traded a variety of goods for sea-otter pelts, food, and artifacts. Cook reported that the Native demand for European products was insatiable:

> Hardly a bit of it [brass] was left in the ships except what belonged to our necessary instruments. Whole suits of clothes were stripped of every button; bureaus of their furniture; and copper kettles, tin cannisters, candlesticks and the like, all went to wreck; so that our American friends got a greater medley and variety of things from us, than any other nations whom we had visited.[7]

The profits that Cook gained from the sale of sea-otter skins in China opened a thriving trade for the Nuu'chah'nulth from the 1780s to the 1820s. British, French, Spanish, and American traders participated in the exchange of goods—usually iron tools—for pelts collected by the Nuu'chah'nulth and other coastal peoples, including the Haida of the Queen Charlotte Islands area. The trade was dominated by the Americans (the "Boston men") and the British ("King George men").

The Natives were hard bargainers who were not dependent on European goods and refused to trade except on their own terms. Like the woodland and parkland nations in the late eighteenth century and the Plains nations well beyond that time, the coastal Natives held the upper hand in the transactions. The maritime trade and the new trade goods it brought into their territories did not appear to have an adverse effect on their institutions; on the contrary, labour-saving devices and metal tools gave the original peoples more time and scope to develop their much-cherished crafts, such as totem poles and masks. The end result was an enhancement of the existing culture rather than an adaptation to the culture of the traders. Indeed, the shipbound traders made no attempt to impose cultural change on the Native peoples—their only interest was in acquiring pelts.

Historians debate the character of the relations between the traders and the coastal nations. Robin Fisher in *Contact and Conflict* argued that because of the Natives' crucial role in the trade, the European traders had little choice but to treat them with consideration. More recently, James R. Gibson has challenged Fisher's claims, demonstrating that the

BIOGRAPHY

A Tale of Two Maquinnas

Maquinna was the chief of the Mowachaht people, a Nuu'chah'nulth group that numbered about 1500, when the Europeans first ventured into Nuu'chah'nulth territory. His first encounter with Europeans came in 1774, when the Spanish, after meeting the Haida, encountered storms and, forced southward, sought shelter in Nootka Sound. Four years later Captain Cook's ships ventured past the Mowachaht summer home at Yuquot, on the southeast of Nootka Island, a large island off the west coast of Vancouver Island. Maquinna sent some of his people to greet the strangers on their boats, and then initiated trade with the British, giving Cook his royal robe of sea-otter skins as a gift.

Maquinna presided over the Mowachaht trade with the Europeans until his death in 1795. While he allowed the Spanish to establish a fortified base on Nootka Sound in the late 1780s, he was eager both to preserve good relations with all the white groups interested in trading with his people and to compel them to recognize Nuu'chah'nulth control over a homeland that Natives had occupied for 4300 years. In 1792 he hosted a meeting of Captain Vancouver for the English and Captain Quadra for the Spanish that settled the two countries' dispute regarding trading rights in the area. Maquinna insisted that Europeans must pay each time they fished in Mowachaht waters or cut trees on their land.

Despite his best efforts, Maquinna could not prevent some traders from treating his people without respect. In 1785, as the trade began in earnest, a ship's captain, in retaliation for a stolen chisel, unleashed a cannon attack on the Nootka Sound people that left 20 dead. That same year Maquinna's successor, who would take the same name at the time of his succession, was scarred permanently by gunpowder placed under him by a ship's crew that had invited him aboard. Meanwhile, the smallpox epidemic a few years earlier, which many Natives correctly associated with the newcomers, had killed about half the Nuu'chah'nulth population.

Outrages occurred periodically, often the result of crews taking a swift and terrible revenge on an entire group because of petty thievery or assault by a few of its members. In turn, the Nuu'chah'nulth were prepared to take a collective revenge on the whites, whom they regarded as having collectively abused Natives even if it was a relatively small number of traders who engaged in murderous behaviour. In 1803, under the second Maquinna's orders, the Mowachaht warriors planned the mur-

der of the crew members of the American ship *Boston*. American ships did not allow armed Natives aboard, but Maquinna's followers, after being strip-searched, overpowered the ship's crew, using paddles and equipment as weapons. They then used weapons aboard to murder all but two of the twenty-seven crew members.

The two men, when they were freed, produced a classic captivity book in which they described in excruciating detail the daily horrors they allegedly faced at the hands of their captors. The book, like others of its sort, was used by American officials and landgrabbers to make Natives appear less than human and therefore unfit to have sovereignty over their traditional lands. Of course, the provocations of the whites and the many cold-blooded murders of Natives were conveniently ignored in such accounts.

Callicum and Maquinna, Nuu'chah'nulth leaders, 1789.
Library and Archives Canada/C27699

European traders often dealt violently with the Natives, precipitating violent responses from the Natives in return. Traders might recognize that they depended on the cooperation of the Native peoples, but racist assumptions about Native inferiority sometimes meant that European attempts at domination obstructed the more profitable course of cooperative relations. "Thus, Euroamerican-Indian relations, initially cordial, soon became strained, with the mutual distaste periodically exploding in violence, mainly owing to prejudging, defrauding, and kidnapping on the part of white traders."[8] While he places more emphasis than Fisher on the violence—including many murders—that occurred, Gibson concedes that the countries involved in the trade placed pressure on individual traders to resolve problems with the Natives since the latter were essential to the trade.

Inland Trade

Not long after the coastal sea-otter trade took off, trade for furs had begun in the British Columbia interior. The first trader to reach this region was Alexander Mackenzie of the North West Company. Unlike the HBC, which could deliver supplies by ships to its posts on Hudson and James bays in the heart of the continent, the Nor'Westers relied on long and expensive overland journeys. Mackenzie, hoping to find a river link between the northern posts and the Pacific, made two voyages, one in 1789 and one in 1793, in search of the elusive route. On the second voyage, he arrived in what is now British Columbia.

As beaver in the interior plains became more scarce, the Nor'Westers began to seriously pursue the idea of trading in the British Columbia interior. The first steps were made with the explorations of David Thompson and Simon Fraser, who, aided by the Natives of the region, provided the NWC with critical knowledge of the area's river systems. Fraser established posts across the Rockies in Carrier and Sekani territories during a journey from 1806 to 1808, and Thompson descended the Columbia to its mouth in 1811, discovering that it offered a satisfactory connection to the coast. Within the central interior of British Columbia, posts such as Fort Fraser, Fort St James, and Fort George became year-round homes to some Nor'Westers. Like their counterparts further east,

Portrait of Alexander Mackenzie by British painter Sir Thomas Lawrence. On July 22, 1793, after a 74-day voyage from Fort Chipewyan, Alexander Mackenzie and his crew of nine became the first Europeans to reach the Pacific Ocean by land. Their voyage was made possible by advice from First Nations peoples along the way regarding the best route to take to reach the ocean.
Library and Archives Canada/C-000138

most of these men formed liaisons with Native women. Although some of them abandoned their Native families when they left the posts, many remained, retiring with their families to Red River or, after its founding in 1843, to Fort Victoria.

CONCLUSION

While the West continued to provide homelands for a variety of First Nations in 1821, much of the region had also become an area of European exploitation for beaver furs and sea-otter pelts. The Natives were partners in the fur trade and as long as competition among the Europeans and good markets for furs prevailed, First Nations significantly influenced the terms of trade. They also retained control over their own territories and maintained traditional religious and cultural practices. After 1821, however, the fur-trade monopoly, declining supplies of furs, and increasing European interest in the West as an area of settlement would all threaten the Natives' dominance in their own homelands.

NOTES

1 R. Cole Harris, *Making Native Space: Colonialism, Resistance, and Reserves in British Columbia* (Vancouver: UBC Press, 2002), 10.

2 Samuel Hearne, *A Journey from Prince of Wales's Fort in Hudson's Bay, to the Northern Ocean . . . In the Years 1769, 1770, 1771 and 1772* (London: A. Strahan and T. Cadell, 1795), 51–52.

3 Maureen K. Lux, *Medicine That Walks: Disease, Medicine, and Canadian Plains Native People, 1880–1940* (Toronto: University of Toronto Press, 2001), 10–11.

4 Cole Harris, "Voices of Disaster: Smallpox around the Strait of Georgia in 1782," *Ethnohistory* 41, 4 (Fall 1994): 595.

5 D. Wayne Moody and Barry Kaye, "Indian Agriculture in the Fur-trade Northwest," *Prairie Forum* 11, 2 (Fall 1986): 176.

6 Lyle Dick, "The Seven Oaks Incident and the Construction of a Historical Tradition, 1816 to 1970," *Journal of the Canadian Historical Association* (n.s.) 2 (1992): 97.

7 James Cook, *A Voyage to the Pacific Ocean in the Years 1776, 1777, 1778, 1779, and 1780 . . .* , vol. 2, ed. John Douglas, cited in J.C.H. King, "The Nootka of Vancouver Island," in *Cook's Voyages and Peoples of the Pacific*, ed. Hugh Cobbe (London: British Museum Publications, 1979), 102.

8 James R. Gibson, *Otter Skins, Boston Ships, and China Goods: The Maritime Fur Trade of the Northwest Coast, 1785–1841* (Montreal: McGill-Queen's University Press, 1992), 171.

RELATED READINGS IN THIS SERIES

From *Foundations: Readings in Pre-Confederation Canadian History*
Carolyn Podruchny, "Unfair Masters and Rascally Servants? Labour Relations among Bourgeois, Clerks and Voyageurs in the Montreal Fur Trade, 1780–1821," 233–53.
Lyle Dick, "The Seven Oaks Incident and the Construction of a Historical Tradition, 1816 to 1970," 254–72.

From Media Companion CD-ROM, Volume I
A Copie of Orders and Instructions to Anthy Hendey
The Emergence of a New Nation
The Métis National Anthem, Composed at the Battle of Seven Oaks, 1815
The Columbia River

SELECTED READING

For the Prairies and Northern Ontario, the period covered in this chapter is surveyed in the early chapters of Gerald Friesen, *The Canadian Prairies: A History* (Toronto: University of Toronto Press, 1987). Also see the opening chapters of the major provincial histories: Howard Palmer with Tamara Palmer, *Alberta: A New History* (Edmonton: Hurtig, 1990); John Archer, *Saskatchewan: A History* (Saskatoon: Western Producer Prairie Books, 1980); and W.L. Morton, *Manitoba: A History* (Toronto: University of Toronto Press, 1957). The early history of British Columbia is the subject of the opening chapters of Margaret Ormsby, *British Columbia: A History* (Toronto: Macmillan, 1976), and Jean Barman, *The West beyond the West: A History of British Columbia* (Toronto: University of Toronto Press, 1996).

For Native peoples, a good place to start is chapters 11 and 12 of Arthur J. Ray, *I Have Lived Here Since the World Began: An Illustrated History of Canada's Native People* (Toronto: Lester/Key Porter, 1996) or the parallel chapters in the textbooks by Olive P. Dickason and J.R. Miller mentioned in Chapter 2. Several essay collections focus on Prairie and Northern Canadian Native peoples, particularly R. Bruce Morrison and C. Roderick Wilson, eds., *Native Peoples: The Canadian Experience* (Toronto: McClelland and Stewart, 1986). Philip Drucker, *Cultures of the North Pacific Coast* (San Francisco: Chander Publishing, 1965) outlines the pre-contact history of Pacific Coast Natives. Mike Robinson, *Sea Otter Chiefs* (Calgary: Bayeux Arts, 1996) provides background on the coastal Native leaders in the early years of contact.

Among excellent studies of the religious and cultural life of Native peoples are Jennifer Brown and Robert Brightman, eds., *The Orders of the Dreamed: George Nelson on Cree and Northern Ojibwa Religion and Myth* (Winnipeg: University of Manitoba Press, 1988), and David G. Mandelbaum, *The Plains Cree: An Ethnographic, Historical and Comparative Study* (Regina: Canadian Plains Research Centre, 1979).

Studies of the impact of the fur trade on major Native societies include Robin Fisher, *Contact and Conflict: Indian-European Relations in British Columbia, 1774–1890* (Vancouver: UBC Press, 1979); Theodore Binnema, *Common and Contested Ground: A Human and Environmental History of the Northwestern Plains* (Norman: University of Oklahoma Press, 2001); Arthur J. Ray, *Indians in the Fur Trade: Their Role as Trappers, Hunters, and Middlemen in the Lands Southwest of Hudson Bay, 1660–1870* (Toronto: University of Toronto Press, 1974); Laura Peers, *The Ojibwa of Western Canada, 1780–1870* (St Paul: Minnesota Historical Society Press, 1994); Charles A. Bishop, *The Northern Ojibwa and the Fur Trade: An Historical and Ecological Study* (Toronto: Holt, Rinehart and Winston, 1974); Oscar Lewis, *The Effects of White Contact upon Blackfoot Culture with Special Reference to the Role of the Fur Trade* (Seattle: American Ethnological Society, 1942); John S. Milloy, *The Plains Cree: Trade, Diplomacy and War* (Winnipeg: University of Manitoba Press, 1990); and Paul C. Thistle, *Indian-European Trade Relations in the Lower Saskatchewan River Region to 1840* (Winnipeg: University of Manitoba Press, 1986).

A good short introduction to the fur trade is Frits Pannekoek, *The Fur Trade and Western Canadian Society, 1670–1870* (Ottawa: Canadian Historical Association, 1987). A lengthier but highly readable account is Daniel Francis, *Battle for the West: Fur Traders and the Birth of Western Canada* (Edmonton: Hurtig, 1982). On the West Coast trade, see James Gibson, *Otter Skins, Boston Ships and China Goods: The Maritime Fur Trade of the Northwest Coast, 1785–1841* (Montreal: McGill-Queen's University Press, 1992), and Richard Mackie, *Trading beyond the Mountains: The British Fur Trade on the Pacific, 1793–1843* (Vancouver: UBC Press, 1996). On the northern trade, see Kerry Abel, *Drum Songs: Glimpses of Dene History* (Montreal: McGill-Queen's

University Press, 1993). The Hudson's Bay Company's history to 1870 is surveyed in Glyndwr Williams, "Highlights of the First 200 Years of the Hudson's Bay Company," *The Beaver*, special issue (Autumn 1970). A detailed account of the company's history is E.E. Rich, *The Hudson's Bay Company*, 3 vols. (Toronto: Hudson's Bay Records Society, 1960).

On key explorers and explorations, see Robert M. Galois, ed., *A Voyage to the North West Side of America: The Journals of James Colnett, 1786–1789* (Vancouver: UBC Press, 2003); Barry M. Gough, *First across the Continent: Sir Alexander Mackenzie* (Norman: University of Oklahoma Press, 1997); Samuel Hearne, *Journals of Samuel Hearne and Philip Turner Between the Years 1792 and 1794*, ed. J.B. Tyrell (Toronto: Greenwood, 1934); and J.B. Tyrrell, ed., *David Thompson's Narrative of His Explorations in Western America, 1784–1812* (New York: Greenwood Press, 1968). Two excellent accounts of women in the fur trade are Sylvia Van Kirk, *"Many Tender Ties": Women in Fur Trade Society in Western Canada, 1670–1870* (Winnipeg: Watson and Dwyer, 1980), and Jennifer S.H. Brown, *Strangers in Blood: Fur Trade Company Families in the Indian Country* (Vancouver: UBC Press, 1980).

Barry Kaye, "The Red River Settlement: Lord Selkirk's Isolated Colony in the Wilderness," *Prairie Forum* 11, 1 (Spring 1986): 1–20 outlines how a decision was made to establish a colony at the forks of the Red and Assiniboine rivers. A biography of the founder of the Red River colony is Lucille H. Campey, *The Silver Chief: Lord Selkirk and the Scottish Pioneers of Belfast, Baldoon, and Red River* (Toronto: National Heritage Books, 2003). The confrontation between the settlement and the Métis is detailed in Margaret Macleod and W.L. Morton, *Cuthbert Grant of Grantown: Warden of the Plains of Red River* (Toronto: McClelland and Stewart, 1974). A critique of their account and the historical tradition within which it was written is in Lyle Dick, "The Seven Oaks Incident and the Construction of a Historical Tradition, 1816 to 1870," *Journal of the Canadian Historical Association* (n.s.) 2 (1992): 91–113. A critical reflection on the history of the Métis is Laurier Turgeon, *Patrimoines Métisses. Contextes coloniaux et postcoloniaux* (Sainte-Foy and Paris: Éditions de la Maison des sciences de l'homme, 2003).

WEBLINKS

HUDSON'S BAY COMPANY
www.solon.org/Constitutions/Canada/English/PreConfederation/hbc_charter_1670.html

For the text of the HBC charter, see this site.

DAVID THOMPSON
www.collectionscanada.ca/explorers/h24-1650-e.html

The Library and Archives Canada site contains a brief biography of Thompson along with listings of his papers and journals.

Part III Summary

By 1821, the success of British settlement and enterprise in the northern half of North America was evident. The British presence in the region until the late 1740s had been limited to a small military and civilian establishment in Nova Scotia, small fishing communities in Newfoundland, and a few posts on Hudson Bay. Eighty years later the demography of Newfoundland, Nova Scotia, Prince Edward Island, New Brunswick, and Upper Canada reflected the attraction of British North America to both British and Anglo-American emigrants. While Lower Canada was still largely inhabited by the Canadiens and the West was mainly home to its First Nations, the imperial government dominated the former while English-speaking fur traders exercised growing control over the latter. Peace with the Americans after 1814 removed fears of external threats to Britain's remaining North American possessions, but efforts of colonial administrators to impose imperial economic control and the British social order on the monarchy's curious mix of North American subjects would meet many challenges.

MATURING COLONIAL SOCIETIES, 1815–1867

Between 1815 and 1867 the British North American colonies and territories went their separate ways but were drawing closer in culture and values. The Atlantic colonies and the Canadas grew in population and political maturity. On the West Coast, the colonies of Vancouver Island (1849) and British Columbia (1858) were carved out of the vast territory under the jurisdiction of the Hudson's Bay Company, which was increasingly feeling the impact of outside influences and the growing power of the Métis. Most communities were beginning to build churches, schools, and charitable organizations to sustain an increasingly vibrant social and intellectual life. When Great Britain dismantled the mercantile system in the 1840s and began reshaping the apparatus of colonial governance, British North Americans faced a common crisis: how to adjust to a world where old colonial empires were crumbling and new industrial empires were emerging.

CHAPTER 13

The Maritime Colonies, 1815-1867

Timeline

1820   Cape Breton annexed to Nova Scotia; Bank of New Brunswick founded

1821–23   Thomas McCulloch publishes *The Stepsure Letters*

1823   Lawrence Kavanagh, a Roman Catholic, takes a seat in Nova Scotia legislature

1824   Julia Beckwith publishes *St Ursula's Convent*

1825   Great Miramichi fire

1826   General Mining Association established to develop Nova Scotia coal resources

1829   Catholic Emancipation

1833   British Parliament passes act to abolish slavery throughout Empire

1835   Joseph Howe defends himself against charges of libel

1836   Thomas Chandler publishes *The Clockmaker*

1842   Webster-Ashburton Treaty

1846   Great Britain adopts free trade policy

1848   Nova Scotia becomes first colony in Empire to achieve responsible government

1851   *Marco Polo* launched

1852   PEI legislature passes region's first Free School Act

1854–66   Reciprocity Treaty

In 1842, Joseph Malli, chief of the Mi'kmaq on the Restigouche River in New Brunswick, travelled to England in an effort to get the British authorities to do something to stop incoming settlers from stealing Native lands. His statement, which was recorded, said in part:

When the Superiority over the Territories in which we were born passed out of the hands of the French into those of the British, We—the Mic-Macs of the Restigouche River were in possession of a Tract of Country, the quiet and undistinguished holding of which was secured to us by a written Deed. —The care of that Deed We entrusted to our Christian Priest. —He lost it.

About 50 years ago a white man of the name of Mann came to us,—and asked our leave to build a Hut for him to sleep in when he came to fish—We said "No! If we allow you to build the Hut, you will keep Pigs and Sheep—We Indians have many Dogs—the Dogs will worry the Pigs & Sheep and bad consequences will spring up." —Mann did build his Hut, and we did not use force to expel him from our Reserve. —After some time Mann claimed a large Tract of our Reserve as his own.[1]

In the half-century following the Napoleonic Wars, the Maritime colonies of Nova Scotia, New Brunswick, and Prince Edward Island experienced unprecedented levels of population growth and institutional development. The Native people in the region fared badly in this context. No longer a military threat, they were pushed to the margins of society, at best the objects of charity, at worst easy targets for exploitation by rapacious immigrants. They nevertheless continued to fight for their rights and, when ignored by local authorities, took their grievances directly to the Colonial Office. While their petitions often received a sympathetic hearing in Great Britain, Colonial Secretaries were reluctant to impose their views on the colonists who were increasingly demanding "responsible government," which, among other things, would give them power to control policy for Chief Malli and the people he represented.

DEFINING THE MARITIMES

The geographical perimeters of the Maritimes that still exist today were set in this period. After functioning as a separate colonial jurisdiction since 1784, Cape Breton was re-annexed to Nova Scotia in 1820. The Colonial Office's justification for this administrative decision was failure of the officials at Sydney to call an assembly. Given the prejudices of the time, it was difficult to do so in a colony settled primarily by Scots, Irish, and Acadians, most of whom were Roman Catholic and spoke either French or Gaelic.

New Brunswick's border with the United States, in contention since the American Revolution, proved difficult to establish. Despite continuing efforts, the identity of the St Croix River, part of the boundary defined by the peace treaty, was only determined in 1798 when the site of Champlain's seventeenth-century settlement was located. The Webster-

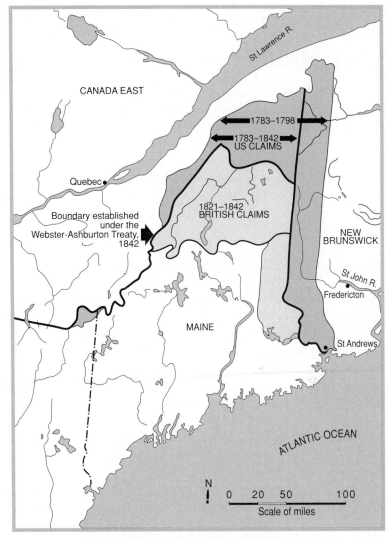

MAP 13.1 Maine-New Brunswick boundary claims

Ashburton Treaty, named after the principal negotiators, finally put an end to wrangling over territory in the Aroostook-Madawaska region on the upper St John River in 1842. The division of the disputed territory, which left a hump of land between New Brunswick and the Eastern Townships, came as a disappointment to New Brunswickers, who had hoped for a more direct link to the Canadas.

POPULATION GROWTH

The Maritimes caught the advance wave of British immigration washing up on the shores of North America in the first half of the nineteenth century.

Oral History

One of the most valuable sources for information about ordinary people is oral history. Family lore, ballads, and superstitions, passed down through generations, can often open a window on how people in the past thought about themselves. As with written documents, historians must be careful about how they interpret oral sources. The ballads produced by the Highland Scottish immigrants who came to the Atlantic region provide a useful case study of the problems and potential of oral history.

The Scots, especially the Gaelic-speaking Highlanders, drew upon a rich and complex cultural heritage. As they moved to new locations around the world, they composed poems and songs to commemorate the often difficult and painful emigrant experience. Historians who consult only one or two of these ballads might make the mistake of assuming that there was only one point of view on the migration process. As the work of Margaret MacDonell illustrates, nothing could be further from the truth. While many bards lamented that they ever came to North America, others found in the New World the freedom to re-establish a way of life that was fast being swept away in Britain. A person's point of view, it seems, depended upon his or her political perspective and motivation in coming to the New World.

Among the Selkirk settlers on Prince Edward Island was Calum Bàn MacMhannain (1758–1829) from the Isle of Skye. The extortions of the "bailie," or bailiff, and intermittent plague among his cattle induced him to emigrate to North America with his wife and six children. For MacMhannain, the island was a haven from the oppressive conditions of his native Scotland:

> By Mary, for a very long time
> we remained in that land;
> although we could raise sufficient there,
> many a calamity and loss
> plagued these at times,
> so that they vanished into the mists on the mountain.
> Although we might go to market
> and sell our herd,
> for which we got a fair price
> the bailie would come around
> with the cruel summons
> and extort the entire sum from us. . . .

> But if you ever go
> over the sea
> bring my greetings to my friends.
> Urge them without delay
> to flee the rents
> and come out as soon as opportune for them.
> If they could find a time
> and means to come over
> they would not be beholden to MacDonald.
> They would get land
> in which to sow crops,
> and potatoes and barley would grow very well there.
> This is the isle of contentment
> where we are now.
> Our seed is fruitful here;
> oats grow
> and wheat, in full bloom,
> turnip, cabbage, and peas.
> Sugar from trees
> may be had free here;
> we have it in large chunks.
> There is fresh red rum
> in every dwelling and shop,
> abundant as the stream, being imbibed here.

In contrast, another bard, known only as a MacLean from Raasay, had a different perspective on the Prince Edward Island experience. With the entrepreneur Samuel Cunard as his landlord and a rent collector named Peters, conditions were as oppressive in North America as in Scotland.

> I am lonely here
> in Murray Harbour not knowing English
> it is not what I have been accustomed to,
> for I always spoke Gaelic.
> My neighbours and I
> used to chat at length together;
> here I see only scoundrels,
> and I do not understand their language.
> I am offended at my relatives
> who came before me;
> they did not tell me about this place
> and how it has tried them.
> Going through the wilderness

there is nothing but a blazed trail
this is truly a lonesome place
for one who lives by himself.
A matter of grave concern,
as you may surmise,
is the want of footwear and clothing
for each one who needs them.
No one can procure anything
unless he wrests it from the forest.
The length of winter is depressing;

it is fully half one's lifetime. . . .
We left there
and came out here
thinking we would receive consideration,
and that the rent would not be so exacting.
But Peters is oppressing us,
and, if he doesn't die,
we must leave this place
and Cunard, himself a beast.[2]

Following the Napoleonic Wars, a recession brought unemployment for thousands of civilians as well as former soldiers and sailors. This was only one factor pushing people out of Great Britain. By the end of the eighteenth century, the Industrial Revolution, and the new middle class that benefited from it, were beginning to transform social arrangements. Tenant farmers, artisans, and rural gentry were forced to seek ways of supplementing their income and shoring up their crumbling status.

The most dramatic collapse of social organization took place in recently conquered regions of the British Isles. Following their defeat by the British army at Culloden in 1746, clan chieftains in the Scottish Highlands became oppressive landlords, forcing their dependants to emigrate or be reduced to penury. The kelp industry, on which many Highland Scots depended, was also in a state of collapse. Since most of the Highlanders were Roman Catholic, they were excluded from the political processes that governed their lives. Religious discrimination also plagued the Irish, who had become reluctant British subjects by the Act of Union in 1801. For the Roman Catholic peasantry in Ireland, the combination of a growing population, periodic famines, and political oppression was a powerful stimulus to emigration.

Even people who had excellent prospects in Europe were often pulled by the opportunities that North America seemed to offer. Merchants eager to expand their operations, farmers with visions of being gentlemen, young families determined to make a better life for their children, and any number of adventurers and ne'er-do-wells turned their sights on British North America. Many immigrants brought traditional values with them, spurred by the desire for economic and spiritual "independence" as much as by a thirst for wealth. Others were converts to the values of industrial capitalism, more anxious to "get ahead" than to re-establish a way of life rapidly disappearing in Britain.

The Scots

By the end of the eighteenth century, the forces gaining momentum during the previous 50 years had come together to increase the tide of emigration from Scotland. The Scots took up land throughout the Maritime region, but their presence was particularly concentrated in eastern Nova Scotia, Cape Breton, and Prince Edward Island. Between 1785 and 1849, nearly 40 000 Scots arrived in Nova Scotia, which finally became home to a population reflecting its seventeenth-century name.

The most ambitious Scottish settlement scheme was sponsored by Thomas Douglas, Earl of Selkirk, who in 1803 brought 800 Highlanders to the Orwell-Point Prim area of Prince Edward Island. Scots were also prominent in mercantile circles throughout the region. Scots dominated the import-export trade and the timber trade, and were counted among the major shipbuilders in the region. Fraser and Thom on the Miramichi was one of the most successful Scottish timber and shipbuilding firms, with its operations attracting labour from the old country to a region hitherto dominated by Mi'kmaq and Acadians.

In addition to a strong attachment to the land, the Scots brought their religious values, including the

Roman Catholic traditions of the Highlanders and Presbyterian beliefs that flourished mainly in the Lowlands. They also planted the Scottish reverence for education in the Maritime region. Thomas McCulloch, a Presbyterian minister who settled in Pictou, founded Pictou Academy, one of the most respected schools in British North America. A widely acclaimed natural scientist, McCulloch also wrote *The Stepsure Letters* (1821–23), one of the first works of fiction produced in British North America.

The Irish

Following the end of the Napoleonic Wars, young Irish men and a few women escaping the poverty and oppression of their native island boarded fishing vessels bound for Newfoundland and then made their way to the Maritimes. The expansion of the timber trade in New Brunswick offered direct passage in one of the empty timber vessels sailing to the Miramichi or Saint John. When periodic famines raged in Ireland, timber ports in the Maritimes were awash with destitute Irish families.

While the Irish Protestants were quickly assimilated into the dominant Anglo-Protestant culture of the Maritime colonies, the Roman Catholic Irish remained distinct, separated by their religion, history, and, for many, Gaelic language. The Irish became tenant farmers on Prince Edward Island, harvested New Brunswick forests, and worked as domestic servants. By mid-century, they had penetrated virtually every corner of the Maritime region and constituted more than half the population of Saint John and Fredericton.

The Irish gradually emerged as an important factor in the political life of all the colonies. On Prince Edward Island, Irish tenant farmers resorted to tactics learned in their homeland to resist hated Protestant proprietors. Issues defined in Ireland, such as Catholic rights and repeal of the 1801 Act of Union, were commonly debated in colonial settings. Institutions organized around Irish concerns quickly made their appearance. In all three Maritime colonies, Orange Orders and Protestant Alliances could be found aligned against Roman Catholic organizations with names such as Ribbon, Repeal, and St Patrick's.

Diversity in the Maritime Mosaic

Between 1817 and 1822, ships carrying Welsh settlers also arrived in the region. Like the Scots and Irish, the Welsh were pushed from their homes by population pressures and pulled by the prospects of a better life in North America. Although never a large portion of the incoming tide of immigrants, they were easily singled out for their distinctive costumes, Welsh tongue, and, in many cases, dissenting Baptist heritage.

Nineteenth-century censuses show that the Maritime colonies also received immigrants from mainland Europe, Africa, and Asia—people who, as crew members, occasionally disembarked from ships in one of the many ports in the region. These individuals were usually quickly absorbed into the larger society through marriage and left only their names and perhaps a court case or two as evidence of their presence.

By the mid-nineteenth century, the three Maritime colonies, with a population of over 500 000, had reached their limits of pre-industrial settlement. Most of Europe's emigrating millions would thereafter bypass the region for western frontiers, and Maritimers themselves joined the exodus, lured by the notion of richer land, warmer climates, and better opportunities. The region was also losing population to the new industrial frontier centred in New England. As early as the 1840s, Thomas Chandler Haliburton, the Nova Scotia-born author of *The Clockmaker* (1836) and *The Old Judge* (1849), observed that his province was a land of "comers and goers."

THE COMMERCIAL ECONOMY

In the first half of the nineteenth century the Maritime economy went from strength to strength, buoyed by an increasingly productive commercial economy. Following the Napoleonic Wars, a recession wreaked hardship on rich and poor alike, but by the 1820s conditions had improved. Colonial staples of fish, foodstuffs, and timber found markets in an expanding global economy, and Maritime ships could be found flogging their cargoes in ports throughout the world.

Shipbuilding, financed by British and colonial capitalists, emerged as the most important manufacturing endeavour in the Maritimes. By 1825, Saint John had become the major shipbuilding centre, but there were shipyards scattered along the region's ample coastline. Over the next 25 years, the Maritimes became a major producer of ocean-going vessels for sale in Britain and elsewhere. Ships such as the *Marco Polo*, built in Saint John in 1851, broke world speed records and helped to make the region's shipbuilding skills better known in international circles. Smaller coastal and fishing vessels were built by the thousands. Between 1815 and 1860, more than two million tonnes of shipping were built in the Maritime provinces. This was nearly three times the shipping produced in the Canadas and almost 40 percent of Britain's output in the same period.

Shipbuilding at Yarmouth.
Library and Archives Canada/PA32404

In addition to building and selling vessels, merchants in the Maritimes became involved in the carrying trade. Initially, most of their vessels carried local staples such as timber or fish. When shipping capacity outstripped the resources of the region, the merchants found cargoes elsewhere. By mid-century, sailing ships

BIOGRAPHY

Enos Collins

One of Nova Scotia's most successful businessmen, Enos Collins (1774–1871) got his start during the French Revolutionary and Napoleonic Wars. The second of 26 children born to a Liverpool, Nova Scotia, merchant, Enos was captain of a schooner at the age of 20. In 1799, he turned from trade to privateering, serving on the famed *Charles Mary Wentworth*. Investing his capital in vessels trading out of Liverpool, he made a handsome profit running the French blockade to supply the British army on the Iberian peninsula.

In 1811, Collins moved to Halifax, where he engaged in shipping and privateering. Collins was part-owner of the *Liverpool Packet* and, with his partner Joseph Allison, did well in the prize courts.

After the war, Collins diversified his activities into everything from currency trading to whaling. His public and private activities consolidated his growing status. In 1822, he was appointed to a seat on the colony's council, which gave him considerable political influence. He married Margaret Halliburton, the eldest daughter of a member of the council, and lived in Gorsebrook, a fine estate in the south end of the city. Collins was prominent among the founders of the Halifax Banking Company, which became known as "Collins' Bank."

His influence in the political and economic life of the colony and his conservative opposition to the democratic tendencies of the age soon drew criticism from the reform movement led by Joseph Howe. In 1840, Collins retired from the council and retreated into his private life of family and business. The confederation movement caused the aging Collins to break with the Conservatives and publicly support the anti-confederates. Like many other merchants in the region, he saw the union as the death-knell to the commercial empire that had financed his fortune. When he died in 1871, Collins left an estate worth over $6 million and was reputed to be one of the richest men in British North America.

from the Maritimes were plying the seven seas, full participants in the rapid expansion of the carrying trade that occurred in the mid-nineteenth century.

The region's mineral wealth also came under intense development in this period. In 1826, the London-based General Mining Association was created to develop Nova Scotia's mineral resources, over which it had a virtual monopoly. The company brought skilled miners to the coalfields of Cape Breton and Pictou County and introduced modern technology, including steam-driven machinery and vessels. In 1839, it constructed the first railway line in the Maritimes, which carried coal from Albion Mines (now Stellarton) to Pictou harbour.

Building on its timber and shipping activities, Saint John emerged as the major industrial centre in the Maritimes, the value of its foundry, footwear, and clothing industries surpassing that of shipbuilding by the 1860s. Halifax, too, developed an industrial base, specializing in food processing industries such as brewing, distilling, and sugar refining. For both cities,

the West Indies trade was a critical factor in the supply of raw materials such as sugar, spices, and rum.

The founding of banking institutions testifies to the attempts of the region's mercantile elite to organize their wealth for systematic investment. In Saint John, the Bank of New Brunswick (1820) and the Commercial Bank (1834) dominated financial activities. Halifax supported two banks, the Halifax Banking Company (1825) and the Bank of Nova Scotia (1832). Smaller communities in the region also began mobilizing their capital, sometimes in branches of already established banks but more often in locally incorporated operations.

The British mercantile system was finally eclipsed in the wake of the Irish famine of 1845. In order to import foodstuffs as cheaply as possible, the British Parliament suspended its long-standing preferential duties on grain, precipitating a revolution in British economic policy. Between 1846 and 1849, Britain began dismantling its entire system of colonial preferences and abolished the Navigation Acts.

Market Wharf and Ferry Landing, Halifax, *by William H. Eagar.*
Royal Ontario Museum/Canadiana/955.218.4

Notwithstanding the cries of gloom and doom in merchant circles—and especially among those whose fortunes were tied to the timber trade—the free trade "crisis" did not immediately change the structure of the colonial economies. Timber, fish, foodstuffs, and sailing ships continued to find markets in Britain's informal economic empire.

THE DOMESTIC ECONOMY

Although the world of staple trade and colonial shipping touched the lives of people in the Maritimes both directly and indirectly, the seasonal rhythms of household production determined most people's general well-being prior to 1850. Pre-industrial families engaged in a variety of activities that included farming, fishing and hunting, building houses and barns, spinning and weaving wool, making and repairing clothing, preparing and preserving food, and bearing and rearing children. Pioneers made their own furniture and crafted shoes, harnesses, and carriages for their

horses. Travellers in the region, most of them accustomed to more sophisticated urban settings, often remarked on the self-sufficiency of the "bluenoses," who could turn their hands to a variety of skills.

Women's work in pre-industrial society was largely confined to the domestic realm, where most of the food and clothing were produced. By the mid-nineteenth century, colonial census takers began documenting home-based production. Over 1.5 million kilograms of butter, 296 000 kilograms of cheese, and over 20 000 kilograms of maple sugar as well as over a million yards of cloth and flannels were produced in Nova Scotia in 1851. In fishing communities women were often involved in the shore-based processing of fish. Women's paid labour usually took the form of domestic service in the homes of other women where they learned and practised housewifery skills.

Clearing the land was a daunting task for most pioneer settlers. They assaulted the forests as if trees were an enemy to be conquered. Despite the lessons learned in Britain, where most of the productive

Clearing the town plot, Stanley, New Brunswick, 1834, **by W.P. Kay.**
Library and Archives Canada/C17

forests were gone and hunting had become a sport reserved for the aristocracy, immigrants showed little interest in conservation. In their haste to establish themselves, they cut down giant hardwood stands and burned the stumps, a process often leading to runaway fires that destroyed both the forests and those who inhabited them. Walter Johnstone, a Scottish visitor to Prince Edward Island, remarked in 1820, "Burnt woods are to be seen in the neighbourhood of almost every settlement, some of them of considerable magnitude."[3] The greatest disaster of this kind took place on the Miramichi in 1825, when fire consumed over two million hectares of forests and took the lives of 160 people and countless animals.

The speed with which European immigrants killed off wild animals is one of the most remarkable features of the colonization process. As early as 1794, the Nova Scotia government felt compelled to pass a law to protect grouse and black duck, both facing extinction. Moose had virtually disappeared from New Brunswick by the 1820s. According to Peter Fisher, New Brunswick's first historian, they "were found in great abundance when the loyalists first came to the province" but "were wantonly destroyed, being hunted for the skin, while their carcasses were left in the woods, a few only being used for food."[4] Although laws had been enacted for the preservation of moose, they were not enforced.

Class and Culture

European class distinctions prevailed in the Maritime colonies and in some cases were actually enhanced by colonial conditions. This was particularly the case for skilled artisans, whose status was rapidly declining in Europe under the impact of the Industrial Revolution. In the colonies, the demand for the products and services of an artisan class was actually expanding. Women in colonial cities could eke out a living making hats and dresses for the local elite, while the services of blacksmiths, carpenters, and millers were widely used. As T.W. Acheson has shown in the context of Saint John, the artisan class rose to prominence in the first half of the nineteenth century, and a few of their number would be in a position to transcend their class when new techniques of production and capital accumulation made it possible to turn their shops into industrial enterprises.[5]

The colonies also supported an administrative and professional class of doctors, lawyers, clergy, politicians, and military officers. Together with the great wholesale and export merchants, they made up the elite of colonial society. In the early years of settlement, this class consisted almost exclusively of immigrants from Britain and the United States, but native-born elites soon asserted themselves. As citizens of the British Empire, young men in the colonies had a broad scope for their career ambitions. Those who were highly successful, such as shipping magnate Samuel Cunard and author Thomas Chandler Haliburton, often retired to Great Britain once they could afford to do so.

On the other side of the social scale, landless labourers, many of them recent immigrants, and the dependent poor, including the very old and very young as well as the mentally challenged and physically disabled, lived a precarious existence. Their ranks fluctuated, and any number of disasters—fires, crop failures, economic cycles, and even the onset of winter—set the relief lists soaring. In December 1850, the *Saint John Morning News* noted this Dickensian scene:

> Winter is a terrible enemy to the destitute in this most rigorous climate. None but those who experience it, can tell the amount of suffering there is in this City, during five months of the year, among women and children. We see the pauper in the streets, in tattered garb and attenuated form, and he passes by and out of mind in a moment. Could we follow him to his inhospitable abode, and see his little ones crouching around a single brand of fire, to keep themselves warm, and witness the scanty meal of which they are to partake, we should soon begin to learn something of the dark shades of human life and incline towards charity.[6]

Social Relations in Pre-Industrial Society

In colonial society, all its members—men and women, rich and poor, immigrant and native-born—were bound together by the mercantile and domestic economies, which functioned on barter and mutual dependence as much as on hard currency. Women's work was performed within the context of the family, where, by law, the male head of the household controlled the wealth of his wife and children. Both the fisheries and timber trade nurtured the "truck system" in which merchants provided their labourers with the equipment and provisions they needed for the season's work in return for the product of their labour. Many workers never saw their wages and were perpetually bound to their merchant-supplier by a web of debt.

The same system often prevailed in farming communities, where merchants held mortgages on indebted farms. In Prince Edward Island, rents to proprietors were notoriously in arrears, and tenants could be—though they rarely were—forcibly ejected from their lands. The region's Aboriginal population, having incorporated European society into traditional seasonal rhythms, was now part of the network of dependency. Each spring, Native women emerged from their winter retreats with quill boxes and woven baskets to sell in the urban markets, while Native men made axe handles and brooms and found work during the peak season as guides, loggers, and dock workers.

What is most obvious about these economic relationships is a fundamental inequality. Patriarchy, the belief that men should have power over women and children, and paternalism, the practice by which people in authority rule benevolently but intrusively over those below them on the social scale, encouraged duty and deference in colonial society. Women and children were socialized to obey the male head of the household, and members of the labouring class deferred to their social superiors. Both patriarchy and social inequality came under strong attack in the nineteenth century, and the more recent British immigrants often complained that colonials failed to show proper respect for those above them on the social scale.

RELIGION

Perhaps no single source of identity in colonial society was more important than organized religion. By the mid-nineteenth century, churches were sprouting like mushrooms across the Maritime landscape. Religious affiliation, of course, had been a vital political issue in western society since the Reformation, but in the nineteenth century both the Protestant and Roman Catholic churches became more aggressive in their pursuit of converts and in their attempts to influence the behaviour of their adherents. In the Maritimes this new religious energy was, for some communities, an integrative force, but just as often it spawned divisions that were reflected in every aspect of colonial life.

The political emancipation of Roman Catholics was one of the most important developments in this period. Laws preventing Roman Catholics from voting, acquiring land, and worshipping in public had been abolished in the Maritimes as early as the 1780s, but Catholics could still not hold public office. This ban was first lifted in 1823 for Lawrence Kavanagh, a Cape Breton merchant elected to the Nova Scotia Assembly. In 1829, Great Britain removed restrictions on the civil rights of Roman Catholics at home and throughout the empire. At the same time, the number of Roman Catholics was growing dramatically, and the missionary nature of their church was giving way to more formal structures. The Maritime provinces remained under the jurisdiction of the bishop of Quebec until 1817, when Edmund Burke was named bishop of Nova Scotia. In 1829, a separate bishop was appointed for New Brunswick and Prince Edward Island. These administrative changes marked the beginning of a reinvigorated Roman Catholicism in the Maritime colonies.

Evangelical Awakening

Another significant development in this period was the rise of evangelicalism, a movement that swept Europe and North America in the eighteenth and early nineteenth centuries. Those who embraced evangelicalism emphasized individual piety, personal "conversion," and direct communication with God. Such views defied the notions of hierarchy and social order advocated by the "established" Anglican, Presbyterian, and Roman Catholic churches and paralleled the secular demand for greater personal freedom and democratic consent that had found expression in the American and French revolutions. In the Maritimes, Baptist and Methodist churches grew more rapidly than any other denominations. Even the Halifax elite were attracted by the message preached by the Baptists. St Paul's Anglican Church was split in two by religious controversy in the 1820s, with the result that some of the city's leading families became Baptists.

The public expression of the evangelical spirit was a transformed personal life. Although salvation could not be bought through good works, "saved" individuals were expected to show outward manifestations of their reformed spiritual state. It was not long before evangelicals also turned their reforming zeal on society. Largely in self-defence, Anglicans, Presbyterians, and Roman Catholics were also caught up in the reforming spirit of the age. Not surprisingly, the areas traditionally dominated by the church—education, charity, and personal behaviour—became arenas for public controversy.

Religion and Society

For people of evangelical persuasion, formal education was more than a vehicle for teaching "the basics" of reading, writing, and cyphering; it offered a structured way of imparting morality and civic virtues. In the early nineteenth century, education in the Maritimes was offered in a variety of institutions, many of them sponsored by colonial churches, both Protestant and Catholic. The Madras school system, so called because it was developed in India, used older students as tutors to younger ones, and was promoted by the Church of England in the region. In the 1830s the Sunday school movement became popular, particularly among Methodists, Presbyterians, and Baptists.

By the mid-nineteenth century, reformers were beginning to advocate the establishment of a uniform state-supported "common" education system like the ones that existed in Ireland, Massachusetts, and Prussia. Their efforts were frustrated by opposition from those who feared the cultural and financial costs of such a move. Concerned for their success at the polls, most politicians preferred to provide grants to locally generated schools rather than to attempt to impose a single, centralized system upon their reluctant constituents.

In the area of higher education, the churches emerged triumphant. Between 1838 and 1855, the foundations of no less than six universities were laid in the Maritime colonies: Prince of Wales and St Dunstan's in Prince Edward Island; Acadia, St Mary's, and St Francis Xavier in Nova Scotia; and Mount Allison in New Brunswick. Each was associated with a religious denomination, as had been the earlier Anglican institutions—King's College in Windsor, Nova Scotia, and the College of New Brunswick in Fredericton.

Dalhousie College, founded in 1818 by Lieutenant-Governor Dalhousie as a non-denominational institution, became narrowly Presbyterian in its faculty-hiring practices and drew fire from the outlying regions for its Halifax location. Reform politician Joseph Howe tried to forestall the fragmentation of higher education in Nova Scotia by introducing a bill for one state-supported university in Halifax. He earned only the antipathy of his opponents, who resented his assertion that supporters of small denominational colleges were "four-eyed lawyers," "eloquent wiseacres," and "sap-headed shingle merchants."

By the 1840s, most of the religious denominations in the region sponsored their own newspapers, which debated global and local political events as well as religious questions. Churches also emerged as important dispensers of charity in a society characterized by rampant poverty and disaster. In urban centres, orphanages, hospitals, and shelters were usually church-sponsored institutions. Evangelical churches were among the first to develop home and overseas missions. In 1845, Maritime Baptists sent Richard Burpee to India and, in the following year, the Presbyterian Church of Nova Scotia agreed to send John Geddes to the Hebrides.

In addition to educational, charitable, and mission activities, the church served as the focus for various reform movements in colonial society. The most successful by far was the temperance movement, which from its beginnings in the late 1820s soon engulfed the region. Even the Anglican and Roman Catholic churches encouraged temperance among their followers, although they were much less likely than their evangelical counterparts to countenance total prohibition of alcoholic beverages as a solution to society's ills. According to temperance advocates, excessive drinking undermined family life and was both a waste of money and a detriment to hard work.

Religious Conflict

The church was the one institution in colonial society where men and women, rich and poor, old and young met together. Nevertheless, churches revealed the status of their members in not-so-subtle ways. In many colonial churches, the renting of pews still permitted

Richard Preston.
Black Cultural Centre, Dartmouth, NS

the rich to sit closer to the pulpit. Women were sometimes relegated to a separate section of the church. People of colour were almost always set apart. The black Baptists of Nova Scotia, never fully accepted by their white co-religionists, formed separate churches and associations under the leadership of such men as the Reverend Richard Preston, an emigrant from the United States who studied for the ministry in Britain.

In the early nineteenth century, the gulf separating Protestant and Roman Catholic was nearly as wide as that separating the races. Tensions often erupted in violence. On 12 July 1847, the anniversary of the Battle of the Boyne, 300 Irish Catholics battled Protestants in Woodstock, New Brunswick, resulting in 10 deaths. Two years later, an even bloodier confrontation rocked the Catholic enclave of York Point in Saint John. In Prince Edward Island, where the numbers of Protestants and Catholics were nearly equal, the religious factor figured prominently in political struggles.

Harmony did not always prevail within Protestant and Roman Catholic ranks. Presbyterianism was racked by divisions between the established Church of Scotland and various secessionist groups. So deeply did these divisions go that in 1845 the sheriff erected a barrier over two metres high across Pictou's main street to keep the warring factions apart. Roman Catholics were also divided among themselves, usually along ethnic lines. With Natives, Acadians, Scots, and Irish all practising Roman Catholicism, there was little hope for unity either in language or administration.

EMERGING POLITICAL CULTURES

Political developments in the Maritimes, as elsewhere in British North America, reflected social tensions and changing economic relationships. At the formal level, the colonies moved along the continuum from imperial dependency to representative and responsible government. The latter refers to a system in which the executive council (cabinet) is drawn from the majority party in the elected assembly and requires a majority of votes in the assembly to pass its legislation. As this definition implies, it is the political system that, with some modification, exists in Canada today. The road to responsible government was not always an easy one. Nor was it necessarily the democratic triumph that is often portrayed. Only a relatively small number of men emerged as the power brokers under responsible government, and their values were revealed in the laws they imposed on the society they governed.

Colonial politics evolved within the larger framework of western political thought. In Europe, the divine right of kings and the concentration of power in the hands of a small hereditary landed elite, bolstered by a state-supported church and a standing army, were being challenged by the rising middle class. Its demand that power be shared among all men with a stake in society—usually defined as those possessing property or wealth—was a popular rallying cry in both the American and French revolutions. By the nineteenth century, wider concepts of democracy were being advanced. Why not give every man—and even women—an equal political voice? Indeed, why not create a society in which equality of condition, not just equality of opportunity, prevailed? In the Maritime colonies, as in much of the North Atlantic world, political discussions were informed by these three perspectives: conservatism, liberalism, and socialism.

When calling for political reforms, colonial politicians could draw upon the practical experience of an evolving parliamentary democracy in Great Britain and a full-fledged republican system in the United States. The British Chartist movement, with its demands for a broader franchise and reforms to stop political corruption and intimidation, appealed to many British North American reformers. On the European continent, popular unrest flared in 1830 and 1848, threatening monarchs and inspiring revolutionary tracts such as the *Communist Manifesto*, written by Karl Marx in 1848. Those more remote from formal political processes also took lessons from their American and European counterparts. The Irish movement for repeal of the Union of 1801 became a model for mobilizing mass support for a political cause and was closely watched by Irish Catholics in the Maritime colonies. The British labour movement, still in its infancy, offered practical ideas about how ordinary people could exert influence.

For colonials who lamented the erosion of traditional institutions, European conservatism served as a source of inspiration. Tories, clinging to their beliefs in hierarchy and tradition, were still a force to be reckoned with in Great Britain, while the papacy, emerging from a century of retreat, sounded the clarion call to all Roman Catholics to resist the "sins" of liberalism and socialism.

Prince Edward Island

On Prince Edward Island, the land question was the animating force of political life. During the first decade of the nineteenth century, Irish lawyer James Palmer and Rhode Island Loyalist William Haszard led an organization known as the Loyal Electors, which criticized the corruption of the official coterie around Lieutenant-Governor J.F.W. DesBarres (1805–13). Local authorities and absentee proprietors used their influence to have Palmer dismissed from his public offices. Postwar efforts to make the proprietorial system work ended in failure and frustration for both proprietors and tenants.

In 1831, William Cooper, a former land agent for absentee proprietor Lord James Townsend, won a hard-fought election for a seat in the island legislature on a platform of "our country's freedom and farmers' rights." He soon emerged as leader of the Escheat Movement, which won an overwhelming victory in the 1838 election. When Cooper travelled to London to plead his case for a general escheat, or cancellation, of the proprietary grants, he was refused even a hearing from Colonial Secretary Lord John Russell. Thereafter, reform on the island focused on responsible government as the only means of achieving a satisfactory conclusion to the interminable land question.

New Brunswick

In New Brunswick, the timber trade dominated the political process. The revenues from the sale, leasing, and licensing of Crown lands, spent at the lieutenant-governor's prerogative, became the object of the assembly's reform efforts and were a prize worth fighting for. The issue became more contentious

Trotting Match on the Ice—Prince Edward Island, **by Henry Buckton Laurence.**
Confederation Centre Art Gallery and Museum, Charlottetown, PEI

with the appointment of Thomas Baillie as commissioner of Crown lands in 1824. Charged with bringing bureaucratic efficiency to the administration of Crown lands, Baillie alienated virtually everyone in the colony while chalking up vast surpluses in the colonial treasury. In 1833, when the Colonial Office decided to divide the council into legislative and executive branches, Thomas Baillie headed the list of appointments to the new Executive Council.

Charles Simonds of Saint John led opposition to appointed officials in government, and in 1837 the assembly agreed to a compromise worked out the previous year with the Colonial Office. In return for a "civil list" guaranteeing the salaries of civil servants, including the hated Thomas Baillie, the revenues from Crown lands would be turned over to the assembly's disposal. At the same time, Colonial Secretary Lord Glenelg's injunction to New Brunswick Lieutenant-Governor Sir John Harvey to choose councillors who had the confidence of the assembly relieved the new Executive Council of the dead weight of lifetime appointments. With Simonds the chief adviser to the lieutenant-governor, New Brunswick had achieved one of the most important conditions for the operation of responsible government: executive responsibility to the majority in the assembly.

Nova Scotia

Resentment against appointed colonial officials, who held their positions virtually for life, was also a cause of complaint in Nova Scotia. In 1835, Joseph Howe successfully defended himself against a charge of libel when he published a letter criticizing the colony's appointed magistrates in his newspaper, the *Novascotian*. Riding on his popular acclaim, he won a seat in the assembly and used it to continue his battle for political reform. Perhaps more than any other colonial politician, Howe knew what he wanted: the same constitutional rights for British subjects in the colonies as they enjoyed at home.

This was an audacious request and one that seemed incompatible with imperial control of the colonies. Nevertheless, Howe pressed his case in London and applauded the recommendations of Lord Durham, who had been sent to report on the British North American colonies following the 1837 rebellions in the Canadas. In 1839, when Lord John Russell stubbornly refused to concede the principle of responsible government as recommended by Durham, Howe expounded his position in a series of public letters to the colonial secretary. "Every poor boy in Nova Scotia . . . knows that he has the same rights to the honours and emoluments of office as he would have if he lived in Britain or the United States," Howe concluded. "And he feels, that while the great honours of the empire are almost beyond his reach, he ought to have a chance of dispensing the patronage and guiding the administration of his native country without any sacrifice of principle or diminution of self-respect."[7]

Responsible Government

By the time Howe was writing his letters to Lord Russell, Britain had split the old council into executive and legislative councils, and the principle of permanent executive appointments had been abandoned. Before responsible government could become a reality, two more changes were required. First, it was necessary, as a general principle, for members of the executive council to have the support of the majority party in the assembly and to resign when they had lost the assembly's confidence by a vote in the House or in a general election. Second, it was necessary for the lieutenant-governor to defer to the recommendations of his cabinet advisers and, like the monarch in Britain, withdraw from the daily routine of political life.

For these principles to be accepted, changes had to occur both in Britain and the colonies. The party system in the colonies was rudimentary at best, as was the system of cabinet responsibility in the executive council. Both the party system and bureaucratic processes began to take shape in the turbulent political atmosphere of the 1840s. Meanwhile, imperial reluctance to cut the colonial apron strings was reduced by the adoption of free trade in 1846. Political reform was not tied directly to economic reform—British colonies inhabited primarily by people of colour were stripped of representative government in this period—but free trade undermined one of the major rationales for maintaining control over colonies where white settlers were in the majority. With growing support in the colonies as well as in Great Britain for reform in colonial administration, the stage was set for a major turning point in British colonial history.

In 1847, Nova Scotia's recently-appointed lieutenant-governor, Sir John Harvey, was instructed by Colonial Secretary Lord Grey to choose his advisers from the party that commanded a majority in the assembly. The Reformers were victorious in an election held later that year and they stood firm in their resolve to take exclusive control of the reins of power. Early in 1848, a Liberal government under the leadership of James Boyle Uniacke became the first "responsible" administration in the British Empire.

The process by which political institutions evolved was different in each of the Maritime colonies, but the end result was the same. By 1851, responsible government, by which the executive authority was drawn from and responsible to an elected colonial assembly, came into effect throughout the Maritimes. This did not mean that the colonies were politically independent. Indeed, imperial authority was exercised

in a variety of ways. The Colonial Office still kept a watchful administrative eye over colonial politics; the British Parliament continued to legislate on matters relating to defence, foreign policy, and constitutional amendment; and the Privy Council in Britain remained the final court of appeal for the colonies. Another century would pass before these ties of empire would be fully dissolved in "British" North America.

Responsible Government in Action

Responsible government represented the official transfer of power from the British to the colonial middle class. In some ways, it was a clever tactical move binding the colonies ever closer to Britain, which was steadily extending the boundaries of its informal empire based on trade and naval power. The significance of responsible government lay in its potential.

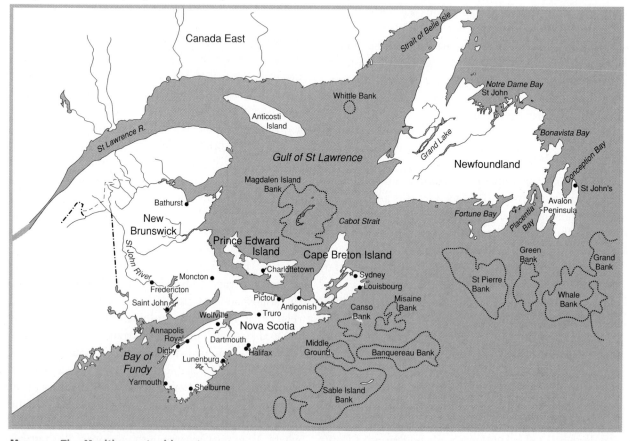

MAP 13.2 The Maritimes at mid-century.
Adapted from *Canada before Confederation: A Study in Historical Geography*, by R. Cole Harris and John Warkentin. Copyright © 1974 by Oxford University Press Inc.

After it was granted, colonial politicians had a much wider scope for using the powers of the state for achieving their own ends.

Most of the Maritime colonies used their newly won powers to symbolically lay to rest deeply entrenched claims to privilege. In Nova Scotia, for example, the legislature repealed the law banning trade unions, revoked the special privileges of the Church of England, and put an end to the General Mining Association's monopoly over the colony's mineral resources. The New Brunswick assembly transformed King's College, an Anglican institution, into the secular University of New Brunswick, introduced the secret ballot at election time, and even experimented with the prohibition of alcohol. According to historian Ian Robertson, Prince Edward Island had the most "far-reaching agenda of any reform government in the region."[8] Reform leaders George Coles and Edward Whelan failed to solve the land question but they managed to introduce the first Free Schools Act

in the Maritimes in 1852 and to extend voting privileges to a larger segment of the tenant population.

Although responsible government did not immediately alter the power structure in the Maritime colonies, it coincided with a debate over who could participate in the democratic process. Under representative government, the Maritime colonies had adopted a broad franchise that extended the vote to all "freeholders." In the 1850s, the franchise was extended to include most male ratepayers, whether they owned or rented property. Meanwhile, women were disfranchised by law in all the British North American colonies between 1832 and 1851. Aboriginal peoples were in effect disqualified by virtue of their poverty, but the Nova Scotia government made it legal, specifically denying the franchise to Natives and paupers in 1854. In practice, less than a quarter of the population in the Maritimes was legally entitled to vote in the mid-nineteenth century, and even fewer people were eligible to run for public office.

MORE TO THE STORY

Joseph Howe on Trial, 1835

The struggle for political reform in British North America was often led by journalists. Using their newspapers as a forum for their views, journalists helped to persuade an increasingly literate public that the representative system of government, where the real power was held by appointed officials, was corrupt, inefficient, and heavy-handed. Authorities often tried to silence their journalistic critics by launching lawsuits, using physical violence, or even resorting to deportation. By the 1830s such tactics could no longer be employed without proving the very points raised by their critics.

Joseph Howe's famous libel trial of 1835 was a major turning point in the struggle between conservative and reform forces in Nova Scotia. The son of a Loyalist, Howe at an early age assisted his father in his duties as postmaster general and king's printer. In 1828 young Howe took over the *Novascotian* and soon made it a leading newspaper in the colony. Howe was initially a conservative politically but the more he investigated the political system the less he liked it. On 1 January 1835, he published a letter claiming that "the Magistracy and Police have, by one stratagem or other, taken from the pockets of the people, in over exactions, fines, etc. etc., a sum that

would exceed in the gross amount of £30,000." As a result of this accusation, he was charged with criminal libel.

According to the law of the day, it was indeed libelous to publish anything that was designed to degrade a person or disturb the public peace, and the truth of the charge could not be used as a defence. Howe decided to plead his own case, a calculated move that enabled him to use unorthodox arguments to appeal to the jury. Describing a number of specific cases in which the behaviour of appointed officials was clearly improper, he argued that he would have failed in his duty of keeping the peace if he had not brought these practices to public attention. He went on to make his case one that championed freedom of the press, stating that, "while I live, Nova Scotia shall have the blessing of an open and unshackled press."[9] The jury disregarded the law as stated by the judge and principal prosecutor and took only 10 minutes to declare Howe, "Not Guilty." The case helped to launch Howe's political career. In the 1836 election he won a seat in the assembly and became a leading figure in the Reform Party that led the fight for responsible government.

INTELLECTUAL AWAKENING

The achievement of responsible government was only one of the symptoms of the reform spirit sweeping western society in the early years of the nineteenth century. Perched on the margins of the North Atlantic world, colonial citizens were full participants in debates over social change. Their newspapers, college professors, and urban literati were alive to the intellectual currents of the age. It was often only a matter of a few years or even a few months before movements in Britain or the United States had their impact and their imitators in the Maritime colonies. Travelling lecturers, speaking on a wide range of subjects, were enthusiastically received. Ambitious young men from the colonies travelled to Britain and the United States to be educated as doctors, scientists, and philosophers, and many of them returned home to practise or to teach their new-found knowledge in the local colleges.

One of the most influential organizations to be transplanted from Britain was the Mechanics' Institute. Founded in Scotland in 1823 as a vehicle for scientific education among the artisan class, mechanics' institutes took root in the Maritime region in the 1830s. Patronized by the upwardly mobile professional class in cities such as Saint John and Halifax, they helped to spread the doctrine of self-help and encouraged a growing interest in literary and scientific pursuits.

In the first half of the nineteenth century, the readership for both regional and international literature grew rapidly. Colonial newspapers carried British and North American authors in serial form, making Walter Scott, Frances Trollope, and Charles Dickens as well as local authors easily accessible to colonials. Libraries and bookstores could be found in most urban centres. Although cheap pirated reprints of popular fiction flourished briefly in the early 1840s, they were quickly suppressed by copyright laws.

Colonial authors were also coming into their own. In 1824, Julia Catherine Beckwith of Fredericton became the first native-born British North American novelist with the publication of *St Ursula's Convent*, written when she was 17. Following publication of his two-volume history of Nova Scotia in 1829, Judge Thomas Chandler Haliburton turned to satire in his Sam Slick series, which won him international acclaim. The growing interest in natural history

Thomas Chandler Haliburton.
Webster Canadiana Collection/W647/New Brunswick Museum, Saint John

inspired Nova Scotia artist Maria Morris to publish, in collaboration with pioneer naturalist Titus Smith, a book entitled *Wildflowers of Nova Scotia* in 1839. New England poet Henry Wadsworth Longfellow—who never visited the Maritimes—immortalized the deportation of the Acadians with his poem "Evangeline," published in 1847. Although this had not been his goal, the poem helped to spark a new sense of collective identity among Acadians in the Maritimes and elsewhere.

The intellectual awakening in the region was often practical in its manifestations. In 1818, John Young, a Scottish merchant in Halifax, wrote a series of letters under the pen name of "Agricola" in which he encouraged scientific methods in agriculture. As a result of his efforts and financial assistance from the government, agricultural societies were established throughout Nova Scotia in the 1820s. Farmers experimented with new varieties of crops and breeds of livestock, hoping to profit from expanding farm surpluses. With the growth of the timber trade and shipping in the Maritimes, the market for farm products increased dramatically, providing an incentive to agricultural innovation.

The Maritime Economy: The Legacy of Mercantilism in the Maritimes

The legacy of mercantilism in the Maritimes was a mixed one. As early as 1825, New Brunswick historian Peter Fisher, author of the *First History of New Brunswick*, offered a scathing attack on the exploitative nature of mercantilism:

> The persons principally engaged in shipping the timber have been strangers who have taken no interest in the welfare of the country; but have merely occupied a spot to make what they could in the shortest possible time. Some have done well, and others have had to quit the trade: but whether they won or lost the capital of the country has been wasted, and no improvement of any consequence made to compensate for it, or to secure a source of trade for the inhabitants, when the lumber shall fail. Instead of seeing towns built, farms improved, and the country cleared and stocked with the reasonable returns of so great a trade; the forests are stripped and nothing left in prospect, but the gloomy apprehension when the timber is gone of sinking into insignificance and poverty. . . . These are some of the causes that have and still do operate against the prosperity of the country. Men who take no interest in the welfare of the province, continue to sap and prey on its resources.[10]

Other contemporary observers remarked upon the negative impact of the timber trade on colonial agriculture. Lieutenant-Colonel Joseph Gubbins, inspecting the New Brunswick militia in 1811, noted: "The labouring class devote much time to this lucrative employment which would be much better bestowed on their farms."[11]

Following the collapse of the Maritime region's industrial economy in the twentieth century, scholars began to see the mercantile era in a somewhat different light. Political economist Harold Innis, perhaps reflecting the general nostalgia for the "age of sail" in the Maritimes, wrote in 1930: "Nothing . . . has been a more serious blow to the development of that section of the Dominion than the decay of the industry of shipbuilding. . . . The competition of iron and steel destroyed a magnificent achievement, an integration of capital and labour, of lumbering, fishing and agriculture, on which rested a progressive community life."[12]

Although there is little doubt that staples exploitation stimulated economic growth of a specific kind, most historians agree with Fisher and Gubbins that the timber trade and the shipbuild-

ing industry helped to retard agricultural and industrial development in the Atlantic colonies. In their study of the shipping industry in the Maritimes, for instance, historians Eric W. Sager and Gerald Panting argue persuasively that the economic and social structures inherited from the region's mercantile past contributed to the unequal integration of the Maritime region into the North American industrial economy following Confederation.[13]

To a considerable extent, the sheer success of shipbuilding prior to the 1870s diverted the attention of merchants in the region from other avenues of industrial investment. Moreover, staples exploitation, shipbuilding, and shipping reinforced pre-industrial modes of production and seasonal rhythms, making a full-scale transition to a modern industrial economy difficult. In many parts of the Maritimes, people worked part of the year in mercantile industries and then retreated to the family farm, where a subsistence existence was always an alternative to wage labour. Without a landless working class driven by desperation to take low wages and poor working conditions, it was difficult for the region to compete in the race for industrial ascendancy.

Colonial dependency also remained long after the Navigation Acts had been swept away. Shipbuilders and timber merchants, many of them representing British-based companies, used their influence to import the tools of their trade and the cargoes for their vessels rather than supporting legislation that would encourage the growth of local industries. The Maritimes thus failed to develop what economists call the "backward linkages" of their activities. Sails, metal fittings, and engines were imported, as were cheap foodstuffs to feed the crews employed on the ships and in the lumber woods. When wood gave way to iron as the preferred fabric of ship construction, the Atlantic colonies had relatively few industries that would survive the transition.

The question, nevertheless, remains: Why did Maritime entrepreneurs not invest in the iron ships that were beginning to dominate their trade? Evidence suggests that they, like other business leaders in the period, were attracted to investment frontiers elsewhere, or shifted their interest to textiles, transportation, and iron rails. As the mercantile era gave way to industrialization, the activities of staple exploitation, shipbuilding, and shipping remained linked, and they all collapsed together, leaving the Maritimes strapped in a "great coastal nation with a small merchant navy."[14]

As in economic and political life, the Maritime colonies by the middle of the nineteenth century were on the brink of a new age of cultural maturity. Nearly three-quarters of the inhabitants in the region were native-born, and the sense of colonial identity was strong. For Joseph Howe, one of the colony's most enthusiastic patriots, time was all that was required to solve the problems posed by limited cultural identities: "You who owe your origins to other lands cannot resist the conviction that, as you loved them, so will your children love this: and though the second place in their hearts may be filled by merry England, romantic Scotland or the verdant fields of Erin, the first and highest will be occupied by the little province where they drew their earliest breath, and which claims from them filial reverence and care."[15]

Conclusion

Joseph Howe underestimated the tenacity of cultural differences, but his optimism was understandable. Like the British Isles, the Maritime colonies were poised on the edge of a great continent. They had seemingly endless fish and forest resources and an abundance of coal and iron, the essential ingredients of the industrial age. What could stop them from becoming the brightest jewels in the British colonial empire or even from developing an empire that would rival that of Britain itself?

Notes

1 "Statement of the Indian Delegation, 23 June 1842," cited in *Source Materials Relating to the New Brunswick Indian*, ed. W.D. Hamilton and W.A. Spray (Fredericton: Centennial Print and Litho Ltd., 1976), 112.

2 Margaret MacDonell, *The Emigrant Experience: Songs of Highland Emigrants in North America* (Toronto: University of Toronto Press, 1982), 105–12, 118–25.

3 D.C. Harvey, ed., *Journeys to the Island of St John or Prince Edward Island, 1775–1832* (Toronto: Macmillan, 1955), 104.

4 Peter Fisher, *The First History of New Brunswick* (1825; reprinted Woodstock, NB: Non-Entity Press, 1981), 17.

5 T.W. Acheson, *Saint John: The Making of a Colonial Urban Community* (Toronto: University of Toronto Press, 1985).

6 Judith Fingard, "The Winter's Tale: The Seasonal Contours of Pre-Industrial Poverty in British North America, 1815–1860," *Canadian Historical Association Historical Papers* (1974): 66.

7 Howe's fourth Letter to Lord John Russell, 1839, cited in *The Speeches and Letters of Joseph Howe*, ed. J.A. Chisholm (Halifax: n.p., 1909), 266.

8 Ian Ross Robertson, "The 1850s: Maturity and Reform," in *The Atlantic Region to Confederation: A History*, ed. Phillip A. Buckner and John G. Reid, (Toronto: University of Toronto Press, 1994), 344.

9 Cited in D.C. Harvey, *Joseph Howe and Local Patriotism* (Winnipeg, 1921), reprinted in *Joseph Howe: Opportunist? Man of Vision? Frustrated Politician?* ed. George Rawlyk (Toronto: Copp Clark, 1967), 44.

10 Fisher, 73.

11 Howard Temperley, ed., *Gubbins' New Brunswick Journals, 1811 and 1813* (Fredericton: New Brunswick Heritage Publications, 1980), 5.

12 C.R. Fay and H.A. Innis, "The Maritime Provinces," *The Cambridge History of the British Empire*, vol. 6 (New York: Macmillan, 1930), 663.

13 Eric W. Sager with Gerald E. Panting, *Maritime Capital: The Shipping Industry in Atlantic Canada, 1820–1914* (Montreal: McGill-Queen's University Press, 1990), 7.

14 Sager with Panting, 210.

15 J. Murray Beck, *Politics of Nova Scotia*, vol. 1, 1710–1896 (Halifax: Four East Publications, 1985), 109.

RELATED READINGS IN THIS SERIES

From *Foundations: Readings in Pre-Confederation Canadian History*

Ian Ross Robertson, "Reform, Literacy, and the Lease: The Prince Edward Island Free Education Act of 1852," 276–90. Gail Campbell, "The Most Restrictive Franchise in British North America? A Case Study," 291–312.

From Media Companion CD-ROM, Volume I

Louisa Collins Diary, 1815
Webster-Ashburton Treaty of 1842
To the Tenantry and the Other Inhabitants of the Island of Prince Edward
Protestant Organization

SELECTED READING

General regional histories include Margaret R. Conrad and James K. Hiller, *Atlantic Canada: A Region in the Making* (Toronto: Oxford University Press, 2001); Phillip A. Buckner and John G. Reid, eds., *The Atlantic Region to Confederation: A History* (Toronto: University of Toronto Press, 1994); and W.S. MacNutt, *The Atlantic Provinces: The Emergence of Colonial Society, 1712–1857* (Toronto: McClelland and Stewart, 1965). George A. Rawlyk, ed., *Historical Essays on the Atlantic Provinces* (Ottawa: Carleton University Press, 1967) includes many of the now "classic" essays on the region. P.A. Buckner and David Frank, eds., *The Acadiensis Reader: Atlantic Canada before Confederation*, 2nd ed., vol. 1 (Fredericton: Acadiensis Press, 1988) offers a sample of more recent scholarship on the pre-Confederation period. The chapter on "The Atlantic Region" in R. Cole Harris and John Warkentin, *Canada before Confederation* (Toronto: Oxford University Press, 1974) provides a useful overview.

Provincial histories include W.S. MacNutt, *New Brunswick: A History, 1784–1867* (Toronto: Macmillan, 1984); Graeme Wynn, *Timber Colony: A Historical Geography of Early-Nineteenth-Century New Brunswick* (Toronto: University of Toronto Press, 1981); Andrew Hill Clark, *Three Centuries and the Island* (Toronto: University of Toronto Press, 1959); and J.M. Bumsted, *Land, Settlement and Politics on Eighteenth-Century Prince Edward Island* (Montreal: McGill-Queen's University Press, 1987). On Cape Breton, see Donald Macgillivray and Brian Tennyson, eds., *Cape Breton Historical Essays* (Sydney, NS: University College of Cape Breton Press, 1980); Stephen Hornsby, *Nineteenth-Century Cape Breton: A Historical Geography* (Montreal: McGill-Queen's University Press, 1992); and two books edited by Kenneth Donovan: *Cape Breton at 200: Historical Essays in Honour of the Island's Bicentennial, 1785–1985* (Sydney, NS: University College of Cape Breton Press, 1985) and *The Island: New Perspectives on Cape Breton's History, 1713–1975* (Fredericton: Acadiensis Press, 1990). Urban developments are discussed in T.W. Acheson, *Saint John: The Making of a Colonial Urban Community* (Toronto: University of Toronto Press, 1985), and

Judith Fingard, Janet Guildford, and David Sutherland, *Halifax: The First 250 Years* (Halifax: Formac, 1999).

Aboriginal history is covered in L.S.F. Upton, *Micmacs and Colonists: Indian-White Relations in the Maritimes, 1713–1867* (Vancouver: UBC Press, 1979); Jennifer Reid, *Myth, Symbol, and Colonial Encounter: British and Mi'kmaq in Acadia, 1700–1867* (Ottawa: University of Ottawa Press, 1995); Daniel N. Paul, *We Were Not the Savages: A Mi'kmaq Perspective on the Collision between Europe and North American Civilizations*, rev. ed. (Halifax: Fernwood, 2000); and William C. Wicken, *Mi'kmaq Treaties on Trial: History, Land, and Donald Marshall Junior* (Toronto: University of Toronto Press, 2002). Two articles by Judith Fingard describe aspects of Protestant missionary activity directed toward Native peoples in this period: "English Humanitarianism and the Colonial Mind: Walter Bromley in Nova Scotia, 1813–1825," *Canadian Historical Review* 54, 2 (June 1973): 123–51 and "The New England Company and the New Brunswick Indians, 1786–1826: A Comment on the Colonial Perversion of British Benevolence," *Acadiensis* 1, 2 (Spring 1972): 29–42.

Acadian history in this period is covered in Nicolas Landry and Nicole Lang, *Histoire de l'Acadie* (Sillery: Septentrion, 2001) and Jean Daigle, ed., *Acadia of the Maritimes: Thematic Studies* (Moncton: Chaire d'études acadiennes, Université de Moncton, 1995). The history of blacks in the region is covered in Robin W. Winks, *The Blacks in Canada: A History*, 2nd ed. (Montreal and Kingston: McGill-Queen's University Press, 1997); Bridglal Pachai, *Beneath the Clouds of the Promised Land: The Survival of Nova Scotia Blacks*, vol. II: *1800–1989* (Halifax: The Black Educators Association of Nova Scotia, 1990); W.A. Spray, *The Blacks in New Brunswick* (Fredericton: Brunswick Press, 1972); and Jim Hornsby, *Black Islanders: Prince Edward Island's Historical Black Community* (Charlottetown: Institute of Island Studies, 1991).

Aspects of Scottish settlement in this period are discussed in D. Campbell and R.A. MacLean, *Beyond the Atlantic Roar: A Study of Nova Scotia Scots* (Toronto: McClelland and

Stewart, 1974). On the Irish, see Peter Toner, ed., *New Ireland Remembered: Historical Essays on the Irish in New Brunswick* (Fredericton: New Ireland Press, 1988), and Thomas P. Power, ed., *The Irish in Atlantic Canada, 1780–1900* (Fredericton: New Ireland Press, 1991). On Welsh settlement in the Maritimes, see Peter Thomas, *Strangers from a Secret Land: The Voyage of the Brif "Albion" and the Founding of the First Welsh Settlements in Canada* (Toronto: University of Toronto Press, 1986).

Women in the region are the subject of Janet Guildford and Suzanne Morton, eds., *Separate Spheres: Women's Worlds in the 19th-Century Maritimes* (Fredericton: Acadiensis Press, 1994), and Sylvia Hamilton, "Naming Names, Naming Ourselves: A Survey of Early Black Women in Nova Scotia," in *"We're Rooted Here and They Can't Pull Us Up": Essays in African Canadian Women's History*, ed. Peggy Bristow et al. (Toronto: University of Toronto Press, 1994), 13–40.

The impact of sea-based industries on the Atlantic region is explored in two books by Eric Sager: *Seafaring Labour: The Merchant Marine in Atlantic Canada* (Montreal: McGill-Queen's University Press, 1989) and *Maritime Capital: The Shipping Industry in Atlantic Canada, 1820–1914* (Montreal: McGill-Queen's University Press, 1990), and two by Rosemary Ommer: *Merchant Credit and Labour Strategies in Historical Perspective* (Fredericton: Acadiensis Press, 1990) and *From Outpost to Outport: A Structural Analysis of the Jersey-Gaspé Cod Fishery, 1767–1886* (Montreal: McGill-Queen's University Press, 1991). A Canadian Historical Association booklet by Eric W. Sager and Lewis R. Fischer, *Shipping and Shipbuilding in Atlantic Canada, 1820–1914* (Ottawa: Canadian Historical Association, 1986) offers a convenient summary of general trends relating to shipbuilding. The fisheries are the subject of James E. Candow and Carol Corbin, eds., *How Deep is the Ocean? Historical Essays on Canada's Atlantic Fishery* (Sydney: University College of Cape Breton Press, 1997).

The politics of pre-Confederation Nova Scotia have been described in J. Murray Beck, *Politics of Nova Scotia*, vol. 1, *1710–1896* (Tantallon, NS: Four East Publications, 1985). Beck's earlier work, *The Government of Nova Scotia* (Toronto: University of Toronto Press, 1957) offers detailed information on the structures of colonial government, and his two-volume biography, *Joseph Howe* (Montreal: McGill-Queen's University Press, 1982, 1984), is by far the most thorough study undertaken of a Maritime politician in this period. See also Brian Cuthbertson, *Johnny Bluenose at the Polls: Epic Nova Scotian Election Battles, 1758–1848* (Halifax: Formac,

1994). The political implications of the land question in Prince Edward Island are summarized in Ian Ross Robertson's introduction to *The Prince Edward Island Land Commission of 1860* (Fredericton: Acadiensis Press, 1988) and his book *The Tenant League of Prince Edward Island, 1864–1867: Leasehold Tenure in the New World* (Toronto: University of Toronto Press, 1996). The Maritime context of imperial developments is clearly outlined in P.A. Buckner, *The Transition to Responsible Government: British Policy in British North America, 1815–1850* (Westport, CT: Greenwood, 1985).

Social and cultural developments in the Atlantic colonies have yet to be fully explored. George Rawlyk, *Ravaged by the Spirit: Religious Revivals, Baptists and Henry Alline* (Montreal: McGill-Queen's University Press, 1984) traces the roots of religious revivalism in the region. Jan Noel, in *Canada Dry: Temperance Crusades before Confederation* (Toronto: University of Toronto Press, 1995), examines the early history of the temperance movement. Scott W. See explores religious violence in *Riots in New Brunswick: Orange Nativism and Social Violence in the 1840s* (Toronto: University of Toronto Press, 1993), and Judith Fingard examines local aspects of a larger reality in pre-industrial society in "The Relief of the Unemployed Poor in Saint John, Halifax, and St John's, 1815–1860," *Acadiensis* 1, 5 (Autumn 1975): 32–53. The same subject is described in Fingard's "The Winter's Tale: The Seasonal Contours of Pre-industrial Poverty in British North America," *Canadian Historical Association Historical Papers* (1974): 65–94. Douglas Baldwin and Thomas Spira explore aspects of mid-nineteenth-century society in *Gaslights, Epidemics and Vagabond Cows: Charlottetown in the Victorian Era* (Charlottetown: Ragweed Press, 1988).

A good place to start looking for an understanding of literary development in the region is Fred Cogswell, "Literary Activity in the Maritime Provinces, 1815–1880," in *Literary History of Canada: Canadian Literature in English*, ed. Carl Klinck (Toronto: University of Toronto Press, 1976) and Gwendolyn Davies, *Studies in Maritime Literary History* (Fredericton: Acadiensis Press, 1991). An interesting perspective on the European vision of Nova Scotia can be found in Mary Sparling, *Great Expectations: The European Vision of Nova Scotia, 1749–1848* (Halifax: Mount Saint Vincent University, 1980). Ruth Holmes Whitehead, *Micmac Quillwork* (Halifax: Nova Scotia Museum, 1982) offers a detailed analysis of an important feature of Mi'kmaq economic and material life.

WEBLINKS

WEBSTER-ASHBURTON TREATY

www.yale.edu/lawweb/avalon/diplomacy/britian/
brtreaty.htm

The Avalon Project at the Yale Law School offers the text of the treaty and related documents at this address.

THE HIGHLAND SCOTTISH

www.chebucto.ns.ca/Heritage/FSCNS/Scots_NS/
About_Clans/HtySctNS.html

This site, History of the Scots in New Scotland (Nova Scotia), has internal links to related material.

"EVANGELINE"

www.ac.wwu.edu/~jay/pages/evangel.html

For the story behind "Evangeline," and links to Longfellow and Acadian history, see this site.

PARTRIDGE ISLAND

www.saintjohn.nbcc.nb.ca/~Heritage/PartridgeIsland/
sectionindex.htm

This site offers documentary material on the history of Partridge Island.

CHAPTER 14

Newfoundland and Labrador, 1815–1855

Timeline

1791	Supreme Court established in Newfoundland
1804–05	Religious revival in Labrador
1807	The *Royal Gazette and Newfoundland Advertiser* begins publication
1816	Disastrous fire in St John's
1820	Court cases of Landrigan and Butler
1825	Sir Thomas Cochrane appointed first civil governor
1829	Death of Shanawdithit, the last Beothuk
1830	Hebron established by Moravians
1832	Newfoundland granted representative government
1842–48	Amalgamated legislature
1855	Responsible government granted

"We . . . look to other causes for our neglected condition, than the intentional policy of the parent state; and we are induced to believe that it has been owing solely to the exigencies of the war, and the more pressing demands of the empire upon the attention of your Majesty's government. But we humbly hope that the time is at length arrived when the state of this island will be taken into consideration, and some system adopted which may be more in unison with the altered condition of these extensive, populous, and valuable possessions of your Majesty's Crown.

"Your Petitioners therefore most humbly pray your Majesty will take their case into your most gracious consideration, and endow Newfoundland with all the rights and privileges of your Majesty's other transatlantic possessions, and especially to the cause of the Courts of Justice to be reformed, so that the laws may be administered to them by competent judges."[1]

Newfoundland and Labrador were the first areas of North America to experience European exploration and exploitation; they were among the last to enjoy the benefits of civilian government. As this 1818 petition from aggrieved Newfoundlanders attests, the reasons for this paradox are complex. The French and Napoleonic Wars served as an excuse but were not the cause for what Patrick O'Flaherty calls Great Britain's "studied neglect" of its closest British North American possession.[2] While it was certainly the case that the Beothuk, Innu, and Inuit who lived in Newfoundland and Labrador soon became hostile to all intruders, they were not sufficiently numerous or powerful to prevent Great Britain from introducing representative institutions in the region. The lack of good agricultural land contributed to the unwillingness of British authorities to see Newfoundland and Labrador as colonies like the others, but geography alone did not seal their fate. As with most of its overseas possessions, Great Britain calculated colonial policy in Newfoundland and Labrador with imperial interests in mind, and it would take persistent colonial pressure and new attitudes toward governance to bring about political reform.

The lack of representative institutions, historian Jerry Bannister reminds us, does not mean that Newfoundland and Labrador were without institutions of government before 1832. He argues that after the mid-eighteenth century the colony had an effective system of naval government and customary practices that only came under assault when reformers began to mobilize a growing middle class to support political change.[3]

THE COLONIAL CONDITION

As we have seen in previous chapters, France recognized Great Britain's possession of Newfoundland in the Treaty of Utrecht of 1713. The coast of Labrador (along with the Magdalen Islands and Anticosti) was attached to Newfoundland's jurisdiction in 1763, but became part of the enlarged colony of Quebec by the Quebec Act in 1774. In 1809 Labrador was restored to Newfoundland, an administrative decision that reflected the difficulty of governing coastal Labrador from Quebec and the growing involvement of Newfoundlanders in the Labrador fishery. No attempt was made at the time to survey Labrador's inland boundary.

Although the French relinquished all territorial claims in North America outside of St Pierre and Miquelon in 1763, they were granted the right to fish along the "French Shore" of the island of Newfoundland. The extent of the French Shore was variously defined, but following the French and Napoleonic Wars it was confirmed as running from Cape St John on Notre Dame Bay around the Northern Peninsula and along the west coast to Cape Ray. By the Anglo-American Convention of 1818, the United States had also been granted access to the

inshore waters of Labrador and large portions of the west and south coasts of Newfoundland (see Map 14.1).

Since Newfoundland and Labrador were not deemed to be colonies, their inhabitants were not consulted when these concessions were made. British authorities governed the region as a naval state and had little interest in making it a colony like the others in British North America. Meanwhile, the conditions that supported such a policy were gradually undermined. European settlement took firm root on the island of Newfoundland in the eighteenth century. Following the Seven Years' War, the coast of Labrador began to attract an increasing number of fishers, fur traders, missionaries, and servants. The growth of a Newfoundland-based fishery eventually attracted a resident merchant community. In this changing context, the lack of representative institutions increasingly became a major cause for grievance.

THE MIGRATORY FISHERY AND SETTLEMENT

The cod fisheries shaped the institutional development of colonial Newfoundland. Every spring since the early sixteenth century, thousands of men had used the island as a base for their fishing operations. Following time-honoured custom, the captain of the first ship to arrive in a given harbour assumed the power to settle disputes and maintain order. This policy remained in place after Great Britain assumed authority over the entire island in 1713. Beginning in 1729, governors were appointed to Newfoundland and a rudimentary judicial system with justices of the peace and constables was established, but fishing admirals, theoretically at least, still retained their powers during the summer months.

Meanwhile the great merchant families of the "West Country" of England were growing rich by exploiting the Newfoundland fishery. Operating out of such ports as Poole, Dartmouth, and Bristol, the West Country merchants developed a seasonal round that began with the winter outfitting of ships and the hiring of labour. If their home ports failed to provide enough hired hands, vessels bound for the Newfoundland fisheries in late March and April stopped in southern Ireland at ports such as Waterford and Cork to hire additional crew. A May arrival gave captains time to find the best fishing rooms (shore bases) and to supervise the construction or repair of stages (platforms where fish were processed and equipment stored), flakes (wooden platforms where fish were dried), and sheds to store their equipment. The summer months were devoted to catching and curing fish before the trip home in September and October. Over the winter, shore facilities were vulnerable to vandalism from both Europeans and Beothuk and, during wartime, from enemy ships.

The migratory fishery inevitably led to settlement. By leaving behind a few servants, the West Country merchants would protect their property, ensure a good "room" for the next fishing season, and perhaps extend the time devoted to fishing. These servants could also be encouraged to cut timber for fuel and construction over the winter months and manage meadows and gardens to provide food for the summer sojourners. They might even diversify their merchant's interests by catching fur-bearing animals and seals.

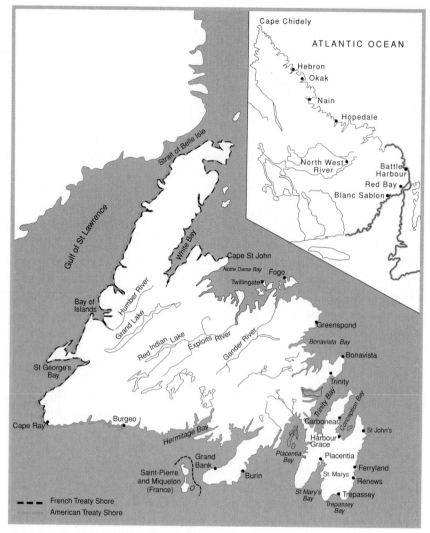

MAP 14.1 Newfoundland and Labrador.

From the early days of discovery, immigrants also arrived in Newfoundland on their own initiative, their goal being to process fish and sell their product to the merchants. Known as "planters," they often began as "by-boatmen"—small boat owners who arrived each spring as passengers, fished with their hired servants, sold the fish to the "sacks" (fishing ships), and left their boats behind when they returned to England in the fall. Inevitably, both the by-boatmen and their servants often took up residency in Newfoundland. Conception Bay, with its timber and potential for farming, was the first area to attract planters, but by 1750, permanent communities had taken root along the bay-studded coasts south and northwest of St John's.

In the second half of the eighteenth century, several developments brought further increases to the resident population. First, the potato, which became an important food staple in this period, proved to be a valuable source of vitamin C that warded off the dreaded scurvy. Second, the growth of British trade to Quebec following the conquest brought more vessels to Newfoundland, whose residents remained dependent on imported foodstuffs and other commodities. Together, these factors created a more stable environment for settlement.

The wars of the late eighteenth and early nineteenth centuries encouraged more immigration, and finally tipped the balance of fishery production in favour of the residents of Newfoundland. By that time English and Scottish merchants had also found it profitable to locate on the island. The biggest concentration of merchants was in St John's, which was fast emerging as the great entrepôt of the British fisheries and a major distribution centre for imported foodstuffs and manufactured goods. Most of the communities in the outlying areas, known as "outports," had a local merchant who supplied the settlers and bought the year's catch from resident fishing families.

Following the French and Napoleonic Wars, expanding markets for saltfish and seal oil stimulated investment and immigration. By 1827 the island of Newfoundland was home to over 57 000 people. This figure more than doubled to 122 000 in the next 30 years. In addition, at least 10 000 French fishers arrived seasonally on the north and west coasts, where a small but cosmopolitan population—from France, England, the Maritimes and other parts of Newfoundland—migrated to serve the French sojourners who were not legally permitted to become permanent settlers. An even larger number of American fishers appeared each spring in Newfoundland waters.

Immigration and Society

The vast majority of immigrants to Newfoundland came from either western England or southern Ireland. Like the people who flocked to other regions of North America, they were pushed out of their homeland by economic pressures and lured by the dream of economic security. The island's proximity to Great Britain, its exemption from immigrant regulations affecting other colonies, and the relatively high wages offered in the fishery made it a desirable destination for people with little money. Newfoundland might have more than its share of fog and rocky soil, but its cod was a free resource for those willing to put in the labour to exploit it.

The distribution of settlers in the colony reflected the patterns of mercantile activity in Newfoundland. For example, the port of Poole, which drew labour from its hinterland in Dorset and from the Waterford area in Ireland, supplied many of the settlers for Bonavista Bay. The port of Dartmouth depended more on Irish labour, making its Ferryland base a largely Roman Catholic area. The Irish were also numerous in Conception Bay, and gradually developed an independent fishery on the south coast of the Avalon Peninsula. By 1815 two-thirds of St John's population of nearly 10 000 was Irish. As a result of this migration pattern, Newfoundland attracted an almost equal number of English and Irish, Protestant and Roman Catholic immigrants.

Three-quarters of the immigrants were young men between the ages of 18 and 25, many of them indentured servants recruited by merchants under contract. Most of the female immigrants came as domestic servants from England and Ireland. Being in short supply, the women in Newfoundland communities married at a much younger age than men, over a quarter between the ages of 16 and 20. Weddings were often performed in November after the fishing season came to an end. Intermarriage between Protestants and Roman Catholics was discouraged on both sides.

As in other pre-industrial colonial societies, personal well-being in Newfoundland depended on a strong family economy. Men working in the Newfoundland fishery might spend a few winters in Newfoundland but were unlikely to make it their permanent home unless they could attract a marriage partner. Women were responsible for producing much of the food and clothing necessary for survival over the long, cold Newfoundland winters and raised the children who, at an early age, became valued workers in the family fisheries. Women also often served as the "skipper of the shore-crew," overseeing the drying and packing of fish.[4]

THE SALTFISH TRADE

Efforts to diversify Newfoundland's economy in the nineteenth century failed to dislodge the cod fishery as the primary industry in the colony. In exchange for salted cod, Newfoundlanders could import the food, clothing, and manufactured goods necessary for survival. The extent of Newfoundland's dependency was starkly revealed in the 1840s and 1850s when blight and bad weather spelled disaster for the potato crop on both sides of the North Atlantic. In many Newfoundland communities, only relief saved people from starvation.

No other British North American colony was so dependent upon imported food or a single staple product. The saltfish economy made Newfoundland unique in another way as well. Unlike the other British North American colonies, which traded primarily with Great Britain and the United States, Newfoundland's export trade was largely to southern Europe, Brazil, and the Caribbean. Saltfish was the major source of protein of the poor in countries with warm climates. Its advantages were obvious: it was cheap, easily transported, and slow to spoil.

During the French and Napoleonic Wars, the profits to be made in the salt cod fishery turned retailers, tavernkeepers, and artisans into merchants. Watchmaker Benjamin Bowering, for example, became one of St John's most successful fish merchants in this period and gradually diversified his activities to include the retailing of imported products. From 1815 to 1914 Newfoundlanders exported on the average 1 million hundredweights of saltfish a year,

testimony to the continuing demand for the product and the amazing fertility of the lowly cod.

In the nineteenth century, especially prior to 1866, when transatlantic telegraphic communications were inaugurated, the negotiating of prices and markets was a complicated process. Newfoundland merchants usually sold saltfish through agents based in distant ports, a factor that contributed to the concentration of the trade in the hands of a relatively small number of merchants in St John's. By the early nineteenth century the structure of dependence that came to dominate the saltfish industry was quickly taking shape. Merchants provided outport fishing families with supplies and in payment took the complete catch in the fall. As a result many fishing families rarely received cash for their labour and often sank hopelessly into debt to their merchant supplier.

The success of the saltfish industry was at once a blessing and a curse for Newfoundlanders. At the mercy of periodic poor fishing seasons, international

MORE TO THE STORY

The Seal Fishery

Economic diversification in Newfoundland came primarily in the form of another sea-based industry. In the 1790s Newfoundlanders began to exploit the seal fishery. North Atlantic harp seals visit coastal Newfoundland and Labrador in the late winter and early spring to feed and give birth to their calves on the ice floes before moving into the Arctic. In addition to their skins, seals yielded a fatty blubber that was rendered into oil for lighting and lubricants. The demand for seal oil expanded dramatically in the early nineteenth century. Although the seal fishery was a brutal and dangerous enterprise, it offered both adventure and profit. Newfoundlanders were quick to pursue the opportunities available primarily to those who wintered in the colony.

In a report on the 1804 season, Governor Erasmus Gower summarized the new industry:

> The fishery commences about the middle of March and continues till the early part of May. The Merchants or owners of the vessels, who are at the whole expense of the outfits, receive one half the proceeds of the voyage, the other half is divided in equal portions among the

Crew, who generally clear from £5 to £25 each man; and though the success of the voyage is precarious, yet the personal interest which the men feel in it stimulates them to encounter the most inclement weather, and expose themselves to the most immanent dangers, and instances last spring occurred of Crews, who were taken off the wrecks of vessels that were crushed between the ice, and brought home, having procured other vessels and made a successful voyage. The owners' profits are generally sufficient to defray the expense of fitting out the same vessel in the Cod Fishery, which commences about the time of her return from sealing.[5]

As the profits from sealing grew, crews began to challenge efforts to exploit them. Sealers went on strike in Carbonear and Harbour Grace in 1832, demanding payment in cash instead of kind. The imposition of high berthing fees for sealing vessels led hundreds of men to march in protest in St John's in 1842 and in Harbour Main and Brigus in 1845. These were the first labour actions in Newfoundland and, not

St John's fleet departing for the seal fishery, c. 1860. As this image indicates, the sealers were obliged to cut channels in the harbour ice so that the vessels could be towed to open water.
Courtesy of Centre for Newfoundland Studies Archives, Queen Elizabeth II Library, Memorial University of Newfoundland

surprisingly, they brought a mixed reaction. The editor of the *Ledger* concluded in 1842 that there was "nothing illegal in a number of people peaceably assembling together to determine for themselves the wages which they may agree to receive for their labour," but "when they proceed to offer threats, and to use personal violence by way of compelling others to accede to their views and to join their number . . . it evidently becomes a conspiracy of a most dangerous character, which it is of the utmost importance instantly to suppress by the strong arm of the law."[6]

The numbers of men engaged in sealing and the significance of the industry to the Newfoundland economy made the "ice hunters" a force to be reckoned with. At its height in the 1850s the sealing industry employed 14 000 men and accounted for nearly a quarter of the colony's exports by value. In the 1860s merchants turned to steamers to increase both yields and profits, a process that centralized the industry in St John's and Conception Bay and reduced the number of men involved in the hunt. The industry declined at the end of the century with the rise of the petroleum industry, the introduction of electricity, and decreasing herds.

market conditions, competition from other saltfish producing countries, and the quality of their fish cure, everyone in Newfoundland depended on the success or failure of the cod fishery.

CLASS AND SOCIETY

By the beginning of the nineteenth century, Newfoundland had developed a unique class structure, constructed around the principal participants in the fishery: merchants, planters, and servants. Merchants were those who engaged in the saltfish trade and gradually expanded their operations to include fish oil, seal skins, and seal oil. Planters dominated the resident fishery, setting up their own stages, flakes, and sheds. Servants worked for merchants and planters, rather than for themselves.

Both planters and servants were dependent on the merchant for their supplies and markets for their catch. While similar dependence between merchants and producers existed in other colonies, Newfoundlanders had few options for making a living other than the fish-

eries. The client-patron relationship, known as the "truck system," therefore became a central feature of Newfoundland society, and one that few could escape.

Most scholars have few good words to say for the truck system and the merchants who are accused of manipulating it and perpetuating it to their advantage. Historian Sean Cadigan takes another perspective, arguing that the rise of the truck system and the household-based fishery was a practical accommodation to the realities of Newfoundland's limited resource base. What is clear, he argues, is that reformers struggling for colonial self-government exaggerated the role of the merchants in impoverishing the fishery and preventing agricultural development to secure political support.[8]

Such an argument was effective because of the way society developed in Newfoundland. Both Irish and English settlers became planters, and there were many Protestants among the propertyless servant class, but the merchants were mostly English and Protestant. As mercantile power concentrated in St John's, the island's commercial, military, and political

VOICES FROM THE PAST

Drowning a Dog, 1846

People in pre-industrial British North America relied on domesticated animals—primarily dogs, oxen, and horses—to help them do their work. In the nineteenth century, critics began commenting on the cruelty with which animals were treated and began forming organizations such as the Society for the Prevention of Cruelty Towards Animals. In 1846, Philip Togue, a native of Carbonear, Conception Bay, published this graphic description of the treatment of animals in his native province:

> No animal in Newfoundland is a greater sufferer from man than the dog. The animal is employed during the winter season in drawing timber from the woods, and he supplies the place of a horse in the performance of several duties. I have frequently seen one of those noble creatures drawing three seals (about one hundred and thirty pounds weight) for a distance of four miles over huge rugged masses of ice, safe to land. In drawing wood the poor animal is frequently burdened beyond

his strength, and compelled to proceed by the most barbarous treatment. Of the cruel conduct of many an unfeeling master I have often been a witness, and I have seen the poor creatures left dead on the side of the road. . . .

> I well remember seeing some boys taking a poor dog to drown him. It is almost general practice in Newfoundland that after the poor animal has faithfully served his master, and is no longer able to draw wood, there is a large stone sufficient to sink him, fastened firmly around his neck, and he is then thrown into the sea to die. The boys were engaged in this most cruel and unfeeling practice when I saw them, but in this instance instead of taking him to sea, where there was deep water, they were endeavouring to drown him in a brook with hardly sufficient water to cover the poor animal. The owner of the dog was looking on, and appeared pleased to see his children practicing such cruelty.[7]

centre, people in the outports were increasingly pitted against the capital. The coincidence of class, culture, religion, and geography laid the foundations for a vigorous political culture.

POLITICAL CONFLICT

By the eighteenth century Newfoundland was developing a well-deserved reputation for skulduggery and violence. It was also the site of spectacular smuggling activities, mostly with vessels from France and New England. Although fishing admirals continued to enforce English laws during the summer months, their handling of cases was often harsh and open to corruption. Governors were notable by their absence, preferring to leave the island when autumn arrived. During the winter, people were left to their own devices and justices of the peace coped as best they could with problems as they arose.

A Supreme Court was finally established in 1791 to deal with both civil and criminal matters. As first Chief Justice, Oxford-educated barrister John Reeves urged British authorities to establish a legislature so that laws could be made to address local conditions. He also produced the *History of the Government of the Island of Newfoundland* (1795), in which he highlighted the role of the West Country merchants in retarding the colony's political development. Although there was much truth to Reeves's analysis, it is also the case that many colonial officials in Newfoundland, as elsewhere in British North America, liked the system as it was. So, too, did some members of the Protestant merchant community, who feared what an elected assembly might do, especially if Roman Catholics were given the right to vote, as they had been in the Maritimes and the Canadas.

During the Napoleonic Wars, any complacency about the lack of representative government was swept away. The colony's first newspaper, the *Royal Gazette and Newfoundland Advertiser*, was established in 1807 by John Ryan, a Loyalist who arrived in St John's from New Brunswick. Other newspapers followed in its wake. As the population increased, especially in St John's, uncertainty about land tenure created havoc. The land issue and other problems—notably the lack of schools and legal provisions for the poor—became the substance of a petition to the Prince Regent in 1811.

One of the authors of this document was Dr William Carson, a recent immigrant from Scotland. His devotion to liberalism was surpassed only by his determination to make Newfoundland rise to what he saw as its unlimited potential. Quick of wit and pen, he played a major role in convincing Newfoundlanders that representative government, security of land tenure, and the full range of English civil rights were long overdue.

A lingering post-war depression, compounded by several years of poor fish catches and a disastrous fire in St John's in 1816, resulted in many bankruptcies and much human misery. With immigrants arriving in larger numbers than ever, most of them from Ireland, social tensions intensified. Sporadic looting of merchant property and hungry mobs demanding provisions in communities such as St John's, Carbonear, and Harbour Grace made officials uneasy. Although the British Parliament granted relief, it refused to consider political concessions.

In 1820 two separate court cases brought matters to a head. Indebted Irish fishers James Landrigan and Philip Butler were each convicted of contempt of court in refusing to respond to the magistrates' summons to appear in court and surrender their property. After some difficulty—in response to a constable's demands, Landrigan's wife Sarah threatened "to blow his brains out"—their property was seized and both men were sentenced to receive 36 lashes with a cat-o'-nine-tails. Many people were outraged by what they saw as an unjustified overreaction on the part of officialdom. Backed by the reformers, Landrigan and Butler sued the magistrates for assault and false imprisonment. They were unsuccessful, but the scandal served as a catalyst for change.

The reform movement in the colony was led by Dr Carson and by Irish-born merchant Patrick Morris, and promoted by two reform newspapers, the *Newfoundland Sentinel* and the *Public Ledger*. While an elected legislature was not immediately forthcoming, other reforms were implemented. In 1824–25, circuit courts were instituted and Newfoundland was declared a Crown colony. Sir Thomas Cochrane became the first civil governor in 1825. Cochrane ruled with an appointed council and lived in grand style, building an elegant Government House in St John's that still houses Newfoundland's lieutenant-governor. He also

MORE TO THE STORY

Mummering

In Newfoundland, Old World cultural practices were sometimes adapted to new purposes. Such is the case with mummering, an Irish custom that was transported to Newfoundland. During the period between Christmas and Twelfth Night, people donned masks and bizarre clothing, disguised their voices, and paraded throughout the community, performing strange antics in the homes of their neighbours. A typical folk ritual to shake off the restraints of everyday identity and obligations, it sometimes became an occasion for expressing hostile class and cultural feelings among the "lower orders." This was especially the case in mid-nineteenth-century St John's, where social tensions ran higher than in most outport communities. In 1861, it was made illegal to appear as a mummer, masked or otherwise disguised, in the public streets, but the custom of "visits" by mummers still prevails in many areas of Newfoundland.

Mummers, as depicted in *The Evening of the Twelfth Day Fifty Years Ago—Prescott Stret* [sic], painted at the end of the nineteenth century by J.W. Hayward.
Courtesy of Harold Hayward, great-grandson. Photo courtesy of the Art Gallery of Newfoundland and Labrador (MUN Photographic Services)

set about building roads to connect St John's to nearby districts and providing relief to the destitute.

Inevitably, the cost of Cochrane's administration greatly outstripped the income from leases of public land and customs revenue. This situation prompted colonial officials to seek ways of convincing Newfoundlanders to tax themselves for colonial "improvements." Meanwhile both civil and religious leaders in the colony—most notably Bishop Fleming, who presided over a growing Roman Catholic flock—continued to push for representative government.

When Great Britain itself began to broaden its electoral base though Catholic Emancipation in 1829 and the Reform Bill of 1832, it became even more difficult to deny similar rights to colonies settled by British populations. Newfoundland was granted representative government in 1832 with a broad male franchise. Every man who owned or occupied a house for at least one year was eligible to vote and after two years could run for elected office. As in most of British North America, political parties in Newfoundland took the names of their British counterparts. The Reformers or Liberals drew support primarily from Irish Roman Catholic voters, while the Conservatives represented English Protestant interests.

During the early years of representative government, the Reformers dominated the elected assembly, which inevitably came in conflict with the appointed council dominated by Conservatives. The Colonial Office tried to mute divisions in 1842 by creating an amalgamated legislature, in which a portion of the members were appointed rather than elected. But the time for treating Newfoundland as an exception among the British North American colonies was fast disappearing. Full representative government was restored in 1848. Once it was clear that responsible government did not lead to chaos in the Maritimes and the Canadas, it was granted in Newfoundland as well in 1855.

The first administration under responsible government was headed by the Liberals under Philip Little. A Prince Edward Islander who had moved to Newfoundland in 1844 to practise law, Little included two Protestants in his cabinet but there was no denying the influence of the Roman Catholic Church in the new administration. The Roman Catholic bishop, John Mullock, intervened directly in political matters and priests often managed elections in the outports. Although the Liberals won the 1859 election, the lieutenant-governor, Sir Alexander Bannerman, dismissed the administration, now under John Kent, claiming corruption in the dispensing of relief monies. The ensuing 1861 election was bitterly fought, especially in the Conception Bay area. In St John's, rival factions came to blows and troops fired on the crowd, killing three people and wounding twenty more.

This tragedy finally brought compromise. Mullock and other religious leaders in the colony voluntarily withdrew from political activity, and the Conservatives who won the election, carrying all Protestant constituencies, offered cabinet positions to a number of Roman Catholic politicians. Premier Hugh Hoyles tried to move beyond religious divisions by pursing policies that would lead to economic and social development in the colony and by dispensing patronage with an even hand. Thus, within a decade of the granting of responsible government, Newfoundland began to escape the sectarian violence that might have made it another Ulster.

The Town and Harbour of St John's from Signal Hill, 1831, by William Edgar. By the time this image was painted, St John's had emerged as a great commercial entrepôt, a major naval base, and the political capital of the colony. It was also the refuge of discharged servants, known as "dieters," who wrought havoc in the community when the fisheries failed and unemployment escalated.
Pyall, Henry/Library and Archives Canada/C-041605

LABRADOR

People in Labrador would wait another century before voting in a democratic election. Although attached to Newfoundland, its resident European population was small and widely scattered. Moreover, English men—fur traders and fishers who made up the majority of immigrants—were as likely to conform to the practices of the Innu and Inuit as they were to force Western values upon peoples who outnumbered them.

At the beginning of the nineteenth century, the most significant European presence in the region consisted of the Moravian missionaries based at Nain (1771), Okak (1776), and Hopedale (1782). Their primary goal was to Christianize the Inuit. To achieve it, they combined their mission work with trade in the hope that the Inuit would abandon their longtime custom of travelling each summer to the Strait of Belle Isle to trade with, and steal from, the fishers.

Despite the many difficulties they encountered, including the hostility of Native religious leaders, or *angekut*, the Moravians prevailed. The close connec-tion that the missionaries established between spiritual conversion and trade no doubt was a critical factor, but the Christian message also had its appeal. In 1804–05 a religious revival yielded a number of converts, most of them women, who responded to the power and independence that the new religion seemed to offer them. Mission schools, which both boys and girls attended, taught Native languages. When famine and disease struck, the missionaries offered relief and med-ical treatment.

The mission communities gradually expanded to include a large population of Christian Inuit. Encouraged by their initial successes and competition from external forces, the Moravians established a base at Hebron in 1830. The Moravian economic ascen-dancy in northern Labrador was challenged by the Hudson's Bay Company, which built trading posts at Rigolet, North West River, and Cartwright in the 1830s. By mid-century the Moravians also had compe-tition for Inuit souls with the arrival of Methodist and Roman Catholic missionaries, who made seasonal appearances on the south coast to serve an immigrant

Nain, 1884. Established in 1771, Nain was the first Moravian mission in Labrador.
R. Bell/Library and Archives Canada/C-089544

population. The Moravian mission at Zoar, founded in the mid-1860s, served both Inuit and immigrants, and increasingly a mixed-blood population.

As in Newfoundland, a growing number of fishers and traders made Labrador their base of operations. By the 1860s there was an English "settler" population of about 1600 living along the coast from Blanc Sablon, through the Strait of Belle Isle, and "down" the shore to Sandwich Bay. During the summer they were supplemented by 30 000 "floaters" and "stationers," engaged in the fisheries. The Innu of Labrador, who had only seasonal contact with Europeans after the fur trade frontier moved up the St Lawrence in the seventeenth century, began to enter into a closer relationship with the settlers.

In 1863, the Colonial Office recommended a representative for Labrador in the Newfoundland Assembly, but Premier Hugh Hoyles rejected the idea. The reason for his reluctance is not clear, though the prospect of conducting elections in the far-flung Labrador territory may well have been a daunting one. He did, however, establish a court and a customs collector for the region. Since there was no organized movement in Labrador for representation in St John's, it remained, as did the communities on the French Treaty Shore, outside of the formal political framework.

The Labrador Middle Ground

The presence of Europeans and their manufactured goods gradually transformed the lives of Inuit and Innu. Like other areas of North America, Labrador was increasingly becoming a middle ground where European and Aboriginal cultures coexisted and intertwined. Christianity blended with Native religious beliefs. Intermarriage among Aboriginal women and European fur traders and fishers became common practice. By the mid-nineteenth century the Innu and Inuit were increasingly found living around mission stations and trading posts during the winter months. Time-honoured seasonal rhythms of hunting and fishing continued, but they were altered to accommodate the European commercial cycle.

Lydia Campbell, born Lydia Brooks in Hamilton Inlet in 1819, represents the transitional generation, half Inuit and half European, in her lineage, beliefs, and practices. Still tending her rabbit traps at the age

of 75 in 1894, Campbell reported that her sister Hannah, then 80 years old, was even more ambitious: "She hunts fresh meat, and chops holes in 3 foot ice this very winter and catches trout with her hook, enough for her household." Despite the survival of such skills, Campbell knew that she had witnessed a critical turning point in the history of the Labrador Inuit. "How tall and pretty that first race of Eskimo was, and so lively," she reminisced about her childhood. "In that time the Eskimos was very plentiful all along the shore and islands but now there is only 6 or 7 families."

She concluded that they had been reduced by "the cursed drink and tobacco smoking," a view shaped by her Methodist faith and its injunctions against drinking and smoking. Disease had also taken its toll, spreading quickly through mission settlements. In 1827 measles cut a swath through the Inuit of Nain and Hopedale, leaving the survivors dependent on the missionaries for food. A more sedentary lifestyle and the depletion of resources led to periodic famines. Lydia Campbell remembered a time when "everything was plentiful," including white whales, walruses, and white bears. "People could stand on the rocks and hook fish ashore on the beach and spear the salmon that was swimming along the shore," she recalled. Her father, an Englishman, told her that when he arrived in Labrador early in the nineteenth century, "they would have to wait until the tide would turn for to clear the fish and caplin away before they could row through them."[9] Such abundance was squandered during Campbell's lifetime as Native and newcomer competed for success in the commercial economy.

THE FATE OF THE BEOTHUK

While the Innu and Inuit of Labrador survived the impact of European immigration, the Beothuk on the island of Newfoundland did not. After more than three centuries of continuous European contact, they became extinct. Their story is a particularly tragic one.

Prior to contact with Europeans, the Beothuk relied heavily on river and ocean resources for survival. They frequented the coasts during the summer months, seeking fish, as well as seabirds and their eggs, to provide variety in their diets. No doubt it was during their summer sojourns that they met Europeans.

In the sixteenth century, the Beothuk traded with French and Basque fishers. John Guy recorded meeting Beothuk in Trinity Bay in 1612, who greeted him enthusiastically and waved skins hoisted on poles. Such friendly relations did not last. Because the Beothuk pilfered metal items, sails, and other manufactured goods left behind by fishing crews, they had little need for direct trade with Europeans.

Like the fisheries, the fur trade that developed in Newfoundland was conducted by Europeans, not Native peoples. These industries therefore pitted the two cultures against each other rather than encouraging alliances. Nor did the Beothuk develop alliances with other Aboriginal peoples. Hostile relations with Innu and Inuit around the Strait of Belle Isle were typical also of interaction with the Mi'kmaq who by the second half of the eighteenth century were competing with the Beothuk for Newfoundland's resources. Unlike Labrador, Newfoundland had no missionary endeavour to help moderate the negative impact of European and intertribal competition.

Hounded from their favourite coastal locations by the fishers, who saw them as dangerous thieves, the Beothuk retreated to the interior, where their living conditions deteriorated. Diseases, carried by the goods they scavenged and occasional contact with Europeans, easily ravaged a people whose diets no longer sustained good health. By the second half of the eighteenth century, humanitarians were beginning to raise questions about the condition of the Beothuk. Stories of piteous deaths from hunger and disease as well as outright murder by fur traders and fishers gradually drew the attention of authorities.

Governor Palliser tried, without success, to make friendly contact with the Beothuk. In 1768 Lieutenant John Cartwright led an expedition up the Exploits River, where Beothuk were known to live, but found only abandoned camps. Subsequent efforts to capture a Beothuk who might serve as a go-between to establish friendly relations proved both dangerous and futile. In 1810–11, David Buchan led an expedition to Red Indian Lake, where he managed to surprise a small camp of Beothuk. Two men who stayed behind while Buchan went downriver to fetch presents were found decapitated when he returned. Although the governor ordered no reprisals, the Beothuk continued to resist contact. They also continued to raid settle-

ments for the metal goods they needed for their spears, harpoon blades, and arrowheads.

In 1818 John Peyton Jr lost 150 pounds' worth of gear when the Beothuk conducted a successful raid on his salmon boat and cargo at Lower Sandy Point on the Bay of Exploits. Shanawdithit, who had been a member of the raiding party, later told Peyton that for several days they had watched all his movements from a tree on a ridge behind his house. When Peyton last inspected his wharf, the Beothuk were already hidden in their canoe beneath it, keeping perfectly motionless so that he would not notice their presence.

Peyton led an expedition to regain his property and, he claimed, to establish regular trading relations with the Beothuk. Although his motives are difficult to determine and the evidence elusive, it seems that he also wanted to take a Beothuk prisoner as a means of opening communication with others. He succeeded in capturing a Beothuk woman named Demasduit in

This watercolour of Demasduit, known as Mary March by her captors, was painted in 1819 by Lady Henrietta Hamilton, the wife of the governor of Newfoundland. It is the only known life portrait of a Beothuk.
Library and Archives Canada/C28544

BIOGRAPHY

Shanawdithit

Little is known about Shanawdithit's short life. Born around 1801, she was apparently the niece of Demasduit's husband, Nonosbawsut. By her own account, she was present at the meeting with David Buchan's expedition in 1811 and among those who absconded with John Peyton's boat in 1818. She witnessed the capture of Demasduit at Red Indian Lake in 1819 and the murder of her uncle and his daughter by fur traders James Carey and Stephen Adams late in 1822. Shanawdithit herself escaped capture until 1823, when she, along with her mother and sister, found in a starving condition, were captured at Badger Bay.

The women were brought to Peyton at Exploits Island, and Peyton took them to St John's. There they attracted much attention. The Reverend William Wilson recorded his impressions: "The ladies had dressed them in English garb," he observed, "but over their dresses they all had on their, to them indispensable, deer-skin shawl." The youngest, Shanawdithit, renamed Nancy or Nancy April by her captors, was fascinated by her new surroundings. She decorated her forehead and arms with tinsel and coloured paper, chased onlookers, and was curious about the townfolk's material possessions. When she was given pencil and paper, Wilson reported, "she was in raptures. She made a few marks on the paper, apparently to try the pencil, then in one flourish she drew a deer perfectly."[10]

Following a brief sojourn in the interior and the death of her mother and sister in 1823, Shanawdithit was taken into the Peyton household, where she spent the next five years. There she worked as a servant for her keep and developed a close relationship with Peyton's three young children but reportedly refused to be pushed around. Occasionally, she would go into the woods, where she claimed to have talked to her mother and sister. While she tolerated her captors, she was afraid of

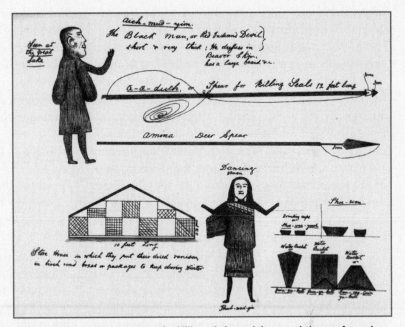

Shanawdithit's pictures of spears for killing whales and deer, smokehouses for curing meat, storehouses for winter supplies, a dancing woman, and a devil clad in beaver skin reflect the cultural practices and beliefs of her people.
Library and Archives Canada/C87698

the Mi'kmaq, who increasingly dominated the interior of the island, reporting that one, "bad Noel boss," had shot her while she was washing venison, wounding her in the back and legs.

In the last year of her life, Shanawdithit was taken to St John's, where she lived with William Eppes Cormack, president of the recently established Beothuk Institution. This organization was too late to save the Beothuk from extinction, but it was largely because of Cormack's efforts that Shanawdithit's knowledge of her people was preserved. She helped Cormack develop a Beothuk vocabulary and drew sketches depicting the culture of her people as she knew it. Even in death, she continued to satisfy the curiosity of the people who had inadvertently brought the Beothuk to such a sad end. Before her body was interred in a St John's military cemetery in 1829, her skull and scalp were removed by Dr Carson, who performed the autopsy, to be sent to the Royal Society of Physicians in London.

March 1819, but only after a bloody confrontation in which her husband, Nonosbawsut, was killed and her recently born baby left behind to die. Known as Mary March by her captors, Demasduit herself soon died of tuberculosis. Her body was returned to the deserted encampment of her people in February 1820.

In 1823, three Beothuk women, a mother and her two daughters, were seized by fur traders and brought to St John's. Here, too, the husband and father died in the encounter, falling through the ice in a desperate attempt to rescue his family. After spending a few months in St John's, where they attracted much attention, the women were returned to the interior. Unable to survive there, they soon reappeared on the coast, where the mother and one of her daughters died. The surviving daughter, Shanawdithit, died six years later, in 1829. As far as we know, she was the last Beothuk on the island of Newfoundland.

Ralph Pastore and George M. Story note that the tragic story of the Beothuk often suffers from wild exaggerations. According to them, the Beothuk were never "hunted for sport and massacred in large numbers." They died "because they were few in number to begin with, because they had no resistance to European diseases, and because Newfoundland was a fishing colony, which almost by definition, lacked enough of the sort of white men who wanted or needed to keep Indians alive."[11] Ingeborg Marshall is less forgiving, noting "prejudice, a total disregard for the rights and needs of the native population, and ruthlessness and brutality on the side of the English" as factors in the demise of the Beothuk. Nevertheless, she also argues that the Beothuk were not totally helpless victims of circumstances, their "withdrawal and their commitment to revenge" indicating that they made their own choices. Marshall concludes that the Beothuk were "a heroic people who valued their independence and traditions above all and were prepared to face hostilities and possible annihilation rather than be subjugated. They therefore rank alongside those North American native groups who are renowned for their courage in the defence of their territory and cultural integrity."[12]

CONCLUSION

Between 1815 and 1855 Newfoundland became a colony like others in British North America, with an elected assembly and an executive responsible to it. In other respects Newfoundland differed considerably from the Maritimes and Canada. Its dependence on the cod fishery and sealing made it highly vulnerable to international market conditions and created a social organization characterized by the dependence of fishing families on merchant credit. Nevertheless, while the fish and seals lasted, there were fortunes to be made and Newfoundland emerged as a significant player in the global commercial economy. In this period, Labrador remained the preserve of the Innu and Inuit and the merchants and missionaries upon whom they increasingly depended. Meanwhile the Beothuk, who were unable to reach accommodation with European immigrants, became extinct, a testimony to the extreme consequences of colonization.

NOTES

1 "A Plea for Reform: the Case of James Landergan (1818)," cited in *By Great Waters: A Newfoundland and Labrador Anthology*, ed. Peter Neary and Patrick O'Flaherty (Toronto: University of Toronto Press, 1974), 69.

2 Patrick O'Flaherty, *Old Newfoundland: A History to 1843* (St John's: Long Beach Press, 1999), 63.

3 Jerry Bannister, *The Rule of the Admirals: Laws, Custom, and Naval Government in Newfoundland, 1699–1832* (Toronto: University of Toronto Press, 2003), 6.

4 Marilyn Porter, "'She was Skipper of the Shore-Crew': Notes on the Sexual Division of Labour in Newfoundland," *Labour/Le Travail* 15 (1985): 105–23.

5 Cited in Shannon Ryan, *The Ice Hunters: A History of Newfoundland Sealing to 1914* (St John's: Breakwater Press, 1994), 58.

6 Ryan, 330–31.

7 Peter Toque, *Wandering Thoughts and Solitary Hours* (London, 1846), cited in *By Great Waters: A Newfoundland and Labrador Anthology*, ed. Peter Neary and Patrick O'Flaherty (Toronto: University of Toronto Press, 1974), 93.

8 Sean T. Cadigan, *Hope and Deception in Conception Bay: Merchant–Settler Relations in Newfoundland, 1785–1855* (Toronto: University of Toronto Press, 1995).

9 Lydia Campbell, *Sketches of Labrador Life* (Happy Valley: The Days, 1984), n.p.

10 L.S.F. Upton, "The Extermination of the Beothuk of Newfoundland," *Canadian Historical Review* 58, 2 (1977): 133–53.

11 Ralph T. Pastore and G.M. Story, "Shawnadithit," *Dictionary of Canadian Biography*, vol. 6, *1821–1835* (Toronto: University of Toronto Press, 1987), 708.

12 Ingeborg Marshall, *A History and Ethnography of the Beothuk* (Montreal and Kingston: McGill-Queen's University Press, 1996), 445.

Related Readings in This Series

From *Foundations: Readings in Pre-Confederation Canadian History*

Jerry Bannister, "The Campaign for Representative Government in Newfoundland," 313–36.
Ralph Pastore, "The Collapse of the Beothuk World," 337–48.

From **Media Companion CD-ROM, Volume I**

The Women of Labrador
Indentured Servants
Extracts from the Report of the Committee Appointed to Inquire into the State of Trade to Newfoundland, 1793
Extract of a Letter from St John's, 1811

Selected Reading

The history of Newfoundland and Labrador is covered in general Atlantic regional studies mentioned in the previous chapter. Surveys of Newfoundland and Labrador history include Frederick W. Rowe, *History of Newfoundland and Labrador* (Toronto: McGraw-Hill Ryerson, 1980), and Peter Neary and Patrick O'Flaherty, *Part of the Main: An Illustrated History of Newfoundland and Labrador* (St John's: Breakwater Books, 1983). The early history of the colony is analyzed in Jerry Bannister, *The Rule of the Admirals: Laws, Custom, and Naval Government in Newfoundland, 1699–1832* (Toronto: University of Toronto Press, 2003); Patrick O'Flaherty, *Old Newfoundland: A History to 1843* (St John's: Long Beach Press, 1999); Sean Cadigan, *Hope and Deception in Conception Bay: Merchant-Settler Relations in Newfoundland, 1785–1855* (Toronto: University of Toronto Press, 1985); and Keith Matthews, *Lectures on the History of Newfoundland, 1500–1830* (St John's: Breakwater Books, 1988). See also relevant essays in James Hiller and Peter Neary, eds., *Newfoundland in the Nineteenth and Twentieth Centuries: Essays in Interpretation* (Toronto: University of Toronto Press, 1980), and Rosemary E. Ommer, ed., *Merchant Credit & Labour Strategies in Historical Perspective* (Fredericton: Acadiensis Press, 1990). Primary documents are published in Peter Neary and Patrick O'Flaherty, eds., *By Great Waters: A Newfoundland and Labrador Anthology* (Toronto: University of Toronto Press, 1974), and R.G. Moyles, *"Complaints is Many and Various But the Odd Divil Likes It"* (Toronto: Peter Martin Associates, 1975). See also Patrick O'Flaherty, *The Rock Observed: Studies in the Literature of Newfoundland* (Toronto: University of Toronto Press, 1979).

Specific studies on immigration and settlement in Newfoundland include W. Gordon Handcock, *"Soe longe as there comes noe women": Origins of English Settlement in Newfoundland* (1989; reprint, Milton, ON: Global Heritage Press, 2000), and John J. Mannion, ed., *The Peopling of Newfoundland: Essays in Historical Geography* (St John's: Institute for Social and Economic Research, 1977). For the history of St John's, see Patrick O'Neill, *The Story of St. John's, Newfoundland* (Erin, ON: Boston Mills Press, 1975). On the saltfish trade and sealing in this period see two books by Shannon Ryan, *Fish out of Water: The Newfoundland Saltfish Trade, 1814–1914* (St John's: Breakwater, 1986) and *The Ice Hunters: A History of Newfoundland Sealing to 1914* (St. John's: Breakwater, 1984). The cod itself is the focus of a delightful study by Mark Kurlansky, *Cod: A Biography of the Fish that Changed the World* (New York: Alfred A Knopf, 1997). The folk custom of mummering is explored in Herbert Halpert and G.M. Storey, eds., *Christmas Mummering in Newfoundland* (Toronto: University of Toronto Press, 1969). A splendid resource that explores Newfoundland culture through the province's colourful language is G.M. Story et al., *Dictionary of Newfoundland English* (Toronto: University of Toronto Press, 1982).

Newfoundland politics in the mid-nineteenth century is the subject of Gertrude Gunn, *The Political History of Newfoundland, 1832–1864* (Toronto: University of Toronto Press, 1966). For the Beothuk, see Ingeborg Marshall, *The History and Ethnography of the Beothuk* (Montreal and Kingston: McGill-Queen's University Press, 1996), and Ralph Pastore, *Shanawdithit's People* (St John's: Atlantic

Archaeology, 1992) and "The Collapse of the Beothuk World," *Acadiensis* 19, 1 (Autumn 1989): 52–71. The Aboriginal peoples of Labrador are discussed in Robert McGhee, *The Native Peoples of Atlantic Canada* (Toronto: McClelland and Stewart, 1974) and *Ancient Peoples of the Arctic* (Vancouver: University of British Columbia Press, 1996); Helge Kleivan, *The Eskimos of Northeast Labrador: A History of Eskimo-White Relations, 1771–1955* (Oslo: Norsk Polarinstitutt, 1966), and José Mailhot, *The People of Sheshatshit: In the Land of the Innu* (St John's: Institute for Social and Economic Research, 1997).

Women are the focus of Linda Kealey, ed., *Pursuing Equality: Historical Perspectives on Women in Newfoundland and Labrador* (St John's: Institute for Social and Economic Research, 1993), and Marilyn Porter, *Place and Persistence in the Lives of Newfoundland Women* (Aldershot: Avebury, 1993).

WEBLINKS

MARITIME HISTORY

www.mun.ca/mha/index.php

The Maritime History Archive at Memorial University, Newfoundland, lists its holdings on this page. Included are parish records, photographs, maps, and mercantile records.

RELIGION, SOCIETY, AND CULTURE IN NEWFOUNDLAND AND LABRADOR

www.ucs.mun.ca/~hrollman/

Visit this site for information and links.

SALT FISHERIES

collections.ic.gc.ca/fisheries/main.asp?frame=on

This is the Newfoundland Salt Fisheries digital exhibit. A wealth of information in both image and text form is available, with numerous related links.

NEWFOUNDLAND AND LABRADOR HERITAGE

www.heritage.nf.ca

This excellent resource contains a vast amount of information about the heritage of Newfoundland and Labrador, broadly grouped under the headings Natural Environment, Aboriginal Peoples, Society, Economy and Culture, Exploration and Settlement, Politics and Government, and Arts.

CHAPTER 15

The Canadas: Economy and Society, 1815–1850s

Timeline

▶ 1816	First provision of government subsidies for community schools in Upper Canada
▶ 1817	Montreal women form Female Benevolent Society
▶ 1829	African Americans found community of Wilberforce in Upper Canada
▶ 1830	Ogle Gowan establishes Grand Orange Lodge of British North America
▶ 1832	Cholera epidemic
▶ 1834	Another outbreak of cholera; incorporation of city of Toronto
▶ 1842	Formation of Montreal Board of Trade
▶ 1847	Masters and Servants Act in Upper Canada

"[T]he wool thus obtained was washed, picked, carded and spun by the good wives on their little wheels, which had been brought out from their old homes. This wool was then woven into durable homespun by some of the emigrants who were weavers from Scotland and had their looms with them. The men wore gray homespun for rough working suits—with brown for gala days—while the women and girls had gray flannel proms and skirts, with ones of checked woolen goods woven into tasteful patterns for better occasions. The dyeing materials used were mostly of nature's providing ... The men wore linen shirts of home spinning, sometimes checked blue and white ones for working. All the better suits were made by a tailor who went from house to house to ply his trade ... A shoemaker always came once a year to every home, going from house to house carrying his tools and implements."[1]

This description of life in Perth, Upper Canada, by a pioneer invokes an image of life in the Canadas in the early nineteenth century as characterized by nearly self-sufficient farm households that produced enough to support a small artisan class as well. Certainly, for many Upper and Lower Canadians, that was the ideal. While some attained it and might write to their relatives that "here we are laird ourselves," the Church of Scotland magazine noted in 1838 that there were "thousands upon thousands in this vast uncultivated territory, struggling with the hardships and penury of new settlements, and with whom years of constant toil must pass away, ere they can hope to attain any thing beyond the merest necessities of life."[2]

Contrasts abounded in the British North American colonies. In Lower Canada's seigneurial belt most farmers were tenants, many of them living a marginal existence. Even Upper Canada, touted as a land of opportunity in the early nineteenth century, was bedeviled by unequal access to land and government favour. Discontent reached such a pitch that rebellions broke out in both Upper and Lower Canada in 1837–38. The uprisings prompted British authorities to pass the Act of Union in 1840, creating an uneasy political entity: the United Canadas. Forced to cope with two increasingly different societies called Canada East and Canada West, the government of the colony—both before and after responsible government was granted in 1848—never worked well. In this chapter we will look at the economic and social conditions that served as a context for rebellion and responsible government, which will be discussed in the following chapter.

POSTWAR MIGRATION

Like the Atlantic colonies, the Canadas following the War of 1812 were no longer the preferred destination of immigrants from the United States. An exception to this generalization was African Americans. Upper Canada, where Simcoe had introduced an act in 1793 to gradually eliminate slavery, became home to free blacks and refugee slaves who crossed the border to settle near Windsor and Niagara Falls. Most black immigrants settled in white communities, but there were also attempts to organize group settlements. For example, in 1829, near London, Ontario, African-American immigrants founded the community of Wilberforce, named after a prominent British abolitionist. By the 1860s there were an estimated 23 000 blacks living in Canada West.

Upper Canada was the destination of many of the nearly one million people who emigrated from Great Britain to British North America between 1815 and 1850. By 1842, one-third of the people in the colony had been born in the British Isles. Of these, one-half came from Ireland, one-quarter from Scotland, and one-quarter from England and Wales. Only about 50 000 immigrants from Britain settled in Lower Canada from 1815 to 1850, and the high francophone birth rate in that province prevented the new arrivals

from significantly reducing the French-speaking proportion of the population.

The Canadas attracted people in Great Britain who had been marginalized by a changing economy. Most of the people who migrated to Upper and Lower Canada were small landowners or tenants, not paupers. Recent research has also established that, contrary to earlier beliefs, the migrants did not come to the Canadas as individuals, abandoning relatives and friends in a search for a better life. Rather, many of them emigrated as extended family and community groups and were often joined by kin from home. Only the filling up of the good farmland in the Canadas by the mid-1850s caused the migratory chain to break.

A few immigrants benefited from the monetary assistance Britain provided sporadically to emigrants willing to go to the colonies. When the British government offered assisted passage to a group of Scots wishing to settle in Glengarry County, Upper Canada, in 1815, four Highland parishes provided about half of the total group of 800 émigrés. Most of the other passengers were from the Glasgow area, where people were most likely to see advertisements for assisted emigration. Some 80 percent of the Highland Glengarry group were farmers; only 20 percent were labourers. The weak representation of the landless is not surprising: settlers were required to repay some of the costs of their transport, and a mandatory deposit was enough to weed out the very poor.

A few of Great Britain's poor managed to scrape together the cost of an uncomfortable passage in the steerage of a transatlantic vessel. Because they lacked capital, connections, and sometimes the skills necessary to prosper in their new home, their lot was often a difficult one. Irish Catholics figured largely in this group. Some of the Irish poor eventually managed to escape poverty in the countryside of Upper Canada. In Montague Township, Lanark County, Irish newcomers in the 1840s were mainly squatters. In 1852, fully 30 percent of them still lived in shanties. By 1861, however, as a result of families and neighbours working closely together, only 1 percent lived in shanties, and a majority owned the land they occupied.

In the cities and the lumber camps, poverty was more commonplace. While the authorities and British upper-class writers who commented on the Canadas believed that any industrious "head of family" would

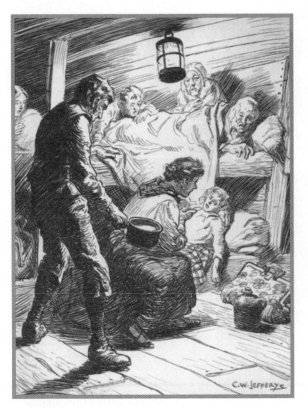

Immigrants aboard ship in the 1820s.
Charles William Jefferys/Library and Archives Canada/C73435

quickly be able to buy land, many could never do so. They were forced to eke out a living in a town or city. As in the countryside, a disproportionate number of the urban and industrial poor were Irish Catholics who—even though they were not of the poorest class at home—often arrived penniless after they had paid the costs of passage to Canada. In Leeds Township, successful Irish-Catholic farmers disdained the poor Irish-Catholic workers in Gananoque and maintained their own church rather than associate with their poor compatriots in the parish church in town.

The emigration experience was often tragic. In 1832, a large group of military pensioners were persuaded to exchange their pensions for a lump sum of money and land in the Canadian bush. Anna Brownell Jameson, an upper-class British woman whose husband was Upper Canada's attorney general, was shocked in 1836 to find a hamlet at Penetanguishene peopled with old, sick veterans, many unable to farm. Since the area had no roads, those who could farm had difficulty taking their produce to market. Jameson was

appalled that "men who fought our battles in Egypt, Spain, and France" were living in shacks, often reduced to begging in order to survive.[3]

IMMIGRANT RECEPTION

The arrival of immigrants created social tensions. The newcomers were rivals for land and jobs, and often brought cultural values that offended the local residents. In the Ottawa Valley, Irish labourers were notorious for using violence to force employers to hire them, although the Canadiens were generally regarded as more skilful and industrious. In the late 1830s and early 1840s, wealthy timber merchant Peter Aylen, seeking personal control of the valley, led the Irish in open warfare against the French-speaking lumbermen. The so-called Shiners' War continued until Aylen unleashed his troops on the respectable middle-class Protestant citizens of Bytown (now Ottawa), who then used state authority to stop the armed Irish-French confrontations.

Quebec City was the most common port of entry for immigrants to the Canadas, and therefore Lower Canadians were most vulnerable to the diseases that the immigrants brought with them. A cholera epidemic swept through Britain in 1831 and arrived in British North America with infected immigrants the following year. The cramped, unsanitary conditions on the ships spread cholera among the passengers. On shore, poor water systems and urban filth resulted in rapid contamination of a terrified population. In 1832, health officials reported 5820 cholera deaths in Lower Canada, most of them immigrants leaving ships and Canadiens in Quebec and Montreal. By contrast, only about 504 people succumbed to the disease in Upper Canada. Two years later, another outbreak claimed 2358 victims in Lower Canada, compared with 555 in Upper Canada and 320 in Nova Scotia.

After the 1832 epidemic, new arrivals were immediately taken to an improvised quarantine station downriver from Quebec City at Grosse Île. Only those not infected with the deadly disease were allowed to go on to their destinations. Despite this precaution, there were far too many arrivals at the port of Quebec for the quarantine to prove effective: from 1833 to 1837, an average of over 20 000 immigrants landed at Quebec each year. The spread of cholera caused city

The Cholera Epidemic, 1832, by Joseph Légaré.
© National Gallery of Canada

residents in particular to despise new arrivals. Communities in both Lower Canada and Upper Canada often blocked off their roads to keep out possibly infected immigrants.

While disease and economic rivalries fuelled tension between immigrants and the settled population, old-country hatreds afflicted the immigrants themselves. This was particularly the case among the Irish. Ogle R. Gowan, an Irish Protestant immigrant to Brockville, Upper Canada, in 1829, was a major figure in transplanting Irish religious feuds to British North American soil. A younger son of the gentry, he had not inherited land and had earned his living in Dublin as a writer of anti-Catholic tracts. In 1830, Gowan established the Grand Orange Lodge of British North America, with himself as head.

The Orangemen in Ireland were devoted to maintaining Protestant ascendancy over Roman Catholics. Although the Canadian Orange Order would eventually serve its members as a social club and even an insurance company, its anti-Catholic roots permeated its being. By 1833, there were ninety-one lodges in Upper Canada and eight in Lower Canada, with a combined membership of 10 000. The order claimed 100 000 members in British North America by 1860. Orange employers and union members associated with their own group and favoured Protestants over Catholics for jobs and for political and community offices. Clashes between the Orange and the Green on days of importance to the two Irish religious groups were frequent throughout the second half of the nineteenth century.

NATIVE PEOPLES IN THE CANADAS

Immigration had a direct impact on Native peoples, who found themselves deprived of their land base and the game upon which many of them depended for their livelihood. As long as Native peoples in areas close to the American border were valued as military allies, the government placed some restriction on white settlement. After the War of 1812, British authorities hoped to resolve future disputes with the United States through diplomacy rather than war and had less need to cultivate the Natives as military allies. Groups such as the Ojibwa of southern Ontario were seen as a nuisance who stood in the way of the agricultural development of a British colony.

To protect Aboriginal peoples from the greed of land-hungry settlers, the government established reserves. Humanitarians in Britain and the Canadas believed that assimilation of First Nations into a Christian culture with agricultural and commercial values was the best hope for their survival. On reserves, Natives could live under the tutelage of missionaries and learn to become good farmers and good Christians. Some Native peoples responded to the new situation by moving north and west to continue their lives as self-sufficient hunters or to participate in the fur trade. Others accepted that their old ways were passing and tried to accommodate the new order by moving onto the reserves and establishing farms. They often embraced Christianity because their ancient religion had been tied so closely to their lived experience while the Christian religion seemed to suit the European lifestyle to which many now aspired.

Famine in Ireland

The Irish were the largest single ethnic group to immigrate to British North America in the first half of the nineteenth century. Presbyterian Irish, the majority in the northern area of Ireland known as Ulster, were among the first to leave in large numbers after the French Revolutionary and Napoleonic Wars. Anglican small farmers and Roman Catholic tenants soon joined the exodus. Until the early nineteenth century, Roman Catholics in Ireland possessed few civil rights. Agitation for "Catholic emancipation" finally ended in victory in 1829 when Roman Catholics throughout the British Empire were granted the right to vote and hold public office, but the hated Act of Union of 1801 was still in effect and most Roman Catholic Irish remained tenant farmers on land owned by Protestant landlords.

The potato, a North American import, had become the staple crop of tenant families, and it sustained them well in good years. Between 1780 and 1840, the population of Ireland grew from four to eight million. Unfortunately, overdependence on one food source made life precarious when blight or bad weather destroyed the crop. Famine years in 1817, 1821, 1825, 1829, and much of the 1830s offered incontrovertible evidence that the rapidly expanding Irish population could no longer be sustained through traditional agricultural methods and feudal class relations. Between 1825 and 1845, at least 450 000 Irish landed in British North America, about one-third of them moving on to the United States.

These emigrants were the lucky ones. Tragedy finally struck in 1845 when a new strain of potato blight invaded Ireland. By 1848, over 800 000 people had died of starvation and disease. Another million had moved overseas and still more had migrated to other areas of Great Britain. Nearly half of the five million who remained in Ireland were living on soup and meal provided by the British authorities. At the height of the famine one officer wrote an account that appeared in the London *Times*:

> Fever, dissentry, and starvation stare you in the face everywhere—children of ten and nine years old I have

mistaken for decrepit old women, their faces wrinkled, their bodies bent and distorted in pain, the eyes looking like those of a corpse. Bodies are found lifeless, lying on their mothers' bosoms. I tell you one thing which struck me as particularly horrible: a dead woman was found lying on the road with a dead infant on her breast, the child having bitten the nipple of the mother right through in trying to derive nourishment from the wretched body. Dogs feed on the half-buried dead, and the rats are commonly known to tear people to pieces who, though still alive, are too weak to cry out. . . . Instead of following us, beggars throw themselves on their knees before us, holding up their dead infants to our sight.[4]

The outpouring of Ireland's starving and disease-ridden masses created short-term problems for the communities that received them. Over 300 000 Irish refugees came to British North America between 1845 and 1850, most of them entering through quarantine stations at Grosse Île in the St Lawrence and Partridge Island, near Saint John, New Brunswick. Subject to resentment, discrimination, and exploitation, they intensified ethnic, class, and religious tensions throughout North America simply by their presence. They also carried a particularly virulent strain of fever that decimated both their own numbers and the people with whom they came in contact.

The Irish understandably reciprocated the hatred expressed against them, and soon the "anglophobia" that characterized the slums of Dublin and the devastated Irish countryside appeared full-blown in the greater Ireland overseas. In the 1850s, the disaffected Irish spawned an organization that was determined to lift the yoke of British oppression by any means possible. Known popularly as the Fenians, the Irish Republican Brotherhood and Clan-na-Gael had supporters on both sides of the Atlantic. They were a force to be reckoned with in American and British political life and even played a role in the confederation movement in Canada.

Beginning in the 1820s reserves for Natives became part of Upper Canadian land surrender agreements. In practice, these agreements were often violated because the government, responsible both for helping immigrants to get settled and for protecting Native rights, generally favoured the former when the interests of the groups clashed. An "Indian Affairs" commission appointed by the Legislative Assembly of

The St Regis reserve, an Iroquois reserve, in the early nineteenth century, near Cornwall, Ontario, as rendered by John Bartlet.
Library and Archives Canada/C40312

Canada in 1856 wrote unapologetically: "The hardy pioneer who in advance of his fellows plunges with a half sullen resolution into the forest, determined to make a home for himself, is not likely to be over scrupulous in respecting reserved lands."[5]

UPPER CANADA: THE COUNTRYSIDE

In the first half of the nineteenth century, most immigrants to Upper Canada wanted to acquire land and develop a farm. Ownership of land was an achievement for immigrants who had been tenants or farm labourers in Britain, but it was often an elusive goal. Many families failed to accumulate the capital to buy land or, where land was free, the implements and seed to clear land and start a farm. In Peel County in 1835, for example, a quarter of all householders were tenants or squatters. In the rural areas of Home District in 1851, 67.8 percent of the men of labouring age were landless. Without roots, landless labour ranged far and wide in search of work.

Those who did own land took years to prosper, with at best modest surpluses as a source of income for purchasing off-farm goods. Wheat, the major exportable crop, provided an average income per

household of only about $25 in 1830. By the 1840s, when wheat exports increased about 500 percent, many farm families began to rise above subsistence. About half of the cash income on the farms before 1850 came not from exported wheat but from other products sold in local markets. Farmers on Lake Ontario raised pigs to satisfy local markets for pork; western Upper Canada farmers produced rye, tobacco, and barley; farmers in eastern Upper Canada sold ashes and lumber; women everywhere sold surpluses of milk, butter, and eggs.

Men's labour, which involved the clearing of land and producing marketable crops, was essential to the achievement of an improved standard of living through participation in the commercial economy. A farmer working on his own could, on average, clear only four hectares per year. A large family all working the land could clear ten hectares in a year. It took years until a pioneer farm family cleared enough land to allow it to have surpluses.

Women produced the goods for household consumption that allowed the family to meet its basic needs and sold surpluses from the dairy, garden, and loom. They also produced the next generation. Before mid-century, the average Upper Canadian woman bore six children, and women tended to have children at home with them for most of their lives. In 1851, two of every ten women who died between the ages of 15 and 50 died in childbirth. The Peel County records show that 40 percent of the women starting families there in the 1850s were dead before all their children had reached adulthood.

The number of tasks a farm woman could undertake was limited by the resources available to her, by the time required for each of the jobs, and by her total responsibility for the upbringing of children. With the prosperity of the farm household so dependent upon the farm wife, it is not surprising that—as a contemporary commentator reported—a woman was "prized in this country according to her usefulness; and a

Shingwaukonse

Born either at Sault Ste Marie or Mackinac about 1773, Shingwaukonse or Little Pine was an Ojibwa who spent much of his early life in the fur trade, guiding brigades in the northwest. A warrior, he fought on the British side during the War of 1812. Though he was a leader of his people for much of the period after 1820, he only became a head chief in 1836 upon the death of Kaygosh, his mentor in the *midewiwin*.

Even before that, Shingwaukonse had begun to forge alliances with missionaries and government agents whom he regarded as sympathetic to Native efforts to control their own lands. While he recognized that the Ojibwa had to adapt to the European settler society that was replacing the fur-trading society that posed less of a threat to Native possession of their lands, Shingwaukonse strongly defended his people's cultural values and practices. His goal became the establishment of a diversified, sustainable economy. In his efforts to blend old and new, he recruited Métis farmers to settle within Ojibwa lands and train the Ojibwa to follow European farming methods. He also persuaded the Hudson's Bay Company to conclude an agreement in 1834 to keep American free traders out of the Native fishery. Realizing that education in European ways would give Natives a better chance to control their own affairs in the transition to new economic ways, Shingwaukonse pressed government officials and missionaries to establish schools for the Ojibwa.

When Upper Canadian businessmen learned of mine deposits, especially copper, in the Sault, they convinced the legislature of the United Provinces of Canada to allow them to exploit these resources. Government officials ordered the Ojibwa of the region to relocate on Manitoulin Island. Shingwaukonse spoke neither English nor French, and was illiterate. Nonetheless, he pooled a group of allies, Native and non-Native, in an effort to negotiate acceptable locations for mines and adequate royalties for the First Nations owners of the lands on which the mines would be located. His position on the issue of Ojibwa-European relations was translated into a press release that said in part:

> The Great Spirit, we think, placed these rich mines on our lands, for the benefit of his red children, so that their rising generations might get support from them when the animals of the woods should have grown too scarce for our subsistence. We will carry out, therefore the good object of our Father, the Great Spirit. We will sell you lands, if you will give us what is right and at the same time, we want pay for every pound of mineral that has been taken off our lands, as well as for that which may hereafter be carried away.[6]

Among Shingwaukonse's allies were independent prospectors, including Toronto lawyer Allan Macdonell. Macdonell had negotiated a royalty arrangement on a copper mine with Shingwaukonse in 1848, and accepted the Ojibwa chief's claims that his people had to control the cutting of timber within their territories for their long-term survival. Macdonell and several other whites and Métis joined with the Ojibwa in autumn, 1849, to peacefully force the operators of a mine at Mica Bay to leave. In the spring, Shingwaukonse and other Native leaders were jailed for leading this action against a company whose mining claims were recognized by the legislature. Macdonell's efforts led to a full pardon in 1851.

The legislature responded in 1853 with a law that could lead to a jail sentence of up to five years for anyone found guilty of "inciting Indians or half-breeds." Macdonell and other sympathetic whites broke off their alliance with Shingwaukonse. Though the government responded to the militancy of Shingwaukonse and other chiefs with treaties that, on the surface, met Native demands, few promises made to the Natives were fulfilled.

Shingwaukonse was about 80 and ailing in 1853, but he remained a fighter to the end. Having enlarged the economic base of his territory, he pressed the legislature of the Canadas to allow dispossessed Ojibwa within American-controlled territories to resettle at the Sault. When the legislature turned him down, he raised funds for a trip to Britain to persuade Queen Victoria to support his position. But he died before he could make the voyage, leaving a legacy of purposeful but peaceful First Nations efforts to maintain sovereignty over their lands while accepting the presence of the Europeans and the need to blend First Nations and European ways of organizing society.

thriving young settler will marry a clever industrious girl, who has a reputation for being a good spinner and knitter, than one who has nothing but a pretty face to recommend her."[7]

Despite her crucial economic role, a woman was legally subordinate to the husband, father, or even brother for whom she performed labour. The husband's right to dispose of the family property was limited only by a widow's legal claim to one-third of it, and most men willed their farm homes to a son, grandson, or son-in-law. In Peel County, at mid-century, only one-quarter of widows received a separate inheritance from their husbands. The others became boarders in the homes of a male heir. Wills generally indicated what provisions the heir was to make for the widow, and over 20 percent of the documents explicitly forbade the widow to remarry, on pain of being forced to surrender the property her labour had helped to create.

Small children may have been a burden to their mother, but older children were put to work both inside the farm home and outside in the fields. Boys or girls around the age of 10 could expect to spend much of their day looking after younger siblings or helping their mother with tasks, from cleaning house to gardening. A 15-year-old girl would join her mother in a full range of tasks, while a 15-year-old boy worked in the fields with his father. Infancy, then, was followed not by a long period of playful childhood but by an apprenticeship to farm work. The unpaid labour of older children was an essential element in a household economy that left little room for hiring farm labourers or house servants.

Poor families often hired out their children from about the age of seven or eight to gain additional income. Others "adopted out" their children—that is, indentured them to other families in a formal contract that outlined the duties of the child, proscriptions on the child's leisure activities, and the responsibilities of the family utilizing the child's labour. For example, in 1855, Catherine Aiken, age five, was apprenticed as a domestic to a farm family outside Toronto. Her indenture would last 16 years. During that period she was obliged to perform domestic duties at the hours required by her employer. In her leisure time, she was forbidden to frequent taverns or playhouses. The employer, apart from providing food and lodgings,

was to ensure that she received two years of schooling. At the end of her "apprenticeship," Catherine was to be awarded two cows, a feather bed, and linens.

Most pioneer farm families gave education a low priority. After 1816, a community that built a school and hired a teacher could obtain provincial subsidies, but it had to assess fees to make up the shortfall between school operating costs and the government grant. In the 1830s, the fee was $2 or $3 per quarter, plus firewood in winter months. Often farmers did not have the money to pay these fees and did not feel they could spare their children's time on education—much less their own time in transporting children to and from school. As late as 1851, Prescott County reported only 7 and 17 percent of French-speaking and English-speaking children respectively, aged 5 to 16, attending school. By contrast, 39 percent of children in that age group in Hamilton attended school that same year, reflecting the greater importance urban families attached to education's importance in the work world.

UPPER CANADA: THE CITIES AND TOWNS

In 1851, only 15 percent of Upper Canadians lived in urban communities of 1000 people or more. Five towns contained half of this population, with the rest spread out between thirty-three centres. York was a government centre, Kingston the site of an important military garrison, and Bytown the heart of a thriving timber industry. Most towns served the needs of the rural population and moved rural surpluses to export markets. The relatively small urban population reflected the modest purchasing power of the farmers, the limited impact of exports and imports, and the insignificance of the urban economy in pre-industrial society.

York—which became incorporated as the city of Toronto in 1834—was the fastest-growing centre because of its location in the Home District, the colony's most prosperous rural area. From only 2235 people in 1828, Toronto's population grew to 12 571 in 1838 and over 30 000 in 1851. By that time, perhaps one in four persons employed outside the home worked in manufacturing or processing. The existence of factories producing spices, syrup, glue, oil cloth, and patent leather indicated that the increased wheat

King Street East, Toronto, 1835.
Metropolitan Toronto Reference Library/J. Ross Robertson Collection/T10248

sales of the 1840s were creating a domestic market for a wider array of products. By contrast, Kingston, the largest town before the 1830s, was centre to a relatively poor agricultural area and failed to develop an important manufacturing sector despite its relatively large population (over 10 000 in 1851).

Hamilton's population, meanwhile, grew from 1400 in 1833 to 4300 in 1842 and 14 000 in 1851 as its agricultural hinterland expanded. The city's reputation as a centre for iron products was established with the opening of the Gurney stove-works in 1843 and of several other foundries in the early 1850s. In 1851 a Hamilton carriage factory employing 131 workers was one of Upper Canada's largest industrial plants. A cloth factory in Cobourg with 175 workers and a Dundas foundry with 120 completed the list of factories in the province employing over 100 persons that year. In addition, London was already establishing itself as a brewing centre: both Thomas Carling and John K. Labatt launched businesses there in the 1840s.

CLASS, CULTURE, AND CONFLICT IN UPPER CANADA

In the countryside, where few were wealthy, the sharpest social division was between landowners and labourers. The landless workers were generally forced to search for employment or for cheap available land. In towns, particularly the larger ones, a more complex class structure asserted itself early on. Towns were home not only to the wealthy, who received land grants, government jobs, and contracts, but also to the poor, who could not afford to obtain land and so took whatever labouring jobs they could find. In between were small shopkeepers, artisans, carters, professionals, and, by 1850, an increasing number of skilled tradesmen, who worked in the small plants of the nascent manufacturing sector.

The wealthy lived in substantial brick homes. The poor lived in rented wooden shacks densely packed together—places that burned like matchsticks when a fire started. In poor and middling families, the work of maintaining the household was shared by family members; the wealthy hired servants, usually young immigrants. The rich, groaning about the general insubordination of servants in North America relative to their British counterparts, paid the help poorly and housed them in tiny rooms. Women in poor families and widows often worked as charwomen, washerwomen, or pedlars. Children broke stones for roads, took labouring and servant jobs, or worked with their parents as pedlars, cleaners, or beggars.

Canal construction provided perhaps 8000 or 9000 men with seasonal work annually, but the wages were low and both living and working conditions unsafe. According to John Mactaggart, a British engineer who was clerk of the works on the Rideau Canal from 1826 to 1828, "One tenth of all the poor Irish emigrants who come to Canada perish during the first two years they are in the country."[8] In Bytown, reported Mactaggart, the Irish labourers "burrow into the sand-hills; smoke is seen to issue out of holes which are opened to answer the purpose of chimneys."[9] Many of the workers suffered from frostbite, contracted malaria from drinking swamp waters, and were injured or even killed in explosions when tree stumps were blasted.

Reflecting the ethnic prejudices of the time, Mactaggart blamed the Irish for their own problems, saying that they did not properly learn how to do their jobs and that they knew little about sanitation. In practice, as historian William Wylie observes, immigrant workers were the victims of ruthless exploitation as subcontractors competed for jobs by setting aside the least money possible for pay, training, and supervision of workers. Challenging the standard view that anyone who wanted to start a farm or small business could do so, Wylie writes: "The economic future of the workers was bleak. The evidence suggests that few wage-earners on the Rideau were able to save much from their earnings. While some may have become struggling farmers, artisans, or shopkeepers, the majority had to continue competing for jobs with successive annual waves of immigrants."[10]

It was this competition for jobs that produced the Shiners' War of the 1830s and the battles between Irish workers from Munster and Connaught on canal construction in the 1840s. Since the wages of the Irish workers could barely sustain life, there were times when they cooperated among themselves in strikes for higher wages or for payment of overdue wages. Troops were often used to quash these strikes. The authorities, defending the employers, argued that the strikes were the result of an Irish proclivity to violence rather than a justifiable attempt to seek redress of grievances. Responding to complaints from the lumber merchants in Upper Canada, the government legislated a Masters and Servants Act in 1847 that provided fines and jail sentences for employees who left a job before their employment contract had expired.

Lasting unions of labourers were difficult to organize in an economic climate in which jobs were short-term and workers easily replaced by new immigrants. Although skilled workers such as printers and moulders managed to form trade unions, these organizations remained small. They served more as cooperative insurance companies for members' families in case of illness or death than as organizations to negotiate contracts with recalcitrant employers. Only 56 strikes were recorded in the Canadas from 1815 to 1849, an indication that few workers were organized and that those who were could rarely challenge their employers directly.

By the 1840s, there was begrudging recognition from most reformers that at least some of the poor were victims of circumstance rather than creatures of sloth and intemperance. Houses of industry, providing shelter and food to the "deserving poor," opened in cities. Unless they were too old, very young, or infirm, most of the inmates of these institutions were required to work for their supper and bed. The Toronto House of Industry, for example, apprenticed children to respectable country folk in hopes that the youngsters would become sober and industrious. In its first year of operation, this institution provided relief to one-twelfth of the city's residents and one-seventh of its children. Kingston's House of Industry opened in December 1847 and admitted 183 persons the first month, 175 of them Irish. Of the total of 183, 47 were widows and 63 were children under 10.

One of the characteristics that distinguished the "deserving" from the "undeserving" poor was the use of alcohol. Temperance advocates pointed to the baleful consequences of alcoholism for many families, particularly the abuse of women and children by drunken men, and the mismanagement of the family's income by spending scarce funds on liquor. Throughout British North America, there was popular support for the temperance movement. If the records of the tem-

Built in 1842, the Oakville Temperance Hall (of which just the façade is left) was one of the first such structures built in Canada West. The temperance movement opened halls to provide people with alternative meeting places to the tavern.
Library and Archives Canada/PA87397

perance organizations are to be believed, a quarter to a third of the adult population of the Canadas had taken the pledge in the 1840s to forswear alcohol. Toronto's temperance society, founded in 1839, had 1300 members by 1841. Yet such numbers did not mean that the city's drinkers were forced to imbibe on the sly, away from their disapproving neighbours. In 1846, Toronto had almost 500 beer shops, 200 retailers of spirits, and an estimated 150 unlicensed taverns to serve a population of about 20 000 souls. Clearly, those who drank often drank to excess.

RELIGION, LEISURE, AND THE REGULATION OF MORALITY IN UPPER CANADA

Cooperation among members of different Protestant denominations in the establishment of schools, charities, and temperance societies suggested a degree of religious toleration—although intolerance was also evident. For instance, Church of England leaders in the colony campaigned for establishment of their church to the exclusion of all others. This policy was consistent with British practice but was rejected by other denominations, whose members refused to accept that their institutions were inferior in rights and privileges to the "established" church.

Among the largely rural population, the early pioneer farm families were mainly preoccupied with the arduous tasks of clearing forest and planting crops. With few entertainments available, Methodist circuit riders from the United States found a ready audience when they ventured into the Upper Canadian bush. They won many adherents, including Egerton Ryerson and his two brothers, the sons of Anglican Loyalists in Vittoria, a few miles inland from Lake Erie.

In 1841, the four Methodist sects that emerged in Upper Canada could claim the adherence of about 17 percent of the Canadian population. Another 22 percent identified with the Church of England, 20 percent with the Church of Scotland and dissenting Presbyterian sects, and 12 percent with Roman Catholicism. Baptists, Quakers, Lutherans, Congregationalists, Mennonites, and Tunkers (a pacifist sect with origins similar to the Mennonites) all had their followings, along with several smaller sects. About 10 percent of the population either failed to describe their religion to the census taker or indicated no affiliation with a particular religious group.

Religion was important in the lives of most Upper Canadians. Splits within Methodism and Presbyterianism over beliefs and rituals indicated that church attendance was more than a mere social formality for many people. Belief systems promoted by various churches were the principles by which many people lived their lives. Churches were also important social institutions. In an age when the state offered little or no help, networks among co-religionists assured families of a helping hand when illness or tragedy struck.

The price for the spiritual and material support that membership in a church provided was often limits on personal privacy. Methodists, Presbyterians, and Baptists imposed strict disciplinary codes on their members and relied on reports by parishioners to reveal when the church's moral code had been infringed. While drinking in moderation might be allowed, someone accused of public drunkenness on several occasions might face excommunication by the Baptists or Presbyterians.

Accusations of sexual impropriety, which included all sexual relations outside of marriage, often split congregations. According to the records of the Wicklow Baptist Church for July 1849, church members were asked to give a verdict based on little more than local gossip: "Sister Nancy Finton charge[d] Sister Matilda Gleason with having carnal connection with Hiram Card in the same bed that she was in and she had told it before the World and it had become public talk. . . . Both women [were] brought before the Church to give their account of the incident. Members were split in their opinion as to who was the guilty party."[11] Such gossip could be oppressive for many people: women especially were more likely to be condemned as "fallen" and beyond redemption for sexual offences. Yet the weight of community condemnation could also provide support for some women and children who were victims of domestic violence.

Religion and politics were often closely intertwined. In the period before Britain conceded a large measure of colonial self-government, the Anglican Church leaders formed part of a governing clique that included the large landowners and government officials. They regarded calls for popular control of the legislature as tantamount to treason, accusing democrats of wanting to take Upper Canada out of the British orbit to join the American republic. Above all, they defended their church's privileged position as the "established church," meaning that it received state funds for schools and missions while other religious denominations had to raise such funds privately.

For many radicals in Upper Canada, it was precisely the issue of having to support an established church that strengthened their conviction in favour of popular democracy. The large population of Scottish Presbyterian Seceders who emigrated to Upper Canada after 1815 had a long history of battling English encroachments on their religious and national independence. They identified easily with calls for Upper Canada to enjoy equality among religions and an end to British interference in the political life of the colony. William Lyon Mackenzie, the leading radical, was a Presbyterian who formulated his demands for

change in secular language reminiscent of the American revolutionaries of the 1770s. But many of his Scottish-born compatriots agreed with his proposals for change less because of an identification with American democratic thought than because they seemed consistent with religious and nationalist views that they had developed in their homeland.[12]

In addition to church condemnation, communities in both Upper Canada and Lower Canada had other extra-legal means of imposing conformity. Charivaris, for example, could be used to convey disapproval or give pause to people who might consider offending community norms. The churches might agree to solemnize a marriage that conventional thinking deemed "ill-assorted," but the masses sometimes demonstrated their own less tolerant viewpoint.

The state also played a role in attempting to force individuals to conform to community moral standards. Although homosexuality was a capital crime under

VOICES FROM THE PAST

Susanna Moodie Describes an Upper Canadian Charivari

In the 1830s, quoting a neighbour's report, author Susanna Moodie provided a detailed description of a charivari in her book *Roughing It in the Bush*:

> When an old man marries a young wife, or an old woman a young husband, or two old people, who ought to be thinking of their graves, enter for the second or third time into the holy estate of wedlock, as the priest calls it, all the idle young fellows in the neighbourhood meet together to charivari them. For this purpose they disguise themselves, blackening their faces, putting their clothes on hind part before, and wearing horrible masks, with grotesque caps on their heads, adorned with cocks' feathers and bells. They then form in a regular body, and proceed to the bridegroom's house, to the sound of tin kettles, horns and drums, cracked fiddles, and all the discordant instruments they can collect together. Thus equipped, they surround the house where the wedding is held, just at the hour when the happy couple are supposed to be about to retire to rest—beating upon the door with clubs and staves, and demand-

ing of the bridegroom admittance to drink the bride's health, or in lieu thereof to receive a certain sum of money to treat the band at the nearest tavern.

> If the bridegroom refuses to appear and grant their request, they commence the horrible din you heard, firing guns charged with peas against the doors and windows, rattling old pots and kettles, and abusing him for his stinginess in no measured terms. Sometimes they break open the doors, and seize upon the bridegroom. . . . I have known many fatal accidents arise out of an imprudent refusal to satisfy the demands of the assailants.[13]

Moodie's neighbour observed that mob justice sometimes had an ugly side. In one instance a mob, seeking to penalize a black barber for marrying a local Irishwoman, dragged him nearly naked from his wedding bed and rode him upon a rail. The ordeal resulted in the death of the victim, but no one was brought to trial.

British law, the records of court cases in Upper Canada suggest that gay males in the army, the elite, and the middle class had secret networks. Those caught faced the loss of their careers and long jail sentences. In 1842, Samuel Moore, lance corporal, and Patrick Kelly, private, of the 89th Regiment of Foot, were discovered making love and were tried and sentenced to hang for "sodomy." They did not hang, but they both spent long terms in Kingston Penitentiary.

LOWER CANADA: THE COUNTRYSIDE

While the farming population in Upper Canada was gradually being drawn into the emerging international capitalist economy, where they sold their farm surpluses, rural society in Lower Canada was developing along different lines. Farmers in Lower Canada were increasingly becoming part of the larger economy as sellers of their labour, particularly to the timber companies. In rural Quebec in 1851, there were almost as many agricultural labourers (63 365) as farmers (78 437), testimony to the fact that the seigneurial system could no longer accommodate the growing rural population.

Between 1815 and 1840, the French-Canadian population in Lower Canada increased by 250 000. Habitants resisted subdivision of small plots of land among their children, aware that the land would not support anyone if a holding fell much below 125 hectares. Older sons tended to become the only heirs to land, and their younger brothers were forced either to move elsewhere in search of land or find work as agricultural labourers, forestry workers, or fishers. Daughters could marry a landholder, become domestics, or move away from home.

In the 1830s, many habitants moved to the Eastern Townships, and the French-Canadian component of the population of this once predominantly English area increased to almost a third by 1844. Settlement also occurred in places once considered too poor agriculturally for colonization. The Saguenay, the Mauricie, and the Ottawa River regions were settled as "agro-forestry" areas, where, it was hoped, forestry income would allow families to survive on marginal agricultural land. New seigneuries opened in Malbaie, but the land there was hilly and

farmers survived by fishing and working for forestry companies.

After 1830, the expanding textile mills of New England offered an escape to landless men and women unable to find remunerative employment within Lower Canada. By 1850, what had begun as a trickle became a flood of émigrés, and by 1900 an estimated 700 000 French Canadians had left for the United States. Their willingness to leave raises questions about popular notions that French Canadians in the nineteenth century were poor because they lacked a capacity for risk taking. What they lacked was capital and good land. The soils of Lower Canada were generally poorer than the land in Upper Canada, especially western Upper Canada, and had become exhausted from years of questionable agricultural practices, particularly the lack of crop rotation.

The situation in Lower Canada was not unique: soil-exhausting agriculture was practised everywhere in North America and had, for example, turned the farmers of the Atlantic seaboard of the United States into net importers of wheat. In the United States, the usual solution to lowered productivity from agricultural land was to move west to new areas where the same poor practices could be followed anew. Such an option was unavailable to the Canadiens, who were not encouraged to take up lands in the upper province and were therefore forced to live with the consequences of their poor agricultural practices.

Changes in crops reflected the agricultural crisis. Wheat had accounted for 60 to 70 percent of agricultural production in Lower Canada in 1800, and a record export of one million bushels in 1802 indicated the crop's economic importance to the province. By 1831, wheat accounted for 21 percent of agricultural production, and Lower Canada was a large importer of wheat. Wheat-fly infestations ravaged crops in the 1830s, and by 1844 wheat provided only 4.4 percent of total agricultural revenue.

Oats and potatoes replaced wheat in both the farmers' diet and their off-farm sales. These products were sold mainly in local markets and provided less revenue than wheat had once done. But wheat yields were too low to make its continued cultivation outside a few areas profitable. Habitants also raised more sheep, pigs, and cows than before, but limited capital and small farms restricted the potential of the livestock

Making maple sugar, Lower Canada, c. 1837.
P.J. Bainbrigge/Library and Archives Canada/C131921

industry in Lower Canada. Capital was required to buy high-quality livestock and supplies of feed and to build better winter shelter for animals.

Instead of capital, the habitants had debts. Unable to achieve self-sufficiency on their small plots of land, they bought goods, seeds, and animal feed on credit from local merchants, both English-speaking and French-speaking. The merchants bought the habitants' crop surpluses as partial payment for debts incurred, paying low prices for products in good crop years and then holding on to them to sell dearly in poor crop years. Repayment of debts to merchants as well as dues to seigneurs and the various levies of the church created a treadmill of debt throughout the entire seigneurial belt. In the political arena, seigneurs such as Louis-Joseph Papineau castigated heartless landlords, but in their own affairs they forgave no debtors. Habitants without cash paid seigneurs back in kind, whether by working on their buildings, roads, and manors, in upkeep of their sawmills and dykes, or by supplying construction materials, animals, and furs.

Life on credit also characterized the agro-forestry frontier. In the Saguenay, the William Price Company controlled the local forestry sector and paid workers in credits at a company store rather than in cash. The farmers were dependent on the company for employment because its forest reserves were large enough to block agricultural expansion. When Jean-Baptiste Honorat came to the Saguenay in 1844, sent by the archbishop of Quebec to be the superior of an Oblate mission, he denounced the subordination of the settlers to a capitalist enterprise and of agriculture to forestry. The archbishop responded by removing him from the region in 1849.

Feudal exploitation by seigneurs and clergy, along with capitalist exploitation by merchants and lumber companies, left habitants vulnerable to bankruptcy when crops failed, as they did at least six times between 1813 and 1837. The Journals of the Legislative Assembly in 1833 claimed that in the Quebec district a third of the population had nothing to eat and another third could not afford to buy enough food to tide themselves over until the next harvest. While further credit allowed most people to scrape through, many left the land to escape an endless debt cycle. By the 1830s, the habitant diet had potatoes rather than bread at its centre and was neither as varied nor as nutritious as it had been a generation earlier. Potatoes, peas, maple sugar, and pork were the basic staples.

When the overcrowding, poor crops, and debt caused habitant men to seek off-farm work, habitant women stayed on the land, doing all the farm work as well as caring for the children and discharging their other domestic responsibilities. Women born in 1825 would, on average, bear eight children, as had women in the *ancien régime*; but women born in 1845 would reduce this average to six, as families practised birth control, despite the church's opposition.

To reduce the household's dependence on markets and credit, women tried to produce items the family needed for survival. Families raised sheep so that the women could make the family's clothing, and they raised pigs so they did not have to purchase meat. These activities improved the farm family's economic situation, but they could not solve all the problems

Map 15.1 The United Province of Canada, 1851.

created when neither the land base nor other resources for total self-sufficiency were available.

The people who decided to stay in the rural areas in Lower Canada depended to a large extent on the continued British demand for squared timber. The forest industry at least created seasonal employment, albeit at low wages. There were 727 sawmills in operation in the province in 1831 and 911 in 1844. Farmers produced staves, hoops, and barrel ends for local and export markets. For the most part, however, they simply hired out their labour as loggers and rafts-men, and the families attempted to eke out a living from the men's wages and women's household and farm production.

In general, while the period from 1815 to 1850 witnessed a gradual improvement in living conditions in Upper Canada for its hard-working farmers, it also saw a significant deterioration in living standards for rural Canadiens. In 1851, the average farm in Upper Canada could boast a net value of production twice that of a Lower Canadian farm and sold about four times as much in the market.

Lower Canada: The Cities and Towns

As in Canada West, only 15 percent of the population in Canada East lived in towns and cities with over 1000 residents in 1851. Two centres accounted for three-quarters of this population: Montreal and Quebec. Montreal was British North America's largest city. After 1815, Irish and Scottish immigrants bolstered the Anglo-American component of the population enough that from 1835 to 1865 the majority of Montreal's population were anglophones. The city benefited from British mercantilist policies that ended only in the late 1840s, when free trade became the new British economic religion. Before that time, Americans shipped their wheat to Britain through Montreal to avoid paying British customs duties. Wheat from Upper Canada also passed through Montreal. When railways were built in the 1850s, Montreal served as the headquarters of the Grand Trunk Railway, which played a key role in American-Canadian trade beginning in the late 1850s.

View of Montreal, c. 1835, by W.H. Bartlett.
Library and Archives Canada/C-002342

The mercantile community of Montreal formed a committee of trade in 1821 and a board of trade in 1842. A society apart, Montreal's merchant capitalists lived in huge mansions in exclusive neighbourhoods. They rubbed elbows at curling, hunt, cricket, and racquet clubs, the Horticultural Society and the Mercantile Library, the Anglican and Presbyterian churches, and Tory political meetings. Their English-language newspapers, the *Gazette* (unilingual after 1816), the *Canadian Courant and Montreal Advertiser* (1807–34), the *Montreal Herald* (1811–1957), and the *Daily Advertiser* (1833–34), among others, extolled capitalist values and scoffed at the peasant mentality of legislators unwilling to raise taxes to pay for canals and roads that would ignite commerce.

French Canadians were poor cousins within Montreal's middle class, but their presence among property owners was noticeable. One of the biggest landowners was Denis-Benjamin Viger, cousin to Louis-Joseph Papineau and a Parti canadien politician. Viger rented commercial properties and in 1825 was the second-biggest property renter in Montreal after Pierre Berthelet, who let 23 properties to 61 tenants and also rented out 300 cast-iron stoves in the winter.

French speakers were also a minority of Quebec City's mercantile elite. Much of that city's steady growth, from about 8500 in 1795 to over 42 000 in 1851, was the result of the expansion of port facilities to handle increased timber exports. It was the lack of return cargoes for the timber ships that led their owners to rent space to British immigrants for the return journey. The timber trade and shipping also stimulated the construction of shipyards: in 1851, seven shipyards employed 1338 persons.

Men of Scottish origin dominated the shipyards and the timber trade. English-speaking merchants also controlled civic administration in the two cities. Their main concern was to maintain low property taxes, the source of civic revenues; they neglected streets and drains and ignored the threat of disease and fire. St Roch, the working-class area of Quebec City, had mud roads, wooden drains that easily broke, and wooden homes crowded close together. Poor drainage meant contaminated water, and death rates were higher in the poor areas than in the prosperous ones. In 1845, two huge fires left 20 000 people, or half the population, in Quebec City homeless. A major fire in Montreal in 1852 razed 1100 homes, leaving one-sixth of the population without shelter.

In both Quebec City and Montreal, people were beginning to band together in a variety of associations. In the 1830s and 1840s, tailors, shoemakers, bakers, carpenters, printers, mechanics, firefighters, painters, stonecutters, and milkmen all organized for mutual protection and very occasionally went on strike. French-speaking professionals and small businessmen also organized, especially in Montreal. In the 1830s, apart from the Parti patriote (the name for the Parti canadien after 1826), there were nationalist societies such as La Société Saint-Jean Baptiste and the Société aide-toi et ciel t'aidera. The Irish formed the St Patrick's Society. In the 1840s, the Instituts Canadiens became centres for intellectual exchange, their offices serving as libraries, newsrooms, and conference halls all rolled into one.

CLASS, CULTURE, AND RELIGION IN LOWER CANADA

In Lower Canada, Roman Catholicism claimed the adherence of the majority of French Canadians. Before the rebellions of 1837 and 1838, the influence of the Roman Catholic Church was waning, both in the urban and rural areas. From one cleric for every 355 residents in 1760, by 1830 the priest-to-population ratio had fallen to one for every 1834. In Montreal, only 36 percent of parishioners took Easter communion, and regular attendance was far smaller.

Inspired by the return of the Jesuits to Canada East in the 1840s and a quickening of religious devotion throughout colonial society at mid-century, the Roman Catholic Church made a comeback. More French Canadians opted to become priests and nuns. By the 1860s attendance of parishioners at Easter communion was nearly universal. The church established newspapers and associations to reassert its influence and counter the liberalizing tendencies of the Instituts Canadiens. Led by energetic bishops such as Jean-Jacques Lartigue and his successor, Ignace Bourget, in Montreal, the church successfully marginalized political-nationalist reform elements that had once dominated the province's political discourse.

Even before the church achieved its influential political role, its pre-eminence in social welfare for Catholics was largely unchallenged. Social welfare services and hospitals continued to be the responsibility of the religious orders, especially the female ones, whose growing numbers after the 1840s meant expanded services. The Soeurs de la Charité de l'Hôpital-Général of Montreal, for example, cared for the sick and poor as well as for foundlings. Priests were also involved in charitable services through the St Vincent de Paul Societies, which collected donations in the parishes to be used to aid the destitute.

In the English-speaking community, women also began to dominate social services, which until the 1840s were operated by private charity organizations. In 1817, upper-class women in Montreal organized the Female Benevolent Society, which established the Montreal General Hospital four years later; the Female Compassionate Society, to assist married women in childbirth, in 1822; the Montreal Protestant Orphan Asylum in 1822; and the Ladies' Benevolent Society, which helped destitute women, in 1824. While well-off women often felt genuine compassion for those they aided, this attitude was often mixed with contempt. Like their husbands and fathers, they insisted that these needy people were profligate and intemperate rather than victims of poor pay and seasonal work.

The poor took help from whatever quarter offered it. Every winter, people struggled to find enough money to buy food and firewood and hoped they would be spared the smallpox, diphtheria, and measles that killed off many of the youngest and oldest members of the population. Maria Louisa Beleau was not spared during the severe winter of 1816–17. The daughter of a single mother, she died in a home that was described by a witness at her inquest:

> The hovel in which the deceased had lived, with her mother, and two sisters, is not fit for a stable. It is open in many parts of the roof and on all sides. There is no other floor than the bare earth. It is a mere wooden stall: it has no window nor any chimney. In the middle is a shallow hole made in the earth, in which there are marks of a fire having been made; and the smoke escaped through the open parts of the roof and sides. When I was there on Tuesday last, there was no fire in the hole.[14]

For those barely scraping by, the political issues that animated middle-class discourse would have seemed esoteric. It was the "national question," rather than the means of alleviating poverty, that often dominated legislative debates. Historians disagree about the extent to which nationalism penetrated the popular consciousness of French Canadians. There is little doubt that the middle class of teachers, clergy, civil servants, journalists, and artists came to see themselves as the natural leaders of a French-Canadian Catholic nation that lacked either political independence or economic control in Lower Canada.

From the elite point of view, the lower-class French Canadians needed to be reformed. They spoke an impoverished French, read vulgar literature when they read at all, and had common pastimes of gambling, drinking, and fighting that they had picked up from a North American frontier environment. The elites wanted to "Europeanize a North American popular culture,"[15] but the masses had other ideas. When a Special Council was created to govern Lower Canada for several years after the 1837 Rebellion, social reform was one of its major goals. It set regulations for the operation of taverns, the clearing of winter roads, and even the design of sleighs, and established a rural police force to enforce the rules. The habitants and townspeople defied regulations that they found inconvenient, even at the expense of fines and jail sentences. They would not abide meddling new-comers telling them how to design their winter vehicles or when they could drink.

CONCLUSION

Superficially, the societies of the Canadas changed little in the first half of the nineteenth century. Most people still farmed, and trade activity centred on a few exportable natural products such as wheat and timber. Beneath the surface, however, much had changed. By the 1850s most farmers in the Canadas were dependent on market exchanges for a growing portion of the products they used. In Canada West, this typically meant that a farm family sold about two-thirds of what it produced, using the proceeds to buy farm equipment and household items. In Canada East, it meant that farmers without saleable surpluses had to supplement their farm income with off-farm waged work, usually in the timbering trade. Towns and cities in the Canadas grew because of increased foreign demand for Canadian staples and increased domestic demand for manufactures. In both rural and urban communities class and cultural divisions defined the social fabric. These social divisions would create political divisions—manifested most dramatically in the rebellions of the late 1830s.

NOTES

1 Françoise Noël, *Family Life and Sociability in Upper and Lower Canada, 1780–1870: A View from Diaries and Family Correspondence* (Montreal: McGill-Queen's University Press, 2003), 93.

2 Peter A. Russell, "Forest into Farmland: Upper Canadian Clearing Rates, 1822–1839," in *Historical Essays on Upper Canada: New Perspectives*, ed. J.K. Johnson and Bruce G. Wilson (Ottawa: Carleton University Press, 1989), 132, 143.

3 Anna Brownell Jameson, *Winter Studies and Summer Rambles in Canada: Selections* (Toronto: McClelland and Stewart, 1965), 167.

4 Cited in Donald Mackay, *Flight from Famine: The Coming of the Irish to Canada* (Toronto: McClelland and Stewart, 1990), 245.

5 Arthur J. Ray, *I Have Lived Here Since the World Began: An Illustrated History of Canada's Native Peoples* (Toronto: Lester/Key Porter, 1996), 158.

6 Janet L. Chute, "A Unifying Vision: Shingwaukonse's Plan for the Future of the Great Lakes Ojibwa," *Journal of the Canadian Historical Association*, New Series 7 (1996): 69.

7 Catharine Parr Traill, *The Backwoods of Canada* (1836; reprinted Toronto: McClelland and Stewart, 1959), 185.

8 Quoted in *Upper Canada in the 1830s*, ed. Virginia R. Robeson (Toronto: OISE, 1977), 14.

9 Ibid.

10 William T.N. Wylie, "Labour and the Construction of the Rideau Canal, 1826–1832," *Labour/Le Travail* 11 (Spring 1983): 29.

11 Lynne Marks, "Religion, Leisure, and Working-Class Identity," in *Labouring Lives: Work and Workers in Nineteenth-Century Ontario*, ed. Paul Craven (Toronto: University of Toronto Press, 1995), 288.

12 Michael Gauvreau, "Covenanter Democracy: Scottish Popular Religion, Ethnicity, and the Varieties of Politico-religious Dissent in Upper Canada, 1815–1841," *Histoire Sociale/Social History*, 36, 71 (May 2003): 55–84..

13 Susanna Moodie, *Roughing It in the Bush; or, Life in Canada*, ed. Elizabeth Thompson (Ottawa: Tecumseh Press, 1997), 152.

14 Quoted in Judith Fingard, "The Winter's Tale: The Seasonal Contours of Pre-Industrial Poverty in British North America, 1815–1860," *Canadian Historical Association Historical Papers* (1974): 72.

15 Gérard Bouchard, "Une Nation, deux cultures: Continuités et ruptures dans la pensée québécoise traditionelle (1840–1960)," in *La construction d'une culture: Le Québec et l'Amérique française*, sous la direction de Gérard Bouchard avec la collaboration de Serge Courville (Quebec: Les Presses de l'Université Laval, 1993), 13.

RELATED READINGS IN THIS SERIES

From *Foundations: Readings in Pre-Confederation Canadian History*

Marjorie Griffin Cohen, "Division of Labour in a Staple-Exporting Economy," 349–69.

From **Media Companion CD-ROM, Volume I**

James Winnett's Appointment as Superintendent of the Six Nations

Irish Emigrants, 1851

Roughing It in the Bush or Life in Canada

To the Earl of Elgin, Governor General of British North America, 1847

SELECTED READING

In addition to sources cited in earlier chapters, the social history of early Ontario is examined in a variety of excellent essays in J.K. Johnson and B. Wilson, eds., *Historical Essays on Upper Canada: New Perspectives* (Ottawa: Carleton University Press, 1989) and an earlier volume, *Historical Essays on Upper Canada* (Ottawa: Carleton University Press, 1975). Another important study is Peter A. Russell, *Attitudes to Social Structure and Mobility in Upper Canada, 1815–1840: "Here We Are Laird Ourselves"* (Lewiston, NY: Edwin Mellen Press, 1990). More recent work includes J. David Wood, *Making Ontario: Agricultural Colonization and Landscape Re-creation before the Railway* (Montreal: McGill-Queen's University Press, 2000), and Neil Forkey, *Shaping the Upper Canadian Frontier: Environment, Society, and Culture in the Trent Valley* (Calgary: University of Calgary Press, 2002). The voices of the immigrants are heard in Wendy Cameron, Sheila Haines, and Mary McDougall Maude, eds., *English Immigrant Voices: Labourers' Letters from Upper Canada in the 1830s* (Montreal: McGill-Queen's University Press, 2000), and Wendy Cameron and Mary McDougall Maude, *Assisting Emigration to Upper Canada: The Petworth Project, 1832–1837* (Montreal: McGill-Queen's University Press, 2000). On elite formation in the colony, see J.K. Johnson, *Becoming Prominent: Regional Leadership in Upper Canada, 1791–1841* (Montreal: McGill-Queen's University Press, 1989), and Bruce Wilson, *The Enterprises of Robert Hamilton: A Study of Wealth and Influence in Early Upper Canada* (Ottawa: Carleton University Press, 1983). The social lives of the upper classes in the two Canadas are explored in Françoise Noël, *Family Life and Sociability in Upper and Lower Canada, 1780–1870: A View from Diaries and Family Correspondence* (Montreal: McGill-Queen's University Press, 2003). Also useful in revealing the social history of the colony are the contemporary observations by Susanna Moodie, *Roughing It in the Bush* (Ottawa: Carleton University Press, 1970), and by Catharine Parr Traill, *The Backwoods of Canada* (Toronto: McClelland and Stewart, 1959).

In addition to the sources in Chapter 11 on economic and social development in Upper Canada, see John Clarke, *Land, Power and Economics on the Frontier of Upper Canada* (Montreal: McGill-Queen's University Press, 2001), and Marjorie Griffin Cohen, *Women's Work, Markets, and Economic Development in Nineteenth-Century Ontario* (Toronto: University of Toronto Press, 1988). A fictional account that has considerable insight regarding social class and gender in Upper Canada is Margaret Atwood, *Alias Grace* (Toronto: McClelland and Stewart, 1996).

There are several excellent works on Irish immigrants, including Donald Harmon Akenson, *The Irish in Ontario: A Study in Rural History* (Montreal: McGill-Queen's University Press, 1984), and Bruce S. Elliott, *Irish Migrants in the*

Canadas: A New Approach (Montreal: McGill-Queen's University Press, 1988). Robin Winks, *The Blacks in Canadian History*, 2nd ed. (Montreal: McGill-Queen's University Press, 1997) contains information on a smaller but more immediately visible group of immigrants. On Scottish immigrants, see Marianne Maclean, "Achd an Righ: A Highland Response to the Assisted Emigration of 1815," *Canadian Papers in Rural History* 5 (1986): 181–97. Irish conflict with other groups is the subject of Michael S. Cross, "The Shiners' War: Social Violence in the Ottawa Valley in the 1830s," *Canadian Historical Review* 54, 1 (1973): 1–26, while the article by Ruth Bleasdale in Johnson, *Historical Essays on Upper Canada* (1989) deals with the importance of ethnic solidarity among Irish workers in responding to harsh employment conditions. Working conditions generally are the subject of William T.N. Wylie, "Labour and the Construction of the Rideau Canal, 1826–1832," *Labour/Le Travail* 11 (Spring 1983): 7–29.

Two good community studies with information regarding landholding patterns that is suggestive for the entire province are David Gagan, *Hopeful Travellers: Families, Land, and Social Change in Mid-Victorian Peel County, Canada West* (Toronto: University of Toronto Press, 1981), and Leo A. Johnson, "Land Policy, Population Growth, and Social Structure in the Home District, 1793–1851," *Ontario History* 69 (1977): 151–68. The most detailed urban study is Michael Katz, *The People of Hamilton, Canada West: Family and Class in a Mid-Nineteenth-Century City* (Cambridge: Harvard University Press, 1975). See also Gordon Darroch and Lee Saltow, *Property and Inequality in Victorian Ontario: Structural Patterns and Cultural Communities in the 1871 Census* (Toronto: University of Toronto Press, 1994).

On religion, see Michael Gauvreau, *The Evangelical Century* (Montreal: McGill-Queen's University Press, 1991); William Westfall, *Two Worlds: The Protestant Culture of Nineteenth Century Ontario* (Montreal: McGill-Queen's University Press, 1989); Curtis Fahey, *In His Name: The Anglican Experience in Upper Canada, 1791–1854* (Ottawa: Carleton University Press, 1991); J.W. Grant, *A Profusion of Spires: Religion in Nineteenth-Century Ontario* (Toronto: University of Toronto Press, 1988); J.L.H. Henderson, ed., *John Strachan: Documents and Opinions* (Toronto: McClelland and Stewart, 1969); Nancy Christie, ed., *Households of Faith: Family, Gender and Community* (Montreal: McGill-Queen's University Press, 2002); and Terence J. Fay, *A History of Canadian Catholics: Gallicanism, Romanism, and Canadians* (Montreal: McGill-Queen's University Press, 2002).

On Native peoples, see Peter S. Schmalz, *The Ojibwa of Southern Ontario* (Toronto: University of Toronto Press,

1991). The temperance movement is detailed in Jan Noel, *Canada Dry: Temperance Crusades before Confederation* (Toronto: University of Toronto Press, 1995). On leisure, Patricia Jasen, *Wild Things: Nature, Culture, and Tourism in Ontario, 1790–1914* (Toronto: University of Toronto Press, 1995) is useful. On legal history, see John C. Weaver, *Crimes, Constables, and Courts: Order and Transgression in a Canadian City, 1816–1970* (Montreal: McGill-Queen's University Press, 1995).

For Lower Canada, John A. Dickinson and Brian Young, *A Short History of Quebec*, 2nd ed. (Toronto: Copp Clark Pitman, 1993), chapters 4 and 5, provides a vivid account of life in nineteenth-century Quebec. The Clio Collective, *Quebec Women: A History*, trans. Roger Gannon and Rosalind Gill (Toronto: Women's Press, 1987), chapters 3–7, summarizes much of the literature on women in Lower Canada. See also sources cited in Chapter 12 of this text.

Case studies of community development are found in Peter Gossage, *Families in Transition: Industry and Population in Saint-Hyacinthe* (Montreal: McGill-Queen's University Press, 1999); Gérard Bouchard, *Quelque Arpents d'Amérique: Population, économie, famille au Saguenay, 1838–1971* (Montreal: Boréal, 1996); John I. Little, *Crofters and Habitants: Settler Society and Culture in a Quebec Township, 1848–1881* (Montreal: McGill-Queen's University Press, 1992) and *Nationalism, Capitalism and Colonization in Nineteenth-Century Quebec: The Upper St Francis District* (Montreal and Kingston: McGill-Queen's University Press, 1989); Allan Greer, *Peasant, Lord, and Merchant: Rural Society in Three Quebec Parishes, 1740–1840* (Toronto: University of Toronto Press, 1985); Claude Baribeau, *La seigneurie de la Petite Nation, 1801–1854: le rôle économique et social du seigneur* (Hull, QC: Éditions Asticou, 1983); Normand Seguin, *La conquête du sol au 19e siècle* (Montreal: Boréal Express, 1977), and René Hardy, *La sidérurgie dans le monde rural: les hauts fourneaux du Québec au XIXe siècle* (Saint-Foy: Les Presses de l'Université Laval, 1995). The reasons for Quebec's slow agricultural development relative to Ontario's are explored in John McCallum, *Unequal Beginnings: Agriculture and Economic Development in Quebec and Ontario until 1870* (Toronto: University of Toronto Press, 1980). The changing economy of Canada East after the rebellion is discussed in Gerald J.J. Tulchinsky, *The River Barons: Montreal Businessmen and the Growth of Industry and Transportation, 1837–1853* (Toronto: University of Toronto Press, 1977). On the English-speaking minority, see Ronald Rudin, *The Forgotten Quebecers: A History of English-Speaking Quebec, 1759–1980* (Quebec: Institut québécois de recherche sur la culture, 1985) and J.I. Little, *The Child Letters: Public and Private Life in a Canadian Merchant-Politician's Family, 1841–1845* (Montreal: McGill-

Queen's University Press, 1995), and Richard W. Vaudry, *Anglicans and the Atlantic World: High Churchmen, Evangelicals, and the Quebec Connection* (Montreal: McGill-Queen's University Press, 2003).

The impact of epidemic disease on British North America, particularly Lower Canada, is assessed in Geoffrey Bilson, *A Darkened House: Cholera in Nineteenth-Century Canada* (Toronto: University of Toronto Press, 1980), and

André Charbonneau and André Sevigny, *1847: Grosse Île: A Record of Daily Events* (Ottawa: Parks Canada, 1997). The dismal conditions of urban life that aided in the spread of disease are the subject of David-Thiery Ruddel and Marie La France, "Québec, 1785–1840: problèmes de croissance d'une ville coloniale," *Histoire sociale/Social History* 18, 36 (1985): 315–33.

WEBLINKS

GROSSE ÎLE

www.pc.gc.ca/lhn-nhs/qc/grosseile/index_e.asp

This Parks Canada site offers historical material and links relating to Grosse Île.

RIDEAU CANAL

www.rideau-info.com/canal/history/hist-canal.html

For a history of the canal, with some rather personal commentary, check out this site.

METHODISM

www.mb-soft.com/believe/text/methodis.htm

For a brief history of the movement and an abbreviated bibliography, see this site.

CHAPTER 16

Rebellions and Responsible Government in the Canadas, 1815–1860

Timeline

1815	Election of Louis-Joseph Papineau as Speaker in Lower Canadian Assembly
1819	Banishment of Robert Gourlay from Upper Canada
1833	Major crop failure in Lower Canada
1834	92 Resolutions passed in Lower Canadian Assembly; Upper Canadian Assembly endorses Report of Committee on Grievances
1836	Controversial Conservative win in Upper Canadian Assembly elections
1837	Russell's Ten Resolutions; another crop failure in Lower Canada
1837–38	Rebellions in Lower and Upper Canada
1839	Lord Durham's report
1840	Act of Union
1848	Responsible government in United Province of Canada
1849	Rebellion Losses Bill
1854	Abolition of seigneurial system and clergy reserves

Saint-Jean-Baptiste Day was a well-entrenched Roman Catholic feast day in Quebec from the time of New France. But in 1834, Ludger Duvernay, a Montreal *Patriote* leader, gave it a new twist. The editor of La Minerve and Assembly member for Lachenaie, Duvernay called upon Patriote supporters to organize banquets with the political theme of popular control of the legislature. This democratic emphasis was linked to French-Canadian nationalism, and Duvernay dubbed the Catholic holiday "la fête nationale." For the next three years, June 25 was a day of both celebration and political protest throughout most French-speaking areas of Lower Canada. After the Rebellion of 1837, Duvernay became a fugitive in the United States for five years. The Roman Catholic Church reasserted its control over the day, and made temperance, rather than popular sovereignty, the theme of Jean-Baptiste Day.[1]

This chapter describes the conditions and events that led to open rebellion in the Canadas in 1837 and 1838. As we shall see, by no means everyone supported the rebellions. Moderates among the reform forces in the Canadas balked at resorting to revolution to achieve their ends, and many of the revolutionaries continued to embrace conservative social values. Still, the radicals in the two Canadas shared a perspective favouring a society of small property holders governed by democratically chosen representatives. It was a vision that they shared with most of their American neighbours and with an increasing number of Europeans, who, from the French Revolution onward, organized, with varying degrees of success, to replace rule by a privileged elite with popular rule. Their opponents defended a hierarchical social and political order in which power was placed in the hands of a governor and his advisers—all appointed by the British Crown—as the safeguard of social stability. Although the rebellions were defeated, they forced Great Britain to reassess its relationship with its colonies. By 1848 "responsible government," which gave more power to the elected members of the Assembly, had been granted to the United Canadas, but only after a decade of turmoil.

THE ROAD TO REBELLION IN LOWER CANADA

The agricultural crisis in Lower Canada, coupled with the frustration of a Canadien middle class excluded from the Executive and Legislative councils, provided a backdrop to the rebellions in that colony in 1837 and 1838. Following the War of 1812, the Parti canadien began to agitate for political reform that would reduce the power of appointed officials in the colony. A creation of the new middle class of French-speaking lawyers, doctors, and newspapermen, the Parti canadien proved popular with the habitants because it campaigned for the opening of new seigneuries outside the seigneurial belt.

By the 1830s access to land in Lower Canada had become a hot political issue. Overcrowding on the seigneuries was leading to a lower standard of living and pressure to emigrate in many rural areas of the colony. Between 1795 and 1840 almost seven million hectares of land in the Eastern Townships passed into the hands of speculators, a policy that angered land-starved habitant families.

Some historians have labelled the rebellion as a "feudal reaction" because the Parti canadien supported the seigneurial system over freehold tenure. No doubt many habitants would have preferred freehold tenure, but they were in no position to accumulate the cash required to pay a speculator for land. They blamed the government for condemning them to landlessness and supported the Parti canadien because it supported habitant demands for access to undeveloped lands in the hands of speculators.

Even English-speaking settlers in the Eastern Townships, while hesitant about supporting French-Canadian political organizations, opposed the government's policies, complaining about government corruption and the lack of useable roads. A farmer in the New Glasgow settlement, writing to the editor of the Montreal *Gazette* in 1824, described a road where the water was three feet deep in May and June, adding that "although our roads are left in this state, the person who contracted to make them is said to have received £1000 of the public money for this job."[2]

The Parti canadien, which changed its name to Parti patriote in 1826, handily won all elections for the House of Assembly. In 1827 it won 90 percent of the Assembly seats. Its stature had been raised significantly in 1822 when it joined with the clergy to fend off a proposal by the British government to unite Lower Canada and Upper Canada into one province. English-speaking merchants in Lower Canada and their allies in London had been responsible for pressing for a union of the two provinces to reduce the influence of Canadien representatives in the Assembly.

To the merchants, the members of the Assembly majority were opponents of commerce. They balked at proposals for state-funded canal construction on the St Lawrence and demanded grants of new seigneuries before they would approve road-building expenditures for the Eastern Townships. With the completion of the Erie Canal in 1825, a development that gave New York State an advantage over Montreal in shipping, the clamour of the Montreal merchants for canal expenditures grew louder, and their resolve to oppose Assembly demands for more power in colonial politics stiffened.

The leading English-speaking merchants, along with the French-speaking merchants favoured by the governors, were labelled the Château Clique because they could often be found at the Château St-Louis, the governor's residence in Quebec City. As in Upper Canada, a small merchant-dominated group appeared to monopolize government appointments at all levels except the elected Assembly. This privileged group, it seemed, had the ear of the governor, and received all the Crown land grants and government contracts.

Louis-Joseph Papineau and his colleagues initially stressed that the Roman Catholic Church, the seigneurial system, and the French language and culture were fundamental aspects of the nationality of their people. They defended these three elements against all perceived attacks. In the 1830s, the Parti patriote program began to change. The refusal of governors to respond to the Assembly's demands and Bishop Plessis' coziness with the governing clique perhaps helped to push the Parti patriote in a more radical direction. The party's leaders were also influenced by developments in Europe and the United States, which were advancing the cause of liberalism.

While Papineau remained a defender of the seigneurial system, he and other leaders were increasingly drawn to American republicanism and the democratic ideal of a government controlled by the people. They also began to question the authority of the Roman Catholic Church in such areas as education. In 1829, the Assembly voted to establish schools that it would control, supervise, and partly finance. This policy flew in the face of efforts by Bishop Plessis to keep education under the control of curés and church-wardens. By 1836, there were over 1500 "secular" schools, a situation that horrified Plessis' successor, Bishop Jean-Jacques Lartigue.

In 1834, Papineau put forward in the Assembly a set of 92 resolutions designed to make the authority of an electoral majority supreme. The resolutions demanded an Executive Council chosen by the Assembly, an elected Legislative Council, and the Assembly's approval of civil service appointments and salaries. The resolutions made thinly veiled threats that if Britain did not accept their proposals, the Canadiens would demand independence from the British Empire.

While the Assembly passed the resolutions by a vote of 56 to 23, 17 of the "nay" votes came from Patriotes who refused to embrace the radicalism of their leader. During the Assembly elections that year, the Patriote leadership ensured that none of these moderates—or backsliders as the radicals perceived them—were renominated as Patriotes. The new Assembly, with 78 Patriotes in an elected group of 88, was adamant in its calls for an end to government by an appointed British colonial clique in the Executive and Legislative councils.

The Patriotes drew most of their support from the French-speaking population, but they were not ethnically exclusive. Irish settlers, angry with land speculators, and English-speaking democrats joined their ranks. In 1834 Dr Edmund O'Callaghan and Dr Wolfred Nelson won election in French-Canadian ridings under the Patriote banner. At the same time, the party's growing radicalism prompted the defection of some of its earlier English-speaking supporters. John Neilson, editor of the Quebec *Gazette*, for example, had supported Papineau's party and served in the Assembly during the period when the party concentrated its attention on defence of traditional francophone institutions within the British Empire. The new emphasis on republican virtues repelled a man who firmly believed in the monarchical system.

Lord Matthew Whitworth-Aylmer, the governor from 1830 to 1835, attempted to reduce Assembly influence. To provide the Executive Council with the revenue it needed to meet the costs of the civil list without requiring Assembly approval, he sold over 2.1 million hectares of uncultivated land to the British American Land Company. His action appalled Patriote supporters and crystallized the popular view that the government wished to deny ordinary people both land and democracy. Such policies only increased the determination of the Patriotes to use whatever powers the Assembly could muster to challenge scheming colonial governors.

Tired of continued obstructionism by the Lower Canadian Assembly, Colonial Secretary Lord John Russell decided to act. In March 1837 he issued 10 resolutions approved by the British Parliament, which permitted the new Lower Canadian governor, Lord Gosford, to appropriate provincial revenue without the authority of the elected Assembly. Russell also rejected calls for an elected Legislative Council and confirmed the title of the British American Land Company to the lands it was selling at prohibitive prices. For many Patriote leaders, this marked the end of the constitutional avenue to reform. They resolved to overthrow British rule by a campaign of civil disobedience if possible, by violence if necessary.

By the summer of 1837, tensions were running high. English-speaking defenders of the government who had formed paramilitary loyalist associations, such as the Doric Club in Montreal, tried to break up

Patriote meetings. The Patriotes responded with the creation of a paramilitary organization of their own, the *Fils de la liberté*. Meanwhile, Lord Gosford, following Russell's orders, dismissed the Assembly for refusing to vote support for long-term funding of civil servants appointed by the governor. The Patriote central committee responded with a call for a constitutional convention for Lower Canada in December 1837, to be preceded by an economic boycott, large rallies, and petitions.

The Patriote women's associations led the boycott movement, organizing women to replace bought clothing with homespun and the purchase of manufactured goods only from merchants known to be Patriote supporters. The women also made bullets and cartridges. In the parish of St Antoine, in September, 250 women held a party that, according to the *Vindicator*, the English-language newspaper that supported the Patriotes, used only locally produced items. Nonetheless the Patriotes were not supporters of greater rights for women. Indeed, they had joined the government members (often called Tories after their British counterparts) of the Assembly in 1834 to place an absolute legislative ban on women's right to vote.

As it became clear that the boycott was having no effect on the government's resolve to resist the demands of the Assembly majority, the Patriotes stepped up their pressures with a campaign against minor officials. They called on all justices of the peace and militia captains and battalion lieutenants to resign their posts. These men had all been appointed by the governor, acting on the advice of local authorities. The Patriotes were not above using violence or the threat of violence to force the resignations. In the parish of St Athanase on the upper Richelieu, Captain Louis Bessette, a wealthy habitant, at first resisted demands that he resign his militia commission. He soon changed his mind when a small gang of armed men chopped down a maypole on his property. The armed men were soon joined by a larger group of masked men who threw stones and lumps of frozen earth at Bessette's home.

The government was determined to stop what it regarded as Patriote subversion. A street battle in Montreal between the Doric Club and the Fils de la liberté on 6 November became Gosford's pretext for calling in troops from the other British North

The Beauharnois Rebels, 1838, a painting by Jane Ellice. Many of the captured rebels were deported to New South Wales in today's Australia.
Library and Archives Canada/C-013392

American colonies to suppress the protest movement. Gosford ordered the arrest of Papineau and other Patriote leaders. When Papineau fled to the United States, many of his supporters began to lose some of their patriotic zeal. For the Patriote leadership, however, the die had been cast. They interpreted the government's actions to mean that further peaceful protest would be suppressed. So they resorted to armed rebellion, relying on contingency plans made several months earlier.

On 23 November, a mainly habitant Patriote army under Wolfred Nelson defeated British troops at St Denis on the Richelieu River, but they could not follow up their victory. Two days later, the British defeated the Patriotes who had mobilized at St Charles farther south on the Richelieu. They destroyed St Denis on 1 December and two weeks later sacked St Eustache, leaving 58 Patriotes dead and 60 homes burned. Two days afterward, British forces burned and looted the village of St Benoît, and the first rebellion was over. Martial law was declared, and more Patriote leaders fled south of the border.

In the United States, a core of exiles led by Wolfred Nelson's brother Robert organized the Frères chasseurs and proposed a more militant program to gather popular support for another uprising. It included an end to all seigneurial dues, with lands to be handed freely to the habitants, a promise that alienated Papineau. The rebels entered Lower Canada in November 1838 and gathered about 4000 insurgents, but they were no match for the British troops. The Iroquois of Kahnawaké joined the attack on the Patriotes. Though the Five Nations had their own grievances with the government, they decided to make common cause against the rebels after the latter invaded Kahnawaké on their march to Montreal.

Determined to prevent future attempts at rebellion, the British forces went on a rampage of looting and burning of farms and houses in Patriote strongholds in the Montreal area and on the Richelieu. The government also arrested 850 Patriotes for their roles in the rebellions. Twelve of them were hanged, fifty-eight deported to Australian penal colonies, and two

banished. The Australian exiles produced the haunting folksong "Un canadien errant," which described the pain of banishment and would inspire generations of Quebec nationalists.

The military failure and the absence of revolts in the Quebec district, the Ottawa valley, and the Gaspé have caused some historians to question the extent of support for the rebels. The church, long estranged from the Patriotes, who had become supporters of the separation of church and state and of democracy generally, condemned the rebellions and ordered its flock to be obedient to the British. The strength of British arms along with church authority helped to limit the spread of the rebellions.

REBELLION IN UPPER CANADA

Upper Canadians also experienced social unrest leading to rebellion in the 1830s. In the wake of the War of 1812, conservative values became strongly entrenched in Upper Canada. Government leaders equated political reform with American republicanism and used the threat of American expansion to suppress dissent. For a time, American immigration to Upper Canada was actively discouraged and the political and property rights of American-born residents in the colony were called into question. Anyone who advocated political reform was accused of sowing disunity, which could weaken Upper Canada's ability to resist future American attacks. So, for example, the banishment of Robert Gourlay, a recent Scottish immigrant, in 1819, demonstrated the limits of tolerance. Gourlay had organized township meetings to record settlers' complaints about the system of land grants in the colony, with a view to holding a colony-wide convention to address the issue. When he published the proceedings of a settlers' meeting in Niagara that had been drawn up as a petition to the Prince Regent, members of the elite charged him with seditious libel. Twice charged and twice

British troops on the march from Fredericton to Quebec, 1837.
Metropolitan Toronto Reference Library/Ross Robertson Collection/2238

acquitted by juries that accepted his claim that he was upholding citizens' rights to petition their monarch, he was banished by the government anyway.

Opponents of the government accused it of having created an oligarchy, which the reformers called the Family Compact. Historians have disagreed about the appropriateness of the term "Family Compact." Some claim that the term misleadingly implies that the members of the oligarchy were interrelated and located in one geographical area. They note that there were small cliques exercising local power throughout the province and that their members were not, at least initially, related by blood. By contrast, a recent study of land-holding in Upper Canada concludes that members of the Compact "were linked at various levels of patronage and geographically in a series of regional layers. The layers were held together not only by ties of sentiment but by political position, by family and economic linkage, and perhaps by shared ethnicity and education among the governing elite."[3] This colonial oligarchy was favoured by most of the lieutenant-governors and monopolized government positions, government contracts, and large land grants. Its members saw themselves as the gentlemen of the colony, a class akin to the British aristocracy. To their opponents, they were pretentious and corrupt beneficiaries of undeserved patronage.

The Family Compact resisted growing opposition demands after 1815 for land reforms, secularization of clergy reserves (or at least their distribution among all religious denominations), and greater power for the elected Assembly. In Assembly elections, the oligarchy could count on significant support from British immigrants against the allegedly pro-American Reformers. Leaders of the Roman Catholic Church, who feared the consequences for a religious minority of majoritarian rule espoused by the Reformers, also supported the status quo. By the 1830s, an uneasy electoral alliance existed between the Family Compact and the Orange Order, the Roman Catholic hierarchy, and some moderate Reformers.

In the Assembly, Reform members had difficulty uniting as a cohesive party, although they did share some common objectives. One such goal was the defence of the civil rights of Upper Canada's American-born population. Bishop Strachan and his supporters called into question the property rights of

"aliens" and, by inference, the voting rights for American émigrés of the post-Loyalist period. Only British intervention in 1828 settled this issue in the immigrants' favour. The clergy reserves issue also briefly united Reformers, causing conservative reformers such as Egerton Ryerson, a leader of one of the Methodist churches, to make common cause with radical politicians. Indications in the early 1830s that Britain would move to resolve the reserves question caused Ryerson, who rejected popular democracy in terms similar to those used by the Family Compact, to break with his former allies.

In the 1830s, two poles of reform were to be found in the Assembly. One, associated with Dr W.W. Baldwin and his son Robert, called for a continued role for Britain in colonial government and even accepted an appointed Executive Council as long as the members had the support of a majority in the elected Assembly. Radical Reformers supported the notion of a cabinet drawn from the majority group in the legislature but believed its achievement would be only a half-measure of reform. Led by William Lyon Mackenzie, Marshall Spring Bidwell, and Dr John Rolph, the radicals wanted the Executive Council, like the Assembly, to be an elected body with the lieutenant-governor reduced to a figurehead. They also wanted to fill other government positions in the colony through election rather than appointment.

As in Lower Canada, when the Reformers controlled the Upper Canadian Assembly, they were reluctant to pass money bills, most notably the civil list, which authorized the salaries of the lieutenant-governor's appointees. The administration demanded that the list be voted for long periods, such as the reign of a particular sovereign, so that its patronage efforts would not be continuously thwarted by elected Assembly members.

Given its support from a large percentage of new British immigrants, the governing clique had no need to fear, as it did in Lower Canada, the constant dominance of the Assembly by Reform members. The squabbling Reformers lost their majority in 1830, regained it in 1834, and lost it again in 1836. The win by the Tories in 1836 was controversial. Sir Francis Bond Head, a gentleman-adventurer who became lieutenant-governor in late 1835, was less willing than some of his predecessors to attempt to reconcile the

Papineau and Mackenzie: Rebels with a Cause

LOUIS-JOSEPH PAPINEAU

Louis-Joseph Papineau was born in 1786, the son of a notary who served in the Assembly and purchased a seigneury in 1801. He studied law before following his father into politics. Elected to the Assembly in June 1808, Papineau quickly rose to leadership positions within the Parti canadien, and was chosen by the Assembly majority as Speaker in 1815, a position he held until 1837.

Papineau served as a militia captain in the War of 1812, and until the late 1820s supported British parliamentary institutions, arguing that rule by an Assembly majority would be consistent with British political traditions.

In 1822, Papineau and John Neilson led a delegation to London to oppose British plans to unite the two Canadas. Papineau soured on British institutions and became more enamoured of American democracy as he tired of the contempt with which the British-appointed lieutenant governors treated resolutions passed by the people's representatives in the Assembly.

In many ways, Papineau's views seemed a bundle of contradictions. By 1837, he was a republican, a democrat, and an anticlerical nationalist who denounced Britain's political and economic oppression of Lower Canadians. Yet he was also a vigorous supporter of the seigneurial system. After purchasing his father's seigneury in 1817, he had become lord of the manor to about 300 people, a number that swelled as a result of both migration and births to over 3000 in 1852. He was not an ideal master. In an analysis of Petite Nation, Papineau's seigneury on the north shore of the Ottawa River, Claude Baribeau concludes: "On the one hand, he took part in a feudal type of exploitation that he condemned elsewhere; on the other, he gave to anglophone capitalists the responsibility of exploiting the forestry resources of his seigneury, commercializing agriculture and to an extent proletarianizing his people, activities that he reproached elsewhere as an agrarian, anti-capitalist nationalist."[4] The contradictions in his personal life aside, there is little doubt that he spoke for a Lower Canadian majority in rejecting the notion of land as simply capitalist real estate to be bought and sold for whatever price speculators believed it could fetch.

Reluctant to turn to armed force in 1837, Papineau played little role in the military side of the rebellion. He fled to the

Louis-Joseph Papineau.
Library and Archives Canada/C21005

United States and attempted both there and in France to encourage official efforts to dislodge Britain from Canada. His efforts met with little success. Amnestied in 1844, Papineau returned to Quebec in 1845. He was re-elected to the Assembly in 1847 and remained there until 1854, serving as an inspiration for the opposition group that became the Parti rouge. At the same time he supervised the construction of a manor house inspired by castles on the Loire River, to which he retired from politics in 1854, the year the seigneurial system was abolished. He died at his manor house at Montebello in 1871.

WILLIAM LYON MACKENZIE

Born in 1795 in Dundee, Scotland, Mackenzie came from a poor farming background. He received a modest business education and in 1820 set sail for Upper Canada, seeking advancement beyond the modest clerical jobs he had found at home. Four years of shopkeeping later, he started the *Colonial Advocate* in Queenston in 1824, moving his family (which eventually included seven children) and the paper to York later that year.

The *Advocate* became the leading voice of the radicals in the colony, particularly after several younger members of the elite destroyed Mackenzie's printing press in 1826. Elected to the Assembly in 1828, he was expelled five times by the Tory majority for allegedly libelling them, but he was always re-elected in the subsequent by-election. Mackenzie regarded the Compact as a collection of corrupt, pompous individuals whose public high-mindedness concealed an attachment to the public trough.

Against Tory assertions of the need for a hierarchical society where each person knew his or her place, Mackenzie extolled a society of small farmers and small businessmen of relatively equal wealth and equal opportunities for education. Influenced, like Papineau, by romanticized notions of what the United States represented, Mackenzie railed against land speculators, special privileges for the Church of England, corporate entities such as the Compact-controlled Bank of Upper Canada, and a myriad of policies that he blamed for the creation of a system of social classes in Upper Canada.

Elected the first mayor of Toronto in 1834, Mackenzie reached the peak of his influence in the Assembly the following year when the reformers won an electoral majority. He published his Seventh Report of the Committee on Grievances, demanding that elected politicians rather than British appointees have power in the colony. When the reformers lost their majority and Mackenzie his seat in the 1836 election orchestrated by Governor Head, Mackenzie abandoned any hope of peaceful change. He made preparations for armed resistance, coordinating his efforts to a degree with Papineau with whom he corresponded frequently.

William Lyon Mackenzie.
Library and Archives Canada/C1993, detail

After the rebellion failed, Mackenzie fled to the United States and attempted to organize exiles on Navy Island in the Niagara River for an invasion of Upper Canada. This earned him 11 months in prison in Rochester, New York, and disillusioned him regarding the Americans' concern for spreading democracy. Allowed to return to Canada in 1849, Mackenzie was re-elected to the Assembly in 1851 and continued to press for radical reforms until illness forced his retirement in 1858. He died in 1861.

competing claims of Compact and Reformers. Faced with a truculent Assembly in 1836, he dissolved it and called new elections.

Head made a mockery of the election. He blackmailed voters who wished their constituencies to receive roads and other government expenditures, and he condoned bullying tactics by Orangemen at the polls and dubious procedures by government-appointed returning officers. After the election, only 17 Reformers held their seats in the 63-member Assembly. Convinced that Head's tactics had produced this result, the Reformers were livid. There was great bitterness at Head's scare-mongering when he claimed throughout the election that a vote for the Reformers was a vote for annexation to the United States.

Moderate Reformers such as Robert Baldwin, while appalled by Head, believed that they would eventually achieve political change in Upper Canada if they bided their time and continued to apply pressure in London. The radicals were less sanguine. They took particular aim at Head's announcement of the endowment of 57 Anglican rectories, a decision made but not announced by his predecessor in his last days of office. They also attacked Head's dismissals of government officials who were apparently sympathetic to the Reform cause.

Like Papineau, Mackenzie gradually became convinced of the need for a break between Upper Canada and Britain and concluded that this should be achieved by the use of violence if necessary. The behaviour of British authorities helped to drive him to this position. When Lord Goderich, the colonial secretary, ordered Lieutenant-Governor Sir John Colborne to begin charging all immigrants for land, his reasoning demonstrated Britain's distaste for the egalitarian principles espoused by Mackenzie and his associates. Goderich wrote:

> I know not how to propound in plainer terms than I have already done . . . the necessity that there should be in every society a class of laborers as well as a class of capitalists or land-owners. The high rate of wages and the scarcity of labour is the complaint of every growing Society. To force that condition artificially, by tempting into the class of Landowners those who would naturally remain laborers, appears to me a course opposed to the dearest interests of the Colony . . . because, as I have stated, to the good of every society a supply of Labour and a division of employment must be indispensable.[5]

As in Lower Canada, the land issue in Upper Canada provoked resentment that could be focused on the political elite. While new settlers were increasingly forced to buy land or move to remote areas of the colony, speculators were able to purchase choice lands relatively cheaply. The Upper Canadian government in 1826 sold 3.5 million hectares of Crown reserves at a low price to the Canada Land Company, headed by John Galt. Later Galt's company bought another

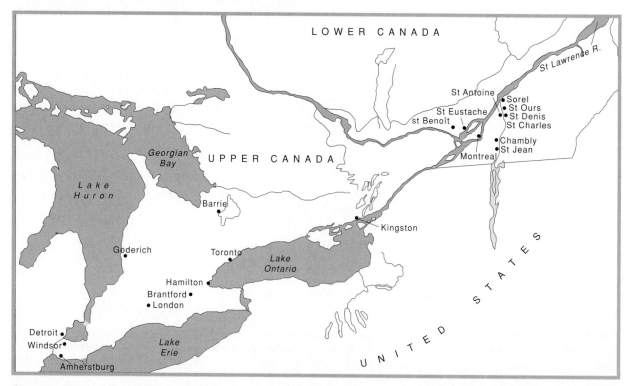

MAP 16.1 Sites of the 1837–38 rebellion.

2.8 million hectares along Lake Huron, the so-called Huron Tract. To the Reformers, already riled by the grants of land to Family Compact members and their supporters, the sale of land to a new group of speculators added insult to injury.

By the fall of 1837, Mackenzie believed that an armed uprising would be necessary to bring his vision of a frontier agrarian democracy into being. His newspaper, now called *The Constitution* (formerly the *Colonial Advocate*), presented a blueprint for the state of Upper Canada that was modelled on the American constitution. However, the planning for a rebellion, undertaken mainly in the taverns of republican publicans in the Home District, was amateurish and confused. Convinced by his oratory that the government was planning to confiscate their land, many Reformers joined Mackenzie's cause out of sheer desperation.

The departure of Upper Canadian troops to quell the rebellion in Lower Canada gave Mackenzie and his confederates the chance they were waiting for. With Toronto now largely unprotected, the chances of military success seemed within their grasp. Mackenzie's original plan was to seize a large cache of government arms in Toronto on 7 December. Due to developments in Lower Canada, his lieutenants, in his absence, decided to push the date ahead to the 4th, gathering men at Montgomery's Tavern north of Toronto for the assault on the capital. But news of the change of date did not reach all the rebels, and confusion about the timing of the uprising limited the number of men available to take Toronto.

Unfortunately for the rebels, the gathering on the 4th tipped off loyalists in the area, who warned Governor Head of the insurgency. He was able to assemble 1500 volunteers, and reports of the size of this force caused many of the rebels to abandon Mackenzie. On the fateful Thursday, Mackenzie's ragtag army therefore numbered only about 400 men and they were quickly dispersed.

Word of rebellion in the Home District spread to the London District, where, as in the Toronto area, American-born settlers proved to be the most willing to take up arms. Inevitably, given the communications of the period, the news arrived in distorted form. Rumours circulated in the London area that Mackenzie's forces were in control in the capital and that government loyalists, assisted by the violence-prone Orangemen, were planning to arrest local Reformers. To forestall the latter event, Dr Charles Duncombe hurriedly organized local Reformers to make a stand, but pro-government volunteers, better armed than their opponents, carried the day.

The rebellion in Upper Canada resulted in 885 arrests, with 422 of them in the Home District, 163 in the London District, 90 in Gore (which included the present-day cities of Hamilton, Guelph, Kitchener, and Brantford), and 75 in Midland (which included Kingston). Most of those arrested were established farmers or tradesmen, men neither wealthy nor poor.

EXECUTION OF LOUNT AND MATTHEWS.

Upper Canadian rebels Samuel Lount and Peter Matthews were hanged in 1838. After the execution, Lount's widow, Elizabeth, wrote a public letter accusing Chief Justice John Beverley Robinson of callousness and treachery in her husband's death. Her letter, which raged against "the series of hardships brought upon me and my orphan children by you, and others of the tory party of Canada," was one of the few pieces of writing by a woman that was to appear in the Reform press.
Library and Archives Canada/C1242

For their part in the rebellion, two men were hanged: Samuel Lount, a blacksmith, and Peter Matthews, a farmer. While Lount hailed from Pennsylvania, Matthews was a veteran of the War of 1812 on the British side. Another rebel, Colonel A.G.W. Van Egmond, a veteran of the Napoleonic Wars, had settled in the Huron Tract and complained bitterly that the Canada Land Company provided no services to settlers. Cajoled by Mackenzie to serve as military leader of the rebels, the 65-year-old colonel was imprisoned for his role in the rebellion despite his status as a war hero.

Mackenzie and other rebel leaders fled to the United States. Artisans, small farmers, and labourers in the United States, who opposed growing tendencies in their own country toward social inequality, sympathized with the "republican" cause of the rebels in the Canadas, that is with their call for democratic control over their lives rather than rule by foreigners. With the help of sympathetic Americans, the exiles formed Hunters' Lodges and conducted border raids on Upper Canada in hopes of rallying opposition within the colony. But a combination of British troops, lack of popular enthusiasm, and the unwillingness of the American government to alienate Britain by supporting the rebels doomed their efforts at a new rebellion. In Upper Canada in 1838, 156 men were imprisoned, 99 deported, and 18 hanged for continuing to foment rebellion. At least 30 people, mostly rebels, were killed when radicals in exile in the United States, aided by their American sympathizers, attacked a militia barracks in Windsor.

ASSESSING THE REBELLIONS

The rebellions of the 1830s can be explained in several ways: as class struggles, ethnic struggles, and ideological conflicts. The rebellions pitted social classes against one another and had economic roots in the complaints of farmers, labourers, and the landless against the entrenched oligarchies of Upper and Lower Canada. The importance of middle-class leadership in the rebellions of both provinces, as well as the role of the prominent seigneur Papineau in Lower Canada, suggests that explanations stressing only the oppression of the majority may partly miss the mark. Elements of the middle class and even of the wealthy were suspicious of grasping landowners and a political oligarchy.

In Lower Canada, the class struggle had an ethnic character because most of the elite were of British descent and most of the rebels of French descent. The prominent presence of English speakers on the rebel side and French speakers on the government side suggests the need for caution in employing an ethnic explanation for the Lower Canadian rebellions. Because the mass of rural people suffering from economic dislocation were francophone, the ethnic division could hardly be other than what it was.

Although material interests motivated the various actors in the rebellion drama, ideas were also important. The rebels were influenced by the example of American democracy, British notions of parliamentary rule, and the anticlericalism evident in the French revolutions of 1789 and 1830. The ruling elites followed the model of British society in which social classes were rigidly stratified to create social stability. But even in Great Britain, ideas about society and governance were changing.

THE STRUGGLE FOR RESPONSIBLE GOVERNMENT

In 1838, John George Lambton, Earl of Durham, was named governor-general of the Canadas. He was asked to prepare a report on the causes of the rebellions and to suggest ways of avoiding recurrences. Heir to collieries in Newcastle, England, he was, like many capitalists, suspicious of aristocratic landowners, who were widely blamed for high food costs that in turn led to high labour costs in factories. After spending only a few months in the colonies, he produced a report early in 1839. Two of its main recommendations were union of Lower Canada and Upper Canada, and the granting of responsible government.

Durham was impressed with the moderate Reformers of Upper Canada, who shared his vision of a society organized not on the Compact's principles of rigid social hierarchy but on the basis of the individual's pursuit of profit unhindered by unnecessary monopolies. He blamed the Family Compact for the colony's slow development, accepting the Reformers' view that undeveloped land held for speculative purposes hindered the progress of the colony. Responsible government, Durham felt, would weaken the power of the landholding, office-holding oligarchy and allow market forces to prevail in Upper Canada. To ensure that an elected government in the Canadas would not harm British interests, he recommended that Britain retain control over foreign relations, trade, and the distribution of public lands.

Durham's partial embrace of the Upper Canadian reform perspective, or at least its more moderate version, was not matched by sympathy for Lower Canadian reformers. After spending a mere eight days in Lower Canada, Durham concluded that the rebellion there had been largely an ethnic issue. He claimed to have found "two nations warring in the bosom of a single state."[6] Ignoring the conservatism of colonial policy and the extent to which the Patriotes had embraced liberal political ideology, Durham blamed Lower Canada's economic problems on the reactionary prejudices of the Canadiens.

An ethnocentric Englishman, Durham regarded the French Canadians as backward. He believed that anything that tended to assimilate them to British Protestant values would be for their benefit as individuals. Indeed, as a supporter of individual liberties he placed no value on the protection of the collective liberties of a subordinate group. From his point of view, an amalgamation of the two Canadas and the granting of official status to only the English language constituted no attack on liberty. Instead it would be a step along the road to material advancement for the Canadiens.

In 1840, the British Parliament passed the Act of Union, which created the United Province of Canada. Durham's call for responsible government was, however, rejected. The governor would continue to appoint members to the Executive and Legislative councils according to his own perception of which individuals could best be counted upon to reflect British colonial interests. The elected Assembly would remain a relatively powerless body. The institutional structure that prevailed before the rebellions had been restored, except that where there had been two governors, two Executive Councils, two Legislative Councils, and two Assemblies, there would now be only one of each.

The union was unpopular in both Canadas. Although Assembly seats were divided equally between the two Canadas so that Upper Canada would not suffer because of its smaller population, Upper Canadians generally feared French and Catholic domination. Lower Canadians, for their part, were convinced that union was a plot to achieve their assimilation—a goal that Durham had openly recommended.

Despite these fears, reform was in the air and gradually won the day. With the radicals routed by the defeat of the rebellions, moderate reformers in the two Canadas joined forces in support of Durham's vision of a progressive capitalist society. The Reformers in Canada West were led by Robert Baldwin, a Toronto lawyer, and railway promoter Francis Hincks. In Canada East, Louis-Hippolyte LaFontaine, a lawyer and former Patriote who had not taken part in the rebellions, was the major proponent of an alliance with Upper Canadian Reformers.

LaFontaine's political position was carefully calculated. He argued that by winning responsible government and ensuring the formation of a progressive administration requiring Canadien cooperation, the French culture of Lower Canada could be preserved despite Durham's wishes. Initially regarded as a traitor for proposing these views, LaFontaine failed to win a Lower Canadian riding in the Assembly elections of 1841. Once it became clear that Britain would not allow Lower Canada to exist as a separate province, LaFontaine's option began to appear realistic, if not entirely palatable, to his compatriots.

The reform alliance demonstrated considerable strength in Assembly elections through the 1840s, but successive governors proved unwilling to grant the degree of colonial autonomy implied in the phrase "responsible government." Lord Sydenham (1840–41), Sir Charles Bagot (1841–43), and Sir Charles Metcalfe (1843–46) attempted, in varying degrees, to retain the former powers of the lieutenant-governors, although Bagot in particular was prepared to go a long way to meet the Reformers' demands for some degree of power sharing.

Metcalfe's successor, Lord Elgin, arrived at a time when British trade and colonial policy were in the process of a significant transformation, most notably in the economic realm, with the abandonment of imperial protectionism in favour of free trade. This alteration in trade policy reflected a fundamental

VOICES FROM THE PAST

A School Lesson in the 1840s

Every Boy's Own Book, a school text in use in Canada West in the 1840s, provides clues to particular social values that educational authorities hoped children would absorb. The text attempted to convey to young people definite views about monarchy, imperialism, patriarchy, and democracy.

> "Great Britain–a power to which Rome in the height of her glory is not to be compared, which had dotted the whole earth with her possessions and military posts–whose morning drum follows the Sun, and keeping company with his beams, circles the globe daily with one continuous and unbroken strain of the martial airs of England."–Daniel Webster.
>
> Lesson 1st.
>
> Adam, the first King, as well as the first man, was the father of his own subjects, and when the eldest son succeeded to his father's authority, he succeeded also to his title of father, and hence the style of father is given to this day to all Kings, which points remarkably to the origin of Government, or Kingship, in the time of man's innocency in Eden, which God first instituted there, both in nature and by positive command. And therefore we owe to our Sovereign the same obedience, which Adam's children or subjects paid to him, for God's commands and institutions descend through all ages to the end of time, and Government is of the same necessity and obligation now, as it was when it was first imposed by God, and it is equally "his ordinance" now, as it was then.

If Government and its succession was ordained by God himself,–then it is as natural that it should succeed in the same track as for the sun to proceed in his diurnal course.

There are but three kinds of Government. When the sovereign power is vested in one person it is called a Monarchy: if in all the nobles it is called an Aristocracy, or an Oligarchy if confined to a few of these: if an Assembly of the people have the chief authority, it is called a Democracy or a Republic.*

Of all the different species of Governments, the Monarchical is the most ancient and natural, originating at first in parental authority, hence Kings are called the fathers of their people. . .

Democracy on the other hand, is that form of Government, which irrespective of the obligation of law and custom, places the present will of the populace above all restraint, and of course leaves the general weal entirely at the mercy of that, which is more fickle and capricious, than the winds of heaven.

* Note. In strictness of language, a great difference exists between a Republic and a Democracy. Properly speaking, the term Republic, is more justly applicable to Great Britain than to any other nation on earth, for although it may be objected, that one of its pillars is Monarchy, yet it is very evident, that the whole tendency and practice of the British system is Republican, that is impartially respective of the general good.[7]

change in attitude toward the white-settler colonies. Britain no longer considered it necessary to control their internal political processes. Elgin became the agent of this new British attitude in the Canadas. After elections held in 1848 returned a large reform majority in the two sections of the United Canadas, Elgin called upon LaFontaine and Robert Baldwin to form a ministry. The power of patronage, once in the hands of the governor, was handed over to an Executive Council (cabinet) that enjoyed a majority in the elected Assembly.

Traditionally in English-Canadian historical writing, the achievement of "responsible government" in British North America is regarded as a watershed. It meant that Great Britain accepted the right of the colonies to a large degree of internal self-rule and would allow the party system, which had in any case been active in the Canadas before the rebellions, to achieve legitimacy. For many nationalists in Canada East, however, the main political objective was not the achievement of responsible government but the dissolution of the union of Upper and Lower Canada decreed by Britain in 1840.

RESPONSIBLE GOVERNMENT IN ACTION

The government of LaFontaine and Baldwin, unlike its predecessors in both the pre-union and union periods, could claim to have a mandate from the electors. How faithfully it fulfilled that mandate is debatable. As apostles of economic progress, LaFontaine and Baldwin, while in opposition, had supported the completion of the St Lawrence canals at taxpayers' expense. In office they showed their eagerness for the state to play a positive role in the transportation revolution. They placed the Guarantee Act before the legislature in 1849, pledging the government's credit for half the bonds of any railroad over 120 kilometres in length after half the line was built. While the provisions of this act were restricted in 1851 to the three railways then under construction, later guarantees were also given to the Grand Trunk Railway, the most ambitious of the pre-Confederation railway schemes. The boards of the favoured railway companies and the membership of Canadian cabinets in the 1850s bore striking resemblances. Cynics claimed that the unelected cliques who had previously handed themselves free or cheap land had now been replaced by an elected clique who used their offices to support pet railway projects and other industrial and commercial endeavours.

The Tories, believing that they had been abandoned by Britain, were outraged. First the trade laws that gave protected markets to Canadian products and encouraged Americans to ship through Canadian ports had been abandoned. Then the political power of the oligarchy had been destroyed. In 1849, Lord Elgin agreed to sign into law a legislative motion called the Rebellion Losses Bill, which provided compensation for Lower Canadians, including rebels, whose property had been damaged in 1837 or 1838 (an earlier bill gave similar compensation to Upper Canadians, whose losses were much smaller than those of Lower Canadians). The bill caused the conservative forces to explode in anger. A Tory mob in Montreal attacked the Parliament building, then located in that city, and burned it to the ground.

By 1854, the old oligarchy and the upstarts of 1848 found they had more in common than they once believed. Agrarian reformers known as the Clear Grits, whose views harkened back to the perspectives of the pre-rebellion radical reformers, had won several seats in Canada West in 1851. This group denounced the moderate Reformers for their support of big business interests and extolled free trade and inexpensive government.

A new Reform alliance gradually emerged around George Brown, editor of the *Globe* and a businessman and land speculator in the Toronto area. Brown embraced the Clear Grits' calls for cheaper government and free trade, but he rejected their anti-business bias. His denunciations of the legislature's attempts to impose publicly supported Catholic schools on Canada West helped him gain a dominant position among English-speaking Reformers. By the end of the 1850s, Brown's Reform Party had eclipsed the more radical Clear Grit movement.

The emergence of the new Reform coalition in Canada West exposed the Baldwin-Hincks alliance as Tories in disguise. Hincks replaced Baldwin as head of the Canada West half of the coalition government in 1851, but by 1854 Brown's Reformers and Clear Grits held the majority of Canada West seats, with a new group of moderate Conservatives constituting a respectable minority and the Hincksites reduced to a rump. The LaFontaine group, now led by A.N. Morin and E.P. Taché and generally referred to as the Bleus to distinguish them from the radical reformers, who were labelled the Rouges, held an overwhelming number of seats in Canada East. But the Hincksites provided too small a group of partners from Canada West to form a stable government.

The Bleus agreed to join a coalition with the Conservatives led by the "laird of Hamilton," Allan MacNab. A charter member of the old Family Compact, MacNab had extensive land, railroad, and other business interests. He had played an active role in crushing the rebellions in Canada West and he strongly opposed the march toward responsible government. Over time, he begrudgingly accepted the need to implement political change. "Railways are my politics," he allegedly responded when asked how he could join forces with his old political enemies. On the whole, economic development was creating new political alliances, and out of these alliances embryonic political parties emerged: the Conservatives wanted the state to help underwrite private economic development, while

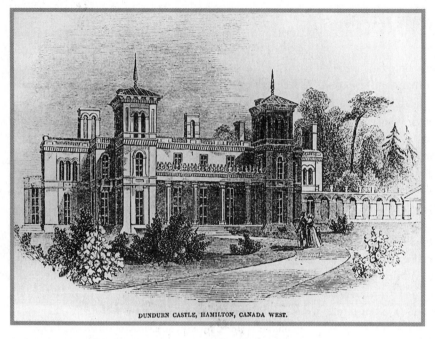

Dundurn Castle, Allan MacNab's home.
Courtesy of Dundurn Castle, Department of Culture and Recreation, Corporation of the City of Hamilton

the Liberals favoured more modest state involvement. Appropriately, the new administration assumed the label Liberal-Conservative.

The Conservatives of the 1840s and 1850s consisted partly of the old Compact politicians. They also included other strong supporters of the British tie, people who after the granting of responsible government were difficult to distinguish from the Baldwin-Hincks group of Reformers. They, too, were involved in the new manufacturing firms, railways, and insurance companies that began to spring up in the 1840s and 1850s in Canada West. A rising star in their ranks, after his election to the Assembly for the constituency of Kingston in 1844, was John A. Macdonald, a young lawyer-businessman. In 1857, Macdonald replaced MacNab as the leader from Canada West in the governing Liberal-Conservative coalition.

Macdonald's opposite number was George-Étienne Cartier, a former Patriote turned wealthy lawyer whose corporate links typified the dramatic change from feudal to capitalist connections among the leading French-Canadian politicians. His clients included the Grand Trunk Railway, the Seminary of Montreal, the French government, and various insurance, mining, and railway companies, and he had extensive investments in property and banks.

Industrial capitalists and their lawyers in Canada East were predominantly English-speaking, and the French-speaking element of this group formed a minuscule proportion of the Quebec population. The francophone elite's dominance in Canada East politics was the result of the shrewd informal alliance their leaders made with the hierarchy of the Catholic Church. The Bleus militantly defended church control of both Catholic education in the United Province of Canada and social services, marriage, and the family life of Catholics in Canada East. In return, the clergy thundered against the Rouges and other political opponents of the Bleus who defended separation of church and state.

For Cartier, the leading Bleu, the alliance with Quebec's dour clergymen appears to have been opportunistic. While as a politician he stressed the need to confirm the church's right to govern the moral lives of its adherents, he did not submit his own private life to church control—he had an opulent lifestyle and lived openly in a common-law relationship with his wife's cousin. The church, in turn, was pleased with Cartier's political services and did not intrude upon his private affairs.

The Rouges were the spiritual heirs of the radicals of 1837 and 1838. Supporters of free trade and of a property-owning democracy, they joined the Reformers of Canada West in attacking the governing coalition's decisions that granted government moneys to special interests. The Rouges favoured low taxes and complete separation of church and state, including an end to public support of church-controlled schools. Strongest in Montreal, the Rouges had important allies in the Violettes, based in Quebec City. The Violettes were moderate liberals who shared the Rouges' economic policies but trod gently on issues involving the church. The church's resurgence in the

George-Étienne Cartier.
Library and Archives Canada/C2728

countryside in the period after the rebellions limited Reform penetration outside the cities, and the combined strength of the Rouges and Violettes, while impressive in vote totals, was not enough to prevent the Bleus from winning the lion's share of the seats in Canada East in the pre-Confederation period.

LAND AND THE CHANGING POLITICAL ORDER

Two pieces of legislation passed in 1854 demonstrate the ways in which the combination of responsible government and the rise of industrial capitalism forced changes in the thinking of conservative politicians. The abolition of the clergy reserves ended the Church of England's status as the established church in the Canadas, a status that had entitled the church to special state subsidies. At the same time, the abolition of seigneurial tenure made all Lower Canadian farms saleable commodities.

Some historians have argued that the decision of the government of the United Province of Canada to require habitant compensation of seigneurs removed funds from the rural economy that habitants might otherwise have used to modernize their operations.

Such a drain on the potential investment income of farmers was at cross-purposes with the needs of the new industrial system, but the agenda of the political elite was not always determined exclusively by the interests of capital. While this elite, which included a number of seigneurs, wanted to promote industry, they would support no actions that appeared to be attacks on property rights.

EDUCATION FOR A NEW SOCIETY

One area in which the role of the state changed significantly in the mid-nineteenth century was education. Before the 1840s, only a minority of children had formal schooling. The state had no control over the curriculum and had no right to tell parents how their children should be educated. In the era of responsible government, education became the focus of public debate and political action. With literacy increasingly a factor in economic development, the state assumed greater control over who should be educated and what they should learn.

From the earliest days of European settlement, the elite made an effort to see that their children received formal instruction. They either sent their children, at considerable cost, to private schools or hired tutors for home instruction. By the nineteenth century, locally run classical colleges, such as the Collège de Montréal, and grammar schools, such as Upper Canada College in Toronto, provided education for the sons of the elite. The curriculum in these institutions included Greek, Latin, and rhetoric, the "basics" for the professions of theology, law, and medicine. Although Upper Canada's grammar schools received state subsidies, they served only a tiny minority of the population. In 1839, there were only 300 pupils enrolled in grammar schools in a colony that was home to over 200 000 children under the age of 16. A further 14 776 Upper Canadian children attended common schools, which were sustained with the help of grants from the state.

Both Conservatives and Reformers favoured the expansion of the common school system, but they differed on how public education should be financed. Conservatives called for a special property tax to fund education, while Reformers favoured using the proceeds from the sale of clergy reserves, which after 1840 were divided among the various denominations, with the Church of England receiving a disproportionate share. In Lower Canada, the Roman Catholic Church struggled to retain control over education, but it was hampered in its efforts to expand educational facilities by a lack of funds.

Politics also played a role in the way higher education developed in the United Canadas. As in the Atlantic region, the Church of England attempted to establish a university—King's College in Toronto—under its exclusive control. This plan was roundly attacked by other denominations, which insisted upon establishing their own colleges and upon having access to any public moneys made available for higher education. In the 1840s, the Methodists established Victoria College in Cobourg and the Church of Scotland founded Queen's College in Kingston. As early as 1843, Robert Baldwin introduced a University Bill, which would transform the Anglican-controlled King's College into a non-sectarian arts college known as the University of Toronto, with which other denominational colleges might affiliate. Baldwin finally saw his bill passed in 1849. Contrary to Baldwin's wishes, denominationalism survived in the affiliated colleges of the University of Toronto and reasserted itself later in the century when Queen's went its separate way and the Baptists established McMaster University. In Canada East, linguistic and religious differences were responsible for the emergence of three universities: Université Laval in Quebec City, McGill University in Montreal, and Bishops University in the Eastern Townships.

CONCLUSION

By the late 1840s, parliamentary democracy had been established in the Canadas, but it did not live up to expectations held by radicals in the 1830s. While most radical theorists believed in a society of virtually equal property-holders whose political representatives would fight against privileges for the few, the legislature of the 1850s was dominated by wealthy capitalists and lawyers, tiny groups within the general population. Yet the need to be elected guaranteed that they could not operate as the oligarchies before 1837 did. They might use their positions in the legislature to aid their own business projects, but they also had to be attentive to voter concerns. Measures such as greater state aid to schools and the abolition of clergy reserves and the seigneurial system in 1854, while serving the interests of a nascent capitalism, were also attempts to respond to popular grievances. The rebels of the 1830s might regard the legislature of the 1850s as a travesty of the democratic ideal, but they could be rightly proud that they had forced Britain to take an important step in granting popular control over government.

A HISTORIOGRAPHICAL DEBATE

Causes of the Rebellion in Lower Canada

What were the causes of the Rebellion of 1837–38 in Lower Canada? Historians, often using many of the same documents, have provided dramatically different accounts of the events leading to the rebellion, the key demands of the rebels, and ultimately the character of the society that was in rebellion against the British conquerors. Two poles of the debate are represented by Fernand Ouellet and Allan Greer.

Fernand Ouellet stresses two elements in explaining the outbreak of the rebellion and its large degree of habitant support in the rural region of the District of Montreal. First, he emphasizes the determination of the Patriote leadership, mainly French-Canadian petit-bourgeois men, to assert not only the political independence of the French-Canadian nation but also their right, as the better-educated or more affluent members of that nation, to hold political power. Second, he asserts that the habitants supported the Patriote program because they were suffering from acute poverty as a result of a series of agricultural crises. The habitants blamed these recurring crises on government policy that allowed large numbers of anglophone agricultural immigrants into the colony but did little to help habitants open new lands for a burgeoning population.

In Ouellet's opinion, the Patriotes were elitists and reactionaries who hoped to reinforce the feudal structures that predated the conquest. Their goal was to usurp power from the English and the minority of French-Canadians who supported the British program for a capitalist land-holding system and commercial society. Ouellet argues that the Patriotes opportunistically used the language of democracy to further their cause and that, in reality, they opposed the extension of the franchise to the landless—a growing group in the colony—and turned back efforts by habitants to have feudal dues abolished. When the British government refused to respond to their demands, the Patriotes, according to Ouellet, used intimidation and violence to break Britain's control over local power structures. They then called local "democratic" assemblies to support the Patriote program, cynically manipulating these meetings by providing predetermined resolutions and brooking no debate. In analyzing the Patriote motivation, Ouellet's sympathies generally appear to be with the government. Ouellet attributes habitant support for the Patriote cause to anti-government discontent accompanying the sustained agricultural crisis in Lower Canada. While Ouellet in no way minimizes the poverty of the habitants, he tends to attribute their plight to their own unwillingness to change outdated agricultural practices, not to specific policies pursued by the colonial government.[8]

Allan Greer presents the Patriotes primarily as democrats rather than nationalists. He believes they should be viewed, like the Upper Canadian rebels, as supporters of representative democracy in opposition to authoritarian rule. Patriote views reflected the republican and democratic spirit that had taken hold of much of Europe and the Americas since the American and French revolutions.

The habitants as well had imbibed something of that spirit, and it was Britain's efforts to limit or destroy Lower Canada's evolution toward democracy that mobilized habitant opposition to British rule. Greer sees poverty as a secondary cause and notes that most of the fighting occurred in the Montreal region, which was more prosperous than the rest of the colony. He argues that "to understand the habitants in the Rebellion, we must look at the habitants."[9] As they demonstrated in the popular assemblies, the habitants were interested in popular control of government—or, at least, male popular control. They were neither pro-capitalism nor pro-feudalism; like the settlers of Upper Canada, their goal was to achieve self-sufficiency. They fought feudal exactions that they regarded as excessive, but they had every reason as tenants to oppose the campaign of seigneurs, many of whom were English, for the right of landlords to do whatever they wished with their land.

Greer regards the Patriotes as the intellectual leaders of the revolt but insists that the habitants had long played an independent political role in Quebec and continued to do so during the rebellion. The habitants, he argues, exercised a degree of control over government-appointed militia officers through popular ceremonies approving investitures. Moreover, they circumvented the authority of both the curés and justices of the peace by imposing their own notions of justice on individuals through charivaris and ostracism. They spontaneously made use of such measures of popular control to enforce their campaign for non-compliance with British rule in the months leading to the rebellion.

Greer suggests that the Patriote leaders provided intellectual direction for the habitants but did not control the events that produced the military conflict between Britain and the rebels. He argues that the Patriotes were democrats first and nationalists second, and that they attempted to rally anglophones as well as francophones in their campaign for a more democratic system of government. Such attempts were unsuccessful because anglophones, especially recent immigrants, largely viewed the Patriotes as French Canadians opposing British rule. With their support thus restricted to francophone districts, the Patriotes often combined appeals to democracy with appeals to nationhood.

One might almost wonder whether Ouellet and Greer are writing about the same colony. Clearly, historical sources regarding Lower Canada during the rebellion and the period leading up to it lend themselves to several interpretations. For example, Greer makes use of the resolutions passed by the various assemblies to posit the view that a relatively homogeneous habitant population had developed a particular view of the problems facing their colony and the best ways of resolving them. Ouellet, by contrast, suggests that such a uniformity of views must have been stage-managed by the Patriote leadership. Greer challenges such a view, arguing that the habitants would not go along with, much less take up arms to defend, a revolution whose course they had little chance to influence. Ouellet maintains that habitant participation resulted from their frustration with government policies that they blamed for poverty that left many on the brink of starvation. The details of the Patriote program were less important to them than the fact that the Patriotes were fellow French Canadians who promised them some relief from their economic hardships if the *maudits anglais* were defeated.

NOTES

1 Alan Gordon, *Making Public Pasts: The Contested Terrain of Montreal's Public Memories, 1891–1930* (Montreal and Kingston: McGill-Queen's University Press, 2001), 164.

2 Montreal *Gazette*, 10 Nov. 1824, reprinted in Michael S. Cross, ed., *The Workingman in the Nineteenth Century* (Toronto: Oxford University Press, 1974), 17.

3 John Clarke, *Land, Power, and Economics on the Frontier of Upper Canada* (Montreal and Kingston: McGill-Queen's University Press, 2001), 381.

4 Translated from Claude Baribeau, *La seigneurie de la Petite-Nation 1801–1859: Le rôle économique et social du seigneur* (Hull, QC: Éditions Asticou, 1983), 112.

5 Quoted in Leo Johnson, "Land Policy, Population Growth, and Social Structure in the Home District, 1793–1851," *Ontario History* 63, 1 (March 1971): 57–58.

6 *Lord Durham's Report: An Abridgement of Report on the Affairs of British North America*, ed. Gerald M. Craig (Toronto: McClelland and Stewart, 1963), 23.

7 From John George Bridges, *The Every Boy's Own Book, or a Digest of the British Constitution, Compiled and Arranged for the Use of Schools and Private Families* (Ottawa, 1842), reprinted in *Family, School and Society in Nineteenth-Century Canada*, ed. Alison L. Prentice and Susan E. Houston (Toronto: Oxford University Press, 1975), 23–24.

8 Fernand Ouellet's views are developed in *Lower Canada 1791–1840: Social Change and Nationalism* (Toronto: McClelland and Stewart, 1980) and *Economic and Social History of Quebec* (Toronto: Macmillan, 1981). His response to Greer's interpretation of Lower Canadian social, political, and economic developments is found in a review essay in *Histoire sociale/Social History* 28, 56 (Nov. 1996): 541–54.

9 Allan Greer, *The Patriots and the People: The Rebellion of 1837 in Rural Lower Canada* (Toronto: University of Toronto Press, 1993), xi.

RELATED READINGS IN THIS SERIES

From *Foundations: Readings in Pre-Confederation Canadian History*

Allan Greer, "Parish Republics," 370–89.
"William Lyon Mackenzie's Draft Constitution, 15 November 1837," 390–93.

From Media Companion CD-ROM, Volume I

Lord John Russell's Ten Resolutions, 1837
W. L. Mackenzie's Appeal to Arms
Letter from Louis-Joseph Papineau to Wilmot, December 16, 1822

SELECTED READING

See also Selected Reading for Chapter 15.

On Upper Canadian politics, Gerald Craig's *Upper Canada: The Formative Years* (Toronto: McClelland and Stewart, 1963) is informative but conservative. The rebel view is presented forcefully in Stanley Ryerson, *Unequal Union: Confederation and the Roots of Conflict in the Canadas, 1815–1873*, 2nd ed. (Toronto: Progress Books, 1983). An attempt to gauge popular thinking regarding public issues of this period is Jeffrey L. McNairn's *Public Opinion and Deliberative Democracy* (Toronto: University of Toronto Press, 2000). Events leading to the Rebellions of 1837 and 1838 and the conduct of the rebellions are outlined in Colin Read and Ronald J. Stagg, eds., *The Rebellion of 1837 in Upper Canada: A Collection of Documents* (Toronto: Champlain Society, 1985), and Colin Read, *The Rising in Western Upper Canada, 1837–1838* (Toronto: University of Toronto Press, 1982).

For Lower Canada, the causes of the 1837–38 rebellions are explored in Jean-Paul Bernard, *Les rébellions de 1837–1838* (Montreal: Boréal Express, 1983) and in the works by Ouellet and Creighton cited in Chapter 11. More favourable treatment of the unsuccessful revolutionaries is found in Allan Greer, *The Patriots and the People: The Rebellion of 1837 in Rural Lower Canada* (Toronto: University of Toronto Press, 1993); Gérard Filteau, *Histoire des Patriotes* (Sillery, QC: Septentrion, 2003); and Stanley Ryerson, *Unequal Union*. Ouellet's *Louis-Joseph Papineau: A Divided Soul* (Ottawa: Canadian Historical Association, 1964) provides a brief biography of the key Patriote. Events of the rebellions are outlined in Elinor Kyte Senior, *Redcoats and Patriotes: The Rebellions in Lower Canada* (Montreal: McGill-Queen's University Press, 1981). The involvement of American democrats in efforts to overthrow British rule in the Canadas is discussed in Andrew Bonthius, "The Patriot War of 1837–1838: Locofocoism with a Gun?," *Labour/Le Travail*, 52 (Fall 2003): 9–43. On the treatment of the defeated rebels, see Beverley Boissery, *A Deep Sense of Wrong: The Treason Trials of Lower Canadian Rebels after the 1838 Rebellion* (Toronto: Dundurn, 1995).

The politics of the 1840s and 1850s are discussed in Derek Pollard and Ged Martin, eds., *Canada 1849* (Edinburgh: University of Edinburgh Press, 2001); J.M.S. Careless, *The Union of the Canadas: The Growth of Canadian Institutions 1841–1857* (Toronto: McClelland and Stewart, 1967), and Jacques Monet, *The Last Cannon Shot: A Study of French-Canadian Nationalism, 1837–1850* (Toronto: University of Toronto Press, 1969). Monet's positive assessment of the post-rebellion political elite contrasts with Brian Young's critical evaluation of a key member in *George-Étienne Cartier: Montreal Bourgeois* (Montreal: McGill-Queen's University Press, 1981). A continuing rebel tradition is discussed in Jean-Paul Bernard, *Les Rouges: libéralisme, nationalisme et anticlericalisme au milieu du XIXe siècle* (Montreal: Les Presses de l'Université du Québec, 1971),

and Allan Greer, "The Birth of the Police in Canada," in *Colonial Leviathan: State Formation in Mid-Nineteenth-Century Canada*, ed. Allan Greer and Ian Radforth (Toronto: University of Toronto Press, 1992), 17–49. On Lord Durham, see Janet Ajzenstat, *The Political Thought of Lord Durham* (Montreal: McGill-Queen's University Press, 1988). The causes and character of educational changes are treated somewhat differently in Susan Houston and Alison Prentice, *Schooling and Scholars in Nineteenth-Century Ontario* (Toronto: University of Toronto Press, 1988), and Bruce Curtis, *Building the Educational State: Canada West, 1836–1871* (London, ON: Althouse, 1988). The emergence of universities in Upper Canada is chronicled in A.B. McKillop, *Matters of Mind: The University in Ontario, 1791–1851* (Toronto: University of Toronto Press, 1994), and Martin L. Friedland, *The University of Toronto: A History* (Toronto: University of Toronto Press, 2002). Rural responses to taxation levied to support public schools and municipal government in Canada East are explored in Wendie Nelson, "'Rage against the Dying of the Light': Interpreting the Guerre des Éteignoirs," *Canadian Historical Review* 81, 4 (December 2000): 551–81.

WEBLINKS

1837 Rebellion

www.edunetconnect.com/cat/rebellions/index.html

This site offers information on nearly every aspect of the rebellion: biographical information on the leaders, timelines, issues that provoked the conflict, and consequences.

Lord Durham

www.collectionscanada.ca/confederation/h18-2086-e.html

A brief account of Lord Durham's activities as Governor General is offered at this Library and Archives Canada site.

Act of Union 1840

www.collectionscanada.ca/confederation/h18-2954-e.html

The text of the Act of Union is available at this Library and Archives Canada site.

CHAPTER 17

The Northwest, 1821–1860s

Timeline

▶ 1819, Franklin expeditions to find
  1825, Northwest Passage
  1845

▶ 1822   George Simpson becomes
         governor-in-chief of Hudson's
         Bay Company

▶ 1849   Sayer case brings free trade to
         Rupert's Land

▶ 1860   Report of Hind Expedition

▶ 1862   Report of Palliser Expedition

▶ 1863   London bankers buy Hudson's
         Bay Company

Kapitow, later Chief Thunderchild, was a young Cree boy in the 1850s when his people faced a winter of starvation. Game had disappeared from their area, hunger pervaded the people, and wolves killed their dogs during the night. When Kapitow told his father that he had a dream in which bison could be found to the south, his father told him: "Dreams count, my son. The spirits have pitied us and guided us."[1] The move proved profitable, and by spring the tribe had a bountiful food supply once again. Two decades later, such practices had little impact. The buffalo would be gone, and the First Nations and Métis whose lives were based on the buffalo hunt would be forced to make painful adjustments.

Changes in the fur trade, followed by the arrival of European settlers, would make such adjustments more painful still. While Native peoples tried to hold on to their communities and their cultural values, external forces placed severe restrictions on their ability to determine their own fates. This chapter traces the changes that occurred for Natives and whites in the Northwest.

THE FUR-TRADE MONOPOLY PERIOD, 1821–1849

After 1821 the Hudson's Bay Company had a nominal monopoly in the fur trade of Rupert's Land. The company's control was not complete because American traders operated illegally in the HBC's territory and offered an alternative market for those who were prepared to defy the law. Nevertheless, the HBC ascendancy in the region after its amalgamation with the North West Company (NWC) in 1821 allowed it to streamline its operations, institute conservation measures, and rewrite the terms of trade with the Native peoples. The impact on the various Native groups of these new policies varied according to their degree of dependence upon the fur trade.

The new company followed an NWC practice, belatedly introduced in the pre-merger HBC as well, of making field officers partners in the company. Under the new system, the company divided 40 percent of its profits among 25 chief factors and 28 chief traders, with the factors receiving twice as much as the traders. The factors supervised trade districts, while the traders supervised large posts. From 1821 to 1833, chief factors earned average profits of £800 a year while traders received £400 a year.

Chief factors and traders were at the top of a status-and-pay hierarchy. Clerks, just below field officers in the hierarchy, earned £100 a year, although many of them were in charge of posts and expeditions. Apprentice clerks kept the posts' accounts and earned half the salary of full clerks. A variety of engagés were next to the bottom of the hierarchy and held jobs that included postmaster, interpreter, voyageur, and labourer. At the very bottom were apprentice labourers.

Although Métis held an increasing number of company jobs, none was ever named chief factor or trader and few were ever given the position of clerk. Native men served the HBC as members of canoe brigades, provision hunters, and unskilled labourers at posts. Native women produced footwear and canoe sails, planted vegetables, trapped small animals, dressed furs, and preserved fish.

Between 1846 and 1848 artist Paul Kane was lavishly hosted by the HBC officers as he travelled in the Northwest. His paintings portray an image of a harmonious fur-trading society consisting of well-ordered posts for whites and the easy labours of romanticized "noble savages." The reality was much more complex.

From the time of its founding in 1670, the directors of the HBC attempted to control all aspects of the lives of its servants. Employees of the company were expected to attend church, deal with the Natives in a prescribed manner, avoid drunkenness and adultery, and submit their letters to responsible officials for censorship before sending them. Not surprisingly, company employees often flouted their employer's all-encompassing regulations. Officers recorded many instances of drunkenness, insubordination, theft, private trading with Natives, and desertion. Occasionally, company servants beat up or even murdered a superior. Such acts of rebellion never seriously threatened company profits or control over its workforce. A series of fur-trading posts, mostly sparsely staffed, spread over thousands of miles, provided little opportunity for collective protest. Rebellion against a cruel officer or arbitrary rules at one post would be put down before it could spread to others.

As for the First Nations workers, Kane paintings of supermen disguised the extent to which company exploitation harmed their health. Reverend F.G. Stevens described the brutal

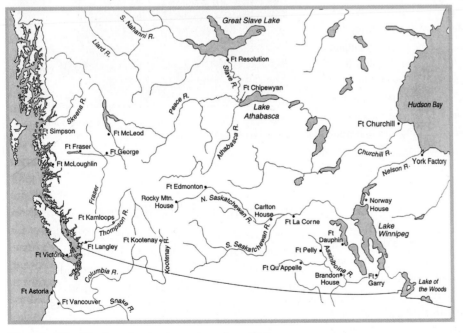

MAP 17.1 The Western fur trade region circa 1850.

MORE TO THE STORY

Life at a Fur-Trading Post

If the Hudson's Bay Company was rigidly hierarchical, the company also had to make concessions to frontier realities. Both tendencies were evident in Fort Edmonton. The fort, originally named Fort Augustus, was built in 1795 on the North Saskatchewan River near today's city of Edmonton. It was designed to compete with Fort George, a nearby post built by the NWC in 1792. After the merger of the two companies, Fort Edmonton became the headquarters for the fur trade of the western prairies. The large two-storey residence where the chief factor lived, with its spacious dining and entertainment areas, provided a marked contrast both to the crowded and cold ramshackle huts where the labourers bunked and the Native tents set up outside the fort's walls.

Each fall, when the fur brigade arrived from York Factory with trade goods, the "Big House" of the chief factor became the scene of an all-night party with dancing and free rum for all the whites at the post. Meanwhile, the Natives—other than the wives of the traders—were kept outside of the fort, its gates locked. When the time came to take care of business, the Natives were allowed to enter, and during an all-day ceremony that followed Native traditions of trade, gifts were exchanged and the peace pipe passed around. Only on the next day could the real trading begin.

After celebrating the completion of their journey from Hudson Bay to the main regional fort, the company employees set off on horseback and by boat to take supplies to the smaller posts in the area. Back at Fort Edmonton, these men hunted buffalo, moose, and deer in the winter while their Native wives, who lived with them inside the fort, prepared snowshoes, shirts, and pemmican for the brigades that would leave in May to carry furs to York Factory. In the spring, voyageurs brought furs from other posts to be inspected at Fort Edmonton and loaded onto boats along with the furs Fort Edmonton's traders received directly from Native trappers. During the summer, employees who were not part of the brigade hunted or joined the women in planting crops and tending livestock.

The Trapper's Bride, oil on canvas, by Alfred Jacob Miller, 1837. Joslyn Art Museum, Omaha, Nebraska

conditions under which Native boatmen worked in northern Manitoba. They carried loads of 200 pounds across each portage, and then they hauled the company's York boats across the portages, using ropes and log rollers. "One day in camp I was concerned to see a man having a bad lung hemorrhage. Next day he was working as usual. Right there I discovered that there were worse conditions of labour than negro slavery."[2]

Monopoly and the Natives

As governor of the northern half of Rupert's Land, Governor George Simpson implemented a policy of substantially reducing the goods exchanged with the First Nations for beaver pelts. In doing so, he recognized that the company's ability to impose its will on the Native peoples was directly proportional to the degree of dependence of specific Native groups on the company. In 1822, after having visited the posts within his district and hearing Indian complaints about low-ered prices, he explained his policies to Andrew Colvile, deputy governor of the HBC.

> Their immediate wants have been fully supplied, but of course the scenes of extravagance are at an end, and it will be a work of time to reconcile them to the new order of things. I have made it my study to examine the nature and character of the Indians and however repugnant it may be to our feelings, I am convinced they must be ruled with a rod of iron, to bring, and keep them in a proper state of subor-dination, and the most certain way to effect this is by letting them feel their dependence upon us. In the Woods and Northern barren grounds this measure ought to be pursued rigidly next year if they do not improve, and no credit, not so much as a load of ammunition given them until they exhibit an inclination to renew their habits of industry. In the plains however this system will not do, as they can live independent of us, and by withholding ammunition, tobacco and spirits, the staple articles of trade, for one year they will recover the use of their Bows and spears and lose sight of their smok-ing and Drinking habits; it will therefore be neces-sary to bring those Tribes round by mild and cau-tious measures which may soon be effected.[3]

The company implemented conservation policies in the area north of the Great Lakes to try to increase the supplies of beaver. Outposts with low volumes of trade were abandoned; steel traps, which made trap-ping easier, were proscribed; and quotas on pelts were imposed at the very moment when the price of trade goods was rising. With game in the region already scarce, the Ojibwa of the area found their dependence on the company heightened at the same time that the company appeared to want their services less and at a cheaper rate. Many Ojibwa, like many Cree and Assiniboine from the northern parklands, simply moved to the Plains where, as Simpson observed, the company felt obliged to remain more magnanimous.

Increasing population pressures soon reduced the number of beaver and buffalo on the Plains and resulted in conservation measures and higher prices for trade goods in that region as well. As historian Arthur Ray observes:

> In spite of the fact that necessity for cooperation prevented any deliberate attempts to destroy the Indians and their cultures by hostile actions, their

traditional life ways were transformed nonetheless. The fur-trade favoured economic specialization. . . . Ultimately, the resource bases upon which these specialized economies developed were destroyed due to over-exploitation. Significantly for Western Canada, this occurred before extensive European settlement began.[4]

Disease continued to fell even the least dependent of First Nations. A smallpox epidemic in 1837–38 wiped out an estimated two-thirds of the 9000 Blackfoot peoples and the 2000 Assiniboine. Some Plains Cree traders were spared a similar fate because the company made use of a new vaccine against small-pox to immunize the Native suppliers at Fort Pelly on the Assiniboine River.

Overexploitation of resources during the fur-trade period was a response to demand in European mar-kets, but it also required Native willingness and ability to supply. The Blackfoot, with their growing emphasis on commercial values, eagerly filled all orders for pemmican given them by the HBC. From the 1830s, they also took advantage of the growing American market for buffalo robes and in the 1840s for buffalo tongues. Women processed the buffalo robes, provid-ing men with an incentive to have several wives in order to increase their share of a lucrative market. Beginning in the mid-1860s, the American market for buffalo hides proved even more lucrative than that for robes. Hides were used as belts in power-transmission systems for factory machinery. Meeting the demand for buffalo hides quickly reduced buffalo numbers almost to the point of extinction. While Natives par-ticipated to a degree in this massacre, their abstention would have made little difference because white buf-falo-hunters were eager to supply the factories' needs. As historian Maureen K. Lux notes, developments in the United States led to the extinction of the Canadian buffalo herds.

> It was in the United States that the carnage began in earnest; after the Civil War ended, the killing moved westward, targeting the bison herds and the Aboriginal people who lived by them. The hunt turned to slaughter, with hide and robe traders concealing themselves in bushes and indiscrimi-nately emptying their repeating rifles into the herds. Ox teams and chains ripped hides from the still-warm flesh. Settlers and railway construction

crews lived off the herds even while they sliced into bison habitat. Hunters, traders, and sportsmen ravaged the southern herds for the increasingly lucrative robe, hide, and (later) bone trade. It has been estimated that a single American firm traded in the slaughter of more than *two-and-a half-million animals annually* from 1870 to 1875. The real pressure on the Canadian herds came when the robe and hide trade opened an overland route south from Blackfoot territory and into the Missouri River trade network.[5]

In 1867, Natives in the Hudson's Bay Company territories could still supply their own needs and the needs of the fur trade from the Canadian herds. But Cree and Assiniboine hunters had been forced to go westward into Blackfoot territory, while the Métis hunted further south in Sioux areas. The result was increasing warfare among Native groups as they competed for a share of a declining resource.

Throughout the history of Native-European contact, the spread of deadly diseases and the disappearance of resources had always predated a willingness on the part of First Nations to question their traditional belief systems and listen to the Christian message of the missionaries. The Northwest was no exception. In 1845, the Oblates, a Roman Catholic congregation of French origin with Canadian headquarters in

George Simpson

Born in Scotland in 1787, George Simpson joined the Hudson's Bay Company in London in 1820 and was sent to the Athabasca country in the dying days of HBC–North West Company rivalry. The following year, after the merger of the two companies, Andrew Colvile used his connections to put his friend in charge of the Northern Department of Rupert's Land. This made him one of two field governors for the company in North America. From 1826 to his death in 1860 Simpson was the sole governor-in-chief of all HBC territories in North America. Although his authority could be countermanded by the governor and board of the company in London, Simpson in practice made company policy in the field. An annual council meeting of all chief factors and traders assisted him in his work, but Simpson ran the council and set his stamp upon company operations in Rupert's Land. With company profits never below 10 percent of invested capital each year from 1826 to 1860, neither the London officers nor Simpson's subordinates had much interest in challenging his autocratic rule.

Rejecting the old paternalism in which fur-trading companies looked after their employees when times were hard or they suffered individual hardships, Simpson was determined not only to trim staff costs but to eliminate gift-giving to Natives in accordance with traditional Native trading practices. He travelled throughout the company's vast territories searching for potential economies. The resulting austerity campaign reduced the HBC's full-time staff from 1983 in 1821 to 827 in 1825, and cut the wages of those workers who remained in the company's employ.

Simpson moved away from Red River in 1833, making Lachine, outside Montreal, his home and Canadian company headquarters. He invested in railway projects and became a pillar of the Montreal establishment. He died at Lachine in 1860.

George Simpson.
William Notman/Library and Archives Canada/C44702

To celebrate a Dog Feast, such as the one depicted here in 1857, the Cree wore coloured blankets, bright handkerchiefs, and ribbons. The feast was held in oblong enclosures set off by willow branches. The short pole in the drawing was placed in the centre, and participants brought offerings to place on an ochre-painted stone at the foot of the pole.
Watercolour by Major George Seton/Library and Archives Canada/C1063

command before running the buffalo. Like the Indians, the Métis seemed able to maintain order through community pressure without resort to formal legal mechanisms.

European influences on the Métis grew dramatically in this period. Both English and French Métis took up farming, planting their crops on lots along the river. Beginning in 1818, Catholic missionaries arrived in Red River, led by Bishop Joseph-Norbert Provencher, and Protestant ministers, particularly Anglicans, soon followed. The Church of England persuaded many English-speaking Métis to practise full-time farming and set up schools to educate their children. Yet many educated English-speaking Métis, who had accepted the church's attempts to assimilate them to Euro-Canadian culture, were frustrated when it became clear that the HBC had no intention of discarding racial barriers in its hiring policy.

Montreal, set up their first mission at Red River. They dispersed quickly through the West, reaching the Columbia River in 1847 and Vancouver Island in 1858.

The Oblates, who were devotees of the pope and who attacked Protestantism relentlessly, were the natural enemies of the Church of England's Church Missionary Society, which denounced Roman Catholicism in similarly extreme terms. Such attitudes softened on the frontier, where there were few white Christians to perpetuate Catholic-Protestant antagonisms. The small numbers of missionaries of these two sects competed in a friendly manner, often commiserating about the difficulty of doing God's work in such an inhospitable environment.

Monopoly and the Métis

The Métis living within and near the Red River settlement also expanded their involvement in the buffalo hunt. By 1860, over 2500 Métis reportedly took part in the hunt, more than a fivefold increase from 40 years earlier. The community used threats of public censure of offenders to enforce various rules for the hunt, such as a prohibition against running the buffalo on Sundays and a requirement to wait for the assigned

Most French-speaking Métis remained more aloof from the HBC than their English-speaking counterparts. As company orders for pemmican and furs fell along with the prices for these products, many Métis, particularly French-speaking ones, began to do business with American traders in direct violation of the HBC rule that only the company could act as a buyer of furs or pemmican within its claimed territories. In 1849, the company charged a Métis trader named Pierre-Guillaume Sayer with infringing the company's trade monopoly by selling furs to American traders. Some 200 armed and furious Métis milled menacingly outside the courthouse as Sayer's trial proceeded. The jury, aware of what was going on outside, found Sayer guilty but recommended mercy on the grounds that he truly believed he had the right to sell furs freely. The HBC then avoided a possible confrontation by dropping the charges. The crowd outside was jubilant: the company monopoly had been broken and trade was now free. It would prove a pyrrhic victory, because both the fur-bearing animals and the buffalo declined drastically over the next 30 years.

The history of the Métis community in the monopoly period was intertwined with the history of the Red River colony, which had developed slowly following the debacle of Seven Oaks. Locusts, drought, and floods took turns and sometimes combined to ruin crops from 1812 to 1826, causing many settlers to leave. Good crops from 1827 to 1835 offered encouragement, but they were followed by several more poor years. Attempts by George Simpson to diversify the colony's economy through an experimental farm, a buffalo-wool company, and the cultivation of hemp and flax all fizzled. Without the meat provided by the Métis hunters, the colonists would have faced starvation. By 1850, the colony's population was estimated at 5000. A majority were Métis; most non-Métis were retired company servants.

Relations among the various groups in the colony were strained by religious, linguistic, and racial divisions. White English speakers tended to be the most prosperous group and more likely to be included by the HBC in political decision making. Although the Métis of both English and French backgrounds experienced discrimination, they sometimes differed among themselves. Many English-speaking Métis abandoned the growing free trade movement in the late 1840s after it was denounced by the Anglican

clergy as an Oblate plot to increase papal power in Assiniboia. Still, English- and French-speaking Métis managed to cooperate in the buffalo hunt, and intermarriages occurred between the two groups.

Initially, membership in the Council of Assiniboia, which served as the governing authority within Rupert's Land, was restricted to former company officers—that is, chief factors and traders—all of them of British or Anglo-Canadian origin. Later, Cuthbert Grant was named to the council. In 1828, Grant had become "Warden of the Plains" for the company he had once fought, charged with preventing the illicit trade of furs in Assiniboia. He was also the founder of Grantown (now St François Xavier), a Métis settlement of several hundred families along the Assiniboine River. Grant's enforcement of the HBC's monopoly did not make him popular among the Métis.

The French-speaking Métis developed a strong sense of being a distinctive community. Their language and religion separated them from other Natives, while their Native heritage separated them from the French. Although their economic activities paralleled those of the English-speaking Métis, many of the English speakers desperately sought respectability in European eyes; the French-speaking Métis largely sought autonomy. Their sense of community was enhanced not only by the Sayer victory, but also by successful battles with the Sioux to the south for con-

Voices from the Past

A View of the Métis

Alexander Ross, patriarch of a large English-speaking Métis family, accompanied the Métis on the buffalo hunt of 1840. He found much to admire, but objected to their hostility to the HBC and white rule.

I must say, I found less selfishness and more liberality among these ordinary men than I had been accustomed to find in higher circles. Their conversation was free, practical and interesting; and the time passed more agreeably than could be expected among such people, till we touched on politics. Like the American peasantry these people are all politicians, but of a peculiar creed, favouring a barbarous

state of society and self-will; for they cordially detest all the laws and restraints of civilized life, believing all men were born to be free. In their own estimation, they are all great men, and wonderfully wise; and so long as they wander about on these wild and lawless expeditions, they will never become a thoroughly civilized people, nor orderly subjects in a civilized community. Feeling their own strength, from being constantly armed, and free from control, they despise all others; but above all, they are marvellously tenacious of their own original habits. They cherish freedom as they cherish life.[6]

trol of major hunting grounds. Among the English-speaking group, racism was becoming more apparent in daily life. The refusal of upper-class white women to associate with the Métis and Native women was a major symptom of the racial antagonism rampant in the colony.

Court cases of the period testify to a hardening of social divisions. In 1850, Mrs Ballenden, Métis wife of the officer in charge of Upper Fort Garry, sued members of the elite for defamatory conspiracy. Charging that these men and women, including judges, sheriffs, clergymen, and doctors, had falsely spread word that she was an adulteress, Mrs Ballenden convinced a jury to award her a substantial sum for damage to her reputation. The English-speaking colonists were bitterly divided throughout the trial, largely along Métis-white lines, with clergymen and their wives being particularly strident in their denunciations of Mrs Ballenden and her supporters. That same year Adam Thom, recorder of Rupert's Land and Assiniboia, who was being sued for failure to pay a bill, objected to French-speaking jurors, including bilingual ones, hearing his case, claiming that they would not understand the nuances of British law. Thom had been editor of the francophobic Montreal *Herald* in the 1830s and had brought his anti-French, anti-Catholic views with him when he came to Red River in 1839. Asked by the HBC to prepare a legal code for the colony, he later acted as a judge and refused to allow the use of French in his court.

VISIONS OF THE NORTHWEST

Promoters of a white, English-speaking Northwest in the colony had important counterparts in both Britain and the United Province of Canada. The rapid agricultural settlement of the American frontier caused first British expansionists and then Canada West expansionists to proclaim the necessity of "civilizing" the northern plains. The state of Minnesota, whose population had grown from 6000 in 1850 to 172 000 in 1860, staked a claim on Assiniboia in 1858; it seemed that only warfare with the Sioux, lasting from 1857 to 1865, slowed down Minnesota's northward advance.

In 1857, John Palliser, a scion of wealthy Irish landowners, convinced the Royal Geographic Society to sponsor a fact-finding expedition through HBC ter-

ritories east of the Rockies. The society, in turn, convinced the British government to foot the bill. Palliser officially reported in 1862 that much of today's Prairie region, particularly the Red River and North Saskatchewan River valleys, was suitable for agricultural settlement. He also identified a fairly large area, stretching from present-day Brandon to the Rocky Mountains and from the forty-ninth to the fifty-second parallel, that he believed to be too dry for successful farming. Henry Youle Hind, a University of Toronto professor of chemistry and geology and the head of an expedition sponsored by the Canadian government in 1857, had reached much the same conclusions. Hind, writing of a "fertile belt" within the HBC territories, stated in his 1860 report:

> It is a physical reality of the highest importance to the interests of British North America that this continuous belt can be settled and cultivated from a few miles west of the Lake of The Woods to the passes of the Rocky Mountains, and any line of communication, whether by waggon road or railroad, passing through it, will eventually enjoy the great advantage of being fed by an agricultural population from one extremity to another.[7]

The Hind and Palliser reports confirmed the view of Canada West expansionists that Rupert's Land could become an agricultural paradise. Toronto's merchant community, concerned about its future as the city's western hinterland filled up, regarded the far-flung territories further west as an extension of that hinterland. The American cities of the eastern seaboard had profited by supplying manufactured products to the farmers of the new western states and territories, and the Toronto businessmen hoped to imitate their success. In this goal, they were led by the most powerful Reformer in Canada West, George Brown, the editor of the *Globe* and a businessman with a variety of speculative investments whose future returns were tied to Toronto's prosperity. The expansionists found sympathetic ears in the British government and financial circles. They also gradually won over the colony's farmers, who were anxious because land for their children could not be found closer to home.

In 1857, a select committee of the British House of Commons accepted in principle Canada West's "just and reasonable wishes" to annex Rupert's Land. As historian Doug Owram notes, "By the end of the

Hind Expedition, 1858.
Library and Archives Canada/C4572

lowing the HBC-NWC merger, the HBC regarded the region as of little importance.

While furs remained readily available in southern regions, the company allocated only a modest quantity of trade goods for the North. The Natives traded both furs and food to the poorly supplied remote posts and in return received flour, tea, sugar, metal implements, beads, blankets, tobacco, and alcohol. Like the early encounters of Aboriginal groups throughout British North America with whites, the Natives of the Mackenzie Valley retained their cultural values and practices in the early period of the fur trade.

The impact of European diseases on the northern peoples was no less devastating than it was on the southern Natives. Infection spread rapidly among Native groups. In the Yukon, for example, epidemics of mumps and scarlet fever occurred even before contact with non-Natives began in the 1840s: Native groups from outside the region, trading with Yukon nations, were carriers of diseases contracted from Europeans. The Native population of the Yukon, estimated to have been between 7000 and 9000 in the immediate pre-contact period, had fallen to about 2600 by the end of the nineteenth century. The Natives remained largely self-sufficient, acquiring mainly luxury goods—knives, guns, iron goods, alcohol—from the Europeans living among them. Despite the ravages of disease, the First Nations of the Yukon would not face a real challenge to the control of their territory before the Klondike gold rush at the close of the century.

decade, the debate on the Hudson's Bay Company had ended, because everyone, including its own officials, accepted the impending end of the fur-trade empire."[8] Of course, that empire was not about to collapse altogether; the northern fur trade would continue to operate for more than a century.

Once it became clear that the HBC's lands would soon be sought by farmers and presumably railway promoters, speculators with little interest in the fur trade began to buy shares in the company. In 1863, London bankers closely associated with the Grand Trunk Railway bought control of the HBC. In one year, the share value of the company rose from £500 000 to £2 000 000. The character of both Western Canada and the HBC was about to change forever.

THE NORTHERN FUR TRADE

In the Mackenzie Valley and the Yukon, the changes affecting the fur-trading regions to the south had no parallel before 1860. Here, as yet, resources had not been significantly depleted, and Europeans had shown no interest in replacing fur trading with economic ventures that would bring new settlement into the area. The fur trade reached the Mackenzie Valley in the 1790s during the period of intense competition between the NWC and the HBC. In the period fol-

THE FRANKLIN EXPEDITION

Meanwhile, the far North still lured European explorers eager to find an elusive "Northwest Passage." The most famous was Englishman Sir John Franklin. In 1819 and again in 1825, Franklin's attempts to penetrate the northern waters ended in failure. Franklin set out again in 1845, but failed to return. Between 1848

The Franklin Expedition.
Library and Archives Canada/C-001403

University of Alberta undertook a scientific and systematic approach to the problem. Their archeological investigations on King William Island unearthed the remains of seven unidentified crew members. Analysis of the bodies seemed to confirm that the survivors had resorted to cannibalism, a controversial issue that the fur trader Rae had first raised in 1854.

Between 1984 and 1986, the remains of three of Franklin's crew members found on Beechy Island, where the expedition had wintered in 1846, were exhumed and examined. One of them was identified as the body of 20-year-old officer John Torrington. Buried in the permafrost, the corpse was almost perfectly preserved. Torrington had apparently died of pneumonia, but the high levels of lead in his blood suggested that he and the others in the expedition may have been slowly poisoned by the containers that held their food supplies.

More recently, David C. Woodman, relying on Inuit oral history, argues that while Franklin's men may have been suffering from lead poisoning, they were more likely killed by a disease common to earlier explorers. According to the Inuit, the bodies of Franklin and his men were found with hard black mouths and emaciated limbs, symptoms of the dreaded scurvy.[9]

and 1859, some 30 rescue missions attempted to find the missing Franklin Expedition. One group, headed by the resourceful Captain Robert McClure, actually traversed the Northwest Passage by foot and sled in a desperate attempt to escape the arctic ice.

Finally in 1857, Lady Franklin sent her own expedition under Captain Leopold McClintock to solve the mystery of her husband's disappearance. Acting on information supplied by the Inuit to Dr John Rae, a fur trader working for the HBC, McClintock searched the shores of King William Island. There he found a stone cairn with a message, dated April 1848, indicating that 24 men, including Franklin, were dead, and that the survivors were heading overland. We now know that they all perished.

Interest in the fate of Franklin and his men did not end with McClintock's discovery. Explorers and scholars continued to search for more clues relating to Franklin's expedition and to debate why these seasoned explorers had failed to survive the rigours of the North. In the early 1980s, anthropologists from the

Conclusion

Expeditions such as those led by Franklin only confirmed what most people believed about the Northwest region generally. A land dominated by a harsh climate and Native peoples, it attracted only small numbers of Europeans. Such a view would soon be challenged. By the 1860s the planned replacement of the fur trade with agriculture on the Plains threatened what remained of Native independence in the Northwest.

Native Women and the Fur Trade

Before 1980, historians studied the fur trade as a virtually all-male affair. That year saw the publication of two books highlighting the role of Native women in the trade. The books, by Sylvia Van Kirk and Jennifer Brown, not only filled in an important gap but also reshaped historical perspectives on the fur trade itself.

Discussion of relations between European men and Native women in earlier histories often reflected traditional European race and gender biases. E.E. Rich's authoritative three-volume history of the Hudson's Bay Company, which appeared from 1958 to 1960, devoted scarcely two out of over fifteen hundred pages of text to the subject. Repeating misunderstandings common since the writings of the Jesuits in the seventeenth century, Rich asserted that Native women were promiscuous and Native men were willing to prostitute their wives and daughters for a bottle of brandy. Despite the HBC's prohibitions against sexual intercourse with Native women, Rich said, "Such behaviour was almost inevitable when active men were quartered for long periods among those with the concepts and habits of the Indians."[10]

While Rich appeared to believe that sexual availability was the only attraction of Native women, he also recognized that "domestic ties to some extent explained the willingness with which men spent year after year at the posts, willingly renewed their engagements, and volunteered to settle there if the Company's Charter were overthrown."[11] For Rich, like other early historians of the fur trade, this incidental observation merited little further

Dene woman with winter's fur catch.
Anglican Church of Canada, General Synod Archives/GS-75-103-53-113

exploration. The real focus of his and similar studies of the fur trade was the leading European male figures in the trade: HBC officials in Canada, partners in the North West Company, explorers, and the like. Family life received scant concern in accounts centred on the public sphere of company business.

Brown and Van Kirk, in contrast, focused on the domestic realm and thereby demonstrated the danger of separating family life from the overall operation of the fur trade. Native women provided their fur-trading husbands with far more than sex, companionship, and babies, although all of these were important. Their unpaid labour was crucial to the fur trade—the women made moccasins and snowshoes, prepared pemmican, fished, collected food supplies such as wild rice and berries, snared small game, tended crops at company posts, and assisted in making and powering canoes. Their knowledge of local language and geography also made them invaluable as interpreters, guides, and diplomats.

The story of Thanadelthur, a Chipewyan woman captured by Cree in 1713, provides an example of the Native woman's diplomatic role. Escaping her captors, Thanadelthur stumbled upon HBC servants and subsequently became the fur company's prime agent in persuading the Cree and Chipewyan of the Churchill River area to cease their hostilities. While Thanadelthur's aim was most likely to bring peace to her own people, she served the HBC's aim of ending a conflict that was reducing the supplies of furs brought to the post.

Van Kirk, relying on fur traders' accounts, concludes that Native women sometimes actively sought alliances with the traders. Many of these women believed that the Europeans offered an easier life with more material goods. Furthermore, their new husbands quickly learned that Native women, more so than European women, enjoyed autonomy within their domestic sphere and brooked no interference from men. Even the trading of furs, often viewed as a male-only activity, tended to be a shared husband-and-wife venture. The Native women, knowing the people who were supplying the furs and often having excellent business acumen, became indispensable to many traders. Madame Lamallice, the wife of the brigade guide at an HBC fort on Lake Athabasca, was the only interpreter in the area and could demand extra rations for her family. She also carried on "her own private trade in pounded meat, beaver tails and moose skins, with a hoarded stock of trade goods, including cloth and ribbons."[12] She threatened that if the HBC tried to stop her trade, she would turn the Natives against the company.

Van Kirk emphasizes that while many Native women were abandoned by fur traders whom they had married *à la façon du pays*, fur-trade society on the whole was characterized by sta-

ble interracial marriages. Yet over time, the female progeny of these marriages, rather than Native women, became the favoured marriage partners of fur traders: "The replacement of the Indian wife by the mixed-blood wife resulted in a widespread and complex pattern of intermarriage among fur-trade families. It produced a close-knit society in which family life was highly valued. James Douglas echoed the sentiments of many of his colleagues when he declared that "without 'the many tender ties' of family, the monotonous life of a fur trader would be unbearable."[13]

Although Native wives tried to pass on their wilderness skills to their children, daughters were often encouraged by their fathers to emulate European examples of what was considered to be ladylike behaviour. Compounding the resultant crisis of identity was the fact that, after the 1820s, the gradual arrival of European women in fur-trade society provoked an unfavourable re-evaluation of Métis wives. Officers began to marry European women, and these new wives snubbed the Métis wives of traders as racially inferior and unladylike, making the Métis women victims of racist and sexist stereotypes. By then, the fur trade itself was in decline and the white wife in the Red River Settlement, like the missionary, "symbolized the coming of a settled agrarian order" where "native women would have little role to play."[14]

The insights of Van Kirk and Brown had a negligible effect on Peter C. Newman, who in the 1980s wrote a lively popular history of the Hudson's Bay Company. In the first volume of his work, Newman gave scant attention to the role of women in the trade and presented a traditional image of larger-than-life male adventurers rather than the family men portrayed by Van Kirk and Brown. The fur traders, he claimed, saw the women as "bits of brown," and he added: "Love-making on the frontier did not carry much emotional baggage, being routinely offered and casually accepted."[15] Academic historians, unlike journalists, largely rejected Newman's approach and conclusions, and the second volume of his study gave more credence to the Van Kirk-Brown thesis.

There is little doubt that including women in the story of the fur trade does far more than sharpen the focus of an existing picture; it changes our image of the trade and the male traders completely. They were not lone adventurers passing through a wilderness for excitement and profit. Rather they were part of a complex interaction between Europeans and Natives, and they led lives that gave them emotional and economic ties to both groups.

NOTES

1 Maureen K. Lux, *Medicine That Walks: Disease, Medicine, and Canadian Plains Native People, 1880–1940* (Toronto: University of Toronto Press, 2001), 21.

2 Quoted in Frank Tough, "Review of Burley, 'Servants of the Honourable Company,'" *Manitoba History* 37 (Spring/Summer 1999): 51.

3 Frederick Merk, ed., *Fur Trade and Empire: George Simpson's Journal* (Cambridge: Harvard University Press, 1968), 179.

4 Arthur J. Ray, *Indians in the Fur Trade: Their Role as Trappers, Hunters, and Middlemen in the Lands Southwest of Hudson Bay, 1660–1870* (Toronto: University of Toronto Press, 1974), 228.

5 Maureen K. Lux, *Medicine That Walks*, 21–22.

6 George Woodcock, *Gabriel Dumont* (Edmonton: Hurtig, 1975) 35–36.

7 Henry Youle Hind, *Narrative of the Canadian Red River Exploring Expedition of 1857 and of the Assiniboine and Saskatchewan Exploring Expedition of 1858*, vol. 1 (London: 1860), 234.

8 Doug Owram, *Promise of Eden: The Canadian Expansionist Movement and the Idea of the West, 1856–1900* (Toronto: University of Toronto Press, 1980), 38.

9 On Sir John Franklin, see Owen Beattie, *Frozen in Time: Unlocking the Secrets of the Franklin Expedition* (New York: Dutton, 1988); David C. Woodman, *Unravelling the Franklin Mystery: Inuit Testimony* (Montreal: McGill-Queen's University Press, 1991); and Leslie H. Neatby, *The Search for the Franklin Expedition* (Edmonton: Hurtig, 1970).

10 E.E. Rich, *The History of the Hudson's Bay Company, 1670–1870*, vol. 1, *1670–1763* (London: Hudson's Bay Records Society, 1958), 605.

11 Ibid.

12 Sylvia Van Kirk, *"Many Tender Ties": Women in Fur Trade Society in Western Canada, 1670–1870* (Winnipeg: Watson and Dwyer, 1980), 84–85.

13 Ibid.

14 Ibid.

15 Peter C. Newman, *Company of Adventurers*, vol. 1 (Markham, ON: Viking, 1985), 205.

RELATED READINGS IN THIS SERIES

From *Foundations: Readings in Pre-Confederation Canadian History*

Sylvia Van Kirk, "The Role of Native Women in the Creation of Fur Trade Society in Western Canada, 1670–1830," 394–400.

From Media Companion CD-ROM, Volume I

The Palliser Papers
Learning to be a Gentlewoman

SELECTED READING

On Hudson's Bay Company organization and officials, see Frederick Merk, ed., *Fur Trade and Empire: George Simpson's Journal* (Cambridge: Harvard University Press, 1968); J.S. Galbraith, *The Little Emperor: Governor Simpson of the Hudson's Bay Company* (Toronto: Macmillan, 1976); and J.G. McGregor, *John Rowand: Czar of the Prairies* (Saskatoon: Western Producer Prairie Books, 1979). Resistance by company employees to HBC authoritarianism is detailed in Edith I. Burley, *Servants of the Honourable Company: Work, Discipline and Conflict in the Hudson's Bay Company, 1770–1879* (Toronto: Oxford University Press, 1997). Two excellent accounts of women in the fur trade are Sylvia Van Kirk, *"Many Tender Ties": Women in Fur Trade Society in Western*

Canada, 1670–1870 (Winnipeg: Watson and Dwyer, 1980), and Jennifer S.H. Brown, *Strangers in Blood: Fur Trade Company Families in Indian Country* (Vancouver: UBC Press, 1980).

The social history of the Red River Settlement is related in J.M. Bumsted, *Trials and Tribulations: The Emergence of Manitoba, 1821–1870* (Winnipeg: Great Plains Publications, 2003); Frits Pannekoek, *A Snug Little Flock: The Social Origins of the Riel Resistance of 1869–1870* (Winnipeg: Watson and Dwyer, 1991). On early colonization generally, see Sarah Carter, *Aboriginal People and Colonizers of Western Canada to 1900* (Toronto: University of Toronto Press, 1999). On the early history of Métis communities in Canada, see Jennifer Brown and Jacqueline Petersen, eds., *The New Peoples: Being and Becoming Métis in North America* (Winnipeg: University of Manitoba Press, 1985). On Red River, see Gerhard Ens, *Homeland to Hinterland: Changing Worlds of the Red River Métis in the Nineteenth Century* (Toronto: University of Toronto Press, 1996). W.L. Morton's introduction to Alexander Begg's *Red River Journal* (Toronto: Champlain Society, 1956) is useful, if dated in its notions of "civilization" and "primitivism." D. Bruce Sealey and Antoine Lussier, in *The Métis: Canada's Forgotten People* (Winnipeg: Pemmican, 1983), present an unabashedly partisan account of Métis life. Conflicts at Red River between French and English speakers, Métis and white, are the subject of Kathryn M. Bindon, "Hudson's Bay Company Law: Adam Thom and the Institution of Order in Rupert's Land 1839–1854," in *Essays in the History of Canadian Law*, vol. 1, ed. David H. Flaherty (Toronto: University of Toronto Press, 1981), 43–87. Barry Cooper's biography, *Alexander Kennedy Isbister: A Respectable Critic of the Honourable Company* (Ottawa: Carleton University Press, 1988) elaborates the conflicts in Red River. On the Métis outside Red River in this period, see J.E. Foster, "The Plains Métis," in R. Bruce Morrison and C. Roderick Wilson, eds., *Native Peoples: The Canadian Experience* (Toronto: McClelland and Stewart, 1986), 375–403, and Foster's "End of the Plains Buffalo," *Alberta* 3, 1 (1992): 61–77.

The goals and attitudes of Canadian expansionists with eyes on the West are detailed in Doug Owram, *Promise of Eden: The Canadian Expansionist Movement and the Idea of the West, 1856–1900* (Toronto: University of Toronto Press, 1980), and Douglas Francis, *Images of the West: Changing Perceptions of the Prairies, 1690–1960* (Saskatoon: Western Producer Prairie Books, 1989). Their American rivals are the subject of Alvin Gluek, *Minnesota and the Manifest Destiny of the Canadian Northwest* (Toronto: University of Toronto Press, 1965). British expansionists are discussed in Irene M. Spry, *The Palliser Expedition: An Account of John Palliser's British North American Expedition, 1857–1860* (Toronto: Macmillan, 1963), and the opening chapters of Vernon Fowke, *The National Policy and the Wheat Economy* (Toronto: University of Toronto Press, 1957). On the Franklin Expedition, see the books mentioned in note 9 in this chapter.

WEBLINKS

JOHN PALLISER
www.canadahistory.com/sections/documents/
palliser_observations.htm

See this site for John Palliser's confidential dispatch of March 1858 to the Secretary of State for the Colonies on the proposed annexation of Rupert's Land.

HENRY YOULE HIND
www.canadahistory.com/sections/documents/
dochind_buffalo_hunt.htm

This page offers an excerpt from Hind's narrative on the buffalo hunt.

SIR JOHN FRANKLIN
www.ric.edu/rpotter/sjfranklin.html

An extensive archive on material relating to the Franklin Expedition is available at this site.

CHAPTER 18

The Pacific Northwest, 1821–1860s

Timeline

1827	Establishment of Fort Langley
1846	Oregon Treaty
1849	Vancouver Island becomes Crown colony
1858	Gold rush on Fraser and Thompson rivers; mainland British Columbia becomes Crown colony
1862	Cariboo gold rush
1866	Vancouver Island and British Columbia colonies merged into one

Te-Kol-a-kan, the elderly blind chief at Nicola Lake, met Indian Superintendent I.W. Powell during his fact-finding trip along the Fraser River in 1874 and informed him of the policies that had come to govern European-First Nations relations in the previous decade:

I have come a long way to meet you. My heart is glad now because I hope you will give us our rights. I had a piece of land which I cultivated for years. A white man named Chartes came and he agreed to work the land with me. We made a ditch and three other settlers came in with him each one taking [pre-empting] 320 acres. They took all my land—all my fences—my house—and told me, go. I said nothing and told my people not to quarrel on this account. I went across the Creek and commenced work on another place. Soon a man named Chapman came and ordered me off and said he had permission from the Government to pre-empt it. I wanted to remain there one year longer but Chapman would not agree to this and told me to go off at once. I have had a bad feeling ever since and so have my people. If I do not get back my land I shall never get over it. All my people have a sick heart because we have no lands and have always been used this way by the whites.[1]

The First Nations of today's British Columbia experienced the beginnings of European settlement in their region largely as dispossession of their lands. Before settlement began, many Native groups in British Columbia participated enthusiastically in the fur trade with the Europeans and exercised a fair degree of control over their relationship with the newcomers. It was a relationship however, that, while it involved considerable intercultural cooperation, was also marked by periodic violence. This chapter explores the relationship of First Nations and Europeans from the period of the later fur trade through to the period of early European settlement in coastal British Columbia.

THE FUR TRADE

At the time of the merger between the Hudson's Bay Company and the North West Company in 1821, the land-based fur trade had displaced the maritime sea-otter trade in HBC account books. The disastrous decline in sea-otter populations by the 1820s meant important changes in the economies of the First Nations that had participated in the maritime trade. Although the Nuu'chah'nulth appear to have adjusted poorly to the changed circumstances, the Haida, eager to maintain the flow of European goods into their villages, proved highly resourceful. They sold the potatoes they had learned to cultivate to mainland Native groups and later to the HBC at Fort Simpson. They also found markets for their wood and argillite carvings and cedar canoes.

Meanwhile, the area west of the Rockies became the focus of intense fur-trade activity. The wealth of untapped furs in the region dictated a strategy opposite to the policy of consolidation that prevailed in the prairie Northwest. Throughout the Columbia Plateau—called New Caledonia—new posts were built. The company also established coastal posts that formed part of the land-based trade.

Fort Vancouver, the HBC's first major post in the Pacific Northwest, was located in what is today the southern part of the state of Washington. Built in 1824 on the south bank of the Columbia River, Fort Vancouver was designed to establish British control over the Oregon territory (today's states of Washington and Oregon), which was also claimed by the United States. Fort Langley, on the Fraser River, erected in 1827, became the first of a number of posts on the Lower Mainland. George Simpson had chosen the site after deciding that a headquarters near the mouth of the Fraser would mean an easier provisioning of the lucrative New Caledonia posts. The company attempted to cement good relations with local First Nations by arranging the marriage of a junior officer with a local chief's daughter.

In 1831, Fort Simpson was established on the northern Pacific coast near today's city of Prince Rupert. The local Tsimshian people were so keen to participate in the fur trade that all nine of their villages on the lower Skeena River moved to the vicinity of the fort. Like their inland counterparts, coastal posts were walled fortresses meant to keep out the Natives when they were not bringing furs to a post. As on the Plains, the company maintained a strict class system at its posts in the Pacific Northwest. An American writer commented in 1834 on the opulence of Chief Factor John McLoughlin's dining hall at Fort Vancouver. Elegant Queen's Ware china and decanters of fine Italian wines on the Chief Factor's table compared dramatically with the simple appointments and fare available to the company's servants. At Fort Okanagan in 1826, the three gentlemen and their small families consumed 799 pounds of venison while the 12 servants and their large families ate only 344 pounds. At many posts, the employees had a diet mainly of dried fish and potatoes.

Forts were staffed by six or seven officers and as many as fifty employees. While the officers were almost invariably of British descent, French-Canadians, Métis, and Hawaiian men made up a large percentage of the lower ranks. The presence of the Hawaiians reflected the HBC's expanding Pacific trade. Most of the men had Native wives, some of whom, in turn, had Native slave women to serve them. Along the Columbia, cultural diversity prevailed, with the languages of the French and Chinook traders mixed with those of other Natives and Europeans.

Staff at the forts, while often at a distance from one another, kept in touch and traded among themselves, using horse trails and waterways as their venues of communication. So, for example, Fort Kamloops traded its horses and dried fish with Fort Alexander and Fort Okanagan, respectively about 30 kilometres north and south of Kamloops. Natives served as mail carriers between posts. Connections with the Hudson Bay area were equally important to these fur-trading outposts. Fur-bearing brigades travelled from the lower Columbia to York Factory via the Athabasca Pass in spring, requiring three months for the journey. On their way back, they were loaded with the supplies for the inland posts that York Factory had received from London.

In the land trade, as in the maritime trade, the fur-company men made no attempt to alter Native cultures. The Native interest in the trade lay in the possibilities for enriching their own cultures rather than in adopting foreign ways. The Europeans were nonetheless often dismayed by the behaviour of their fur-trade partners. To the bewilderment of the possessive Europeans, the Natives often seemed to give or trade away what they had earned from selling furs. In 1826, for example, fur traders at Fort Kamloops watched with puzzlement as Secwepemc chief Court Apatte hosted an all-male feast for 300 of his people and Nlaka'pamax guests. The Nlaka'pamax, with elaborate rituals, gave the Secwepemc horses and guns while the latter gave the Nlaka'pamax guns, robes, beads, and beaver traps.

European values also prompted fur traders to rebuke men of the Plateau nation for allowing women to undertake such strenuous physical tasks as hauling heavy loads of furs and provisions. As a result of the fur trade, Native women's work had intensified. Three days of constant labour were necessary to dress one hide, with the construction of a single tipi requiring 15 to 20 hides. Traders' demand for dressed hides translated into far more time spent on this occupation. At the same time, women had retained their traditional roles in Plateau societies. They gathered the plant foods that still provided the bulk of the food supply, and maintained control over its distribution.

Fur traders tended to regard the Plateau First Nations as destitute compared with Plains nations that owed much of their food to the products of the hunt. Appearing to view large quantities of meat as a necessity to avoid starvation, the Europeans failed to realize that the plant foods provided by the women and the fish provided by the men were more than adequate to maintain a healthy diet. As historian Elizabeth Vibert observes: "the traders' pragmatic purposes constantly interacted with their inherited assumptions and beliefs on the production of their cultural knowledge about Plateau societies."[2]

European diseases limited the extent to which the coastal nations could control their own destiny. In the Columbia Plateau, measles in 1848, influenza in 1849, and smallpox in 1862 decimated entire Native villages. Such an incidence of mortality was too devastating for Native numbers in much of the area to ever recuperate. So great was the grim reaper's harvest that historical geographer Cole Harris, writing in 1985 about the area, blithely stated that Natives had never lived in the Idaho Peaks area in which his family had deep roots. Twelve years and a great deal of research later, Harris admitted that he had fallen into the common trap of assuming that areas without substantial Native populations in recent times had also lacked such populations

Haida village of Skiddegate.
Provincial Archives of British Columbia/HP33784

in the pre-contact period. From this viewpoint, these areas were essentially wilderness before Europeans arrived and "pioneered" their development. "Mine is another example," Harris conceded, "from one who should have known better, of the substitution of wilderness for an erased Native world."[3]

Epidemics also ravaged the coast. In 1835 and 1836, a smallpox epidemic cut a deadly swath, and during that same decade influenza decimated many villages. According to some estimates, the Native population of the Pacific Coast between what is now Alaska and Oregon declined from about 50 000 to 13 000 in the period 1835–43. While the population appeared to recover swiftly, another smallpox epidemic in the 1860s wiped out many communities. The Haida, whose culture flourished during the maritime trade, failed to master European bacilli. From a population of 6000 in 1835, the Haida count fell to only 800 people in 1885.

So many deaths interfered with the coastal Natives' elaborate kinship-based social relations. Everyone in these societies had titles and positions, rights and responsibilities, which were marked out from birth. The inheritance of these rights and titles presumed that most people remained alive long enough to claim their inherited honours. Inevitably, with so many heirs in their graves, new claimants for their titles and property appeared, and a stratification system that had developed over a long period gave way to confusion. There was a large increase in the number of potlatches as contenders for honours tried to establish the legitimacy of their claims.

Yet the resource base of most of the coastal nations remained intact. Because the fur trade brought a comparatively small number of outsiders to their region, it did not produce as significant a breakdown of Native society as would be seen in the subsequent settlement period. Before the 1840s, the HBC had no intention of settling the region. Urged on by George Simpson, the HBC sought to create a coastal fur-trade empire from Alaska to Oregon. Such an empire could only survive if European settlers stayed away.

George Simpson was determined to do whatever was in his power to discourage American settlement in the Oregon territory. This included creating an ecological wasteland as far as fur-bearing animals were concerned. While company policy in the Plains region was to conserve beaver supplies by limiting the number of animals trapped, the policy in the Columbia region was to deliberately overtrap. Simpson reasoned, wrongly as matters turned out, that colonization would only follow a successful fur trade in the area. He noted: "The greatest and best protection we can have from opposition is keeping the country closely hunted as the first step that the American Government will take towards Colonization is through their Indian Traders and if the country becomes exhausted in Fur bearing animals they can have no inducement to proceed thither."[4] By the 1840s, Simpson's policies gave the HBC total control of the fur trade in the Oregon territory.

Before the 1840s the HBC's main interest in the Pacific Northwest was in securing beaver pelts to make felt hats. Other products were also produced when markets were available. The British military purchased bear skins; makers of penknife handles sent orders for deer and stag horns; pharmacists and perfume-makers sought castoreum from beavers' glands; brewers and distillers used a product from the sturgeon's float bladder to clarify their product; and down from certain birds made powder puffs.

THE CLOSE OF THE FUR-TRADE ERA

Simpson's expansionist policies led to conflicts with the United States and Russia, nations which, along with Great Britain, had imperial interests in the region. The Russians were mollified in 1825 when the British conceded that all territory north of 54′ 40″—that is, north of Fort Simpson—would be part of the Russian Empire. The southward push of British interests continued until the 1840s, when James K. Polk successfully contested the American presidency on the belligerent pledge, "Fifty-four Forty or Fight." Once in office Polk proved willing to compromise on his promise to win for the United States the entire coastal region south of Russian-held territory. In 1846 Great Britain and the United States signed the Oregon Treaty establishing the current boundary between the United States and Canada along the forty-ninth parallel.

By this time the company had reluctantly come to the recognition that the beaver trade alone could not guarantee long-term profits. The silk hat had begun to overtake felt hats among the fashion-minded, while American muskrat hats could be sold for less than those made of beaver pelts. In 1847, with inventory piling up, the company sold off its surplus at rates only 10 percent of the price that beaver furs had fetched in 1821.

Nor was the HBC as influential in imperial policy circles as it had once been. The rapid rate of settlement in the American West in the 1840s and 1850s raised concerns that the thinly populated fur-trade empire of the HBC would eventually be seized by the Americans. British settlement would be necessary to secure title to the region. Furthermore, a vocal minority in Canada West was promoting the idea of westward expansion. For these expansionists, the HBC and its fur trade were an anachronism and a barrier to progress. Under such conditions, British authorities began to question both the fur trade and the company that had become synonymous with that industry in British North America.

The new thinking in the Colonial Office was soon reflected in policy relating to Vancouver Island. In January 1848, shipping magnate Samuel Cunard alerted the Admiralty that action must be taken to protect Vancouver Island coal from the Americans. The British government was receptive to this argument, and it soon came to the view that an agriculturally based colony must be established on the island to shore up British control in the area. While HBC field governor George Simpson argued that colonization and the fur trade did not mix, he was overruled by the London governor of the HBC, John Henry Pelly. Pelly indicated to the government that the HBC was willing to colonize Vancouver Island and also to begin extracting its coal.

The company sent instructions to James Douglas, supervisor of HBC territories west of the Rockies, to purchase Native land on Vancouver Island. Under British laws relating to territorial possession, Native land was deemed to include only places where permanent structures had been built and land placed under cultivation. Thus the treaties negotiated with the Native peoples on Vancouver Island excluded most of the fishing and hunting territories that provided them

with their livelihood. Douglas, a veteran HBC employee and father of a large Métis family, encouraged the Natives to become farmers. He also welcomed missionaries who would convert and re-educate the Natives, and he began to employ the Natives as coal miners. About 800 Natives, mainly Kwakwaka'wakw, worked the coal deposits of Fort Rupert, where mining started in 1849 (and proved unsuccessful). They continued to work when Scottish miners, imported by the HBC, struck for better pay and food. When a mine at Nanaimo began operations in 1852, Native men and women were hired to haul coal to the harbour. Native people, once lords of the fur trade, were becoming wage labourers.

In an effort to assert its authority on the West Coast, Great Britain made Vancouver Island a Crown colony in 1849. The HBC was given a 10-year lease of Vancouver Island but the British government named a governor for the colony and required the HBC to recruit permanent settlers of British descent within five years or forfeit its lease. Land sales were to be used to finance roads, churches, schools, and other necessary services. The first governor, Richard Blanshard, a British lawyer, quit after nine months in the position, charging obstruction by the HBC hierarchy.

Blanshard, however, did have HBC support when he launched gunboat assaults on the Newitty at the north end of Vancouver Island and two expeditions against the Cowichan in which he anchored ships outside their territory. While the HBC and Europeans generally regarded Native lands as ripe for European exploitation, the First Nations asserted their sovereignty whenever the Europeans undertook economic activities without seeking approval of the original occupiers of the land.

James Douglas was named the second governor of Vancouver Island in 1851 and was not asked to relinquish his HBC position. Although he established schools, roads, and a courthouse, Douglas opposed democratic institutions, believing that only a small number of men in any society were fit to rule. Instructed by Britain in 1856 to have an assembly elected, Douglas subverted this request by setting a stiff property qualification for voting and holding office, a move that restricted political participation to a fraction of the population. Meanwhile the HBC,

BIOGRAPHY

Sir James Douglas

Born in British Guiana in 1803, James Douglas was the son of a Scottish merchant and his part-African wife. Originally a Nor'Wester, Douglas moved up the ranks in the Hudson's Bay Company to become chief trader at Fort Vancouver in 1835 and chief factor in 1839. The company gave him the responsibility to establish Fort Victoria in 1843 in preparation for a likely forced abandonment of Fort Vancouver to the Americans. In 1846 he was named supervisor of company territories west of the Rockies. Douglas had married Amelia Connolly, the mixed-blood daughter of a chief factor, in 1828. As her husband climbed the status ladder in the company, Amelia challenged racist detractors by adopting the dress and manners of a Victorian lady. She raised a large family, ever-conscious that the norms of fur-trade society required that the Native and African part of their heritage could not be celebrated.

As the company moved toward white settlement and economic diversification on Vancouver Island, Douglas recognized that First Nations would resist encroachments on their homelands. He negotiated 14 treaties with Natives on the island, reserving only 10 acres of land per Native family of five. The Natives agreed because they felt under extreme pressure from the company and settlers.

Douglas became Britain's governor of Vancouver Island in 1851, and later became governor of British Columbia in 1858. By then his land policy had changed. Focusing on establishing British rule over the mainly American newcomers lured by the gold rushes of 1858 and 1862, Douglas spent public funds on roads to link the population centres of a sprawling if thinly populated white colony, and on government and legal institutions to coerce the miners' respect for public authority. Unable to persuade either the British Colonial Office or the colonial legislature to fund his treaty-making policy, Douglas made informal deals with First Nations to set aside reserves. His successors ignored both the treaties and the reserves. In their view, the Proclamation of 1763, which recognized Native rights in all areas with rivers that drained into Hudson Bay, gave British Columbia a geographical exemption from responsibility for recognizing Native possession of land.

James Douglas and Amelia Douglas.
William Notman, Library and Archives Canada/PA611930; British Columbia Archives and Records Service/A-01679

having overtrapped the Pacific region and facing declining demand and prices for furs, increasingly turned to other profit-making ventures. In the central interior, company officials formed the Puget's Sound Agricultural Company, established farms along the Columbia River, and secured a contract in 1841 with the Russian fur traders in the region north of HBC territory for exclusive provisioning of their posts. By 1850, Fort Victoria housed several sawmills that sold lumber to California miners. Both the fort and Esquimalt, a few kilometres away, sold supplies to Royal Navy ships that docked there. Increasing demand for lumber during the Crimean War from 1854 to 1856 further stimulated forest exploitation. The coal mines at Nanaimo had a steady market in the United States. Four manorial farms had been established near Fort Victoria, although it proved difficult to attract labourers on the five-year contracts that were offered.

Victoria in the 1850s.
Glenbow Archives/NA-674-67

GOLD RUSH DAYS

In 1858, reports of company discoveries of gold on the shores of the Fraser and Thompson rivers sparked a gold rush. That year, over 27 000 men left San Francisco ports for British Columbia. Most were transient adventurers who had come to the West Coast in search of gold during the San Francisco rush of 1849. Douglas attempted to control this invasion with decrees forbidding, for example, the entry of foreign vessels on the Fraser River, but the miners questioned the right of an HBC officer to make this kind of regulation. Britain, recognizing the need for imperial rather than company control over both the mainland and the island, cancelled the HBC's lease on Vancouver Island and made the mainland a formal Crown colony. Douglas, after agreeing to resign his HBC posts, was named governor of British Columbia (which then referred only to the mainland) in November 1858, while retaining his position as governor of Vancouver Island. New Westminster, now a suburb of Vancouver, was named the capital of the mainland colony.

Douglas made use of mining licences and judges to control the behaviour of the miners. His main aim was to keep the territory under British control and to fend off any efforts on the part of American immigrants to reverse the boundary treaty of 1846. Part of the plan included construction of about 600 kilometres of highway connecting settlements and gold-mining territories with the capital.

The Royal Engineers planned the capital, erecting government buildings, Holy Trinity Anglican Church, residential areas, and public squares in imitation of their equivalents in British cities. The government buildings included a land registry, a jail, a customs house, a courthouse, and an assay office. Beyond the genteel town centre, however, seedy boarding houses and hotels sprang up, serving men en route to or from the goldfields as well as sailors in port. Here, prostitutes and publicans rather than civil servants in suits plied their trades.

Main street of Barkerville during the gold rush in the 1860s.
Library and Archives Canada/PA-61940

While independent businesses were slowly established in the 1850s, it was the gold rush that challenged the HBC's commercial dominance of the island. The gold rush also changed the sleepy town of Victoria. In a six-week period in 1858, over 200 buildings, mainly businesses, were erected in Victoria. These ramshackle structures, surrounded by a tent town created by the gold-seekers en route to imagined riches, transformed the fort from a tidy, compact village of 300 people to an overcrowded town of 6000. The population would decline by half in a few years as the gold rush ended, leaving empty buildings.

Victoria's decline was modest relative to that of the gold-mining towns themselves. First in the Fraser Canyon and then in the Cariboo region to its north, instant towns of shacks and tents arose. Sometimes the gold miners along the Fraser settled near established fur-trading forts such as Fort Langley and Fort Hope,

but they also set up entirely new communities such as Yale, Boston Bar, and Lytton. The strike of gold in Cariboo, which began in earnest in 1862, produced the instant town of Barkerville, with a population of 10 000 in 1863. Within a few years, these towns had become mere villages or even ghost towns.

The European population on both the mainland and the island was overwhelmingly male. Most settlers and miners were young, single men seeking their fortune and satisfying their sexual desires by visiting the white or Chinese prostitutes who came to work in the area. By 1860, Governor Douglas, determined to create permanent, family based settlements, was advertising in Great Britain for marriage-minded women to come to the colony as domestics. The fur traders who preceded these settlers had generally married locally, but most settlers had little desire to mingle with, much less marry, Native women.

SETTLERS AND RACE RELATIONS

In contrast to most HBC traders, the new settlers and miners were devoid of respect for the coastal Native peoples. Unlike the fur traders, they had no need of the Natives' services and regarded them as competitors for land. For their part, the Native peoples were stunned by the Europeans' penchant for building fences around everything and the viciousness of the settlers' response to anyone who scaled fences in search of food. As historian Robin Fisher notes: "For the settler concerned to establish and defend a beachhead of civilization in the wilderness, the Indian was the symbol of something that he must not allow himself to become. The British colonist established a line of cleavage based on race and would not permit any crossing of that barrier by admitting that the Indian was in any way comparable to western man."[5]

The Natives often resorted to violence in their attempts to prevent their lands from being taken by settlers. In 1844, Cowichan, Songhee, and Clallum destroyed livestock belonging to Fort Victoria and attacked the fort. Beginning in the 1850s, warships were used to put down Native revolts. For example, when the Newitty Indians killed three HBC men on Vancouver Island in 1850, two warships were sent, each to destroy a village when the Newitty refused to surrender the killers to the authorities.

The American gold miners of 1858, some of them veterans of "Indian wars" at home, proved far more vicious than the British with their gunboats. In the Fraser Canyon, they created their own de facto government and ignored the official government's efforts to maintain a degree of order in European-Native relations. Bent on exterminating Natives who stood in their way, miners organized the burning of Native villages and the killing of Natives, including women and children. Better armed than their adversaries, they forced the terrified Natives to agree to peace treaties that alienated Native lands.

By 1860, the First Nations of British Columbia, their numbers already weakened by European diseases, were being quickly dispossessed. Settlers and transients grabbed their land or established mining operations on it. The authorities largely sided with the newcomers. James Douglas had recognized the need for a degree of Native protection, and had negotiated the establishment of reserves with a variety of First Nations. Joseph Trutch, appointed chief commissioner of Lands and Works in 1864, refused to consider recognition of Aboriginal title and drastically cut the size of existing reserves. Neither settlers nor the authorities provided compensation for Native fields, gardens, and houses that settlers pre-empted. The truncated reserves were often left without a source of water and therefore no opportunity for agricultural pursuits. Many Natives were demoralized as their intricate societies collapsed around them. Others, accustomed by the fur trade to notions of trading their labour in exchange for goods, integrated themselves into the resource-based economy that the European settlers established. From the 1850s onward, many Natives worked at commercial fishing, canning, sailing, coal mining, farming, and lumbering. In the early 1860s, for example, five mainly Squamish villages had been established near Burrard Inlet, their male residents working in local sawmills and logging camps.

Integration was often cultural as well as economic. A few Natives cooperated with the new European authorities to prosecute their fellows who had broken the laws decreed by white officials. As the economy that had been interwoven with their religious beliefs unravelled, many Natives proved open to the Christian message that missionaries preached to their communities. The Oblates won converts to Roman Catholicism among the Salish of southern Vancouver Island and the Lower Mainland; the Anglicans had successes among the Tsimshian of Fort Simpson; and the Methodists, relying on the mass camp meetings they had largely abandoned as unrespectable in Canada West, recruited Natives near Victoria, Chiliwack, and Nanaimo, employing a few of their converts as missionaries among their own people. Many other Native peoples held fast to their old traditions and regarded employment in European enterprises as a means to acquire goods for distribution at potlatches rather than as a way to assimilate into European cultural and religious traditions.

Missionaries bemoaned the negative influence of both Native traditionalists and the nominally Christian settlers and gold miners. A few such missionaries followed a path dating back at least to the Jesuits' establishment of Sillery: they founded Native-only Christian communities. The Anglican missionary

Native Views of European Land Claims

In 1860, Gilbert Sproat purchased land in the Alberni district of Vancouver Island, although he needed the aid of two armed vessels to take possession. With loaded cannons aimed at their village, the Nuu'chah'nulth agreed to surrender their village site to Sproat, but they made clear to him that his title to the land was illegitimate in their eyes. Sproat wrote an account of his impression of the confrontation:

> "We see your ships, and hear things that make our hearts grow faint. They say that more King-George-men will soon be here, and will take our land, our firewood, our fishing grounds; that we shall be placed on a little spot, and shall have to do everything according to the fancies of the King-George-men." "Do you believe all this," I asked. "We want your information," said the speaker. "Then," answered I, "it is true that more King-George-men (as they call the English) are coming: they will soon be here; but your land will be bought at a fair price." "We do not wish to sell our land nor our water; let your friends stay in their own coun-try." To which I rejoined: "My great chief, the high chief of the King-George-men, seeing that you do not work your land, orders that you shall sell it. It is of no use to you. The trees you do not need; you will fish and hunt as you do now, and collect firewood, planks for your houses, and cedar for your canoes. The white man will give you work, and buy your fish and oil." "Ah, but we don't care to do as the white men wish." "Whether or not," said I, "the white men will come. All your people know that they are your superiors; they make the things you value. You cannot make muskets, blankets, or bread. The white men will teach your children to read printing, and to be like themselves." "We do not want the white man. He steals what we have. We wish to live as we are."[6]

William Duncan gathered a group of about 50 Tsimshian in Fort Simpson in 1862 and established a settlement called Metlakatla at a former village site across from today's Prince Rupert. The settlement was modelled on a Victorian village and run along authoritarian lines. Duncan established a volunteer police force whose duties included surveillance of the sexual relations, church attendance, and work habits of members of the group.

The face of British Columbia was changing, and not only because of the influx of European settlers. Black and Asian peoples began to arrive in the area in the late 1850s, and both groups confronted the same racist hostility and air of superiority with which the Europeans viewed the Native peoples. The colony's first black residents arrived in Vancouver Island in 1858, escaping restrictive legislation in California. Some farmed or ranched; others found employment as miners, bakers, restaurateurs, merchants, or barbers. Discouraged by prejudice and the harsh conditions of life on Vancouver Island, most of them returned to the United States after the Northern victory in the Civil War appeared to herald a new era of race relations in that country.

The gold mines of the Fraser Valley and the Cariboo Mountains region attracted between 6000 and 7000 Chinese, mainly men, from both California and Hong Kong. They worked as prospectors for gold and jade, importers, fishers, gardeners, labourers, restaurateurs, and handymen. A small number of wives also came; most were married to merchants and worked alongside their husbands. Unmarried Chinese women imported by Chinese merchants worked as servants or prostitutes. Like the blacks, the Chinese learned that economic success did not lead to acceptance by the whites; the norm was segregation in churches, saloons, theatres, and residential areas. As the gold rush ended in the 1860s, most of this first wave of Chinese immigrants departed.

BRITISH COLUMBIA AFTER THE GOLD RUSH

While the gold rushes of 1858 and 1862 proved ephemeral, the beginnings of the post-fur-trade economy were evident in many corners of British Columbia. By 1864, entrepreneurs were salt-curing and canning salmon and sturgeon on the Lower Mainland. Capitalists such as Edward Stamp had received huge concessions of forests covered in Douglas firs and western red cedars. In 1865 he established a steam-powered mill on the south shore of Burrard Inlet. Later known as the Hastings Mill, it had a ready export market in areas along the Pacific Rim. Stamp had a competitor in the water-powered sawmill begun earlier by S.P. Moody and Company. The West Coast's fish and forests became the backbone of the new post-fur-trade economy. Agriculture, by contrast, was inhibited by the presence of the dense forests and by a lack of markets. By 1867, crops were cultivated on only about 445 hectares of the lower Fraser Valley.

The West Coast was also experiencing a communications revolution. During the 1858 gold rush, San Francisco mail steamers began regular trips into Puget Sound. This allowed the British colony on the Pacific to join in the benefits that improved shipping and a railway across the isthmus of Panama had brought to the American Pacific West. Sailing time from Vancouver Island to London was reduced from over 200 days in the 1820s to about 45 days. The telegraph, which made it possible for commercial outposts to link up speedily with major centres and their mercantile information, joined New Westminster to the towns of Washington and Oregon, as well as to San Francisco in 1865. Western Union, the American firm that controlled this telegraph line, extended the line that year over 644 kilometres to reach the Skeena Valley.

POLITICAL DEVELOPMENTS

When British Columbia became a province of the new Dominion of Canada in 1871, the territories that constituted it had less than a century of continuous European contact. The product of HBC influence before the 1850s and Great Britain's desire to placate

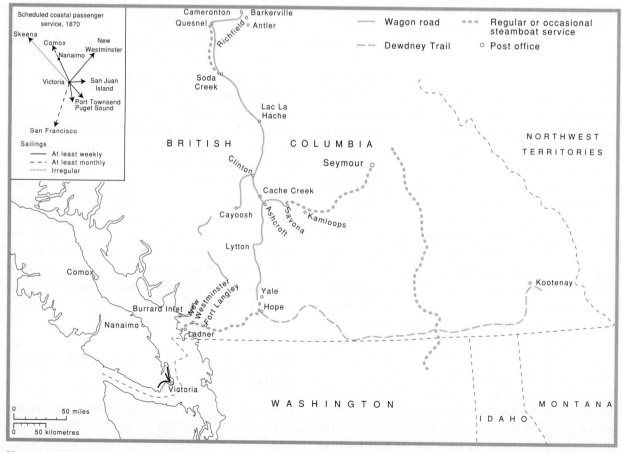

MAP 18.1 British Columbia, 1870.

both company officials and the aggressive Americans, British Columbia was still a colony in formation when the Confederation debate got underway in 1864.

British Columbia experienced a number of boundary changes in the mid-nineteenth century. Before the Oregon Treaty of 1846, what would become British Columbia was a set of trading posts within the Pacific region of HBC operations. Vancouver Island, the mainland coastal area, and New Caledonia, the interior trading posts stretching to the Rocky Mountains, were linked with company operations as far south as Oregon. Britain's desire to maintain friendly relations with the United States government might have led to abandonment of the Pacific altogether to the Americans but for HBC pressures on British politicians not to allow their Pacific fur-trade empire to be dissolved. In the end, Britain's need to pacify both the company and the Americans led to the compromise that ceded the southern areas where Americans had settled in great numbers to the United States, preserving the areas northward for Britain and the HBC.

The HBC then moved its regional capital from Fort Vancouver to Fort Victoria, which in turn became a colonial capital when Vancouver Island became a Crown colony in 1849. Next, the entire mainland became a colony called British Columbia in 1858, with New Westminster as capital. In 1862 Britain made 60 degrees North latitude the northern boundary of British Columbia, and added the Queen Charlotte Islands to its territory. Then, in 1866, motivated by a desire to reduce administrative costs, the British government merged the colonies of Vancouver Island and British Columbia into one colony, without consulting their citizens. The mainland appeared to be the big winner, with the new colony given the name British Columbia and New Westminster being made

the capital. Lobbying by Victoria politicians caused Britain to move the capital to Victoria in 1868. By then John A. Macdonald, the prime minister of the new government of Canada, began wooing the British Columbian colonists to reinvent their colony as a Canadian province.

Throughout these changes, the First Nations people remained the majority of residents of British Columbia. The 1870 Census of Canada, which almost certainly underestimated Native numbers, suggested that over 70 percent of British Columbia's population of 36 247 was Native. It classified 25 percent of the population as White and 4 percent as Asian.

CONCLUSION

The transformation of the Pacific Northwest from 1821 to the 1860s was, in many respects, an accelerated version of what had happened throughout the length and breadth of the rest of today's Canada since the late sixteenth century. An area under the control of its inhabitants of many millennia first became a fur-trading partnership between Europeans and Natives in which real reciprocity was common; then it changed into an area of European colonization and Native dispossession. First Nations peoples attempted to cope with the newcomers, sometimes by becoming their workforce and sometimes by signing peace treaties that supported the rights of the invaders. New settlers, so dismissive of the original inhabitants that they referred to themselves as "pioneers" and the long-inhabited territories around them as "wilderness," had seized the land. While the First Nations would continue to claim the lands the colonizers stole from them, it was the colonizers, not the First Nations, who would, from then on, have the upper hand in shaping the character of British Columbia.

NOTES

1 R. Cole Harris, *Making Native Space: Colonialism, Resistance, and Reserves in British Columbia* (Vancouver: UBC Press, 2002), 83.

2 Elizabeth Vibert, *Traders' Tales: Narratives of Cultural Encounters in the Columbia Plateau, 1807–1846* (Norman: University of Oklahoma Press, 1997), 276.

3 R. Cole Harris, *The Resettlement of British Columbia: Essays on Colonialism and Geographical Change* (Vancouver: UBC Press, 1997), xvi.

4 Lorne Hammond, "Marketing Wildlife: The Hudson's Bay Company and the Pacific Northwest," in *The Invention of Canada: Readings in Pre-Confederation History,*

ed. Chad Gaffield (Toronto: Copp Clark Longman, 1994), 379–401.

5 Robin Fisher, *Contact and Conflict: Indian-European Relations in British Columbia, 1774–1890* (Vancouver: UBC Press, 1977), 93.

6 Quoted in Peter A. Cumming and Neil H. Mickenberg, eds., *Native Rights in Canada* (Toronto: General Publishing, 1972), 175.

RELATED READINGS IN THIS SERIES

From *Foundations: Readings in Pre-Confederation Canadian History*

Adele Perry, "Hardy Backwoodsmen, Wholesome Women, and Steady Families: Immigration and the Construction of a White Society in Colonial British Columbia, 1849–1871," 401–14.

From Media Companion CD-ROM, Volume I

The Oregon Treaty, 1846
Establishment of Trade in British Columbia
The Cariboo
Letter to the Editor—C. Gardiner

SELECTED READING

Overviews of the period discussed in this chapter are found in Jean Barman, *The West beyond the West: A History of British Columbia*, rev. ed. (Toronto: University of Toronto Press, 1996); Margaret A. Ormsby, *British Columbia: A History* (Toronto: Macmillan, 1958); and in the early essays of Patricia Roy, ed., *A History of British Columbia: Selected Readings* (Toronto: Copp Clark Pitman, 1989). On the fur-trading period after 1821, see Robin Fisher, *Contact and Conflict: Indian-European Relations in British Columbia, 1774–1890*, 2nd ed. (Vancouver: UBC Press, 1992); Elizabeth Vibert, *Traders' Tales: Narratives of Cultural Encounters in the Columbia Plateau, 1807–1846* (Norman: University of Oklahoma Press, 1997); James Gibson, *Otter Skins, Boston Ships and China Goods: The Maritime Fur Trade of the Northwest Coast, 1785–1841* (Montreal: McGill-Queen's University Press, 1992); Richard Mackie, *Trading beyond the Mountains: The British Fur Trade on the Pacific, 1793–1843* (Vancouver: UBC Press, 1996); Frederick Merk, ed., *Fur Trade and Empire: George Simpson's Journal* (Cambridge: Harvard University Press, 1968); and Lorne Hammond, "Marketing Wildlife: The Hudson's Bay Company and the Pacific Northwest, 1821–49," *Forest and Conservation History* 37 (January 1993): 14–25. Local documentary studies include Morag McLachlan, *The Fort Langley Journals, 1827–30* (Vancouver: UBC Press, 1998), and Neil J. Sterritt et al., *Tribal Boundaries in the Nass Watershed* (Vancouver: UBC Press, 1998). On the Fraser River gold rush, see Donald J. Hauka, *McGowan's War: The Birth of Modern British Columbia on the Fraser River Gold Fields* (Vancouver: New Star, 2003).

On European-Native relations in the early period of settlement in British Columbia, key works include R. Cole Harris, *Making Native Space: Colonialism, Resistance, and Reserves in British Columbia* (Vancouver: UBC Press, 2002), and *The Resettlement of British Columbia: Essays on Colonialism and Geographical Change* (Vancouver: UBC Press, 1997); Adele Perry, *On the Edge of Empire: Gender, Race and the Making of British Columbia, 1849–1871* (Toronto: University of Toronto Press, 2001); Barry M. Gough, *Gunboat Frontier: British Maritime Authority and Northwest Coast Indians, 1846–1890* (Vancouver: UBC Press, 1983); Paul Tennant, *Aboriginal Peoples and Politics: The Indian Land Question in British Columbia, 1849–1989* (Vancouver: UBC Press, 1990); Tina Loo, *Making Law, Order, and Authority in British Columbia, 1821–1871* (Toronto: University of Toronto Press, 1994); and Hamar Foster, "Letting Go the Bone: The Idea of Indian Title in British Columbia, 1849–1927," in *Essays in the History of Canadian Law*, vol. 6, *British Columbia and the Yukon*, ed. Hamar Foster and John McLaren (Toronto: Osgoode Society for Canadian Legal History, 1995). The impact of epidemics is discussed in Harris, *The Resettlement of British Columbia*, chap. 1, and Robert Galois, "Measles, 1847–1850: The First Modern Epidemic in British Columbia," *BC Studies* 109 (Spring 1996): 31–46. On early settlement more generally, see also Richard S. Mackie, *The Wilderness Profound: Victorian Life on the Gulf of Georgia* (Victoria: Sono Nis Press, 1995), and Graeme Wynn and Timothy Oke, eds., *Vancouver and Its Region* (Vancouver: UBC Press, 1992). The beginnings of the lumber industry in British Columbia are detailed in Gordon Hak, *Turning Trees into Dollars: the British Columbia Coastal Lumber Industry, 1858–1913* (Toronto: University of Toronto Press, 2000).

Studies of visible minority women in early British Columbia include Tamara Adilman, "A Preliminary Sketch of

Chinese Women and Work in British Columbia, 1858–1920," in *Not Just Pin Money: Selected Essays on the History of Women's Work in British Columbia*, eds. Barbara K. Latham and Roberta J. Pazdro (Victoria: Camosum College, 1984), and Sherry

Edmunds-Flett, "19th-Century African-Canadian Women on Vancouver Island," in *Telling Tales: Essays in Western Women's History*, eds. Catherine A. Cavanaugh and Randi R. Warne (Vancouver: UBC Press, 2000).

WEBLINKS

OREGON TREATY

www.pbs.org/weta/thewest/resources/archives/two/oretreat.htm

Articles 1–4 of the Oregon Treaty are available at this site.

1858 GOLD RUSH

www.bcarchives.gov.bc.ca/exhibits/timemach/galler04/frames/maps.htm

This page from the British Columbia archives contains maps of the gold rush regions of 1858.

PART IV SUMMARY

By the 1860s Britain's North American colonies had reached a level of population growth, economic development, and institutional maturity that was scarcely imaginable 50 years earlier. Except in the West, the colonies were virtually self-governing and even in the West, colonial administrations were no longer immune from popular opinion. Economic diversification was everywhere in evidence, from mining in the Hudson's Bay Company territories to the seal fishery in Newfoundland, shipbuilding in the Maritimes, and extensive railway construction in the Canadas. The shift from a pre-industrial society to one based mainly on commercial activities was gradual but inexorable. So, too, it seems, was the continued decline of the Aboriginal peoples, who were excluded from full participation in the dynamic new societies taking root in British North America.

INDUSTRIALIZING CANADA, 1840–1867

Following Great Britain's adoption of free trade and acceptance of colonial self-government in the 1840s, the pace of change increased dramatically in British North America. The Industrial Revolution, symbolized by steam power, railways, and factories, was the catalyst for many of the changes taking place. Not only did industrial capitalism introduce new ways for people to make a living and communicate with each other, it also encouraged new political arrangements among the colonies. Leading businessmen, professionals, and politicians in the Canadas and the Maritimes began to dream of a nation from sea to sea, bound together by railways and political institutions adapted from their British heritage. Despite the very real obstacles in their path, the promoters of "confederation" were successful. A new nation called Canada came into being on 1 July 1867, and within less than a decade had expanded its boundaries to the Pacific Coast.

CHAPTER 19

People and Place at Mid-Century

Timeline

1837–1901	Reign of Queen Victoria
1842	Black colony of Dawn founded in Canada West
1845–52	François-Xavier Garneau publishes *Histoire du Canada*
1846	Theatre Royal founded in Halifax
1847	First telegraph line built linking United Canadas and United States
1849	A lazaretto built in Tracadie, New Brunswick
1850	Fugitive Slave Law passed in United States
1851	St Lawrence Hall opened
1854	Last major cholera epidemic in British North America

I am on my way to Canada
That cold and distant land
The dire effects of slavery
I can no longer stand —
Farewell, old master.
Don't come after me.
I'm on my way to Canada
Where coloured men are free.[1]

Slavery had gradually died out in the British North American colonies in the early nineteenth century and was formally abolished throughout the British Empire by an act of Parliament in 1833. The same was not true in the United States, where many states still condoned slavery. In 1850 the Congress passed the Fugitive Slave Law, permitting slave owners to pursue their "property" into non-slave states. To escape the impact of the law, escaped slaves sought sanctuary in British North America. Canada West, in particular, became a major terminal for the "underground railroad," the name given to an informal network of anti-slavery activists who helped the fugitives on their journey to the cold and distant land that promised freedom.

In British North America, African Americans established schools, churches, and newspapers and contributed to the struggle against slavery in their former homeland. They also continued to experience prejudice, as did most people whose skin was not the same colour as the dominant white majority. Nevertheless, British North Americans of all races and classes were beginning to embrace new values, many of them, such as the opposition to slavery, pioneered by reformers in Great Britain.

As members of the greatest empire the world had yet seen, all of the colonies and territories in 1850 possessed, to a greater or lesser degree, the political, legal, and social institutions of their "mother" country. Queen Victoria, who ascended the British throne in 1837, presided over her realm until her death in 1901. British North Americans became Canadians in the Victorian Age, and their values and institutions still bear the stamp of that remarkable period.

SMALL WORLDS

In 1850, the British North American colonies and territories were a study in contrasts. On the West Coast, the Crown colony of Vancouver Island had only a handful of white settlers and was ruled without an elected assembly. Like the vast northern area that stretched from the Pacific to the Atlantic, Vancouver Island was part of the fur-trade empire of the Hudson's Bay Company. Most of the 100 000 Aboriginal peoples in the great Northwest were tied to the market economy through the company's trading posts. The heart of the Northwest was the sprawling district of Red River, where a growing Métis population was rapidly emerging to challenge the hegemony of HBC officialdom. Over 10 000 Inuit lived in the "true" north but they were loosely, if at all, integrated into European trade networks.

Decimated by disease and loss of traditional habitat, fewer than 25 000 Aboriginal people lived in the whole of eastern British North America, which by 1850 was home to 2.5 million people of European background. The eastern colonies, with their predominantly white population, were characterized by diversity. Divided between English- and French-speaking inhabitants, the United Canadas contained two distinct cultures. Canada West was a rough-and-ready frontier society where nearly half of the people were immigrants, primarily from the British Isles. As in most frontier societies, men outnumbered women, and the proportion of people over 70 years of age was relatively low.

In Canada East, most of the people were Canadian-born, sharing a common heritage in the French migrations of the seventeenth century. In the Atlantic colonies, three out of four people were born in the colonies. Like Canada East, the region had a population profile more balanced in age and gender than Canada West's. More than half of the population of British North America was under 17 years of age, making

Building snowhouses at Cape Fullerton, Hudson Bay.
Reproduced with the permission of the Minister of Public Works and Government Services Canada, 2002, and Courtesy of Natural Resources Canada, Geological Survey of Canada, photo #2901

youth a dominant characteristic of all colonial societies. While Prince Edward Island was the most densely populated colony by virtue of its small size, over three-quarters of white British North Americans were concentrated in the St Lawrence and Great Lakes basin.

COMMUNICATIONS

Sprawled over 7 percent of the Earth's surface, the British North American colonies and territories in 1850 remained isolated from each other. Although people in the Atlantic region might brave the harsh winter seas of the Cabot and Northumberland straits or the Bay of Fundy to reach their closest neighbours, the Canadian ports were frozen for nearly half the year and closed to ocean transport. Overland communication between the United Canadas and territories east or west was confined to ill-marked trails that could be negotiated only by the most intrepid travellers.

By 1850, telegraph and railway communication promised an end to colonial isolation, but the cost of building intercolonial links was prohibitive for a population of less than three million. A telegraph line linking Canada to the American system was completed in 1847, and in the following year New Brunswick was linked with Calais, Maine. Thus, in a roundabout way, Maritimers could communicate telegraphically with Canadians. Underwater cable connected Prince Edward Island to the mainland in 1851 and Newfoundland in 1856. In 1850, a 23-kilometre railway connecting La Prairie on the St Lawrence with St Jean on the Richelieu was the longest railway in the colonies.

While stagecoach service carried passengers and mail to and from major colonial cities, the trunk roads left much to be desired. Stumps, rocks, and potholes commonly threatened to overturn carriages. In spring, raging torrents removed bridges, roadbeds, and even

The Atlantic Telegraph, by Rex Woods. In 1866, the Great Eastern managed to lay an underwater cable between Great Britain and British North America.
Confederation Life Gallery of Canadian History

travellers. Road construction depended largely on statute labour, which men were required to perform every year. As a result, road repair varied according to the density and the enthusiasm of the population in any given area. British North Americans experimented with corduroy roads (made from tree trunks), plank roads (subject to rot), and macadamized roads (crushed rock and gravel), but each had its disadvantages and all were in need of constant repair.

COLONIAL ECONOMIES

In 1851, the vast majority of British North Americans lived in a rural environment, their work regulated by the sun and seasons. Most work also occurred within a family context, the combined labour of all members contributing to the survival of the family unit as a whole. On the fringes of colonial settlement, gangs of men lived in bunkhouses during the winter and returned to towns in the spring with the timber drive. In widely dispersed areas from Sydney to Nanaimo, miners extracted minerals—gypsum, coal, iron, copper—from the bowels of the Earth. Many Aboriginal communities still survived by hunting and gathering but, especially in the eastern colonies, seasonal migrations were increasingly restricted by expanding settlement.

Despite their isolation, most British North Americans had moved beyond the pioneer stage by mid-century. Each region produced a staple that helped to shape its domestic economy: furs in the Northwest, wheat and timber in the Canadas, and fish and timber in the Atlantic colonies. Notwithstanding Britain's adoption of a free trade policy in the 1840s, the expanding empire continued to absorb most of the staples produced in the colonies. The United States was also emerging as a significant market for colonial primary products. By mid-century, too, secondary producers—shipbuilders and fish processors in the Atlantic and St Lawrence regions, and Canadian millers and distillers—were beginning to develop a reputation for quality beyond the boundaries of British North America.

The eastern colonies sustained a vibrant domestic economy that revolved around the family farm and artisan shops. From the countryside came the wool, flax, and foodstuffs that kept colonials clothed and fed.

Most of the furniture, footwear, clothing, and hardware used by British North Americans was crafted in private homes or in shops employing fewer than five people. In every town and village, local blacksmiths forged shoes for horses and nails for carpenters from their stocks of pig iron, while tailors and seamstresses fashioned custom-made suits and dresses, and at least one or two cobblers produced the footwear needed to protect colonial feet from the intractable terrain and cold climate. The construction of more substantial homes, often in the fashionable neoclassical or gothic style, documented the wealth and domestic comfort of a growing number of colonial families in both rural and urban areas of British North America.

While family and community economies displayed varying degrees of self-sufficiency, economic independence eluded most British North Americans. There were still a few families who managed to survive on the products of their own farms and some Native peoples who bartered for luxuries rather than necessities, but people living in the colonies were eager to participate in the commercial economy. Not only did they need to purchase such basic staples as sugar, tea, and spices, but they also wanted to replace their homespun with manufactured cloth and their crude tools and utensils with the increasingly superior output of the factory system.

Commercial activity kept goods and services moving in colonial British North America, but only in the major cities was there any specialization in the wholesale and retail trades. Merchants in towns and villages sold a variety of products, often including farm surpluses, and might also serve as the local postmaster, hotel operator, and political representative. General stores were exactly what the name implies, selling everything from tea and sugar to glassware and crockery. Prices were bargained, and purchases were made through barter or on long-term credit to established customers. Depending on location, merchants sometimes became involved in farming, milling, distilling, lumbering, or fishing.

Most mercantile firms operated on a 12-month cycle, reflecting the rhythms of primary pursuits. Credit radiated out of the British cities of London, Glasgow, and Liverpool, binding backwoods producers, local merchants, and major wholesalers and export dealers in a complex network of economic dependency.

Because merchants operated individually or in partnerships, businesses rarely survived the death of an owner, and bankruptcy meant disaster not only for the business but also for the merchant personally. Most British North Americans, it seems, lived not only in small worlds, but also in uncertain ones.

TOWN AND COUNTRY

The frontier of farm, forest, and fishery contrasted dramatically with the colonial cities, where variety, activity, and congestion prevailed. In 1851, the largest city in British North America was Montreal, with 57 000 people. Quebec City had 42 000 inhabitants and Toronto 30 000. Saint John, with a population of nearly 30 000, was the largest city in the Atlantic region. Most cities in 1850 were little more than overgrown villages. Even Montreal was a "walking" city, its commercial section crowded near the port.

Markets were the centre of urban life. There farm families hawked their produce, and in the nearby streets merchants and artisans sold specialized goods

and services that were unavailable in the rural areas. At mid-century, cities in British North America were building imposing new structures to house their markets and other activities of urban civic life. Bonsecours market in Montreal was, not surprisingly, the biggest of them all.

Unlike their twenty-first-century counterparts, colonial cities were not planned around business and residential activities. Merchants, artisans, and apprentices usually lived and worked in the same building, and the "seedy" side of town was often only a block away from elite business and residential areas. While colonial elites were inclined to build their "estates" on the edge of the city, working people were clustered according to ethnicity and occupation. Census records indicate that widows and single women gravitated to urban areas, where they found more opportunities for making a living than in the countryside.

Despite the opportunities cities offered, they were not always pleasant places to live. Decaying garbage and the excrement of thousands of horses, cows, and pigs filled the streets. Market squares were awash with

Behind Bonsecours Market, Montreal, by William Raphael, a Jewish migrant from Germany.
© National Gallery of Canada

animal carcasses, fish heads, and rotting vegetables. In the lower regions of the town, noxious cesspools accumulated to become a breeding place of foul odours, enormous rats, and dreaded disease. Outdoor toilets still graced the backyards of many urban homes along with pigs, chickens, and even cattle.

By 1850, city councils were beginning to install rudimentary water and sewer systems and street lighting, but even in the most progressive cities, such as Montreal, Quebec, and Saint John, only a few wealthy wards had access to such services. For those unable to afford the cost of indoor plumbing, public wells and private carters provided water. The condition of the water that reached urban dwellers helped to account for a higher death rate in cities than in rural areas.

Major British North American cities boasted a military presence to protect citizens against invasion from without and civil strife from within. Over 10 000 British soldiers were scattered from St John's to Victoria, with Halifax, Montreal, and Kingston serving as the major garrison towns. As well as infusing money into the colonial economy, the military made a substantial contribution to urban social life. Amateur theatre, sports events, and libraries were sponsored by the military, while grog shops, taverns, and prostitution inevitably flourished in the vicinity of the barracks.

Civilian British North Americans also shouldered a responsibility for defence. Every able-bodied man between 16 and 60 (except for judges, Quakers, and "lunatics") could be called out for militia duty, theoretically providing an impressive force of over 300 000. In practice, the militia were unarmed, untrained, and unenthusiastic—not usually to be relied upon in time of crisis.

Town and country in British North America were bound together by commercial exchange, which extended to the frontiers of settlement. In the Canadas, Montreal and Toronto were emerging as the focus for road, water, and eventually rail transportation networks to their economic hinterlands, but no city dominated the whole colony. In the Atlantic region, the ocean gave many communities direct communication with the great commercial capitals of the world. Boston, New York, Liverpool, and London therefore competed directly with Halifax, Saint John, Charlottetown, and St John's for economic control over the regional economy. Victoria's closest links

As this picture shows, pigs roamed freely along Sparks Street in Ottawa in the 1860s.
City of Ottawa Archives/CA-0219

were with San Francisco, which was growing by leaps and bounds following the California gold rush of 1849. As the American frontier moved steadily westward, inhabitants of Red River and other centres in the Northwest felt the inexorable pull of their southern neighbour.

THE FAMILY IN TRANSITION

The family in 1850 was still the fundamental economic and social unit of colonial society. Although a few people married at astonishingly young ages, most men remained unmarried until they were 25. The majority of women were over 23 when they married. Protestant Scots tended to marry late and have smaller families, while French-speaking Roman Catholics married earlier and had larger families. Indeed, French-speaking women on the average had nearly twice as many children as English-speaking women. Completed families—that is, families in which both parents lived for the mother's entire childbearing years—were large, averaging seven children in 1851. Married women of normal fertility could expect to have a child every two to three years. Urban women had fewer children than rural women. Aboriginal women also had low fecundity, as did those who suffered from extreme poverty and malnutrition.

At mid-century, the average family size was beginning to decrease. For the rich, too many children brought complicated claims on their estates; for the poor they brought additional stress on the family economy. Although late marriage was the most acceptable form of family limitation, artificial methods of birth control were practised. Douches, condoms, and diaphragms were available by mid-century but not widely used. The rhythm method was inadequately understood, and patent medicines to "regulate" menstruation were highly unreliable and sometimes dangerous to a woman's health. Most married women who wanted to limit the size of their families either abstained from sexual intercourse or practised extended breast-feeding to reduce their fertility.

While there is no question that families were the basic social unit, they often varied widely from the ideal. A significant proportion of British North Americans at any given time (more than 25 percent in most regions) inhabited households extended by the presence of another family, a relative, or boarders. At least 5 percent of British North Americans never married, while a growing proportion of families were headed by women who had been widowed or abandoned by their husbands. Step-parents were common in many family units. Despite biblical and legal injunctions to the contrary, marriage between cousins was considered a positive match in families attempting to retain control of property or other forms of wealth. Throughout British North America, most marriages were endogamous—that is, within the same cultural group. Despite the mixing of peoples, Old World identities remained a strong and enduring feature of colonial life.

LIFE AND DEATH

Death was a constant companion in mid-nineteenth-century British North America. One in five children died before reaching one year of age. In crowded, disease-ridden cities, the rate of infant mortality was even higher. Life expectancy was less than 50 years for both men and women. Those who managed to survive to the age of 20 could still on the average expect to live only to 60. Among the poor, malnutrition was a problem, and the rich often ate such poorly balanced diets that they contracted gout and rickets.

Women of all classes and cultures risked death in childbirth. Home was the place where most women had

their children, aided by the services of an experienced midwife. Only affluent colonials could afford the services of a doctor. Given the dangers associated with bearing children, middle-class British North Americans medicalized the experience in the hope of reducing the incidence of infant and maternal mortality.

British North Americans suffered from periodic epidemics of cholera, typhoid, smallpox, diphtheria, and other contagious diseases. In northern New Brunswick, an outbreak of leprosy among a few Acadian families resulted in government legislation to isolate the victims from their communities. Eighteen lepers were sent to an island in the Miramichi River in 1844. Five years later, they were moved to Tracadie, where the colonial Board of Health had constructed a walled lazaretto for their confinement. The angry inmates burned their building to the ground in 1852, but it was rebuilt and, in the late nineteenth century, Tracadie became the home of other Canadians suffering from the disease.

Most illnesses were treated by home remedies that were often more successful than the bleeding, blistering, and poisonous purges of medical doctors. In 1850 the medical practices of physicians were, for good reasons, widely suspected. Doctors commonly prescribed calomel, a derivative of mercury, and opium for stomach ailments, and continued to believe in the value of bleeding their patients to cure them of their "bad humours." By 1850, the Hippocratic theory that illness was the result of an imbalance among the four humours present in the body—black bile, phlegm, blood, and yellow bile—was gradually being abandoned. Many physicians still subscribed to the miasmatic theory of disease, which held that "miasma," or the poisonous atmosphere from swamps, sewers, and cellars, caused plagues. It was only during the cholera epidemic of 1854 that the connection between illness and polluted drinking water was established, and it was much longer before the germ theory of disease was accepted by medical practitioners.

In 1850, university-trained doctors were on the defensive against "root doctors," homeopaths, and patent-medicine dealers who were gaining wide popularity. Armed with new therapeutic techniques, anesthetics, and antiseptic methods, trained medical doctors in the second half of the nineteenth century moved quickly to professionalize their trade and exclude midwives, herbalists, homeopaths, and "quacks" who threatened their ascendancy. Nurses in colonial society and elsewhere were little more than poorly paid domestic servants. It was only in the mid-1850s that British reformer Florence Nightingale began her long crusade to make nursing a respectable profession.

Public health services in British North America were, at best, rudimentary. Hospitals in 1850 were places where the poor were incarcerated and given medicine and morality in equal doses. As late as 1861 in Kingston General Hospital, 45 percent of the admissions were reported to be suffering from alcohol-related diseases, and most of the babies born in hospitals were to destitute single mothers.

Alcohol was a widely used remedy for both physical and psychological ailments. Although a stiff swig of alcohol was often administered to a patient before surgery, it was used to cure other real and imagined ills as well. The range of possible alcoholic cures was impressive: home-made beer, cider, wine, and distilled liquor were supplemented by almost universal access to commercially produced rum, rye, and beer, the preferred drinks of British North Americans. Nearly all hotels, inns, and general stores sold alcohol, as did the ubiquitous taverns and saloons designed especially for the purpose. Women as well as men sought the soothing effects of alcohol, and even children were introduced to liquor at an early age. The yearly per capita consumption of alcohol by British North Americans was about 27 litres of liquor and beer for every man, woman, and child, considerably more than Canadians drink today.

Given the high incidence of death in colonial society, it is not surprising that much attention was paid to the rituals relating to death and dying. Wakes, funeral processions, and elaborate church services were turned into social occasions where people came together to comfort relatives and friends. In middle-class families, extended periods of mourning were observed, special mourning clothes purchased by the family of the deceased, and separate rooms set aside for experiencing grief.

GENDER AND SOCIETY

The old adage "women to the hearth and men to the plough" was firmly rooted in the pre-industrial division of labour. No distinction in colonial society was more fundamental than that between the sexes. Men and women performed distinct tasks in the colonial economy and were treated differently under the law. Ultimately, separate gender roles, believed to be complementary, were brought together in the family, the basic unit of production in colonial society.

While men and women contributed different skills to the family economy, women were placed in a subordinate position by laws that recognized men as household heads with wives and children as their property. In this patriarchal system, women's sexuality and reproductive powers were carefully controlled. Girls and women were supervised within families, while church, state, and collective community pressure encouraged strict conformity to acceptable sexual behaviour. Women considered to be of easy sexual virtue were publicly ridiculed and socially ostracized, while men who failed to provide for their families or were dominated by their wives were subject to criticism.

There was often great sympathy expressed for single mothers, but their lot was not an easy one. In a curious twist of legal logic, a woman could not sue a man for the support of their child, but her own father could sue the man for the loss of his daughter's services, as well as his personal distress and dishonour. Denied any recourse under the law, children without legal fathers were called "illegitimate" and carried that stigma for life. Fewer than 5 percent of all colonial births were deemed illegitimate, although a considerably higher percentage of first children were born less than nine months after the wedding day.

For young women who found themselves pregnant outside marriage, the alternatives could be grim. Infanticide was the desperate resort of many unwed mothers in the mid-nineteenth century. The bodies of newborn infants were found buried in the snow, inside hollow trees, at the bottoms of wells, under floorboards, in privies and stovepipes, and floating down rivers. The mothers who were caught were usually destitute, unmarried, working-class women with no family to share the burden of their shame or help them raise a child. Unwanted children were often placed in charitable institutions, where the majority of them died. Under the British laws that prevailed in the colonies in the early nineteenth century, anyone convicted of infanticide, abortion, or rape was subject to the death penalty, but lighter sentences for these crimes were gradually being adopted.

Throughout British North America, divorces were difficult to obtain, frowned upon by the church and state as a threat to social stability. Before mid-century, a woman who left her husband received no property settlement, and custody of the children invariably went to the father. A divorce could be granted by a special act of the legislature in cases where the husband was proved to be guilty of incest, sodomy, bestiality, bigamy, or rape of a woman other than his wife (under the law it was impossible for a husband to rape his own wife). Except in Nova Scotia, cruelty was not a legal justification for divorce in British North America: as the head of the family, a man was considered to have the right to inflict physical "discipline" on his wife and children, provided he did not use "excessive force." In the Maritime colonies, the divorce laws, rooted in New England practice, were less rigid than in Canada West, where only five divorces were granted before Confederation. The Custom of Paris was even more stringent and did not recognize divorce at all.

Class Identities

In British North America, class lines lost some of their old world rigidity but they still played a major role in determining individual identity. Class in colonial society was based on kinship, wealth, and relationship to production. Although hereditary privileges were largely absent in North America, access to sources of wealth and power was narrowly restricted. Most people lived in the middle and lower ranks of society and faced a lifetime of unrelenting toil.

Tight little cliques of merchants, professionals, and politicians dominated all aspects of life in the settled colonies. While individual members of the colonial elite might experience failure, as a group they were growing more powerful. Michael Katz's studies show that at mid-century less than 10 percent of the adult men in Hamilton, Canada West, held "virtually all of the resources necessary to the health, well-being, and prosperity" of the rest of the community. "The rulers, the owners, and the rich were by and large the same people."[2]

A middle class of farmers and artisans constituted the "bone and sinew" of colonial society. A term first used in England in 1811, "middle class" was beginning to take on a new, more complex meaning in the nineteenth century as some "producers" in the colonies expanded their operations beyond the family farm and the artisan's shop to emerge as successful entrepreneurs. Respectable artisans in British North America joined fraternal organizations and were elected to city councils. On the lower end of the middle-class spectrum, subsistence farming, fishing, and artisan families struggled to survive, their fate never far removed from the uncertainty of wage dependency.

In both town and country, a class of propertyless labour survived by doing manual work, often on a seasonal basis. Skilled labourers such as printers and ship pilots earned a living wage while unskilled labourers were subject to cycles of boom and bust, the rhythms of the seasons, and payment in kind rather than cash. For some British North Americans, wage labour was only a stage in their life cycle, a chance to earn a little money before returning to the family farm or setting up in business. But for most labourers, these possibilities were receding in a society where class lines had become increasingly rigid.

Education

Social factors in British North America determined who went to school and what they learned once there. For anyone planning to make a living trapping, farming, fishing, or homemaking, formal schooling was far less important than practical experience. The skills of the artisan were acquired through apprenticeship. Boys learned to become good providers by following in their fathers' footsteps; girls learned housewifery skills from their mothers and female relatives and perhaps practised them for a brief period in domestic service before setting up their own households.

Although over 60 percent of British North American youngsters received formal schooling at mid-century, most of these children attended irregularly and for only a few years. Regular and extended school attendance was difficult for the poor, especially in rural areas where children's labour was required on the farm. Protestants, particularly Scots and Americans, sent their children to school more regularly than did French and Irish Catholics. Boys tended to receive more formal education than girls, and they learned different subjects. In the elite private schools, emphasis was placed on Latin, science, mathematics, and philosophy for boys destined for business and the professions, while girls were taught the "ornamental skills" of sewing, music, painting, and polite manners. The growing number of common schools taught the "three Rs" to both boys and girls but offered few of the "frills" found in the private schools.

Despite the uneven educational picture, a majority of British North Americans seem to have been literate. Many of them were taught at home or in the shop. While publicly supported schools increasingly became the choice of parents for educating their children, some families continued to rely on privately operated schools. The elite wanted their children educated separately from the riff-raff, and ordinary folk often had misgivings about the public-school curriculum or the local public-school teacher. In Kingston in 1849, there were 738 children in common schools and 826 in various private schools.

Notwithstanding the patchwork of educational institutions, it was clear to many people by 1850 that formal education was a valuable asset. The founding of colleges testified to the acceptance of learning a living as the way of the future. Even those who remained illiterate acknowledged the growing power of the printed word in their everyday lives. From the census, which was taken in many of the colonies in 1851, to account books, contracts, diaries, prescriptions, and school ledgers, society was increasingly defined in texts, and the advantage was on the side of those who could read them.

CHRISTIANITY AND CULTURE

At mid-century, the Christian religion was the prism through which many British North Americans interpreted their values about class, culture, gender, race, and politics. The new liberal order had insisted on the separation of church and state, but churches remained vibrant voluntary organizations that competed with each other for adherents and influence. In all but the largest towns and cities, a new church was the most prominent building in 1850, the size of the structure a clear indication of the power that a particular denomination held in the community. British North Americans often looked first to their parsons and

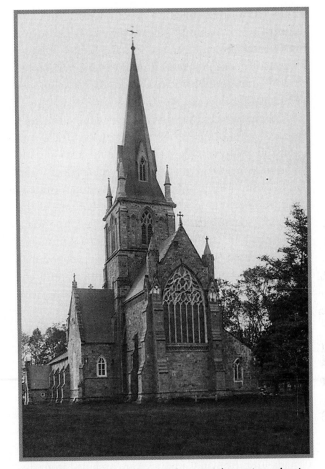

In the mid-nineteenth century, churches were the most prominent public buildings in the colonies. Many churches were designed in the Gothic revival style, which was inspired by a renewed interest in the Gothic architecture of the Middle Ages. Christ Church Cathedral in Fredericton, built between 1845 and 1853, reflected the "correct" ecclesiastic principles in Gothic revival church architecture as perceived by the Anglican Bishop of Fredericton, the Right Reverend John Medley.
New Brunswick Provincial Archives

priests for guidance on secular as well as spiritual matters and usually, though not always, followed their injunctions.

Although most British North Americans claimed to be Christians, they differed considerably in their approach to religious practice. Four out of ten British North Americans were Roman Catholics, but only in Assiniboia and Quebec were Roman Catholics in the majority. Over 40 percent of the population of Newfoundland and Prince Edward Island, a third of New Brunswickers, and one-quarter of Nova Scotians also subscribed to the Roman Catholic faith. Canada West, where Roman Catholics accounted for only

20 percent of the population, was the most Protestant region in British North America. Methodists, Presbyterians, and Anglicans were the largest Protestant denominations. In the western portions of Nova Scotia and New Brunswick, Baptist churches attracted a significant following.

Ethnicity was a major factor determining religious affiliation. People of Aboriginal, French, Irish, and Highland Scottish backgrounds were most commonly found in Roman Catholic churches, while people who had English, Welsh, Lowland Scot, and American heritage were more likely to be adherents of one of the Protestant denominations. Mixed marriages between Protestant and Catholic were frowned upon and in many areas schools were developed along denominational lines to ensure that young people of different religious and ethnic background did not come in close contact in an educational setting.

While religious affiliation was closely tied to ethnic origin, it also had a bearing on class. The Methodists and Baptists, for instance, were particularly adept at winning converts among farmers and artisans. Although Methodists and Baptists could be found among those who had already acquired wealth and status, members of the Church of England and the Church of Scotland were overrepresented among colonial elites. Outside Canada East, Roman Catholics were excluded from the corridors of wealth and power, and throughout British North America Roman Catholics were heavily concentrated in the labouring class.

The impact of cultural differences varied. Nowhere in British North America was there a closer correlation between class, ethnicity, and religion than in Newfoundland, where an overwhelmingly Protestant mercantile elite stood apart from a predominantly (though not exclusively) labouring class of Irish Roman Catholics who caught and cured the fish and did manual work in the mercantile centre of St John's. Similarly, English and Scottish immigrants and native-born anglophones dominated the high-status occupations in New Brunswick, while Irish Catholics made up a disproportionate number of the working class. Conversely, immigrant Irish Catholics in Leeds and Lansdowne townships in Canada West were among the most successful farmers and no more likely to be found among the ranks of the labouring class than their Canadian-born neighbours.

Ethnicity, unlike race, was an invisible identity that could be modified by time, marriage, and deliberate choice. In Charlotte County, New Brunswick, Irish Protestants in the late nineteenth century escaped any negative implications of their ethnic identity in a "Loyalist province" by adopting the more general "English" designation.

RACE AND RACISM

People whose skin was not white suffered most from the smug, small worlds of class and culture in British North America. At mid-century, Indians, Inuit, and blacks made up the majority of people of colour. Few in number, with the exception of the Native population of Rupert's Land, they were relegated to the margins of colonial society and treated with a mixture of disdain and paternalism.

First Nations

In areas where they no longer posed a threat to European settlement, Aboriginal peoples became a cause for concern among administrators and humanitarians. Early-nineteenth-century theories supported a belief in the common origins of human life and the possibilities of "improving" primitive people through education in Christian principles and civilized behaviour. As a result of such thinking, both imperial and colonial administrators encouraged Native peoples to abandon their nomadic existence and to become farmers "like everybody else." This policy soon fell victim to racial biases. At best, it was well-meaning but condescending; at worst, exploitative, fraudulent, and negligent.

The lives of Aboriginal peoples in the colonies varied considerably. In the Grand River area, in Canada West, the Six Nations lived a settled agricultural existence and were reasonably successful in resisting white encroachment on their lands. Nevertheless, the superintendent of Indian affairs invested $38 000 of band money in the failing Grand River Navigation Company (of which the superintendent was a director) without consulting the Six Nations. Like the Mohawk of Caughnawaga (Kahnawaké) near Lachine, most Aboriginal peoples trapped within the confines of white settlement found the world around them changing rapidly in the mid-nineteenth century. They were not only isolated on reserves but also had to contend with constant interference by white bureaucracies.

Aboriginal peoples still dependent upon the hunt moved north and west with the receding fur-trade frontier, but the white bureaucracies followed them there as well. Manitoulin Island in Lake Huron became a centre of Ojibwa settlement in the late 1830s. By 1848, armed skirmishes between Ojibwa and the Quebec Mining Company resulted in a new series of treaties on the boundary separating Canada from the HBC territory, a sign that the fur-trade frontier and a way of life originally identified with the First Nations in eastern British North America was virtually gone.

As in the past, white policy was based on the willingness of Aboriginal peoples to surrender claims to land in return for reserves, annual gifts, and the right to hunt and fish on unoccupied land. The treaties arranged by W.B. Robinson with the Ojibwa in the Upper Great Lakes region in 1850 included several new provisions, reflecting the changing circumstances. Among them were the rights to royalties on any minerals found on their reserves and an "escalator" clause providing for an increase in the annuity payments should the value of the surrendered land increase dramatically.

In the Atlantic colonies by 1850, the fur-trade frontier was little more than a memory. Each summer the Mi'kmaq and Maliseet emerged from their winter retreats to peddle their wares in markets and from

VOICES FROM THE PAST

Great Chief Petrokeshig and Oshawana Speak Their Minds

Although the Christian missionaries sometimes met a hostile reception from Native peoples, they rarely bothered to record the arguments of the people who opposed them. An important exception is the careful account that Father Pierre Chazelle, a Jesuit, kept of his dialogue with the people of Walpole Island. Ojibwa had settled on the small, marsh-covered island in Lake St Clair in the eighteenth century. While they remained the largest group of residents in 1844, when this conversation was recorded, they had been joined by other Native groups dispossessed by westward expansion in the United States. About 700 families lived on the island, with an additional 400 living on the surrounding mainland. As the speeches of Great Chief Petrokeshig and of Oshawana, an 83-year-old warrior, make clear, many traditionalists did not appreciate the coming of the Jesuits, and their mission mysteriously went up in flames in 1849:

> Oshawana: The man with a hat left his island; he crossed the great water, he arrived on our land; he travelled through our forests and over our lakes, and he pursued us everywhere to take from us what belonged to us. And today, his race has multiplied on our great island and has established its customs here. But we, we have become fugitives, destitute and almost annihilated.

> Before, the savage man did not know drunkenness; you, man with a hat, are the one who poured me firewater.

> Thus, the man that lives beyond the great water did not come here to bring us blessings but misfortune. How then could we believe the things he comes to tell us? . . .

> Petrokeshig: . . . As a Savage, I peel the bark of trees and I build myself a cabin. I also look for remedies in the varied plants that the Great Spirit made grow from the earth. I find those that I know and that I want; I boil them in water; I drink and I cease to be sick. The Great Spirit taught this science to my ancestor. He also communicated much more knowledge to him. The blessings he received are great; we do not want to renounce them.

> My brother, you also received great blessings from your Ancestor; but I believe that you did not keep them faithfully, and that is undoubtedly why the Great Spirit sent his son, who came to bestow new blessings on you. However, you did not want to believe him, you mistreated him, you made him die.

> But I, a savage man, did not need his visit, because I have kept my Ancestor's blessings. Neither did he come to my great island. None of us ever heard that he appeared anywhere to teach Wisdom.[3]

door to door in white communities. Sought by collectors throughout the world, Native crafts were prominent among colonial exhibits appearing at the Great Exhibition in London in 1851. Gifted Native artists such as Mary Christianne Paul Morris could earn a reasonable living from their labours.

Despite valiant efforts to live on the margins of white culture, most Aboriginal peoples had a difficult time just surviving. Their numbers declined precipitously in the first half of the nineteenth century, and by all accounts they suffered terribly from tuberculosis, typhus, smallpox, measles, scarlet fever, and whooping cough. Sickness attacked families and whole bands and drained the energy from survivors. Language barriers made it difficult for Aboriginal peoples to express their concerns and to use the court system effectively. Although alcohol took its toll among whites, its effects were particularly noticeable among the Natives, whose lives were more open to public scrutiny.

Treaties gave Aboriginal peoples some legal grounds to use against the relentless encroachment of white settlement on reserve lands. Yet even land guaranteed by treaty had to be defended against the public policy of selling off portions of reserves to make Native administration pay for itself. Aboriginal people who managed to play the white man's game had difficulty functioning within the context of the reserve system. Miramichi chief Barnaby Julien, for instance, leased reserve lands and consequently was deposed by the band on the grounds that he was personally profiting from a communal resource. The likelihood of securing the consent of a whole tribe for commercial transactions was extremely remote.

By mid-century, responsibility for Indian policy was gradually being transferred from British to colonial governments. The colonies were even more reluctant than Britain to spend public money on Aboriginal people. In Nova Scotia, Joseph Howe was appointed first Indian commissioner under colonial legislation of 1842, but the position carried no salary. Not surprisingly his enthusiasm soon flagged. In 1857, the colony ceased special relief payments to the Mi'kmaq and insisted that they be included under the general municipal poor laws.

Church and philanthropic agencies frequently filled the vacuum left by sluggish colonial administrations. In 1845, Methodist minister Peter Jones, son of a white surveyor father and a Mississauga mother, established the Mount Elgin Industrial Institution at Munceytown Reserve, Canada West. The objective of the institution was to inculcate Christian values and the work ethic. While boys learned trades such as shoemaking and carpentry, girls were taught sewing, knitting, spinning, and the general skills of housewifery. In the Maritimes, Silas Rand tried to convert the Mi'kmaq, who had practised Roman Catholicism since the time of the French regime, to the Baptist faith. Rand's evangelical efforts had less of a long-term impact than his work in collecting Mi'kmaq legends and compiling a Mi'kmaq dictionary. In general, the promotion of mission schools, evangelical religion, and useful skills in an environment segregated from the corrupting influences of white society testified to the paternalism of whites and the barriers preventing Aboriginal peoples from full participation in North American society.

Blacks

Discrimination against blacks in British North America was less formal but equally crippling in its impact. Compared with the United States, where slavery was still practised, British North America appeared to be a mecca, and refugees from the United States arrived in substantial numbers throughout the first half of the nineteenth century. They soon separated themselves both from white settlement and from the descendants of the black Loyalists. Blacks had their historical and cultural differences, but in the eyes of whites these were often blurred by the overriding factor of colour.

Notwithstanding strong anti-slavery sentiment in the colonies, the treatment of blacks was characterized by little Christian charity. Some 20 years after the arrival of the black refugees following the War of 1812, land title in Nova Scotia and New Brunswick was still uncertain. When their complaints were eventually addressed, blacks were given small allocations. The grants to their white neighbours were both larger and more efficiently registered. Following the abolition of slavery in the British Empire in 1833, the Nova Scotia Assembly passed "An Act to prevent the Clandestine Landing of Liberated Slaves . . . from Vessels arriving in the Province."

In every area of public life, blacks faced discrimination. Although black men who owned land could vote in British North America, they complained in Nova Scotia that they could not do so without being questioned and browbeaten. They were also denied equal access to public schooling. Only through the initiative of religious and philanthropic societies such as the Society for the Propagation of the Gospel, Dr Bray's Associates, and the Society for Promoting Christian Knowledge were schools provided for blacks.

By the 1830s, Canada West had become the preferred destination for free blacks and refugee slaves who crossed the border to settle near Windsor and Niagara Falls. One of the most publicized efforts to plant a black colony in Canada was initiated in 1842 under the auspices of the British-American Institute. Josiah Henson, a slave who escaped to Upper Canada in 1830, was the moving spirit behind the settlement, located near Chatham. Christened "Dawn," the community attracted over 500 settlers, who raised tobacco, wheat, and coarse grains and engaged in lumbering activities. Believing that separation was the best means of preparing slaves for freedom, the Dawn settlers were served by their own school, church, gristmill, sawmill, and brickyard. The publication of Harriet Beecher Stowe's novel *Uncle Tom's Cabin* in 1851 brought immediate fame to Dawn, because Henson was reputedly the prototype for the character of Uncle Tom.

BIOGRAPHY

Mary Ann Shadd Cary

Born in Wilmington, Delaware, in 1823, Mary Ann Shadd was the eldest child of a free black abolitionist family. She was educated at a Quaker boarding school in Pennsylvania and from 1839 to 1850 worked as a teacher in the United States. Following the passage of the Fugitive Slave Law in 1850, Shadd moved to Windsor, Canada West, where she opened a school with funds provided by the American Missionary Association. She soon became involved in anti-slavery societies and in 1852 published *A Plea for Emigration*, an information manual for African Americans who were interested in moving to Canada West. She was the driving force behind the founding of the *Provincial Freeman*, an anti-slavery weekly newspaper, which published more or less regularly between 1854 and 1858.

An ardent integrationist, Shadd opposed the founding of segregated black communities and schools. After the death of her husband, Thomas Cary, in 1860, she supported herself and her two children by teaching at an interracial school in Chatham. Shadd moved to the United States in 1863 to help recruit volunteers for the Union Army during the American Civil War. Although she returned briefly to Canada West in 1866, she spent most of the rest of her life in the United States. She taught school to support herself while studying law at Harvard, and after graduating in 1883 she set up a practice in Washington, DC. In 1881, she visited Canada to help organize a suffrage campaign. She died in 1893.

Mary Ann Shadd Cary.
Library and Archives Canada/C29977

Following the passage of the Fugitive Slave Act, the number of African Americans moving into Canada West increased, but not in the tens of thousands that historians once claimed. A recent study suggests that the number was much smaller, perhaps 20 percent of a total black population of about 23 000.[4] More than 40 percent of the blacks living in the colony were colonial-born, and most of the black immigrants were free settlers, not runaway slaves.

Whether immigrant or colonial-born, fugitive or free, blacks in Canada West could not escape the cold shoulder of racial prejudice. For example, 400 people gathered in Chatham, Canada West, in August 1849 to protest against a proposed black settlement in the area by the Elgin Association. The citizens of Chatham then passed a resolution stating: "That in the opinion of this meeting, it would be unconstitutional, impolitic and unjust government, to sell large portions of the public domain in SETTLED PARTS of this province, to foreigners, the more so, when such persons belong to a different branch of the human family, and are BLACK."[5] Although the Elgin settlement eventually went ahead, the immigrants continued to experience opposition from their neighbours. In 1850, segregated schools were officially sanctioned in Canada West. Mary Ann Shadd Cary, who in the 1850s edited a newspaper for her people called the *Provincial Freeman*, argued against the separatist tendencies of both whites and blacks, but to little avail.

Abolitionists in Canada West occasionally scored some victories against racism. When John Anderson, a fugitive slave accused of killing his master, was tried in Toronto in 1860, two of the three judges, including Sir John Beverley Robinson, argued that by killing a man Anderson had made himself liable to extradition to the United States to stand trial for his crime. Following massive protests from the international abolitionist community and a threat of intervention by Britain, the case was dismissed on a technicality. Meanwhile, Anderson was taken to Britain by his abolitionist friends and he eventually settled in the West African state of Liberia.

In the middle of the nineteenth century, many slaves made their way to British North America, and freedom, by an informal network of sympathizers in the United States, known collectively as the "underground railroad," who provided shelter, food, and transportation in defiance of the Fugitive Slave Law.
Library and Archives Canada/PA123708

SPORTS AND LEISURE

Most British North Americans had little time for what in the twenty-first century is called leisure activity. Yet weekly and seasonal rhythms incorporated social activity as a break from the monotony of daily toil. The "sabbath" was rigorously observed among those of evangelical persuasion, and church services were important community occasions for all Christians. In rural areas, "bees" brought people together for quilting, building, planting, and harvest activities. Priests and parsons often complained of the drunkenness and immorality that prevailed at rural "frolics" that were popular throughout the colonies, especially among those of Scottish and Irish background.

In urban centres, the military and social elite engaged in organized sports. Colonial cities also sprouted theatres where local amateur players and professional travelling troupes delighted audiences, and appalled evangelicals, with their performances. During winter months, enforced relaxation provided a good opportunity for sleighing parties, weddings, and

extended visits with friends and relatives. Winter travel over well-packed snow or ice was often a welcome alternative to muddy and uncomfortably rough roads in other seasons of the year. Diaries and letters of the colonial middle class often tell of family members reading and writing letters around a flickering candle or oil lamp on a chilly winter's evening.

In 1850, religious holidays had yet to take on the crass materialism that developed later in the century, but most cultural groups formally marked Christmas and Easter as well as the passing of the old year and the arrival of spring. For Aboriginal peoples in the Maritime colonies, the feast of Saint Anne on 26 July was a time to meet at Shubenacadie, Chapel Island, Lennox Island, and Burnt Church to reaffirm their culture. Days devoted to St George, St Patrick, and St Andrew were celebrated by the English, Irish, and Scots respectively. Irish Protestants, and increasingly Protestants generally, remembered the anniversary of the Battle of the Boyne. Many of these cultural events preserved limited identities and made the sense of a larger community identity difficult to establish.

Games, sports, and competitions were part of the festive and communal occasions of all pre-industrial cultures. Unorganized, unsophisticated, and accompanied by drinking and brawling, they were often scenes of cracked heads and hard feelings. In rural areas of British North America, cock-fighting, bearbaiting, horse races, wrestling, and fisticuffs were popular. The colonial elite increasingly criticized such activities. They participated in organized sports, copied, for the most part, from events held among the British aristocracy. Clubs devoted to racing, yachting, rowing, and curling could be found from St John's to Toronto by the mid-nineteenth century and would soon take root in Victoria. Sports developed by Aboriginal peoples, most notably lacrosse and snowshoeing, were also popular in elite circles.

Until the founding of the Canadian Lacrosse Association in 1867, lacrosse was largely confined to Montreal, where a Caughnawaga team first demonstrated the game before a white audience on the St Pierre Race Course in 1834.
Notman Photographic Archives, McCord Museum of Canadian History, Montreal, I-29099

As the largest British North American city, and one with a significant military presence, Montreal emerged as the centre of organized sports. It boasted the first organized club—the Montreal Curling Club—in 1807, the first cricket, lacrosse, hunt, and snowshoeing clubs, and the first specialized sports facilities. Cricket was the game of champions in mid-nineteenth century British North America and Toronto was the cricket capital of British North America, in part because of the influence of the first headmaster of Upper Canada College, which was founded in 1829. Considered a vehicle for teaching elite values, cricket was initially the sport of British immigrants and others who aped British sporting ideology. On 13 July 1836, the editor of the *Toronto Patriot* even claimed that a "cricketer as a matter of course, detests democracy and is staunch in his allegiance to his King." By the 1850s, cricket enjoyed a wide popularity and cricket clubs had mushroomed all over British North America. International matches with American teams began in 1844 and became annual events after 1853.

THE CREATIVE ARTS

British North Americans consumed literature produced abroad and generated some of their own. By 1850, Thomas Chandler Haliburton and Susanna Moodie had gained an international reputation for their work, which consisted primarily of humorous sketches of colonial life. Moodie's sister, Catharine Parr Traill, was one of several British writers who wrote guides for fellow immigrants. Traill's *Backwoods of Canada* (1836) and *The Canadian Settler's Guide* (1855) presented a mixture of sound advice, pious homilies, and natural history that reflected the literary taste of the time.

An intellectual awakening in French Canada was one of the noteworthy cultural developments of the mid-nineteenth century. Following Durham's cruel comment that the French Canadians were a people with no literature and no culture, histories and creative writing appeared to prove the British lord wrong. François-Xavier Garneau's *Histoire du Canada*, which appeared in several volumes between 1845 and 1852, was an inspired piece of scholarship. In the Maritimes, Peter Fisher and Haliburton had also turned their

hands to writing history, and in Canada West, John Richardson published *The War of 1812* in 1842. Robert Christie's *History of the Late Province of Lower Canada*, published in six ponderous volumes, began appearing in 1848.

Magazines published in British North America had a difficult time competing with American publications and colonial newspapers that contained popular works of British and American writers. The *Literary Garland*, based in Montreal, expired in 1851 after a valiant effort to provide a forum for colonial writers. In the same year, Halifax-born poet Mary Eliza Herbert began publishing the *Mayflower*. Devoted to literature for those who wished "to roam a while in the flowery field of romance,—to hold communion with the Muses," it survived for only nine issues and most of the contributions came from Herbert herself.

Despite the paucity of colonial contributors, the reading audience was growing and the pace of intellectual life quickening noticeably. Mechanics' Institutes served as vehicles for literary and scientific discussion among the middle classes in major colonial cities, while branches of the Institut Canadien in Canada East were hotbeds of intellectual debate and literary creativity.

Circuses and travelling shows were popular in the mid-nineteenth century. Even John A. Macdonald was reputed to have briefly joined a travelling troupe in his younger days. A "mud show," so called because of the conditions of the roads, could get around in a horse and wagon convoy, making perhaps little more than 15 or 20 kilometres a day. With the advent of the train, travelling troupes and circuses became grander affairs, with long parades of jugglers, exotic animals, and other weird and wonderful sights parading down the village street from the railway station.

The sublime, exotic, quaint, and unusual were considered appropriate subjects in the romantic age, and British North America, in the eyes of outsiders at least, was a fertile field for the creative imagination. Deemed quaint and romantic, both the Acadians of the Maritimes and the French Canadians in Canada East drew the attention of foreign authors and artists. So, too, did Native peoples. Two Cape Breton "giants," Angus McAskill and Anna Swan, became well-known attractions throughout North America and were courted by American promoter P.T. Barnum,

MORE TO THE STORY

Romantic Art in a Colonial Setting

As in the eighteenth century, artists in early-nineteenth-century British North America were influenced by conventions defined in Europe and increasingly in the United States. Romantic notions of the rural countryside led city-trained artists to produce idealized landscapes to grace the homes of people who could afford to buy artwork. In British North America, this trend was reflected in panoramic views of the rugged colonial terrain and romantic renderings of the supposedly quaint and exotic peoples who lived there.

In their pursuit of subjects that would not offend the buying public, colonial artists often ignored reality. Thus, the Dutch-born artist Cornelius Krieghoff painted happy habitants in colourful costumes at a time when political and economic pressures were eroding seigneurial society. Similarly, the Toronto-based painter Paul Kane, who made his artistic reputation painting the Aboriginal peoples of the western plains, failed to capture the dark side of a world that was being rapidly transformed by outside forces. The work of both men displays a preoccupation with light and colour typical of artists in the romantic era.

One of the most accomplished of colonial artists was Quebec-born Joseph Légaré. His use of light and colour was exceptional, and he turned out landscapes, portraits, and religious subjects to suit the most conventional tastes. At the same time, Légaré was an ardent Patriote who was arrested during the rebellions of 1837–38. Such paintings as *The Cholera Plague, Quebec* (c. 1837) and *After the Fire at Saint-Roch* (1845) testify to his political sensibility and the less romantic side of colonial life.

By the mid-nineteenth century, colonial artists were being forced to adjust to the impact of photography. While the growing middle class continued to buy landscape paintings for their walls, they were now less inclined to have their portraits painted. Instead, people of all classes visited photographic studios, where they sat motionless in front of a bulky mechanical device that "shot" their photographic images. The most successful photographic studio in pre-Confederation British North America was founded by William Notman in Montreal in 1856. Over the next 35 years, Notman established 14 branch studios in Canada and the United States, all managed by his trainees, including three of his sons who followed him into the trade. The 400 000 pictures in the Notman Archives in the McCord Museum at McGill University constitute a national treasure of incalculable value.

The Burning of the Parliament Building, c. 1849, by Joseph Légaré.
McCord Museum of Canadian History, Montreal, M11712

Interior of a French Canadian Farm House, by Cornelius Krieghoff, c. 1856.
Metropolitan Toronto Reference Library/JRR1659

who specialized in the bizarre and unusual. In June 1859, Blondin, the famous French funambulist, walked a tightrope over the even more famous Niagara Falls.

By this time Niagara Falls had emerged as a popular destination for the travelling public not only from within the colony, but also from the United States and Europe. Promoters of the Falls created an image of a sublime, wild, and romantic locale for European travellers. As early as the 1820s, the Falls had lost much of its natural beauty, surrounded as it was by efforts to make money from the growing number of tourists. Entrepreneurs set up hotels, museums, sea gardens, souvenir shops, steamboat services, and coach services, and guidebooks directed tourists through the area. Native women fashioned crafts that they and their children sold to visitors happy to purchase mementoes of such exotic people. Old soldiers served as guides to battle sites of the War of 1812. With the growth of train travel, the Falls became a site for newly married couples who indulged in a new fad called "the honeymoon."

Colonial theatres hosted a variety of functions, including live plays, music concerts, and dramatic readings. Toronto's much-praised St Lawrence Hall was opened in 1851 to accommodate, among other things, the increasing variety of local and international artists. In 1846, Haligonians converted a hay barn into the Theatre Royal, which in the following decade became the Sothern Lyceum, named after E.A. Sothern, whose troupe was located briefly in the city. No British North American writer made a living from producing plays, but a few actors did well on the theatre circuit.

Most plays had conventional themes that appealed to the relatively unsophisticated tastes of the colonial middle class. On occasion sparks flew, as in 1845 when a play entitled *The Provincial Association* by Thomas Hill provoked a riot among the hired hands of the satirized protectionist merchants and politicians of Saint John. Although art was still confined primarily to polite drawing-room sketches—nudes were the source of much head-shaking—a few art teachers survived in the colonies, and art shows were no longer a rare event.

In the mid-nineteenth century, music appealed to a wider audience than most artistic forms. Regimental bands, operas, operettas, symphonies, and choral recitals were well attended. Even in the backwoods, itinerant teachers inspired the formation of singing schools—all the rage in the 1850s—in which the basics of hymn and psalm singing were taught. No Victorian parlour worthy of the name was complete without a pump organ, the perfect accompaniment to hymns and popular tunes. With its elite Grenadier and Coldstream Guards, Quebec City boasted the best band concerts in the colonies.

Those British North Americans too poor or living in regions too remote to attend gala performances made their own music, using their own voices and whatever musical instrument happened to be at hand. Combs, spoons, saws, and stepping feet would serve as reasonable accompaniment if nothing else was available. Many families treasured a violin or harpsichord brought from their homelands, and the very talented could often fashion instruments from local resources.

French Canadians had a rich musical heritage, which was enhanced by European immigrants such as Charles Wugk Sabatier, who arrived from Paris in 1848. A student of the famous Conservatoire de Paris, Sabatier taught Calixa Lavallée, the future composer of *O Canada*. By 1850, Joseph Casavant, who had installed his first church organ in 1840, was already well on his way to establishing a worldwide reputation as an organ manufacturer. Talented British North Americans were also beginning to develop careers that took them outside of their homeland. Emma (Lajeunesse) Albani, a child prodigy destined to become an international singing star, made her debut at the Mechanics' Hall in Montreal in 1856.

CONCLUSION

By the 1850s, the hierarchical class system, unequal distribution of wealth and status, and carefully prescribed roles of men and women that prevailed in much of British North America were increasingly being called into question. Although religious prescription and the ever-present threat of death and disaster tended to encourage fatalism and discourage long-range planning, "free will" was becoming increasingly accepted among the middle class as the basis for making personal decisions. For the poor and powerless, Providence, God's will, or Lady Luck were still acknowledged to have as much influence as human motivation in shaping destiny, but their social superiors would no longer tolerate such a rationalization for their pitiful state. As the values of the new industrial order settled upon the colonial landscape, everyone was called upon to rise to the occasion, and there would be no place for slackers.

A HISTORIOGRAPHICAL DEBATE

Religion and Culture

Religion played an important role in British North American society, but Canadian social historians have been slow to focus on its significance. Marxist scholars had a tendency to dismiss religion as a manifestation of "false consciousness," while early feminist writers either ignored or treated unsympathetically the impact of religion on women's culture. A few intrepid scholars, such as George Rawlyk and his students at Queen's in the 1970s, treated religion seriously enough, but they initially emphasized its conservative rather than revolutionary potential.

Later studies, including several by George Rawlyk himself, offer a new interpretation of the role of religion in colonial society. Instead of serving as a reactionary force, evangelicalism, it is argued, struck at the roots of the divine-right ideology that justified the old aristocratic order.[6]

Historian Michael Gauvreau maintains that the several waves of evangelical fervour that occurred in the North Atlantic world in the nineteenth century "touched and transformed the religion of all social classes." In addition to empowering individuals to shoulder tremendous burdens and make great changes in their lives, evangelicalism had a significant impact on Canadian public life. Evangelicalism, Gauvreau argues, coincided exactly with the decades in which society, ideologies, and institutions took shape in English Canada, and it helped mould new ideologies and institutions in a way impossible in the older societies of Britain and France, and even of the United States.

Gauvreau maintains that evangelicalism was one of the key cultural forces leading to the emergence of the complex of ideas and attitudes that we designate as "modern." "For those who lived through the cataclysmic social and cultural changes of the decades between 1800 and 1870," he argues, evangelicalism "was expressive of their participation in a transatlantic movement of religious revival, which transformed not only personal piety but also values, institutional life and the relationship of the Christian churches to state and society."[7]

Like Gauvreau, John Webster Grant interprets evangelicalism as a "new age" religion that supplied the language, values, and goals for people immersed in the culture of commercial capitalism. The evangelical emphasis on "individual" religious experience and the voluntary association of free individuals prepared people for participation in a variety of organizations, including temperance groups, missionary societies, fraternal groups, and Sunday schools, as well as business enterprises and democratically elected political institutions.[8]

By approaching religions as belief systems rather than institutions, William Westfall shows that people in the nineteenth century were beginning to draw distinctions between the Old World view based on order and the new one based on experience. Anglicans such as Bishop John Strachan feared the political implications of the religious "experience" promoted by the Methodists because it led to rejection of received religion and the leadership of one's social superiors.[9]

Gradually, over the course of the first half of the nineteenth century, the evangelical perspective prevailed and a "Protestant consensus" emerged about how the world worked. Rather than being divinely constructed, as conservative Anglicans and Roman Catholics maintained, or preordained as argued in the Calvinist tradition, the basic elements of human life were now defined as being created through the personal actions of individuals. Ultimately, the state, the economy, and society itself took shape around this consensus. "Responsible" government, "free" enterprise, and "voluntary" association became basic tools that British North Americans used to enter the second half of the nineteenth century.

Historians of religion may have been relegated to the margins in the past, but this is no longer the case. As scholars increasingly focus on culture—the beliefs and practices that define various groups—religion has become a major topic of research. Indeed, Nancy Christie and Michael Gauvreau have recently argued that at least until the 1940s religion was a major cultural resource that people drew upon to conceptualize their identities and served, along with the family, as the dominant source of social discipline in Canadian society.[10] Such claims still have to be proven but they spark debate and encourage historians to undertake further research on the role of religion in Canadian society.

NOTES

1 Cited in Claudette Knight, "Black Parents Speak: Education in Mid-Nineteenth-Century Canada West," *Ontario History* (Dec. 1997): 269.

2 Michael B. Katz, *The People of Hamilton, Canada West: Family and Class in a Mid-Nineteenth-Century City* (Cambridge: Harvard University Press, 1975), 43.

3 Denys Delâge and Helen Hornbeck Tanner, "The Ojibwa-Jesuit Debate at Walpole Island, 1844," in *The Native Imprint: The Contribution of First Peoples to Canada's Character*, vol. 1, *To 1815*, ed. Olive Dickason (Athabasca: Athabasca University Educational Enterprises, 1995), 280, 287–88.

4 Michael Wayne, "The Black Population of Canada West on the Eve of the American Civil War: A Reassessment Based on the Manuscript Census of 1861," *Histoire sociale/Social History* 28, 56 (Nov. 1995): 465–81.

5 Peggy Bristow, "'Whatever you can raise in the ground you can sell it in Chatham': Black Women in Buxton and Chatham, 1850–65," in Peggy Bristow et al., *"We're Rooted Here and They Can't Pull Us Up": Essays in African Canadian Women's History* (Toronto: University of Toronto Press, 1994), 77.

6 See, for example, G.A. Rawlyk, *Ravished by the Spirit: Religious Revivals, Baptists, and Henry Alline* (Montreal: McGill-Queen's University Press, 1984).

7 See the works by Michael Gauvreau, "Beyond the Half-Way House: Evangelicalism and the Shaping of English-Canadian Culture," *Acadiensis* 20, 2 (Spring 1991): 158–77; "Protestantism Transformed: Personal Piety and the Evangelical Social Vision, 1815–1867," in *The Canadian Protestant Experience, 1760–1990*, ed. George A. Rawlyk (Burlington, ON: G.R. Welch, 1990), 48–97; and *The Evangelical Century: College and Creed in English Canada from the Great Revival to the Great Depression* (Montreal: McGill-Queen's University Press, 1991).

8 John Webster Grant, *A Profusion of Spires: Religion in Nineteenth-Century Ontario* (Toronto: University of Toronto Press, 1988).

9 William Westfall, *Two Worlds: The Protestant Culture of Nineteenth-Century Ontario* (Montreal: McGill-Queen's University Press, 1989).

10 Nancy Christie and Michael Gauvreau, "Modalities of Social Authority: Suggesting an Interface for Religious and Social History," *Histoire Sociale/Social History*, 36, 71 (May 2003): 2, 20.

RELATED READINGS IN THIS SERIES

From *Foundations: Readings in Pre-Confederation Canadian History*

Claudette Knight, "Black Parents Speak: Education in Mid-Nineteenth-Century Canada West," 418–29.

From Media Companion CD-ROM, Volume I

Robinson Treaty, 1850
Petition of Coloured People at Preston
Parallel Qualities of the Sexes
Good—Growing out of Evil—Filmorism

SELECTED READING

R.C. Harris and J. Warkentin, *Canada before Confederation* (Toronto: Oxford University Press, 1974), and *The Historical Atlas of Canada*, vol. 2 are the most comprehensive sources for the history of British North America in the mid-nineteenth century. Raw data on the population and production from pre-Confederation censuses are contained in the *Census of Canada, 1871*, vol. 4, and analyzed in M.C. Urquhart and K.A.H. Buckley, eds., *Historical Statistics of Canada* (Cambridge: Cambridge University Press, 1965); F.H. Lacey, ed., *Historical Statistics of Canada*, 2nd ed. (Ottawa: Statistics Canada, 1983); and Jacques Henripin, *Tendances et facteurs de fécondité au Canada* (Ottawa: Ministry of Supply and Services, 1968). Provincial and regional histories cited in earlier chapters also offer detailed information on colonial conditions in the mid-nineteenth century.

Conditions leading to improvements in transportation and urban amenities in this period are described in Norman R. Ball, ed., *Building Canada: A History of Public Works* (Toronto: University of Toronto Press, 1988). The role of the military is the subject of Elinor Kyte Senior, *British Regulars in Montreal: An Imperial Garrison, 1832–1854* (Montreal: McGill-Queen's University Press, 1981), and the early chapters of Desmond Morton, *Canada and War: A Military and Political History* (Toronto: Butterworths, 1981).

Several detailed studies have contributed much to our understanding of social history in the pre-Confederation period: T.W. Acheson's *Saint John: The Making of a Colonial Urban Community* (Toronto: University of Toronto Press, 1985); Donald Akenson, *The Irish in Ontario: A Study in Rural History* (Montreal: McGill-Queen's University Press, 1984); David Gagan, *Hopeful Travellers: Families, Land and Social Change in Mid-Victorian Peel County, Canada West* (Toronto: Ontario Historical Studies Series, 1981); Michael Katz, *The People of Hamilton, Canada West: Family and Class in a Mid-Nineteenth-Century City* (Cambridge: Harvard University Press, 1975); Claude Baribeau, *La seigneurie de la Petite Nation, 1801–1854: Le rôle économique et social du seigneur* (Hull, QC: Asticou, 1983); Normand Séguin, *La Conquête du sol au 19ᵉ siècle* (Montreal: Boréal Express, 1977); and J.I. Little, *Crofters and Habitants: Settler Society, Economy, and Culture in a Quebec Township, 1848–1881* (Montreal: McGill-Queen's University Press, 1991). More general studies of rural life include John McCallum, *Unequal Beginnings: Agriculture and Economic Development in Quebec and Ontario to 1870* (Toronto: University of Toronto Press, 1980), and Marjorie Griffin Cohen, *Women's Work, Markets, and Economic Development in Nineteenth-Century Ontario* (Toronto: University of Toronto Press, 1988).

The working class in the nineteenth century has received considerable attention, most notably in Bryan D. Palmer's *The Working-Class Experience: Rethinking the History of Canadian Labour, 1800–1991*, 2nd ed. (Toronto: McClelland and Stewart, 1992); M.S. Cross, ed., *The Workingman in the Nineteenth Century* (Toronto: Oxford University Press, 1975); and Steven Langdon, *The Emergence of the Working-Class Movement, 1845–1875* (Toronto: New Hogtown, 1975). Class and culture are the subjects of J.I. Cooper, "The Social Structure in Montreal in the 1850s," *Canadian Historical Association, Report* (1956), and Fernand Ouellet, "Libéré ou exploité: le paysan québécois d'avant 1850," *Histoire sociale/Social History* 13, 26 (Nov. 1980): 339–68.

For a discussion of religion in the mid-nineteenth century see Michael Gauvreau, *The Evangelical Century: College and Creed in English Canada from the Great Revival to the Great Depression* (Montreal: McGill-Queen's University Press, 1991); William Westfall, *Two Worlds: The Protestant Culture of Nineteenth-Century Ontario* (Montreal: McGill-Queen's University Press, 1989); John Webster Grant, *A Profusion of Spires: Religion in Nineteenth-Century Ontario* (Toronto: University of Toronto Press, 1988); Jacques Monet, *The Last Cannon Shot: A Study of French-Canadian Nationalism* (Toronto: University of Toronto Press, 1969); Ollivier Hubert, *Sur la terre comme au ciel: la Gestion des rites par l' Église catholique au Québec fin XVIIᵉ siècle–mi-XIXᵉ siè-cle* (Quebec: Les Presses de l' Université Laval, 2000); Christine Hudon, *Prêtres et fidèles dans le Diocèse de Saint-Hyacinthe, 1820–1875* (Quebec: Septentrion, 1996); René Hardy, *Contrôle social et mutation de la culture religieuse au Québec, 1830–1930* (Montreal: Boréal, 1999); Nire Voisine and Jean Hamelin, eds., *Les Ultramontanes Canadiens-français* (Montreal: Boréal Express, 1985); Richard W. Vaudry, *Anglicans and the Atlantic World: High Churchmen, Evangelicals, and the Quebec Connection* (Montreal: McGill-Queen's University Press, 2003); Terrance J. Fay, *A History of Canadian Catholics: Gallicanism, Romanism, and Canadians* (Montreal: McGill-Queen's University Press, 2000); Goldwin French, *Parsons and Politics: The Role of the Wesleyan Methodists in Upper Canada and the Maritimes, 1780–1855* (Toronto: Ryerson Press, 1962); George Rawlyk, *Ravished by the Spirit: Religious Revivals, Baptists, and Henry Alline* (Montreal: McGill-Queen's University Press, 1984), and *Canadian Baptists and Christian Higher Education* (Montreal: McGill-Queen's University Press, 1988); and John S. Moir, *The Church in the British Era: From Conquest to Confederation* (Toronto: McGraw-Hill Ryerson, 1972). Also see several essays in Michael Gauvreau and Ollivier Hubert, eds., *Religion and Social Practice* (Montreal: McGill-Queen's University Press, 2004), and Nancy Christie, ed., *Households of Faith: Family, Gender and Community* (Montreal: McGill-Queen's University Press, 2002). For a discussion of historiographical developments relating to religion and society, see Michael Gauvreau, "Beyond the Half-Way House: Evangelicalism and the Shaping of English-Canadian Culture," *Acadiensis* 20, 2 (Spring 1991): 158–77, and Nancy Christie and Michael Gauvreau, "Modalities of Social Authority: Suggesting an Interface for Religious and Social History," *Histoire Sociale/Social History*, 36, 71 (May 2003): 1–30.

For education in this period, see Susan Houston and Alison Prentice, *Schooling and Scholars in Nineteenth-Century Ontario* (Toronto: University of Toronto Press, 1988); Bruce Curtis, *Building the Educational State: Canada West, 1836–1871* (London, ON: Althouse Press, 1988); Alison Prentice, *The School Promoters: Education and Social Class in Mid-Nineteenth-Century Upper Canada* (Toronto: McClelland and Stewart, 1977); Chad Gaffield, *Language, Schooling, and Cultural Conflict: The Origins of the French-Language Controversy in Ontario* (Montreal: McGill-Queen's University Press, 1987); Paul Axelrod, *The Promise of Schooling, 1800–1914* (Toronto: University of Toronto Press, 1997); J.D. Wilson et al., *Canadian Education: A History* (Toronto: Prentice-Hall, 1970); and Claude Galarneau, *Les collèges classiques au Canada français* (Montreal: Fides, 1978). Gerald Friesen offers a valuable assessment of the relation between technology and society in this and other periods of Canadian history in *Citizens and Nation: An Essay on History, Communication, and Canada* (Toronto: University of Toronto Press, 2000).

Women's experience is summarized in Alison Prentice et al., *Canadian Women: A History*, 2nd ed. (Toronto: Harcourt Brace, 1996); Peggy Bristow et al., *"We're Rooted Here and They Can't Pull Us Up": Essays in African-Canadian Women's History* (Toronto: University of Toronto Press, 1994); Janet Guildford and Suzanne Morton, eds., *Separate Spheres: Women's Worlds in the Nineteenth-Century Maritimes* (Fredericton: Acadiensis Press, 1994); and the Clio Collective, *Quebec Women: A History*, trans. Roger Gannon and Rosalind Gill (Toronto: Women's Press, 1987). See also Françoise Nöel, *Family Life and Sociability in Upper and Lower Canada, 1780–1870: A View from Diaries and Family Correspondence* (Montreal: McGill-Queen's University Press, 2003), and Peter Ward, *Courtship, Love, and Marriage in Nineteenth-Century English Canada* (Montreal: McGill-Queen's University Press, 1990).

In addition to the surveys by Olive Dickason, J.R. Miller, Arthur J. Ray, and L.S.F. Upton, cited earlier, the experience of Aboriginal peoples in this period is discussed in Donald Smith, *The Reverend Peter Jones (Kahkewaquonaby) and the Mississauga Indians* (Toronto: University of Toronto Press, 1987); Robin Fisher, *Contact and Conflict: Indian-European Relations in British Columbia, 1774–1890* (Vancouver: UBC Press, 1992); Ian A.L. Getty and Antoine S. Lussier, eds., *As Long as the Sun Shines and the Rivers Flow: A Reader in Canadian Native Studies* (Vancouver: UBC Press, 1983); Robin Fisher and Kenneth Coates, eds., *Out of the Background: Readings in Canadian Native History*, 2nd ed. (Toronto: Copp Clark, 1996); and Kenneth Coates and William R. Morrison, eds., *Interpreting Canada's North* (Toronto: Copp Clark Pitman, 1989).

The history of blacks in this period is covered in Robin W. Winks, *The Blacks in Canada: A History*, 2nd ed. (Montreal: McGill-Queen's University Press, 1997); Bridglal Pachai, *Beneath the Clouds of the Promised Land: The Survival of Nova Scotia Blacks*, vol. 2: *1800–1989* (Halifax: The Black Educators Association of Nova Scotia, 1990); W.A. Spray, *The Blacks in New Brunswick* (Fredericton: Brunswick Press, 1972); Jim Hornsby, *Black Islanders: Prince Edward Island's Historical Black Community* (Charlottetown: Institute of Island Studies, 1991); Daniel Hill, *The Blacks in Early Canada: The Freedom-Seekers* (Agincourt, ON: Book Society, 1981); and Peggy Bristow et al., *"We're Rooted Here and They Can't Pull Us Up,"* cited above. See also Jason H.

Silverman, "Mary Ann Camberton (Cary) Shadd," *Dictionary of Canadian Biography*, vol. 12, *1891 to 1900* (Toronto: University of Toronto Press, 1990), 960–61.

Sickness and health are discussed in Geoffrey Bilson, *A Darkened House: Cholera in Nineteenth-Century Canada* (Toronto: University of Toronto Press, 1980); Wendy Mitchinson, *The Nature of Their Bodies: Women and Their Doctors in Victorian Canada* (Toronto: University of Toronto Press, 1991); and Charles G. Roland, ed., *Health, Disease and Medicine: Essays in Canadian History* (Toronto: Irwin, 1984).

Sports in the nineteenth century is the focus of Alan Metcalfe, *Canada Learns to Play: The Emergence of Organized Sport, 1807–1914* (Toronto: McClelland and Stewart, 1987); Morris Mott, ed., *Sports in Canada: Historical Readings* (Toronto: Copp Clark Pitman, 1989); and Don Morrow et al., *A Concise History of Sports in Canada* (Toronto: Oxford University Press, 1989).

Aspects of tourism and leisure are discussed in Patricia Jasen, *Wild Things: Nature, Culture, and Tourism in Ontario, 1790–1914* (Toronto: University of Toronto Press, 1995), and Karen Dubinsky, *The Second Greatest Disappointment: A History of Honeymoons and Tourism at Niagara Falls* (Toronto: Between the Lines, 1999).

Literature is discussed in Carl Klinck, *Literary History of Canada* (Toronto: University of Toronto Press, 1976) and Patricia Lockhart Fleming, Gilles Gallichan, and Yvan Lamonde, eds., *History of the Book in Canada*, vol. I (Toronto: University of Toronto Press, 2004). Historiographical developments are the subject of M. Brook Taylor, *Promoters, Patriots, and Partisans: Historiography in Nineteenth-Century English Canada* (Toronto: University of Toronto Press, 1989), and Serge Gagnon, *Quebec and Its Historians* (Montreal: Harvest House, 1982). The architecture of the period is examined in Harold Kalman, *A History of Canadian Architecture*, vol. 1 (Toronto: University of Toronto Press, 1994), and Peter Ennals and Deryck W. Holdsworth, *Homeplace: The Making of the Canadian Dwelling over Three Centuries* (Toronto: University of Toronto Press, 1998). J. Russell Harper has written extensively on nineteenth-century art and artists. A good place to start is his *Painting in Canada: A History* (Toronto: University of Toronto Press, 1977). *The Historical Atlas of Canada*, the *Horizon* series, *Dictionary of Canadian Biography*, and *Canada's Visual History Series* each offer valuable perspectives on aspects of Canadian social and cultural history. See also Sandra Paikowsky, "Landscape Painting in Canada," in *Profiles of Canada*, ed. Kenneth G. Pryke and Walter R. Soderlund (Toronto: Copp Clark Pitman, 1992), 336–45.

WEBLINKS

HIPPOCRATIC THEORY

www.med.virginia.edu/hs-library/historical/antiqua/
textn.htm

For an introduction to the theory that illness was an imbalance of the four humours in the body, see this site on early medicine.

THE UNDERGROUND RAILROAD

http://education.ucdavis.edu/NEW/STC/lesson/
socstud/railroad/title.htm

This site, prepared by two education students at the University of California—Davis, offers two maps of routes used in the underground railroad. Also available are internal links to online resources and a short bibliography.

collections.ic.gc.ca/freedom/page1.htm

This address offers a Canadian perspective on the underground railroad.

SUSANNA MOODIE

www.collectionscanada.ca/moodie-traill/
t1-2100-e.html

This Library and Archives Canada site offers a biography of Moodie with specific reference to her writings.

THOMAS CHANDLER HALIBURTON

www.blupete.com/Hist/BiosNS/1800-67/
Haliburton.htm

A brief biography is available at this site, with internal links to Haliburton's writings and his contemporaries.

EARLY CANADIANA ONLINE

www.canadiana.org

This site consists of several collections, each with a particular scope and focus in Canadian history.

CHAPTER 20

British North America's Revolutionary Age

Timeline

▶ **1844** Provincial Association established in New Brunswick to lobby for higher tariffs

▶ **1846** Great Britain adopts free trade policy

▶ **1849** Annexation Manifesto; Joseph Howe proposes Intercolonial Railway

▶ **1854** Reciprocity Treaty signed

1854–56 Crimean War

1858 Association for the Protection of Canadian Industry established

1859 Grand Trunk Railway completed; Darwin's *The Origin of Species* published

1861–65 American Civil War

T.C. Keefer, an engineer from Canada West, wrote a book entitled *Philosophy of Railroads* in 1850. In it he waxed lyrical about the potential of railways, indicating that they would form a "powerful antidote" to the "state of primitive" existence in the colonies:

> Poverty, indifference, the bigotry or jealousy of religious denominations, local dissensions or political demagogueism may stifle or neutralize the influence of the best intended efforts of an educational system; but that invisible power which has waged successful war with the material elements, will assuredly overcome the prejudices of mental weakness or the designs of mental tyrants. It calls for no cooperation, it waits for no convenient season, but with a restless, rushing, roaring assiduity, it keeps up a constant and unavoidable spirit of enquiry or comparison; and while ministering to the material wants, and appealing to the covetousness of the multitude, it unconsciously, irresistibly, impels them to a more intimate union with their fellow men.[1]

Although the reality of the railway never quite matched the grand promise prophesied by Keefer, it did have a major impact on the British North American colonies. The railway boom of the mid-nineteenth century generated industry in British North America and inspired dreams of bigger and better lines and bigger and better political organizations to sustain them. Among the many supporters of Confederation were railway promoters and politicians, the heroes and villains of British North America's early age of industry.

THE INDUSTRIAL REVOLUTION

In the mid-nineteenth century, British North Americans were conscious of living in an era of rapid change and miraculous events. New ideas, new methods of transportation, and new ways of producing goods and services were quickening the pace of everyday life. The Industrial Revolution was the catalyst for this change. Along with the new economic arrangements, it laid the groundwork for deep social transformation and intellectual departures that challenged virtually everything people had hitherto believed about the Earth and its inhabitants.

The impact of the Industrial Revolution on British North America was distinctive in two respects. First, the colonies experienced the effects of industrialism long before they were industrialized themselves. Second, the timing of British North America's Industrial Revolution coincided with a revolution in communications and values that made its advent all the more "revolutionary." Initially restricted to a few industries and locations, industrial growth inspired

dreams of confederation from the Atlantic to the Pacific, and the fruits of industrialism—most notably the railway—helped to make those dreams a reality.

The Industrial Revolution takes its name from fundamental changes in technology and the organization of production that gradually transformed how people lived. The world's first industrial nation was Great Britain. It pioneered in the application of steam power to machines and machines to production in key sectors of the economy: agriculture, manufacturing, and transportation. In the eighteenth century, developments in mining and metallurgy made Great Britain a leader in the production of pig iron in large quantities and at low costs. British "mechanics," inspired by the possibilities of iron and steam power, experimented with machinery that transformed the labour process. By the end of the eighteenth century, spinning machines and power looms had multiplied textile output in Britain far beyond anything that could be done by human hands. Within a remarkably short time, machines were developed to perform a wide range of tasks, and the volume of manufactured products exploded.

Mechanization also changed how people related to each other. In pre-industrial European society, artisans had retained control of the production process, making a product from start to finish and determining standards and prices through organizations called guilds. With the Industrial Revolution, machines encouraged the division of labour into repetitive tasks; they also encouraged centralization—work was performed at factories where the machines were located, and control of the factory system was centralized in the hands of a few capitalists who could finance such extensive operations. Under the factory system, labourers lost control over their work. Factory owners, if they were competitive and shrewd, became wealthy from their entrepreneurial activities.

There was nothing particularly inevitable about this process, except that commercial societies in Britain and North America had a well-developed exchange

The Dorchester, the locomotive that pulled Canada's first train along the Champlain-St Lawrence line in July 1836, is illustrated in this commemorative stamp issued by Canada Post.
Canada Post Corporation

system that adapted easily to industrialism. Since the fifteenth century, successful merchants, artisans, and farmers in the North Atlantic world had gradually adopted a capitalist perspective. They worked for profit instead of subsistence; they translated all transactions into monetary value; they established structures such as joint-stock companies and banks to accumulate capital; they experimented with new ways of performing traditional tasks; and they developed laws to protect their property and the market system from fraud, piracy, and theft.

As they grew in numbers and wealth, capitalists had little difficulty incorporating people and resources into their exchange processes. They were also adept at convincing governments to pass legislation to protect their new interests. Under the pressure from this new entrepreneurial class, the communal management of land in the countryside, the guild control of industry in the towns, and the privilege of monopoly were all eventually pushed aside to facilitate the new industrial order.

Industrial capitalism transformed Great Britain and eventually the whole world. It introduced a new materialism that challenged traditional spiritual values, encouraged the growth of cities at the expense of the countryside, and created a new class structure based on relationship to production rather than heredity. It redistributed wealth geographically as well as socially and drove a wedge between the public world of work and the private realm of the family. It altered the relationship among men, women, and children and the relationship of human beings to their natural environment.

British North Americans were no strangers to this revolutionary process. They read about the new machines in their newspapers, purchased the products of Britain's factories with their hard-earned cash, and sent an increasing volume of their own raw resources to sustain Britain's expanding industrial economy. The impact of the changing British economy was also felt on colonial policy. As the output of British factories began to dominate world markets, formal colonies became less important to imperial strategy. The rising middle class of industrialists in Britain wanted a policy of laissez-faire, by which they meant fewer taxes and less government intervention in the market economy. Colonies, they argued, were an expensive luxury—at

least those colonies controlled by white settlers, who could be safely left alone to govern themselves. Let the invisible hand of supply and demand be allowed to operate freely, they argued, and Britain would soon conquer the whole world economically rather than militarily. These industrial interests eventually prevailed. For the colonies their success meant free trade and responsible government. The onus was now on British North Americans to decide what economic strategy to pursue.

FREE TRADE, RECIPROCITY, AND PROTECTION

The mercantile community in the colonies was thrown into a tailspin by the commercial revolution of the 1840s, which ushered in free trade throughout the British Empire. Fortunately, it was a good time to experience economic and political crises. The British economy was entering a boom period that would last for over two decades. With typical enthusiasm and success, the Americans had also embarked on the road to industrialization and were gobbling up resources at an amazing rate. The discovery of gold in California, Australia, British Columbia, and New Zealand and the expansion of credit through the banking and insurance companies fuelled the global economy. In addition, the Crimean War (1854–56) in Europe and the Civil War in the United States (1861–65) increased the demand for colonial products. If circumstances had thrust the colonies back on their own devices, the context was favourable for developing strategies appropriate for the industrial age.

While a few merchants, especially those closely tied to the timber and wheat trade, saw annexation to the United States as the solution to their temporarily failing fortunes, others, in particular those involved in the production side of the trading process, advocated a protectionist strategy to develop internal markets. The British-American League, which was formed in 1849 to respond to the perceived economic crisis, included tariff protection as a plank in its platform and called for a union of all British North America as a means of "creating large home markets for the consumption of agricultural products and domestic manufactures."[2]

Still others, eyeing the nearest booming industrial economy, suggested free trade with the United States as the best policy for sustaining British North America's primary industries. Annexation was quickly abandoned by all but the most principled republicans, and a union of British North America still seemed highly impractical. Tariff protection was perceived as an inadequate measure by a business community dominated by mercantile interests. Free trade, perhaps, was an idea whose time had come.

In 1851, the eastern British North American colonies agreed to free trade among themselves in natural products. Three years later, Britain negotiated a reciprocity treaty that provided for the free exchange of natural products between the British North American colonies and the United States. Under the Reciprocity Treaty, which remained in effect from 1855 to 1866, colonial staples such as foodstuffs, wheat, timber, fish, and coal found American markets to supplement their imperial ones, while Americans enjoyed access to the inshore fisheries of the Atlantic region and access to the Great Lakes-St Lawrence canal system.

Economists disagree about the exact impact of the reciprocity agreement on the British North American economy. Even without free trade, the American market was looming ever larger on the British North American horizon. Moreover, the outbreak of the

The Annexation Manifesto

In October 1849, a number of leading Montreal merchants issued a manifesto calling for annexation to the United States. The first paragraph read, in part: "Of all the remedies that have been suggested for the acknowledged and insufferable ills with which our country is afflicted, there remains but one to be considered. . . . this remedy consists in a friendly and peaceful separation from the British connection and a union upon equitable terms with the great North American confederacy of sovereign states." The manifesto also outlined the advantages that the merchants felt would come from such a union:

> The proposed union would render Canada a field for American capital, into which it would enter as freely for the prosecution of public works and private enterprise as into any of the present States. It would equalise the value of real estate upon both sides of the boundary, thereby probably doubling at once the entire present value of property in Canada, whilst, by giving stability to our institutions, and introducing prosperity, it would raise our public corporate and private credit. It would increase our commerce, both with the United States and foreign countries, and would not necessarily diminish to any great extent our intercourse with Great Britain, into which our products would for the most part enter on the same terms as present. It would render our rivers and canals the highway for the immigration to and exports from, the West, to the incalculable benefit of our country. It would also introduce manufacturers into Canada as rapidly as they have been introduced into the northern states; and to Lower Canada especially, where water privileges and labour are abundant and cheap, it would attract manufacturing capital, enhancing the value of property and agricultural produce and giving remunerative employment to what is at present a comparatively non-producing population. Nor would the United States merely furnish the capital for our manufacturers. They would also supply them the most extensive market in the world, without the intervention of a custom house officer. Railways would forthwith be constructed by American capital as feeders for all the great lines now approaching the frontiers; and railway enterprise in general would doubtless be as active and prosperous among us as among our neighbours. The value of our agricultural produce would be raised at once to a par with that of the United States, whilst agricultural implements and many of the necessities of life, such as tea, coffee and sugar, would be greatly reduced in price.[3]

Among those who signed the manifesto were John Abbott, who would one day be a Canadian prime minister, and Alexander Galt, who would serve as finance minister for the United Canadas in the 1850s.

Civil War between the northern and southern states in 1861 stimulated the southern movement of commodities essential for the war effort. The disruption of the American economy resulting from the war would have stimulated British North American trade without a free trade arrangement. What is clear is that the Reciprocity Treaty coupled with the Civil War reinforced north-south lines of trade and gave British North Americans another option in a world of expanding markets.

Despite the widespread support for free trade, protectionists managed to win small victories. Businessmen in Saint John established the Provincial Association in 1844 to lobby the government for a protective tariff policy. Following the introduction of free trade, the New Brunswick legislature raised the tariffs on imported manufactures. In Canada, the tariff was set at 12.5 percent of the value of imports in 1849 and raised even higher in 1858 and 1859. Although the goal was still to raise revenue, or so Finance Minister Alexander Galt argued in 1859, it clearly served to protect local producers from cheaper imports.

Galt's tariff was popular among industrialists in Canada West, who had established the Association for the Protection of Canadian Industry in 1858. In its ranks were agricultural-implements manufacturer Hart Massey, furniture manufacturer Robert Hay, and drug manufacturer William Lyman. Behind a tariff wall, these and other entrepreneurs could develop a "Home Industry" and perhaps become strong enough to compete effectively in other regions of British North America. Countering the free traders who argued that tariffs raised the costs to colonial consumers, Montreal-based journalist D'Arcy McGee maintained that the effect of judicious protection would "not be to make them dear, but to make them here."

TRANSPORTATION

In addition to revolutionizing production techniques, mechanization also inspired new methods of transportation. Steam applied to sea and land transport offered a stronger and more reliable power than wind, water, and animal power. Steamboats became commercially viable in the first decade of the nineteenth century, railways in the 1820s and 1830s. In Britain, industrialization was underway before the transportation revolution wrought by steam, but in British North America the steamboat and the railway accompanied and accelerated the industrialization process.

In 1809, two years after the world's first steamship navigated up the Hudson River in New York State, John Molson, an ambitious Montreal brewer, launched the steamship *Accommodation* in partnership with two Englishmen. Its six-horsepower engine was made at the St Maurice forges. Although the *Accommodation* was a commercial failure, its successors did a roaring trade on the Great Lakes and St Lawrence, and competition for traffic among the "river barons" was keen.

Halifax native Samuel Cunard was the merchant prince of steam service throughout the Atlantic region. In 1830 he joined forces with other merchants in Halifax and Quebec City to run a mail service between the two port cities. This group also sponsored the *Royal*

When the *Royal William* was launched from Quebec shipyards in 1831, it was equipped with steam power as well as sails. It became the first ship to cross the Atlantic using steam engines in 1833, taking 25 days to make the trip from Pictou, Nova Scotia, to Gravesend, England.
J.P. Cockburn/Library and Archives Canada/C12649

William, which in 1833 made one of the first Atlantic crossings under steam. In 1840, when Cunard succeeded in capturing the contract for mail delivery between Britain and North America, steam had come of age in British North America.

By that time, colonials were all agog with the potential of the iron horse. Railways promised to liberate British North Americans from the problems of climate and isolation and fully launch them on the road to progress. In the years between 1852 and 1867, the British North American colonies built over 3200 kilometres of track and sank over $100 million into railways. Much of the capital came from Britain, as did the expertise required to build the new transportation systems. Colonial governments, whatever their political stripe, were obliging in their efforts to support railway development. Joseph Howe was a great railway booster, and the Liberal government in which he served sponsored lines from Halifax to Windsor and Pictou. His Conservative nemesis, Charles Tupper, was equally enthusiastic about the potential of railways in his native province, especially a railroad that would make his Cumberland County constituency the link between Nova Scotia and points north and west.

Meanwhile, New Brunswickers sank money into a railway, grandly labelled the European and North American, which ran between Shediac on the Northumberland Strait and Saint John on the Bay of Fundy. A line connecting St Andrews with Quebec was abandoned in the backwoods of New Brunswick when its promoters ran out of money in 1863. In the United Canadas, politicians of all parties supported railways and, in the 1850s, brought the colony to the brink of bankruptcy with their decision to build the Grand Trunk Railway. When it was completed in 1859, it was the longest railway in the world, stretching from Quebec City to Sarnia and on American lines to Chicago.

In the initial flush of railway enthusiasm, British North American politicians made plans for an intercolonial railway that would link Canadians to an ice-free Atlantic port. Failure to agree on a route or to secure imperial backing caused the expensive project to be abandoned. In the meantime, a Montreal-Portland line, completed in 1853, gave the colony of Canada its much-desired winter port. By the end of the decade, railways crisscrossed the colony, reaching northward to the timber stands of the Ottawa Valley and Lake Huron and linking the market towns of the Ontario peninsula.

Despite the enthusiasm of their promoters, the Grand Trunk and other government-sponsored railways proved a burden to colonial taxpayers. The decision to raise tariffs in both New Brunswick and the Canadas in the 1850s had as much to do with the need to raise revenue to finance the growing railway debt as it did with the protection of colonial producers. In a curious feat of convoluted logic, colonial politicians and promoters argued that the solution to failing railways was more railways—to link the colonies with each other and with American lines, and even with the Pacific Ocean. Only by expanding could railways tap new frontiers and secure the traffic that would make them pay.

The close link between railway promoters and politicians in the United Canadas inevitably led to

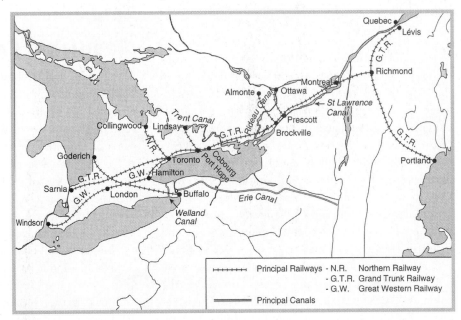

MAP 20.1 Canals and railways in the United Canadas before Confederation.
Adapted from P.G. Cornell et al., *Canada: Unity in Diversity* (Toronto: Holt, Rinehart, and Winston, 1967), 239.

Great Western Railway engine, Hamilton, 1854.
Library and Archives Canada/C-028860

capitalist practices into British North American society. In Montreal, the Grand Trunk, which eventually employed nearly 2000 people and included a wide range of metal-producing shops, was a monument to the industrial era.

British North America's Industrial Revolution came of age with the railway, but its origins can be found in earlier transportation developments. In the 1840s, industries located along the Lachine Canal were near transportation routes and potential hydraulic power. Between 1847 and 1854, $500 000 was invested in 30 industries in Lachine by entrepreneurs from Canada, Britain, and the United States. Mills and factories producing flour, beer, iron, furniture, sewing machines, steam engines, heating and ventilating equipment, paints, rubber, footwear, clothes, and drugs employed nearly 2000 people, who crowded into the nearby suburbs of St Ann, Point St Charles, and Verdun. By 1856, Montrealers boasted that their city was "the best site for a manufacturing city in Canada, perhaps on the Continent."

scandals. Politicians bought shares in railway companies and sat on their boards. Although the line between public and private interests was not then as carefully drawn as it would be later on, the prospect of government leader Francis Hincks making £10 000 on the Great Northern Railway contract in 1854 raised more than a few eyebrows. Hincks was forced to resign over the "Ten Thousand Pound Job" but he did not go to jail, nor was he made to give back the money.

If railways were sometimes a failing and scandalous proposition, they nevertheless fulfilled many of the expectations outlined by their promoters. Areas where the railway ran invariably experienced a quickening of economic pace. In the cities where railway-repair shops were located, heavy industry was given a tremendous boost. Railway companies were Canada's first large-scale integrated corporations. Not only were they transportation companies but they also had the capacity to rebuild and repair lines, to manufacture locomotives and industrial machinery, to store and forward freight, to operate grain elevators and steamships, and to maintain large administrative offices. They were among the largest employers in the colonies. Through their practices relating to management, division of labour, accounting, quality control, and even waste recycling, they introduced advanced

Mobilizing Capital

Money was the lifeblood of capitalism, and channelling money into enterprises with the greatest potential for profit was at the heart of the industrial capitalist system. In pre-industrial British North America, colonial governments, military commissariats, banks, and successful merchants often accumulated large pools of capital, but most major projects, such as Canadian canals and railways, relied on capital from Britain. As late as the 1840s, the Bank of Montreal's paid-up capital stock was smaller than that of the city's military commissariat. Commentators complained about how easily capital was drained out of the colonies to purchase British and American products. If the colonies could substitute their own manufactures for imports, they reasoned, more capital could be invested in colonial enterprises.

Transportation injected large infusions of capital into the colonies, especially in the United Canadas, which led the way in canal and railway building. It was no coincidence that the 1850s saw the rapid development of banks and insurance companies in the colony, and the appearance of a fledgling stock market. Financial institutions also expanded in the Atlantic colonies, where shipbuilding, another transportation industry, helped to fuel economic growth. The output of wooden vessels grew dramatically after 1850 and brought steady returns on capital investment in the major shipping ports such as Saint John well into the 1870s. Shipbuilders and owners often invested their money in industrial concerns, their ships supplying the raw products—cotton, tobacco, flax, wheat, and molasses—required in their mills to produce textiles, sails, rope, spices, biscuits, sugar, and candy.

In the early 1860s, Father George-Antoine Belcourt helped his fellow Prince Edward Island Acadians to establish a banking co-operative, the Farmer's Bank of Rustico.
Prince Edward Island Archives and Records Office

Financial activities also benefited from currency legislation that reduced confusion over exchange. The variety of coins and notes in circulation, including British, Spanish, and American currencies, made transactions cumbersome if not impossible. In the 1850s and 1860s, British North Americans adopted decimal currency, which was both easier to calculate than British pounds and shillings and increasingly popular in the age of reciprocity with the United States.

LABOUR AND INDUSTRY

Without a supply of cheap and willing labour to work in the new factories, the Industrial Revolution would have been stillborn. Two developments, one demographic and the other economic, interacted with each other to guarantee the labour supply needed both in Britain and North America.

Over the course of the eighteenth century, the population of Europe in general and Britain in particular grew dramatically. From a population of five million in 1700, Britain grew to nine million a century later. Higher birth rates, lower death rates, better living standards, more efficient exchange networks, and even improved psychological conditions seem to account for some of the growth. At the same time, overcrowding in the countryside and the commercialization of agriculture pushed people off the land and into the cities to find work. Factory towns, like the colonies, became magnets for the rural dispossessed. Indeed, factory towns and colonies, considered frontiers of opportunity, attracted people whose rural lives were reasonably stable. In 1700, 80 percent of people in Britain made their living in agriculture; by 1800 only 40 percent did so.

Those fleeing the economic dislocation of the Industrial Revolution in Great Britain also found the land frontier disappearing in British North America. Even in Canada West immigrants were confronting the rugged Canadian Shield, which proved an inhospitable barrier to the farmer's plough. It took a lifetime for a pioneer without capital or a large family to make a farm out of tree-covered wilderness. With the free land virtually gone and the cost of labour in British North America relatively high, the capital requirements of farming were steadily mounting. A prosperous farm was still the goal of most immigrants and native-born British North Americans, but it was

Most of the canals in British North America were built by man- and horse-power. In the 1840s, as many as 10 000 men, many of them poor Irish immigrants, worked from dawn to dusk digging, hauling, and quarrying for about 50 cents a day. The workers moved from job to job with their families, who lived in shantytowns that were established near construction sites. Given the poor working and living conditions, it is little wonder that strikes were a frequent occurrence.
Library and Archives Canada/C61471

beyond the reach of many people, who found themselves forced into other occupations. Irish famine immigration in the late 1840s further added to the pool of available labour.

Many immigrant labourers brought with them traditions of resistance against unfair labour practices. Craftsmen, whose skills were often rendered obsolete by the new machines, and work crews, whose livelihood was jeopardized by attempts to lower wages, protested efforts by employers to exploit them. At first, workers tried to destroy the new machines that threatened their traditional practices, as was the case among shoemakers in Montreal when the sewing machine was introduced in 1852. Gradually, workers began organizing to press for better working conditions and a fairer distribution of the profits of mechanized production.

Only skilled labourers could risk joining unions, which were considered seditious conspiracies by factory owners. Unskilled workers, who could easily be replaced, were fired if they were caught trying to organize the shop floor. Only a tiny minority of workers belonged to unions, but whether unionized or not, wage earners were determined not to become slaves to their capitalist masters. On 10 June 1867, just three weeks before the first Dominion Day, over 10 000 workers in Montreal, parading behind the Patriote flag of the Lower Canadian rebels of 1837, took to the street in a show of worker solidarity.

The state assisted the interests of capital by creating conditions conducive to managerial control over labour. Various master and servant acts passed in the colonies included provisions for punishing craftsmen, labourers, and servants who left their jobs. Couched in the language of pre-industrial labour relations, these acts were designed primarily to control servants, timber workers, and ship crews. Nevertheless, they reveal the bias in favour of employers that would continue to prevail in industrial settings and would make labour's lot a difficult one.

LAW AND INDUSTRY

The law was a vital instrument in capital accumulation during the Industrial Revolution. In the colonies, however, legal principles and practices were quickly outdated by the pace of economic change. Based on a belief in eternal principles and natural law, colonial legal systems lacked the extensive laws and trained personnel required to deal with the complexities of commercial transactions. In most colonies, executive councillors sat in judicial capacities, and their lack of specialized legal knowledge coupled with their busy schedules was a growing cause for complaint.

Legal reform followed hard on the heels of responsible government. In most colonial jurisdictions, new laws relating to contracts, partnerships, patents, and property were introduced, while the courts were reorganized to separate executive and judicial functions, to increase efficiency, and to incorporate change into legal decisions. Reform extended beyond commercial law and court procedures to the fundamental basis of law itself. No longer paternalistic and protective in its thrust, the law became an instrument for individual accumulation and economic development.

Nowhere in British North America was legal reform more at issue than in the rapidly developing colony of Canada. In 1849, William Hume Blake, solicitor-general in the Baldwin-LaFontaine administration, introduced legislation to establish a Court of Common Pleas and a Court of Error and Appeals as well as to reform the Court of Queen's Bench and Court of Chancery. The latter was designed to administer jurisprudence to supplement and remedy the limitations and inflexibility of the common law. As chancellor from 1849 to 1862, Blake attempted to inject the principles of freedom and progress into his legal decisions.

Legal reform was not confined solely to English jurisdictions. As early as 1846 the *Revue de législation et de jurisprudence* in Canada East published this revealing statement:

> The conquests which modern society has made in politics, science, the arts, agriculture, industry and commerce necessitate the reform of the old codes which directed the ancient societies. Everywhere, one feels the inadequacy of laws made for an order of ideas and things which no longer exists, and the need to remodel ancient systems and of promulgating new ones, in order to put ourselves at the level of society's progress.[4]

In 1857, George-Étienne Cartier, lawyer and leader of the Bleus in Canada East, introduced bills to make the legal system more centralized and uniform. He also chaired the committee that produced a new Civil Code to replace the antiquated Custom of Paris. The code brought major revisions to contract and labour law. It also introduced changes in the property provisions of family law, abolishing dower rights except in cases where they were formally registered. In practice, this freed husbands from any claims held by their wives and children on family property. Although the Civil Code retained the principle of patriarchy in requiring a husband's permission for a married woman to engage in business, once this permission was granted she was free to conduct her activities as she saw fit.

THE STRUCTURE OF INDUSTRIAL CAPITALISM

The Industrial Revolution proceeded unevenly, its impact varying from sector to sector and from one region to another. Only a few colonial industries, following the precedents set in Britain and the United States, initially lent themselves to large-scale production: metal trades, locomotives, textiles, boots and shoes, furniture, agricultural implements, tobacco, beer and ale, biscuits and bread, candies, carriages, and sails and rope. While most factories adopted techniques for division of labour (as in the shoe industry) or included a number of skills under one roof (as in carriage-making), not all industries relied on steam-powered machinery. Cheap hand labour remained central to the Industrial Revolution and, in certain sectors, such as textiles and cigar-making, guaranteed success against foreign competitors.

Manufacturing in British North America, as elsewhere, tended to be geographically concentrated. Saint John, Montreal, Toronto, and Hamilton led the way in the industrial process. Montreal, with its large domestic market, low-wage structure, and pivotal location in the St Lawrence trading system, was British North America's leading industrial city before

Confederation. Hamilton failed to recover from the recession of the late 1850s and was gradually eclipsed by Toronto as the major industrial city in Canada West. Between 1851 and 1871, Toronto was transformed from a city of artisans to one where over 70 percent of the labour force worked in units of over 30 people. In Atlantic Canada, Saint John emerged as the major manufacturing centre, holding sway over the whole Bay of Fundy basin, which, with over 300 000 people, contained nearly half the Maritime region's population. By the 1860s, the foundry, footwear, and clothing industries in Saint John each exceeded shipbuilding in the value of their output.

In some cases, demand inspired large-scale production—an example being Moirs in Halifax, which had the bread contract for the military stationed in the city. When new technological developments occurred, whole industries were transformed. For instance, the shoe industry in Montreal and Toronto was reorganized within a decade of the introduction of the sewing machine in the early 1850s. External factors also figured prominently in the encouragement of industry. Disruptions caused by the American Civil War, for example, led to tobacco companies locating in Montreal and Toronto.

Entrepreneurs came from every class and culture, although hardly in equal proportions. A few, such as John Molson of Montreal, had a long tradition of capitalist investment in everything from beer to railroads. Many "captains of industry" emerged from the ranks of the merchant class that had accumulated capital in its commercial ventures to invest in new frontiers of opportunity. Successful primary producers and artisans were also in a good position to expand their operations in such areas as milling, tanning, or carriage-making when demand, technology, or sheer luck made it possible to reap a profit. Most of British North America's entrepreneurs were anglophones, many of them recent immigrants from Britain or the United States.

One French-Canadian exception was Augustin Cantin, Montreal's major steamboat builder and the first person to integrate ship construction and marine engineering. By 1856, Cantin's shipyards on the Lachine Canal covered five and a half hectares and included two harbours, a sawmill, and an engine foundry.

British North America's industrial workforce was overwhelmingly male. The milling, woodworking, and metal industries hired men almost exclusively and supervisory positions were reserved for them throughout the industrial structure. Women, both married and single, and children, some as young as eight or nine years of age, were employed in the clothing and tobacco industries and made up a significant proportion of the people hired in printing, footwear, and confectionery work. Women and children also formed the bulk of workers employed in the "sweated trades," the term used to describe industrial tasks performed at home at appallingly low rates. Although the exploitation of women and children in the industrial process was already a cause of concern in Britain when the industrial system was adopted in British North America, it became part of the industrial structure in British North America without much comment.

Young women sorting ore at the Huntington Copper Mining Company Works, Quebec, 1867.
Notman Photographic Archives, McCord Museum of Canadian History, Montreal, N-0000.94.56

The impact of industrial production was quickly felt throughout British North America. In industries where the new processes prevailed, artisans were either thrown out of work or found their jobs radically altered. Erastus Wiman, in the 1863 *Report of the Toronto Board of Trade*, described the transformation in the shoe industry: "Eight years ago there was only one regular traveller from Montreal and one from Toronto who solicited orders from the country trade, and these seldom left the line of the railroad. Now it is no uncommon thing to meet from fifteen to eighteen in a single season—all keenly alive to business, and pushing into all sections of the country, remote or otherwise." Wiman remarked that where shoes had once been made in over a thousand workshops scattered across the colony, now manufacture was concentrated in "eighteen or twenty establishments of the five cities of the provinces."[5]

As Wiman correctly observed, British North Americans had witnessed an economic revolution in the decade of the 1850s. Factories, railways, and new values were now part of the colonial scene. By 1859, even Red River had a steamboat, and on the West Coast fur-trade society was rapidly receding in the wake of the gold rush of 1858. There was nowhere to hide from the transforming processes of the new industrial order.

INTELLECTUAL REVOLUTIONS

The Industrial Revolution was a child of the Age of Enlightenment, a term applied to the dramatic shift in the tenor of European intellectual life in the eighteenth century. Building on developments in science and philosophy that had been gaining momentum since the Renaissance, intellectuals in the eighteenth century called into question the claims of revealed religion and a divinely sanctioned social order. They argued that societies could be studied rationally and scientifically, and that social conditions could be improved by human planning and purposeful action. With enlightened rulers and educated citizens, people could move progressively toward a better society in this world instead of only dreaming of ascending to a heavenly city after they died.

Such ideas, once held by a tiny minority, gradually gained wide acceptance, especially among members of the rising middle class. Scientific innovation was the source of much of their new wealth, and their desire to change antiquated laws and institutions that restricted their advancement was reinforced by the reforming spirit of the age. Since middle-class people were in the vanguard of progressive developments, they saw their values as the only appropriate ones for a vastly improved social order in which they held the reins of power. Separation of church and state, the distinction between public and private lives, equality of opportunity, and social reform would usher in a new era of progress from which all would benefit.

Nothing excited British North Americans as much as the promise and practice of science. It stimulated industry, advanced civilization, filled hours of leisure time, and even, some claimed, brought people closer to God. Just as God had revealed Himself in the written word, it was argued, He was also manifested in the natural world. Natural history, a comprehensive term applied to the general study of science, was popular in educated circles, and natural scientists combed the colonies classifying the flora and fauna, studying geological formations, and finding evidence of God's wisdom, power, and goodness. Practical scientists, most of them amateur tinkerers, were inspired by the applications of their discoveries which, if successful, promised to bring them both wealth and fame. The advancement of science was the most noteworthy intellectual achievement of British North Americans in the nineteenth century, one befitting a new country with a short history and a shallow literary tradition.

Early in the nineteenth century, only a few educated immigrants, such as Thomas McCulloch in Nova Scotia and Charles Fothergill in Upper Canada, had systematically pursued their interest in natural history. By mid-century, science had become a popular movement. Organizations devoted to the study of science were founded in most colonial cities, and large audiences turned out to hear lectures on scientific topics and participate in field trips. Mechanics' Institutes devoted attention to scientific matters, while any university worthy of the name hired a professor of science. Such a professor was required to be an accomplished generalist, teaching subjects that today would include everything from chemistry and physics to biology and geology.

People in rural areas learned about the latest scientific discoveries through newspapers, books, and travelling lecturers. In August 1849, Margaret Dickie of the seaport town of Hantsport, Nova Scotia, noted in her diary that a Mr Giffin from the United States had lectured to packed houses on "Electricity, Galvanism and Magnetism" as well as "Animal Physiology." Not only that, he had also "explained how the telegraph worked."[6] During the time that Dickie was not teaching school or attending to domestic duties, she was reading books on navigation, geography, and the new psychology of phrenology. The practical applications of science were not lost on Dickie— she later became the telegraph operator in Hantsport.

British North Americans not only gobbled up scientific knowledge, but they also helped to advance it.

Andrew Downs, creator of a zoological garden in Halifax in 1847, supplied specimens to museums in Europe and the United States. William Logan, director of the Geological Survey of the Province of Canada, was knighted in 1856 for his pioneer work on the geology of Canada. In the 1860s, Hudson's Bay Company fur traders, at the behest of scientists from the Smithsonian Institution in Washington, DC, began collecting information on everything from birds' eggs to the weather. Scientists such as James Robb at the University of New Brunswick, William Dawson at McGill, and George Lawson at Queen's remained in close contact with the larger scientific community for whom they published their findings.

BIOGRAPHY

J. William Dawson

In 1855, in his book *Acadian Geology*, J. William Dawson (1820–1899) announced that the Maritime region had formed millions of years ago and that giant reptiles once roamed the land. For British North Americans raised on the Christian Bible, such claims seemed not only far-fetched but perhaps even blasphemous.

One of the leading scientists of his generation, Dawson was born in Pictou, Nova Scotia, and educated at Pictou Academy and the University of Edinburgh. He was a pioneer in the field of geology, which was challenging everything people believed about the Earth and its inhabitants.

Dawson's discovery of ancient fossils in the cliffs along the Bay of Fundy helped to establish new theories about the Earth's origins. A committed Presbyterian, Dawson went to great lengths to make geological time agree with Biblical creation accounts and he refused to accept the evolutionary theories that were expounded by his great contemporary Charles Darwin.

Dawson also had a brilliant administrative career. He was appointed Superintendent of Education in Nova Scotia in 1850 and Principal of McGill in 1855, a position he held for 38 years. In addition to making McGill one of the world's leading universities, he taught classes, published 20 books, became the only individual to preside over both the American and British Associations for the Advancement of Science, and helped to establish the Royal Society of Canada in 1882. He was knighted for his public services in 1884.

J. William Dawson.
Notman Photographic Archives, McCord Museum of Canadian History, Montreal/I-99584

British North American inventors also had a wide impact. Abraham Gesner, a medical doctor, geologist, and museum curator in the Maritimes, developed a process for making kerosene oil in 1847 and promptly established a factory on Long Island, New York, to market his product. Ironically, Gesner's process was eclipsed by drilled oil, with the first well dug by James Williams in Enniskillen Township in the late 1850s. In turn, Canada West's boom town, Petrolia, was superseded by oil fields in Ohio and Pennsylvania.

Practical inventions were the stock and trade of British North Americans who, like their southern neighbours, were obsessed with finding better ways of doing things. The timber-crib slide was developed on the Ottawa River in 1829. Robert Foulis, an engineer from New Brunswick, produced the world's first steam fog-whistle, installed in the Partridge Island lighthouse in 1860. Given the abundance of timber in Canada, it is not surprising that the first plank roads were built east of Toronto in the mid-1830s. A variety of patents for steam engines were filed by the "river barons" of the St Lawrence. The failure of Nova Scotia native Charles Fenerty to secure a patent for his method of making paper out of pulverized wood in 1838–39 meant that much of the credit went to others. In any event, the new process heralded the decline of a brisk trade in cotton and linen rags that had hitherto been the major ingredient in paper.

By the mid-nineteenth century, most British North Americans had adjusted to the "age of progress," accepting the new science as part of the larger movement toward a better society. Scientific pronouncements concerning the age of the Earth or aggressive tendencies in the animal kingdom remained consistent with God's purpose for human beings. But when Charles Darwin published *The Origin of Species* in 1859, this complacency was undermined. Darwin's view that all living things had evolved from a single, primitive form of life and had developed by a process of natural selection and survival of the fittest flew in the face of Christianity's human-centred view of creation and the notion of a benevolent God.

As the long debate over "Darwinism" dragged its weary way through the second half of the nineteenth century, most Christians simply accepted the discrepancy between Darwin's findings and divine revelation as a mystery that would be revealed in God's good time. Others became more sceptical about religion, and a few deserted the church for the cold comfort of atheism. Still others attempted to refute Darwin's theories on a scientific basis. Geologist William Dawson of McGill, renowned for his study of fossilized plants and animals in the rock formations along the Bay of Fundy, became one of the world's foremost apologists for the creationist view. Although millions of years old, these fossils showed no evidence of evolutionary development, he argued, a view which, both then and now, offered comfort to the creationists.

CONCLUSION

The industrial and intellectual revolutions of the mid-nineteenth century offered British North Americans both challenges and opportunities. For those who clung to the older notions of class privilege, patriarchal authority, religious certainty, and family self-sufficiency the challenges would be daunting. Even those who embraced new ideas were often disappointed in their practical results. Yet the opportunities continued to beckon. As we will see in the next chapter, British North Americans were determined to embrace them, and in the process laid the social and cultural foundations of the modern age.

NOTES

1 Thomas C. Keefer, "Philosophy of Railroads," in *Philosophy of Railroads and Other Essays*, ed. T.C. Keefer (1850; reprinted Toronto: University of Toronto Press, 1972), 10–11.

2 Cited in Gregory S. Kealey, *Toronto Workers Respond to Industrial Capitalism, 1867–1892* (Toronto: University of Toronto Press, 1980), 6.

3 Cited in Michael Cross, ed., *Free Trade, Annexation and Reciprocity, 1846–1854* (Toronto: Holt, Rinehart, and Winston, 1971), 53–54.

4 Jean-Marie Fecteau, "Prolégomènes à une étude historique des rapports entre l'État et le droit dans la société québécoise, de la fin du XVIIIe siècle à la crise de 1929," *Sociologie et sociétés* 18, 1 (April 1986): 129–38.

5 Cited in Kealey, 23.

6 *Margaret Dickie Michener McCulloch Diary*, typescript, Dalhousie University Archives.

RELATED READINGS IN THIS SERIES

From *Foundations: Readings in Pre-Confederation Canadian History*

Paul Craven and Tom Traves, "Dimensions of Paternalism: Discipline and Culture in Canadian Railway Operations in the 1850s," 448–64.

From Media Companion CD-ROM, Volume I

The Old Blacksmith Shop
Employee Contract for E. & C. Gurney (Hamilton Founders)
The Sweated Trades

SELECTED READING

The classic discussion of the impact of industrialism is Karl Polanyi, *The Great Transformation: The Political and Economic Origins of Our Time* (Boston: Beacon Press, 1957). Canadian studies include Donald Creighton, *The Commercial Empire of the Saint Lawrence, 1760–1850* (Toronto: Macmillan, 1937); Stanley Ryerson, *Unequal Union: Confederation and the Roots of Conflict in the Canadas, 1815–1873* (Toronto: Progress Books, 1968); Gerald Tulchinsky, *The River Barons: Montreal Businessmen and the Growth of Industry and Transportation, 1837–1853* (Toronto: University of Toronto Press, 1977); Douglas McCalla, *The Upper Canada Trade, 1834–1872: A Study of Buchanan's Business* (Toronto: University of Toronto Press, 1979); and T.W. Acheson, *Saint John: The Making of a Colonial Urban Community* (Toronto: University of Toronto Press, 1985). Michael Bliss usefully summarizes the general trends in *Northern Enterprise: Five Centuries of Canadian Business* (Toronto: McClelland and Stewart, 1987). Other general studies include Kenneth Norrie and Douglas Owram, *A History of the Canadian Economy* (Toronto: Harcourt Brace Jovanovich, 1991); W.L. Marr and D.G. Paterson, *Canada: An Economic History* (Toronto: Macmillan, 1980); and W.T. Easterbrook and H.G.J. Aitken, *Canadian Economic History* (Toronto: Macmillan, 1963). A valuable perspective on the industrializing process is offered in the introductory chapters to R.T. Naylor, *The History of Canadian Business*, vol. 1, *1867–1914* (Toronto: Lorimer, 1975); Bryan Palmer, *A Culture in Conflict: Skilled Workers and Industrial Capitalism in Hamilton, Ontario, 1860–1914* (Montreal: McGill-Queen's University Press, 1979); and Gregory S. Kealey, *Toronto Responds to Industrial Capitalism, 1867–1892* (Toronto: University of Toronto Press, 1980). See also Ian McKay, "Capital and Labour in the Halifax Baking and Confectionary Industry during the Last Half of the Nineteenth Century," in *Essays in Canadian Business History*, ed. Tom Traves (Toronto: McClelland and Stewart, 1984), 47–81, and Paul Craven and Tom Traves, "Canadian Railways as Manufacturers, 1850–1880," *Canadian Historical Association Historical Papers* (1983): 254–81.

On legal reform see three volumes of *Essays in the History of Canadian Law* (Toronto: University of Toronto Press, 1981, 1983, and 1990); Peter Waite et al., *Law in a Colonial Society: The Nova Scotia Experience* (Toronto: Carswell, 1984); W. Wesley Pue and Barry Wright, *Canadian Perspectives on Law and Society: Issues in Legal History* (Ottawa: Carleton University Press, 1988); R.C. Macleod, ed., *Lawful Authority: Readings on the History of Criminal Justice in Canada* (Toronto: Copp Clark Pitman, 1988); Constance Backhouse, *Petticoats and Prejudice: Women and Law in Nineteenth-Century Canada* (Toronto: Women's Press, 1991), and "Married Women's Property Law in Nineteenth-Century Canada," in *Canadian Family History: Selected Readings*, ed. Bettina Bradbury (Toronto: Copp Clark Pitman, 1992), 320–59; and R.C.B. Risk, "The Law and the Economy in Mid-Nineteenth-Century Ontario: A Perspective," in *Essays in the History of Canadian Law*, vol. 1, ed. David H. Flaherty (Toronto: University of Toronto Press, 1981), 88–131.

Other studies on nineteenth-century economic development include T.C. Keefer, ed., *Philosophy of Railroads and Other Essays* (1850; reprinted Toronto: University of Toronto Press, 1972); A.A. den Otter, *The Philosophy of Railways: The Transcontinental Railway Idea in British North America* (Toronto: University of Toronto Press, 1997); S.A. Saunders, *The Economic History of the Maritime Provinces* (1939; reprinted Fredericton: Acadiensis Press, 1984); G.N. Tucker, *The Canadian Commercial Revolution, 1845–1851* (Ottawa: Carleton University Press, 1964); D.C. Masters, *The Reciprocity Treaty of 1854* (Toronto: McClelland and Stewart, 1963); John McCallum, *Unequal Beginnings: Agriculture and Economic Development in Quebec and Ontario until 1870* (Toronto: University of Toronto Press, 1980); A.R.M. Lower,

Great Britain's Woodyard: British America and the Timber Trade, 1763–1867 (Montreal: McGill-Queen's University Press, 1973); G.P. de T. Glazebrook, *A History of Transportation in Canada*, vol. 1 (Ottawa: Carleton University Press, 1964); Brian Young, *Promoters and Politicians: The North-Shore Railways in the History of Quebec* (Toronto: University of Toronto Press, 1978); and Jacob Spelt, *Urban Development in South Central Ontario* (Ottawa: Carleton University Press, 1972). The relationship between statistics and developments in this period is the subject of Bruce Curtis, *State Formation, Statistics and the Census of Canada* (Toronto: University of Toronto Press, 2001).

Sources on nineteenth-century intellectual history include Carl Berger, *Science, God, and Nature in Victorian Canada* (Toronto: University of Toronto Press, 1983); Susan Sheets-Pyenson, *John William Dawson: Faith, Hope, and Science* (Montreal: McGill-Queen's University Press, 1996); and several works by A.B. McKillop: *A Disciplined Intelligence: Critical Inquiry and Canadian Thought in the Victorian Era* (Montreal: McGill-Queen's University Press, 1979), *Contours of Canadian Thought* (Toronto: University of Toronto Press, 1987), and "Culture, Intellect, and Context," *Journal of Canadian Studies* 24 (Fall 1989): 7–31.

WEBLINKS

RECIPROCITY TREATY
www.collectionscanada.ca/confederation/
h18-2996-e.html
The text of the treaty is available at the Library and Archives Canada site.

GEOLOGICAL SURVEY OF CANADA
http://gsc.nrcan.gc.ca/index_e.php
Natural Resources Canada maintains this site on the Geological Survey of Canada. Historical and current materials are available.

CRIMEAN WAR
http://www.hillsdale.edu/oldacademics/history/war/
This site provides access to contemporary comment and documents relating to the Crimean conflict.

CHAPTER 21

Society in Transition

Timeline

1845–51 Blight attacks potato crops throughout Europe and North America

1844–76 Egerton Ryerson is superintendent of education in Canada West/Ontario

1848 Women's rights become topic of debate with the Declaration of Sentiments in the United States

1853 Gavazzi Riots in Montreal

1855 Prohibition bill passes in New Brunswick

1856–60 Prince Edward Islanders debate Bible reading in public schools

"[H]ow many souls and bodies of my fellow-men, since the days of Noah . . . have been ruined by the vile practice of drinking! If all men and women were sober, there would not be the twentieth part for gaols [and] lunatic asylums . . . neither would there be children in our streets, or brawls in the family circle. . . . If young men continue as they have commenced, the weeds of woe to mothers and children must forever cease. If all men were abstainers, then schools and churches would soon be filled, and the days of the millennium would be beginning to dawn."[1]

These comments appeared in the April 1852 issue of the *Cadet*, a Montreal temperance magazine. They reflect the optimism about the future that circulated in colonial society. Impressed by the potential of industrial and intellectual progress, many people predicted the end of the ignorance, poverty, and violence that they saw around them. There was talk of reform in politics, in economic policy, and, above all, reform of individuals. Through education and self-discipline, it was argued, people could improve themselves and, together with the new production processes, usher in a new age of material well-being and harmonious human relations.

SOCIETY IN CRISIS

Notwithstanding such expressions of optimism, British North Americans were experiencing a sense of crisis in the mid-nineteenth century. Their economy seemed rudderless and political structures were in a state of chaos. Under the impact of the Industrial Revolution work was being transformed from muscle to machine and even such fundamental concepts as gender and class relations were being called into question. Formal education, once the luxury of the rich, was now increasingly a necessity for getting along in a society where written documents mediated human relationships. Violence and poverty, though not new to colonial society, were taking on startling dimensions. What was the world coming to?

In the face of these challenges, British North Americans advocated sweeping changes. Those advocating reform, mostly members of the rapidly growing middle class who benefited from the new industrial order, maintained that social problems could be eradicated or greatly reduced by careful study and appropriate action. In the name of reform, they urged greater state intervention in the lives of individuals through the passing of new laws and the establishment of bureaucratic structures to enforce them. Eventually, they also began to argue that closer cooperation among the colonies would advance the well-being of British North Americans and lay the foundations for a new nationalism that would spur colonials to even greater achievements.

View of Indian Village on the River St John above Fredericton, February 1832. By mid-century many of the Aboriginal people in the Maritimes and the United Canadas were living on reserves that were often too small to ensure an adequate living.
Library and Archives Canada/C-011076

Poverty in a Cold Climate

Colonial reformers did not exaggerate the conditions that they set out to address. By modern standards, British North Americans in 1850 were materially poor, and those on the bottom of the social ladder lived a precarious existence. Family life, indeed survival itself, was often at stake when unemployment, illness, or other disaster struck. Although cases of death from hunger and exposure were uncommon enough to warrant coverage by colonial newspapers, it is certainly the case that poverty shortened life expectancy and contributed greatly to human suffering.

In the first half of the nineteenth century, poverty, and the diseases that it encouraged, seemed everywhere. Poverty accounted in large measure for the drastic decline in the Aboriginal population of the eastern colonies. It arrived with the immigrants who flooded the colonies as a result of the famine migration of the 1840s. With the onset of winter, seasonal workers were thrown out of work at the very time that the cost of life's necessities—food and fuel—were prohibitively expensive.

The chronically poor lived in substandard housing, sometimes with several families to one room. Due to malnutrition and illness, the poor were less likely to find and keep a wage-paying job. Poverty reduced very old people, pregnant mothers, and dependent children to begging on city streets or from door to door. Even the poor person's best friend and only beast of burden, the dog, showed evidence of the poverty-stricken state of its master.

The poor had few resources to respond to disasters. When the potato blight, which devastated Ireland, also invaded British North America in the 1840s, families living on the margin of subsistence faced starvation. Cape Breton was the scene of widespread famine between 1845 and 1851. Historian Robert Morgan cites the account of one woman from Loch Lomond:

A group of men and women started from L'Ardoise by foot over blazed roads, following the lake and river down as far as Grand River then taking a blazed trail over l'Ardoise Highlands, for some of us were over thirty miles from our homes. The poor women were barefooted and each woman took her knitting along with her and knitted away as they walked over and around the hills, by waterfalls and swamps until they reached the shore, hungry and tired. Each man and woman was supplied with half a barrel of Indian meal, then they cried for something to eat. Mr. Bremner rolled out a barrel of meal and they rolled it to a brook, opened it and poured the water from the brook into the barrel and made raw cakes and passed it around to each person. All ate heartily then each man and woman took their half-barrel on their backs and sang "Ben Dorian" as they left for their homes over the blazed roads.[2]

Although most people responded generously to the plight of famine victims, some were quick to see God's hand in events. The *Presbyterian Witness* in August 1851 pronounced the famine as "a punishment inflicted upon man for his presumption in attempting to introduce disorder into the economy of Nature by giving undue prominence to the Potato."

SOCIAL WELFARE

Social policy relating to the poor in mid-nineteenth-century British North America was a haphazard mixture of public and private initiatives. Although colonial cities maintained jails, almshouses, hospitals, and asylums where the poor could take refuge, attitudes toward poverty restricted those eligible for public assistance. Only the disabled, the old, and the very young were considered "deserving" of charity. The able-bodied poor, who were victims of seasonal-employment patterns, the absence of kinship networks, crude exploitation, or their own human weaknesses, were given little public assistance and even less sympathy.

In rural areas, local assessment for the poor was levied on the ratepayers, a policy that led to parsimony. "Outdoor" relief was handed out begrudgingly. The recipients were often required to do community work—perhaps breaking rock for roads—in return for assistance. It was common in some localities to auction the poor as labourers to the bidder who would agree to provide room and board at the lowest price. Because the poor laws permitted municipalities to "warn out" vagrants from their jurisdiction, poor immigrants often wandered from place to place in search of food and shelter.

Private charity dispensed by church, ethnic, and labour organizations was not accessible to all and rarely adequate to the need. Not surprisingly, therefore, the poor, who often resorted to desperate measures to survive, made up the majority of those who appeared in colonial courts. Minor offences were punished by fines, branding, or the stocks; major offences, such as theft, murder, treason, and mutiny, brought the death penalty or banishment to a penal colony. Although long prison sentences were rare, prisons outside major colonial cities were usually crowded with the poor, criminal, and insane because there were few specialized institutions to house the casualties of pre-industrial life.

A report on prison conditions in Canada East produced by Dr Wolfred Nelson in 1852 is revealing. Women constituted 47 percent of those in Montreal's prisons at that time. According to the sheriff of Montreal, "it is very often the case that people who are simply homeless or devoid of funds are incarcerated. The old, the sick, the infirm and the mad are often sent to prison on the very vague charge of being idle and debauched and for having disturbed the peace." The doctor in the Montreal prison claimed that "The Montreal prison is improperly referred to as simply a prison. . . . One could almost call it a maternity hospital, because so many of the women who go there are pregnant and give birth there. . . . One could call it a children's home since very large numbers of very young children are taken in there."[3]

SOCIAL CONFLICT

In the mid-nineteenth century, violence was a last—and for some a first—resort for expressing frustration with a society based on inequality and uncertainty. Labour disputes, along with an increased incidence of highway robbery and theft in rural areas, testified to the growing complexity and conflict in British North American communities. Those on the margins of organized society frequently used rough justice to challenge the constituted public order. The charivari, a common practice throughout the colonies, was used not only to control private morality and public virtue

Troops were called out to keep the peace in Montreal during the elections of 1832, 1844, 1846, and 1847. Throughout British North America, elections were often accompanied by riots as opposing sides tried to intimidate voters.
Library and Archives Canada/C15494

but also to express the hostility of the underclasses toward their self-styled betters. In Newfoundland, mummering sometimes served a similar purpose. Orange Orders and Ribbon societies clashed on 17 March and the "glorious 12th" in July, bringing regular activities to a standstill.

Authorities often resorted to reading the Riot Act and sending in troops as a means of dispersing a potentially volatile mob. In 1853, when Italian patriot Alessandro Gavazzi gave anti-papal lectures in Montreal, the military were called out to prevent a confrontation between the city's Protestant and Roman Catholic communities. During the confusion following one of Gavazzi's public performances, the police opened fire, killing 10 and wounding 50 people. The military in British North America was more often called in to put down civil disturbances and potential threats to property than to deal with threats from foreign invasion.

Violence punctuated all aspects of colonial life. Because voting was conducted openly, rather than by secret ballot, polling stations at election time were scenes of violence and intimidation. Although duelling was illegal, colonial men still occasionally challenged each other to duels and killed their opponents. Wife-beating was still legally sanctioned. Children were sometimes the victims of their anxiety-ridden elders and

"spare the rod and spoil the child" informed disciplinary policy at both home and school. Even animals bore the brunt of human anger and frustration. The fate of horses, oxen, and dogs, the "beasts of burden" in colonial society, was to work to exhaustion and be shot or abandoned when no longer useful. In the late 1820s, old circus animals were packed into leaky boats and sent over Niagara Falls, while callous onlookers took bets to see which ones and how many would survive.

Seaport towns were noted for their violent and illegal activities. Areas such as Lower Town in Quebec and Water Street in Halifax were separate worlds of crimps (a kind of pimp for sailors), prostitutes, and boarding-house keepers who traded in the labour of sailors and defied sea captains, shipping masters, and local constables who tried to enforce the law. Drunken and disorderly behaviour often brought seamen to colonial courts. Injured victims went to special hospitals established for sailors.

Like raftsmen and soldiers, sailors lived in an all-male environment under repressive and often violent regimes. Green hands, cabin boys, stewards, cooks, and blacks were most likely to be victimized by hard-bitten captains, and all sailors were the victims of the unscrupulous shore-based underworld. Desertion, absence without leave, insubordination, mutiny, and other forms of resistance were common reactions among men for whom extra-legal action was as effective as colonial courts in securing justice. Until the mid-nineteenth century, vice-admiralty courts and local magistrates had often favoured sailors in their battles with captains and shipowners over wages, contracts, and working conditions. With the tightening of marine law and the appointment of stipendiary magistrates in the 1850s, the sailor had little chance of success without the help of an able—and expensive—lawyer.

The elite were equally prepared to use violence as a means of achieving their ends. When public policy failed to meet their approval in 1849, they threw rocks at the governor and burned the Parliament buildings in Montreal. Elites only rarely were driven to such acts of desperation. Because their interests were usually expressed in both the legislatures and the law courts, "respectable" citizens had little need to resort directly to violence. In cities, councils representing property owners appointed marshals and constables to keep the peace, swore in special deputies during emergencies, and in extreme cases could call on the military for assistance. By mid-century, city fathers were beginning to establish full-time police forces and installing street lights to protect the lives and property of the respectable city folk.

THE RAGE FOR REFORM

While reforms were sometimes spearheaded by governments, they were more often the focus of voluntary groups, many of them associated with colonial churches. The growing influence of Christian churches in the lives of British North Americans is one of the major trends of the early industrial age. Although the separation of church and state became an accepted policy in all colonial jurisdictions, it did little to halt the power of organized religion in British North American society. Determined to maintain their intellectual and social influence, church leaders by mid-century were advocating a variety of reforms and taking institutional initiatives to achieve their goals. Attention focused on ignorance, alcoholism, crime, poverty, disease, and racial discrimination. Initially inspired by the evangelical movement, with its strong roots in the rural-farming and urban-artisan communities, the reform impulse soon spread to embrace a wide spectrum of colonial society.

Promoting spiritual rebirth as the vehicle for transforming individuals and society, the evangelical movement was a sharp reaction to the cold rationalism of the Enlightenment. Nevertheless, evangelicals were heirs of the Enlightenment in their commitment to social improvement. In addition to urging personal

MORE TO THE STORY

The Triumph of Civic Policing in Toronto

In the early nineteenth century, policing was the job of a constable and justice of the peace in most colonial jurisdictions. The reform of municipal government at mid-century to manage the growing complexity and violence in urban life led to the creation of a police department and a full-time, paid police force in many colonial cities.

Toronto led the way and served as a model for Canada West. When it was incorporated in 1834, Toronto had a police force consisting of a high bailiff and five constables. By the mid-1850s, the force had grown to 50 officers. The site of 29 riots between 1839 and 1864, many of them involving Orangemen, Toronto gave the police plenty of work to do. They may not have always been impartial in the conduct of their duty. Although each police officer was required to take an oath swearing that he did not belong to any secret society, many officers actually maintained their Orange Lodge membership.

In an effort to remove policing from the political fray, the United Canadas passed legislation in 1858 requiring cities in Canada West to organize boards of police commissioners to supervise police forces. The following year Toronto hired as its chief constable Captain William Stratton Prince, a former British Army officer, to instill military discipline in the force. Prince demanded that his officers be men of high calibre. In one of his reports he stated that the ideal candidate must be in "the prime of manhood, mentally and bodily, shrewd, intelligent and possessed of a good English education" and "far above the class of labourers and equal, if not superior, to the most respectable class of journeymen mechanics. . . ."[4] Prince favoured candidates from Great Britain, particularly Irish Protestants, so the ethnic bias in Toronto's police force was not eradicated.

In 1856, Attorney General John A. Macdonald tried to introduce legislation that would consolidate municipal police forces into a colonial constabulary under a commissioner, but his government fell before the bill could be passed. Municipal opposition to a provincial police force remained strong for the rest of the century. It was not until 1909 that the Ontario Provincial Police came into being.

piety and perfection, evangelicals attempted to create an environment in which spiritual salvation would be more readily accepted. Using Christ's Sermon on the Mount as their inspiration, evangelicals formed missionary societies, fought slavery, encouraged education, founded hospitals for the sick and asylums for the insane, and urged temperance and civic reform. The evangelical impulse was strongest among Methodists, Presbyterians, and Baptists, but it touched all Protestant denominations and was complemented by a revitalized spirituality in the Roman Catholic Church at mid-century.

Colonial churches played a particularly prominent role in the temperance movement. Arguably the first mass movement in Canadian history, temperance in the consumption of alcoholic beverages was an idea whose time had come. People of evangelical leanings in the Maritimes began forming temperance societies in the late 1820s. By 1850 temperance had gained a following among all classes, religions, and cultures, from St John's to Red River.

While temperance in the use of alcohol was encouraged by evangelicals as a means of self-help, it also supposedly offered a solution to what seemed to be the effects of intemperance: crime, insanity, poverty, violence, and the abuse of women and children. Many of the supporters of the movement were those who had little formal power. A female lecturer in Hamilton in 1851 caused a newspaper editor to reflect: "It is a rather novel thing for a female to be engaged in this cause, as a public lecturer, but we can see no valid objection to it. We do not know who could better describe the sad scenes occasioned by intemperance than those who have been its innocent victims."5

In the late 1840s, a secular organization called the Sons of Temperance made its appearance in British North America. With its elaborate rites and rituals, Cadets of Temperance and Cold Water Armies, and divisions for women and children as well as men, the Sons of Temperance drew its members from all denominations and became a potent political force in the era of responsible government. The temperance crusade was so successful that it seemed possible to go one step further—state prohibition of the manufacture and sale of intoxicating beverages. The call for prohibition split the movement between those for and against greater state intervention in the lives of individuals and drew fierce opposition from brewers, distillers, sellers, and drinkers of alcoholic beverages.

In New Brunswick, the prohibition movement was temporarily successful. There, political timing and the influence of the state of Maine, which passed prohibition legislation in 1851, were crucial to events. In 1855, fresh from their success in achieving responsible government, the Liberals, known as "Smashers" because of their views on alcohol, passed a prohibition bill. The problems created by prohibition were quickly revealed. Not only were the regulations difficult to enforce, they precipitated a drastic drop in customs revenues. The governor stepped in, prompting the government to resign. In the ensuing election the "Rummies" beat the Smasher faction in the Liberal Party, including Samuel Leonard Tilley, the Most Worthy Patriarch of the Sons of Temperance in North America, and the offensive legislation was repealed. Other colonies avoided the New Brunswick experience by letting individuals and municipal corporations make the difficult decision on the thorny temperance question.

EDUCATION REFORM

It was not so easy to delegate responsibility for education to individuals and local communities. Acts by colonial legislatures encouraging local initiative in education had led to a hodgepodge of schools. Some were privately sponsored, many church-affiliated, and the whole system lacked the efficiency and uniformity so dear to the hearts of educational reformers. Like temperance, education was expected to accomplish many purposes. Egerton Ryerson, the Methodist superintendent of education for Canada West and Ontario from 1844 to 1876, defined education in 1846 as "not the mere acquisition of certain arts, or of certain branches of knowledge, but that instruction and discipline which qualify and dispose the subjects of it for their appropriate duties and employments of life, as Christians, as persons of business, and also as members of the civil community in which they live."6 Programs in Prussia, Ireland, and the United States to establish systems of non-denominational state-supported schools offered models for colonial reformers to follow.

Only three obstacles stood in the way of success: class, religion, and race. The notion of state-supported schools open to all classes and cultures was, like prohi-

Egerton Ryerson was a Methodist minister who served as superintendent of education in Canada West and Ontario from 1844 to 1876.
Archives of Ontario, 5623

ority in their classrooms, opponents of the system charged that morality could not be divorced from religious instruction. Roman Catholics were particularly wary of state-supported schools, which, with their daily Bible readings and prayers, seemed little more than Protestant schools in disguise.

Between 1856 and 1860, Prince Edward Island's advanced "free" school system was rocked by the question of Bible reading in the schools, which was demanded by the "Protestant Combination" and staunchly opposed by Roman Catholics. A compromise was effected: Bible reading in the common schools was to be mandatory by law, but children who found it offensive could be excused from attendance. In addition to fuelling denominational tensions, the controversy altered the political alignment on the island. A coalition of Tories and evangelicals led by Edward Palmer swept the Liberals and their Roman Catholic supporters from office, in the process creating a party system dangerously divided by religion.

Common-school legislation was so controversial that most colonial administrations championed its cause only at their peril. Nevertheless, Egerton Ryerson managed to achieve most of his objectives during his long tenure in office. Under Ryerson's careful guidance, Canada West adopted general assessment for schools, uniform textbooks, a system of graded subjects, the bureaucratization of administration, and the centralization of power at the expense of local school boards. He also pointed teachers on the path to professionalization through his encouragement of normal-school training, teachers' institutes and associations, and the publication of the *Journal of Education for Upper Canada*.

Theodore Harding Rand, a Nova Scotia Baptist who served as superintendent of education in both Nova Scotia and New Brunswick, followed Ryerson's lead. Despite their opposition to separate schools, both men were forced to accept compromises with the politically powerful Roman Catholics, who insisted that confessional schools be eligible for state support. In contrast, Canada East and Newfoundland, where the Roman Catholic Church and Church of England were strong, made denominational schools the basis for public education. Racial and linguistic differences were also reflected in the public school systems. Both Nova Scotia and Canada West had "Negro Separate Schools."

bition, one that struck terror into the hearts of many British North Americans. The supporters of the idea, again a loose alliance of Protestant middle-class reformers, hoped to establish social harmony through a universal curriculum and a "common" school experience. They also saw obvious benefits for their own children in the implementation of such a system, especially one that they had a hand in designing. In contrast, working-class families feared that schools would take children away from productive labour at home and in the workforce and impose taxes they were ill-equipped to pay. At the other end of the social scale, the colonial elite opposed the "levelling" impact of common schools and the low standards that would surely prevail in such a system.

The question that concerned many British North Americans was the role of religion in a common-school system. While education reformers left little doubt that Christian morality would have a high pri-

Canada West also administered separate schools after 1860 for Algonkian children. In addition, there were bilingual schools where instruction was given in English and one of French, German, or Gaelic.

The education revolution that occurred during the middle decades of the nineteenth century had a profound effect on the course of British North American childhood. Since that time, most children have left home for a significant portion of the day during the "school year" to receive moral and academic training at the hands of a professional teacher, rather than from their parents. Increasingly, that teacher was drawn from the ranks of young women between the ages of 16 and 25—women prepared to work long hours for low wages. In this way, people avoided paying higher taxes for their new educational institutions. The overall effect of this schooling experience on children was to prepare them for the vastly different ways in which they would make their living in a rapidly industrializing British North America.

Reformers of all denominations placed a special emphasis on saving the child, who, it was believed, was the most receptive to socialization. Orphanages, workhouses, and industrial schools were targeted as special agents of social reform because they focused on dependent mothers and their children. As early as 1832, a group of reform-minded women in St John's set up a factory to teach carding, spinning, and net-making to the children of the poor. Saint John established a House of Female Industry in 1834. In the wake of the Irish famine migration of the 1840s, orphanages were established in colonial cities to care for homeless children. Reformers also promoted "reformatories" as alternatives to prisons for juveniles in trouble with the law. It was argued that by separating impressionable youths from hard-bitten criminals and by teaching them appropriate behaviour, they might be "saved" from a life of crime.

THE DISCOVERY OF THE ASYLUM

By 1850, the notion that poverty, criminal behaviour, and mental illness should be cured rather than endured was beginning to gain currency. Emphasis was therefore placed on providing the needy with skills and values necessary for them to become self-supporting citizens. By helping unfortunate people to help themselves, it was argued, society in general and the taxpayer in particular would benefit. Reformers also argued that specialized institutions designed to focus on specific problems would be more effective than the family in achieving the desired results. With appropriate treatment, there was even hope for the rehabilitation of the criminal and the insane, two groups hitherto considered beyond redemption.

Following the lead of Britain, which had instituted a new Poor Law in 1834, urban British North Americans erected Houses of Industry where the poor would not only find shelter but also be taught habits of industry and self-discipline. These institutions were designed to reduce the cost of outdoor relief and avoid the practice of committing the poor to common jails. At the same time, they would offer an ideal setting for moral uplift. In Toronto, private subscriptions led to the construction of a House of Industry in 1836. Since social services were the responsibility of local authorities and continued to remain so after the achievement of responsible government, the reach of reform was limited. Only affluent municipalities, which in practice meant cities, could sustain such asylums for their poor.

Asylums were also built for the treatment of the insane. In 1836, the citizens of Saint John established British North America's first "lunatic asylum," but it housed both the poor and the insane until 1848. The spate

Provincial Lunatic Asylum in Toronto, designed by John G. Howard.
City of Toronto Art Collection

of new asylums in colonial cities at mid-century was inspired by the view motivating the commissioners of the Beauport Asylum near Quebec. They argued that their new institution was a place where the insane could "exchange their chains, gloom and filth for liberty, cheerfulness and cleanliness, where they are subject to the remedial powers and moral influences, and to the mode of treatment in accordance with the most improved principles of the present day."[7] Institutional treatment of the insane was so significant on the reform agenda in Canada West that when the Lunatic Asylum opened its doors in Toronto in 1850 it was the largest building in the colony.

Under the reform impulse, prisons, too, became institutions of reform rather than punishment. The Kingston Penitentiary, which had opened in 1835, was designed "to correct" deviant behaviour by imposing rigid discipline in a closely controlled environment. Like many of the new asylums, Kingston Penitentiary soon came under severe criticism for the harsh treatment of its inmates. Prisoners, who included men, women, and children, were flogged for minor infractions, confined for days to a dark cell, and fed on diets of bread and water. In 1848–49, George Brown chaired a commission of inquiry into conditions at the Kingston Penitentiary that laid bare the cruel and corrupt regime of warden Henry Smith. Brown's charges earned him the undying enmity of John A. Macdonald, in whose constituency the penitentiary was located. They also resulted in the appointment of a paid inspector to investigate prison operations.

By the 1850s, social reform and the institutions it encouraged had run aground on the shoals of denominational rivalry. The high incidence of Roman Catholics among those committed to institutional care prompted Protestants to complain about the costs of treating Roman Catholics and to conclude that social problems were associated with religious belief. In an effort to avoid the proselytizing tendencies of custodians in public institutions, a reinvigorated Roman Catholic Church expanded its social services to assist its own people. Protestants, not to be outdone, established separate institutions for themselves. Most British North American cities in mid-century spawned church-sponsored asylums, hospitals, and hostels, thus creating a patchwork of state, church, and privately supported efforts, vastly uneven in quality and accessible to only a fraction of the potential clients.

The rage for reform among the colonial middle classes in the mid-nineteenth century was motivated by altruism and by the example of their counterparts in Britain and the United States. It also served to disguise the growing disparity between rich and poor that increasingly characterized colonial society. Operating on the democratic belief that self-discipline and education would enable everyone to benefit from the new economic and political order, middle-class reformers made life even more difficult for those excluded from the race for success. Once merely perceived as the world's unfortunates, the poor were attacked for their lack of character and moral fibre. By placing the blame on individuals rather than on the system that created and tolerated inequality, reformers avoided any wholesale critique of the social order that sustained their own affluence.

PUBLIC AND PRIVATE WORLDS

New social values and attitudes toward work also had a profound influence on the family. Home in the pre-industrial world was the centre of work and play, business and politics, religion and education. By the mid-nineteenth century British North Americans were increasingly making a distinction between their public and private lives. The public world of business, paid labour, and politics, it was argued, should be separate from the domestic realm of the family, which should serve as a refuge from the outside world of exploitation and competition.

The impact of these changes was felt first in urban middle-class families, where marriages were based on sentimental as well as economic considerations and where fewer children were being raised. In these families, the work performed by women in the home changed with the introduction of manufactured goods such as textiles, the increasing number of servants, and the tendency to send children to public schools. As the productive and reproductive roles of women decreased, more emphasis was placed on motherhood and household management. Women's spiritual qualities and their capacity for charitable works were also singled out for approval. In Protestant cultures,

Domestic scene, by Cornelius Krieghoff.
Library and Archives Canada/C-011224

as possible. The increased emphasis on childhood and adolescence complemented the emergence of motherhood, which developed new meaning in the privatized world of the family.

Working-class family life was far removed from concerns for privacy and sentimentality. In the working-class district of St Jacques in Montreal, families dependent on wage labour for survival lived a precarious existence. Faced with unemployment, illness, death, and unplanned pregnancy, families were often forced to commit their younger children to the Saint-Alexis Orphanage, run by the Sisters of Providence. The lot of the working-class widow and her children was particularly difficult. Josephine Brousseau, for instance, shared a dwelling with a married couple and a twenty-four-year-old widower and his one-year-old child, while she worked as a washerwoman. She placed her eight-year-old daughter Clara in Saint-Alexis in 1868. By the time she was 12, Clara and her brothers, aged 10 and 14, were working in Macdonald's tobacco factory. The majority of children at Saint-Alexis in the mid-nineteenth century were not technically orphans but had lived in families who were too poor to care for them at home.

Despite objections of middle-class moralists to "working wives," a working-class family could often survive only if more than one of its members engaged in paid labour. Middle-class families might live very well on the income of the male head of household and hire servants to attend to household chores. For the working class, the whole family was the economic unit and the work of wives and children was crucial to family survival. Although a wife's work in the home was not calculated in monetary terms, the family could not survive without her labour at home and, when necessary, in the paid work force. By the same token, children who were not old enough to work threatened the delicately balanced economy of the working-class family.

middle-class women functioned as the unpaid staff of church-sponsored charitable organizations, while Roman Catholic women entered convents in unprecedented numbers. The careful delineation of separate spheres for men and women that had prevailed in the pre-industrial world was thus maintained: men dominated the public sphere with all its attendant opportunities while women were relegated to the private sphere of domesticity and good works.

Life-cycle choices were also being gradually altered to accommodate the new social reality. Both men and women married later, and they spent more time in the paid labour force before they married. Although the work of unmarried women was largely confined to domestic service, new professions such as school-teaching gave educated women experience in the public sphere and the possibility of economic independence outside the institution of marriage. With the delaying of marriage, adolescence—a word coined only in the late nineteenth century—was emerging as a stage in the life cycle of British North Americans. Childhood was also becoming distinct from infancy and adulthood, and children were perceived as innocent and angelic rather than primitive creatures to be socialized to adult behaviour as quickly

The middle-class notion of proper family life, with its carefully defined spheres, nonetheless prevailed in mid-nineteenth-century British North America. As a result the notion that women's place was in the home took on the status of a prescription, rather than a description of where women did their work. The Reverend Robert Sedgewick's lecture to the Young Men's Christian Association in Halifax in 1856 was typical of the patriarchal concern voiced over women's "proper" sphere in colonial society: "The errors and blunders which are interwoven with the subject of women's rights and women's place in modern society are . . . to be traced either to the ignoring of the fact or the omission of the fact that in the economy of nature or rather in the design of God, woman is the complement of man. In defining her sphere and describing her influence, that fact is fundamental." Predictably, for Sedgewick women's "proper sphere" was "the home and whatever is co-relative with the home in the social economy."[8]

WOMEN'S RIGHTS

Sedgewick's outburst was a calculated response to the emergence of the women's rights movement in the United States. There, women involved in the anti-slavery movement soon recognized their own lack of civil rights and began organizing to remove the legal and attitudinal barriers that made women subordinate to men. In 1848, American abolitionist women, led by Elizabeth Cady Stanton and Lucretia Mott, held a convention at Seneca Falls, New York, where a Declaration of Sentiments and Resolutions was adopted. Using the language of the earlier Declaration of Independence, the advocates of women's rights maintained "that all men and women are created equal; that they are endowed by their Creator with certain inalienable rights; that among these are life, liberty, and the pursuit of happiness." They also charged that "the history of mankind is a history of repeated injuries and usurpations on the part of man toward woman, having its direct object the establishment of an absolute tyranny over her."[9] Such views were certain to draw the fire of men whose power was directly challenged by women's rights advocates.

Lacking the spur that the anti-slavery crusade provided for women in the United States, British North American women were slow to organize.

Nevertheless, they were aware of their inequality under the law. Between 1852 and 1857, three groups of women petitioned the legislature in Canada West for reform of laws relating to married women's property. In 1852, a landmark statute passed by the Prince Edward Island legislature permitted cases of seduction to be brought in the name of the woman seduced rather than in the name of the father. A Nova Scotia law of 1857 made divorce easier to obtain on the grounds of desertion or adultery. In Canada West, an 1855 law gave the court discretion to permit mothers to have access to or custody of infant children in cases where judges "saw fit." Subsequent decisions rendered by the courts recognized the enhanced status of motherhood in British North American society.

NATIONALISM AND COLONIAL IDENTITIES

While many British North Americans believed that social reform and rights movements would cure colonial ills, others were inspired by national sentiments that were sweeping the western world. Following the French Revolution and Napoleonic Wars, periodic nationalist uprisings, most notably in 1830 and 1848, rocked European empires. Nationalism fuelled movements to unify the Italian and German states, and in the name of nationalism Irish patriots demanded an end to the hated union between Britain and Ireland. Nationalist rhetoric inspired the "rebels of '37," especially among French Canadians, whose common language, religion, and history provided the basis for a cohesive national identity.

British immigrants brought their cultural identities with them, a confusing mixture of the ethnic, national, and imperial sentiment that prevailed in Great Britain itself. By the mid-nineteenth century, there were voices calling for a larger British North American nationalism to mute class and cultural cleavages. The concept of a united British North America was not new to the mid-nineteenth century. In the late eighteenth century, Loyalists had voiced such sentiments, and Lord Durham had been a recent proponent of the idea. But developments in communication and transportation, coupled with expanded horizons, made a larger national outlook possible—though not, it must be conceded, inevitable.

BIOGRAPHY

Emily Jennings Howard Stowe

British North American women were close observers of the women's movement in the United States. Although there was no colonial equivalent to the Seneca Falls declaration, many British North American women opposed laws and practices that discriminated against them, and they often travelled to the United States to take advantage of educational opportunities denied them at home.

The experience of Emily Jennings reveals the obstacles placed in the path of women seeking equality in the professional sphere. Born in 1831 in Norwich, Upper Canada, Emily was the eldest of six daughters. She and her sisters were raised in the Quaker tradition, which emphasized the freedom and equality of women. A clever student, Emily began teaching school at the age of 15 and saved her income to further her education. Denied admission to the University of Toronto, she took a teaching degree at the Normal School in Toronto in 1854. At the age of 23, she was appointed principal of the Brantford Public School, the first woman to hold such a position in the public school system.

In 1856, she married John Howard Stowe. When her husband became ill with tuberculosis, she decided to become a doctor. Since the University of Toronto's Medical School was closed to women, Stowe studied at the New York Medical College for Women, which two of her sisters had already attended. Upon graduation in 1867, Stowe returned to Canada, where she set up a medical practice.

Stowe's difficulties were not yet over. The College of Physicians and Surgeons of Ontario refused to grant her a licence to practise because she had not attended lectures in an Ontario medical school. Since she was barred from doing so

because of her gender, there was little Stowe could do other than practise illegally and fight for fairer laws. She finally received a licence to practise in 1880. By that time, women were being grudgingly permitted to attend classes in Canadian medical schools, but they still faced ridicule and hostility from male professors and students. Stowe was the moving spirit behind the founding of the Women's Medical College of Toronto in 1883, and in the same year another medical college was opened in Kingston.

In 1876, Stowe also helped to organize the Toronto Women's Literary Club, a polite euphemism for a women's rights organization. Seven years later, the group's name was changed to the Toronto Women's Suffrage Association.

Emily Jennings Howard Stowe.
Library and Archives Canada/C9480

Colonial poets, politicians, and newspapermen were the first to voice lofty national sentiments. Joseph Howe, who practised all three professions, paid tribute to his native "Acadia" in romantic poetry. He also wrote enthusiastically about the potential of British North American unity. In his efforts to garner support for an intercolonial railroad in 1851 he asked his constituents to "stand by me now in this last effort to improve our country, elevate these noble Provinces, and form them into a Nation."[10] Another

passionate British North American nationalist was Thomas D'Arcy McGee. An Irish patriot who had participated in the Irish rebellion of 1848, McGee fled to the United States and in 1857 moved to Montreal. As a newspaperman and later a member of the legislature in the Canadas, McGee became a supporter of a "new Northern nationality" within the larger British imperial context. For McGee, nationalism offered a solution to the ethnic and sectional conflicts that he felt impeded the progress of British

Patriotic Poets

In the mid-nineteenth century colonial writers penned romantic tributes to the land and its people, especially the noble Natives, Acadians, and military heroes. Charles Sangster, for instance, in his poem "The St Lawrence and the Saguenay," tried to praise Wolfe and Montcalm equally:

> Wolfe and Montcalm! Two nobler names ne'er graced
> The page of history, or the hostile plain;
> No braver souls the storm of battle faced,
> Regardless of the danger or the pain.
> They pass'd unto their rest without a stain
> Upon their nature or their generous hearts.
> One graceful column to the noble twain
> Speaks of a nation's gratitude, and starts
> The tear that Valour claims, and Feeling's self imparts.[11]

Nevertheless, Sangster's attitude toward the "courteous, gentle race," expressed later in the poem, was clearly patronizing and condescending to the French Canadians.

The nationalist theme grew dramatically in strength in French Canada, gathering religious overtones as the century progressed. François-Xavier Garneau actually tailored later editions of his *Histoire* to meet clerical criticism of his overt liberalism. Romantic nationalism typical of the French Empire under Napoleon III also found echoes in poems by Octave Crémazie, Antoine Gérin-Lajoie, and Philippe Aubert de Gaspé. Crémazie's "Le Canada," written in 1859, is one of the earliest expressions of French Canada's love for the "fatherland":

> Greetings, O Heaven of my fatherland!
> Greetings, O noble St Lawrence!
> In my softened soul your name
> Flows as an intoxicating perfume.
> O Canada, you son of France,
> Who covered you with her blessings
> You our love, our hope,
> Who will ever forget you?[12]

North America just as they had poisoned the potential of his native Ireland.

As in Ireland, nationalist sentiment posed problems for British North Americans because one patriot's nationalism often proved to be another patriot's bigotry. Safer ground for the new nationalism was the economic potential of the northern half of the continent, which stirred the hearts and imagination of both the romantic idealist and the practical businessman. Such an alternative vision of national destiny came not from across the Atlantic but from south of the border. By mid-century, the Americans were advancing across the continent, dazzling the world with the speed and scope of their economic achievement.

Like their southern neighbours, British North Americans began to argue that it was their manifest destiny to develop their own western frontier. Eyeing Rupert's Land as their next resource frontier, empire builders in Montreal and Toronto dreamed of railways that would link them to their economic hinterland. In 1857, the colony of Canada sent delegates to the commission of inquiry into the Hudson's Bay Company monopoly, where they laid claim to Rupert's Land by virtue of French exploration.

With dramatic suddenness, the notion of a formidable and inaccessible western territory gave way to glowing reports of agricultural potential and unlimited opportunity. Reports of scientific expeditions in the late 1850s dispelled many of the long-held views about the harshness of the climate and encouraged hopes for the industrial, commercial, and agricultural potential of the West. With the Fraser Valley gold rush of 1858, the potential of the West seemed endless. Alexander Morris, who published *The Hudson's Bay and Pacific Territories* in 1859, expressed the optimism of many British North Americans when he described the possibilities offered by westward expansion:

> With two powerful colonies on the Pacific, with another or more in the region between Canada and the Rocky Mountains, with a railway and a telegraph linking the Atlantic and the Pacific and absorbing the newly-opened and fast-developing trade with China and Japan . . . who can doubt of the reality and accuracy of the vision which rises distinctly and clearly before us, as the Great Britannic Empire of the North stands out in all its grandeur.[13]

CONCLUSION

The new industrial order had prompted a few British North Americans to dream big. Why not create a transcontinental nation? The ingredients were there: a shared British heritage, the eagerness of Great Britain to relinquish direct control over its colonies of settlement, the potential of the railway to bring unity across vast distances, the promise of national greatness, and the lure of private profit. All that was needed was a little push and the pieces of the British North American puzzle would fall in place. As we will see in the next chapter, that push would come from a variety of sources in the heady atmosphere of the 1860s.

NOTES

1 Cited in Jan Noel, *Canada Dry: Temperance Crusades before Confederation* (Toronto: University of Toronto Press, 1995), 79.

2 R.J. Morgan, "'Poverty, Wretchedness and Misery': The Great Famine in Cape Breton, 1845–1851," *Nova Scotia Historical Review* 6, 1 (1986): 93.

3 Raymond Boyer, *Les crimes et les châtiments au Canada français* (Montreal: Le Cercle du livre de France, 1966), 477, 482, cited in the Clio Collective, *Quebec Women: A History*, trans. Roger Gannon and Rosalind Gill (Toronto: Women's Press, 1987), 172.

4 Greg Marquis, *Policing Canada's Century: A History of the Canadian Association of Chiefs of Police* (Toronto: University of Toronto Press, 1993), 28.

5 Noel, 101.

6 Cited in Susan Houston, "Politics, Schools, and Change in Upper Canada," *Canadian Historical Review*, 53, 3 (Sept. 1972): 265.

7 Daniel Francis, "Minds in Chains," *Horizon Canada*, vol. 7 (Quebec: Centre for the Study of Teaching Canada, 1987), 1793.

8 Cited in Ramsay Cook and Wendy Mitchinson, eds., *The Proper Sphere: Women's Place in Canadian Society* (Toronto: Oxford University Press, 1976), 8, 19.

9 Aileen S. Kraditor, ed., *Up from the Pedestal: Selected Writings in the History of American Feminism* (New York: Quadrangle, 1968), 184.

10 J. Murray Beck, ed., *Joseph Howe: Voice of Nova Scotia* (Toronto: McClelland and Stewart, 1964), 132.

11 J.M. Bumsted, ed., *Documentary Problems in Canadian History*, vol. 1, *Pre-Confederation* (Georgetown: Irwin-Dorsey Ltd., 1969), 251.

12 Ibid., 256.

13 Alexander Morris, *The Hudson's Bay and Pacific Territories* (Montreal: John Lovell, 1959).

RELATED READINGS IN THIS SERIES

From *Foundations: Readings in Pre-Confederation Canadian History*

Jan Noel, "French Canada Awakens" and "Patriotism and Sackcloth" (excerpts), 465–79.

From **Media Companion CD-ROM, Volume I**

The Role of Religion in the School System
An Act for Remedy in Cases of Seduction
The Magdalene Asylum Annual Meeting

SELECTED READING

See also the readings for Chapter 19.

The plight of poor and easily exploited groups in Victorian society is a major theme in Judith Fingard's *The Dark Side of Life in Victorian Halifax* (Porters Lake, NS: Pottersfield, 1989), *Jack in Port: Sailortowns of Eastern Canada* (Toronto: University of Toronto Press, 1982), and her much-quoted article, "The Winter's Tale: The Seasonal Contours of Pre-Industrial Poverty in British North America, 1815–1860," *Canadian Historical Association Historical Papers* (1974): 65–94. Social reform is discussed in Richard B. Splane, *Social Welfare in Ontario, 1791–1893: A Study of Public Welfare Administration* (Toronto: University of Toronto Press, 1965). See also James E. Moran, *Committed to the State Asylum: Insanity and Society in 19th-Century Quebec and Ontario* (Montreal: McGill-Queen's University Press, 2002). The pre-Confederation temperance movement is treated in

Jan Noel, *Canada Dry: Temperance Crusades before Confederation* (Toronto: University of Toronto Press, 1995), and alcohol use and abuse more generally in Craig Heron, *Booze* (Toronto: Between the Lines, 2003).

Violence in this period is the subject of Scott W. See, *Riots in New Brunswick: Orange Nativism and Social Violence in the 1840s* (Toronto: University of Toronto Press, 1993), and a number of articles, including Kenneth McNaught, "Violence in Canadian History," in *Character and Circumstance: Essays in Honour of Donald Grant Creighton*, ed. John S. Moir (Toronto: Macmillan, 1979), 66–84; Ruth Bleasdale, "Class Conflict on the Canals of Upper Canada in the 1840s," *Labour/Le Travail* 7 (1981): 9–39; and two articles by Michael Cross: "The Shiners' War: Social Violence

in the Ottawa Valley in the 1830s," *Canadian Historical Review* 54, 1 (1973): 1–26, and "The Rebellion Losses Riots in Bytown," in R.C. MacLeod, ed., *Lawful Authority: Readings on the History of Criminal Justice in Canada* (Toronto: Copp Clark Pitman, 1988), 49–63. On policing, see Greg Marquis, *Policing Canada's Century: A History of the Canadian Association of Chiefs of Police* (Toronto: University of Toronto Press, 1993); Peter McGahan, *Crime and Policing in Maritime Canada* (Fredericton: Goose Lane, 1988); and John C. Weaver, *Crimes, Constables and Courts: Order and Transgression in a Canadian City, 1816–1970* (Montreal: McGill-Queen's University Press, 1995).

On religion, education, and literary developments in this period, see Selected Reading in Chapter 19.

WEBLINKS

THOMAS D'ARCY MCGEE

collections.ic.gc.ca/charlottetown/fathers/mcgee.html

This site offers a profile of McGee. Links are available to Library and Archives Canada, and Canadian constitutional documents.

EMILY JENNINGS HOWARD STOWE

http://www.collectionscanada.ca/women/h12-207-e.html

This Library and Archives Canada site offers profiles of Stowe and her daughter, physicians and supporters of women's suffrage.

CHAPTER 22

The Road to Confederation

Timeline

- **1862** Reform ministry formed in United Province of Canada
- **1863** Conservatives win majority in Nova Scotia; election in United Province of Canada produces impasse
- **1864** Pro-Confederation coalition government formed in United Province of Canada; Charlottetown conference; Quebec City conference
- **1865** New Brunswick elects anti-confederate majority; legislature of United Province approves Confederation
- **1866** Fenian raids; New Brunswick elects pro-confederate majority; Nova Scotia legislature approves further negotiations on Confederation; London conference; Reciprocity ends
- **1867** Confederation of New Brunswick, Nova Scotia, Quebec, and Ontario

"But a few months ago, we were steadily advancing towards prosperity, satisfied with the present and confident in the future of the French-Canadian people. Suddenly discouragement, which had never overcome us in our adversity, takes possession of us; our aspirations are now only empty dreams; the labours of a country must be wasted; we must give up our nationality, adapt a new one, greater and nobler, we are told, than our own, but then it will no longer be our own. And why? Because it is our inevitable fate, against which it is of no use to struggle. But have we not already struggled against destiny when we were more feeble than we are now, and have we not triumphed? Let us not give to the world the sad spectacle of a people voluntarily resigning its nationality."[1]

Henri Joly, a member from Canada East in the Legislative Assembly of the United Province of Canada, spoke for many French Canadians when he rose in the Assembly on 20 February 1865 to oppose the idea of a confederation of all the British North American colonies. At a conference in Quebec City in October 1864, delegates from several British North American colonies had hammered out a proposal for political union and agreed to submit the "Confederation" proposal to their respective legislatures. The debate on Confederation in the Assembly of the United Province of Canada stretched from 2 February 1865 to 11 March 1865 and featured long, often raucous sittings. Nor was it only French Canadians who believed that their collective existence would be harmed by the federation that was proposed.

In Nova Scotia, Joseph Howe lamented the attempts by the United Province of Canada to lure the Atlantic colonies into Confederation and ridiculed the notion that "a new nationality" would result from the project. The French and English of the United Province were, in his view, too different in their thinking. "A more unpromising nucleus of a new nation could hardly be found on the face of the earth," he concluded.[2] This chapter explores the arguments of both the proponents and the opponents of Confederation within British North America.

NATION AND COLONY

Influenced by growing nationalist movements in Europe, the United States, and Latin America, British North Americans began in the late 1850s to ponder their future. Should they, too, consider whether they had a grander fate than that of citizens of isolated outposts of the British Empire? The discussion cut several ways. For some British North Americans, it seemed only natural that the colonies form a transcontinental nation to rival their giant southern neighbour. In their eyes, this new political unity would consolidate, not sever, the link with Great Britain. For others, it seemed equally natural that their particular colony—because it had its own history and its own economic interests—declare itself a nation.

Like their European counterparts, supporters of British North American unity were often inspired by dreams of economic development. Although a depression from 1846 to 1849 followed the dismantling of imperial preferences, the 1850s and 1860s witnessed dramatic economic growth in most of the British North American colonies. Responsible government had placed power in the hands of elected representatives who were eager to stimulate even more economic development. They were increasingly convinced that the most direct route to economic growth was through British North American union.

THE CANADAS: ECONOMIC SUCCESS AND POLITICAL IMPASSE

During its brief existence as a political entity, the United Province of Canada experienced steady economic and population growth, but political stability proved elusive. Part of the problem lay in the unequal population growth of the two Canadas. At the time of the union, Lower Canada had a population of 650 000, compared with 450 000 in the upper province. By 1851, owing particularly to the large-scale influx of Irish immigrants, Canada West's population had more than doubled (see Table 22.1). The population of Canada East, by contrast, had risen only to 890 000. Many of the Upper Canadian politicians who in 1840 had decried Lower Canadian complaints about under-representation now believed that representation by population in the legislature of the United Province must replace the equal division of seats provided for in the Act of Union.

By 1861, with population growth in Canada West continuing to outstrip that in Canada East, support for "rep by pop" among Canada West Reformers was matched by French-Canadian resistance to the idea. The claim that democracy demanded representation proportional to population was met by the charge that the undemocratic union of 1840 provided no other means to protect French Catholic rights than a large representation in the Assembly. Capitalizing on sectional tensions, George Brown, a leader of the Reform movement in Canada West, shaped an organization that resembled in embryo a modern political party. Apart from the goal of representation by population, the glue bonding Reformers together was support for annexation of the Northwest to Canada and opposition to public moneys for separate schools and for subsidies to the Grand Trunk Railway.

John A. Macdonald emerged as the leader of an equally organized bloc of Conservative politicians who resisted the Reformers' demands as impediments to an alliance with the majority Bleu group of Canada East. Relying on the skilful use of patronage, sentimental ties to Great Britain, and the importance of the economic link to the St Lawrence River, Macdonald persuaded many voters in Canada West to reject a program of reforms that would alienate the French-speaking majority of Canada East. Increasingly, however, the majority in Canada West preferred the Reformers' message. In 1863, in the last general election for the Legislative Assembly of the United Province of Canada, only 20 of the 65 seats in Canada West went to John A. Macdonald and his supporters.

TABLE 22.1 **Population of British North America, 1851–1871**

	1851	**1861**	**1871**
Ontario	952 004	1 396 091	1 620 851
Quebec	890 261	1 111 566	1 191 516
Nova Scotia	276 854	330 857	387 800
New Brunswick	193 800	252 047	285 594
Prince Edward Island	62 678*	80 857	94 021
Newfoundland†	–	122 638	158 958
British Columbia	55 000	51 524	36 247**
Manitoba	–	–	25 228
Northwest Territories	–	–	48 000

* Figure is from 1848.

† Figures are from 1857 and 1874.

** This figure probably understates the Native population of the province by about 15 000.

Source: "Series A 2-14. Population of Canada by province, census dates, 1851 to 1976," in *Historical Statistics of Canada*, 2nd ed., ed. F.H. Leacy (Ottawa: Minister of Supply and Services, 1983) and James Hiller, "Confederation Defeated: The Newfoundland Election of 1869," in *Newfoundland in the Nineteenth and Twentieth Centuries: Essays in Interpretation*, ed. James Hiller and Peter Neary (Toronto: University of Toronto Press, 1980).

In Canada East, the opponents of the Bleus never won more than 25 of the 65 seats allocated for their province. Divided between the liberal Rouges and independents, the reformist element in Canada East formed neither a coherent party nor an easy ally of the Canada West Reformers. A Reform ministry created in 1862 under the leadership of John Sandfield Macdonald, Brown's chief rival among Canada West Reformers, survived just a year and a half and only by abandoning principles of "rep by pop" and opposition to public support of denominational schools. No French-speaking politician could afford politically to support either the reduction of Canadien legislative representation or the abandonment of their co-religionists in Canada West; and no government, Conservative or Reform, was thinkable without Canadien representation. By 1864, the chances of forming a government acceptable to both halves of the United Province seemed remote. A "double majority"—majority support in each of the two sections of the province—was not constitutionally necessary, but most politicians accepted it as a practical necessity for commanding legitimacy.

The schools issue demonstrated the difficulties facing supporters of a "double majority." In 1841, well before responsible government had been granted, the

Common School Act for Canada West had established the right of religious minorities to share in the provincial grant for schools. In 1853, the Hincks-Morin ministry, relying mainly on the vote of Canada East politicians, strengthened the government's commitment to separate schools in Canada West by explicitly exempting separate-school ratepayers from property taxes for the support of common schools. A majority in Canada West opposed the bill and railed against Canada East politicians who thought they could impose the principle of separate schools upon the United Canadas. Canada West seemed no more reconciled to separate schools 10 years later, when John Sandfield Macdonald was forced to rely on votes from francophone members in Canada East to allow separate schools to license their own teachers.

By the early 1860s, new problems were added to the woes facing the administration of the Canadas. Three railways—the Northern, Great Western, and St Lawrence and Atlantic—received bond guarantees under the Guarantee Act of 1849 from an Assembly filled with railway investors. Three years later, the Assembly chartered and began providing financial guarantees for the Grand Trunk Railway, whose investors included major British banking concerns and the usual crew of Canadian politicians. In 1853, the Grand Trunk, which initially sought only to build lines from Montreal to Hamilton, recognized the need for an Atlantic link and bought, at inflated prices, the assets of the St Lawrence and Atlantic Railway, in which Finance Minister Alexander Galt was a leading figure. By 1859, the Grand Trunk was a nest of corruption and an enormous drain on the public purse.

Only the wealthy could afford to participate in a political life, which offered no salary for an elected member of the Assembly. Responsible government had placed the running of public affairs in the hands of elected officials who barely recognized a boundary between their own and the public's interests. Answering critics within the British American Land Company who thought his foray into politics in 1849 reduced the time he could spend on company matters, Galt said, "I consider the interests of the Company and the country to be identical."[3]

The colony's main source of revenue was a tariff on imported goods. As finance minister, Galt had raised that tariff to a record 15 percent in 1859 to protect

Canadian manufacturers and raise money to pay the growing public debt. Nonetheless, the revenues of the United Canadas could not meet the expenditures necessary to pay interest on existing debts and, at the same time, begin other public works. Increasingly, Canada's British creditors balked at making loans to a colony that could not live within its own means and appeared to have no plans to expand its revenue base.

THE CANADIANS MAKE THEIR MOVE

By 1864, the political and economic impasse caused a coterie of leading Canadian politicians to look to a confederation of the British North American colonies as a solution. At George Brown's instigation, the Assembly appointed a constitutional committee to examine options for the Canadas. In June 1864, the committee issued a report in which 12 of its 15 members called for consideration of a federal union of the British North American colonies.

The idea was not new. Lord Durham had proposed an eventual union of all the colonies in his 1840 report, and Galt had made the same suggestion to the legislature in 1858. Brown had been pushing since 1857 for reform of the political system imposed on Upper and Lower Canada in 1840. In 1860, he introduced a motion into the Assembly favouring the adoption of a federal union: a central government with specific responsibilities for legislation would continue to exist, but provincial governments with their own responsibilities would also be created. Brown hoped that by making the provincial governments powerful enough—for example, by giving them complete control over education—Canada East's ability to impose legislation on Canada West would be greatly reduced. In 1860, no member from Canada East was willing to support a federal union of the Canadas, but the continuing impasse in the legislature gave Brown another chance to achieve his goals.

As editor of the Toronto *Globe*, Brown had been one of the bitterest foes of the conservative regimes that predominated in the 1850s. A booster of his home city, Brown had invested in a variety of mercantile and manufacturing ventures in Toronto. He regarded the Cartier-Macdonald coalition as supporters of the imperial ambitions of Montreal and particularly resented the Grand Trunk as an agent of Montreal interests. Toronto's imperial ambitions, according to Brown and like-minded business people, required less public spending on railway projects centred on Montreal and more attention paid to acquiring the Northwest. As fertile land for settlers disappeared, Toronto merchants seeking new markets began to cry all the louder for acquisition of the Northwest. Farmer families, looking for new agricultural frontiers, echoed the call.

After the release of the Assembly committee's report in June 1864, Brown made the decisive political move that started the ball rolling toward Confederation. He approached George-Étienne Cartier and John A. Macdonald, who were having great difficulty establishing a functioning majority in the Assembly, with the idea of a "Great Coalition" whose goal would be the achievement of British North American Confederation. The coalition would include the supporters of Cartier, Macdonald, and Brown and would thus command a strong majority in both sections of Canada. Only the recalcitrant Rouges would be excluded. Macdonald would remain the government leader for Canada West, with half of the cabinet posts from that section to be filled by Brown and his Reform associates.

John A. Macdonald had been one of three members of the constitutional committee who opposed confederation, partly because he favoured a legislative union over a federal union. He was also lukewarm to the proposal to annex Hudson's Bay Company territories to Canada. But he wanted to remain in office and build a broader base for Toryism in Canada West. He and Cartier quickly came to terms with Brown, and a new ministry dedicated to the idea of a confederation of the British American colonies was sworn in.

It was a strange first step in the creation of a new nation-state. A ministry in one of the colonies of the state-to-be had been formed with the objective of nation-building without a single member having received an electoral mandate for the undertaking. Macdonald was, however, a consummate political organizer whose persuasive skills could only be an asset in promoting his new-found project. Like most leading Canadian politicians of the period, Macdonald was a businessman-politician. Both a workaholic and an alcoholic, he was a lawyer with directorships in bank, insurance, railway, and utility companies in his home constituency of Kingston. His land speculations were spread over a dozen counties of Canada West. Like Brown, he came to view the Northwest as a vast territory awaiting Upper Canadian settlement and the Maritimes as another potential market for Upper Canadian manufactures.

As it happened, the premiers of the Maritime colonies had committed their ministries to consider Maritime union. Happily for Macdonald and the other pro-confederates, the lieutenant-governors of the Maritime colonies were easily persuaded to broaden the scope of their constitutional deliberations to include consideration of a complete British North American union.

GREAT EXPECTATIONS IN THE MARITIMES

In the Atlantic region, Nova Scotia and New Brunswick were the most receptive to the idea of British North American union. The healthy state of the coastal trade, shipbuilding, and the fisheries as well as increased demand for Nova Scotia coal and New Brunswick lumber fattened the treasuries of these two colonies in the 1850s and 1860s. Elected governments, following the Canadian lead, chose to spend much of this money on the building of railways and soon found themselves with revenue shortfalls.

Reformers dominated the Nova Scotia legislature until 1863, when the electorate gave a clear majority to their Conservative opponents. Although serving as premier only from 1860 to 1863, Joseph Howe played a towering role in the Nova Scotia cabinets of the period, always promoting railway projects as the key to increased colonial prosperity. He was largely responsible for the government's decision in the 1850s to place railways built with provincial money under public ownership, in contrast to the other colonies' practice of giving grants and loan guarantees without demanding a direct return to the public purse.

Howe's railway projects were the main cause of a $4.5-million provincial debt accumulated by 1863. His favourite venture was a line linking Halifax to the St

Lawrence, generally referred to as the Intercolonial Railway. As early as 1849 Howe had proposed the Intercolonial at a conference held in Halifax to discuss the implications for the Atlantic colonies of free trade. Howe believed the railway line would provide a valuable military highway for Britain in time of war as well as stimulate British North American trade. Despite local enthusiam for it, the project always failed to attract the necessary capital from British financiers.

The Conservatives continued the Reformers' commitment to public works in Nova Scotia. Particularly after Charles Tupper became premier in early 1864, expenditures began to climb and the provincial debt rose to over $8 million by 1866. Tupper, a medical doctor, had represented Cumberland County since 1855. With substantial investments in the county's coal mines, the Nova Scotia premier believed that the region's future was assured as long as secure markets for its coal and iron resources could be found. Rumours that the Americans, angry at Britain's support of the South during the Civil War, would abrogate the Reciprocity Treaty caused him grave concern about whether Cumberland County would achieve its potential. The Intercolonial might provide Nova Scotia with new markets in New Brunswick and Canada, but the province was in no position financially to proceed. With only 235 kilometres of track laid down by 1867, Nova Scotia had invested $7.5 million in railways and was too deeply in debt to build more.

Railroads were also on the minds of leading New Brunswick politicians. Unable to secure the funds for the Intercolonial in the 1850s, New Brunswick's politicians began to follow a pied piper from Maine named John Alfred Poor, who was promoting a railway to link Maine with New Brunswick and Nova Scotia. When Poor declared bankruptcy in 1855, the colony pressed ahead with a line linking Shediac to Saint John and continued to plan its extension into the United States. A labour shortage had forced the province to import British navvies to build its railway lines, and labour costs plus a variety of technical problems resulted in huge cost overruns. Government patronage in the awarding of contracts also pushed up costs.

In 1861, Premier Charles Fisher had his political career ruined when it was revealed that he had

John A. Macdonald: The Changing Face of Toryism in Canada West

John A. Macdonald was born in Glasgow, Scotland, in 1815 and immigrated to Upper Canada with his parents five years later. The family moved to Kingston, and his father's merchant activities were sufficiently successful for young John A. to attend private and grammar schools. At age 15 he began to article in a Kingston law office, and he was called to the bar in 1836. An active Presbyterian and Kingston clubman, Macdonald became the solicitor for several major financial concerns by the early 1840s. His entry into politics in 1843 began with a successful run for Kingston town council, followed by election to the Assembly in 1844.

When Macdonald was first elected as a Conservative in 1844, he opposed responsible government, the secularization of clergy reserves, the abolition of primogeniture, and the broadening of the franchise. He argued that the democratic changes favoured by Reformers would lead to a weakening of both the British connection and of property rights. Although his support of the British connection and of the propertied classes never waned, he adapted quickly to the introduction of responsible government in 1848. He recognized that pragmatism, patronage, and party organization could keep conservatism alive in an age of democratic competition.

Appointed to the cabinet in 1847, he was Canada West's first minister, chief Conservative strategist, fundraiser, and campaign organizer by 1856. No candidate could be nominated as a Conservative candidate in Canada West without Macdonald's approval. He developed a centralized system of government patronage that guaranteed the personal loyalty of many state employees and recipients of government contracts. Attempting to create a mass base for conservatism, he appealed for support to leaders of disparate groups such as the Orange Order and the Catholic and Methodist churches. He not only dropped his opposition to secularization of clergy reserves but also, as attorney general, steered the government's legislation on the subject through the Assembly in 1854. Such a pragmatic change of heart would be repeated 10 years later when, in the interests of retaining office, he agreed to lead the fight for a Confederation agreement—a project he had denounced just days before becoming one of the leaders of a coalition government formed for the sole end of achieving confederation of the British North American colonies.

John A. Macdonald.

Joseph Howe (left) and George Brown (right).
Nova Scotia Archives and Records Management PANS N-1257 (left); Library and Archives Canada/C9553 (right)

acquired vast areas of Crown land despite a Crown Lands Office regulation forbidding elected officials and civil servants from making such purchases. He was hardly the only legislator to take advantage of the increased market for New Brunswick timber, but he proved a convenient sacrificial lamb.

Fisher's replacement was Samuel Leonard Tilley of Gagetown, son of a Loyalist and the leader of the temperance forces in the 1850s. Tilley had been an apothecary, and his patent medicines and pills had made him one of the wealthiest men in the colony. He wanted to press forward with the Intercolonial, but

with a $5-million railway debt and annual revenues of only $600 000, the legislature voted in 1862 not to undertake any new railway construction.

Prince Edward Island built no railways until 1871, and for a time its Assembly had increasing revenues at its disposal, chiefly because reciprocity increased demand for the island's potatoes and fish. Indeed, in the years 1855 to 1865, exports to the United States as a proportion of all island exports grew from 22 percent to 42 percent. One year later, with reciprocity a thing of the past, the figure fell to 9 percent. The land question still nagged at successive island administrations.

In the 1850s, Liberal premier George Coles used provincial revenues to buy out some of the absentee landlords so that tenants could become landowners. Although the landlords and the Colonial Office resisted his efforts, by 1861 about 40 percent of the island's residents were freeholders.

In 1864, when the Conservative Protestant-dominated government proved slow in pressing for more land reform, a Tenant League was formed. The league crossed denominational barriers, and its members, who supported a tenant takeover of rented land with rates of compensation to landlords to be set by townships, vowed to pay no further rents. Their collective action to resist the rent collectors resulted in the government using soldiers to serve writs on tenants in arrears and to repress the league.

There was less militancy in Newfoundland politics in the 1850s and 1860s. Nevertheless, party loyalties there, as in Prince Edward Island, had a strong denominational flavour, with the Liberals mainly Catholic and the Conservatives exclusively Protestant. In an effort to reduce sectarian tensions, politicians on both sides of the Assembly agreed in the 1860s to provide public support to both Protestant and Catholic schools and to split civil-service positions in proportion to the numbers of Catholics and Protestants.

Newfoundland's flagging economy caused Premier Hugh Hoyles to take an interest in the idea of a union of the Atlantic colonies. Newfoundland, however, was not invited to the conference on Maritime union planned for Charlottetown in 1864.

THE EXTERNAL PRESSURE FOR CONFEDERATION

Politicians in Nova Scotia were most receptive to the idea of restoring "greater Nova Scotia" through some kind of Maritime union, and they took the initiative in suggesting a conference on the issue early in 1864. Although resolutions to send delegates to a Maritime union conference passed easily in both the Nova Scotia and New Brunswick legislatures, the proposal was less enthusiastically received in Prince Edward Island and no action was taken to set a time and place for the meeting. The proposal might well have been shelved completely had the Canadians not intervened with their request late in June to attend any conference that the Maritimers were planning.

The Fathers of Confederation at Charlottetown.
Library and Archives Canada/C-000733

MORE TO THE STORY

Canadians and the American Civil War

An estimated 40 000 to 50 000 British North American men took part in the American Civil War, many of them having emigrated to the United States before the war. While they served on both sides of the conflict, more enlisted in the Northern forces, both because they lived in closer proximity to that region and because they tended to favour the anti-slavery cause. Among them was Calixa Lavallée, later the composer of *O Canada*. Born at Verchères, Quebec, in 1842, Lavallée had lived in the United States since 1857 and enlisted in the Union army in 1861.

A few British North American women also served in the war. A most unusual combatant was Sarah Emma Emmonds. An anti-slavery advocate from New Brunswick, Emmonds posed as a man and enlisted in the Union army in 1861. Apart from her role in combat, Emmonds served the northern cause as a "male" nurse, a spy, and a general's aide. Her former comrades-in-arms did not discover her true identity until a regimental reunion in 1884. By that time, Emmonds had married and settled in the United States.

Sarah Emmonds, nurse and spy in the Union army.
Metropolitan Reference Library, Toronto

By the 1860s, both Liberal and Conservative administrations in Britain favoured shifting costs to colonies. The Colonial Office urged representatives in the colonies to support political unions that could allow colonists to take more responsibility for their own military and administrative needs. Nova Scotia's lieutenant-governor, Richard Graves Macdonnell, and his counterpart in New Brunswick, Arthur Gordon, supported Maritime union. From their upper-class British perspective, colonial assemblies were dominated by pretentious, corrupt politicians. When the Canadians asked to attend a conference on Maritime union, Macdonnell and Gordon did everything in their power to ensure that the event went ahead. In an effort to get the support of the Prince Edward Islanders as well as to make it easier for the Canadians who would come down the St Lawrence by ship, Charlottetown was chosen as the site of the meeting proposed to be held on 1 September 1864.

Edward Cardwell, who became colonial secretary in March 1864, supported the Canadian initiative for the larger union of the British North American colonies. Like his immediate predecessors, he regarded Britain's white-settler colonies as unnecessary financial burdens on the British treasury. The Colonial Office had for some time encouraged its North American colonies, particularly the United Province of Canada, to shoulder a greater share of defence costs. Saddled with railway debts, the Canadian Assembly had made only token gestures to improve the quality and quantity of members in the local militia and to upgrade the equipment that they used.

The defence issue was driven home to British North Americans by the American Civil War, which pitted the slave-holding South against the industrial North. Although many British North Americans were sympathetic to the Northern cause, the Southern Confederates also had their supporters in the colonies, especially among elite circles in cities such as Halifax and Montreal. Public opinion in Great Britain was also divided over the conflict. There were important interests in Britain, especially those involved in the importation of such southern products as cotton and tobacco, who would have been happy to see the Confederacy gain independence. As the war dragged on, a number of incidents on the high seas and along the border helped to increase tensions between Britain and the North and exposed the vulnerability of the British North American colonies.

In November 1861, a Northern naval ship seized the *Trent*, a British steamer en route from Cuba to Britain, and arrested two Confederate agents aboard. The North eventually yielded to Britain's protests and released the two agents, but tensions remained high. Since war with the United States was a distinct possibility, Great Britain sent 15 000 troops to British North America to supplement the 3000 soldiers already stationed there.

During the war, British-built destroyers purchased by the Confederacy, including the *Alabama*, the *Florida*, and the *Shenandoah*, sank over 100 vessels. The North in turn pursued Confederate ships into British waters. In December 1863 they caught the *Chesapeake* off Nova Scotia and arrested the men aboard, touching off a diplomatic furor. Relations between Great Britain and the North were further strained by border raids conducted by southern sympathizers from British North American bases. The Northern government was livid in 1864 when a Montreal magistrate set free Confederate agents who had robbed three banks in St Albans, Vermont, and then crossed back into Canada.

While military goals dominated Colonial Office policy in the period when the colonies debated Confederation, there were also vested economic interests pressing for British North American union. The British financiers who bought the Hudson's Bay Company in 1863 hoped to make a fortune when the expansion-minded Canadians bought the lands of Assiniboia for settlement. But the political impasse in the United Province of Canada and the railway debt were impediments to fast action by Canada on the Northwest. A new union with a strong central government might be more efficient. Other British businessmen, under pressure to lend money to the Intercolonial project, likewise believed that their investments would be safer if British North America were politically united. Otherwise any one of three colonial governments could take actions harmful to

investors' interests. Such British support for union would prove a great asset to the pro-confederates in British North America in overcoming opposition within the various colonies.

THE AMERICAN FACTOR

The love-hate relationship that many British North Americans had with the United States helped to shape some of the debates around Confederation. The notion that the British American colonies could, by uniting, develop a western hinterland that would serve as a market for products manufactured in settled regions was inspired by the experience of the Americans. The northeastern states owed much of their prosperity to the budding markets for their manufactured goods in the new, mainly agricultural states to the west.

The Reciprocity Treaty encouraged the colonies to integrate their economies with that of the United States. As early as 1863, however, the United States had given strong indications that it would not renew the agreement after it expired in 1866. In addressing the assembly of the United Province of Canada that year, George Brown spoke for much of the business community when he stated that he hoped the Americans would not abrogate the treaty. As a supporter of Confederation, though, he expressed confidence that a united British North America would constitute an economic alternative to the integration with the United States offered by reciprocity. Confederation, followed by extensive immigration into the new dominion, would create a large market that would be viable even if the American market were to become less accessible.

Echoing the British government, Brown also told the legislature that Confederation would make it easier for the colonials to defend themselves against any attempt by the Americans to annex Canada by force. Fears of such expansionism were not unfounded. The United States had, in recent memory, forcibly annexed large sections of Mexican territory, and several American states were calling for the annexation of the Hudson's Bay Company's empire in the West. William Seward, secretary of state under President Abraham Lincoln, suggested publicly that British North America would inevitably become part of the United States.

Like many Americans, Seward believed that his country had a "manifest destiny" to absorb all of North America within its boundaries. In 1867, he was responsible for his government's decision to purchase Alaska from the Russians for $7.2 million. Although he did not suggest that the United States should invade its northern neighbour, colonial politicians were convinced that a strong defence was the best deterrent to American expansionism.

PLANNING CONFEDERATION

The Charlottetown conference in September 1864 quickly shelved discussion of Maritime union and focused on Canada's proposal for a British North American federation. The delegates agreed to reassemble in Quebec City one month later to produce a detailed proposal that could be presented to their respective legislatures. Representatives from Newfoundland attended the Quebec conference, where the basis of union was hammered out.

As subsequent events indicate, it was only by chance that the five colonies (six, if the two sections of the United Province of Canada are considered separately) happened to be led by pro-confederate pre-

miers. Two premiers would prove unable to bring their colonies into the union in 1867; a third lost an election over the idea of Confederation in 1865; and the others refused to submit the Confederation proposals to a vote in their colonies.

Macdonald favoured a legislative union of the colonies, a constitutional arrangement that would have wiped out all provincial legislatures. From his point of view, federal unions such as that which prevailed in the United States inevitably fell prey to internal discord of the type that had produced the American Civil War. Despite Macdonald's preference, a legislative union was politically impossible to sell to the Maritime leaders or to the political parties of Canada East.

With a legislative union out of the question, Macdonald sought to ensure the primacy of the central government in a federal union. All important economic and diplomatic matters, he argued, ought to be in federal hands, leaving matters of purely local concern, such as education and care of the indigent, to the provinces.

Cartier and Brown supported Macdonald's position. Once an advocate of a loose federal union, Brown had come to accept the view that the federal government required the greatest powers if it were to be able to carry out national objectives such as the acquisition of the Northwest. The leaders of the Atlantic colonies were generally suspicious of the motives of the Canadians and their centralizing policies. When the delegates from Nova Scotia and New Brunswick met with their counterparts from the United Canadas in London in 1866 for the third and final conference on Confederation, they pushed for modifications to the Quebec Resolutions. Their most significant achievement was the inclusion in the British North America Act of a clause guaranteeing that the Intercolonial Railroad would be constructed "by the Government of Canada." By including the railroad in the constitution,

Quebec City at the time of the Quebec City Conference.
Notman Photographic Archives, McCord Museum of Canadian History, Montreal/I-17501.1

Canadians would not be able to back out of their promise to bind the union together by ties of steel rails.

The plan for Confederation created both a federal government and provincial governments and gave each level of jurisdiction specified powers. The existing colonies would become provinces, with the important exception of the United Province of Canada: each of its two sections would have a separate provincial administration, under the new names of Quebec and Ontario. Representation in the federal assembly (House of Commons) would be proportional to population, and all members in the House of Commons would be elected. To appease complaints from the Maritimes that the smaller provinces would be ignored in such an assembly, the plan also called for an appointed Senate that gave Quebec, Ontario, and the Maritimes equal representation.

The division of powers was finalized in 1866 and confirmed in the British North America Act, which was passed by the British House of Commons in March 1867. It gave the federal government control over a number of areas, including international and interprovincial trade; foreign policy and defence; criminal law; Indian affairs; currency and banking; fisheries; and interprovincial transportation. The provinces in turn would control commerce within their borders, natural resources and public lands, civil law, municipal administration, and education. Federal and provincial governments would split authority in the areas of agriculture and immigration.

Both levels of government would have taxing powers; however, while the federal government's powers in this area were unrestricted, the provinces were limited to direct taxation. Tariffs and excise duties, at the time the source of most income for the various colonies, could be collected only by the federal government. Loss of such revenues would be compensated by a federal per capita grant to the provinces. The federal government would also take over responsibility for paying off principal and interest payments on debts accumulated by the colonies before Confederation, up to a specified limit based on a per capita formula.

A limit on provincial powers regarding education was a provision that enshrined, in perpetuity, educational rights acquired by law or custom before Confederation. This protected the tax-supported separate schools of Canada West and the Protestant schools of Canada East. Attempts by Catholic minorities in the Maritimes to achieve guarantees for equality between secular and confessional schools failed, but provision was made that groups that believed their rights had been violated by a province could ask the federal government for "remedial" legislation.

Like any constitution that divides power between separate levels of government, the British North America Act contained ambiguities. For example, the centralizers managed to include a general clause that allowed the federal level of government to make whatever laws were necessary for maintaining "peace, order and good government" in the new nation, even though that clause seemed to contradict the provinces' right to legislate freely on matters concerning "civil rights and property."

One area given little thought was language. French and English were made official languages in the House of Commons and federal courts, and Quebec was to be recognized as bilingual, but the status of French outside Quebec was ignored. The French-Canadian Bleu leaders believed that the new Quebec government would act as the guarantor of the French language in Quebec and gave little thought to French-speaking people outside Quebec and those who might move out of Quebec after Confederation.

SELLING CONFEDERATION

None of the colonial leaders present at Quebec City had an electoral mandate to support a confederation of the British North American colonies. Given the growing emphasis on "responsible" government and democratic principles, the premiers were obliged to seek either a new electoral mandate to allow their respective provinces to enter Confederation or, at a minimum, a majority vote from their legislatures.

For Premier John Hamilton Gray of Prince Edward Island, a majority vote in the legislature was impossible because his own Conservative Party was divided on the issue. His attorney general, Edward Palmer, a former premier, flatly rejected the idea. To submit the proposal to the electorate would most likely have resulted in electoral defeat and disarray in his party. Gray chose to shelve the idea of Confederation.

Premier Hoyles of Newfoundland was also unable to muster the votes needed in his province's legislature, and the issue was resolved only in 1869 when the electorate decisively rejected a surrender of independence. Newfoundland supporters of union argued that it would provide new markets for local products as well as grants that would allow them to build roads and other public works. The importance of federal subsidies, however, had to be balanced against the likely costs to Newfoundlanders of paying taxes to build mainland railroads. Most St John's and Conception Bay merchants believed that Confederation would mean Canadian competition for the island's home market. They argued that Newfoundland's economy would continue to depend on the sea and on trade with Britain, and they discounted trade possibilities with the rest of British North America—at the time, only 5 percent of Newfoundland's exports went to the other colonies. Irish Catholics, led by the church leaders in Newfoundland, feared that newly won Catholic rights would be threatened within the proposed union. Many of the leaders of the Confederation movement, including Macdonald, had Orange affiliations, which contributed to fears that Confederation was an anti-Catholic plot.

For the mercantile community in Nova Scotia and New Brunswick, the agreement to transfer the right to impose tariffs to the federal government was a major cause for concern. They feared that their international trading and shipping interests would be jeopardized by the protectionist tendencies of the Canadians. Many Maritimers, including those who did not reject the notion of a confederation of the colonies out of hand, were appalled that the Quebec Resolutions granted all

Fenian raid, Fort Erie, Canada West, 1866. Although only a tiny minority of Irish Americans joined the Fenians, British North Americans in undefended border towns considered these armed bands of marauding soldiers to be a real threat to their lives and property.
Library and Archives Canada/C18737

monetary and most fiscal powers to the federal government, which would be dominated by Quebec and Ontario.

The argument that the colonies together could muster the military forces to fend off American invaders struck opponents as spurious: in their view it was the bellicose Canadians who had courted American hostility. Now, via their crushing majority in the House of Commons, the Canadians were about to drag Maritimers into their disputes. Each Atlantic colony had far more trade with the Americans than with the Canadians, and they valued continuing good relations with their southern neighbours more than manufacturing a cozy arrangement with the haughty Canadians.

Premier Tilley, leader of a divided party, agreed to face the New Brunswick electorate in March 1865. The anti-confederates, led by Albert J. Smith, a long-time Smasher politician who had turned against the government even before Confederation became the major political issue, won three-quarters of the legislative seats, but their victory proved short-lived. In spring 1865, the American government gave notice of the abrogation of the Reciprocity Treaty—putting an end to the hopes of New Brunswick anti-confederates, as expressed in the 1865 election, of expanding trade with the United States.

In December, the American wing of the Fenian Brotherhood, a group dedicated to Irish independence, made a raid on New Brunswick from Maine. Some Fenians believed that a takeover of Britain's North American possessions could force Britain to negotiate freedom for Ireland. Fenian raids and rumours of impending raids played a small but significant role in the Confederation drama, sowing fear among all British North Americans and emphasizing their dependence on British protection—protection that the British were loudly indicating could not continue indefinitely. In New Brunswick, Protestant pro-confederates, all the while seeking the support of the Catholic hierarchy for their cause, sowed suspicion among their co-religionists that Irish Catholics in the colony and American Fenians were in league, thus fostering the belief that loyal Protestants should support Confederation.

British backing for Confederation played the major role in unravelling popular opposition to the project in New Brunswick. Lieutenant-Governor Arthur Gordon succeeded in winning support for the union from the Catholic bishops of the province as well as from the timber merchants. He also forced an election in May 1866 and left little doubt in the electorate's mind about what the mother country expected from loyal voters. In that election, Tilley and his confederates carried 33 of the 41 legislative seats.

Like his counterparts in the other Maritime provinces, Premier Tupper of Nova Scotia soon found that he lacked the legislative majority to back Nova Scotia's entry into Confederation on the terms arrived at in Quebec City, and perhaps on any terms. One of his principal arguments was that Confederation would allow the province to use its coal and iron to develop a manufacturing sector, but this carried little weight with people who depended upon a mercantile economy for their profits or wages. While Tupper had powerful supporters, including the colony's Anglican bishop and Roman Catholic archbishop along with three judges of its Supreme Court, he faced almost universal opposition from the merchants. This group soon aligned itself with former premier Joseph Howe.

They had once hated Howe for building publicly owned railways, but now together they worked to create the public pressure needed to block Confederation.

If Tupper had been left to his own devices, the anti-confederates might have carried the day. By March 1865, he had retreated from Confederation to the less radical ground of Maritime union. But the new lieutenant-governor of Nova Scotia, Sir William Fenwick Williams, a Nova Scotia native and British military officer, revived Tupper's resolve. He made clear Britain's rejection of any half-measure and twisted the arms of enough politicians to convince the cautious Tupper to risk a legislative showdown on the issue in April 1866. His task had been aided by Macdonald's assurance in September 1865 that the building of the Intercolonial would be guaranteed in the act of union of the colonies.

The Confederation resolution introduced into the Nova Scotia legislature in April 1866 tactfully made no reference to the Quebec Resolutions or any other specific terms of union. Authorizing only continued negotiation on the issue of British North American union, Tupper's motion won the support of 31 of 50 legislators. The same number also defeated a call for a referendum on the issue.

There was also to be neither a referendum nor an election in the Canadas. None of the leaders of the Great Coalition was a radical democrat. Even Brown, the Reform leader, opposed electoral reforms that would expand the voting base from the approximately one-quarter of all adults over 21 years of age who met the property and gender qualification in Canada West. Macdonald, Cartier, and Brown collectively controlled enough votes to win passage of a motion supporting Confederation both in the Legislative Assembly and in the Legislative Council. Only the size of their victory was in doubt.

The anti-confederate opposition in the United Province was led by A.A. Dorion, the Rouge leader, and John Sandfield Macdonald, the leader of moderate reformers in Canada West. They had different reasons for rejecting the Quebec Resolutions. John Sandfield Macdonald was a lawyer and businessman who had established a political fiefdom among the Scottish Highlanders of Stormont and Glengarry counties. For him, the proposed Confederation was

VOICES FROM THE PAST

The Men Who Voted on Confederation

Historians often depict Confederation as a pageant and the Fathers of Confederation as earnest men of vision engaged in a courageous enterprise. The following contemporary account of the last hours of debate on Confederation in the Assembly of the United Province of Canada provides a less romantic portrait of the making of a new nation. The Assembly members had been debating Confederation from 2 February 1865 to 11 March 1865. The reporter for the *Stratford Beacon* gave his impressions of their behaviour and their condition on the night of their historic vote in favour of Confederation:

The House was in an unmistakably seedy condition, having, as it was positively declared, eaten the saloon keeper clean

out, drunk him entirely dry, and got all the fitful naps of sleep that the benches along the passages could be made to yield. For who cared at one, two, three, and four in the morning, to sit in the House, to hear the stale talk of Mr. Ferguson, of South Simcoe, or to listen even to the polished and pointed sentences of Mr. Huntingdon? Men with the strongest constitutions for Parliamentary twaddle were sick of the debate, and the great bulk of the members were scattered about the building, with an up-all-night, get-tight-in-the-morning air, impatient for the sound of the division bell. It rang at last, at quarter past four, and the jaded representatives of the people swarmed in to the discharge of the most important duty of all their lives.[4]

unacceptable because it detached the Ottawa Valley from the upper St Lawrence by dividing the United Province of Canada into two provinces. The region would exchange the political hegemony of Montreal for that of Toronto, to Macdonald's chagrin.

A.A. Dorion, by contrast, supported the division of the United Province of Canada into two provinces. Like many Canadiens he regretted the loss of a separate Lower Canada that had resulted from the Act of Union in 1840. Although he recognized that Britain was still unlikely to grant Lower Canada independent status, he hoped that something approaching sovereignty might be achieved if a loose federal union between the two sections of the United Province replaced the union. Only the degree of centralization implied in proposals from English-Canadian politicians had prevented the Rouges from supporting earlier plans for a federal union of two provinces. Now, however, not only was a federal union with a strong central government being proposed, but the union was to include the largely English-speaking Atlantic colonies.

Fears that Canada East would be drowned in an English sea aroused Quebec nationalism and allowed the Rouges to get signatures for monster petitions against Confederation. In a speech to the Legislative Assembly during the debate on the Confederation

motion in February 1865, Dorion made a last-ditch attempt to have the political impasse in the Canadas resolved via a loose federal union. Among other things, Dorion invoked a popular theme of anti-confederate spokesmen: the allegedly overweening influence of the Grand Trunk in the project. With a large number of cabinet members involved in the Grand Trunk—including Cartier, the railway's chief solicitor—there is no doubt that the company's prospects played some role in the thinking of the fathers of Confederation. Dorion said, in part:

The Confederation of all the British North American Provinces naturally suggested itself to the Grand Trunk officials as the surest means of bringing with it the construction of the Intercolonial Railway. . . . Such was the origin of their Confederation scheme. The Grand Trunk people are at the bottom of it; and I find that at the last meeting of the Grand Trunk Railway Company, Mr. Watkin did in advance congratulate the shareholders and bond-holders on the bright prospects opening before them, by the enhanced value which will be given to their shares and bonds, by the adoption of the Confederation scheme and the construction of the Intercolonial as part of the scheme.[5]

Dorion no doubt overstated the influence of the Grand Trunk in initiating the Confederation scheme.

A.A. Dorion: The Changing Face of Quebec Liberalism

While Antoine-Aimé Dorion led the anti-Confederation forces in Canada East in the 1860s, he was no radical nationalist in the mould of the Patriotes of 1837. Rather, he was a moderate liberal who recognized the political realities of the post-rebellion period and thus distanced himself from the anticlericalism of the early Rouge leadership and ignored campaigns for complete dissolution of the union of the Canadas. He won considerable support from Montreal's English-speaking electors because he fought for development of the port of Montreal and improved trade with the United States. He had worked with the annexationists of 1849 and, over time, his close association with English speakers showed itself in a loss of facility in his first language.

As the son and grandson of Patriote assemblymen, Dorion had received an education in the classics at the Séminaire de Nicolet in the 1830s before articling in a law firm. Called to the bar in 1844, he became well known in liberal circles in Montreal and in 1849 helped found the Club National Démocratique, an organization committed to universal male suffrage and state support for education. After his election as a Rouge in 1854, Dorion, a practising Catholic, attempted to alleviate church concerns about his party's goals. Nevertheless, church authorities were alarmed by his attempts to cooperate with the Reformers of Canada West, led by George Brown, who was hated by the Catholic hierarchy for his attacks on public subsidies for Catholic schools.

Dorion served in the short-lived pre-Confederation Liberal ministries. In October 1862, he resigned from the Liberal cabinet, accusing its members of being too uncritical of Edward Watkin's proposal for an intercolonial railway. From the late 1850s onward, Dorion had proposed schemes for a federal union of the two sections of the United Province, in all cases granting jurisdiction in most domestic areas to the provinces.

This would give Canada East a great deal of autonomy while recognizing its economic links with Canada West. For Dorion, the Confederation agreement of 1864 represented a repudiation of his notions of a loose federation and of private capital developing privately owned railways without government funds.

Antoine-Aimé Dorion.
Library and Archives Canada/C23599

At the same time, economic arguments were as important as political issues such as "rep by pop" in influencing the Canadian supporters of Confederation. In the Assembly, the confederates argued forcefully that the two Canadas would be the major economic benefactors of Confederation. Galt prophesied that the acquisition and settlement of the western territories would stimulate both manufacturing and mercantile activity in Quebec and Ontario. The Maritimes, too, would provide new markets for what would, after 1867, be Central Canada. Only 3 or 4 percent of New Brunswick's trade was with the Canadas, but the completion of the Intercolonial would, it was predicted, dramatically alter this figure. Ontario farmers, long under George Brown's influence, were particularly receptive to the economic arguments for Confederation because their eyes were fixed westward: Assiniboia would become the first frontier for the new province of Ontario, providing agricultural opportunities for the farmers and farmers' sons who faced hard times in Ontario after the most fertile lands were occupied and much of the soil had been exhausted.

In Canada East, outside of the business circles of the Grand Trunk and the Bank of Montreal, both of which saw Montreal as the metropolitan centre serving a developing West, there was virtually no interest in the Northwest. Not only was it far away, but the Catholic missionaries there had insisted for some time that its soil was inimical to agriculture. The missionaries were perhaps motivated by a desire to keep worldly white Canadiens away from their recent Native converts, who were undoubtedly often puzzled by the contradiction between Christian teachings and behaviour.

Confederation was sold in Canada East on political grounds as much as on its economic potential. To counter the Rouge claim that Confederation meant centralization, Cartier and the Bleus focused on the re-establishment of a separate province of Quebec. That province, because of the powers granted provincial governments, would be able to assure its continued French and Catholic character. The supporters of Confederation emphasized the separation of Canada East from Canada West rather than its union with the Atlantic colonies within a Confederation that also aimed to embrace the Northwest. The confederate cause was also supported by the Catholic Church. Prompted by British encouragement and more particularly by guarantees in the Quebec Resolutions for continued public support of the separate school system in the new province of Ontario, the church put its sub-

MAP 22.1 British North America, 1866.

stantial weight behind the push for Confederation.

In the end, a majority of the elected members from each of the two sections of the Province of Canada voted in favour of Confederation. Even among the French-Canadian members, a small majority supported it. But popular enthusiasm for Confederation was largely confined to Canada West. In Canada East, as in New Brunswick, the acceptance of Confederation seemed to amount more to resignation than to a wholehearted embrace of the concept. The church, the British government, and the dominant political party in Canada East were steadfast in their resolve to see Confederation come about. The nationalist forces in Canada East, humiliated in 1837 and divided over socio-economic policies, no longer had the élan to rally the masses against such formidable foes.

The Canadian elites, having first sponsored the idea of a Confederation of the colonies, were determined to control its shape. When they met with the premiers of New Brunswick and Nova Scotia in late 1866 to frame the final version of the British North

America Act, which would be presented to the British Parliament for approval, they insisted that no substantive changes could be made to the Quebec Resolutions regardless of what Tilley may have promised his electorate. They ensured that Ottawa, announced as the permanent capital of the United Province of Canada on 31 December 1857, would become the capital of the new country. The existing civil service of the United Province provided virtually all of the civil servants for the Dominion of Canada, with only token representation from the two Maritime colonies that had merged with the United Province.

THE MEANING OF CONFEDERATION

The British North America Act was introduced in the British Parliament in March 1867 and passed with little debate. On 1 July 1867, the Dominion of Canada officially came into being. "With the first dawn of this gladsome midsummer morn," trumpeted the Toronto *Globe*, "we hail this birthday of a new nationality. A united British America . . . takes its place among the nations of the world."[6]

What was the character of this "new nationality"? Focusing on railways that would link the former colonies, the supporters of Confederation evoked the progressive spirit of the age. Theirs was a vision of ever-expanding factories, whose goods would move by rail to every corner of the new dominion along with the products of farm, forest, sea, and mines, linking once-separate peoples with bonds of prosperity. Continuing ties with Britain would cement these bonds.

Opponents of the Quebec Resolutions in 1864 usually embraced similar nineteenth-century capitalist notions of progress, and many of them were not averse to a federation on different terms. For them, the vision embodied in the British North America Act was a centralizing force, ignoring regional and linguistic communities. Confederation's supporters retorted that the federation proposals carefully balanced provincial needs with the efficiencies that could be achieved in

Proclamation of Confederation in Market Square, Kingston, 1 July 1867.
Kingston Picture Collection, Queen's University Archives

some areas by central authority. They derided the argument that thinly populated colonies hugging the northern boundaries of the United States had a future as semi-independent entities in an era of capitalist expansionism. In their view, material progress was to be achieved only through the efforts of entrepreneurs acting with the support of the governments of strong nation-states.

Confederation was essentially a top-down exercise. The failure to hold referenda or elections (except in New Brunswick) on the issue or to follow the American example and hold a constitutional convention of elected delegates suggested a continuity with British North America's tradition of limited democracy. In the era of responsible government, the old oligarchies were forced to accept a degree of openness both in government and in the economy, but government remained in the hands of a small group of wealthy white men. Women played no role in the deliberations regarding the new constitution, and the document, not surprisingly, was silent on issues related to gender; in keeping with the times, patriarchy was an assumed part of the "new nationality." First Nations peoples were similarly excluded from participation. The BNA Act recognized their existence only to the extent of giving the federal authorities responsibility for their welfare.

The debates about Confederation in the British American colonies in the 1860s indicated that community identity was as important to many people as the elusive search for prosperity through the creation of a new governmental framework. In the years that followed 1867, there would be echoes of the same debate. Could Quebec's French-speaking majority preserve a national existence within a federal framework? Could the Atlantic provinces and later the western territories have enough say in the deliberations of the federal government to protect the interests of their regions? Would provinces have the powers and financial resources they needed to promote economic development and the social well-being of their people? As time went by, these issues would be joined by the concerns of Natives, women, working people, and non-British immigrants regarding the social values underlying the pact devised by the political leaders of the 1860s.

CONCLUSION

From the beginnings of human occupation of what is now Canada, the peoples living there had shaped a multitude of societies, sometimes in harmony with nature, sometimes in blind disregard of nature's limits. Collectively they would also shape the "new nationality"—in reality a gathering of nationalities within a single nation-state. The sun that shone brilliantly in clear blue skies over most of the new nation-state on 1 July 1867 seemed to announce new beginnings; but the people who, on that day, became citizens of Canada were not marked out for a particular destiny. Rather they would continue to shape their own destinies, both in concert and in conflict with others. Confederation on 1 July 1867 was simply a document and a territorial map; in the days and years following, the peoples of the new nation-state would define, through their struggles, the ever-evolving shape of the new nation.

Economic Elites and Confederation

The emergence of Canada as a modern state is inevitably a part of the spread of industrialism and capitalism. Confederation became an effective credit institution with the demands for long-term securities that accompanied the spread of industrialism especially as shown in transportation. The rise of Canada was in a sense the result of the demand for adequate imperial cost accounting, which arose with Gladstonian Liberalism.[7]

This unlovely account of the Canadian Confederation movement was provided in 1933 by Harold Innis, the dean of Canada's economic historians. According to Innis, British financial interests required the creation of the Canadian state to ensure that railway investments in British North America would be protected. While much of the historical work on Confederation focuses on political arguments and personalities, most scholars agree that economic elites and economic arguments provided the real impetus for the Confederation movement. They differ, however, on whether British or Canadian capitalists had the greatest impact on that movement.

The economic historian Vernon Fowke, while acknowledging the role of Canadian and Maritime economic interests in pursuing a Confederation agreement, also stresses the role of British capitalists in promoting the project. According to Fowke, the British politician-businessman E.W. Watkin exemplified imperial attitudes to the economic potential of Confederation. Watkin "accepted the task of salvaging the finances of the newly constructed Grand Trunk Railway for its British owners," but only after "exacting the pledge that the Imperial government would give consideration to a scheme for the union of the British American colonies to be followed eventually by a railway from coast to coast."[8] Fowke says that Watkin's influence was evident in the Quebec City round of negotiations, which devised the terms of the new constitution. Watkin also led the groups that bought the controlling interest in the Hudson's Bay Company in 1863, removing that firm as a possible obstacle to a takeover of the territories north and west of the United Province of Canada.

For Watkin, a railway across Canada would be simply a means of linking British trade with China, Japan, India, and California and a stimulus to natural development (mainly resource extraction). Above all, he foresaw the Grand Trunk

Railway surviving because of the international commerce that this company would come to handle. Railway investors within Canada and the Maritimes, generally men with important political connections, also saw economic merit in the notion of a British North American federation. In Canada, the impending end of reciprocity and the prospect of having to rely on the tiny population base of British North America caused many businessmen to look to Confederation to produce a viable alternative to existing economic arrangements. But what alternative did they seek?

Economic historian R.T. Naylor argues that the Canadian promoters of Confederation, much like their British counterparts, envisioned profitable exploitation of resources rather than the development of manufacturing as the aim of the new nation:

> Far from being the response of a rising industrial capitalism striving to break down intercolonial tariff walls, Confederation and the national policy were the work of the descendants of the mercantile class which had aligned itself with the Colonial Office in 1837 to crush the indigenous petite bourgeoisie and nascent industrialists. . . . The direct line of descent runs from merchant capital, not to industrial capital but to banking and finance, railways, utilities, land speculation, and so on.[9]

This characterization of the Canadian business interests supporting Confederation has been contested. The railway companies were vertically integrated operations involved not only in moving goods but also in a great deal of manufacturing activity. The Grand Trunk and the Great Western built rail cars and locomotives as well as the machinery required in railway construction.

Apart from the railway executives, whose interests appear to have been both industrial and commercial, there were many businessmen prominent in the Confederation movement whose interests seemed to straddle mercantile and manufacturing activity. George Brown and Charles Tupper, as businessmen, were certainly in this category.

As for those whose main field of activity was manufacturing, key elements favoured the project for British North American unity. In Saint John, for example, most of the principal manufacturers as well as the master tradesmen signed a pro-

Confederation address, which a local newspaper reproduced before the Confederation election in the colony in 1865. The signatories believed that the railway construction promised in the Quebec Resolutions would "enable our rising manufacturers to take a firm stand, and instead of the periodical stagnation of trade caused by the fluctuations of our only articles of export—Lumber and Ships—we shall have manufactures that will be a continual source of prosperity, not affected by the changes in the European Market, and giving our working people employment all the year round."[10] By contrast, small manufacturers in Prince Edward Island and parts of Nova Scotia resisted plans for a common British North American market as a threat to local tariffs and therefore local and international markets.

It is difficult to draw a clear dividing line between business supporters and opponents of Confederation. Each side of the debate contained both small and big businessmen as well as manufacturers and mercantilists. Attitudes to publicly subsidized railway projects, however, based on the perceived usefulness of such projects to a particular business, were often pivotal in the positions taken on Confederation: those who believed that railway extension held the key to their economic futures were usually supporters of Confederation, while advocates of laissez-faire railway development usually opposed union of the colonies, at least on the terms proposed in the Quebec Resolutions.

NOTES

1 Janet Ajzenstat, Paul Romney, Ian Gentles, and William D. Gairdner, *Canada's Founding Debates* (Toronto: University of Toronto Press, 2003), 234.

2 Quoted in James L. Sturgis, "The Opposition to Confederation in Nova Scotia, 1864–1868," in *The Causes of Canadian Confederation*, ed. Ged Martin (Fredericton: Acadiensis Press, 1990), 125.

3 A.A. den Otter, *Civilizing the West: The Galts and the Development of Western Canada* (Edmonton: University of Alberta Press, 1982), 15.

4 P.B. Waite, ed., *The Confederation Debates in the Province of Canada, 1865* (Toronto: McClelland and Stewart, 1963), 86–90.

5 P.B. Waite, *The Life and Times of Confederation, 1864–1867: Politics, Newspapers, and the Union of British North America* (Toronto: University of Toronto Press, 1962), 156.

6 Waite, *The Life and Times of Confederation*, 322.

7 Quoted in Tom Traves, "Business-Government Relations in Canadian History," in *Government and Enterprise in Canada*, ed. K.J. Rea and Nelson Wiseman (Toronto: Methuen, 1985), 13–14.

8 Vernon C. Fowke, *The National Policy and the Wheat Economy* (Toronto: University of Toronto Press, 1973), 31.

9 R.T. Naylor, "The Rise and Fall of the Third Commercial Empire of the St Lawrence," in *Capitalism and the National Question in Canada*, ed. Gary Teeple (Toronto: University of Toronto Press, 1972), 16.

10 Quoted in Rosemarie Langhout, "About Face," *Horizons Canada* 53 (1986): 1252.

RELATED READINGS IN THIS SERIES

From *Foundations: Readings in Pre-Confederation Canadian History*

Ged Martin, "The Case against Canadian Confederation," 480–99.
"The British North America Act, 1867," 500–06.

From Media Companion CD-ROM, Volume I

George Brown Describes the Charlottetown Conference, 1864
The *Chesapeake* Affair
The *Trent* Affair
The Latest Terms
The Botheration Scheme
No Confederation!
The Quebec Resolutions, October 1864

Selected Reading

The words of the politicians as they debated Confederation, with emphasis on the pro-Confederation side, are found in Janet Ajzenstat, Paul Romney, Ian Gentles, and William D. Gairdner, *Canada's Founding Debates* (Toronto: University of Toronto Press, 2003). The political and economic history of the pre-Confederation and early post-Confederation years is surveyed in W.L. Morton, *The Critical Years: The Union of British North America, 1857–1873* (Toronto: McClelland and Stewart, 1964). Stanley Ryerson's *Unequal Union: Roots of Crisis in the Canadas* (Toronto: Progress Books, 1968) provides a Marxist perspective on the period. Insights into the state of the public accounts in the United Province of Canada and its influence on political developments are found in Michael Piva, *The Borrowing Process: Public Finance in the Province of Canada, 1840–1867* (Ottawa: University of Ottawa Press, 1992). The years immediately preceding Confederation are examined closely in P.B. Waite, *The Life and Times of Confederation, 1864–1867: Politics, Newspapers, and the Union of British North America* (Toronto: University of Toronto Press, 1962) and Donald Creighton, *The Road to Confederation: The Emergence of Canada 1863–1867* (Toronto: Macmillan, 1964). Several important essays on Confederation itself appear in Ramsay Cook, ed., *Confederation* (Toronto: University of Toronto Press, 1967) and Ged Martin, ed., *The Causes of Canadian Confederation* (Fredericton: Acadiensis Press, 1990). See also Phillip A. Buckner, "The 1860s: An End and a Beginning," in *The Atlantic Region to Confederation: A History*, ed. Phillip A. Buckner and John G. Reid (Toronto: University of Toronto Press, 1994). On Canadians' attitudes toward slavery and the American Civil War, see Tom Brooks and Robert Trueman, *Anxious for a Little War: The Involvement of Canadians in the Civil War in the United States* (Toronto: WWEC, 1993); Allen P. Stouffer, *The Light of Nature and the Law of God: Antislavery in Ontario, 1833–1877* (Montreal: McGill-Queen's University Press, 1992); and Greg Marquis, *In Armageddon's Shadow: The Civil War and Canada's Maritime Provinces* (Halifax: Gorsebrook Research Institute for Atlantic Canadian Studies, St Mary's University; Montreal: McGill-Queen's University Press, 1998).

Quebec attitudes to Confederation are discussed in A.I. Silver, *The French-Canadian Idea of Confederation, 1864–1900* (Toronto: University of Toronto Press, 1982). Quebec society at the time of Confederation is analyzed in Paul-André Linteau, René Durocher, and Jean-Claude Robert, *Quebec: A History, 1867–1929* (Toronto: Lorimer, 1983). The key Quebec pro-confederate politicians are the subjects of critical biographies: Brian Young, *George-Étienne Cartier:*

Montreal Bourgeois (Montreal: McGill-Queen's University Press, 1981) and A.A. den Otter, *Civilizing the West: The Galts and the Development of Western Canada* (Edmonton: University of Alberta Press, 1982). Ontario's key Confederation politicians are also the subjects of biographies. The major biography of John A. Macdonald is D.G. Creighton's laudatory two-volume *John A. Macdonald* (Toronto: Macmillan, 1965), much of which is cast into question by other works in this bibliography. George Brown's political and journalistic career is traced in a two-part biography, *Brown of the Globe* (Toronto: Macmillan, 1959), by J.M.S. Careless. The politics of Canada West more generally are outlined in J.M.S. Careless, ed., *The Pre-Confederation Premiers: Ontario Government Leaders, 1841–1867* (Toronto: University of Toronto Press, 1980).

Two books edited by George Rawlyk, *The Atlantic Provinces and the Problem of Confederation* (St John's: Breakwater, 1980) and *Historical Essays on the Atlantic Provinces* (Ottawa: Carleton University Press, 1967), contain articles on the Confederation period. Economic conditions in the region are treated in S.A. Saunders, *The Economic History of the Maritime Provinces* (Fredericton: Acadiensis Press, 1984). *Nova Scotia and Confederation, 1864–74*, by Kenneth G. Pryke (Toronto: University of Toronto Press, 1979) provides detail on Nova Scotia politics in the 1860s and 1870s. The leading anti-confederate is portrayed in J. Murray Beck, *Joseph Howe*, vol. 2, *The Briton Becomes Canadian, 1848–1873* (Montreal: McGill-Queen's University Press, 1983). New Brunswick politics during this period are discussed in W.S. MacNutt, *New Brunswick: A History, 1784–1867* (Toronto: Macmillan, 1984); William M. Baker, "Squelching the Disloyal, Fenian-Sympathizing Brood: T.W. Anglin and Confederation in New Brunswick, 1865–1866," *Canadian Historical Review* 55, 2 (June 1974): 141–58; William M. Baker, *Timothy Warren Anglin, 1822–1896: Irish Catholic Canadian* (Toronto: University of Toronto Press, 1977); and Alfred G. Bailey, "The Basis and Persistence of Opposition to Confederation in New Brunswick," *Canadian Historical Review* 23, 4 (Dec. 1942): 374–97. Prince Edward Island politics are discussed in Ian Ross Robertson, "Prince Edward Island Politics in the 1860s," *Acadiensis* 15, 1 (Autumn 1985): 35–58; David Weale and Harry Baglole, *The Island and Confederation: The End of an Era* (Summerside, PEI: Williams and Crue, 1973); and F.W.P. Bolger, *Prince Edward Island and Confederation* (Charlottetown: St Dunstan's University Press, 1964). On Newfoundland's rejection of Confederation, see James Hiller, "Confederation Defeated: The Newfoundland Election of 1869," in *Newfoundland in the Nineteenth and*

Twentieth Centuries: Essays in Interpretation, ed. James Hiller and Peter Neary (Toronto: University of Toronto Press, 1980): 67–94. Newfoundland politics in the period are dis- cussed in S.J. Noel, *Politics of Newfoundland* (Toronto: University of Toronto Press, 1971).

WEBLINKS

GEORGE-ÉTIENNE CARTIER

collections.ic.gc.ca/charlottetown/fathers/cartier.html

This site on the Charlottetown Conference of 1864 offers a profile of Cartier. Numerous internal links are available.

SAMUEL LEONARD TILLEY

collections.ic.gc.ca/charlottetown/fathers/tilley.html

This site offers a brief profile of Tilley and his political career.

CONFEDERATION

www.nlc-bnc.ca/2/18/index-e.html

This site describes the path to Canadian Confederation, noting the influence of the American Civil War. It contains links to relevant historical documents, key terms, notable public figures, a bibliography, and maps outlining the changing shape of Canada from the seventeenth century to the present.

AMERICAN CIVIL WAR

www.cwc.lsu.edu/cwc/civlink.htm

The site of the United States Civil War Center contains a list of over 7000 thematic links to Civil War resources on the Internet.

GEORGE BROWN

http://collections.ic.gc.ca/charlottetown/fathers/brown. html

This site provides an overview of George Brown's career, the Charlottetown Conference, and several useful links.

Part V Summary

The years preceding Confederation were marked by an increasing emphasis on individualism and the virtues of the marketplace as well as by a growing reliance on the state to promote economic development and social compliance with the ways of the new economic order. Huge public expenditures on railways represented the outstanding example of the state's economic role, while its social thrust was evident in public schools, asylums, and legal reform. In their private lives, British North Americans struggled to reconcile traditional religious beliefs and social values with new concepts represented by Darwinism, consumerism, and class conflict. For many British North Americans, the solution to social problems and colonial underdevelopment lay in developing the apparently inexhaustible economic potential of their resource-rich territories. Each colony tried this strategy on its own, but as the financial costs became clear, the attraction of uniting the colonies into a new nation devoted to economic progress attracted growing support. Although the Confederation exercise demonstrated the extent to which colonial elites dominated the political process in the age of responsible government, it also pointed to the processes and problems that would continue to prevail, for better and for worse, in the new Dominion of Canada.

INDEX

A

Abbott, John, 361
Aboriginal culture
    Canadian Shield First Nations, 15–18
    of change and adaptation, 9–10
    childrearing in, 13
    collective sharing in, 18
    creation myths, 9, 17
    diversity, 9
    divorce, 13
    female infanticide, 14
    First Nations of Atlantic and Gulf
      region, 14–15
    Great Lakes-St Lawrence Lowlands
      First Nations, 20–23
    homosexuality in, 13
    hunting, 10, 16, 19
    impact of epidemics, 321
    Interior Plains First Nations, 18–20
    and intermarriages, 213
    Iroquoian-speaking peoples, 9–10
    land in, 18
    language groupings, 9
    marriage, 17
    North's First Nations, 25–26
    polygamy, 211
    potlatch, 23–24
    relationship with environment, 11, 12
    sexuality, 13, 17
    slavery, 13
    spiritual belief system, 11–16, 18, 19,
      22, 24
    Sun Dance, 20
    trade, 12–13, 21
    Western Cordillera First
      Nations, 23–25
Aboriginal-European relations
    early contact, 34, 50–55, 57
    European views of Native society, 43,
      60, 69–210
    French alliances, 58, 111–112,
      141–142
    fur trade, 115, 208–211, 217–219
    impact of Native culture on
      colonists, 77
    intermarriages, 77, 212–213, 315
    See also Métis
    Iroquois, 86, 106
    Native impressions of European soci-
      ety, 61
    resource depletion and, 67
    skill of Native trappers and, 57
    trade in firearms, 68, 209

    Treaty of Montreal, 108
    violence, 209, 218, 219
Aboriginal lands
    Native control of, 269
    Natives' views of European
      claims, 326–327
    pre-emption of, 332
    Proclamation of 1763 and, 163–164,
      323
    reserves, 267
    in southern Ontario, 185
    value of, 345
    Vancouver Island, 322, 323
    violation of agreements, 184, 267–323,
      332, 344–345
Aboriginal peoples
    and American Revolutionary
      War, 174, 175
    and Articles of Capitulation, 156
    and assimilation, 68, 266, 344
    and cessation of British territories, 184
    and Christianity, 50–61, 69–70,
      256–257, 266, 326–327
    and Confederation debate, 407
    decimation of, 42, 43, 44, 212
    diseases and epidemics, 44, 212, 307,
      312, 320–321, 346
    economic dispossession, 332, 344–375
    economy, 337
    and education, 69, 269
    in Labrador, 257–260
    leadership, 269
    Loyalists, 185
    and missionaries, 345
    Native trade rivalries, 207, 258
    in New France, 87, 122–123
    origins of, 9
    Pacific coast, 335
    population, 9, 335
    Portuguese traders and, 42
    resistance, 332
    resource depletion and, 67, 307–308
    segregated schools, 380
    Spanish conquistadores and, 42–43
    sports, 349
    Treaty of Utrecht and, 145
    and voting rights, 239
    wage labour, 305, 306–306, 322, 332
Aboriginal warfare
    arrival of firearms and, 57
    casualties, 17
    competition for hunting grounds, 17,
      19
    Dutch allies, 58

    French allies, 58
    "mourning wars," 13
    Native alliances, 17, 21, 22
    nature of, 13
    prisoners, 13, 23
    slaves, 24
    trade rivalries, 72
Aboriginal women
    in Athapaskan society, 25
    in Blackfoot society, 20, 211
    in Carrier society, 25
    economic role of, 13, 16
    fur-trade wives, 305, 306, 314–315,
      319
    in Haida society, 24
    in Innu society, 16, 69
    in Iroquoian societies, 21
    labour, 16, 21, 24, 320
    in Ojibwa society, 16, 17
    role in religious activities, 13
    shamans, 16
    slaves, 24
    in Tsimshian society, 24
Abortion, 341
Absolutism
    of Louis XIV, 84–85
    and royal government, 85–89
Acadia
    agriculture, 88
    and British control, 142–145
    civil war in, 65–67
    founding of, 56–57
    Mi'kmaq hostilities, 144–145, 146
    royal government in, 87–88
    1654 seizure by New Englanders, 67
    Treaty of Utrecht and, 109, 142, 145
    War of the Spanish Succession in, 109
Acadian forest region, 4
Acadians, 114
    deportation of, 149–152
    and French appeals to re-relo-
      cate, 113, 114
    leprosy outbreak, 340
    "Massacre of Grand Pré" and, 146
    neutrality, 144
Acosta, Mathieu d', 56
Act of Union, 295
Act of Union (1801), 190, 228
Adolescence, concept of, 16–383
Advocate, 291
Agricultural society, rise of, 31
Agriculture
    Aboriginal, 9, 21, 216
    agricultural societies, 240

agro-forestry, 275, 276, 277
  corn, 216
  dykeland, 88
  and interest in the Northwest, 311
  in Lower Canada, 275–277
  Maritimes, 4
  in New France, 76, 126
    See also Seigneurialism
  soil exhaustion, 275
  in Upper Canada, 268–270, 275, 277
  wheat, 337
Alabama, 398
Albanel, Charles, 105
Albani, Emma, 352
Alcohol
  and Aboriginal peoples, 67, 68
  abuse, 346
  consumption, 273, 341
  and fur trade, 104
  and social problems, 272–273
  See also Temperance movement
Alexander, Sir William, 57
Algonquin, French allies, 58
Allan, John, 176
Allison, Joseph, 229
American Civil War, 397, 398
American colonies, population, 79
American Missionary Association, 347
American Revolution, 172–178
  colonial grievances, 172
Amherst, Jeffrey, 153, 154, 164
Amundsen, Roald, 52
Anderson, John, 348
Angélique, Marie-Joseph, 134
Anglo-American Convention of
  1818, 198, 247
Animals, cruelty to, 252, 377
Anishinabeg, 185
Annexation, 360, 361
Anti-confederates
  in New Brunswick, 401–402
  in Newfoundland, 401
  in Nova Scotia, 402
  in Prince Edward Island, 400
  in United Canadas, 403
Anti-Semitism, 39, 191
Anville, Duc d', 146
Appalachians, 4
Argall, Samuel, 57
Arnold, Benedict, 173
Arrêts de Marly, 97
Art, 351, 352
Articles of Capitulation, 156
Assiniboine, 18, 112, 212
Association for the Protection of Canadian
  Industry, 362
Asylums, 381–382
Athapaskans, 25
Atlantic and Gulf region, 4
Aubert de Gaspé, Philippe, 386
Aulnay, Charles de Menou d', 65–67

Axtell, James, 8
Aylen, Peter, 265
Aztec empire, destruction of, 42–43

B

Baillie, Thomas, 237
Baldwin, Robert, 289, 295, 300
Baldwin, W.W., 289
Baldwin-Hincks alliance, 295, 297
Baldwin-LaFontaine government, 297,
  367
Ball, John, 183
Ballad, as oral sources, 226–227
Banalités, 97
Banking, 230
Bank of Montreal, 364
Bank of New Brunswick, 230
Bannerman, Sir Alexander, 255
Bannister, Jerry, 247
Baptists, 183, 233, 234, 273, 344
Baribeau, Claude, 290
Barkley, Murray, 183
Barnum, P.T., 350
Bartering, 337
Basque cod fishery, 50
Basque whalers, 51–53
Battle of Put-in-Bay, 195
Battle of Queenston Heights, 193, 195
Battle of Sainte-Foy, 156
Battle of Saratoga, 174
Battle of the Boyne, anniversary of, 235
Battle of the Plains of Abraham, 154–156
Beauharnois, Charles de, 134
Beckwith, Julia Catherine, 240
Bédard, Pierre, 192
"Bees," work, 349
Bégon, Élisabeth, 124, 125
Belcher, Jonathan, 163
Beleau, Maria Louisa, 279
Beothuk, 14–22, 257–260
Berczy, William, 201
Bering, Vitus, 217
Bernon, Gabriel, 92
Berthelet, Pierre, 278
Bessette, Louis, 287
Biard, Pierre, 56
Bidwell, Marshall Spring, 289
Biencourt, Charles de, 56, 57
Bigot, François, 126, 132, 133
Birchtown, 183
Birth control, 34, 276, 340
Birthing experience, 128, 340, 341
Bishops University, 300
Black Death, 31–32
Black experience
  American immigration, 264, 348
  in Atlantic colonies, 346–347
    See also Loyalists
  British North American settle-
    ments, 334
  in Canada West, 347–348

  of discrimination, 346–348
  education, 347, 381
  emigration to Sierra Leone, 183, 197
  Loyalists, 182, 183, 197
  religion, 183, 235
  Vancouver Island community, 327
  West Indian immigration, 197
Blackfoot, 10, 18–19, 20, 210–211, 212
Blainville, Pierre-Joseph Céloron, 147
Blake, William, 367
Blanchet, François, 192
Blanshard, Richard, 322
Bleus, 297
  alliance with Conservatives, 297–298
  Cartier as leader, 298
  and Catholic Church, 298
Blood, 19, 211
Bodega y Quadra, Francisco de la, 217
Boreal forest, 4
Boscawen, Edward, 153
Boston Tea Party, 172
Boullé, Hélène, 58, 136
Bourgeois, Claude, 151
Bourgeoys, Marguerite, 70–136
Bourget, Ignace, 279
Bowering, Benjamin, 250
Braddock, Edward, 149
Bradstreet, John, 144, 153–154
Bradstreet, Simon, 144
Brant, Joseph, 174–175
Brant, Molly, 174–175
Braudel, Fernand, 42
Brébeuf, Jean de, 69
Briand, Jean-Olivier, 165
British American Land Company, 286
British-American League, 360
British Columbia
  amalgamation with Vancouver
    Island, 329
  creation of, 324
  economic development, 327–328
  gold rush, 324–325
  race relations, 326–327
British North America
  colonial economies, 337
  communications, 336–337
  currency, 365
  economy of, 337–338
  health, 340–341
  poverty, 375–376
  religion, 343–344
  residual powers, 400
  social welfare, 376
  urban life, 338–339
British North America Act, 399–400
  act of British Parliament, 406
  division of powers, 400
  French language, 400
  minority rights, 400
  taxation, 400
British Royal African Company, 45

Brock, Isaac, 193
Brown, George, 297, 311, 382
  and Confederation debate, 398–399
  and federal system, 399
  proposal of confederation, 392
  and "rep by pop," 390
Brown, Jennifer, 314
Brown, William, 216
Brûle, Étienne, 59
Brunet, Michel, 177
Buffalo
  Blackfoot dependence on, 211, 323
  extinction of herds, 307–308
  hunt, 309, 325
  trade in robes, 307–308
Buffalo pound, 10
Bumsted, J.M., 171
Bungi, 213
Burke, Edmund, 233
Burpee, Richard, 233
Business
  and annexation, 361
  capitalists, 359–360, 368
  and Confederation, 398, 401, 402,
    408–409
  credit, 276
  and expansion of the state, 37
  investments, 365
  mercantile firms, 337
  merchants of New France, 131–132
  and protectionism, 362
  St John's merchants, 250, 252–253
  "truck system," 250, 252
  West Country merchants, 247–248
Butler, Philip, 253
Bytown (Ottawa), economy, 270

C

Cabot, John, 43, 50
Cadet, Joseph, 132
Cadigan, Sean, 252
Cadillac, Antoine Laumet de
  Lamothe, 108
Cady, Elizabeth, 384
Cajuns, 152
Callbeck, Phillips, 176
Calvert, Sir George, 53–54
Cameron, Duncan, 214–215
Campbell, Lydia, 257
Campeau, Lucien, 78
Canada, during French regime, 58
  See also New France
Canada Land Company, 292
Canadian Shield, 4
Canal construction, 271–272
Cantin, Augustin, 368
Cape Breton
  new colony, 184
  re-annexed to Nova Scotia, 225
Capitalism
  capital, 364–365

industrialism and, 359–360
Capuchins, 67–111
Cardwell, Edward, 397
Cariboo gold rush, 325
Carignan-Salières regiment, 86, 87
Carleton, Guy, 167, 173, 186
Carlos III (king of Spain), 217
Carmelites, 111
Carrier, 25
Carson, William, 253
Cartier, George-Étienne, 367, 392
  and federal system, 399
  and idea of Confederation, 392
  as leader of the *Bleus*, 298
Cartier, Jacques, 55
Cary, Mary Ann Shad, 347, 348
Casson, François Dollier de, 105
Catholic Emancipation, 233, 254
Censitaires, 97
Champlain, Samuel de, 56, 58, 74
Charitable Irish Society, 199
Charivari, 59–274, 128, 274–296, 376
Charles II (king of England), 105
Charles I (king of England), 61
Charlottetown conference, 399
Chartist movement, 236
Chartrand, René, 147
Château Clique, 285
Chazelle, Pierre, 345
Chesapeake, 197, 398
Children
  and childhood, 16–383
  childrearing, 13, 33, 34, 129
  corporal punishment, 129, 377
  death rate, 128
  and family economy, 270
  illegitimacy rates, 127
  labour, 34, 270, 271, 368
  and poverty, 383
  unwanted, 341
Chipewyan, 210, 212
Christie, Robert, 350
Church of England, 183, 199, 234,
  273–274, 299, 327–344
Church of Scotland, 273, 344
Cipolla, Carlo, 33
Circuses, 350
Cities. *See* Urban centres
Civil law, 166, 187
Civil service, of federal government, 406
Class
  Loyalists, 182
  Newfoundland society, 252
  and religion, 344
  and social structure of Lower
    Canada, 278, 279
  and social structure of Upper
    Canada, 271
  and violence, 376–378
Clear Grits, 297
Clergy reserves, 289, 299

Coates, Colin, 107
Cochrane, Sir Thomas, 199, 253–254
Code Noir, 134
Cod fishery
  "by-boatmen," 248
  "dry fishery, 50
  European demand and, 50
  European fishery, 43, 50–52, 88
  export markets, 250
  St John's merchants and, 248–249
  saltfish trade, 249–250
  "truck system," 250, 252
  West Country merchants
    and, 247–248
Coercive Acts, 172
Colbert, Jean-Baptiste, 85, 88, 90, 94, 95,
  96
Colborne, Sir John, 292
Coles, George, 239, 396
College of New Brunswick, 234
Collins, Enos, 229
Colonial Advocate, 291
Colonization, purpose of, 37–38, 48
Coltman, William Bachelor, 215
Columbus, Christopher, 42, 43
Colvile, Andrew, 307, 308
Comingo, Joseph Brown, 201
Commercial Bank, 230
Compagnie de la Nouvelle France. *See*
  Company of One Hundred Associates
  (Compagnie des Cents Associés)
Compagnie de l'Île Saint-Jean, 114
Compagnie des Indes, 110–117
Compagnie du Saint-Sacrement, 75
Company of One Hundred Associates
  (Compagnie des Cents Associés), 61, 74,
  79
Confederation
  arguments for, 390, 404–405
  British Colonial Office and, 397
  business interests and, 398, 401, 402,
    408–409
  Canada East and, 403–405
  Charlottetown conference, 399
  and defence against American expan-
    sion, 397–398, 399
  economic arguments, 404–405
  nationalism and, 384–386
  nature of, 406–407
  New Brunswick and, 401–402
  Newfoundland and, 401
  Nova Scotia and, 401, 402
  political impasse and, 390–392
  Prince Edward Island and, 400
  Quebec Resolutions, 399–401,
    405–406
  re-establishment of separate
    Quebec, 405
  terms of Maritime colonies, 399–400
  United Canadas and, 402–406
  and western colonization, 404–405

Congés, 105
Connolly, Amelia, 323
Conquest
  and economic policy, 165–166
  and French laws, 165
  historical interpretations of, 176–177
  and Native lands, 163–164
  and Native policy, 163
  and Quebec, 164–167
  and repatriation, 164
Conservatives
  alliance with *Bleus*, 297
  alliance with Liberals, 298
Constitutional Act, 1791, 187–188
Continental shelf, 4
Cook, James, 171, 200, 217
Cooper, William, 236
Copernicus, Nicolaus, 40
Cormack, William Eppes, 259
Cornwallis, Charles, 176
Cornwallis, Edward, 146
Cortés, Hernándo, 42–43
Corvée, 135
Cost Salish, 23
Côte, 98
Coureurs de bois, 104, 105, 108, 127
Coyne, Henry, 183
Craig, James, 192
Credit, 337
Cree, 10, 18–19, 112, 212
Crémazie, Octave, 386
Cricket, 350
Crime, poverty and, 376
Crosby, Alfred W., 44
Crowe, Keith J., 26
Crowley, Terrence, 99, 136
Crowne, William, 67
Crown reserves, 89
Cruikshank, Julie, 10
Cugnet, François-Étienne, 116
Cumberland House, 208
Cunard, Samuel, 226, 227, 232, 322, 362
Cupidon, Jean-Baptiste, 134
Curling, 350
Custom of Paris
  and divorce, 342
  in New France, 91

D

Dakota, 112
Dalhousie College, 234
Darwin, Charles, 371
Davies, Thomas, 200
Davis, Ralph, 36
Dawson, William, 370
Death, and dying, 128
Defence, 339
Dekanawidah, 22
Delgamuukw case, 10
Demasduit, 258–260, 259

Democracy, political ferment
  and, 235–236
Demography, 121
Dene, 209
Denonville, Marquis de, 106
Denys, Nicholas, 66
DesBarres, J.F.W., 200, 236
Descartes, René, 40
"Deserving" poor, 272–273, 376
Detroit
  and fur trade, 112
  surrender of, 185
Diaz, Bartolomeu, 41
Dieskau, Jean-Armand, Baron de, 149
Dinwiddie, Robert, 149
Divorce, 342, 384
Doane, Edmund, 169
Doane, Elizabeth, 169
Dr Bray's Associates, 347
Dongan, Thomas, 106
Donnacona, 55
Doric Club, 287, 295
Dorion, A.A., 402, 403
Douglas, James, 315, 322–323, 325
Downs, Andrew, 370
Drake, Sir Francis, 217
Droit de seigneur, 134
"Dry fishery," 50
Duelling, 377
Dumont, Micheline, 136
Duncan, William, 327
Duncombe, Charles, 293
Duquesne, Ange de Menneville, 147, 149
Duquesnel, Le Prévost, 145
Durham, John George Lambton, Earl
  of, 294–295
Dutch West India Company, 45

E

East India Company, 53
Eccles, William J., 99
"Ecozones," 3
Eddy, Jonathan, 176
Edict of Nantes, 92
Education
  Aboriginal peoples, 69, 70–71, 269,
    346
  black experience, 347, 380–381
  classical colleges, 191
  common schools, 299, 379–380
  constitutional protection, 400
  farm families and, 270
  gender and, 125, 201, 342–343
  grammar schools, 299
  higher education, 234, 239, 300
  Loyalist contribution to, 199
  Madras school system, 234
  in New France, 92
  racial segregation, 347, 380
  reform, 239, 379–381

  and religion, 234, 380
  school attendance, 342–343
  school funding, 286
  separate schools, 380
  textbooks, 296
Edward, Prince (later Duke of Kent), 202
Eirik the Red, 49
Elections, violence, 377
Elgin, James Bruce, 8th Earl of, 296, 297
Emmonds, Sarah Emma, 397
Entertainment, popular, 350–352
Environmental degradation
  colonization and, 232
  population increase and, 35
Epidemics, 31–32, 44, 212, 265–321, 340
Escheat Movement, 236
Ethnicity
  entrepreneurs, 368
  and family size, 339
  Montreal mercantile community, 278
  Newfoundland society, 252
  and religion, 344
  and social structure of Lower
    Canada, 278–279
Ethnohistory, and oral tradition, 8–9
Europe, early modern
  See also Peasantry
  the church in, 38–40
  epidemics, 31–32
  inventions, 41
  life expectancy, 33
  population, 32–33
  Renaissance, 40–41
  standard of living, 36
  transition to, 31–32
Evangelicalism, 183, 233
Evolution, theory of, 371
Exploration
  Asian legends of, 49
  and European expansion, 41–45
  Holland, 45
  Northwest Passage to Asia, 50–52
  route to Pacific Ocean, 111
  Spanish, 42–43
  See also France, and age of exploration;
    Great Britain, and age of exploration

F

Factory system, 359
Family
  economy, 86, 249, 268–270, 277, 383
  household production, 35, 231–232,
    337
  inheritance, 126, 129
  middle-class, 382
  New France, 127–129
  nuclear, 34
  patriarchal, 129
  and patronage, 129
  size, 128, 268, 276, 339–340

structure of households, 340
violence, 377
working-class, 383
See also Children; Marriage
Family Compact, 289
Famine, 32, 375, 376
Feast of the Dead, 21
Female Benevolent Society, 279
Fenerty, Charles, 371
Fenian raids, 402
Ferryland, 54
Feudalism, 31
Fidler, Peter, 215
Filles du roi, 86–87, 121
Fils de famille, 122
Fils de la liberté, 287, 295
Financial institutions, 364–365
First Continental Congress, 173
First Nations. *See* Aboriginal peoples
Fisher, Charles, 217–219, 393
Fisher, Peter, 241, 350
Fisheries, 337
Fishing admirals, 247, 253
Five Nations Confederacy, 22
See also Iroquois
Fléché, Jessé, 56
Fleming, Bishop, 254
Florida, 398
Forest regions, 3
Fort Alexander, 319
Fort Beauséjour, 146, 149
Fort Bourbon, 111
Fort Carillon, 154
Fort Dauphin, 111
Fort Duquesne, 149
Fort Edmonton, 306
Fort Fraser, 219
Fort Frédéric, 149, 154
Fort Frontenac, 154
Fort George, 219
Fort Kamloops, 319
Fort Langley, 319
Fort La Reine, 111
Fort Maurepas, 111
Fort Necessity, 149
Fort Niagara, 149, 154
Fort Okanagam, 319
Fort Pascoyac, 112
Fort Rouge, 111
Fort Rouillé, 147, 154
Fort St Charles, 111
Fort St James, 219
Fort St Pierre, 111
Fort Vancouver, 319
Fort Victoria, 324
Fort William Henry, 152
Fort York, 106
Fothergill, Charles, 369
Foulis, Robert, 371
Foundlings, in New France, 124

Fowke, Vernon, 408
France
absolutism, 84–85
and age of exploration, 22
and American Revolutionary War, 218
colonial policy, 108
colonization, 45, 51, 55–61
exploration of continental North
America, 105
mercantilism, 95–96
Francheville, François Poulin de, 116
Franchise, 187, 239, 402
Francis I (king of France), 37, 55
Franklin Expedition, 312–313
Franquet, Louis, 117
Fraser, Simon, 219
Fraser and Thom, 227
Fraser gold rush, 324
Free Schools Act, 239
Free trade
British colonial policy, 360
with United States, 361–362
Frégault, Guy, 99, 177
French Canadian nationalism, class
and, 191–192, 280
French cod fishery, 50, 88
French Shore, 247
Frères Hospitaliers, 92, 113
Frobisher, Martin, 52
Frontenac, Louis de Baude, Compte
de, 105, 106–107
Frontier, and metropolis, 65
Fur trade
American traders, 304
BC interior, 219
buffalo robes, 307–308
and cultural change, 207, 208–211
and disease, 212
European fashion and, 51
French, 73–104–105, 106–107,
111–112, 114–115
French diplomacy, 142
French interpreters, 60
illicit trade, 115
intermediaries in, 72
Iroquois hostilities, 106
labour for, 135
in Labrador, 258
life at trading posts, 306
marriage, 127–128, 219
Métis and, 213
Montreal merchants, 207–208, 412
See also North West Company (NWC)
and Native culture, 320
and Native trade rivalries, 258
northern, 209, 312
northwest expansion, 111–112
origins of, 51
in Pacific Northwest, 319–321
quality of trade items, 115

rivalries in the northwest, 206–208
St Lawrence, 57
shrewdness of Native traders, 115, 217
skill of Native trappers, 57
and trade rivalries, 72
and violence, 209, 218, 219
west cost, 217–219
See also Hudson's Bay Company (HBC)
Fu-sang, 49

G
Gage, Thomas, 172
Galileo Galilei, 40
Galinée, René de Bréhant de, 105
Gallicanism, 92
Galt, Alexander, 361, 362, 391
Galt, John, 292
Gama, Vasco da, 42
Garneau, François-Xavier, 176, 350, 386
Garnier, Charles, 68
Gaulin, Antoine, 145
Gauthier, Jean-François, 124
Gavazzi, Alessandro, 377
Geddes, John, 233
Gender
cult of domesticity, 189
and education, 125, 201, 342–343
and social mores, 341–342
General Mining Association, 230, 239
General stores, 337
George, David, 183
Gérin-Lajoie, Antoine, 386
Gesner, Abraham, 371
Gibson, James R., 217–219
Gilbert, Sir Humphrey, 52
Ginseng, 117
Glenelg, Lord, 237
Goderich, Lord, 292
Gold rush, 324, 325, 326
Gordon, Arthur, 397, 402
Gosford, Lord, 286
Gourlay, Robert, 198, 288
Governor
and Constitutional Act, 1791, 89
in New France, 89–90
Gower, Erasmus, 250
Grandfontaine, Hector d'Andigne de, 88
Grand River Navigation Company, 344
Grand Trunk Railway, 297, 312, 363,
408
Grant, Cuthbert, 215
Grass, Michael, 185
Gray, John Hamilton, 400
Great Britain
and age of exploration, 43–45
and Confederation, 397
and Maritime union, 397
mercantilism, 230–231
and Pacific Northwest, 321–322
relations with US, 397–398

and responsible government, 237–238, 296

Great Britsin, and free trade, 360
Great Lakes-St Lawrence Lowlands, 5
Great Northern Railway, 364
Greer, Allan, 127, 128, 301–351
Grey, Lord, 238
Groseilliers, Médard Chouart, Sieur des, 105
Groulx, Lionel, 99, 177
Guarantee Act, 297, 391
Gubbins, Joseph, 241
Guercheville, Marquise de, 56, 136
Guerilla warfare, 108
Guerrilla warfare, 146, 147, 149, 153, 159
Guilds, 35
Guy, John, 258

H

Haida, 23, 319
Haldimand, Frederick, 174, 184, 185
Haliburton, Thomas Chandler, 232, 240, 350
Halifax
  banking, 230
  buildings, 199
  early society, 148
  founded, 146
  industrial centre, 230
Halifax Banking Company, 229, 230
Halliburton, Margaret, 229
Hamelin, Jean, 177
Hamilton
  economy, 271
  as manufacturing centre, 368
Handicraft production, 337
Harmon, Daniel, 211
Harris, Cole, 320
Hart, Ezekiel, 191
Hart, Samuel, 191
Harvey, Sir John, 237, 238
Haszard, William, 236
Havy, François, 132
Hay, Robert, 362
Head, Sir Francis Bond, 289–292, 293
Hébert, Louis, 56
Heidenreich, Conrad, 78
Henday, Anthony, 112, 207
Henri IV (king of France), 56
Henry, Alexander, 216
Herbert, Mary Eliza, 350
Herjolfsson, Bjarni, 49
Herne, Samuel, 210
Hiawatha, 22
Highland Scots, 227–230, 227
Hincks, Francis, 295, 297, 364
Hind, Henry Youle, 311
History
  interpretation in, 73
  and oral sources, 8–9, 226–227

written sources and, 8, 10
Hochelaga, 55
Hocquart, Gille, 116
Holland, and colonization, 45
Holland, Samuel, 200
Homes, styles, 337
Homosexuality, 13, 274–275
Honorat, Jean-Baptiste, 276
Hopson, Peregrine, 146
Horses, and Native peoples, 207, 210
Hôtel-Dieu, 70
Houses of Industry, 272, 381
Howe, John, 199
Howe, Joseph, 234, 346, 363, 385
  anti-confederate, 402
  libel trial, 239
  and railways, 393
  and responsible government, 237
Hoyles, Hugh, 255, 257, 396
Hudson, Henry, 52
Hudson's Bay Company (HBC)
  Aboriginal employees, 305, 306–306
  amalgamation with NWC, 215–216, 305
  business practices, 306–307
  charter, 105
  chief factors and chief traders, 305, 308
  clerks, 305
  coal mines, 322, 324
  communication lines, 319–320
  competition from French fur trade, 112, 206–207
  conservation policy, 307
  control by Grand Trunk Railway, 312, 408
  economic diversification, 322–324
  employee discipline, 305
  under George Simpson, 308
  and intermarriages, 212–213
  in Labrador, 256–257
  and Oregon territory, 321
  organizational hierarchy, 305, 319
  original trade strategy, 206
  overexploitation of resources, 307, 308
  overtrapping, policy of, 321
  and Pacific Northwest, 321–324, 329
  and race, 324
  shipping strategy, 105
  and Vancouver Island, 335
  workforce, 305, 319
Hull, William, 193
Hunt, George, 78
Hunters' Lodges, 294
Huntingdonians, 183
Huron, 21, 22
  Algonquin and French allies, 58
  Christianity and, 71–72
  wars with Iroquois, 71–74, 72
Huronia, destruction of, 72

Huron Tract, 292–293
Hutchinson, Thomas, 172

I

Iberville, Pierre Le Moyne d', 90, 106, 108
Ice Age, 2, 3
Île Royale (Île du Cap-Breton), 109, 113
Île Saint-Jean (Prince Edward Island), 109, 114
Illinois country, 106, 111
Illnesses, treatment of, 340–341
Immigrants
  Chinese, 327
  diseases and epidemics, 265
  Irish, 228
  and land ownership, 268
  in New France, 122, 127
  and Rebellion of 1837-38, 289
  Scots, 171, 227–228
  sectarian rivalry, 266
  Welsh, 228
Immigration
  chain migration, 264
  cod fishery and, 247–249
  post-1812 (1815–1850), 264–266
  potato famine, 267, 375
  rural economic dislocation and, 365
  See also Black experience
Industrialism
  factory system, 359
  impact of, 368–369
  Industrial Revolution, 358–359
  and legal reform, 366–367
  surplus labour, 365–366
  uneven pace of, 367–368
Industrial Revolution, 359–360
Infanticide, 341
Inglis, Charles, 199
Innis, Harold, 241, 408
Innu, 15, 16, 69, 87
Intellectual life, 350
Intendant, 90, 91
Intercolonial Railway, 199, 393, 395, 399
Interior Plains, 4
Interior Salish, 25
Inuit, and European contact, 257, 258
Irish Catholics, 228, 264–265, 344
Irish Protestants, 228
  See also Orange Order
Iroquois
  constitution, 22
  Dutch allies, 58
  and European rivalry, 142
  Five Nations Confederacy, 22–28
  French relations, 86, 106
  peace with Huron, Abenaki, and Ottawa (1700), 108
  wars with Huron, 71–74

J

Jaenen, Cornelius, 78, 99
James I (king of England), 57
Jarvis, Samuel, 188
Jarvis, William, 188
Jay's Treaty, 185
Jessup, Edward, 185
Jesuit Relations, 61
Jesuits, 40, 67–69, 94, 111
Johnson, Guy, 164
Johnson, John, 185
Johnson, William, 164
Jolliet, Louis, 105
Jones, Peter, 346
Journeymen, 133
Julien, Barnaby, 346
Julien, John, 184
Jummonville, Joseph de, 149

K

Kane, Paul, 305, 351
Karsefni, Thorfinn, 49
Kavanagh, Lawrence, 233
Kelly, Patrick, 275
Kelm, Mary-Ellen, 44
Kent, John, 255
King, Boston, 183
King's College (New Brunswick), 239
King's College (Toronto), 300
King's College (Windsor, Nova Scotia), 199, 234
Kingston, economy, 189, 270–271
Kirke, David, 53, 61
Kirke, Sarah, 53
Knowles, Norman, 183
Krieghoff, Cornelius, 351
Kutenai, 25

L

La Barre, Joseph Antoine Lefebvre de, 106
Labour
    agricultural crisis and, 192
    disputes, 250–377
    fur trade, 135, 192, 305, 319
    indentured, 76, 135
    Irish workers, 265, 313–314
    landlessness and, 35, 271, 275
    seasonal workers, 192
    violence, 265
    workers resistance, 366
    workforce, 368, 373
Labrador, 172, 247, 256–260
    Beothuk relations, 257–260
    cultural contact, 257
    economy, 256–257
    missionaries, 256–257
La Corne, Louis, 112
Lacrosse, 17, 349

Ladies' Benevolent Society, 279
Lafitau, Joseph-François, 117
LaFontaine, Louis-Hippolyte, 295
La Galissonière, Roland Michel Barrin, Compte de, 147
La Jonquière, Jacques Pierre de Taffanel, 112
Lalement, Jérome, 68
Landrigan, James, 253
Land speculation, 285, 292
Lane, Michael, 171
L'Anse-aux-Meadows, 49
La Peltrie, Marie-Madeleine de, 71
La Ronde, Denys, 116
Lartigue, Jean-Jacques, 279, 286
La Salle, René-Robert, Chevalier de, 105–106
La Tour, Agathe Saint-Étienne, 144
La Tour, Charles de, 56, 57, 66–67
La Tour, Claude de Saint-Étienne de, 56, 57
La Tour, Marie de, 66
Laval, Bishop, 75, 92, 134
Lavallée, Caixa, 352, 397
La Vérendrye, Pierre Gautier de Varennes et de, 111–112
Law
    French inquisitorial system, 91
    and industry, 367
Law, John, 110
Lawrence, Charles, 146, 150, 151
Leacock, Eleanor, 16
League of Augsburg, 106
Le Borgne, Emmanuel, 67
Le Caron, Joseph, 60
Lefebvre, Jean, 132
Légaré, Joseph, 351
Le Jeune, Paul, 69
Le Loutre, Louis, 145, 146
Le Moyne, Charles, 90
Leonardo de Vinci, 40
Lescarbot, Marc, 56
Lettre de cachet, 122
Lévis, Chevalier de, 156
Lillooet, 25
Literacy, 343
Literature, 240, 350
Little, Philip, 255
Liverpool Packet, 196
Lods et ventes, 97
Logan, William, 370
London and Bristol Company, 52–53
London (Upper Canada), economy, 271
Longueuil, Charles Le Moyne de, 90
Louisbourg, 113–114, 123, 145–146
Louisiana, 108, 110–111
Louis XIII (king of France), 61, 91, 92
Louis XIV (king of France), 37, 84–85, 105, 106, 108, 109
Louis XV (king of France), 109, 111

Lower Canada
    anglophone population, 190–191
    and Constitutional Act, 187
    and creation of united province, 295
    Durham Report and, 286–295
    English merchants, 190
    freehold tenure, 191
    French-speaking majority, 191–192
    land grants, 190
    legislature, 89–90
    patronage, 190
    Rebellion of 1837-38, 285–288
    rural society, 275–277
    social structure, 277–280
    urban centres, 277–279
    and War of 1812, 195–196
Loyal Electors, 236
Loyalists
    diversity among, 182
    emigration from United States, 181
    "late Loyalists," 186
    myth, 202–203
    settlement, 184–187
Loyola, Ignatius, 40
Luther, Martin, 38
Lux, Maureen K., 44, 307
Lyman, William, 362

M

Macdonald, John A., 350, 378, 382
    business interests, 392
    and Canada East, 390
    and federal system, 399
    and idea of Confederation, 392
    and legislative union, 399
    succeeds MacNab as Conservative leader, 298
    Toryism, 394
Macdonald, John Sanfield, 391
MacDonell, Margaret, 226
Macdonnell, Miles, 214–215
Macdonnell, Richard Graves, 397
Machiavelli, Niccolò, 40
Mackenzie, Alexander, 207, 219
Mackenzie, William Lyon, 289, 292, 293, 294
MacNab, Allan, 297
Madras school system, 234
Magazine publishing, 350
Maillard, Pierre-Antoine-Simon, 145, 146
Maisonnat, Marie Madeleine, 144
Maliseet, 15, 57, 67–68
Mance, Jeanne, 70, 136
Maquinnas I, 218
Maquinnas II, 218
Marie de l'Incarnation, 69, 71, 93, 136
Maritimes
    Acadian forest region, 4
    agriculture, 4

and American Revolutionary War, 174–178
Catholicism in, 233
charity, 234
class and culture, 232
colonial identity, 242
communications, 336
economy, 196, 228–231, 241, 337
education, 234
emigration, 228
immigration, 225–228
intellectual life, 240
legacy of mercantilism, 241
Loyalists, 184
population, 228, 335, 336
pre-industrial social relations, 232–233
reform movement, 235–239
region, 225–228
religion, 233–235
responsible government, 238, 239
sectarian rivalry, 235
and War of 1812, 196–197
Maritime union, 396–397
Maroons, 197
Marquette, Jacques, 105
Marriage
age at, 127, 339
à la façon du pays, 128
à la gaumine, 128
contracts, 129
delaying, 383
endogamy, 340
European-Native, 77, 211–213, 315
length of, 128
middle class, 382
of mix-blood women, 213, 315
in New France, 87, 127
peasants, 34
remarriage, 127–128
slaves, 134
weddings, 128
Marshall, Ingeborg, 260
Marx, Karl, 236
Masonic Lodge, 199
"Massacre of Grand Pré," 146
Massé, Énemond, 56
Massey, Hart, 362
Masters and Servants Act, 272
Matthews, Peter, 293–294
Mauger, Joshua, 148, 169
McAskill, Angus, 350
McClintock, Leopold, 313
McClure, Robert, 313
McCulloch, Thomas, 228, 369
McDougall, John, 19
McGee, D'Arcy, 362, 385
McGill University, 300
McLoughlin, John, 319
McMaster University, 300
Mechanics' Institutes, 240, 350

Medicine
practice of, 340
professionalization of, 340
and women, 385
Membertou, 56
Mercantilism, French policy, 95–96
Mercenaries, 32
Merici, Angela, 40
Methodism, 183, 233, 234, 256, 273, 326, 344
Métis, 309–311, 335
and buffalo hunt, 325
distinctive culture, 213
English-speaking, 213, 309
French-speaking, 213, 309–311
and HBC trade monopoly, 309–310
identity, 212
and Miles Macdonnell, 214–215
origins, 211–213
and racism, 213
women, 213
Metlakatla, 327
Metropolis, and frontier, 65
Meulles, Jacques, 96
Miasmatic theory of disease, 340
Michif, 213
Michilimackinac, 104, 112, 193
Middle class
birthing experience, 340
French Canadians, 191–192
marriages, 382
and political reform, 235–236
and responsible government, 238–239
and social reform, 280, 375
standard of living, 383
See also Social elites
Midewiwin (Grand Medicine Society), 17
Mi'kmaq, 14–21, 14–57, 67, 144–145, 152, 163, 258, 346
Militia, 147, 339
Missionaries
Catholic, 39–40, 256
female religious orders, 69–70
in Huronia, 59–60, 68
in Labrador, 256–257
in Northwest, 308–309
in Pacific colonies, 255–327
views of Native society, 60
women, 40
Mob violence, 377
Mohawk, 185
Molson, John, 362, 368
Monarchs
absolutism, 84–85
and nobility, 32
power of, 37
Monckton, Robert, 149
Montagnais. *See* Innu
Montcalm, Louis-Joseph, Marquis de, 152, 153, 154, 155, 159

Montezuma, 42
Montgomery, Richard, 173
Montreal
anglophone population, 277, 278, 279
economic centre, 277
French Canadian population, 278
during French regime, 123
manufacturing, 368
mercantile community, 278
population, 338
social welfare, 279
Montreal Gazette, 199
Montreal merchants, in fur trade, 207–208
Montreal Protestant Orphan Asylum, 279
Montreal Society, 199
Monts, Pierre du Gua de, 56
Moodie, Susanna, 274, 350
Moore, Samuel, 275
Moravian missionaries, in Labrador, 256–257
Morgan, Robert, 375
Morin, A.N., 297
Morris, Maria, 240
Morris, Mary Christianne Paul, 346
Morris, Patrick, 253
Motin, Jeanne, 67
Mott, Lucretia, 384
Mount Allison University, 234
Mount Elgin Industrial Institution, 346
Mullock, John, 255
Mummering, 254, 377
Murrant, John, 183
Murray, James, 156, 165, 166, 167
Music, 352
Myth, 183

N

Naskapi. *See* Innu
Nationalism
British North American unity, 384–386
and colonial identities, 384–386
Nation-states, emergence of, 37
Natural history, interest in, 124, 240, 369, 370
See also Science, interest in
Naval state, 247
Naylor, R.T., 408
Ned, Annie, 10
Neilson, John, 286
Nelson, Wolfred, 286, 376
Neutral, 20, 22
Newark, 189, 195
New Brunswick
and American Revolutionary War, 176
1812 boom conditions, 196
borders, 225
Confederation debate, 401–402
creation of, 184

and Maritime union, 396
political reform, 236–237
prohibition movement, 379
public debt, 395
railways, 363, 393
tariffs, 362, 363
New Caledonia, 319
Newfoundland, 246–255
American fishing rights, 247
and American Revolutionary War, 174
boreal forest, 4
British colonization, 52–54
class structure, 252
Confederation debate, 401
dependence on cod fishery, 249–252
franchise, 254
French fishing rights, 247
under French regime, 88–89
immigration patterns, 248–249
judicial system, 247, 253
and Labrador, 172, 198, 247, 256–260
naval state, 247
Palliser's Act, 172
reform movement, 253–254
religious divisions, 249, 255
representative government, 254
responsible government, 254–255
Royal Proclamation of 1763
and, 163–164
sectarian politics, 396
settlement, 248–249
shore-based fishery, 171
Treaty of Utrecht and, 109
and War of 1812, 197–198
War of the Spanish Succession in, 108
See also Cod fishery
New France
artisans, 133
arts, 124
coal resources, 116
colonial administration, 89–90
colonial elite, 131
colonization of, 74–75, 77–79
corruption in, 89, 116, 132
defence, 86, 115
diet, 77
family policy, 86–87
government, 74
governor general and local
governors, 89–90
habitants, 125–127
immigration, 75
industry, 115–116
inheritance practices, 126
intendant, 90, 91
labour shortages, 135–137
land grants, 75, 76
law and order, 91–92
mercantilism and, 95–96
merchants, 131–132

military spending, 115
paternalism, 90–91
population distribution, 76
religion, 18–75, 92–95
renewed Iroquois hostility, 106
slavery, 133–134
social mobility, 131
social structure, 130–135
society in, 77, 99, 130
Sovereign Council, 90, 91, 123
specie shortage, 96–97, 109
Newman, Peter C., 315
New Netherlands, 45
New Westminster, 324
Niagara Falls, as tourist attraction, 352
Nightingale, Florence, 341
92 Resolutions, 286
Nobel, Arthur, 146
Nobility, in New France, 131
Noblesse d'épée (de sang), 85
Noblesse de robe, 85
Noel, Jan, 136
Nonosbawsut, 259, 260
Norse presence, in North America, 49
North, the, 5–6
Northwest
expansionist interest in, 311–312
missionaries in, 308–309
North West Company (NWC)
amalgamation with HBC, 215–216
in BC interior, 219
competition with HBC, 208
formation of, 208
and Selkirk settlement, 214–215
and violence, 209
Notman, William, 351
Nova Scotia
and American Revolutionary War, 174
Confederation debate, 401, 402
diversity, 170
Loyalists, 182
and Maritime union, 396
mining, 230
New England immigrants, 169
public debt, 393
railways, 363, 393
reform movement, 237–238, 239
Scots, 227
Nova Scotia Magazine, 199
Nursing, 341
Nuu'chah'nulth (Nootka), 23, 24, 217, 218

O

Oblates, 308–326
O'Callaghan, Edmund, 286
O Canada, 352
Ochiltree, Lord, 57
O'Flaherty, Patrick, 246
Ohio Company, 149

Ohio Valley
French defence of, 147–149
and settlement frontier, 168
Tecumseh's uprising, 193
Ojibwa, 10, 15, 16–17, 73–112, 209–210, 212, 216, 345
O'Neill, Charles, 99
Oral sources, 8–9, 226–227
Orange Order, 266
Ordre de Bon Temps, 56
Oregon Treaty, 321
Orléans, Phillipe, Duc d', 109, 110
Orphanages
social reform movement and, 381
working-class children, 383
Osborn, Henry, 143
Oshawana, 345
Ottawa, chosen as capital, 406
Ottawa (First Nation), 108–216
Ouellet, Fernand, 177, 300–351, 301–351
Owram, Doug, 311

P

Palliser, John, 311
Palliser's Act, 172
Palmer, Edward, 236, 380, 400
Panting, Gerald, 241
Papineau, Louis-Joseph, 191, 278, 286, 287
Parkman, Francis, 99, 177
Parti canadien, 191–192, 285
popular support, 285, 286
See also Parti patriote
Parti patriote, 279
and Catholic Church, 286
and Rebellion of 1837-38, 285–288
Party system, 237
Passamaquoddy, 163
Pastore, Ralph, 260
Paternalism, 90–91, 99, 233
Patriarchy, 233
Patterson, Walter, 170
Peasantry
Canadian, 125–127
economic life, 34, 35
and labour market, 31–32, 35
leisure, 34–35
life cycle, 34–35
revolts, 33
serfs, 9
wars and, 32–33
Peigan, 19
Pelly, John Henry, 322
Pemmican, 211, 214, 215
Pepperell, William, 145
Perez, Juan, 217
Perkins, Cato, 183
Perry, Oliver, 193
Petrokeshig, Chief, 345
Petun, 21

Peyton, John, Jr, 258–259
Phillips, Richard, 143, 144
Phips, Sir William, 106
Photography, 351
Physiographic regions, 3, 4–5
    Atlantic and Gulf region, 4
    Canadian Shield, 4
    Great Lakes-St Lawrence Lowlands, 5
    Interior Plains, 4
    North, the, 5–6
    Western Cordillera, 5
Picquet, Abbé, 147
Pisan, Christine de, 40
Pitt, William, 153
Placentia, 88–89
"Planters," 248, 252
Plateau First Nations, 320
Plessis, Joseph-Octave, 196, 286
Police, policing, 378
Polk, James K., 321
Pond, Peter, 174, 207
Pontchartrain, Jerome de, 145
Pontiac, 162, 164
Poor, John Alfred, 393
Popular classes
    sports, 349
    violence, 376–377
Port Royal, 56
Portuguese cod fishery, 50
Portuguese exploration, and trade, 41–42
Portuguese walrus-hunters, 51
Potato, food staple, 248
Potato famine, 249, 267
Potlach, 23–24, 25
Poutrincourt, Jean de, et de Saint-Just, 56
Poverty, 375–376
    among immigrants, 264–265
    birthing experience, 341
    and childbearing, 339
    and health, 340
    and incarceration, 376
    landless labourers, 232
    living conditions, 279–283
    rural, 276
    and social reform movement, 381–382
    and social welfare, 376
Pre-industrial social relations, 232–233
Presbyterianism, 234, 235, 273
Preston, Richard, 235
Prevost, Sir George, 195
Prince, William Stratton, 378
Prince Edward Island
    Confederation debate, 400–401
    education reform, 239, 380
    Escheat Movement, 236
    land reform question, 395–396
    and Maritime union, 396
    political reform, 236, 239
    population, 336
    reciprocity, impact of, 395

Selkirk settlers, 227
    tenant farmers, 228
Prince of Wales, 234
Prisons, and social reform movement, 382
Privateering, 176, 196
Proctor, Henry, 195
Prostitution
    in New France, 124
    poverty and, 192
Protectionism, 360–361, 362
Prouville, Alexandre de, 86
Provincial Academy of Arts and Sciences, 199
Provincial Association (New Brunswick), 362
Puget Sound Agricultural Company, 324
Puritans, and colonization, 45

Q

Quadra, Juan Francisco. *See* Bodega y Quadra, Francisco de la
Quartering Act, 172
Quebec
    and American Revolutionary War, 173–174
    boundaries, 164–168
    British merchants, 166–167
    under British military rule, 164–166
    civilian rule, 166–167
    civil right for Catholics, 166
    English merchants, 168, 186
    inflation, 166
    Loyalists, 182, 186
    resentment over Loyalist land grants, 186
    traditional elites, 167–168, 174
Quebec Act, 1775, 167–168
Quebec City
    during French regime, 122–123, 124
    population, 338
    port of entry for immigrants, 265
    siege of, 153–156
Quebec Gazette, 199
Quebec Mining Company, 345
Quebec Resolutions, 399–401, 405–406
Queen's College, 300

R

Racism
    Aboriginal experience, 332, 344–346
    black experience, 346–348
    in fur trade, 213
    Métis experience, 310–311
    race and, 323, 344–348
    slavery and, 42, 133
Radisson, Pierre-Esprit, 105
Rae, John, 313
Railways, 336
    cost of, 363–364
    government bond guarantees, 297, 391

and politicians, 391
    and promise of economic development, 393
    and public debt, 393, 395
Rand, Silas, 346
Rand, Theodore Harding, 380
Rang, 98
Rape, 341–342
Ray, Arthur, 307
Raynal, Abbé, 117
Razilly, Isaac de, 65
Rebellion Losses Bill, 297
Rebellions of 1937-38, 285–294
    agricultural crisis and, 285
    anti-American sentiment, 288
    armed conflict, 287–288, 293–294
    demand for land reforms, 288–289, 292–293
    ethnicity and, 286
    Family Compact, 289
    grievances, 285–286, 289, 291–292
    in Lower Canada, 285–288, 300–351
    nature of, 294
    political reform and, 286, 289
    republicanism, 286
    in Upper Canada, 288–293
Reciprocity Treaty, 361–362, 398
Récollets, 59–60, 67, 94, 113
Red River
    district, 335
    economy, 324–325
    founding of settlement, 213–215
    linguistic and religious divisions, 309, 310
    Métis community, 309–311
    population influx, 216
    racial divisions, 310–311
Red River cart, 213
Reeves, John, 253
Reform Bill of 1832 (Britain), 254
Reformers
    Baldwin-Lafontaine alliance, 295–296
    moderates, 289, 292, 295
    radicals, 289, 292
    and Rebellion of 1837-38, 289–294
Reform movement
    in Canada East, 391
    in Newfoundland, 253–254
    in Nova Scotia, 237–238
Reform Party
    Francis Hincks, leadership, 297
    George Brown and, 297
    internal politics, 297
    and railway subsidies, 390
    and separate schools, 390
Religion
    and culture, 343–344
    and Darwinism, 371
    ethnicity and, 344
    evangelicalism, 183, 233

holidays, 349
intolerance, 39
and politics, 273–274
Reformation, 38–39
"sabbath," observance of, 349
sectarian rivalry, 235, 266, 376
separate schools, 380
and social inequality, 235
and social mores, 273
and social reform, 234, 378–379
Sunday school movement, 234
syncretic practices, 68
and Upper Canadian society, 273–275
Renaissance, 40–41
Repentigny, Agathe de Saint-Père,
Madame de, 96
Representation by population ("rep by
pop"), 390, 400
Representative government, 239
Responsible government
and democracy, 239
Durham Report and, 286, 295
middle class and, 238
in Newfoundland, 254–255
principles of, 235, 237
in United Canada, 295–296
Rich, E.E., 314
Richardson, John, 350
Richelieu, Cardinal, 61, 65
Ricter, Daniel, 78
Rideau Canal, 198
Riots. See Mob violence
Roads, 336–337
Robb, James, 370
Roberval, Jean-François de La Rocque
de, 55
Robin Hood Society, 199
Robinson, Sir John Beverley, 348
Robinson, W. B., 345
Roche, Marquis Troilus de la, 51
Rolph, John, 289
Roma, Jean-Pierre, 114
Roman Catholic Church
and charity, 92
classical colleges, 191
class system, 131
and Confederation, 401, 402, 405
and Conquest, 165
Gallicanism, 92, 94
influence of, 279
and Newfoundland politics, 255
in New France, 92–95
Quebec Act and, 167–168
and Rebellion of 1837-38, 289
and Reformation, 38–39
and social reform, 382
and War of 1812, 195–196
Roman Catholicism
and Articles of Capitulation, 156
in British North America, 343–344

class and ethnicity, 344
divisions within, 235
Rouges, 392
anti-confederates, 403
political program, 298
and reform movement, 391
Rouvillière, Marie-Catherine de Villebois
de la, 125
Royal Proclamation of 1763, 163–164,
172
Roybon, Madeleine de, d'Alonne, 86
Rupert's Land
British North American nationalism
and, 21–386
HBC charter, 105
Rush-Bagot Agreement, 198
Russell, Lord John, 236, 237, 286
Russian presence, on Pacific coast, 217
Ryan, John, 253
Ryan, Shannon, 198
Ryerson, Egerton, 289, 379, 380

S

Sabatier, Charles Wugk, 352
Sagard, Gabriel, 60, 68
Sager, Eric W., 241
Sailors, violence, 377
Sainte-Pierre, Jacques, 149
Ste-Marie-Among-the-Hurons, 68
Saint John
baking, 230
industrial centre, 230
manufacturing, 368
population, 338
Saint-Lusson, Daumont de, 105
Saint-Pierre, Jacques Le Gardeur de, 112,
114
Saint-Sauveur, 56–57
St Dunstan's, 234
St Francis Xavier University, 234
St John's Island
and American Revolutionary War, 174
colonial settlement, 170–171
lottery of 1767, 170
and Loyalists, 184
and War of 1812, 196
See also Île Saint-Jean (Prince Edward
Island)
St Mary's University, 234
St Maurice ironworks, 116
St Patrick's Society, 279
St-Pierre and Miquelon, 156, 197, 247
St Vincent de Paul Societies, 279
Saint-Vallier, Jean-Baptiste de la Croix
de, 94
Salaberry, Charles, 196
Sangster, Charles, 386
Sarrazin, Michael, 124
Saunders, Charles, 154
Sayer, Pierre-Guillaume, 309

Scammell, G. V., 42
Science, interest in, 369–371
Sealers strike, 250–251
Seal fishery, 250–251
Seamen, labour disputes, 377
Second Continental Congress, 173
Secord, Laura, 197
Secret ballot, introduction of, 239
Sedgwick, Robert, 67
Séguin, Maurice, 177
Seigneurialism
abolition of, 299
agricultural crisis, 192–193
under British rule, 166, 167
censitaires (*see* Seigneurialism, habitants)
crops, 275–276
farms, 125
habitants, 97, 125–127, 276–277
houses, 126
labour, 135
landholding, 75, 76–77, 97–98
merchant credit, 276
objectives of system, 97
population pressure and, 192, 275
poverty, 276
seasonal wage labour, 126, 192
and social structure, 98
status of seigneur, 98–100
strip-like tenant grants, 97–98
Sekani, 25
Selkirk, Thomas Douglas, Earl of, 227
Selkirk settlement, 213–214
Semple, Robert, 215
Seven Oaks, armed conflict at, 215
Seven Years' War, 152–153
Seward, William, 398–399
Sexuality
homosexuality, 274–275
social mores and, 127–128, 273, 341
Shanawdithit, 258, 259, 260
Shannon, 197
Sheaffe, Hale, 193
Shelburne (Nova Scotia), 182, 183
Shenandoah, 398
Shiners' War, 265, 272
Shingwaukonse, 269
Shipbuilding, 115–116, 196, 229–241, 365
Shipping, 196, 229
Shirley, William, 144, 145, 149
Short, Richard, 200
Shuswap, 25
Sillery, mission at, 68
Simcoe, John Graves, 188, 189
Simpson, George, 308, 319, 321, 322
Sioui, Georges, 78
Sioux, 10
Six Nations, 185, 344
Slavery
abolition of, 264, 334
in Aboriginal culture, 13, 24

African, 43, 111
in Articles of Capitulation, 156
Code Noir, 134
in early modern Europe, 36
Loyalists, 182
in New France, 133–134
Portuguese trade, 42
and racism, 42, 134
Slaves
Aboriginal, 13, 24, 43, 106, 134
African, 42, 134
life expectancy, 134
marriage, 134
price of slaves, 134
resistance, 134–135
sexual exploitation of, 134
Smith, Albert J., 401
Smith, Henry, 382
Smith, Titus, 240
Smith, William, 199
Social elites
and charity, 279
education, 299, 342–343
Montreal mercantile community, 278
and religion, 344
residence, 338
sports, 349, 350
Upper Canada, 188
violence, 377–378
See also Middle class
Social reform
and children, 381
and the indigent, 381–382
middle class and, 280, 375
temperance movement, 234, 379
See also Education, reform
Social welfare, 376
Catholic Church, 279
"deserving" poor and, 272–273
Société de Notre-Dame, 75
Société Saint-Jean Baptiste, 279
Society for Promoting Christian
Knowledge, 347
Society for the Propagation of the
Gospel, 347
Soeurs de la Charité de l'Hôpital-Général
of Montreal, 279
Soeurs de la Congrégation de Notre-
Dame, 70–113
Soeurs Grises, 92, 124
Soeurs Hospitalières, 70
Sons of Liberty, 172
Sons of Temperance, 379
Southern Kwakiutl, 23
Sovereign Council, 90, 91, 123
Spain
and American Revolutionary War, 218
exploration, 42–43
on Pacific coast, 217

Spanish cod fishery, 50
Spanish exploration, and imperial-
ism, 42–43
Spear thrower, 10
Spice trade, 41
Sports, and leisure, 349–350
Sproat, Gilbert, 327
Stadacona, 55
Stage service, 337
Stamp Act, 172
Steamship service, 362
Stevens, F. G., 305
Stewart, Robert, 171
Story, George M., 260
Stowe, Emily Jennings Howard, 385
Stowe, John Howard, 385
Strachan, John, 289
Strikes, 272
Subercase, Daniel d'Auger de, 108, 109
Sulpicians, 94
Sulte, Benjamin, 176
Sun Dance, 211
Sunday school movement, 234
Swan, Anna, 350

T

Taché, E.P., 297
Tadoussac, 57, 61
Talon, Jean, 95–96, 105
Tariffs. See Protectionism
Teachers, teaching, women, 381, 383
Tecumseh, 193, 276
Telegraph communication, 336
Temperance movement, 234, 379
Temple, Thomas, 67
Tenant League, 396
Theatre, 352
Thirty Years' War, 33
Thompson, David, 219
Thorpe, Robert, 190
Thule people, 25
Tilley, Samuel Leonard, 379, 395, 402
Timber resources, 337
Tories, 236
Toronto
capital, 189
economy, 270–271
manufacturing, 368
population, 338
Torrington, John, 313
Towsend, Lord James, 236
Tracy, Marquis de, 86
Trade fraternities, in New France, 133
Trade monopoly, de Monts, 56
Traill, Catharine Parr, 350
Treaty of 1726, 145, 146
Treaty of 1752, 146
Treaty of Aix-la-Chapelle, 146
Treaty of Breda, 67

Treaty of Ghent, 198
Treaty of Montreal, 108
Treaty of Paris, 156, 166
Treaty of Ryswick, 106
Treaty of Saint-Germain-en-Laye, 61
Treaty of Utrecht, 109, 142, 247
Trent incident, 398
Trigger, Bruce, 10, 78
Trofimenkoff, Susan Mann, 176
Troupes de la Marine, 111, 149
Troupes de Terre, 149
Troyes, Chevalier de, 105
Trutch, Joseph, 332
Tsimshian, 23
Tupper, Charles, 363

U

"Underground railroad," 348
Uniacke, James Boyle, 238
Unions, 272
United Canadas
communications, 336
Confederate debate, 403–406
creation of, 295
population, 335
public debt, 392
railways, 363–364
responsible government, 295–296
sectional tensions, 390–391
separate schools question, 391
tariffs, 362, 363, 391
United States, export market, 337
Université Laval, 300
University Bill, 300
University of New Brunswick, 239
Upper Canada
capital, 189
and Constitutional Act, 187–188
and creation of united province, 295
legislature, 89–90
local government, 189
Loyalists, 185
patronage, 189
political culture, 188, 198
Rebellion of 1837–1838, 288–291
religion, 273–275
rural society, 268–270
social structure, 188–189, 271
urban centres, 270–271
War of 1812, 193–195, 196
Upper Canada College, 350
Urban centres
defence and security, 339
as economic centres, 339
health, 340, 341
and industrialism, 367–368
lack of sanitation, 338
markets, 338
in New France, 76–77, 122–123

seaport towns, 377
social order, 35–36
Ursulines, 40, 69, 111

V

Van Alstine, Peter, 185
Vancouver, George, 212
Vancouver Island
amalgamation with British
Columbia, 329
colonization of, 322
Crown colony, 335
economy, 337
gold rush conditions, 325
Van Egmond, A.G.W., 294
Van Kirk, Sylvia, 314, 315
Vaudreuil, Philippe de Rigaud, 108,
135–137
Vaudreuil, Pierre de Rigaud, 132–412,
149, 153–156, 159
Vaughan, Sir William, 53
Verchères, Madeleine de, 107, 136
Vibert, Elizabeth, 320
Victoria, 325, 329
Victoria College, 300
Victoria (queen of England), 334
Viger, Denis-Benjamin, 278
Virginia colony, 43–45
Villiers, Louis Coulon de, 146
Violettes, political program, 298–299
Virginia Company, 53
Voltigeurs, 196

W

Walker, Sir Hovenden, 109
War of 1812
causes, 193
in Lower Canada, 195–196
and Maritimes, 196–197
mythology, 197
native allies, 193
and Newfoundland, 197–198
suppression of dissent, 198
in Upper Canada, 193–195, 196
War of the League of Augsburg, 106–107
War of the Spanish Succession, 108–109
Warren, Peter, 145
Washington, D.C., razed, 195
Washington, George, 149, 168
Watkin, E.W., 408
Webster-Ashburton Treaty, 225
Weeks, William, 190
Wentworth, Sir John, 199
West Country merchants, and cod
fishery, 247–248
Western Cordillera, 5
Whaling, 51
Whelan, Edward, 239
White, Richard, 162
Whitworth-Aylmer, Matthew, Lord, 286
Wicken, William, 145
Wiesner, Merry E., 36
Wilkinson, Moses, 183
Willcocks, Joseph, 190
William Price Company, 276
Williams, James, 371
Williams, Sir William Fenwick, 402
Wilson, William, 259
Winman, Erastus, 369
Winniett, William, 144
Winslow, John, 151
Witchcraft, the church and, 93
Wolfe, James, 154, 155
Women
birthing experience, 128, 268, 340,
341
and charitable work, 382–383
and commercial life of New
France, 132
and Confederation debate, 407
death rate, 128
disfranchised, 239
and divorce, 342, 384
in early modern Europe, 36–41
families headed by, 340
of fisher families, 249
franchise, 187
and gender equality, 384
guilds and, 36
industrial workforce, 368
missionaries, 40
in New France, 86–87, 136
paid work, 192, 231, 271, 381, 383
property rights, 270
and Rebellion of 1837-38, 287
single mothers, 341
unpaid labour, 216, 231, 249,
268–279, 277
unwanted pregnancies, 341
See also Aboriginal women; Gender;
Marriage; Sexuality, social mores and
Woodman, David C., 313
Written documents, as historical
sources, 8, 10
Wulstukwuik, 144–145, 146, 163
Wylie, William, 272

X

XY Company, 209

Y

York. *See* Toronto
Young, John, 240
Youville, Marguerite d', 124, 134